PHILIP WEBB

In gratitude to John Brandon-Jones, his wife Helen,
and my husband Harry Vernon Kirk

Published in Great Britain in 2005 by Wiley-Academy, a division of John Wiley & Sons Ltd
The Atrium, Southern Gate, Chichester, West Sussex PO19 8SQ, England
Telephone (+44) 1243 779777
Email (for orders and customer service enquiries): cs-books@wiley.co.uk
Visit our Home Page on www.wileyeurope.com or www.wiley.com

Cover: Standen, East Grinstead
Frontispiece: Red House, Upton Bexleyheath

Other Wiley Editorial Offices

John Wiley & Sons Inc., 111 River Street, Hoboken, NJ 07030, USA
Jossey-Bass, 989 Market Street, San Francisco, CA 94103-1741, USA
Wiley-VCH Verlag GmbH, Boschstr. 12, D-69469 Weinheim, Germany
John Wiley & Sons Australia Ltd, 33 Park Road, Milton, Queensland 4064, Australia
John Wiley & Sons (Asia) Pte Ltd, 2 Clementi Loop #02-01, Jin Xing Distripark, Singapore 129809
John Wiley & Sons Canada Ltd, 22 Worcester Road, Etobicoke, Ontario, Canada M9W 1L1

ISBN 0471987085 (Cloth)
ISBN 0470868082 (Paperback)

Executive Commissioning Editor: Helen Castle
Editorial and Design Management: Mariangela Palazzi-Williams
Picture Research and Editorial Assistance: Famida Rasheed

Designed by Liz Sephton
Printed and bound in Italy by Conti Tipocolor

PHILIP WEBB

Pioneer of Arts & Crafts Architecture

SHEILA KIRK
with photography by Martin Charles

WILEY-ACADEMY

CONTENTS

INTRODUCTION

Philip Webb (1831–1915) was the avant-garde English architect whose philosophy and work had the greatest influence upon the architects of the Arts and Crafts movement. There were other pioneers – including Shaw, Voysey, and MacLaren – but Webb influenced most of them to a degree, too. His first commission, Red House (designed for William Morris between 1858 and 1859), is now widely regarded as the first Arts and Crafts building although it predates by a quarter of a century the coining of the term by its younger practitioners. Webb himself never applied the term to his work or to his approach to architecture because he wished to avoid even a tenuous connection with an architectural style; instead, he developed a philosophy of design that is relevant to this day, and that will be valid at any time in any country with a heritage of traditional buildings. In collaboration with Morris at Red House, he also set a new pattern for garden design that endured throughout much of the twentieth century and which still has emulators today.

A quiet, unassuming man who avoided the limelight assiduously, Webb had a prodigious effect on architects and architecture, of the Modern as well as the Arts and Crafts movement, although he never published his philosophy or his buildings. Through his work for Morris, Marshall, Faulkner & Co, Webb influenced the design of interiors, furniture, and various crafts including plasterwork and wood carving; and through the Society for the Protection of Ancient Buildings, which he helped William Morris to found, he became an important figure in the history of conservation, making the sympathetic repair and enlargement of old buildings rather than their rebuilding a part of Arts and Crafts practice. The society became his unofficial and informal 'school' of practical building, through which he directly influenced the thinking and the new buildings of many young Arts and Crafts architects. Largely through the work of his followers – amongst whom were Lethaby, Prior, Baillie Scott, Blow, Gimson, Lutyens, and Mackintosh – Webb's approach spread throughout Britain and into mainland Europe and North America.

After the imposition of the Palladian style in the early eighteenth century, new architecture had become a matter of designing on paper according to the conventions of one or another style from the past without regard for the materials and other conditions of the country or specific district. Webb's aim was to make it a matter of simple but excellent building once again, based on common sense, practicality, and honesty, and on national and local architectural traditions. He devised a challenging approach to architectural design that offered strong principles and firm guidelines, as well as ample freedom for individual creativity. When followed, his approach – which he hoped would also be adopted in other countries – would produce vigorous, inventive buildings that, through experiments in the use of materials, the design of details, and the adoption of worthy new technology, would allow the national architectural tradition to develop further. His approach required that a building and all its details form a consistent whole, in harmony with its surroundings through being fitted into the site rather than standing upon it, and by its design reflecting the character of the site as well as that of local buildings. To achieve this harmony, it would be necessary to avoid obtrusive, ephemerally fashionable, and self-advertising designs. Webb emphasized the value of handwork and the need to ensure the survival of traditional crafts, both of which were seemingly under threat of extinction through the use of machines. By relying for the pleasing effect of exteriors to a great extent on the texture and colours of materials instead of upon style motifs and ornament, he increased the importance of the everyday labour of the builder's workmen, and thus encouraged their pride and pleasure in it.

Webb's design philosophy and buildings influenced the architecture of the Modern movement

Opposite *Philip Webb (1831–1915), watercolour, by Charles Fairfax Murray, 1873 (National Portrait Gallery, London)*

PHILIP WEBB
ÆTAT·273·

despite the latter's embracing of the machine aesthetic, and although its International style was the antithesis of his celebration, reflection, and development of the native building tradition. That he was cited as a Modernist pioneer in the twentieth century led many people to assume that this was Webb's major or only sphere of influence. Coupled with his steadfast avoidance of publicity, this resulted in the extent of his influence on Arts and Crafts architects not being fully understood (though it had been appreciated and acknowledged during his lifetime), and in comparatively little being written about him and very few of his buildings illustrated.

My interest in Webb and in the Arts and Crafts movement was stimulated by the Open University course 'Architecture and Design 1890–1939', and was increased by my having been a potter with my own studio whilst my children were young, by my earlier architectural training, and by my knowledge and admiration of English vernacular buildings. The origin of the book lies in my post-graduate research into Webb's work in the north east of England for Sir Lowthian Bell, his family, and their iron-founding firm. It became obvious that a thorough study of even this limited topic was impossible without looking into Webb's life, his design philosophy, and his work for other clients. Clearly there was enough unpublished primary material for a new biography of Webb, for which there was a need. My final thesis was submitted successfully in 1990 for a PhD degree from the University of Newcastle upon Tyne, where I subsequently spent six years teaching part-time (chiefly on the history of Arts & Crafts architecture) whilst continuing my research. Following the addition of a considerable amount of further material – particularly on Webb's non-domestic buildings and on his work for Morris & Co – the dissertation has been rewritten as this book. It is the first fully detailed and systematic investigation of Webb's life, philosophy, and the whole of his work, and it is aimed at the wider public as well as the academic world.

Despite my keen interest in and burgeoning admiration for Webb's work, when I began the research in late 1979 I had no suspicion that it might prove to be so fascinating and important that he would occupy a large slice of my life. My husband,

Harry – who has been a great source of practical help, particularly by criticizing rough drafts and checking final chapters – has had to live with him too; he and the rest of our family have borne Webb with commendable patience, all the while giving me great and much appreciated encouragement (the long list of others who have helped appears at the end of the book).

Webb's personal life has been covered separately from his work because, for him, architecture was his life. The rest of it was singularly uneventful. In order to pursue his personal mission to improve contemporary architecture, he lived simply and never married; this ensured that a high income was unnecessary, and thereby enabled him to refuse commissions for which he would not have had time to design all the details himself. Consequently, the chambers he had taken in London in 1864 sufficed until his retirement from practice. He made no major changes to his approach once it was fully developed, and he applied it to all types and sizes of buildings; so, for convenience, these have been grouped in chapters according to category, but all, with his major enlargements and alterations, are listed chronologically in the Catalogue of Architectural Works. Dates given are those of designing (dates of construction are given in the catalogue), and names are those in use in Webb's time, with present-day nomenclature in parentheses.

Webb never set down his design philosophy systematically but it has proved possible to elucidate it from his papers (listed in the Bibliography), in particular from comments in his many letters to clients, builders, younger architects, friends, and acquaintances; from his buildings; from his disciple William Richard Lethaby's *Philip Webb and his Work* (written in 1925 as a series of articles for the *Builder*, and published unchanged in book form in 1935) and the notes he made for it; and from a large quantity of information kindly provided by the late John Brandon-Jones, some of which had been imparted by other friends of Webb. John's most kindly permitting me to make copies of much of his collection of Webb's papers has been and will continue to be a great boon. Contemporary and more recent books and articles (to the authors of which I give thanks) have also been drawn upon to set Webb in the context of his times.

Chapter 1

THE EARLY YEARS

Oxford, a small and beautiful town at the time, relatively little changed since the fifteenth century, had a great influence on the architect Philip Webb (1831–1915), who was born and brought up there. Apart from some roughcast smaller dwellings, all the buildings, including the castle, cathedral, colleges, and water mill, were walled and mostly roofed in grey limestone. A few collegiate buildings had been built in the Baroque style in the late seventeenth and early eighteenth centuries, but there were no large commercial blocks or industrial works and, until Webb was sixteen, there was no railway. He was to be in practice in London from 1859 until the end of 1900 but it was Oxford that had a deep effect on the thinking that governed his approaches to the design of new buildings and to the preservation of old ones. In turn, these approaches were to exercise a wide influence on the architects of the Arts and Crafts movement during the last two decades of the nineteenth century and first fifteen years or so of the twentieth century.

Webb's early childhood was secure and happy. The second son and one of the eleven children of Charles Webb (c. 1795–1848), a general practitioner and physician, he was born at number 1 Beaumont Street on 12 January 1831. Named Phillippe after the French monarch and Speakman after his mother Elizabeth's family, he always used the English form of his first name and ignored the second. When he was about three years of age, his family moved to what had once been the Oxford home of the Dukes of Marlborough, number 15 St Giles'. This large house and its gardens, courtyards and outbuildings, with the grounds of the adjacent St John's College, provided satisfying playgrounds for the child, who found interest and excitement in the everyday life of the town and its annual highlights such as St Giles's Fair. As he grew older, he became fascinated by the architecture of Oxford, by the cottages as well as the colleges and churches, an interest that was to become a lifelong passion for old buildings of all types and

ages. The needless alteration, between 1852 and 1853, of the spire of St Mary's Church in Oxford alerted him to the urgent need to preserve the architectural heritage in the face of public apathy, a crusade with which he would eventually be deeply involved. His love for Oxford never waned, and decades later he affirmed that all his life had been 'coloured and even trained by its fashioning'.[1]

Accompanying his father on his rounds outside the city, Philip was introduced to what became another passion: the unspoilt English countryside, 'full of exquisite beauty and thousands of lovely beasts', and dotted with old buildings that were like open history books, living records of centuries of human endeavour.[2] This acute consciousness of the continuity and unity of the English landscape also had a significant impact on Webb's thinking. His close friend and biographer, the architect William Richard Lethaby (1857–1931), recalled how Webb and William Morris (1834–96) had shared a rare 'religious love for England', beyond that of anyone else, and 'not a vague or abstract love, or possessive pride and patriotism, but affection and even worship for the very earth, trees, fields, animals, ploughs, wagons and buildings – yes, and the weather, too'.[3] The English countryside was never to fail Webb as a source of inspiration and solace.

Dr Charles Webb seemingly inherited some of the artistic ability of his father, Thomas Webb, a renowned medallist of Webb and Hardman, Birmingham, who in the early nineteenth century produced amazingly neat and accurate portraits of important men and was considered to be 'amongst the very first of modern medallists in the class of busts'.[4] Dr Webb encouraged his own son to sketch the plants and animals they saw on their travels, and secured tuition for him from a skilled botanical artist of Oxford, a Mrs Richardson; these early sketches have not survived, but Philip Webb's later drawings of birds and animals are beautiful as well as skilful, and it is regrettable that he never fulfilled his ambition to illustrate a natural history.[5] He treasured his copy of the Reverend Mr Cotes's *The History of British Birds* (1797) for its wood engravings by Thomas Bewick, and deeply admired Albrecht Dürer's drawings, which he found uplifting – in contrast to the depressing work of Rembrandt, whom he termed a 'master of human gloom and hellish ugliness'.[6] With great significance for his future work, his sketching and his study of the work of Dürer and Bewick developed Webb's interest in texture, an interest deepened during his architectural training and by doing the exercises, based on old vernacular buildings, in *Lessons on Art* (1849) by the painter James Duffield Harding.[7] Webb also sketched the horses that were part of his family's daily life. As a child he had his own pony, and eventually he became a fine horseman and an authority on every aspect of the animal, including the design of stables and the use of the horse in painting and sculpture. During his working life, Webb was to find horse-riding both soothing and stimulating to the mind and, in his last years when too much stiffened by rheumatism to ride, would derive great pleasure from watching the Arabian horses in the field behind his cottage.[8]

The happiest years of Webb's childhood came to an abrupt end when at just eight years of age he became a boarding pupil at Aynho Grammar School in the Northamptonshire village of Aynho, some twelve miles from his beloved Oxford. The school had been founded in 1654, and its buildings had

Left Number 15 St Giles', Oxford: Webb's home until he began training as an architect

changed little since that date. Set in almost an acre of land, they consisted of a master's house with two living rooms, two bedrooms, a kitchen and three attics, and an adjacent schoolroom with a dormitory above. In Webb's time it was somewhat in decline through competition from the local national school, but there were probably about twenty pupils, around half of them boarders, chiefly sons of farmers and local tradesmen, with whom he had little in common.[9] Sorely missing his home and Oxford, he was deeply unhappy at the school, where he felt imprisoned. In later years he referred to such establishments as 'boy farms'.[10] Despite his misery, Aynho gave him a sound education and a lifelong love of reading, and taught him to be content with a minimum of worldly goods, to appreciate his home, to be self-sufficient, and to respect the liberty of the individual.

Apparently for no other reason than his liking for privacy, partly innate and probably increased by having so many siblings and by his years at the school, Webb was reticent about his family. He did record in 1869 that it was his mother who instilled in him the Protestant ethic, the belief in the supreme importance of work, which 'kept people out of trouble and mischief'.[11] Possibly she also taught him about Christianity, as throughout his life he was a 'lover of Jesus of Nazareth' and a follower of his principles, though in adulthood he apparently became an agnostic, at least for some years.[12] Doubtless his mother encouraged Webb's kindly and sympathetic nature, and gave him his great respect for truth, which he sought in all things including architecture.

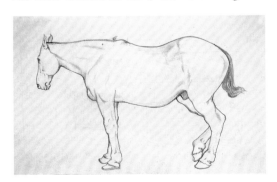

Left Webb's sketch of a horse, from his sketchbook (Private Collection)

Right Aynho Grammar
School, built c. 1654, from
an old print

When Webb was seventeen, his father died, and
he and his brothers had to choose a career that would
earn them a secure living. All four became successful
– Harry as a general practitioner in Welwyn, Percy in
the Anglican Church, Frank as a brewer, and Philip
as an influential architect. Philip Webb had hoped to
become a painter but in an early demonstration of his
reliance on common sense, a faculty he prized highly,
he abandoned this dream because, as he recorded,
'there was not so much need for painting as for
building'.[13] Having such a great interest in buildings
of all ages, he chose architecture, which by then had
become a suitable profession for a middle-class man.
Furthermore, the building industry at the time was
generally booming, despite short periods of
recession.[14] Oxford was a major centre of the current
revival of church building, associated with the
Tractarian movement. Perhaps the young man hoped
to become a designer of Gothic Revival churches, in
which pursuit his extensive knowledge of medieval
ecclesiastical buildings would have been of
inestimable benefit. In the event, Webb would
become a sought-after designer of dwellings, a house
architect, who built only one church and one chapel.

In 1849, Webb began serving his articles with the
architect John W Billing (1817–63) in Reading, then
an unspoilt small market town, where he became
involved with churches and parsonages, Georgian
houses, and small workshops, and with farmhouses
and farm buildings in the surrounding district. Billing
was the borough surveyor, a member of the Oxford
Architectural and Historical Society (often known as
the Oxford Architectural Society) and of the
Statistical Society. He might have known the Webb
family or been recommended as a suitable instructor
by a mutual acquaintance. An inventor of
improvements to chimneys, flues, stoves and
fireplaces, Billing was deeply interested in the
practicalities of building. Whilst Webb was with him,

in addition to the many run-of-the-mill jobs typical
of a small-town practice, Billing designed the Savings
Bank (1849) and Holy Trinity School (1852) in
Reading, and the vicarage at Sandhurst, Berkshire,
and rebuilt Tetworth church, Oxfordshire. The
Savings Bank, and the Victoria Square houses he had
designed earlier, were in the Classical idiom, which
he termed 'Italianate'; the rest were in the Gothic
style.[15] Webb's one surviving student notebook
shows that Billing gave him a sound practical
grounding in both the 'Italianate' and Gothic manner
of design and construction.[16] This broadly based
training, reinforced by his own open-minded attitude
and the eighteenth-century buildings amongst and on
which he worked and lived in as a child, would
eventually release Webb from the straitjacket of
Gothic revivalism which bound the thinking and work
of many of his contemporaries. Billing and Webb
developed a mutual respect, and Webb stayed on as an
assistant for two years after finishing his articles.
Presumably seeking new pastures and better prospects,
Webb left in April 1854, at twenty-three years of age,
to join the practice of Bidlake and Lovatt in
Wolverhampton, armed with five years of office
experience and a fine testimonial, in which Billing
praised the 'assiduity and perseverance' with which he
had pursued his studies and vouched that in the 'best
school of drawing and designing' Webb had been 'very
successful, particularly in the several Gothic styles'.[17]

Wolverhampton proved to be far from pastoral
and only too appallingly new. Webb encountered
modern industry for the first time and found, under
what he saw as black 'clouds of prosperity', a volcano
of factories pouring forth a lava of row upon repeated
row of terraced dwellings which engulfed the
countryside and its ancient villages.[18] The sight of this
despoilment seared his spirit as severely as it did the
landscape, and his reaction to it affected his thinking
and his work. As Lethaby put it, all 'Webb's future
life was shaped by the thought of this and that – of
old and new – of Oxford and Wolverhampton'.[19]
After only four weeks Webb secured a new post, the
reduction by half of his salary of £2 a week being of
no matter against the unutterable relief of returning
to his beloved Oxford, where on 16 May 1854 he
began working for the Diocesan Architect, George
Edmund Street (1824–81), near his old home.[20]
Webb had nailed his colours – art and beauty before
reward, whatever the personal cost – to the mast,
from which he was never to lower them.

He probably thought his future was secure, as Street (who had trained under Owen Browne Carter in Winchester before becoming an assistant of Sir George Gilbert Scott (1811–78)) was one of the architects most esteemed by the Ecclesiological Society which, in the early 1850s, effectively controlled the most advanced sector of English architecture, the High Victorian Gothic movement. It is possible that Webb already knew Street before entering his office. If not, perhaps Billing, a fellow member with Street of the Oxford Architectural Society, introduced Webb to him at Sandhurst, where construction of Billing's vicarage coincided with that of Street's nearby St. Michael's church; or possibly he recommended Webb to Street on learning of the latter's need for an assistant. Whatever the case, Street found that Webb was indeed a first-rate chief assistant, one who was conscientious and capable, and who shared his own liking for hard work and passion for medieval buildings and the natural world. After only twelve months he doubled Webb's salary to £100 a year.[21] In his employer, Webb found a new friend only seven years older than himself. He quickly settled back into the life of the town, working in the street of his birth, probably living with his widowed mother, and resuming old delights such as swimming in the river. He joined the Oxford Architectural Society in June 1856, borrowing the subscription fee from his brothers Harry and Percy.[22]

Street believed that three-fifths of the poetry of a building lay in its minor details, so he designed every part of his buildings himself; his assistants merely finished his pencil drawings in ink.[23] Ultimately Webb followed this practice himself, but meanwhile he must have been deeply frustrated by the embargo on design. However, working for Street, one of the acknowledged leaders of the High Victorian Gothic movement, was far from unpleasant. Street expected his assistants and pupils to work as hard as himself, though not in the evenings as he did, but he was a fair and cheerful employer whose prodigious output ensured constant variety and, for his assistants, frequent surveying trips around Oxfordshire and beyond, including to London. Earnest effort was relieved by joking and high jinks. Webb found his sense of fun at loggerheads with his conscientiousness, and had a little difficulty in ensuring that his juniors finished their drawings.[24] The work of the office was stimulating, and whilst Webb was with Street he would have been involved with all the buildings his employer designed and built, which included several churches, vicarages, and village schools, and the Theological College, Cuddesdon (designed 1852), Street's first important building. Webb also worked on Street's competition drawings. Those of 1855 for Lille Cathedral were placed second, those of 1856 for the English Memorial Church in Constantinople also came second but the church was eventually built to Street's amended design, and those of 1857 for the Government Offices in London were unplaced. Whilst Webb was his assistant, Street gave lectures and wrote papers, several of which appeared in the *Ecclesiologist* (the important journal of the Ecclesiological Society) and published his successful and influential book on Italian polychromatic medieval buildings, *Brick and Marble in the Middle Ages, Notes of a Tour in the North of Italy* (1855).[25]

Street was an admirer of Augustus Welby Northmore Pugin (1812–52), who had pioneered the nineteenth-century crusade to reunite the decorative crafts with architecture, and had revived several dead

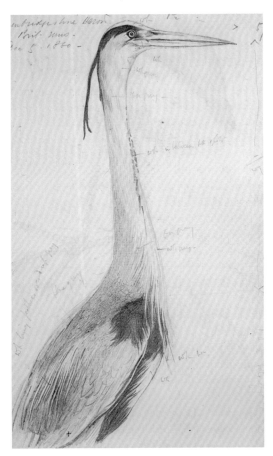

Left Webb's drawing of a heron, from Webb's sketchbook (Private Collection)

or debased arts. Street, too, believed that all the decorative arts for a building should be designed and executed by the architect. He made himself an expert in several of these arts, and was co-author of a book on ecclesiastical embroidery. In a move that gave this confirmed Gothic revivalist an important influence on the Arts and Crafts movement, at his instigation Philip Webb and Street's new pupil William Morris, who were to become the movement's most influential pioneers, took up various crafts including embroidery, illuminating, clay-modelling, carving, and wood-engraving (which Morris had tried already and which Webb found foreign to his aptitude).[26]

William Morris had originally intended to enter the Church with his friend and fellow Oxford undergraduate Edward Burne-Jones (1833–98) after they had graduated from Oxford. A major part of the attraction it held for them came from the beauty of its medieval churches and early music, and the colour and pageantry of the ancient ritual then being revived. Their attention having been drawn already to the aims of the Pre-Raphaelite painters and the beauty of great Gothic buildings by the words of John Ruskin (1819–1900), they went on a tour of French cathedrals in 1855 with another friend, William Fulford. At the end of it, deeply impressed and enthused by their findings and by the seven Pre-Raphaelite paintings they saw on exhibition in Paris, Morris and Burne-Jones decided to devote their lives to art – Burne-Jones to painting and Morris to

architecture. After taking his degree, Morris began his architectural training in January 1856, having apprenticed himself to Street, to whom he might have been introduced or commended by the Reverend Frederick Barlow Guy, who had tutored Morris for the university entrance exam and was a fellow member with Street of the Oxford Architectural Society. Morris already had some knowledge of and love for English Gothic churches, perhaps induced by Guy, and this, with his veneration of the English countryside and old villages, formed an instant point of contact with Webb, whom he met at Street's office and who had been put in charge of his training.[27] They quickly formed a close friendship which would endure until Morris died and which was to have important repercussions on English architecture, interior design, and the preservation of the architectural heritage.[28]

Morris found the routine in Street's office uncongenial, and learning how to do measured drawings of architectural details difficult and tedious. He spent much time writing poetry instead of studying. Webb provided pleasure, however, by introducing him to his own favourite nooks and crannies of Oxford and, often in connection with his work, taking him to see old churches in the district. Morris also enjoyed their shared leisure pursuits, which included swimming and riding as well as tackling various handicrafts. Twice Webb visited Morris's home, Water House (now the William Morris Gallery) in Walthamstow, from which they explored Epping Forest on horseback.[29] There were similarities in their backgrounds. Their fathers were of similar status – Morris's was a discount broker – and though not equally wealthy, each of them provided his family with a large, comfortable home but died during his son's youth. Both boys were deeply unhappy at school, perhaps blaming their banishment in part on the large number of their siblings: Morris was the oldest boy of nine surviving children. Webb, who had to earn his living, fortunately found his vocation at the first attempt. He had been self-supporting for four years when he met Morris, whose several-hundred-pounds-a-year income from his inheritance allowed him to make some false starts in life.

Their personalities were complementary. Morris, usually somewhat unkempt, was mercurial, rebellious, vehement, and prone to sudden enthusiasms which he pursued with an egotism Webb described as 'amusing and childlike', and to sudden violent rages in which he sometimes damaged himself and the furniture.[30] Webb, a tall, slim man with a serious, intelligent and kindly expression, was extremely reticent, of equable temper, self-controlled, slow to form or change his beliefs, and careful of his appearance. Both men were steadfast on matters of principle, loyal, sincere, lacking in pettiness, and wholly without pretence, with a strong aversion to the artificiality of formal social occasions. Each found in the other a source of inspiration, encouragement, and support. Though only three years his senior, Webb had a valuable steadying influence on Morris and, as Webb told another close friend in 1888, it was a 'good corrective' to his own 'melancholy temperament' to 'rub shoulders with Morris's hearty love-of-lifedness'.[31]

Webb and Morris held most of their ideas on art and life in common apart from the matter of English Baroque architecture. Morris's love for medieval buildings had evolved into such a deep passion that he could not countenance the notion that any other architectural forms might approach them in beauty. His dislike of post-Reformation Classicism amounted almost to hatred, and he spoke of the buildings of Sir Christopher Wren (1632–1723) and his peers as belonging to 'the ignorance'.[32] Webb told Lethaby that though Morris knew Wren's St Paul's Cathedral was a great work, it was 'not his kind of art' and he would not 'allow good in what he thinks wrong'.[33] Morris remained convinced to the end of his life that for it to be good, living architecture, 'the form, as well as the spirit, must be Gothic'.[34] Webb, whilst concurring that medieval Gothic architecture at its best was of unassailable beauty, could appreciate good proportions, right use of materials, and excellent craftsmanship in buildings of any age. In 1888, he told his friend William Hale White (1831–1913) that he had 'quarrelled and rejoiced' with Morris for many years.[35] They differed on no other major matter, so their squabbles must have been about English seventeenth- and early-eighteenth-century architecture, and perhaps occasionally about Webb's own work because, as will be demonstrated, his open mind and Billing's training allowed him to develop a design approach which took inspiration for new designs from Elizabethan, Jacobean, and English Baroque buildings as well as from medieval ones.

Back in August 1856, Street had moved his office to Montagu Place in London, taking Webb and Morris with him. Webb took a room, first in Liverpool Street, and then in number 41 Great Ormond Street, Morris lived briefly in Upper Gordon Street before joining Burne-Jones, who had been in London since May, in rooms at number 17 Red Lion Square. When Burne-Jones had first met Webb, he had been surprised to find Webb much his own age, Morris having described his instructor as a kind and 'very fine old fellow in the office'.[36] Dante Gabriel Rossetti (1828–82), who had persuaded his young admirer Burne-Jones to leave Oxford for painting without first taking his degree, now turned his influence on Morris, whose poetry he had admired in the *Oxford and Cambridge Magazine* earlier that year before meeting its author.[37] Rossetti confirmed Morris's view that English poetry had reached its peak, and by July 1856 had persuaded him that there were great deeds yet to be done in painting and that Morris had the ability to do them. For a time, Morris worked in Street's office during the day and spent the evenings at life class with Burne-Jones, but after serving just a few months of his articles, he left Street before the end of the year to become a full-time painter. Financially secure and attracted by the unconventional life of artists, Morris abandoned architecture, as Webb told Lethaby, because 'he found he could not get into contact with it; it had to be done at second hand'.[38] In other words, in architecture, the designer of an item did not make the object, did not execute the design with his own hands.

The Pre-Raphaelite Brotherhood, founded in 1848, had disbanded by 1856; but a wider circle of painters, centred round Rossetti, had espoused its ideal of portraying people and events in the colours and attitudes of real life instead of the formal conventionalized postures and arrangements, with colour subordinated to drawing, demanded by the Royal Academy. Several architects were attracted to the circle. This was not surprising for, as Street pointed out, there were parallels between Pre-Raphaelite goals and those of the Gothic Revival architects: both groups had turned their backs on post-Renaissance art to seek inspiration in medieval art, and both had adopted the rich colours of that period against the blandness of neoclassical buildings and paintings.[39] Webb soon became one of the circle and a friend of Rossetti, who often called on him in the evening, when they talked freely. He tried to make Webb into a painter too, but only managed to persuade him to attend a life-drawing class where the architect carefully measured the dimensions of the human model, to Burne-Jones's lasting amusement.[40] Webb was as fervent a fighter for the revival of art – which included architecture, of course – as were the painters. In 1899, he told Hale White that this cause had been the backbone of his life.[41] In a letter to Rossetti of 1866, Webb said he was sure Rossetti would agree that:

> anyone who wishes to follow art with advantage to the world and with hope of competing with art gone before, must be very severe in the liability of disturbance from collateral causes, such as payment, popularity – position &c – none of these are of necessity ruinous to art, but they do often ruin the workman.[42]

Webb was to pursue his branch of art with fervour and without swerving from these principles for the whole of his working life.

Webb personified the ideal – based on the character of the hero in Charlotte Yonge's *The Heir of Redclyffe* (1853) – that Morris and Burne-Jones had adopted as undergraduates, which embodied conscientiousness, truthfulness, earnestness, courtesy, enthusiasm, and high ideals of honour and friendship. Webb was honourable, immensely kind, and utterly truthful, unable to abide deceit of any kind. He felt keenly his friends' joys and troubles, as well as the wider woes of his nation and mankind, and would help anyone down on his luck, even if short of money himself – always insisting that the loans were gifts, repayable only if good fortune came. He passed on to needy younger architects any commissions he was too busy to undertake. When asked for his opinion about a new or proposed building, he gave encouraging advice and constructive criticism if he felt it would be welcomed, but if he could find nothing good to say, he said nothing, even in his private notebooks. In 1873 he helped one Frances Hohenthal, who had suffered severe hindrances of some kind, to emigrate to Canada and get a good job there, probably as an upper servant; the following year he paid the cost of a pupil teacher to temporarily replace Alice Burbridge, a young friend or relation of his housekeeper, so that she could look after her dying mother; and during his last years in practice, when losing money and with few savings, he gave one of his sisters £10 each month.[43] Even when ill and in pain himself, he wrote long, consoling and stimulating letters to Hale White and to another close friend, the painter George Price Boyce (1826–97), during their frequent bouts of depression. He helped Mrs Boyce during and after her husband's long final illness, and when Charles Faulkner (d. 1892), another close friend, became bedridden, he visited him almost every evening until the invalid died three-and-a-half years later.[44] After setting up his Kelmscott Press in 1891, Morris insisted on giving Webb a copy of every book he published but, in another instance of his kindly forethought, Webb always bought a second costly copy to lend to friends so that Morris would not suffer through this generosity. Sydney Carlyle Cockerell (1867–1962), secretary to Morris's Kelmscott Press from 1891 to 1896, recalled Morris saying that Webb was 'the best man that he had ever known', to which Cockerell had added: 'there are very few of those who were privileged to know him who would not say the same'.[45]

Webb's letters, rich in quotations, Latin tags, and perceptive comments on literature, paintings and painters, philosophy, music, politics, and social organisation, amongst many other subjects, show that he was a well-read man with an enquiring mind. In 1866, he told Rossetti that ever since fate had kindly made him acquainted with the group, he had always thought that for him to be considered as one of such a company there must be something about his 'mental constitution which excused the seeming disparity', and that this was largely because he had the 'capacity for understanding' them.[46] Events were to show that Webb was the intellectual equal of Morris and the rest of the group, despite his slight feeling of inferiority in this respect.

Right *Sir Edward Coley Burne-Jones,* 1st Bt, (1833–98), pencil, by George Howard. 9th Earl of Carlisle, c. 1875 (National Portrait Gallery, London)

Meanwhile, for six months in 1858 he attended the Class of Design of the Architectural Association, as he had done in 1856 when, probably for the first time, Webb met Richard Norman Shaw (1831–1912), his exact contemporary, with whom he struck up a lifelong though not close friendship, and who was shortly to follow in his footsteps as Street's chief clerk.[47] Webb's designs for a public fountain and a covered market for a country town appeared in the association's 1858 Architectural Exhibition, and were selected for 'peculiar praise' by the reviewer in the *Ecclesiologist*, who thought that the market revealed 'a rather close, but successful study of Mr. Street's style'.[48] The Royal Academy's exhibition of the same year included Webb's scheme for the 'Interior of a Town Church'; a reviewer in the *Builder* noted that it resembled Street's churches in character and like them was 'marked generally by invention, and often by attendant beauty in the details'.[49] A reviewer in the *Ecclesiologist* commended the 'bold conception' of the church roof and found in the 'manipulation of the design great dexterity in the imitation of Mr. Street's style; and in the building itself study profitably made in his school', and ended by saying that the ecclesiologists had 'high hopes of Mr. Webb, only let him while young avoid the snare of excessive originality'.[50] This was high praise for a young architect, signifying future success if he obeyed the tenets of the Ecclesiological Society. Webb must have been dismayed rather than uplifted by the last review because to him copying was anathema, and by 1858 he was no longer in sympathy with Street's revivalist ideals.

Webb admired many things about Street and his work, enough indeed to allow him to put reticence aside and write the entry on Street in the *Dictionary of National Biography*. With typical modesty, he said he had joined Street as a pupil though, in fact, he had completed his articles two years previously.[51] In Webb's view, Street was 'everything that was honourable, and industrious beyond words, a very able architect according to his lights'; by 1858, however, the lights of the Gothic Revival had dimmed for the younger man who, despite the invention and originality of Street's work, was soon to leave him, having decided, as Lethaby recorded, that 'modern medievalism was an open contradiction'.[52] Webb deplored the use of foreign Gothic elements and inspirations in England, for which Street was partly to blame through his work

and influential book *Brick and Marble*, and he was gravely upset by the revivalists' so-called restoration of ancient churches whereby much original fabric was being destroyed. Webb was 27, experienced in office and site management and in the construction and supervision of many types and sizes of building. Despite an increase of salary to £160 a year in May 1858, it was time to test his own ideas and powers of invention, but he had neither capital nor commissions with which to set up practice.[53]

Fortunately, he met a number of potential clients through the Pre-Raphaelite circle and its Hogarth Club, founded in 1858. The club was a social gathering-place where the artists could meet their patrons and painters from out of London, and a forum and alternative or additional vehicle to the Royal Academy for the exhibition of work. Webb was elected a member in January 1859, and became a trustee of the 1860 exhibition.[54] The club was dissolved in December 1861 but for three years it brought him into close contact with many painters, sculptors, architects, poets, writers, and art patrons. Membership was divided into two categories: 'artistic' and 'non-artistic'. Amongst the former were: George Boyce, and George Frederic Watts (1817–1904) and his two young protégés Valentine Cameron Prinsep (1838–1904) and John Roddam Spencer Stanhope (1829–1908), for each of whom Webb would design a studio-house in the 1860s or early 1870s; Rossetti and Robert Braithwaite

Martineau for whom also Webb was to design studios; Ruskin, Morris, Burne-Jones, Ford Madox Brown (1821–93), and Arthur Hughes (1832–1915). Several architects were members in this class, including Street and his friends William White (1825–1900) and George Frederick Bodley (1827–1907); the latter became a close friend of Webb for several years. The non-artistic class comprised industrialists, professional men, poets, and writers, including Thomas Carlyle (1795–1881) and two men for each of whom Webb would later design a country house, Francis Dukinfield Palmer Astley (1825–1868) and William James Gillum (1827–1910). Webb's first commission, however, came from William Morris, not through the club but through their well-established comradeship.

In 1857, in Oxford, Morris had met his future wife and become involved in what would prove to be his vocation: interior design. Rossetti had enlisted his help, and that of Burne-Jones, John Hungerford Pollen (1820–1902), Hughes, Prinsep, and Stanhope, in painting the upper walls of the Union Debating Hall, a building designed and recently completed by his friend the architect Benjamin Woodward.[55] Ultimately the paintings were a disaster: the wall spaces were unsuited to the subjects, which were

derived from Sir Thomas Malory's Arthurian prose collection *Le Morte d'Arthur* (c. 1470); the drawing was poor; some panels were never finished; and the damp, ill-prepared walls soon ruined the brilliant colours. Morris's painting of the roof, with which Webb helped occasionally at weekends, fared little better; but the design was attractive, assured and appropriate. Whilst staying in Oxford to do the work, Rossetti, Hughes, and Morris introduced themselves to Jane Burden (1839–1914), the daughter of a local groom, because Rossetti wished to paint her portrait. Morris fell in love with her and she, though not reciprocating the emotion, seized the chance to improve her situation and accepted his proposal of marriage.[56] Burne-Jones was already engaged to marry Georgiana Macdonald (1840–1920), as was Rossetti to Elizabeth Siddall. Whilst they were undergraduates, Morris and Burne-Jones had dreamed of founding a monastic establishment, and had called themselves the Brotherhood. After they decided against careers in the Church, this had mutated into a celibate community devoted to art. In 1858, the dream was amended again, this time in order to accommodate their and Rossetti's future wives. Morris decided to build a house in which the dream would be realized on a part-time basis. It was to be in the country, partly to please Webb and doubtless to enable Jane to become accustomed to her new status away from curious eyes.[57]

Morris and Webb first discussed the new house in August 1858 during a holiday in France – Webb's first trip abroad.[58] His previous vacations had been sketching tours of medieval buildings: inspecting cathedrals in the south of England in 1856; and, in 1857, a five-week study of cathedrals, churches, and monastic remains in northern England and southern Scotland. Studying and sketching ancient architecture was also the object of the 1858 holiday. Webb and Morris were joined on the excursion by Faulkner, a Fellow and Mathematical Tutor of University College, Oxford, who had met Morris when they were undergraduates through Burne-Jones who, like Faulkner, came from Birmingham. Faulkner's lifelong friendship with Webb possibly began when they were helping to paint the Debating Hall. Taking almost a month to do it, the three friends rowed from Paris to Caudebec in a boat sent over from Oxford that had arrived with a hole in it, to Morris's fury. They hoisted sail in favourable winds, slept at inns, and stopped to explore towns and to make short excursions. It was an unusual and adventurous holiday, involving not only the studying of medieval architecture but also hilarious battles with soda-water syphons, a leaking boat, being stranded in a lock because Morris had angered the lock-keeper, and a narrow escape from being shipwrecked by the tidal bore. By the time Webb returned and joined his mother for a week in Ilfracombe, he had added an awareness of many French churches, castles, and town houses to his already extensive knowledge of British buildings. The most memorable, he found, were the cathedrals of Pontoise and Rouen, and the collegiate churches of Notre-Dame at Poissy and Mantes, especially the latter, with its 'appearance of gaunt amplitude (making it look a veritable Noah's Ark)', which he admired greatly.[59]

On his return to England, Morris bought an old orchard at Upton in Kent, a county he loved, where there was a nearby railway station from which to travel to and from London. Webb moved to a room in number 7 Great Ormond Street in September on his return from France, and started designing the house. The drawings were ready by April 1859 and, in late summer the following year, Morris and his wife moved into their new home, which they named Red House because of the colour of its bricks. Rossetti preferred to refer to it as Hog's Hole, which to his delight was the name of nearby cottages.

Red House (see chapter 2) demonstrated Webb's technical expertise and design skills to the members of the Pre-Raphaelite circle and the Hogarth Club. The interest they showed, and probably their promises of commissions in the near future, encouraged Webb to set up on his own, though he still lacked capital. On 29 April 1859, he told Street that he wished to leave, and he did so on 27 May the same year.[60] He had already bought a drawing-board, T-square, and measuring tape, in order to prepare the drawings for Red House but it took three more years to acquire all he needed for his office, necessitating the selling of his old clothes, a treasured pen-and-ink drawing, and a photograph of a painting by Henry Wallis. Technical books, such as Gwilt's *Encyclopaedia and Waterlow's Specification*, were needed to supplement Webb's 1850 edition of Parker's *Glossary of Terms*, and clothes suitable for a professional man's wear in town and country had to be bought, including hats for all occasions.[61] No fee for designing Red House

appears in Webb's account book. It is very likely that Morris offered one and Webb refused to take it. His reticence and fierce personal pride, in which renown and financial success played no part, always prevented him from allowing anyone outside his family to know about his occasional financial problems, though he never pretended to be well-to-do. He adhered always to the principles he outlined to Rossetti in 1866, and as a result he sometimes found it difficult to make ends meet. After the first year or two, this was not through shortage of work but through his insistence on designing every detail, however small and apparently insignificant, of each of his buildings himself with great care, and on spending several days before he started the design work on studying the specific site and the ways local materials had been used in old nearby structures. Stanhope commissioned Webb to design his house Sandroyd at Cobham in Surrey in 1860 (see chapter 5), and Gillum commissioned a terrace of shops and dwellings, numbers 91–101 Worship Street in London in 1861 (see chapter 11), but Webb's account book shows no income during his first two years in business. Until he could submit his bills twelve months after the buildings were finished, he was kept afloat by loans from his mother and brothers, who had to help him again in some of the years when his practice made a loss despite his renown.

Chapter 2

RED HOUSE
Upton, Bexleyheath (1858–9)

The old orchard that Morris had purchased satisfied both the client and the architect on aesthetic, romantic, and practical grounds.[1] It was in the type of gently undulating countryside that Morris liked best, in the hamlet of Upton near the then undeveloped Bexley Heath in Kent (now Bexleyheath in London), with the remains of an ancient abbey nearby and, just to the north, Watling Street, the Pilgrims' Way from London to Canterbury, of which Chaucer had written. Abbey Wood railway station being only three miles away, travelling to and from London would be relatively easy. The plot was the right size, and the old fruit trees would make a new garden look established immediately. Morris had had only a few months of training, under Webb, in Street's office, chiefly spent in learning to make measured drawings, so he knew nothing about designing or constructing buildings.[2] Naturally, he turned to Webb, whose general views on art were the same as his own, and who was an architect with plenty of practical, on-site experience, albeit without a building to his name.

Webb designed the building but Morris was responsible for the interior decoration. Morris told Andreas Scheu years later that he had got a friend to build him a 'house very mediaeval in spirit' and had set himself to decorate it.[3] After their marriage on 26 April 1859 and their six-week wedding tour, Morris and his bride Jane (Janey) lived in furnished rooms a few doors from Webb's room in Great Ormond Street, a proximity that would facilitate consultation between client and architect. As the contract and the drawings that formed part of it had been signed earlier in April by Webb and the chosen builder, these discussions must have been about minor details and fittings, and schemes for the interior decoration. However, Webb would have considered Morris's perceived needs and wishes most carefully from the start. He was never to fail to do this for his clients, and he always bore in mind the fact that they, not he, were to live or work in the building, but he insisted on sole responsibility for matters of design. Morris threw his energy into planning the decoration and furnishing of his house, which he intended to make into the small 'Palace of Art' that had long been one of his dreams.[4] Almost every item needed for furnishing and decorating the house was to be specially designed and made because, as Morris told another friend years later, he and his 'friend the architect especially' had found that 'all the minor arts were in a state of complete degradation', particularly in England.[5] Mackail, Morris's early biographer, recorded that 'much of the furniture was specially designed by Webb and executed under his eye: the great oak dining-table, other tables, chairs, cupboards, massive copper candlesticks, fire-dogs, and table glass of extreme beauty'.[6]

Delays on the part of the builder William Kent led Webb to issue the first of his many 'stiff letters' to builders in June. The work was 'proceeding in a most irregular and unsatisfactory manner', he complained. He ordered Kent to 'send a competent general foreman of the works at once' or be himself 'continually on the ground, to attend to the directions', and to 'see that the building is done to my satisfaction'.[7] After this, the work proceeded quickly and satisfactorily, partly perhaps because the Morrises had rented a nearby house so that Morris could be on site daily and would, of course, report any delays to the architect. They moved into their new home in late summer 1860 and, in the autumn, Burne-Jones and Rossetti with their wives, and Charles Faulkner, spent several weeks at Red House helping to decorate it. Other friends helped when they could. Working creatively together, the highly talented and enthusiastic young men were again enjoying the companionship and mutual stimulation that they had found when decorating the Oxford Union. At Red House, where they also lived together, the dream brotherhood in its amended form was fulfilled, albeit only on a part-time basis. From Saturdays to Mondays and during some longer

periods, life at Red House became a thoroughly enjoyable mixture of conviviality, practical joking, playing games on the bowling-green in the garden, painting works of art, decorating the walls, ceilings and woodwork of the house, and designing furniture and other household items, or embroidering hangings for the rooms.[8] With a housekeeper and three maids to take care of all household matters, the women of the circle were able to share this unconventional creative life. However, Janey and Georgiana (Georgie) Burne-Jones soon found, to the latter's great disappointment, that the advent of their children severely constrained their freedom to do this;[9] and sadly, Rossetti's wife Elizabeth died in 1862.

Working together on Red House was so enjoyable that the friends decided to set up a firm to design and make similar artefacts to commission and for the market, and thereby to attempt to improve the decorative arts in England and reunite them with architecture. Morris, Marshall, Faulkner & Co. (the

Above Red House (1858–1859; constructed 1859–60), Upton, Bexley Heath (Bexleyheath), Kent: the west front

Above Red House: the entrance (north) front

Building of the amended scheme was to have begun in the spring of 1865. Unfortunately, Georgie suffered a life-threatening scarlet fever that caused the premature birth and death of her second son; the expenditure these misfortunes incurred, and the lack of income through Burne-Jones being unable to work for several months, forced them to withdraw from the project, to their and Morris's grief.[11] A chill caused by a wet journey to London had led to Morris becoming bedridden for many weeks with rheumatic fever during Georgie's illness; and after it, he found the long journeys exhausting. With the utmost reluctance, he put his beloved palace of art, with its decoration uncompleted, on the market in the summer of 1865. He took Janey, who was by then embroiled in a love affair with Rossetti, and their two small daughters to live in London, at number 26 Queen Square, which also provided the necessary extra premises for the firm. Morris's despair must have been deep. He could never bring himself to see Red House again, and he never built another palace of art. However, he had discovered his role in life during his time there. He abandoned thoughts of becoming a painter, and instead devoted most of the rest of his life to improving the decorative arts and reuniting them with architecture, through the firm that ironically had been the cause of him having to lose the house, and through its later manifestation, Morris & Co. From 1871, he was able to take solace from holiday times in Kelmscott Manor, a delightful, unpretentious stone manor house of the Elizabethan period with seventeenth-century additions, and many gables and mullioned windows, on the bank of the Thames near Lechlade in Oxfordshire, on which he and Rossetti took a lease. When the family moved to their final London home in 1879, a less congenial eighteenth-century building in Hammersmith, also on the banks of the Thames, he named it Kelmscott House.

Red House was conceived and designed as a permanent family home and workplace for a painter, a studio-house large enough to accommodate artist friends and their wives for considerable periods. Georgie recorded years later that the new dwelling was 'so designed that additions could be made without difficulty, and to this idea it owed part of its form', which suggests that from the start Morris hoped that some of the friends would eventually make it their permanent home.[12] The house was L-shaped, with a well court between the two wings, around which it could easily be extended, and was

subject of chapter 3) was founded in 1861, the partners being Morris, Webb, Burne-Jones, Rossetti, Madox Brown, Charles Faulkner, and Brown's friend Peter Paul Marshall (1830–1900). Workshops were established in London. By 1864, larger premises for the firm had become essential and Morris, who had worked daily in London since 1861 and was becoming increasingly dependent on income from the business, was finding the commuting tiring and time-consuming. It was decided to move the workshops to Upton, and to extend Red House to accommodate the Burne-Jones family. Webb designed an additional wing that if built would result in the two dwellings being under one roof but each with its own entrance, with the garden and court in common and Morris's studio becoming the Burne-Jones's drawing room. Burne-Jones found the design 'so beautiful that life seemed to have no more in it to desire'; it was too ambitious, however, and had to be modified.[10]

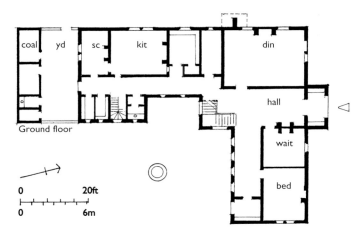

coal | yd | sc | kit | din
hall
wait
bed

Ground floor

0   20ft

0   6m

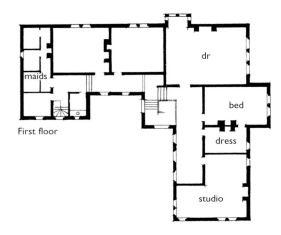

maids

First floor

dr

bed

dress

studio

Above Red House: plans of the ground and first floors

aligned slightly east of north in the middle of the site, which was bounded to the north by the approach road. The entrance was on the north front, and the main rooms in the two two-storey wings faced outwards across the gardens; the passages flanked the well court, and a pyramid-roofed stair tower, topped by a louvre and weathervane, acted as a pivot between the wings. The dining and drawing rooms, on the ground and first floor respectively, occupied the western end of the north wing. Left of the hall on the ground floor was a waiting room for potential patrons and perhaps models, though these were usually members of the household. A wide well-lit passage, presumably intended for the display of paintings on viewing days, led from the hall (from which it is now separated by a glazed screen apparently installed after the Morrises left the house) to the inset garden porch that was romantically named the Pilgrims' Rest by Morris, past a bedroom for bachelor friends, sensibly positioned on the ground floor to prevent late-night revels from disturbing the household. The passage was repeated on the first floor, where it led past the main bedroom over the entrance porch, and the dressing room, to the L-shaped studio, on the first floor for the best light, and positioned where it could have windows on the north, east and south walls.[13] High-level light came from a circular window in the east gable and a dormer on an inner slope of the double roof, and was reflected by the inclined planes of the ceiling. The west wing housed the west-facing kitchen and other domestic offices, and the narrow secondary staircase with winders, and ended in a small kitchen yard. It included, on the first floor, two family bedrooms, the housekeeper's bedroom, and the maids' room, which was divided by curtains into three and lit by a large hipped dormer in the cat-slide roof. The house had no bathrooms or central heating, which at the time were considered inessential luxuries; but, fairly unusually, it had water closets (WCs), serviced by a tank in the roof to which water was pumped. As was then customary, the men's closet was on the ground floor, the women's on the first and the maids' in the kitchen yard.

Red House was not at all like the square Georgian boxes with slate lids that Morris and Webb despised. It was a well-controlled, beautifully composed and proportioned assemblage of varied parts, unified by the strong colouring of the red bricks of the walls and red clay tiles of the striking roofs. The combination of gables, hips and half-hips, dormers, ridges at right angles and ridges in parallel, a cat-slide, a variety of coping and eaves details, a pyramid stair tower, and a wellhead that repeated the lines of the tower roof, effectively constitutes a sampler of roofing forms. Powerful chimneys, on the outer walls as Pugin had urged, with canted sides, tumbled brick setbacks, and shaped terracotta tops, punctuated the roofs. Most of the windows were vertically sliding sashes, which Webb believed gave better ventilation than cheaper but draughty casements. The triple lancets of the drawing room, however, did have casements, which folded inwards, possibly at Morris's request. The major rooms overlooked the gardens, with views of sunlit countryside to the north from the drawing room, which received late afternoon and evening sunshine through the oriel window. The windows had segmental arches inside and out, except the circular ones, which had them only in the interior. Some had a pointed relieving arch, and others were grouped together and recessed under a wider pointed arch.

These arches modelled the wall plane and cast delineating shadows. The sloping brick sills were to become a characteristic of Webb's brick buildings.

Inside the house, in the medieval manner but without Gothic detailing, were arches and chimneypieces in the same red brick as the external walls. Unpainted wooden arris-beads around openings, exposed timber lintels, and some exposed roofing timbers, with bolts on view, echoed the timber-framing of the wellhead, and red clay quarry tiles in the hall and ground-floor passages did the same for the roofing material. The unusually wide hall terminated in a fine oak main staircase, above which the roof timbers of the tower were exposed. The staircase had strikingly attractive tall polygonal newel posts, and a simple close-boarded balustrade with circular holes for children to peep through; the construction of the stairs was exposed under the upper flight. The solid door from the porch was framed and boarded, and painted on the inside with geometric patterns in bright colours. The door to the garden porch was similar, but those of the major rooms on both storeys were six-panelled, and those of less important rooms were ledged, braced, and battened. The high-backed hall settle-cum-press, designed by Webb and still in place, has paintings by Morris on the cupboard doors.[14] Like the rest of the furniture Webb designed for the house, the settle was exceptionally strong in order to withstand Morris, who suffered from sudden muscular spasms which caused the frames of less robust seating to split apart. As Morris banged his tankard on tables when excited and was in the habit of whittling away the edge if kept waiting for his victuals, Webb had the tops of the two long matching oak dining tables bound in scoured iron fixed with clout-headed nails.[15] One table was kept in the hall, except when forming a T with the other in the dining room at feast times.

The dominant fitting in the dining room was the tall, brick fireplace, with a pointed relieving arch, a

Below Red House: from the east

herringbone tympanum, and old, blue-and-white tiles in the jambs; Webb's dresser (now plain but originally embellished with rich painted decoration) was effectively a fitting because of its massive size and weight.[16] The triple gables with trefoils of this piece joined the tiny crenellations on the staircase newels, and some simple scallops and notches on upper rails of panelling and the ends of lintels, in being the only purely ornamental details of the building itself, apart from the stained glass in some of the gallery windows on both floors, some of which had jolly birds and flowers painted by Webb.[17] There were no moulded cornices, skirtings, or architraves.

The sloping plaster ceiling of the drawing room extended into the roof space but it had no exposed braces or trusses in the medieval manner; the plain plaster ceiling followed the line of the scissor-trusses and raised tie-beams (the narrow strips of wood seen in twentieth-century photographs were added by later owners). The huge settle, which had been made to Morris's design for his and Burne-Jones's rooms in Red Lion Square, was adapted by Webb into a minstrels' gallery that prosaically gave access to the roof space of the west wing, and romantically served as a musician's gallery at Christmas. It also featured in the frequent high-spirited horseplay of the friends, on one occasion being the vantage point from which Charles Faulkner pelted Morris with apples until he unintentionally gave him a black eye. The dominant fitting, however, was Webb's tall, hooded, red-brick chimneypiece, an inventive reinterpretation of those in medieval great halls, with brick jambs rubbed into a D-shape. The rubbed and gauged brick arch of this and other fireplaces in the house reflected the external arches of the windows. The chimneypiece depended for its effect upon its overall shape and the pattern made by the bricks; undoubtedly it would have had a robust open grate of iron designed by Webb, perhaps with turned and knobbed posts, like the one he was soon to design for number 26 Queen Square, London.[18] The window-seated oriel with leaded lights of small diamond-shaped panes formed an intimate sitting area that also admitted southerly light into the room.

Webb had provided as simple a background as possible in order to give free rein to Morris and his schemes for the decoration of the house. The dining room was to have had a deep frieze of twelve embroidery panels, each bearing a figure in appliqué designed by Morris and depicting a Classical or

Arthurian heroine; a single tree was to have separated each pair of figures. The scheme was never completed, though a number of unfinished panels survive, including the St Catherine worked by Jane Morris.[19] The hall and drawing room were to have been painted by Burne-Jones, who recalled that as they talked of decorating the house, plans grew apace, with a 'romance for the drawing-room, a great favourite of ours called Sir Degrevaunt', and 'subjects of Troy for the hall, and a great ship carrying Greek heroes'.[20] He designed seven pictures from the poem and painted three of them that summer and autumn in tempera, which were hung in the drawing room and which still survive today; but the remaining four and the hall murals were not realized. The figures in the murals illustrating the Classical legend were to have been portrayed in medieval dress, and their ship – the only part of the scheme that was actually designed – would have been a fourteenth-century warship. These anomalies might have been decided upon in part to suit the rest of the decoration but they also demonstrated the extent of the hold that

Above Red House: the first-floor passage, looking east

Right Red House: a stained-glass window in the first-floor passage

the Middle Ages had on Morris and Burne-Jones.[21] Morris painted hangings with trees, parrots, and labels bearing his motto 'If I can', to hang below Burne-Jones's paintings in the drawing room, and Rossetti painted the doors of the enormous settle with figures illustrating Dante's *The Salutation of Beatrice*.[22] The ceiling of this room was painted by the Morrises with a repeating pattern of briar roses, but most ceilings

Right Red House: the ground-floor passage, looking east

in the house were painted with small geometrical patterns, some of which were probably inspired by pargeting seen in East Anglia. The lines of the patterns were pricked into the plaster to enable inexperienced painters such as Faulkner to do the work, and to facilitate future repainting.

There were no fitted carpets or wallpapers in the house, ironically in the case of the latter, as Morris was soon to become renowned as a designer and supplier of wallpaper. For himself, however, he preferred hangings or murals, or white distemper. Rugs from the East were to be used throughout, and all the bedrooms were intended to have hangings embroidered to Morris's designs, some of which were completed, including those for the main bedroom, in indigo blue wool serge with simple floral motifs.

The grounds of Red House are bounded by a high red-brick wall with close-boarded gates, which gives a sense of safety and seclusion. The garden was designed by Webb with Morris's help, according to Morris's daughter May.[23] Maintained by three gardeners, it was based on the gardens depicted in the medieval illuminated manuscripts that fascinated both Morris and Webb, and on which Morris based the garden he had described in 1856 in 'The Story of an Unknown Church', in the *Oxford and Cambridge Magazine*.[24] Lawns were created to the north and west of the house, the one to the west being a bowling green, and almost all the old fruit tress were saved. Between the road and the eastern part of the north wing, a large square enclosed by hedges was divided into four flowerbeds by rose-covered wattle fences. The beds, with entrances between each and bordered with lavender and rosemary, effectively formed small rooms within a larger room. The informally planted flowers were the old indigenous varieties that Morris had listed in 1856, and included lilies in midsummer and sunflowers in autumn. Georgie Burne-Jones recalled that the Pilgrims' Rest, lined with tiles designed by her husband, served as a 'small garden room', with a 'solid table in it, painted red' and a fitted bench where they 'sat and talked or looked out into the well court, of which two sides were formed by the house and the other two by a tall rose-trellis'.[25] 'This little court,' she continued, 'with its beautiful high-roofed brick well in the centre summed up the feeling of the whole place.' The court formed another outdoor room, and in his design for the

central wellhead Webb had made a most attractive feature and important compositional element out of a practical necessity. The small stable, in the north-east corner of the grounds, was built in red brick with a timber-framed, brick-nogged gable which, with the sides of the maids' bedroom dormer that it echoed, were the only references Webb made to the medieval building traditions of Kent. As with the wellhead, the stable had pragmatic and romantic connotations.

It housed three horses and a wagonette designed by Webb and made in Bexley, in which family and friends travelled to and from the station and explored the surrounding countryside, when its light frame covered with American cloth and lined with chintz hangings sometimes led local people to think that a travelling show was approaching.[26]

The house and garden were designed together and the designs were implemented at the same time.

with outdoor rooms, became almost obligatory features of Arts and Crafts gardens.

In the late nineteenth century, Red House came to be considered (as is still the case) the first Arts and Crafts house, which by implication means that it was believed to be a revolutionary building. Morris's friends, other laymen, and many architects – especially the young ones – believed that it was revolutionary in being built in red brick, an understandable mistake to make as the house was a startling contrast to the multifarious stuccoed villas and terraces of London. However, it was by no means the first red-brick house to be built in England in the nineteenth century. Pugin had used red brick for his first building, St Marie's Grange, Alderbury, the house he designed for himself and his family in 1835, over two decades before Red House was built; he employed it for many later buildings – the Bishop's House, Birmingham, for instance.[28] Also in brick were some of the country houses in the neo-Tudor and so-called 'Jacobethan' styles – popular in the middle third of the nineteenth century – by William Burn (1780–1870), Edward Blore (1787–1879), Anthony Salvin (1799–1881), and their followers.[29] Ruskin, in 'The Poetry of Architecture', a series of articles published in 1837 and 1838, had called for the use of materials suited to the terrain: for stone in hilly districts, and brick in flat country.[30] Street's book *Brick and Marble in the Middle Ages* (1855) increased the Gothic revivalists' interest in brick.[31] The use of it was also encouraged by reactions, including those of Pugin and Ruskin, against Regency stucco; by the need to combat the effects of soot in towns; by the repeal of the brick tax in 1850; and by the need of the Anglican Church to build a large number of churches and schools quickly and cheaply in the expanding towns and cities.

Red House, from the time of construction until the middle of the twentieth century, was mistakenly believed also to be revolutionary in form. This misapprehension is understandable, however, as the precedents were little known; at the time they were built, attention was given to the new churches, not the parsonages.[32] The Anglicans' need to build quickly and cheaply had resulted in vicarages, schools, and cottages being built in a simple manner, stripped of most – or, in the case of small cottages, all – Gothic ornament, and without any of the exaggerated rusticity of the Picturesque *cottage orné*. This so-called 'parsonage' style or manner was

They formed a unified whole, which was enhanced by the powerful chimneys and stair tower that pinned down the building, and the sweeping diagonals of the steep roof planes that, like the climbing plants, linked it to the ground. Webb disliked the brashness of newly built walls, so he probably suggested the extensive use of climbing plants on the house, and he may also have chosen some of the varieties, as his knowledge of plants was already wide, thanks to his father and his own botanical drawing teacher.

The garden of Red House, designed more than two decades before the name of the movement was introduced, is considered to be the first Arts and Crafts garden.[27] The highly unusual, formally arranged garden, with medieval connotations and outdoor rooms, beautiful wellhead, open porches, bowling green, rose-trellises, and orchard, suited the romantic outlook of the day and became very popular, increasingly so from the mid-1880s as the next generation of architects and designers began to come under Webb's and Morris's influence. Boldly bracketed timbers under a tiled roof, usually as covered ways and archways rather than wellheads, featured in most of Webb's later house designs and,

introduced by William Butterfield (1814–1900) in the 1840s, and quickly adopted by Street, William White, and other leading Gothic revivalists.[33] As Street's chief assistant, Webb had been involved with some of these buildings, in which simple vernacular forms were chosen to express the architectural hierarchy of church, vicarage, school, and cottage, as well as for economy and a long, maintenance-free life. By 1858, Webb had lost hope of any great architecture coming from the Gothic Revival or, indeed, from any revival of a past style. Though he liked and respected Street, Webb's thinking on architectural design now had more affinity with that of Butterfield, whom Webb had probably met through the Oxford Architectural Society, of which Butterfield too was a member. Butterfield's approach was less antiquarian and, in Lethaby's words, he viewed Gothic as a 'logical system and an essence not a source of cribs'.[34] He had served a two-year apprenticeship with a builder, the best preliminary training for an architect in the opinion of Webb, who had studied Butterfield's work in London and elsewhere, including the vicarages and cottages at Alvechurch (1855), Great Bookham (1856), and Baldersby (from 1855), and had come to admire the combination of innovation and common sense embodied in his work.[35] An indication of the strength of his admiration is that on declining to be considered for the job himself, Webb recommended Butterfield as the architect for the new Examination Schools in his beloved home town as the only 'architect living who […] could do something which would not severely hurt Oxford'.[36]

Butterfield was seventeen years Webb's senior but they had much in common. Both were bachelors who lived for their work, scorned professional bodies and publicity, and believed architecture to be a matter of good building rather than exhibition drawings, and whose aim was to design buildings that were clearly of their own time, not historical pastiches. Eventually, they were to become close enough to criticize one another's buildings freely, with Butterfield welcoming Webb's 'intelligent but far too favourable criticism'.[37]

When designing Red House in 1858, Webb had looked for inspiration to the only mid-nineteenth-century architecture he truly admired: the vicarages, village schools, and cottages of Butterfield and Street, which had been influenced by Pugin. As a result, Red House is essentially a 'parsonage'-manner

Left Laverstoke Parsonage, Hampshire (1858), by G E Street; designed whilst Webb was working for Street, this building suggests that Webb's views were influencing Street as well as vice versa, though Webb would have found these barge-boards too elaborate

building, with elements chiefly inspired by Butterfield. Butterfield had already used some sash windows, for instance; and the composition, modelling of the roofs, and details of the chimneys of Red House reflect his work. The oriel supported on a pier probably originated in old English examples though it resembles that of Butterfield's Alvechurch Rectory, and though the stair tower has been thought to be French-inspired, its bell-cage is very like that on the ridge of Butterfield's school at Great Bookham, a building Webb had sketched.[38] The dormer window in the maids' bedroom and the row of round windows of the first-floor gallery certainly do reflect buildings seen in France by Webb and Morris during their boating holiday, however. The clerestory fenestration of the church at Mantes inspired the circular windows.

Left Red House: the dining-room fireplace

Opposite Red House: the
main staircase, the landing,
and ceiling of the tower,
bearing the original
decoration

So Red House was not revolutionary in form, but
it appears to have been the first 'parsonage'-manner
house to be built for a middle-class gentleman's own
use, and the first house of its size to be built in this
manner without any Gothic ornament. It has no
cusped window headings or Gothic mouldings such
as appear on Butterfield's vicarages. Webb had rejected
Ruskin's contention in *The Seven Lamps of Architecture*
that a building without ornament is not architecture,[39]
and he had taken heed of the warning in the
Ecclesiologist in 1858 against excessive originality. These
factors, coupled with his own liking for simplicity,
ensured that he kept his inventive capabilities severely
under control. Red House has just enough modelling
and patterning to avoid the ostentation of the over-
plain, which Webb abhorred. It is an unsurpassed
masterpiece of the 'parsonage' manner.

In later years, Webb often told his chief assistant,
George Jack, that he never wanted to see or hear
about Red House again and that no architect ought
to be allowed to build a house until he was forty; and
to Lethaby he spoke disparagingly of his first
buildings as being of his 'Gothic days', although
when Charles Eastlake asked him for samples to
include in *A History of the Gothic Revival* (1872),
Webb refused on the grounds that his work did not
'properly come under the category of the "Gothic
Revival in England"'.[40] Perhaps Webb thought with
hindsight that Red House looked a little too much
like a rectory and – judging by the fact that he soon
began to use simply moulded architraves – that some
of its interior finishes could have been improved. He
would certainly have regretted its embodiment of
French influences because, within a year or two of
designing Red House, he had become convinced
that – in any country – new buildings should reflect,
but not copy, only the traditional national and local
architecture. The house was not timber-framed,
which is probably the foremost architectural tradition
of Kent; and though the use of brick had been
widespread in the county from the sixteenth century,
Webb ignored the brick of the immediate area,
which was yellow-brown in colour, and brought in
red bricks from elsewhere. The design for the
proposed enlargement demonstrates that by 1864 he
was paying greater attention to local vernacular
buildings, a subject that had interested him since his
youth. Three of the upper walls were to have been
timber-framed, those to the east and south being
hung with red tiles, and the western wall facing
Morris's service wing having brick-nogged panels
and an oak-framed oriel.

Webb would also have become aware that the
house had some minor faults. Although the
arrangement of the rooms, major and minor, was
convenient for all who lived and worked in the
building, the housekeeper's and maids' bedrooms
were very mean, and the latter lacked a view. The
fruit trees could be seen above the high sills of the
kitchen windows but because they faced west, the
room was at its hottest just when the evening meal
was being prepared. The narrow secondary staircase
with winders would have been a hindrance to maids
carrying wide trays or heavy jugs of hot water. The
north-facing orientation of the drawing room,
though doubtless arranged to protect the envisaged
paintings and hangings, had clearly become a source

Above Red House: the drawing-room oriel

first-floor solars, of course, and in the thirteenth century halls on the upper floor were fairly common, for example Old Soar, Plaxtol, Kent (c. 1290). Red House and Alvechurch Rectory each have L-shaped plans but, Red House having fewer rooms, Webb was able to place his passages on the outer walls, where they received natural light, in a room-and-passage arrangement such as that used by Pugin in two wings of the U-shaped Bishop's House, which also had a stair tower in the angle between the wings.[42] As Red House was designed for easy extension, and Webb's later schemes for doing so further enclosed the well court and continued the ground-floor passage along its eastern side, Webb clearly had a medieval cloister in mind. Red House was highly unusual in having a living hall, complete with a fireplace, settle, long dining table and several chairs. At least one great hall in a Gothic Revival country house had already been furnished as a living room but to utilise the entrance-cum-stair hall as such in a smaller house was not common, perhaps even unique, in 1858, though some earlier houses of comparable size did have large stair halls, including Pugin's The Grange.

As Red House had been influenced to a degree by Pugin, Butterfield, and Street, the position and relative importance of each room might have been expected to be obvious externally. The drawing room is expressed on the exterior by having its own roof, the highest one; and the main staircase, the hub of the house, is expressed by its large windows and pyramid-roofed tower. However, the maids' staircase, drawing room, studio, kitchen, and adjacent pantry, all have windows with similar pointed relieving arches, and from the outside the studio appears to be two distinct rooms. Webb was clearly not overly concerned with revealing the use or hierarchy of rooms on the exterior. The many window and roof shapes could be interpreted as deliberate Ruskinian changefulness but Webb has imposed a sense of order and rhythm, and the window sizes are always related to the volume and use of the rooms they serve. Even the problem of scale presented by large studio windows has been solved satisfactorily by combining two sashes of domestic size under a pointed arch with a circular light in the tympanum.

Although it was not illustrated in the architectural press for many years, Red House was widely known amongst artistic and literary circles in London from

of regret, as Webb had never repeated it, even though too much sunlight in such rooms was considered undesirable at the time. Red House is, in fact, adequately lit even on a dull day in winter. Some of the chimneys had to be heightened in 1861 to prevent smoking; Webb took the greatest pains to ensure his flues worked well in all his later buildings.

The plan of Red House was also considered to be revolutionary during the second half of the nineteenth and the early decades of the twentieth century. In fact, L-shaped plans had featured already in some of the parsonages. Webb's plan is strikingly similar to that of Butterfield's Alvechurch Rectory (Hereford and Worcestershire) designed just three years earlier, though the latter did not have a first-floor drawing room; the Bishop's House by Pugin did have one, however, and it was partly in the roof like Webb's.[41] Many medieval English houses had

the time it was built, and quite soon thereafter in America. The Morrises kept open house for their friends, many of whom were prominent members of those circles. Amongst those who visited them were the architects William Burges (1827–81), Robert Edis (1839–1927), and Bodley. Shaw and Street would have known all about the building through their friend Webb, of course. Swinburne, Tennyson, and Boyce knew the house, Browning and his wife were kept informed of the progress of building and decorating it, and Rossetti wrote of it to Ruskin's friend, Professor C E Norton of Cambridge, Massachusetts, and described it as being a 'noble work in every way and more a poem than a house […] but an admirable place to live in too'.[43]

During the 1890s and early 1900s, Red House and its garden became known to a younger generation of architects and designers. The first published description apparently occurred in 1897, after which it featured in many papers and books.[44] Webb's young admirers would seek it out, of course; other architects and designers would learn of it through the *Studio*, and no doubt many of them would visit the editor, Charles Holme, at the house. The reuniting of the decorative arts with architecture, which had governed the interior design of the house and culminated in the founding of Morris, Marshall, Faulkner & Co., became a major governing principle of the Arts and Crafts movement. The part-time community of painters living and working together at Red House presaged the Arts and Crafts communities that were established around the turn of the century: for example the Guild of Handicraft founded in 1888 in London by Charles Robert Ashbee (1863–1942), and moved to the Cotswolds in 1901. From the early 1890s, the L-shaped, room-and-passage plan of Red House, in

several cases including a stair tower as a fulcrum, was adopted for many Arts and Crafts houses, including influential examples by Lethaby, Charles Francis Annesley Voysey (1857–1941), Mackay Hugh Baillie Scott (1865–1945), and Charles Rennie Mackintosh (1868–1928).[45]

The plan of Red House, the essential simplicity, straightforwardness, and practicality of the building, and the dependence upon good workmanship, composition and proportions, and the qualities of materials, instead of upon style motifs and exterior ornament, had a wide influence on Arts and Crafts architects in Britain. Ultimately, Webb's later buildings, and the approach to architectural design that governed them, which he developed during the 1860s, had a much greater impact.[46] However, the Arts and Crafts architects and those who promulgated their work regarded Red House as a new beginning, and venerated it as such. The influential writer Lawrence Weaver, for example, in 1922 made Red House the subject of the first chapter in his *Small*

Country Houses of Today because it was a 'fresh starting-point for domestic architecture, of which the importance cannot be exaggerated', and stood for a 'new epoch of new ideals and practices'.[47]

Hermann Muthesius, who described and illustrated it in his highly influential *Das englische Haus*, also saw Red House as a new beginning. In the second edition (1908–11), he describes it as being 'highly important in the history of art' because it was the 'first private house of the new artistic culture, the first house to be conceived and built as a unified whole inside and out, the very first example in the history of the modern house', with a revolutionary interior and an exterior that was 'unique in its time'.[48] Muthesius, like Weaver, seems to have been unaware of Pugin's simple houses and presbyteries, or of Butterfield's and Street's parsonages. Largely through Muthesius's book, Red House became known in mainland Europe, where it influenced Arts and Crafts architects and, in due course and because of the same factors, the development of the architecture of the Modern movement, of which Webb came to be regarded as a pioneer.

When it was built in 1859, Red House was an early example of a new type of middle-class dwelling, the small house in the country, made possible by the increasing prosperity of that class and by the recently expanded railway network. It was also an example of a relatively new category of building, the studio-house individually designed for a specific artist, and it was the first of these to be designed for a gentleman who hoped to become a professional painter but was not yet an established one. It was unique also at the time in being intended for use by the owner's artist friends during weekends and holiday periods. It was not as revolutionary in design and plan as was thought but it was an unsurpassed and masterly interpretation of the 'parsonage' manner. Exceptionally well built, warm and welcoming on the outside, informal and spacious within, and not in the least grand or pretentious, Red House fulfilled Morris's needs, and those of his family and close companions, on practical, visual, and emotional grounds. An astonishingly assured first building, with which Webb achieved his aim of creating a consistent whole, it demonstrated that his training and experience had honed his intuitive feeling for good composition and

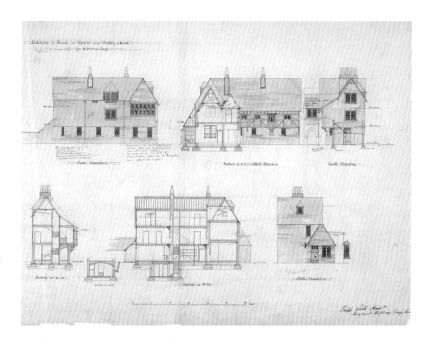

pleasing proportions, and that he knew how to use contrasts of line and volume to impart liveliness. With his first commission, Webb had proved that a building without ornament could be an outstandingly fine work of architecture.

Red House has been fortunate in always having had appreciative owners, who have looked after it well and made only minimal changes to it. During the second half of the twentieth century, it was owned successively by three architects and their spouses, the last being Edward Hollamby and his wife Doris, who became tenants in 1952 and owners of the house in 1964.[49] The Hollambys regularly showed members of the public round the house, and with the aim of ensuring the continuance of this after their time, the Red House (Bexleyheath) Trust was established in 1998. Hollamby died in 1999 and, thanks to the efforts of the Red House trustees, the future of the building and regular public access to it and its garden was secured in 2003, when it was acquired by the National Trust, with the aid of donors and benefactors. Some of the original decoration remains, with Webb's fittings and a couple of large pieces of his furniture. Morris and Webb would doubtless have been surprised and amused to know that an increasing horde of pilgrims comes to the district to see not Canterbury Cathedral, but Red House.

Above Red House: one of Webb's drawings of 1864 for the proposed extension to accommodate Edward Burne-Jones and his family (Victoria & Albert Museum / V&A Images)

Opposite Red House: the wellhead, with the garden porch – the Pilgrims' Rest – behind it on the right

Chapter 3

MORRIS, MARSHALL, FAULKNER & CO

Morris, Marshall, Faulkner & Co., or the Firm as its partners termed it informally, was established in April 1861 with William Morris, poet and painter, in overall control. As Morris's first biographer Mackail noted in 1899, the monastery of Morris's and Burne-Jones's Oxford dreams had been realized as a workshop and the Brotherhood had become a firm registered under the Companies Acts.[1] Morris's six partners were: the artists Edward Burne-Jones, Dante Gabriel Rossetti, and Ford Madox Brown; Charles Faulkner, who had left his post as a Mathematical Tutor and Fellow of University College, Oxford, to study civil engineering in London; Peter Paul Marshall, a surveyor, sanitary engineer, amateur painter, and close friend of Madox Brown; and Philip Webb, the architect, who with typical modesty ensured that his name did not form part of that of the firm.[2] Each partner would pursue his own independent career, in Morris's case as a poet and a painter, and when called upon would work for the Firm on commissioned designs and products for the

Below The round table designed by Webb c. 1860, almost certainly for Red House (Collection of the Society of Antiquaries of London, at Kelmscott Manor)

market. It appears from his letter to F B Guy, the private tutor who had coached Morris for matriculation to Oxford, that Morris had had the basic idea for some time, probably from the hilarious days he and his friends had spent decorating the Union Debating Hall.[3] Working together for the Firm, designing and making by hand well-designed artefacts which they hoped to make available to the relatively poor as well as the wealthy, they would also be actively pursuing their crusade for the improvement of art and the reunification of the fine and decorative arts.

A prospectus was issued, stating that the partners, 'described as 'Fine Art Workmen', having found the want of some one place, where they could either obtain or get produced work of a genuine and beautiful character' proposed to supply artwork and goods designed by themselves and made under their supervision, in various fields: the mural decoration of 'dwelling-houses, churches or public buildings'; architectural carving; stained glass; all branches of metal work, including jewellery; furniture in natural wood, or wood enhanced with other materials; embroidery of all kinds; stamped leather, and work in similar materials; and 'every article necessary for domestic use'.[4] In 1861 and the following year, to raise capital for the Firm, Morris sold some of his thirteen Devon Great Consol shares to his mother, who had given them to him when he reached twenty-one and who now loaned the £100 with which the Firm started trading. The other partners each took a £20 share and put forward £1. Morris was to receive an annual salary of £150 as the general manager, and Faulkner the same as bookkeeper and business manager.

The Firm was not the first to be established with the aim of improving the decorative arts. Concern had been expressed since the 1840s about the low standard of design of many British machine-made goods compared to those of some other northern European countries, and attempts had been made to improve matters. Henry Cole (1808–82), for example, the first director of the South Kensington Museum and an initiator and organiser of the Great Exhibition of 1851 and later the controlling secretary and reformer of the Government Schools of Design, believed that the standard could be improved by the establishing of an association of designers and artists, by better teaching of design, and through the greater involvement of the designers in the manufacturing process. He founded the short-lived Summerley's Art Manufactures in 1847 with the aim of improving public taste and the design of machine-made goods by providing manufacturers with good designs by himself and other artists and designers.

Morris and his partners had no intention of becoming involved in any way with machine production in factories. These self-styled artists were to design and make or closely supervise the making of the Firm's goods by hand, using medieval techniques. In this, Pugin had preceded them by over three decades, by establishing in 1829 a firm to produce furniture and decorative details by hand to his designs, using similar techniques. Unfortunately, the business failed in 1831 because of the high cost of such methods. However, he later worked in association with three trusted craftsmen whose individual firms executed his designs. From the late 1830s, John Hardman executed Pugin's designs in metalwork (chiefly ecclesiastical) and stained glass; and in the 1840s J G Crace the, interior decorator, made his wallpaper and textiles and much of his furniture (the firms of Gillow, Myers, and Holland also made Pugin furniture), and Herbert Minton executed his designs for ceramics, including tiles. In these ventures, Pugin successfully demonstrated that by combining hand-finishing techniques with up-to-date and carefully supervised machine production, decorative artefacts of good design and high quality could be produced at a price that made them available to a wider market.[5] As a result of Pugin's efforts, the Morris firm from the start had stiff competition from established businesses that specialized in high-quality stained glass and church and domestic furnishings, including those of Hardman, Crace, and Minton, and in the case of stained glass, Clayton and Bell.

After Pugin's early death in 1852, his lead in the Gothic Revival had been taken by Ruskin, under whose influence many of the revivalists, failing to learn from Pugin's experience, came to believe that the only way to improve the decorative crafts lay in the complete rejection of machine-made products. Ruskin contended that medieval decorative art was lively and beautiful because the craftsmen, working to their own designs, had imparted to the artefact something of their enjoyment in doing the work. Machine-made goods in his view were worthless because they carried no trace of the human mind and hand.[6] Morris and his partners concurred with him in these matters, hence the resolve to produce their artefacts by hand. Under Ruskin's influence, the concept of art as being the expression of man's pleasure in his work rather than a luxury had become a fundamental element of Webb's and of Morris's thinking. 'Living art – after all is said – is but a representation of right living,' Webb later informed Lethaby.[7]

The partners were fascinated by the notion of medieval artists and craftsmen working together, with shared enthusiasm and beliefs, on a church that would celebrate their combined talents and enjoyment in the work and would be an ecclesiastical palace of folk art for the people. Through the Firm, by designing stained-glass windows and embroidered altar cloths, and by painting the fittings and ceilings of chancels, the partners too would be creating art for the benefit and enjoyment of local communities whilst satisfying their strong need for individual freedom through their independent careers. It was a matter of common sense to concentrate initially on ecclesiastical decorative art if the Firm were to be a success. The great upsurge of vitality in the Anglican

Above A candlestick designed by Webb for Morris, Marshall, Faulkner & Co., from a photograph by the author (the candlestick is in the Collection of the Society of Antiquaries of London, at Kelmscott Manor)

Left A hand-blown glass goblet, with coiled decoration; Webb created this design in 1860 for Morris, and James Powell & Sons made a set for Red House in 1861, the year this firm began making them for Morris, Marshall, Faulkner & Co. (William Morris Gallery, London)

Church and the rapid growth of industrial towns meant that hundreds of new churches were being built in England and Wales, and countless old ones were being refurbished.[8] The partners were acquainted with Ruskin and many of the Gothic Revival architects through the Hogarth Club, and Webb, a member of the influential Oxford Architectural and History Society, already knew three of the leading Gothic revivalists, namely Street and Bodley,[9] of whom he was a close friend, and Butterfield. The partners took advantage of this opportunity and the Firm soon became known for its ecclesiastical stained glass and decoration.

All the partners except perhaps Marshall had had some experience in the decorative arts by 1861. Madox Brown had designed furniture, and both he and Burne-Jones had designed stained-glass windows for James Powell and Sons. Webb, and for a shorter time Morris, had had practical experience in various handicrafts whilst with Street, and Morris had designed a few items of furniture for the lodgings he shared in London with Burne-Jones. Webb, who had been trained by Billing to design in various different materials, had had furniture, candlesticks, stained glass, and table glass made to his designs for Red

House. However, it was clear that skilled help with the painting and firing of stained glass, and the making of furniture, would be necessary from the start. George Campfield, an experienced glass painter whom Rossetti had met at the Working Men's College, was taken on in 1861 after his ability had been tested by Webb, who was knowledgeable about the making of stained glass.[10] Charles Holloway, a fret glazier, was engaged the same year, with three apprentices from the nearby Industrial Home for Destitute Boys, one of the managers of which was Major (later Colonel) Gillum, the Hogarth Club member for whom Webb had already designed a cottage.[11] Twelve men and boys were working in the Firm's London workshop in Red Lion Square by 1862, and the partners were taking an active part in the production of other goods. As early as 1861, Webb's jewellery designs were being executed by an independent jeweller working in the same premises, his table glasses were being made by Powell & Sons, and a local cabinetmaker, a Mr Curwen, was executing his furniture designs.[12]

The partners' womenfolk also played an active role in the production process. Georgiana Burne-Jones, who before her marriage had studied drawing at the Government School of Design in Kensington; Jane Morris and her sister Elizabeth Burden; Faulkner's sisters Lucy, who helped with the Firm's work until around 1870, chiefly by painting figures on tiles, and Kate; and George Campfield's wife, all helped to produce the Firm's goods, mainly the embroidered items and painted tiles.[13] Female outworkers laboured under them and, from a very young age, Morris's daughters Jenny (b. 1861) and May (b. 1862) were embroidering, too. Miss Burden and Kate Faulkner (d. 1898) worked for Morris for many years. Kate also worked freelance for other establishments, but for the Firm and its later manifestation she designed painted pottery, wallpapers, and probably textiles, and executed ornament in gilded or silvered gesso on the panels of Webb's coved settles, and on grand pianos, at least one of the last to the designs of Webb, who referred to her as 'that most excellent of workwomen'.[14] A fine example of their joint work in gesso is the many-panelled, silvered and lacquered reredos of 1886 for the Whitelands College Chapel (then in Chelsea, now in Wandsworth), which includes four panels bearing the symbols of the Evangelists.[15]

The Firm may not have been the first of its kind

Right A goblet, with ornamental prunts, designed by Webb in 1862 for manufacture by James Powell & Sons (Birmingham Museums & Art Gallery)

Above Three tiles painted with a hare, a raven, and a cockerel, to Webb's designs of 1869 for the first and third, and 1870 for the second (Nether Hall, Pakenham, Suffolk)

but it appears to have been unique at the time in involving middle-class women in this way. In the 1860s, it simply was not done for middle-class wives to work for monetary reward, and for the unfortunate spinsters of this class who lacked family support, there were few congenial ways to earn their living. With her humble background, Jane Morris might not have seen anything unusual in being able to join in the communal work with the men, but it could only have happened in an artistic group, indeed perhaps only in this particular one, with its unique respect for the freedom of individuals of both sexes. Better education in the arts, particularly the decorative arts, and consequently more agreeable careers for those in need of them, became available to the women of the next generation in part as a result of the work of the pioneering women of the Firm.[16]

Although Morris was officially the general manager and knew something of commerce, his father having been a leading London discount broker, only Webb had actual business experience, namely seven years of helping to run first Billing's and then Street's office and two years conducting his own practice. Not surprisingly, he played a vital role in getting the designs finished and executed, more or less on time, throughout the early years of the Firm. In Street's office, he had controlled an ebullient bunch of young assistants and pupils; for the Firm, he managed to get the necessary work done by a group of individualists who, despite their enthusiasm, were also absorbed to a high degree in their own chosen careers. He probably had to browbeat them severely to get sufficient items ready for the 1862 International Exhibition at South Kensington. The Firm enjoyed considerable success at the exhibition, selling almost £150 worth of goods, being offered

several commissions, and receiving commendatory medals for the exhibits on its two stands – stained glass and painted furniture respectively – as well as both favourable and unfavourable criticism.[17]

In November 1862, Morris designed his first wallpaper, *Trellis*, on which the birds were drawn by Webb; because of the failure of an attempt to print it in oils, it was not the first to reach the market.[18] The inadequate size of the workshops forced Morris to have the Firm's wallpapers printed by Jeffreys of Islington. By 1864, the range of products had increased, and larger premises were needed. The scheme for moving the Firm's workshops to Upton and adding a wing to Red House for Burne-Jones and his family having been abandoned, chiefly because the needy painter felt there was more chance of receiving commissions in London, where Morris, with his private income depleted and himself

Left Whitelands College Chapel, Chelsea (now in Wandsworth), London: the emblem of St John in the reredos of 1886, decorated by Kate Faulkner to Webb's design

Above 'Trellis', the first wallpaper to be designed for Morris, Marshall, Faulkner & Co. (in 1862 by William Morris, with birds by Webb); it was printed by Jeffrey & Co. for the Firm from 1864

debilitated by rheumatic fever and deeply upset by his wife's burgeoning love affair with Rossetti, and his family had to move in 1865 so that he would be able to devote more time to the business. Soon thereafter, the dyeing, weaving, and printing of textiles, which were to become the staple productions of the Firm, were taking place at number 26 Queen Square, a large Queen Anne house in Bloomsbury, which had become the Morris family home, and the showroom, office, and workshop of the Firm.[19]

George Warington Taylor (1835–70) was appointed business manager of the Firm in 1865, Faulkner no longer being able to devote time to the accounts, having returned to teaching at Oxford the previous year. Taylor had come to know the partners well since introducing himself to Morris at Red House around 1860. Knowledgeable and cultured, educated at Eton but having fallen on hard times, Taylor proved to be an efficient and expert manager of the Firm, the products of which he had been an enthusiastic admirer since the beginning, as his letters to his friend the architect Edward Robert Robson (1836–1917) reveal.[20] Unfortunately for Webb, however, Taylor's tuberculosis forced him to move to Hastings for the sea air in 1866, so Webb had to take up his hectoring role again, constantly urged on by letters from Taylor. Having on several occasions demanded that Webb ask his partners to retrench, in a letter to him of 1869 Taylor criticised Burne-Jones, Morris and Rossetti for egging one another on to

'every kind of useless expense' to the extent that the balance sheets were 'strained to the last penny'. He went on to urge Webb to inspect the books almost weekly. 'We want from you vigorous, stern action, if the firm is to be saved,' he thundered; and added, 'If you do not act no one else will.'[21] Webb did act as requested, and his unstinting efforts on the Firm's and Taylor's behalf made it possible for the latter to remain as manager until his early death in 1870.

At Taylor's urging, the partners voted Webb '£80 per an. as consulting manager of the firm' in 1867 in recognition of his work.[22] Webb must have demurred as Taylor, having previously chided him for never asking for as much as a design had cost him to produce, told Webb by letter that he could no longer allow him to work for the Firm for over five hours a week without payment.[23] In order that Taylor might get a living and Morris extra money, it was absolutely necessary to be able to appeal to Webb on business matters, Taylor wrote, and added that they could not 'move a step' without his professional architectural assistance. Therefore, unless Webb agreed to be paid, the Firm must 'come to a stop' because sponging upon him was degrading. Webb concurred but left the money in the Firm's coffers to keep it on a sounder footing, even though his own financial position at the time was not good. Despite doing all its architectural work, a great deal of designing in almost all fields and, in the early years, many managerial tasks, his earnings from the Firm averaged only £43 a year but with them he was able to buy furniture and fabrics, beer and wine, cheaply through the business.[24] The fact that he was not paid at nearly such a high rate for his designs as were Burne-Jones and Rossetti would not worry Webb in the least because he always preferred to give more than he received.

After Taylor died, George Wardle (d. 1910), who had joined the Firm as a draughtsman and had become a close friend of Webb, was appointed general manager. Webb was busy in his own practice by then but he continued to serve as consulting architect and chief furniture designer. In December 1873, however, he told Morris by letter that although he did not doubt the Firm's stability it was an unfair state of affairs that he, Webb, no longer having any control over the business, should be in a position to benefit from its success or to become involved in any adversity that might befall it. He therefore proposed to withdraw from the Firm 'as a mercantile partnership', whilst keeping to the 'friendly and artistic conjunction' so long as he could be of any use to it. In a postscript, he gave Morris permission to use the letter or part of it in telling the other partners of his, Webb's, proposal, and added that any proportion of shares belonging to him should remain in the business so long as required, at a small rate of interest.[25] Webb's wish not to benefit from the work of others is not surprising because he disapproved of unearned income but it was completely out of character for him to be concerned about possible disadvantages to himself. Therefore, it is likely that in writing his letter, Webb hoped to smooth Morris's way towards having the Firm dissolved and re-formed in his, Morris's, ownership.[26] This course of action might have been suggested to Morris by Webb, who would have known of his friend's increasing financial problems if only by noting that Morris had begun at last to heed Taylor's demands that he curb his habitual over-spending on books, wine, and lavish entertainment of friends, and devote all his attention to the Firm. Whatever the case, meetings to discuss the dissolving of the Firm took place in 1874, sometimes with solicitors present because Rossetti, Brown, and Marshall strongly opposed the proposal. After thirteen years of being liable, with the other partners, for any debts the Firm might have accrued, they resented being cut off from the profits just when it seemed about to become extremely successful in the field of domestic interior decoration. Webb, Burne-Jones, and Faulkner made no claims on the business, in order to help Morris. Webb also renounced the arrears of salary voted to him in 1867, though the £640 due would have made his own practice more secure.[27] After considerable acrimony, it was announced on 31 March 1875 that the Firm would be dissolved and reformed under the name Morris & Co., with Morris as sole proprietor. The three disgruntled partners each received £1000 from him in compensation for loss of profits. In the case of Rossetti, Morris probably paid up with relief. Having already ousted him from the joint tenancy of Kelmscott Manor, which the two men had taken partly so that Rossetti and Jane could spend some time together in privacy, Morris would no longer have to be in contact with this betrayer of good fellowship.[28]

Webb provided product designs when called upon to do so until Morris died in 1896 but not nearly as many as he had made for the Firm. He secured many important interior decoration commissions for Morris & Co. from his own clients, most of whom bought many of the Firm's products, and he continued to provide the encouragement and comradeship on which Morris depended. Morris paid royalties on repeated designs to Webb, who handled any necessary architectural work for his friend's firm when necessary. Burne-Jones produced designs for stained glass on request. The new firm rapidly achieved financial success, and by the mid-1880s it had become the most famous interior design firm in Europe and North America.

Morris, Marshall, Faulkner & Co. had faced stiff competition in the ecclesiastical field during its early days. Pugin and others had revived medieval methods of making coloured glass in the 1840s, and of treating stained glass as a mosaic in contrast to the painting of pictures on clear glass that had become popular in the eighteenth century. Well-designed stained glass of high quality was already available in 1861. However, the Gothic revivalist architects who knew the partners of the Firm well could be certain that with so many painters involved, the designs and colours of the windows were likely to be good. Equally importantly, they could trust their peer Webb to ensure that the glass would be in harmony with the character and detailing of the building, would not dominate the interior, and would admit enough light to illuminate the architectural details as well as the hymn books.

Webb's good friend Bodley, having seen the early panels made for the 1862 exhibition where the high quality led some critics to believe that they were of reused medieval glass, commissioned the Firm to design and make the windows for his church of All Saints, Selsley, Gloucestershire (1859–62) in 1861 and the following year for his St Michael and All Angels, Brighton (1858–62) and St Martin's-on-the-Hill, Scarborough (1861–63). As was to become customary, Webb inspected the buildings, measured the window openings, designed and made a coloured drawing of the overall arrangement taking into account the character and design of the building as a whole, and prepared the larger-scale drawings. Inspired by the windows of Merton College Chapel, Oxford of c. 1294, and by those in the nave aisles of York Minster of c. 1310–20, he placed the richly coloured figure panels at a convenient height to be read and surrounded them with clear glass quarries bearing a delicate pattern in a pale colour.[29] Effectively, three horizontal bands ran round the interior,

Below All Saints, Selsley, Gloucestershire: the rose window (1862) in the west wall, illustrating *The Creation*, with three circular tracery lights designed by Webb (numbers 1, 6, and 8, clockwise from the top: *The Spirit of God on the Waters*; *Birds and Fishes*; *Adam Naming the Beasts*); the others are assumed to be by William Morris

unifying the windows and counterbalancing the vertical lines of the architecture, the upper and lower ones admitting ample light even though each quarry bore a delicate pattern in a pale colour. Burne-Jones and Rossetti designed most of the early figure panels, which Morris and Webb combined into what Webb termed a consistent whole, despite the differences in treatment. The quarries, much of the background patternwork, the canopies and pedestals for the figures, the lettering and layout of inscriptions, the

symbols of the Evangelists, and many of the tracery lights, were designed by Webb from 1861 until 1869, when his involvement began to decrease through pressure of work in his practice. Charles Sewter, in his detailed study of the Firm's and Morris & Co.'s glass, considers that Webb's 'pattern-work and borders have a distinction unmatched elsewhere in nineteenth-century stained glass'; and he avers that when Webb's planning ceased to appear in the Firm's windows 'something irretrievable was lost'.[30]

All Webb's designs for stained glass exhibit great confidence and a thorough understanding of the medium and its qualities, and his brush drawings in sepia for the animals demonstrate a skilful and pleasing surety of hand. His admirable lettering looks fresh today after well over a century. Webb's circular *Adam Naming the Animals* for the west window at Selsley is particularly good, with a fine lion and deer, and the many simply drawn yet full-of-life animals and birds in his smaller tracery lights or within his partners' figure panels, are delightful, notably the bear being tickled by Adam in Madox Brown's west lancet window at Scarborough.[31] May Morris considered that the Evangelist symbols in the Scarborough north aisle windows were the most vigorous and distinguished she had seen in old or new work, and she rightly praised Webb for filling the round spaces 'dextrously with living curves arranged without contortion', and with real creatures rather than heraldic emblems.[32] Normally, Morris added the colour to his partners' monochrome cartoons for the figure panels but in the first two years, in cases where all or several windows were to be provided by the Firm, including the first three commissions, Webb indicated the major colours on his layout drawings, which suggests that he might have had some say in choosing them.[33]

The lead cames holding together the pieces of coloured glass formed part of the design of the windows in the medieval tradition and, at Webb's insistence, the necessary grid of strong iron supports was frankly revealed instead of being hidden behind the darker glass. Coloured glass of medieval quality made by Powell and Sons was used but the painting and re-firing of it was done in the Firm's own workshops. Despite the belief of some contemporary critics, the partners used medieval windows as inspirations for new designs, not as copybooks, and their work was much more inventive than was generally appreciated. It is not surprising that the borders, quarries, and patternwork designed by Webb for the east windows of the south aisle of Bodley's Brighton church, for example, are not in a Gothic style, as he had decided before he left Street in 1859 that modern Gothic was a contradiction in terms. However, designing to suit the character of the specific church afterwards led him to feel that sometimes the result had been too overtly Gothic, as for example his canopies in the windows of 1865 for St Giles' Church in Camberwell, London, which had

been designed in 1844 by Sir George Gilbert Scott.[34] In 1872, the Firm was asked to design, make, and insert stained glass into the windows of the chapel in Castle Howard, North Yorkshire (1699). For this, one of his last stained-glass schemes, Webb designed inventive Classical canopies to suit the grand pillared interior, and placed the new glass into hinged panels to give the congregation a better view of them and to avoid disrupting the symmetrical exterior elevation of the west wing, which Sir Thomas Robinson (c. 1702–77) had added to the great edifice otherwise designed by Sir John Vanbrugh (1664–1726).[35]

Under Webb's influence, the early windows of the Firm had a calm simplicity missing in some contemporary stained glass, a simplicity that ensured the glass would not swamp the architectural details of the interior. Webb's sensitive approach, coupled with his ensuring of the admission of sufficient light to reveal and enhance the details, secured further commissions for the Firm from Gothic Revival architects. After 1869, without Webb in control of the overall scheme, the general character of the windows, whilst undoubtedly beautiful, under Burne-Jones's increased influence became less appropriate for an architectural element and more like paintings. It is more elaborate, with sumptuous colouring and vigorously curving figures filling the whole of the lights. The fact that Webb had always been aware of the inherent danger in Burne-Jones's pictorial approach is revealed by his explanation to Powell of 1904 that though the Firm's glass was good

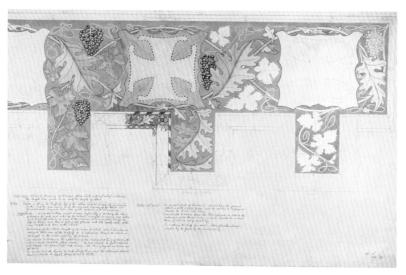

Above The Rochester Diocesan Deaconess Institution Chapel (1896–97): one of Webb's drawings (dated 1898–99; pencil, ink, and watercolour) for the embroidered altar frontal, which was worked by May Morris (Victoria & Albert Museum / V&A Images)

in comparison with such work by others, it was only a partial success as 'it never could be right good craftsmen's glass, because there were no draughtsmen who could translate the beautiful pictures into effective painting for glass', and because it had been impossible for Morris himself to make the glass that was used.[36] The east window of Webb's St Martin's, Brampton, Cumbria (1874–75), is a beautiful example of a Morris & Co. window of the 1880s. Commissioned in 1880 by the Honourable George Howard (1843–1911) as a memorial to his father, it has fifteen panels, each designed specially by Burne-Jones.[37] Loyal as ever, from first accepting the commission, Webb had shared the vicar's intention that any stained glass in the church would be by Morris & Co., and he had made the interior sufficiently light to accommodate it (see chapter 12).

In being autonomous works of art rather than a part of the whole, the windows of Morris & Co. were often not fully in harmony with the architecture of a church. Consequently, the leading Gothic revivalists, including Street, Sir George Gilbert Scott, and John Pollard Seddon (1827–1906), began commissioning windows from elsewhere. Morris's decision in 1877 to cease supplying stained glass for use in medieval churches (apart from those in which one or more of his windows were already installed), although prompted chiefly by his wish to discourage so-called 'restorations' (see chapter 8), suggests that he was aware of the slight incongruity.[38] In spite of this, however, Morris & Co. remained famous for its stained glass until the firm was dissolved after the Second World War.

The Firm undertook the decoration of church interiors in its early years, a fine example being the work in Bodley's St Martin's-on-the-Hill, Scarborough (1861–63) where Webb and Morris designed and painted the chancel ceiling. Webb spent six days on the painting. Campfield painted the figures on the ten panels of the pulpit to the designs of Morris, Rossetti and Madox Brown, and the canopies for the figures and patterns on the frame to Webb's designs.[39] Other ecclesiastical decoration by the Firm includes the chancel ceiling of Bodley's Brighton church, with a repeating pattern of white flowers and red foliage which Webb spent five days painting, and the ceiling (1867) of Jesus College Chapel, Cambridge, with striking heraldic and symbolic panels by Webb, an extremely good heraldic artist, who designed all the Firm's work in this field.[40] The women embroidered altar cloths for the Firm, presumably including the one designed by Morris for St Martin's-on-the-Hill in 1862, which reflects the patterns of the ceiling.[41] In 1898 and 1899, after Morris's death, Webb designed an altar cloth, of which May Morris embroidered the super-frontal, for the chapel he had designed between 1896 and 1897 for Morris's sister, Mrs Isabella Gilmore, Head Deaconess of the Rochester Diocesan Deaconess Institution, Clapham Common. The super-frontal has golden crosses surrounded by trailing stylized oak leaves and vines in their natural colours on a red ground; the rising and falling of the lower border follows the lines of the framing and panels of the oak altar, which Webb had also designed (the chapel and Webb's fittings are covered in chapter 12).[42] His technical notes on the drawing for the frontal show that in the decorative arts, as in the building crafts, Webb had not only an instinctive feeling for materials but also an unsurpassed knowledge of them and of the ways in which they could be worked. In view of this and the years of experience he had had before he met Morris, and the fact that Morris's few months of architectural training were under his charge, it was probably Webb as much as or more than Street who turned Morris's attention to the importance of materials and of having a sound knowledge of how to work them.

The Firm received two prestigious London commissions in 1866, which were to make its reputation as interior decorators of important rooms. They were for the decoration of the Armoury and Tapestry Room of St James's Palace, and of the so-called Green Dining Room in the South Kensington

Museum (now the Victoria and Albert Museum). Webb was responsible for making measured drawings of the rooms, and for designing the overall schemes and almost all the patternwork, including the ceilings, as well as for supervising the work at both venues. Webb devised a scheme for the Armoury that was rich enough not to be overwhelmed by the weaponry arranged in patterns on the upper walls. The cornice, the woodwork, and the existing fireplace, are painted black with patternwork in gold offset by brightly coloured highlights. The reticulated pattern of foliage on the panels of the dado forms a base heavy enough to balance visually the weight of the weapons, whilst the gleam of the polished metal of the latter and the gilded patterning makes the whole an unusual but appropriately impressive interior for a minor state room. In the Tapestry Room, too, all the woodwork is painted black and patterned in gold. The designs on the doors repeat those of the Armoury but the dado pattern is of a similar character to the border of the tapestries. The fireplace, patterned in gold and red, has scrolling

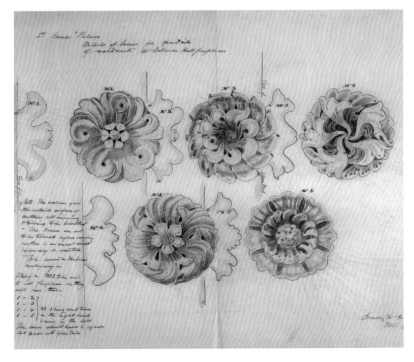

Above The Green Dining Room, South Kensington Museum (now the V&A), decorated by Morris, Marshall, Faulkner & Co. between 1866 and 1869; Webb designed the panelling, the moulded plaster ornament on the upper walls, and the frieze, and he and Morris collaborated on the designs for the painting of the ceiling (Victoria & Albert Museum / V&A Images)

foliage terminating in a lion's head in the spandrels of the Tudor arch. The palace work was done at the request of William Cowper (later Lord Mount-Temple), the first Commissioner of Public Works who, fortuitously, was a friend of Rossetti. Clearly satisfied with the result, Cowper asked the later firm Morris & Co. to undertake further work at the palace in the late 1870s and early 1880s.[43]

Webb prepared the measured drawings for the Green Dining Room of the museum, and designed the frieze that is modelled in relief with a dog chasing a hare, based on a sculpture he had seen on the font in the cathedral of Newcastle upon Tyne. The frieze is painted in red, green and gold, and the patternwork of the ceiling in yellowish brown on a flatted white ground. The wall panels, with green olive branches in relief on a pale blue ground, and the panelled green dado, with fruit branches painted on a gold ground in its upper panels, were also done to his designs. Burne-Jones was responsible for the

small figures in the panels that are interspersed with them, and for the figures in the stained-glass windows, which have animal and flower quarries and canopies by Webb. Although the work was costly, it was intended to be durable; it has proved to be so, having had to be completely repainted only once.[44]

Appropriately, Webb's schemes for the palace apartments and the Green Dining Room were unlike his ordinary domestic interiors. He took just as much care with the domestic work, however. As well as measuring the walls and ceilings and preparing working drawings for any necessary alterations in any rooms the Firm undertook to decorate, Webb designed all the fireplaces, grates, and fitted furniture, including bookcases, sideboards, and china cupboards. He advised on suitable decoration, and chose a selection of the Firm's wallpapers, fabrics, and paints from which the client made the final choice. He took charge of the arrangement and hanging of paintings and curtains, ensuring that the latter were hung simply, so that the architectural detail would not be obscured.

His own taste being simpler and lighter than Morris's, Webb preferred the Firm's quieter wallpapers and fabrics, offset by woodwork painted 'flatted white' or a pale colour to match the ground of the paper or textile. In the mid-1860s, he introduced white-painted panelling, which he was to favour henceforth, in the drawing room of his first country house, Arisaig House, Inverness-shire, Scotland (see chapter 7).[45] Morris was directly involved with the decoration of parts of Webb's Rounton Grange, North Yorkshire (1871–72; see chapter 7), in which the drawing room had a darker, richer scheme, with a panelled dado painted a soft blue-green, indigo blue silk damask on the walls and the upholstered seating, a floriated ceiling and frieze painted by Morris himself and repeating the indigo of the walls, and a beautiful carpet designed by Morris and woven at Merton Abbey, with curling leaves in green, parchment, and blues, with touches of crimson, on a blue ground with a predominantly crimson border.[46] Webb gave the room six large vertical sash windows, three of them in one bay, to ensure that it would have sufficient light for such a scheme. It was whilst working at Rounton that Morris turned on the industrialist Isaac Lowthian Bell (1816–1904) like a mad animal and made his celebrated and incredibly discourteous complaint about having to spend his life 'in ministering to the swinish luxury of the rich', which Bell took in astonishingly good part.[47]

The large town mansion-cum-studio-house, number 1 Palace Green, Kensington (1867–68; see chapter 5), designed by Webb for his young clients, George Howard and his wife Rosalind (1845–1921), was decorated throughout by the Firm and Morris & Co. during the 1870s and early 1880s. Despite the size and importance of the building, Webb avoided grandeur completely in the interiors, for which he designed all the modelled friezes and ceiling patterns except those in the dining room. The lower walls of this room had white panelling with an upper row of panels patterned by Morris in red and silver on a gold ground, on the rail below which he lettered verses from his poems. The most striking feature was the Burne-Jones *Cupid and Psyche* frieze for which the room became renowned. After it was finished, the panelling was repainted peacock green at the request

of the artist, to reduce its contrast with the rich but dark frieze. The ceiling and beams, and the brackets that were supported on Webb's typically strong corbels, bore floriated ornament painted by Morris in soft colours. The fireplace, with one of Webb's pillared grates of the Queen Square pattern, had a pedimented overmantel and eared lintel, whilst the sideboard was housed under a pointed arch – details which, with the bracketed beams, made this probably his most eclectic room, though in fact he had not adopted eclecticism. Having rejected all revivals of past styles, Webb viewed pointed arches simply as one of the ways of creating an opening. However, from this time onwards he seldom employed them, presumably having recognized that in the eyes of the public they would always be associated with the Gothic style. The Howards' drawing room had a ceiling patterned in soft yellow on flatted white to a Webb design rather similar to that of the Green Dining Room, and a fireplace

Above Number 1 Palace Green, Kensington, London (designed by Webb, 1867–68): the diningroom, showing Webb's panelling, fireplace, and grate of the Queen Square type, and painted decoration by Morris, and the frieze by Burne-Jones (*Studio*, vol. 15, 1899)

Above Number 1 Holland Park, Kensington, London (enlarged by Webb and decorated by Morris & Co.1879–83, demolished 1953): the original dining room, with new fittings designed by Webb and ornamented by Walter Crane (Reproduced by permission of English Heritage. NMR)

with a bracketed mantel and panelled overmantel such as were to become characteristic, although Webb designed each one individually.[48]

Morris & Co. also decorated Webb's 1879 extension of number 1 Holland Park, London, for the wealthy Greek, Alexander Ionides. The dining room was particularly notable. Webb's fireplace, in sober Purbeck marble as a foil to the old Persian tiles in its jambs, and his sideboard, an unusual canopied recess built out from the wall, were decorated by the artist Walter Crane (1845–1915) with silvered and clear-lacquered gesso work in so elaborate a manner that Webb must surely have been displeased.[49] The

unusual smoking room that he added in 1889 demonstrated how richness could be achieved in a far more sophisticated manner by exploiting the qualities of English marbles in simple ways. A cornice projecting below windows revealed the near-translucency of the material; wall panels emphasized its several colours and beautiful markings; and carved alabaster capitals on the marble columns of the seating recess added subtle contrasts of texture.[50]

The furniture of Morris, Marshall, Faulkner & Co. had achieved renown before that of its decoration of domestic interiors. Webb was the chief furniture designer from the beginning, not surprisingly as he had had the most experience in designing in wood through his architectural training and the work for Red House. As explained in chapter 1, Webb's furniture for Red House had to be hefty in order to withstand possible damage by Morris. Some of Webb's early pieces for the Firm were similarly extra strong because he and his partners, who often entertained Morris, intended to use the company's products in their homes. Webb designed cabinets with large plain doors on which the partners illustrated medieval legends, these painted cabinets being an early speciality of the Firm.[51] The doors and the lack of mouldings tend to make the pieces look heavy. The St George Cabinet (1861–62), painted by Morris, is an example. Webb treated it as a black-lacquered cabinet on a brown stand with turned legs and distinctive braces. The design was criticised in the *Building News* for the division into parts and for the 'studied affectation' of having metal door pulls

Left Number 1 Holland Park: the main staircase, designed by Webb, 1879 (Reproduced by permission of English Heritage. NMR)

Left Number 1 Holland Park: the smokingroom or waiting room, designed by Webb in 1889–90 (Reproduced by permission of English Heritage. NMR)

and escutcheons on the surface of the painted panels.[52] In 1861 or early 1862, John Pollard Seddon asked the Firm to paint the panels of the King René's Honeymoon Cabinet, which he had designed for his own use; this massive piece has a much more elaborate carcass than the St. George Cabinet.[53]

The partners' passion for medieval art was evident in their early designs. However, like the High Victorian Gothic architects in the 1860s and Webb in his early buildings, all the partners tried to reinterpret medieval art for their own day, using ancient examples as inspirations for new designs. The inspirations for the early furniture came chiefly from illuminated medieval manuscripts, and from Pugin's and Street's simple domestic pieces, and Butterfield's church fittings. Like Butterfield, Street had been greatly influenced by Pugin, and he would certainly have discussed Pugin's work and writings with Webb

and Morris whilst they were his chief assistant and pupil respectively. Street had been greatly influenced by Pugin, to whose work he certainly would have introduced Webb and Morris.

As with the stained glass, the inventiveness of the Firm's furniture was not generally understood at the time. Webb's early pieces have no overtly Gothic ornament yet they do call to mind the Middle Ages, in the case of some cabinets because of the pictures painted on them. Two features are of particular note. First, the unusual detail whereby a circular vertical member emerges from a square base, which appears on the Prioress's Tale Wardrobe – designed in early 1857 for Burne-Jones, who painted on it scenes from Chaucer – and on the feet of the handsome side table designed in c. 1865 for the same artist.[54] Second, the extending of vertical members above the body of

Below Kelmscott House, Hammersmith, London (the home of Morris and his family): the drawing room, with the Prioress's Tale Wardrobe (1858, designed by Webb and painted by Burne-Jones as a wedding present for the Morrises) and Webb's early settle (c. 1860), and also two of his adjustable armchairs, which were manufactured by Morris, Marshall, Faulkner & Co. from c. 1866 (William Morris Gallery, London)

a piece, at first as truncated pyramids, as seen in the Backgammon Players' Cabinet, shown in 1862, and foot.[55]

Webb extended the side members of the seat of one early chair sufficiently to allow the inclusion of two struts between them and the chair-back, and thus utilized the weight of the sitter to help to support the back. The chair, ebonized and with gilded banding, was exhibited with other furniture by the Firm in the Medieval Court of the 1862 International Exhibition where it drew praise for the innovative construction from Dr Christopher Dresser (1834–1904), the designer and influential writer on art.[56] The chair (now at Kelmscott Manor) and the settle by Rossetti that was also in the exhibition are interesting in that whilst not being copyist, and in the case of the chair echoing English vernacular pieces, they reveal the early influence of Japanese artefacts, which was soon to appear in the work of other designers, notably Edward William Godwin (1833–86).[57] Extended vertical members were to feature in several later pieces by the Firm, and in the work of Arthur Heygate Mackmurdo (1851–1942) and Voysey.

Webb never aimed for a primitive, rustic effect. He insisted on good workmanship, and on a smooth but not highly polished finish. His furniture was English in character, without being in any particular English style. Despite its relative simplicity, it was more sophisticated than Madox Brown's joiner-type bedroom pieces, and more innovative than the eighteenth-century-influenced items that George Jack, Webb's chief assistant, would design for Morris & Co. after he succeeded Webb as chief furniture designer in 1890.[58] Jack's designs, some dating from before 1890, although deeply influenced by Webb, always tended to be more elaborate. Where Webb would occasionally permit a little carved ornament, such as a beautiful cornice based on the periwinkle plant on a memorial cabinet of c. 1880, Jack would carve the entire front of a cabinet or cover the whole with inlaid ornament.[59]

In parallel with the increasing sophistication of the woodwork in his interiors, all Webb's furniture had become lighter by the mid-1860s. George Warington Taylor might have had some influence on this but he had admired Webb's furniture since seeing it at Red House in 1860 for what he termed its 'delicate tender' quality.[60] One or two of the early lighter pieces are rather spindly looking but Webb soon got the balance right. By the late 1860s, the

painters by then being too busy to decorate furniture for so little reward, he was able to concentrate on exploiting the inherent qualities of the timber, accented only by simple architectural mouldings. His furniture, waxed to bring out the grain rather than being lacquered black or stained as hitherto, became notable for its good proportions, for the direct use of the material without style motifs or veneers, and

Above The St George Cabinet, designed by Webb and painted by Morris, c. 1861–62 (Victoria & Albert Museum / V&A Images)

Left An ebonised armchair, with a strutted back and gilded bands, designed by Webb in 1861–62; Morris retained this chair for his own home (Collection of the Society of Antiquaries of London, at Kelmscott Manor)

Above A painted sideboard, with ebonised wood, painted decoration, and stamped leather panels, designed by Webb c. 1862 (Victoria & Albert Museum /V&A Images)

Below A rectangular table in oak, designed by Webb c. 1865 for the Burne-Joneses (Victoria & Albert Museum /V&A Images)

for the subtle way the structure was made part of the design. The care he took to ensure that each piece would be entirely right for its purpose is evident. His partly upholstered sofas and armchairs, including a chair with an adjustable back developed from a vernacular Sussex example drawn to his attention by Taylor, are more comfortable than many later Arts and Crafts examples.[61]

Webb designed tables and chairs of many types for the Firm as well as settles and sofas, a circular

settee, sideboards, cabinets for mementoes and games, screens, bookcases, music stands, beds, dressing tables, and framed looking glasses.[62] Smaller items include the official York Diocesan Stamp candlesticks, lamps, metal handles for furniture, jewellery, drinking glasses, embroideries, pottery, and patterns for use on leather panels and white-glazed tiles, which he sometimes painted himself in the early years. Inspirations for the patterns included the signs of the zodiac, flora and fauna, and old Delft and Persian tiles. His large tiles featuring, individually, a hare, rabbit, and raven, in blue on white, are particularly admirable.[63] Webb contributed designs in more fields than any of his partners, and his designs demonstrate the versatility of his creative power.

As with his architecture and his furniture, he exploited the qualities of the material and the effects of the way it would be worked, always designing for the chosen material rather than choosing a material to suit the design. His table glass, for instance, made by Powell & Sons, included various elegant drinking glasses that were obviously made by blowing not moulding, some of them having simple ornament in the form of prunts attached by the blower. These glasses were strikingly simple for their date, yet could only be made by an expert craftsman. They were probably inspired by seventeenth- and eighteenth-century examples from mainland Europe in the South Kensington Museum, an establishment Webb visited regularly.[64] In his early decorative art as in his first building, he had not yet become averse to using sources from other countries.

Except for a few embroideries, which were mostly ecclesiastical and included an altar cloth of 1868 for Llandaff Cathedral, Webb did not design textiles or, apparently, wallpapers, but as the wildlife artist amongst the partners he was responsible for all the birds and animals that appeared in the Firm's early textiles and in some later ones.[65] Examples include the lifelike deer and a delightful flock of small birds in the embroidered frieze designed in 1874–76 by Burne-Jones and Morris for the dining room of Rounton Grange.[66] His beautiful, sensitive studies in watercolour of a lion, fox, peacock, and raven are masterpieces of wildlife illustration; they formed the basis of Morris & Co.'s important *The Forest* tapestry, designed for Webb's country house Clouds (see chapter 7) in 1886 but rejected; made the following year, it was bought by Alexander Ionides for the sitting room of number 1 Holland Park, London.[67]

The Morris look became a fashion, mentioned as such in contemporary novels. However, it was an unusually popular and long-lasting one, not least because of the high quality of design and workmanship of the products of the Firm, and of its successor, most of which represented good value for money; and also because the interiors had an almost timeless English character, thanks to Webb's pleasing fittings and beautiful furniture, and often to his quiet colour schemes. The owners of small houses in the country, the new category of dwelling made possible by the increasing prosperity of the middle classes and the extensive railway network, favoured the Morris look (which suited all sizes and types of houses as Walter Crane noted perceptively in 1911), and it was popular with the residents, including several artists and writers, of the pioneering Bedford Park, an estate of small well-designed houses in Turnham Green, London (late 1870s to early 1880s).[68]

The wide extent of Webb's contribution to the success of Morris, Marshall, Faulkner & Co. and towards the improvement of the decorative arts in general was known at the time but it was played down by his friends, including Morris, because of Webb's intense dislike of praise and his equally strong desire to avoid publicity.[69] In 1900, Arthur Beresford Pite (1861–1934), Professor of Architecture at the Royal College of Art, acknowledged that in internal detail and decoration, Webb for a 'long generation' had been 'foremost in directing and giving tendency to the revival of the decorative crafts'.[70] Webb directly influenced several young architects, notably those who established cabinetmaking workshops in the Cotswolds in the 1890s and early years of the twentieth century (see chapter 8), and long after his retirement his influence was still being exerted indirectly on interior decoration and furniture design, as well as architecture, through the work of his Arts and Crafts disciples, and through the illustration and commendation of his own work in books on domestic architecture and decoration written for the educated public. As late as 1922, for example, Lawrence Weaver devoted the first chapter of *Small Country Houses of Today* to Webb's Red House (1858–59) and his second to Webb's Coneyhurst, Surrey (1883; see chapter 11).[71]

There are two paradoxical aspects of the aims and work of Morris, Marshall, Faulkner & Co. The first is that the partners' aim of making high-quality domestic goods available to all the populace was doomed to failure from the start because of the high costs of the handwork they were determined to revive. The stained-glass windows of the Firm were a step towards art for all in being made to delight and benefit all worshippers whether rich or poor, which undoubtedly they did, but its handmade household goods were too costly for the working classes. The dire poverty of the most disadvantaged meant that they could not buy any new products, whether made by hand or machine. In the late 1870s and 1880s, however, by following Pugin's example of using carefully supervised machine production, Morris brought some of the products of Morris & Co., including woven textiles and carpets, within the reach of the less well-to-do, which was the best that could be done without great social changes such as he and Webb hoped to help bring about after becoming active socialists in the early 1880s (see chapter 10).

The second paradox is that despite the partners' acceptance of Ruskin's belief that there could be no real improvement in art until ordinary craftsmen were free to design their own work, as he and they believed had been the case in the Middle Ages, the craftsmen of Morris, Marshall, Faulkner & Co. had

Below An oak sideboard, designed by Webb around the late 1860s and manufactured by Morris, Marshall, Faulkner & Co. (Fischer Fine Art Ltd)

to work to designs made by the partners. The reasons for this were twofold: the partners had a strong urge to design the items themselves, and they concurred with Ruskin's contention that as since the Renaissance commercialism had curtailed craftsmen's freedom to design their own work, their creative faculties had atrophied to the point that by the nineteenth century they were incapable of producing good designs. These paradoxes are also apparent in the work of the Arts and Crafts architects and designers.

By the late 1870s and early 1880s, young architects, artists, and designers, in London especially, were beginning to adopt the ideals and aims of Ruskin and Morris, and to join the crusade to improve and raise the status of the decorative crafts and reunite them with architecture and the fine arts. Many of the recruits became members of the Art Workers' Guild (AWG), established in 1884 as a forum for debate, exchange of ideas, and lectures. The AWG and the Society for the Protection of Ancient Buildings founded by Morris and Webb in 1877 (see chapter 8) became the two major focal points of the Arts and Crafts movement. The guild had developed from the St George's Society founded in 1883 for monthly discussions on art and architecture by a group of Richard Norman Shaw's assistants and pupils – Lethaby being a prominent one – who revered Morris for his inspirational work in reviving the decorative arts and his great skill as a designer of two-dimensional work, and who, with other young architects, were looking to Webb for an approach to architectural design that had strong ideals and was not based on a style revival. In 1886, a splinter group of the AWG formed the Arts and Crafts Exhibition Society, to publicise the ideals and aims of the expanding movement that took its name from that of the society, which held its first exhibition – a great success – in 1888 (neither Webb

nor Shaw joined the AWG but they did exhibit in the society's shows). Following the example of the AWG and the society, similar guilds of architects, artists, and designers, were established in other towns, thus disseminating the ideology of the Arts and Crafts movement. Ashbee set up his Guild and School of Handicraft in London in 1888, inspired by Ruskin's ideals and the Firm's example, and by the Century Guild, which Mackmurdo, similarly influenced, had established in 1882; and a small group of AWG members – Lethaby, Ernest Gimson (1864–1919), Sidney Barnsley (1865–1926), Reginald Blomfield (1856–1942), and Mervyn Macartney (1853–1932) – followed suit by establishing the short-lived Kenton & Co. in 1890.

Arts and Crafts ideals and practice were taken into the countryside by various charitable organisations set up chiefly by middle-class philanthropists, many of them women, with the aim of reviving the traditional village crafts and providing training in them as a means of earning a living for artisans who were out of reach of the training that was now available in towns, an example being the highly influential Home Arts and Industries Association established in the same year as the AWG. Some architects and many middle-class designer-craftsmen established workshops in the countryside and in small market towns, and took on apprentices. In 1902, Ashbee moved his Guild of Handicraft, with its craftsmen and their families, to Chipping Campden in Gloucestershire, where he provided craft tuition for local people.

The Arts and Crafts movement did not fade away completely in the twentieth century under the twin assaults of Modern movement architecture and mass-production as is sometimes thought. The workshops of designer-craftsmen in many fields thrived and multiplied in the English countryside and small market towns throughout the twentieth century and,

Below *The Forest* tapestry, designed by Morris and John Henry Dearle, with animals by Webb, woven in 1887 (Victoria & Albert Museum /V&A Images)

happily, continue to do so today. Many of the owners learned their trade through serving an apprenticeship with an established craftsman, the method that Webb recommended as the best possible training. In the early twenty-first century, a few craftsmen work entirely by hand but for others, notably cabinetmakers, use of machines in the first stages of the work enables them to offer beautifully designed and crafted pieces, usually made to commission, at about the same cost as or less than the good-quality mass-produced furniture offered by high-street retailers.[72]

Although Morris, Marshall, Faulkner & Co. was not the only firm involved in its revival, the history of handcraftsmanship in the twentieth century and the state of it in the early years of the present century might have been very different, with the revived skills having been lost once more, had not the products of the Firm and of Morris & Co., and the enthusiasm and expertise of Morris and Webb, inspired the Arts and Crafts architects, designers, and

craftsmen. Undoubtedly, Morris was the most important of the Firm's partners. He devoted the most time and money to the business and, after a slow start, he became an extremely good business manager. He was an important reviver of lost or debased decorative arts and a highly talented designer of two-dimensional products, as his many wallpaper and textile designs still in production testify. However, without Philip Webb – who through his own practice influenced Arts and Crafts architecture, fittings, and furniture, and ornamental work in wood, in metal, and in plaster (as is shown in several later chapters) – as its part-time manager, architectural adviser, designer in all fields, and provider of patrons, the Firm might have been a very short-lived venture instead of becoming one of the foremost and most influential producers of art furnishings; and its later manifestation, Morris & Co., the most renowned interior decoration firm of its time, on the Continent and in the USA as well as in Britain, might never have been established.

Above Standen, East Grinstead, Sussex (designed by Webb, 1891): the morning room, decorated by Morris & Co

Chapter 4

THE MIDDLE YEARS

Philip Webb left number 7 Great Ormond Street in the spring of 1864 and moved into second-floor rooms in a late-seventeenth-century house, number 1 Raymond Buildings, Gray's Inn, after making careful calculations to ensure he could afford the rent of £60 a year and seventeen shillings a week for the housekeeper, Mrs Long.[1] As well as cleaning the rooms, Mrs Long would cook his meals and, presumably, would also be paid by other occupants of the building for the same services. Like many others in the area, the building was divided into chambers that were chiefly occupied by barristers. Webb referred to Gray's Inn as his 'lawful district'. His living-room office was decorated and furnished through the Firm, probably with the *Venetian* wallpaper and curtains of blue lining fabric, and with its Sussex chairs, a Dutch cabinet, a huge old French bookcase, an oak table with scrubbed top, and a long drawing table in front of the window. From this room, with its blue-and-white pottery, and a number of small paintings by his friends, he looked out onto his 'seven acres of city paradise', the Gray's Inn gardens and trees.[2] As he never married or needed larger business premises, he was able to live and work in these chambers until he retired in January 1901.

Working in the way he did, designing every detail of his buildings himself, he needed only one or two assistants. He had only part-time help until 1869, when George Basset became his chief assistant. After Basset left in 1884, George Jack (1855–1931), who had served his articles in Glasgow and worked for C G Vinall before moving to Webb's office in 1882, took his position. From the late 1860s, Webb was a respected and renowned architect but his annual earnings averaged a mere £562 against expenses of about £347 excluding his living costs. He made a loss in fourteen of his forty-two years in business, and failed to meet his personal living costs in a further four. George Jack took a gamble in 1891 when he accepted a change in salary from £241 a year to £156 plus a variable share in the profits; by

1893 he was owed £393 in arrears because of cash-flow problems.[3] Webb did not submit his bill until twelve months after a building was completed, and only a small number of clients, including Stanhope, Gillum, and Lowthian Bell, paid sums on account, although this was customary at the time in the case of large buildings. Webb worked for four years on his largest country house, Clouds in Wiltshire (designed 1877–80) before the client, the Honourable Percy Scawen Wyndham (1835–1911), paid a penny, though he knew that the architect had turned away many other jobs to concentrate on his house, and even then he did so only at the architect's request.[4] The tax gatherers could not believe that the income of such a well-known architect was so much lower than that of his fellows. Shaw's income, for example, approached £2,000 in 1870 and by 1880 was more than twice that figure.[5] It was not surprising, therefore, that Webb should be called upon to explain matters in person to the tax inspectors more than once. In 1896, his own statement of accounts was ignored; the resulting ridiculously high income tax demand, based on an official's estimate, stung him into a bitter reply. 'I really cannot understand,' he wrote, 'why so many attempts should be made to convict me of dishonesty.'[6]

Despite what most of his peers would have regarded as financial failure, Webb was content. Overall he made enough for his modest needs with a little over to help others. He despised those who lived idly on unearned income, and believed that only public bodies should be allowed to lend at interest. However, accepting that he had to live according to the times, he eventually saved almost £2,000 for his retirement, and invested it in a Bank of England Warrant.[7] Ironically, Morris and Burne-Jones made sizeable fortunes in what at the outset had seemed to be much more highly speculative careers.

Webb's architectural career had begun partly as an expedient; but long before 1864 it had become, as it was to remain, the centre of his life. As an elderly man, he told Sydney Cockerell that the reason he had never married was because he had never had enough money to keep a wife in the state to which she would have been accustomed.[8] Had the wish to marry not been less than his passion for architecture, Webb could have earned more money simply by allowing experienced assistants to design some details of his buildings. Significantly, marriage had not been included in his 1866 list of things to be given up for the sake of following 'art with advantage to the world'.[9] In 1867 or 1868, Warington Taylor chided Webb for paying so much attention to 'that fair haired girl in Pentonville' that he had no time to visit Taylor; in a following letter, he invited Webb to bring the girl to spend a long weekend with himself and his wife at Hastings.[10] This girl, whose identity is not known, might have rejected Webb, of course, but it seems more likely that when their relationship began to threaten his freedom to work in the way he wished, he chose independence.

The unhappiness in the marriages of several of his friends, particularly those of Taylor, Morris, Rossetti, and Burne-Jones, probably helped him to make this decision. Morris was made deeply unhappy by his wife's affairs with Rossetti (whose own wife had died from an overdose of laudanum) and with the landowner, traveller, and poet, Wilfrid Scawen Blunt (1840–1922). Georgiana Burne-Jones was greatly distressed by her husband's several liaisons, and Taylor's wife absconded for a time with her lover. In 1868, a bitter Taylor warned Webb, who probably heeded the advice, that any man enthusiastic about his work should remain celibate because women lacked enthusiasm and were miserable when their men became absorbed in their jobs.[11] In later years Webb used phrases such as 'freedom from the bondage of women', and averred that Venus, goddess of love, killed as many men as Mars, god of war; and he attended only one marriage ceremony, by accident when trapped in an old church by a wedding party of total strangers.[12]

Webb could probably have supported a wife from the working classes, with less expensive tastes and needs than women of his own class. Several men in the Pre-Raphaelite circle married such women, including Morris, whose wife was the daughter of a groom, and Taylor, whose wife worked in an eel-pie shop. Webb was not a snob, but he was too fastidious and courtly to have been content with an initially rather rough-mannered companion, and his

respect for the liberty of the individual would have hindered any attempt to educate her or inculcate his own standards. When the dying Taylor requested him to keep his wife in order by acting as her trustee after his death, Webb felt bound to refuse. 'I have the strongest dislike,' he explained, 'to preaching one doctrine and practising the opposite.'[13]

He liked children but, as he told George Howard, he had no desire for any of his own.[14] Perhaps he had had a surfeit with his own younger siblings. Certainly he would have observed how the advent of his friends' offspring brought with it interruptions to their working and thinking, and that it prevented their wives from pursuing their artistic careers and diminished the companionship they had had hitherto with their husbands and friends. Furthermore, with his innate empathy, he too would have been worried by the occasional ill health of these children, and deeply grieved by the deaths of any of them. Morris

Above *Philip Webb,* a sepia portrait, by Charles Fairfax Murray, c. 1869 (from a photograph in Webb's collection; his photographs are in a Private Collection)

suffered lasting distress after his elder daughter Jenny developed severe epilepsy, for instance, and one child of the Taylors and one of the Burne-Joneses died, whilst Rossetti and his wife's infant was stillborn.

Webb cherished his close friendships with several women, however, particularly those with Georgiana Burne-Jones, Jane Morris, and Kate, the sister of Charles Faulkner. Kate, who never married and might have been the fair-haired girl, worked with Webb on the Firm's projects. After her brother died, Webb took the responsibility for her welfare.[15] Burne-Jones was possibly referring to Kate when he told Rosalind Howard in 1882 or 1883 that if he had what Webb had – 'some one utterly devoted to me and caring enough about me to live solitary for my sake' – he would not be so doleful.[16] For many years Webb also had a close friendship and exchanged remarkably frank letters with Rosalind Howard, an aristocrat in her own right and, as the wife of George Howard, the future Countess of Carlisle. However, Webb liked to spend a good deal of time on his own, so he was probably more content and at ease with affection than with stronger passions. Affection, a quality for which he had a 'high regard', left him free to work as he pleased and to spend every other Sunday in solitary and valuable 'reflection and purging of mind'.[17]

Perhaps to a large degree a result of his loneliness at Aynho, Webb placed the highest possible value on good companionship. Sincere friendships joined the English countryside, old buildings, books, music, drawings, and paintings as the most precious things in life, indeed perhaps the most valuable of all. 'Fellowship is Life, lack of Fellowship is Death,' Webb informed Lethaby, and in 1902 he told Cockerell that he, Webb, had had 'the unutterable boon of gaining the "inmost love", of some seven or eight of the best of human souls!'.[18] They were the Morrises, the Burne-Joneses, the Boyces, and Charles and Kate Faulkner. Other close friends were Hale White, Warington Taylor, George Wardle (the manager successively of the Firm and of Morris & Co.), and Spencer Stanhope; the Howards, Lowthian Bell and his son Thomas Hugh Bell (1844–1931); and Webb's own brother Harry, older sister Sarah (c. 1826–1922) and younger sister Caroline (d. 1909). In later years, they were joined by Lethaby; Cockerell, who became Director of the Fitzwilliam Museum, Cambridge; Emery Walker (1851–1933) the typographical expert, and the young architects

Sidney Barnsley and his brother Ernest (1863–1926), Detmar Blow (1867–1939), Ernest Gimson, Charles Canning Winmill (1865–1945), Alfred H Powell (1865–1960), George Jack, and Hugh Thackeray Turner (1853–1937). Webb also amassed a wide circle of acquaintances that encompassed eminent people from many different fields.

He spent alternate Sundays in Welwyn, Hertfordshire, at the home of his bachelor brother Harry and their unmarried sisters, Caroline and Sarah. Caroline kept Webb's clothes in order. By early 1881, their home was in New Place, the house and surgery in Welwyn which Philip had designed for Harry between 1877 and 1878. Working in the garden and walking in the surrounding countryside with his family gave Webb beneficial strenuous exercise. He also played on the bowling green and made sketches of the garden plants for use later in decorative work. In London, where the seven-acre paradise of Gray's Inn was a daily substitute for the Hertfordshire countryside, he supplemented these sketches with others done at the British and the South Kensington museums, and his drawings of the animals and birds made in the Regent's Park zoological gardens.[19]

By the time he moved to Gray's Inn, Webb's tastes were fully formed. Fortunately they were simple and inexpensive. Musical evenings at friends' homes cost nothing and, though tickets had to be purchased for concerts and the theatre, when he dined out with his companions afterwards, or after a game of 'American bowls', it was inexpensively at a public house.[20] Friends frequently joined him in the evenings for 'pipes and beer', or a simple supper and cigars; at low cost, beer was purchased from his brewer brother Frank, and wine through the Firm.[21] Webb's idea of a 'dinner fit for an alderman' was a grouse with a bottle of fine burgundy, followed by a 'morsel of cream cheese [...] a cup of good coffee and small glass of excellent brandy'.[22] In 1872, when Webb mistakenly thanked George Howard for grouse sent by someone else, Howard immediately dispatched another brace; an embarrassed Webb enjoyed the joke against himself, as he did again in 1873 when, having refused tickets for a concert from Rosalind Howard, he found them unobtainable elsewhere.[23] In general, he disliked being given presents because he hated to feel beholden to anyone.

It was Webb's belief that greed was the chief characteristic of the nineteenth century. Pretentious or extravagant display, to which he was naturally antipathetic, joined ugliness and shoddiness in being symptomatic of the era. 'Our aim should be to live so as to consume the least possible, yet without impoverishment,' he told Lethaby in 1898.[24] Webb fulfilled his aim. In forty-five years in London all that he amassed, apart from necessities of furniture and equipment, was a moderate number of books; a quantity of useful or pleasing cuttings and prints from architectural journals, *The Times*, and the *Saturday Review*; three or four paintings, drawings, or prints by artist friends; a print of the Sistine Chapel frescoes; two small models of Michelangelo's sculptures, and a print of the portrait of the great artist.[25] Webb bought little, but what he did buy was of the finest quality and design. He went to an excellent and expensive tailor, had his boots custom made and his braces stitched to his own design, and purchased the best snuff for himself and – though a non-smoker until he took to a pipe during his retirement – the finest cigars, which he habitually carried for his friends.[26]

When Rosalind Howard, sharing the view of most of his friends, told Webb by letter that his life was too austere, he replied that the austerity consisted in him 'enjoying every luxury both of mind and matter' which he was capable of digesting, with the added 'delight, of being taken – under the circumstances – for an austere & virtuous person.'[27] After reading some of Webb's letters, Dame Laurentia McLachlan, Abbess of Stanbrook, decided, as she told her friend Sydney Cockerell, that there was 'something of the monk in Webb, such a sane estimate of worldly things and comforts, and, ruling all, a splendid and consistent worship of goodness, beauty and truth in every sphere'.[28] Describing to Boyce a visit to Mount Grace Priory, Webb wrote that he found the idea of being a Carthusian monk attractive, with his 'separate room and fireplace', but that, because the rule of the order would not allow him to read 'Dumas or Carlyle' or to 'laugh very loud over Mrs Gamp' or attempt to sing 'snatches of Don Giovanni', he felt he had better stick to Gray's Inn, where the occupants were not so particular.[29]

Music, to which he had probably been introduced when a child or later by Street, was another abiding source of joy to Webb, who was knowledgeable on the subject but played no instrument. Beethoven, Mozart, Haydn, Handel, Gluck, and Bach, in that order, were his favourite composers, but he also enjoyed the work of Berlioz

and Wagner and the unsophisticated country-dance tunes played by village fiddlers. He attended concerts frequently throughout his London years, usually with Boyce, and he often listened to recitals by musicians playing in their own or his friends' homes. Warington Taylor, for example, invited him to supper and afterwards to hear a twenty-four-year-old American pianist, Edward Dannreuther – who later became renowned – playing Beethoven and Wagner in his own rooms. Webb had an unusual ability to verbally convey the story and emotion of an opera with great vividness, as Morris's daughter May testified. When she and Jenny were young, Webb introduced them to Mozart on his musical box before taking them to hear a performance of the master's *Don Giovanni*.[30]

Morris apparently did not like concerts and Webb lacked the passion for poetry felt by Morris, Burne-Jones and Rossetti. He told Hale White that he had 'no natural turn' for poetry and therefore read relatively little of it in contrast to his devouring of all good prose.[31] He read everything on architecture, past and present, on which he could lay hands, and he shared his friends' delight in medieval manuscripts, Malory's *Le Morte d'Arthur*, and the works of Dante, Dickens, Dumas, Shakespeare, Sir Walter Scott, and Surtees, amongst others. Webb read books recommended by his 'first-class literary tasters', who included Morris, Hale White, Taylor, and Wardle.[32] He also made his own discoveries, however, and before becoming one of the Pre-Raphaelite group was familiar with the works of some of the authors it admired most of all, notably Ruskin's influential *Stones of Venice,* which Webb purchased in 1855 before he knew Morris.[33] Lethaby, a scholar himself, had the highest respect for Webb's intelligence and felt that the 'thought of the world' was packed into his bookcase; he remembered Webb reading philosophical works, biographies, and novels, including works by George Sand, Auerbach, Reade, Defoe, Emily Brontë, Tolstoy, and Meinhold, and he recalled the architect's habit of seasoning his talk and letters with quotations from Dickens, Dumas, Scott, Borrow, and others.[34] Webb's letters reveal his admiration of Blake, Borrow, Bunyan, Cobbett, Euripides, Homer, Keats, Lamb, Lewes, Newman, Plato, St Francis, and Tennyson, for example, and show that he thought deeply about what the thinkers had to say. When books such as Carlyle's *Frederick the Great* and Balzac's *Les Chouans* opened his eyes to a particular epoch and country, Webb read them several times to get a picture of the period and of the 'lie of the land in its natural form, and of the human handiwork indenting it'.[35] Lethaby noted that where

he and others treated books 'like "water laid on" to shelves', to Webb 'they were persons', loved and known intimately.[36] When his dear old friend Kate Faulkner died in 1910, Webb found solace in Wordsworth's poetry, and told Hale White that, even in old age, books that are 'masterpieces of human expression' are 'like the landscape in front of our window in the country, never failing though never changed' and never failing in their 'mission to bless'.[37]

He disliked large social gatherings, small talk, and gossip but greatly enjoyed quiet conversation with a seriously thoughtful friend, and delighted in a hearty laugh, which he considered good for the health. He took a full part in convivial evenings with good friends, with plenty of wine, beer, and jokes, when his fine sense of humour and keen wit came to the fore. Webb was in great demand as a dinner guest, though he seldom chose to dine out in his later years. When visiting works in progress necessitated an overnight stay with clients, his company in the evening was appreciated greatly. Lowthian Bell's daughter Mary (Maisie) told Rosalind Howard in 1874 that Webb's presence, with that of her brother,

Below Webb's drawing of a plan chest for his own use, 1879 (Private Collection)

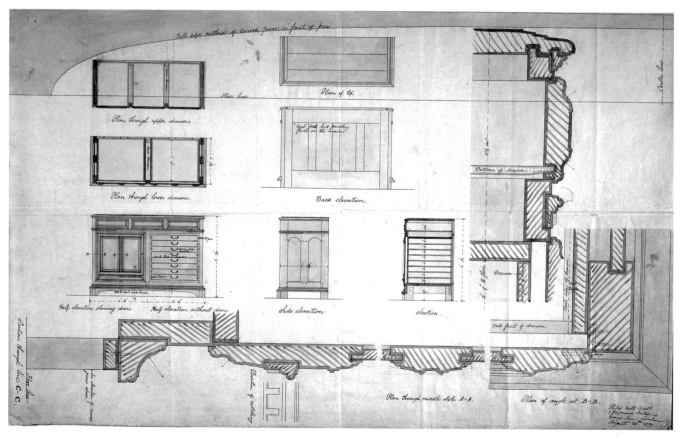

Hugh, and sister, Ada, would ensure a merry party at dinner.[38] Sometimes Webb stayed a day or two longer than duty demanded in the country homes of his clients. In the mid-1860s when Arisaig House was under construction on the west coast of Scotland, he had to spend several days at a time there because it was a remote and difficult place to reach. He was chiefly occupied on the site but he also accompanied the client Francis Astley and his offspring on excursions into the hills and along the coastline, on foot, on horseback, or by boat. In general, however, he loathed country-house life. He found it restrictive and dull because, as he told Hale White,

> the resource of honest jesting retort is out of the question there; partly because it wd. not be understood, & partly because the place wd. become even duller from the ill concealed disgust at "bad manners". I confess that when my business — as it often has — sends me into that atmosphere, the ill-bred but highly relieving jest must out, or I shd. burst.[39]

Webb never joined a large house party, and whenever possible when staying at a country house, he would escape on horseback with his sketchbook to enjoy the surrounding countryside and ancient buildings. He told Rosalind Howard, with whom he stayed at her husband's country seat, Naworth Castle in Cumbria, when inspecting work in progress on the building or others in the district, that although personal friendships flourished in country houses, it was extremely boring when the house was 'full of stupid people'.[40] Far more to his taste were the two or three days that he usually managed to spend annually at Kelmscott Manor after Morris and Rossetti took the lease in 1871. Morris and Faulkner were often there with him, when the friends would happily fish or boat on the adjacent Thames, and explore the neighbouring district.[41]

Webb found his work so interesting and fulfilling as well as time-consuming that during his forty-two years in practice on his own he took only six longer holidays. These comprised a week in the Lake District in 1859 with his brother Harry; a trip to France (his second visit) with the Morrises and Taylor in 1866, during which after a spell in Paris they drove from Sens to Troyes, stopping to study and sketch old buildings on the way; a week or two in Scotland in 1871; a month's rest at Kelmscott Manor in 1875 after overworking and again in 1876; and a recuperative winter in Italy in 1884–85. In 1888, Webb convalesced for several weeks on a farm in Surrey, High Upfolds near Cranleigh, which had been carefully chosen to be within easy reach of several of his houses under construction in the district so that he could keep an eye on them.[42]

Early in 1884, Webb decided that if he were ever to see Italy it must be in that year, a resolve strengthened when his doctor ordered a complete rest. With the office in the capable hands of George Jack, he left London on 9 November and travelled through Belgium to Basle, accompanied as far as Brussels by George Wardle, inspecting art galleries and old buildings along the way, as he was to do in Italy. At Lugano he was met by another friend, the painter Charles Fairfax Murray, with whom he explored Como and Milan before staying with him in Florence for some weeks. During this time, he visited Spencer Stanhope (who had moved to Florence for his health), took lessons in Italian with little success, and visited the Uffizi galleries and the eleventh- and twelfth-century church of San Miniato al Monte. Webb made an excursion to Pisa from Florence, and then in January 1885, he went via Siena and Orvieto to Rome, where for five weeks he lodged in the same building as the historian and archaeologist John Henry Middleton, with whom he explored the city and the Campagna. Webb returned to Florence by way of Assisi, Perugia, and Arezzo and, after a week or so there, he visited Bologna and Ravenna en route to Venice. He spent three weeks in Venice before travelling to Vicenza, Verona, and finally Milan, from whence he left for home on 6 April 1885.[43]

Predictably, the vacation aroused guilt in Webb, who felt that he was 'somewhat of an idle man, living on the sweat of the labours of poverty'.[44] 'I feel rather like a fish out of water,' he told George Jack, 'wanting the support of my daily work which has become so much a habit with me that I do not feel at home without the stay of it.'[45] So that Jack was not too heavily taxed, in Florence and Rome Webb worked each morning on some of the final minor details for Clouds, which was then nearing completion. This made him 'feel less like a middleman amusing himself while the poorer were working for him', and saved him from becoming 'savage and moody under the press of staring at and wondering over the vast wreck of ancient art strewn over' Italy.[46]

He was 'driven almost to desperation by the multitude and variety of things' that could not be

CHAPTER 4

'passed by hastily without extreme folly' and by the little available time for sketching and returning to 'things that should be knawed at and not bolted'.[47] 'I thought to pay but general heed to pictures, but I find they lay hold irresistibly,' he told Boyce.[48] In Belgium, he had been particularly attracted to the work of Van Eyck; in Italy it was that of Giotto, Benozzo Gozzoli, the 'good and great' Fra Angelico, and the 'great of the great' Mantegna, which most appealed, together with Michelangelo's Sistine Chapel ceiling in the Vatican which, despite the naturalism that made it 'all wrong as decorative art', he found the 'most beautiful and comforting' object amongst 'thousands of other wonderful things', a 'great boon' to the world, a 'triumph of art, imagination and beauty'.[49] However, he considered that the *Judgement* at the east end of the chapel, done later in Michelangelo's life, demonstrated the conventionalizing element which had made this painter the 'greatest of all the leaders in the destruction of simplicity in art' after his earlier simplicity had given way to consciousness of style.[50] Stylistic conventions, which he spent his life battling against in contemporary architecture and which he believed had begun to be cultivated deliberately during the Renaissance, were for Webb the major and highly reprehensible feature of Renaissance art. He was sickened by the attention paid in Italy to the 'extraordinary skill, artificial in an artificial time', of Raphael.[51]

As for Italian architecture, Webb found the ancient ruins in Rome wonderful but brutal because most of them were of palaces of emperors or priests not houses of ordinary folk, whilst the splendid buildings of the Renaissance were 'brutal in their magnificence'.[52] He did admire the Pantheon, however, into which he bribed his way when it was officially closed. He admired Michelangelo's San Lorenzo Library in Florence but considered St Peter's Cathedral in Rome a 'mistake from first to last', a mistake which even that great artist had been unable to 'lick into satisfactory shape'.[53] He respected Brunelleschi's work, which he did not class as being truly of the Renaissance. Webb particularly admired the construction of Brunelleschi's Duomo (the dome, 1420–30, of Florence Cathedral), a triumph of innovative engineering, which he had studied in books before investigating it at close quarters. Medieval buildings gave him the greatest delight, however. 'After having been made melancholy by

the skilful but dismal skill of the great Palladio I turned to the beautiful bits of mediaeval work,' he reminisced later.[54] In Venice, for instance, where Webb found the Renaissance architecture cold and formal, the town houses of the Middle Ages made him feel less regret than usual at not being back at work.

His Italian tour had little if any effect on Webb's own architecture. From the early 1860s, he had always followed his own tenet that architects should take inspiration for new work from traditional national and local buildings of the particular country. It has been suggested that his later work was influenced by the Byzantine churches he saw in Italy during 1884 and 1885, and that Byzantine influence is discernible in his ornament at Clouds.[55] If this were indeed so, the influence was exercised subconsciously. Webb told Boyce he was pleased that he had designed Clouds before he left England because 'if there be any part of it bearable no one will be able to say that the good of it came of my seeing Italy'.[56] His use of simple geometric shapes, and his emphasis on materials rather than ornament, had always given his work a robust vigour akin to that of Byzantine buildings, which he admired for this quality before his Italian tour, but which he also found in the Romanesque architecture of England. Many of his buildings had at least one bold round arch, with several more in the interior, and those which formed a major feature of Bell Brothers Offices, Middlesbrough (built 1889 to 1891) were designed between 1881 and 1883, before he went to

Above Webb's slide rule and bamboo measuring rods (Private Collection)

Opposite Kelmscott Manor, Kelmscott, Oxfordshire: William Morris's country home from 1871, in which Webb spent brief holidays

Italy. Lethaby recorded that, in the case of flat ornament, Webb believed that the shapes in the white ground should turn it into a 'mosaic-like pattern effective at a distance'.[57] This was more likely to have been inspired by Celtic and Romanesque work studied in Britain than by the rather similar Byzantine designs.

The Italian countryside pleased Webb, particularly the garden-like landscape of the northern plain and the view from Spencer Stanhope's hillside villa. 'How different the English and Italian landscape are and yet how equally beautiful', he told Boyce.[58] Although he had enjoyed his holiday, Webb disliked travelling and so he probably reached home with considerable relief. The tour having cost less than expected, he spent the surplus on a painting for New Place, a watercolour by Boyce of an English scene.[59] Clearly, Italy had not supplanted England in Webb's affections.

Webb had to spend many days each year travelling to inspect sites and buildings in course of construction. With pragmatic good sense, he travelled by rail to save time, in spite of his deep dislike of the 'fretful rolling of wheels' and his fundamental disapproval of the railway system, which he considered had desecrated the countryside, destroyed local building traditions by making the same materials cheaply and widely available, and made industrialization possible.[60] The railway network in the second half of the nineteenth century was so extensive and the trains so frequent, however, that in the course of a single day he could visit two or more of his building sites in different counties and get back to London in the evening.

Unfortunately, Webb's winter in Italy had no permanent effect on his health, which had been generally good until the 1880s, apart from frequent headaches and at least one bout of liver trouble. He suffered serious illnesses in 1884, 1885, and 1887, probably all being some type of rheumatism. The 1887 bout continued into the following year, when it kept him indoors for three months and necessitated nursing care; this happened again in 1889, when a severe attack of rheumatic fever left him with chronic rheumatism, chiefly in his arms, to the end of his life. His brother had cared for him at Welwyn during less serious indispositions, but in 1894 Webb had to spend three weeks in hospital, probably due to rheumatism. He was a cheerful patient, and passed the sleepless nights in telling stories and fables to his night nurse, a 'highly *respectable* person', with whom there was much joking and laughter, especially when Morris called whilst they were at dinner.[61]

Apart from occasional holidays and illnesses, and the troubles, ill health and in some cases deaths of friends, and a few trials and tribulations in his professional work, Webb's life during his years in practice was calm and contented. The worst setback in his practice was the gutting by fire in 1889 of his largest house, Clouds, just over three years after it was first occupied. Weary months had to be spent in reinstating the building, during which much other work had to be put aside.

In 1884, five years before the Clouds catastrophe, the Art Workers' Guild had been founded by a group of young architects, who were mostly from Shaw's office but were already admirers of Webb's architecture and approach to design, together with some designers and craftsmen. They were inspired by Ruskin's and Morris's ideals on decorative art, and by Morris's work in this field. The guild – which has never ceased to flourish – became the central forum of the Arts and Crafts movement in Britain. The founders of the guild were dedicated to improving art and to removing the distinction between the fine and the decorative arts, just as those of Morris, Marshall, Faulkner & Co. had been twenty-three years earlier. Membership of the guild was by election. Morris was elected, of course, and became Master in 1892. Webb did not join, however. On being approached the same year, undoubtedly not for the first time, he declined the invitation, explaining that he had many reasons for doing so but the one that had helped him to a decision was that he was 'not a craftsman' and he was too old to set about making himself one.[62] He went on to say that he hoped the young architect members would become craftsmen and thus 'lift the "profession" out of the slough in which it sticks', and that he hoped all the other craftsman members would be able to 'drop the misleading title of "designer"'. He disliked the term 'designer' because he believed that the only way to become a craftsman of any type was to learn through an apprenticeship, and that the only way to become a good architect was to serve an apprenticeship with a builder as well as with an experienced architect. He had made up for his own lack of such an apprenticeship by learning everything he could about the various building crafts and about the ways of working all types of building materials, and he habitually urged young architects to gain experience with a good builder.

In the late 1880s, great disquiet had arisen amongst architects about the question of whether or not architecture should become a closed profession, entered only through examinations. The leaders of the RIBA were in favour of registration, partly out of self-interest, so long as the institute controlled the register and the examinations. Many architects, however, including members and non-members, were vociferously opposed to registration through examination because they considered that creative power, or design ability, could not be measured. This faction included Webb, who never joined the RIBA, which had no architectural training school, because he considered that its chief aim was to improve the status of its members. He signed the letter protesting against registration which appeared in *The Times* on 31 March 1891, but this appears to have been the sum of his active involvement. Not surprisingly in view of his determined avoidance of publicity, there is no essay by Webb in the book *Architecture: a Profession or an Art*, which was edited by Richard Norman Shaw and Thomas Graham Jackson (1835–1924), the leaders of the campaign against registration. The chief effect of the book was that it unintentionally drew attention to the poor quality of some architectural training. Webb himself did a great deal to increase the right and just reputation, and ironically the status, of architects by giving a first-class service to his clients on both the practical and art sides of architecture, and by encouraging his disciples to do likewise.[63]

A short hiatus occurred in Webb's working life when he was called to serve as a juror in the trial of Dr Leander Starr Jameson, the southern African statesman. On 29 December 1895, Jameson had led a raid into the Transvaal, with five hundred cavalry, in the interests of the British settlers and with hope of bringing the province under British rule. The raid failed, and Jameson was captured and sent to London for trial, where he was found guilty and sentenced to fifteen months in jail, a punishment that Webb, an opponent of all wars and oppression, probably considered too lenient.

Only two events occurring during his years in practice had a major effect on his life. Webb became involved in the first through his love of old buildings, and in the second through his wish to improve art and the lot of the people by making art a part of everyday life as it had been in the Middle Ages. In both cases, his enthusiasm for the cause led him to go against his inclination by joining institutions, and to abandon to a degree his avoidance of publicity. The first event (covered in chapter 8) was the founding of the Society for the Protection of Ancient Buildings (SPAB) in 1877 by Morris, closely aided by Webb himself. The second (covered in chapter 10) was his becoming an active socialist in 1883 by joining what would soon become the Socialist Democratic Federation. Through the SPAB, Webb would actively strive for the rest of his life to save the architectural heritage; through the Federation and later the Socialist League, he would work equally actively for a few years towards a social revolution which, if it were as violent as was expected, paradoxically threatened to damage parts of that heritage.

Chapter 5

THE STUDIO-HOUSES, AND THE 'QUEEN ANNE' STYLE

The first studio-houses to be designed for individual artists appear to have been the semi-detached numbers 27 and 28 Hyde Park Gardens, designed by Richard Redgrave for himself and Charles Cope in 1841, before the time was ripe for the idea to be taken up by others.[1] By the late 1850s, artists, and particularly painters, were becoming more prosperous, largely because of the newly wealthy middle-class art collectors. A specially designed building, combining home and workplace, in which patrons could be entertained and paintings exhibited, and which would itself either demonstrate their success or, hopefully, contribute to it, was very appealing. Red House quickly became known to many painters after the Morrises moved into it, and Webb was soon commissioned to design studio-houses for artists who were familiar with it.

More pleasing than its precedents by Butterfield and Street, and devoid of the overt Gothic detail of their vicarages of a similar size, Red House had shown Webb to be a master of the 'parsonage style'. His later studio-houses demonstrate the development of his own approach to design, as he began to use fewer pointed arches, to include a little more multiplication of detail by modelling wall planes, and to reflect the local vernacular. Certain factors that would become characteristic of his work were evident in Red House, however. These were: the primacy of achieving a convenient plan; the espousal of simplicity and common-sense practicality; the creation of what he termed a 'consistent whole' of similar character without and within, with all fronts of equal importance, each detail having a purpose and being related to the whole; the expressing of the plan externally only where to do so would help the composition; the dependence for visual effect on good composition and proportion, 'movement', contrasts of line and volume, and first and foremost on good building, instead of upon a revival of a particular style (see chapter 6). Prominent roofs and chimneys, dynamic gables and sash windows –

sometimes placed in bays or oriels and always with white frames and where appropriate sloping brick sills – were to appear in almost all his buildings, as would well-lit rooms of a pleasing variety of sizes and shapes, those on the upper floor often being partly in the roof.

Sandroyd, Fairmile, Cobham, Surrey

Webb's second studio-house, Sandroyd (now Benfleet Hall) near Cobham in Surrey, was commissioned, designed, and partly built in 1860 before Red House was finished. The client was John Spencer Stanhope, whose mother Lady Stanhope was a daughter of the Earl of Leicester. Stanhope had been allowed to take up painting as a career, an almost unthinkable one for an aristocrat at the time, because he was the second son not his father's heir and, as he suffered from chronic asthma, joining the army was not a possibility. He became the pupil of George Frederic Watts after his mother had inspected the artist and his work and concluded that Watts seemed to be a 'delightful person' whose paintings 'must be the result of a highly religious mind'.[2] After Stanhope married Elizabeth Dawson (a widowed granddaughter of the third Earl of Egremont) who had a young child, his London rooms were inadequate. He bought a large site on a well-wooded hillside at Fairmile in Surrey, where it was hoped the country air would alleviate his complaint, and commissioned a studio-house from his good friend and fellow Hogarth Club member Webb, with whom he had much in common, including a love for wildlife and ancient buildings.

Just as he would constantly urge his future followers to do, Webb exploited the possibilities of the site, which sloped towards the north and west, in which directions were fine views. He kept costly excavation to a minimum by making the house tall and narrow, and placing the cellars partly above ground under the drawing room at the northern end of the building. He used the rising ground to shelter

and partly enclose the entrance court, and put the stables on flatter ground below the house so as not to obstruct the view. To obtain the best prospects and doubtless to protect the decoration, Webb placed the dining room facing west, an orientation disapproved of at the time, and made the building only one room deep at the northern end, creating a drawing room that had windows and good prospects on all sides but the south. A large stair-hall reduced the passage area and provided an extra living room, improving upon that of Red House by having a sitting area with direct lighting and in being well sheltered from draughts by an inset, closed porch. A living hall, derived from the medieval great hall and

Above Sandroyd (Benfleet Hall), Fairmile, Cobham, Surrey (1860, constructed 1860–61): the entrance (east) front, with part of the domestic offices added by Webb in 1864

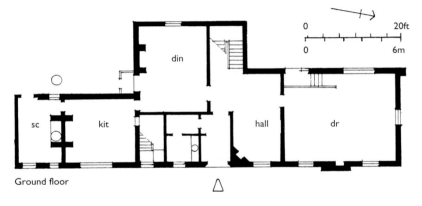

Ground floor

Above Sandroyd: plan of the ground floor

Right Sandroyd: the garden (west) front, showing on the left Webb's enlargement at the drawing-room end (1870)

introduced on a large scale by Paxton & Stokes at Mentmore in 1850, was most unusual in a dwelling of the size of Sandroyd in 1860.[3] Elizabeth Stanhope did not paint, so there was no need here for the studio to be near the drawing-room. The second floor was occupied by two well-lit studios connected by double doors, a waiting room, wc, and models' dressing room. The domestic offices (which were enlarged by Webb in 1864) and the servants' quarters and first-floor nursery suite were in the two-storey southern end of the house.

Sandroyd was as well composed as Red House.

Right Sandroyd: the main staircase in 1962, with stained glass above it containing some birds by Webb, based on fifteenth-century types (Photograph: Surrey County Council)

It, too, was built of red bricks and roofed in red clay tiles, and had similar forms and details, an exception being the major feature of the entrance front – a large timber-framed, brick-nogged gable, which resembled that by Butterfield on the north front of Alvechurch vicarage (1855).[4] It housed the main studio window, usefully disguising its scale, and drew attention to the entrance below it. Other notable features included the tympana of the several pointed arches with herringbone brickwork like that of the dining-room chimneypiece at Red House, and on the west front an emphasized brick mullion between two sashes, an item with which Webb would experiment often in later work. In 1870, he substantially increased the accommodation by doubling the thickness of the house at the north-west corner; doing this destroyed the initial simplicity of the west front and made it rather ponderous, and over-crowded at the centre. Recalling the house as first built, Burne-Jones described it as 'just a bit over-severe' but, as Webb had envisaged, climbing plants soon softened this and ameliorated its harsh red newness.[5]

The interior details, including some pointed, exposed-brick arches, were also similar to those of Red House, but the fireplaces, with grates by Webb and in some cases tiles by William De Morgan, were not as boldly pleasing as those of the earlier house. At the foot of the main staircase, which had a simply boarded oak balustrade, was a bracketed oak arch with stained-glass panels above, bearing patterns and jolly birds by Webb. Elizabeth Stanhope left the decoration and furnishing of the house to her husband. As it is known that he loved bright colours and later filled his villa in Italy with paintings, hangings, and embroideries, and furniture designed and painted by himself, the whole a mass of brilliant hues of pink, rose, gold, and azure blue, it can be assumed that Sandroyd had, or was intended to have, an interior as rich and colourful as that which was envisaged for Red House.[6]

Elements of Sandroyd that were to feature frequently in Webb's future houses include the cloakroom off the hall, the garden porches off the dining room and drawing room, and the dentilated bargeboards of the studio gable. He rarely used timber framing so prominently again, probably in part because it became a feature of houses in Shaw's picturesque Old English style, in which it was not always used honestly.

Unfortunately, Stanhope's ill health forced him to leave Sandroyd soon after the 1870 addition was completed, and subsequently to spend most of the year in Italy. Sandroyd was sold, and became the home of a school for boys and later, under the name Benfleet Hall, of a finishing school for girls. In the 1950s, a fire led to temporary dereliction after a period of neglect; the house was saved by becoming a listed building and subsequently was subdivided into flats and two cottage wings. Externally, it is now almost as Webb left it but the interior lacks several of his fittings.

Number 1 (14) Holland Park Road, Kensington, London

After Sandroyd was completed, Webb was chiefly occupied for a couple of years on the Worship Street dwellings and shops in London designed in 1861 for Major Gillum (see chapter 9) and his first country mansion Arisaig House in Scotland of 1863 (see chapter 7). In 1864 he accepted the commission to design his third studio-house, number 1 (now 14) Holland Park Road, Kensington, for his friend, Valentine Prinsep, whom he had probably met originally, as he apparently did Stanhope, during the decorating of the Oxford Union Debating Hall.

Encouraged by Watts, who had become his unofficial tutor, Prinsep had abandoned his training for the Indian civil service in which his father had served, to be a painter. Eventually, he was successful in this field and as a playwright but it was his father who paid for the studio-house that was anticipatory rather than celebratory of his son's achievements.

In 1864, Val Prinsep took a lease on a large plot near Little Holland House, the home of his parents, and there the studio-house in which he would live for the rest of his life was built the following year. Enlargement was envisaged from the start, the east wall being left blank, apart from a temporarily blocked doorway, for the purpose. Webb minimized the initial cost by skilfully making the house very compact, using basement kitchen and offices in the traditional London manner, dispensing with a drawing room as Prinsep had no wife to make one a necessity, and grouping the major ground-floor rooms round a central hall. The major rooms overlooked the large garden, including the high-ceilinged studio which, with a WC and the models' dressing room, occupied the whole of the first floor.

Below Number 1 (14) Holland Park Road: plans of the basement, and the ground, first, and second floors

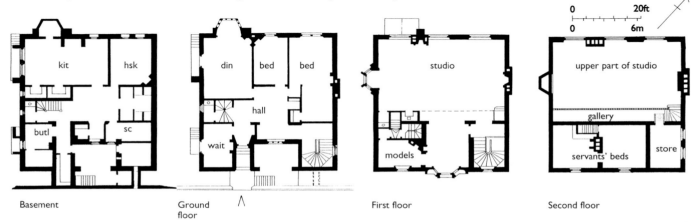

Basement

Ground floor

First floor

Second floor

Right Number 1 (14)
Holland Park Road: a detail
of the entrance front (south-
east), showing parts of the
enlargements by Webb of
1876–77 and 1892–93

The studio had a gallery at second-floor level from which Prinsep, described by George Du Maurier as a 'tender rollicking Hercules', could paint the upper parts of his pictures, which were on the same heroic scale as himself.[7] The plan exhibited what was to be an occasional anomaly in Webb's otherwise deeply considerate attitude to the welfare of servants. In their staircases, he was apt to indulge his penchant for spiral newel stairs, or narrow partly winding stairs, which stemmed from his liking for castles; obviously he had no appreciation for the obstacle they presented to long-skirted maids carrying heavy trays. In 1880, writing in the *Building News*, the critic Frederick Stephens considered that Prinsep's dining room and front door could be easily served via the spiral staircase from the basement.[8] Many servants of the day must have laboured under extreme difficulties if this constituted convenience.

The exterior of the gabled, red-brick, red-tiled house was well composed and proportioned, and of an extremely simple design, astonishingly so when first built. Even the entrance was played down, being an inset open porch with a narrow pointed arch. In an article of 1866 in the *Building News*, the architect Edward Godwin admired Prinsep's house chiefly for its 'beauty of skyline and pleasing arrangement of gabled mass', the very things which in his view were lacking in the adjacent 'altogether unsatisfactory' studio-house, also designed in 1864, by George Aitchison (1825–1910) for Frederick Leighton (1830–96).[9] Again ignoring the external expression of the plan, Webb gave the studio two pointed-arch

windows, each in its own gable, and two windows of domestic size, one of them being an oriel supported by a buttress more attractively detailed than that of Red House. New elements here, inspired by but not copied from old English buildings, include the simple brick pilaster strips derived from those on some late-Tudor towers; a bold combined string-cum-sill in angled and corbelled brickwork derived from those of late-seventeenth-century houses; and slab-like chimneys with tall red pots and a string course of angled bricks. The canted bay window under a gabled roof, added to the dining room as the house was being built and perhaps derived from Butterfield's high-level example at Milton Ernest Hall, would appear again in later Webb experiments.[10] At the turn of the century, Charles Voysey and Frank Lloyd Wright (1867–1959) were to make great play with this combination.

Inside the house, unlike at Red House, the internal arches were plastered, except in the basement; and doors had simple architraves. The Firm's wallpapers and curtain fabrics were used in almost every room, and the dados and door panels of major rooms and the boarded balustrade of the main staircase were covered in Japanese 'leather paper'. Most of the woodwork was painted dark brown but in the dining room it was dark green as a foil to Prinsep's collection of blue-and-white china.[11]

In 1876, having been asked to record the

Below Number 1 (14)
Holland Park Road: Webb's
plans of the basement and
ground floor of the old
house and the new wing of
1892–93 (RIBA Library
Photographs Collection)

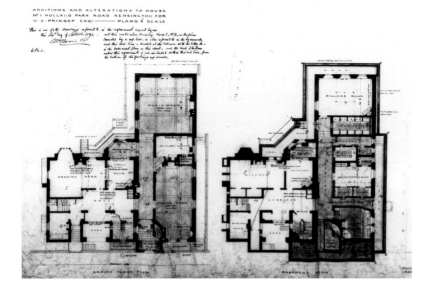

ceremony that was to be held the following year in India to celebrate Queen Victoria's accession to the title of Empress, and no longer having the facilities of Little Holland House as his parents had left London, Prinsep asked Webb to enlarge the studio and increase the accommodation of his house. At minimal cost, Webb created a drawing room by turning the guest room into a dining room and the dining room into a drawing room; and he added a second studio linked to the first by double doors, and two second-floor bedrooms and a storeroom for the studio, by throwing an arch at first-floor level over the open area between the two projecting gables of the entrance front. The balustrade and floor of the gallery in the original studio were made to fold back and rise, respectively, to permit the transfer from one studio to the other of the three large canvases, hinged like a triptych, of Prinsep's twenty-seven-feet-long record of the important event.

Prinsep married in 1884, and in 1892, after his wife Florence had inherited a fortune from her father Frederick Leyland, a Liverpool ship-owner and Pre-Raphaelite patron, he asked Webb to almost double the size of the house. The new accommodation included a large music room over a basement billiard room, a new dining room, and several bedrooms, and incorporated electric lighting and many finishes and fittings in costly materials, including the music room fireplace carved to Webb's design by the sculptor Laurence Turner. On the street front, the hitherto rather odd-looking parapet, added to the right-hand gable in 1876, became the central feature of a symmetrical attic storey which, with a new entrance bay echoing that of the 1876 oriel window, created a balanced elevation which clearly had been envisaged since at least that date.

The opulent fittings and finishes of the new rooms, and those inserted in the original block, did not reflect the taste of Webb, who provided them with great reluctance. Prinsep and his wife probably aimed to equal the magnificence of the Arab Hall added by Aitchison between 1876 and 1879 to Leighton's house next door.[12] Webb must have felt justified as well as annoyed when a quantity of marble flooring, insisted upon by Mrs Prinsep against his advice, arrived from France in a damaged condition.

The use of double glazing for the studio windows in 1864, and of concrete-encased steel beams and a concrete vault for a first-floor passage in 1892, demonstrate Webb's readiness to use new technology if it improved upon older methods. Should this prove not to be the case, then he would abandon it. He heated Prinsep's large studio with a stove but installed central heating in the rest of the building. The latter was found to be inefficient, and so by 1880 had been abandoned in favour of coal fires, which Webb had concluded were the healthiest form of domestic heating when well managed and if closed grates were used.[13] The plenitude of servants made it possible for him to restrict central heating to the circulation areas in several later houses. Number 1 Holland Park Road survives, but defaced and lacking most of Webb's fittings, having been made into flats in 1948.

Number 1 Palace Green, Kensington, London

Between 1867 and 1868, Webb designed his fourth studio-house, number 1 Palace Green, Kensington,

Below Number 1 Palace Green, Kensington, London (1867–68, constructed 1868–70): the entrance (east) front

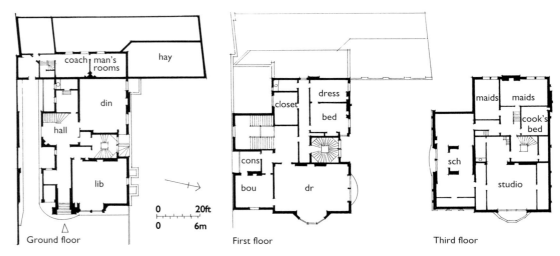

Ground floor   First floor   Third floor

London, for another aristocratic painter, George Howard, later the ninth Earl of Carlisle. As a young man, Howard was expected to be the eventual heir, though four brothers, one of them his father, stood between him and the title; this gave him the chance and time to follow his ambition to be a successful painter against the wishes of his family. In 1864, he married the Honourable Rosalind Stanley, who had been introduced to the Little Holland House circle of painters and writers by her sister Blanche, the Countess of Airlie, but who was disquieted by her husband's wish to become a professional painter; nevertheless she gave him considerable support for many years.[14] In early 1867, the young couple asked Webb, whom they had certainly known since the previous autumn, to design a combined studio-house and town mansion which was also to be the home of George's father, the Honourable Charles Howard, MP.[15] Webb had not yet built a large house in England, but the Howards had inspected Prinsep's house twice and probably would have seen Webb's recent additions to Washington Hall (see chapter 9), the home of their close friends, Lowthian Bell's offspring, and would have known of Stanhope's Sandroyd and, as the owner Francis Astley was a Stanley family friend, of Arisaig House.[16] George Howard bought the lease of a site near Kensington Palace (1695–96) from the Crown in March, after inspecting it with Webb and ascertaining that the Commissioners of Woods and Forests would have no objection to red brick, which had been used for the neo-Queen Anne house on the adjoining plot designed by Frederick Hering in 1860 to 1862 for William Makepeace Thackeray.[17] In August, Webb

submitted his design for the necessary approval of the Commissioners' architect-surveyor, James Pennethorne (1801–71) and invited tenders from six reputable London builders.

Webb was not anticipating any problems with Pennethorne because, as he shortly afterwards explained to George Howard, when designing the house he had 'taken particular pains to avoid anythink [sic] like obtrusive or erratic design', and had 'endeavoured to keep the artistic impression of the Palace neighbourhood always in mind subject only to the necessity of a modern difference'.[18] Unfortunately Pennethorne, a much older man than Webb, thoroughly disliked Webb's design, including the large gable facing the street as had been traditional in the Middle Ages. He told Charles Gore, the First Commissioner, that the proposed building would be 'perfectly hideous' and 'far inferior' to houses already erected on the estate, and in a letter to Webb he objected to the 'mass of red brick without relief of any kind' and said that the house as proposed was of a design unsuited to the locality and 'would not assimilate with others built of late years on the Estate'.[19] Webb, deeply wounded by such insults to his professional ability, countered that no intimation had been given of the need to follow the 'disgracefully heterogeneous forms and colours' of the recent stuccoed Italianate houses in 'new and more carefully considered work' which sought to respect the true character of the neighbourhood and its earlier buildings.[20] He insisted that his choice of materials – a 'full coloured red brick, with pure bright red gauged brick mouldings, arches, string-courses, cornices, &c with the addition of white Portland stone, white sash frames, lead and grey slates'—comprised the 'very best and most harmoniously coloured materials to be used in London', materials which had been used by Sir Christopher Wren [the designer of the Palace] and his peers in buildings that still displayed a 'perfectly delightful effect' despite the 'accumulated soot and dirt'. He pointed out that these and 'many other architects of acknowledged artistic power' had constantly employed the sash windows that Pennethorne found unattractive in Webb's design, with 'great simplicity & breadth of effect'; this supported his own opinion that 'for most purposes of modern convenience' there was 'no form of window so suitable for English town architecture'. He expressed his surprise that Pennethorne was hindering the erection of a building which, whatever its demerits, possessed 'some character and originality, tempered with reverential attention to the works of acknowledged masters of the art of Architecture' and 'certainly framed with a wish to avoid adding another insult to this irreperably [sic] injured neighbourhood'.

Gore supported Pennethorne's objections, however, and when called in as independent referees, so did the architects Salvin and Thomas Henry Wyatt (1807–80), not surprisingly in the latter's case as in the 1840s he had designed some of the nearby houses. Webb took the involvement of these architects as yet another insult but he regarded their inability to categorize his style as a sincere compliment.[21] At Webb's suggestion, made because he did not wish to cause the Howards further trouble, Butterfield was asked to prepare a new design but, as Howard reported to Gore, he refused because, firstly, he considered that Webb had had a 'great injustice done to him' and, secondly, he did not wish to 'place his work under the control of Mr Pennethorne's taste'.[22] Early in 1868, Webb reluctantly redesigned the gable, added more Portland stone dressings, and enlarged the porch as requested. Pennethorne then demanded that what he termed the cornice but what to Webb was the 'gauged brick band or string course', be replaced in stone; Webb refused to do this because for him this band, combined with the pilasters of the brick parapet above it, was the 'chief feature in the design' and he believed that to obey the 'arbitrary rule of another professional', even were he a genius, in such a matter of detail, 'would not improve the work of any architect who had taken pains to make his design

a consistent whole'.[23] Referee Wyatt, though angered by Webb's remark that if his amended design possessed 'any character & proper simplicity' it would again be rejected, offered to meet Webb, who must have apologized, as the design, complete with the brick string course, was finally approved on 30 March 1868.[24] Building began in June, only to be stopped at ground level by the new Metropolitan Board of Works, which had concerns about the drains; however, the new problems caused little delay, as by then Webb had learned the value of tact.[25] This was just as well because with this commission he had another source of interference that was new to him: a client's wife who took as keen an interest in every aspect of the new building as her husband. He stood up with spirit to Rosalind Howard's domineering manner but consulted her about interior details and fulfilled her requests whenever he considered them wise. They soon became good friends. The house was completed by 1870, Pennethorne's interference having raised its cost by about £1,300.[26]

To create as large a garden as possible for children, Webb made the building tall and compact, with basement kitchens, a first-floor drawing room in the London manner, and a carriage-way running through the building to the stable yard at the rear. The primary staircase served only the first floor. The position of the nursery suite on this floor near the main bedroom was unorthodox; it must have been considered eccentric at the time but it fulfilled the wishes of Rosalind Howard.

Left Number 1 Palace Green: detail of garden (north) front

An unusual secondary stair, rising around a polygon within a square, served the upper floors and was the route patrons took to the studio, which models reached by the servants' staircase. The studio was placed on the third floor to gain the best light, and had a balcony overlooking the street for taking the air or smoking and, more prosaically, an adjacent WC.

The height of the house, considerably greater than that of neighbouring buildings, was accentuated by a three-storey bay window with a steep gable above it on the entrance front; by large chimneys that defined the perimeter of the walls above the parapet; and by two tall pointed-arch recesses, on the north and south fronts respectively. Almost certainly, the latter would have been inspired by similar arches inserted c. 1820 into the fifteenth-century Hermitage Castle in Liddesdale, Scotland. To avoid an awkward junction with the porch, the bay window was rectangular on the ground floor before being corbelled out to become canted on the first floor. The north recess sheltered the open stair to the garden from the dining room, and Webb bridged it below the arch to form a passage from the major bedroom to the dressing room. Shaw was to use a similar but round-arched recess in 1883 at number 180 Queen's Gate.[27]

Between 1873 and 1874, Webb created on the third floor a large schoolroom, which extended beyond the two massive chimneys of the south front, by bridging the deep recess between them with a large pointed arch above the level of the first-floor conservatory. This addition, evidently envisaged at an early stage as there is no record of Webb being

paid for it at a later date, had a balcony with a simple wrought-iron balustrade and a gable with a bold segmental arch over the window of the bedroom-cum-workroom of the lady's maid above the schoolroom. The top of this gable, as on the entrance front, had blocks of Portland stone outlined in red brick headers, a most attractive and innovative feature.

This building revealed Webb's burgeoning liking for symmetry, and his interest in reflecting the character of local buildings – which, in the case of the Howards' house, led to an enhancement of his appreciation of the work of the English Baroque architects that had begun in the early 1860s, and, ironically further stimulated by Pennethorne, of their use of brick walls with stone dressings. Webb's design for the Howards' house, even before amendment, demonstrated that he had become totally convinced of the need for the multiplication of detail in order to avoid the ostentation of the over-plain (see chapter 6). In putting this into practice, he had revealed his already great mastery of materials, exploiting and contrasting their various qualities in inventive, sophisticated, and attractive details, as he did again in 1868 with the London office building, number 19 Lincoln's Inn Fields (see chapter 12). To the critic George Morris, the knowledge of brick displayed by Webb in Howard's house was a 'revelation'.[28]

The interior decoration by Morris & Co. of number 1 Palace Green has already been described (see chapter 3). It took many years to complete as funds were available only sporadically but eventually it displayed a unity of unpretentious design entirely in keeping with the architecture, according to George Morris.[29] The Howards were very pleased with their house. They asked Webb make design additions to the family seat, Naworth Castle, Brampton, Cumbria, and to design houses for the agent and the vicar (see chapter 11), and they were instrumental in his being commissioned to design St Martin's Church, Brampton (see chapter 12). In later years, after learning about her husband's long-standing love affair with Maisie Stanley, Lowthian Bell's daughter and the wife of her own brother Lyulph. Rosalind found that number 1 Palace Green bore too many poignant memories; after her husband's death in 1911, she sold the lease.[30] Subsequently, after all Webb's fittings had been removed, the building was turned into flats. Happily, the exterior retains both its character and its detail, despite the insertion of some windows in the north front.

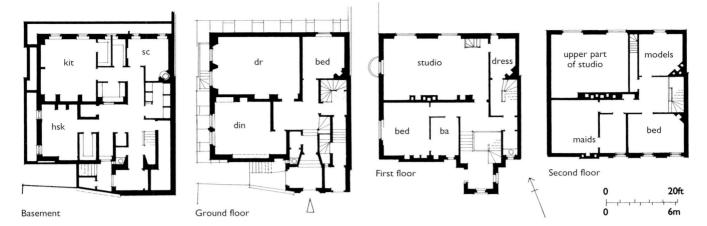

kit	sc	dr	bed
hsk		din	

Basement   Ground floor

studio	dress	upper part of studio	models
bed	ba	maids	bed

First floor   Second floor

0   20ft

0   6m

West House, Glebe Place, Chelsea, London

Webb's fifth studio house, West House in Chelsea, London, designed in 1868, was a much more modest building. His close friend George Price Boyce, encouraged by David Cox and Henry Tanworth Wells, left architecture for painting in 1849, supported by his wealthy father, a London wine merchant and erstwhile pawnbroker. By 1868, when he had to leave his London rooms, Boyce was enjoying a modest success, so he purchased the lease on part of the garden of the Chelsea Rectory, and asked Webb to design a studio-house.[31] Though Boyce had lodged in the same house as Burges for some years, he preferred Webb's simplicity to Burges's elaborate Gothic fantasy. The drawings were completed in October, construction took place the following year, and in March 1870 Boyce moved into the house, in which he would spend the remainder of his life, and to which in 1876 he added a short wing, occasioned by his marriage and designed by Webb.

To retain as large a garden as possible, the house was built on the street boundary, and given basement offices. The dining room and parlour on the ground floor faced west into the garden, and most of the first floor was occupied by the studio, which had a small balcony for fresh air, and a gallery which improved on Prinsep's by being at right angles to the chief light source. The models' dressing room was approached by the backstairs in what for propriety's sake had become the approved manner.

West House, another red-brick, red-tiled building, was positioned in the angle of the L-shaped Glebe Place, facing south down one leg of it, the side fronting the rector's garden being windowless for privacy. In appearance, it was as unpretentious and quietly dignified as the neighbouring Queen Anne

houses that it reflected. Rubbed and gauged brick string-sills and cornices, and recessed panels modelled the wall planes. All the windows except the bull's-eye of the WC, had segmental-arched sashes with no relieving arches, and the chimney on the south front had angled flues inspired by sixteenth-century examples. Repeating a feature of his country house Church Hill House, East Barnet (see chapter 7), designed earlier in 1868, Webb extended the landing over the porch, creating a gracious resting place

Above West House: plans of the basement and the ground, first, and second floors

Below West House, Glebe Place, Chelsea, London (1868, constructed 1869–70): the entrance (south-west) front, with the 1876 addition on the left (from a photograph in Webb's collection)

inside, adding 'movement' to the elevation, and echoing the main hipped roof with a small version.[32] The large segmental-topped windows of the studio, in two of the triple gables on the north front, had a more domestic air than those of Prinsep's house, and gained the more valuable, shadowless north light. On the west front, the two-storey bay window, in which gas pipes had a supporting role (as one had for the studio balcony) was one of the most idiosyncratic of Webb's bay-window experiments.[33] Later ones would be simpler, Webb presumably having decided that multiplication of detail had gone a little too far on West House.

The 1876 extension, added to the blind part of the entrance front, consisted of a dressing room above an open, brick-vaulted passage built over the housekeeper's external staircase. Hefty pediments sat

Below West House: the studio (from a photograph in Webb's collection)

rather awkwardly over the pointed arches of the passage and, above another of Webb's bands or string courses of corbelled bricks, the face of the walls was modelled like battlements – an innovative detail probably inspired by the crenellations of the peles, ancient defensive tower houses common to both sides of the border between England and Scotland, with which Webb was familiar.

The interior of the house was as charming and modest as the exterior. The lack of embellishments suited Boyce's collections of simple old furniture and china, much of it blue-and-white, and of silverware, etchings, and ancient and modern paintings. The studio was furnished in part as a living room, complete with a piano painted by Burne-Jones and possibly designed by Webb. The garden, like that of Red House, was full of old-fashioned flowers, and had a bowling green and dovecot. Espalier fruit trees edged a lawn with a mulberry tree at the centre, and vines and other climbers clothed the house and the old surrounding walls. Arthur E Street, son of the renowned architect for whom Webb had been chief assistant, described West House as a whole, with much justification, as being 'full of a perfectly natural and unforced individuality, which belongs, perhaps, to no other modern English architect's work'.[34] In the twentieth century, it was extended sympathetically to the north, and various changes were made to the interior but much of the exterior is unchanged.

The Briary, Freshwater, Isle of Wight

In 1872, George Frederic Watts commissioned Webb's sixth and last studio-house, the Briary. Twenty years earlier, having found Little Holland House for Thoby and Sara Prinsep, he had gone there to stay for a few days but, finding it easier to paint when cosseted by Sara, he had never left. In 1871, however, the Prinseps' lease of Little Holland House ended and it was clear that the land would soon be sold for redevelopment. Aware of the Prinseps' loss of fortune, partly through futile attempts to get Thoby into Parliament, Watts decided to build a studio-house in the Isle of Wight for the couple and himself. He bought several acres on the outskirts of Freshwater, between the homes of his friends the poet Alfred Tennyson and his wife, and Julia Margaret Cameron, the renowned photographer and sister of Sara, and her husband. Webb designed the house, named the Briary after the wild roses in the local hedgerows, in early 1872; construction began in the summer, and was completed by autumn the following year but not without problems.[35] As Watts was to pay for the Briary by painting portraits, an activity he disliked, to save him the cost of employing a clerk of works, with his agreement Webb employed the London builder John Tyerman who had constructed West House and whom he believed he could trust to do good work without constant supervision.[36] All did not go well, however, Watts blamed his architect unjustly, and so, after ensuring that the house had been completed satisfactorily, Webb refused to accept any fee (see chapter 13).[37]

Though deeply upset, Webb kept a dignified silence over the sad affair and managed to remain on cordial terms with Watts, to whom, ultimately, he owed the commissions from Stanhope and Prinsep, and various ones for alterations from wealthy Greek families. The Briary, conveniently arranged, comfortable, and unpretentious, for some years became part of the daily round of the Prinseps, Camerons, and Tennysons.[38] Watts, however, was there only in winter as he had soon found it necessary to be in London during the summer. He commissioned Frederick P Cockerell (1833–78) to design a second studio-house, number 6 Melbury Road, Kensington; the undistinguished building was erected in 1875 on part of Val Prinsep's garden.[39]

The Briary had a three-storey, south-facing family block, entered at its narrow end like Easneye

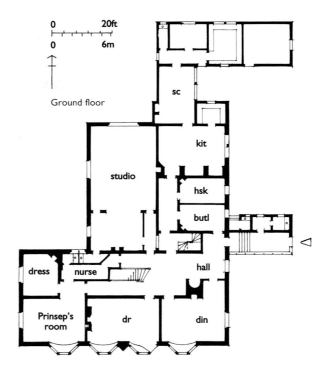

(1867), designed by Alfred Waterhouse (1830–1905), through a gabled and glazed porch.[40] Behind the block were two parallel, contiguous ranges, one containing a vast studio, the other the kitchen, the butler's and housekeeper's rooms, and, on the first floor, the servants' bedrooms. Thoby Prinsep was ill and almost blind but his room was the evening gathering place of family and friends; so, on the ground floor, Webb created an invalid suite which could be shut off when necessary simply by closing a door and had its main room in the south-west corner of the house where it received maximum sunlight. The drawing room and dining room also faced south in what had become Webb's customary manner. The large living hall, a welcome item in a house always full of guests, ensured a compact plan which, with the relatively simple roofs, kept costs low. In Watts's vast studio, an area below the gallery could be curtained off to form a private sitting room. A tall west window, protected from glare by the deep eaves above it, permitted the egress of large paintings, and a huge window provided the desirable north light.

Surrounded by lawns and tall elms, the Briary was described in 1897 as one of the most interesting and attractive houses in Freshwater.[41] Webb reflected the local vernacular by using local red bricks and roof tiles, and covering the gables and dormers with white-painted weatherboarding, but he ignored the

thatch of nearby cottages because he considered it archaic. He continued his experiments with partial symmetry, and with groups of identical gables, which had begun with pairs on Arisaig House and number 1 Holland Park Road. The Briary had three small gables on the servants' wing. By roofing the bay windows on the south front with a continuous, tiled lean-to, he created a veranda, probably at the request of the Prinseps, who had been accustomed to them in India; it formed a shaded sitting area and allowed the major rooms to have south light without risk of damaging the furnishings. As the studio windows could not be seen in conjunction with the domestic sashes, their great size presented no problem. The house was furnished with the Prinseps' collection of antiques, paintings, and china, much of it brought from India.[42] The Briary was destroyed by fire in 1934, after which it was rebuilt to a different design.

The so-called 'Queen Anne' style

All Webb's studio-houses were influential, particularly on the 'Queen Anne' style. The Briary was no exception, even though it was tucked away on the Isle of Wight. Known to a large number of people from many fields, including architects, artists, writers, poets, politicians, the aristocratic group known as the 'Souls', of which two of Sara Prinsep's granddaughters were prominent figures, and American visitors seeking Tennyson's haunts, it widened Webb's renown and increased the popularity of verandas.

Back in the late 1860s, Sandroyd, number 1 Holland Park Road, and West House, being well known to the erstwhile members of the Hogarth Club and the Little Holland House circle, encouraged other painters to commission studio-houses from other architects. Prinsep's house and Aitchison's Leighton House next door, both of 1864, were the first two studio-houses in what, over the next fifteen years, became the Holland Park colony of artists, with Watts at its centre. Webb's simple, well-composed house differed greatly from Aitchison's Italianate one but they were alike in being of red brick and having a galleried studio as the major room, and this became the pattern for the other studio-houses.

Number 1 Palace Green, a large house on an important site near Kensington Palace and therefore bound to attract attention, had the widest influence of Webb's studio-houses. The design of this town mansion-cum-artist's house was revolutionary in its pleasing general form and in its attractive details, and yet it was in harmony with the older buildings of the immediate area. It had an appropriate dignity, and a suitable amount of detail, albeit a little more than Webb had first envisaged, for a London house of its size and position, without being in the slightest grandiose. It had an English air but was neither an historical pastiche nor a deliberate assemblage of eclectic elements and, by the intention of the architect, it was not in any recognizable style. It was still exerting its influence over thirty years after it was built. In 1900, for instance, in 'A Review of the Tendencies of the Modern School of Architecture', a paper read before the RIBA, Professor Pite of the Royal College of Art cited it as an excellent example of the art of Webb, whose work he commended to those who sought 'encouragement from current buildings of real life and progress'.[43]

In designing number 1 Palace Green to reflect and be in harmony with the older houses of the Palace neighbourhood, Webb had unwittingly determined much of the character of the 'Queen Anne' style, in which several of the Holland Park studio-houses would be built. Apart from the use of Portland stone for some details, his chosen list of materials – dark red brick, brighter gauged red-brick dressings, tile-hung gables (employed on Prinsep's house), simple brick pilasters, grey lead, grey slates, and white-painted woodwork – and several of his features including segmental arches, sash windows, simple brick pilasters, aprons, and cornices, were quickly adopted by other architects for work in London and in other towns.[44] The 'Queen Anne' style was not a neo-Baroque revival but, in Mark Girouard's inimitable words, a 'cocktail, with a little genuine Queen Anne in it, a little Dutch, a little Flemish, a squeeze of Robert Adam, a generous dash of Wren, and a touch of François Ier'.[45] Webb, who disapproved of importing alien elements (see chapter 6), had contributed only English components.

The new style became popular for town houses and public buildings such as schools and colleges from the 1870s into the next century, particularly in London and in seaside resorts. It suited the lighter taste of a new generation of the prosperous middle classes, the members of which were cultivating its artistic sensibilities and in some cases had turned away from the hefty neo-Gothic or grandiose Classical houses of their parents. The other pioneers and early practitioners of the new style were well acquainted with Webb and his work. They included Shaw, William Eden Nesfield (1835–88), Bodley, Robson, John James Stevenson (1831–1908), Jackson, George Gilbert Scott junior (1839–97), Robert James Johnson (1832–92), Robert William Edis (1839–1927) and Basil Champneys (1842–1935).[46] Nesfield's Lodge at Kew Gardens suggests that he was thinking on the same lines to Webb in 1867, that is of allowing local buildings to determine character, but as Andrew Saint has pointed out, Nesfield delighted in style and decided on it almost whimsically, and his invention had petered out by 1870.[47] Bodley's St Martin's Vicarage, Scarborough (1866–67) and small country house Cefn Bryntalch, Montgomeryshire (1868) – which resembles Sandroyd (1860) in its expanses of plain brick wall, its high-level timber-framed gable, and its tall, rather gaunt look from certain angles – show that in the

1860s he and Webb were in tune; but Bodley, too, was fundamentally a style man.[48]

In the hands of others and with contributions from others, the manner Webb employed for his London studio-houses had become a style used to determine character and appearance regardless of that of nearby older buildings; a style which emphasized deliberately quaint features, and which, as a member of the American Institute of Architects noted, was 'open to the suspicion of a certain striving after picturesqueness, at the expense of good construction'.[49] Webb deplored this, of course, and repudiated the new style. In 1886, when Percy Wyndham referred to his country house Clouds as the 'house of the age', the architect demurred, explaining why as follows:

> There are two classes of houses which would rightly come under that title in England. The first is the majority one, the natural style of a 'shoddy period' of which the houses in Tyburnia, Belgravia, Victoria Street &c and their kind in the country give the type & might be called Victorian. [...] The second is the non-natural class of which the first mediaeval style is represented by – say, the Law Courts – the scholastic, by the British museum; the showy, by the club houses &c and the Dilettante-picturesque, by the (so-called) Queen Anne style. All these styles are exceedingly artificial, and have been worked and run to death by lively fashion.[50]

As 'Dilettante' to Webb meant 'having no sincerity in it', and as in his view to be 'picturesque' was to be essentially unreal, this was a major condemnation.[51]

Left Queen Anne's Grove, Bedford Park, Turnham Green, London: a terrace of houses by Richard Norman Shaw

Chapter 6

WEBB'S APPROACH TO ARCHITECTURAL DESIGN AND ITS INFLUENCE

Introduction

Philip Webb neither adopted a recognized style nor invented a new one. During his first years in practice, various influences from his background, training, investigation, and reading, coupled with his own thinking and practical experimenting, his independent and open-minded outlook, extensive knowledge of building construction and materials, and his total disregard of fashion, led him to develop an approach to architectural design through which he escaped from the morass of style-consciousness that held fast most if not all his fellow architects. This avant-garde approach, upon which he based all his buildings, was to exert a wide influence on other architects, particularly on those of the next generation, who became known as the Arts and Crafts architects.

Several major factors governed Webb's approach: his great love for the English landscape and its old buildings; the disgust and anger inspired in him by the effects of commercialism on the decorative arts and of heavy industries upon the landscape; his wide knowledge of all types of traditional buildings and their materials in Britain; his appreciation of the beauty of simple vernacular buildings; and his understanding of English architecture as a common tradition of good building, which had readily adopted worthwhile innovations and which in later centuries had retained much of the inventiveness of medieval work until its development was halted by the imposition of the alien Palladian style. Other governing influences include: the theories of the critics of industrialization; Webb's broad training and practical experience as Billing's pupil and assistant; his further experience with Street and admiration for his work; his even greater admiration for that of Butterfield; and his interest in the work of Sir John Vanbrugh and his peers. Webb was influenced also by some of the contentions of Pugin and of Ruskin, by the Romantic movement's antipathy to rules and emphasis on individual freedom and on the ordinary,

everyday things of life, and almost certainly by the medieval scholastic theory of architecture, which stressed an open-minded approach to each new building.

Webb never set down his approach to architectural design systematically. This chapter, after an indication of mid-nineteenth-century architectural thinking, is therefore a detailed investigation and explanation of his thinking and design philosophy, based chiefly on a long and close study of his business documents, including letters; his many letters to close friends; and his buildings. It includes a comparison of his design approach with that of Richard Norman Shaw, who also influenced Arts and Crafts architects, though to a lesser extent than Webb.

It is important when considering Webb's attitude to the aesthetic or art side of architecture to bear in mind two important factors. The first is that he had an unsurpassed knowledge of the practicalities of building, and of the capabilities and inherent qualities of materials, and the ways in which they could be worked. The second is that he steadfastly refused to consider the appearance of a proposed building until he had thoroughly inspected the site, made himself familiar with the traditional building forms and materials of the specific district, and considered the client's way of life and every practical need, and until he had arrived at a convenient plan that would fulfil all those needs (Webb's planning is covered in the chapters on his buildings, in chapter 7 in particular).

Mid-nineteenth-century architectural aims

In the mid-nineteenth century, there was considerable disquiet as to whether or not architecture was following the right path. Architects in Britain were roughly divided into three schools: the Classicists, the Gothic revivalists, and those willing to design in either style according to their clients' wishes. In the 1840s, a few architects had begun to hope that a new style for the age would

develop from a combination of Gothic and Classical elements coupled with new technology. In the same decade, under the influence of the Ecclesiological Society (which until 1846 was the Cambridge Camden Society) and its journal the Ecclesiologist, and of Ruskin and Street, the Gothic revivalist architects of the Church of England began to aim for a developed form of Gothic to replace the archaeological form of the style, through an amalgam of elements from English and Continental medieval architecture, Italian in particular. In the 1850s, two or three English architects suggested that architecture

Above Willinghurst, Surrey (1886–89), carefully positioned by Webb to merge into the landscape

ought to be more a matter of building than of designing according to a particular style, but they found it impossible to escape from the consciousness of style. In 1850, for example, John Pollard Seddon urged architects to think in these terms; but later he became a reviver of Perpendicular Gothic. By 1860, in theory though not in practice, some of the Gothic revivalists were proposing to countenance the use of the lintel and the round arch as well as the pointed arch in what they hoped would become a universal, developed, and evolutionary Gothic style, based on what they termed 'Progressive Eclecticism'.[1]

Webb's rejection of style revivals and attempts to create new styles

Webb had no wish to celebrate the industrialized society of his day by creating a style for the age, whether one based on a combination of the Classical and Gothic idioms or an entirely new one. Indeed, he believed that to create a totally new style was impossible because as nothing could be created out of thin air, so to speak, every new thing must of necessity be based to a degree on something that already exists or has existed.[2] By 1858, influenced in part by Ruskin, he had concluded that it was futile to hope for great architecture from a revival of the Gothic or of any other style, developed or archaeological, once the creative spirit of its creators and their way of life had been lost. Styles that had been developed to suit the conditions of a particular country could not be entirely successful in different circumstances. The 'Greek manner', for instance, as Webb explained to Hale White, was unsuited to their country because its 'simplicity & severity could not be brought out under an English sunlight'; only in a 'perfectly pure atmosphere by moonlight' could the 'nicety of the detail, & shadowing of recess' be 'clearly seen in its sharpness & serenity' in England.[3]

Webb had come to know Ruskin well in London, probably after meeting him in 1856 when Webb became a fellow member of the Oxford Architectural Society.[4] Webb accepted by no means all Ruskin's theories but he valued him for having opened the eyes of so many people to the beauty of architecture, and he found it 'hard that all thoughtful people' were 'not more drawn by the great good' in Ruskin rather than being 'repulsed by his weaker side'.[5] Believing that all great architectures of the past had been 'noble customary ways of building, naturally developed by the craftsmen engaged in the actual works',[6] Webb accepted Ruskin's belief that the glory of medieval Gothic architecture stemmed from the expression of the creative spirit of its craftsmen, who had been allowed to execute their own designs and had done so with enjoyment and pride. He also agreed with Ruskin that by forcing craftsmen to work to the designs of others during and since the Renaissance, commercialism had caused their creative faculty to atrophy and impaired their ability to judge the quality of their work.

Webb could not accept Ruskin's belief that great architecture would result from a revival of the Gothic styles because he, Webb, had become convinced that good, living Gothic architecture could never be created in the nineteenth century when the vital stimulus of working for a society for which art was a part of everyday life had been lost, the damage to the craftsman's creative power had made him 'more of a mere mechanic than ever he was before', and, importantly, architects were no longer knowledgeable about the practicalities of building.[7] After studying buildings of all ages and styles, Webb had concluded that as their inventive powers began to decline during the Renaissance, architects had turned to copying past styles and, under the pressure of commercialism, had ceased to do their own work thoroughly; by the nineteenth century they had lost touch with the realities of building and had become unwilling and 'ill-fitted to deal with buildings where scientific and practical knowledge is required'.[8] Commercialism and the reviving of styles from the past had turned architecture from a folk art with a living, developing tradition, handed down from one generation to another with each one making inventive contributions, into a poor and lifeless affair of copybooks and exhibition drawings. The Gothic revivalists 'worked on a sand-hill', he averred, and many of the results were contemptible 'childish efforts' of 'wasted labour'.[9]

In the 1860s, Webb's use of round and pointed arches in the same building, and of pointed arches with vertical sliding sashes, led some of those who did not understand his approach to believe mistakenly that he was pioneering the Progressive Eclectic style. Beresford Hope, who popularized the idea of this style, believed that it would be a type of architecture which, 'though called medieval', would be 'modern and progressive'.[10] Webb's buildings, with sources of inspiration taken from a wide range of English architecture from medieval Gothic to major and minor early-eighteenth-century buildings, were not medieval, though they were certainly eclectic, modern, and progressive. However, they did not result from designing according to a style but from an approach to architectural design in which style had no part. They were not amalgams of details cribbed from earlier structures; Webb chose a round, pointed, or segmental arch, and similarly all other elements, entirely according to what would best suit the position in the specific building. All were simply answers to building needs for Webb.

In the 1860s, however (as explained in chapter 5), Webb unintentionally became a major pioneer of an urban eclectic style, the so-called 'Queen Anne' style, through designing his London buildings to be in harmony with older neighbouring structures – although, along with all the other styles of the late-nineteenth century, he repudiated it because it had become a fashionable picturesque style, with recognized motifs, which was being applied without regard to local architectural character. Through its widespread popularity from the mid-1870s until the end of the century, the 'Queen Anne' style killed the hope of a universal Gothic style, whether developed or archaeological, and ultimately its eclecticism encouraged the development and popularity of the Neo-Baroque and Neo-Georgian styles.[11]

Webb's architectural aim

By the time he set up his practice in 1859, Webb had decided that the only hope of good architecture lay in a return to good building, entirely without thought of style, whether new or revived. He is unlikely to have heard Seddon's lecture, as he was with Billing in Reading at the time, but he probably discussed the matter with Seddon after he came to know him in London in the late 1850s.[12] By then, however, Webb had probably made his decision to reject all style revivals and to concentrate instead on good simple building founded upon common sense, good composition, and pleasing proportions.

In the late 1850s, as he explained to Lethaby years later, Webb resolved to see whether it might be possible to make 'modern architecture in some way genuine' again, and pleasant without pretences of style.[13] To do this, he concluded – as he maintained to the end – that the only hope of good, genuine architecture lay in 'putting all the brains into simple but excellent building', founded upon common sense by which he set great store, and in making it 'fitting for the climate and other

characteristic qualities of this garden-like country'.[14] He hoped that if all architects and builders were similarly to recognize architecture as the art of good, simple building not of style, and to act accordingly, a living tradition would again develop, which might in due course produce great architecture.

Simplicity

Webb had an innate liking for simplicity. Believing beauty in all its forms to be an 'enemy to all excess', he always found it necessary to excuse the elaboration of French medieval edifices despite his admiration of them.[15] They contained the 'essence of red wine', not of 'ale or mead!' like the 'comparatively rustic' English Gothic buildings that he preferred, especially those of the chaste Early English period, including Cleeve Abbey, which was 'so very lovely and gentle in its perfect simplicity of dignified art'.[16] He had begun to recognize the beauty of humble vernacular buildings when accompanying his father on his countryside rounds; his appreciation was increased through his own copying of J D Harding's sketches and his admiration for the works of the English watercolourists, including his friend Boyce. Coupled with his liking for simplicity, this appreciation led him to regard as a 'fallacy' Ruskin's contention in *Seven Lamps of Architecture* that no building without ornament could be a work of architecture.[17] For this and other reasons explained below, Webb resolved to keep the use of ornament in his work to an absolute minimum. 'I will lick my best soul-work out of simplicity,' he assured Morris in 1896 near the end of his career but expressing an intention held from the beginning.[18] Several comments in Webb's letters refer to his finding the work done to his designs 'very simple & unostentatious & therefore satisfactory'.[19] 'I never begin to be satisfied until my work looks commonplace,' he told Lethaby, by which he did not mean undistinguished or mediocre but restrained as opposed to ostentatious and exhibitionist.[20] George Jack, his chief assistant for many years, recognized this appreciation of the value of the commonplace as a keynote in the development of Webb's philosophy.[21]

Protecting the landscape and townscape

Webb's love for old buildings and the English landscape led him to believe that it was an architect's duty to protect it by ensuring that all new buildings would blend unobtrusively and harmoniously into their surroundings. In this, he was influenced by the threat posed to the landscape, villages, and market towns of England by the new heavy industries. He had become acutely aware of this during his brief time in Wolverhampton and through reading the works of the critics of the industrialized society, notably of Cobbett and Carlyle (there is more on the critics' influence in chapter 10).

The root of architecture lay in the land, he believed; without love of the land, no good work could be done.[22] He loved the English landscape as it was, and did not seek to change it. In this, his understanding of the desirable relationship between buildings and the landscape differed from that of the eighteenth-century English landscape garden theorists, who were willing to change the surroundings radically to fit their new buildings.[23] He fitted each of his houses in the countryside into the particular site and, by allowing the character of old local buildings in the district largely to determine that of the new one, he took the recommendation of the designers of English landscape gardens – that a building should reflect the character of its immediate site – a step further. Much of the harmony of the pre-industrial urban and rural landscape was due to the use of certain building forms and local materials in any given district. By echoing some of these local vernacular forms and using the same locally available materials, and by taking 'particular pains to avoid anything like obtrusive or erratic design' and never to 'err on the side of ostentation', Webb made his buildings subservient to the surroundings, avoided what he termed the 'leprosy of modern vulgar ostentation', and prevented them from 'blasting the view' and being an 'eyesore to all the country round'.[24] As he put it to Boyce with reference to Coneyhurst, Surrey (1883; see chapter 11), he spent a considerable time scratching his head to see how he could 'least mar the site with the coming house'.[25]

Throughout his career, Webb steadfastly refused to discuss the likely appearance of a building, on which he always insisted on having autonomy of design, until he had spent hours, sometimes days, in becoming familiar with every detail of the site and of many existing structures nearby.[26] By allowing the character of a site largely to determine that of each of his houses in the country, and its topography to decide the overall layout – that is, the arrangement of the main block, domestic offices, kitchen yard, stables, and coach house – Webb had created a design

guideline as helpful as but much less restricting than that of designing according to a recognized style. He referred to designing in this way as 'mastering the *possibility* of a site', which he repeatedly urged younger architects to do.[27] He could be termed 'Possibility' Webb.

An open-minded approach

Allowing the site and local buildings to determine character meant that each commission required an open-minded approach such as that which in the Middle Ages had formed part of the scholastic philosophy with which Webb was familiar, doubtless through the work of its spokesman St Thomas Aquinas (c. 1227–74).[28] Medieval scholastic theory contended that art was a practical matter, and therefore designing anything without a practical end in view was useless; and that, as the end would be different for each work, the form of each work was unpredictable and so there could be no rules for the creation of beauty – only conditions of beauty, such as integrity, proportion or harmony, and the clear expression of the purpose of a building.[29] It is likely that scholastic theory had considerable influence on Webb's early thinking, as his approach to architectural design was in accord with it, and to this extent it could be said that he worked in the spirit of Gothic but without employing its letter.

The influence of the Romantic writers

Webb's undertaking to return architecture to the realities of good rational building, away from copying or developing past styles, and his reflection of the local vernacular buildings, equate with Wordsworth's attempt to turn poetry from conventions of style and language back to recording and reflecting on the natural world and everyday life; and with the work of Sir Walter Scott, whom Webb described as 'one of the forerunners of the present movement (now being rather vulgarized) for greater simplicity and naturalness'.[30] Wordsworth's protests against the use of unsuitable buildings in the Lake District and praise of the humble cottages of the region almost certainly increased Webb's interest in vernacular buildings, an interest that was in line with the general tendency of his time to regard primitive art as better than that of cultured man bound by rules and conventions.[31] He was not attracted to them because they were primitive in the sense of being crude. To Webb, most vernacular structures embodied good building, admirable for its practicality, ingenuity, simplicity, and beauty. They retained something of the spirit of medieval architecture, architecture which had been 'always communal and had something for all from the ecstasy of holiness to coarse humour, fairy-fancy, stern-sense, grace and strength', and which had been produced by communities in which craftsmen had used their imagination and skill for the benefit of all – communities that had been more truly civilized than that of his own day.[32]

Reflection of vernacular buildings: local methods and materials

In the late eighteenth and early nineteenth century, the *cottages ornés* of the Picturesque movement – such as those by John Nash (1752–1835) at Blaise Hamlet, near Bristol (1811) – incorporated vernacular forms which were applied in a pictorial and often exaggeratedly rustic manner. As John Brandon-Jones pointed out in 1955, George Devey (1820–86), who had received some perfunctory tuition in drawing from John Sell Cotman (1782–1842) and might have been taught to paint by Harding, was using local materials and structural methods a few years before Webb.[33] Whereas Webb sought reality, however, Devey employed the local vernacular skilfully and deliberately to make his cottages look old and his country houses as if built piecemeal over generations. As he avoided publicity, Devey's work was not well known; but Webb was probably aware of it, perhaps through George Boyce.[34]

Reflecting but not copying the old buildings of a district demanded a detailed knowledge of the qualities and capabilities of local materials and the ways in which they had been worked. Fortunately, in the 1850s and 1860s Webb was able to supplement his extensive knowledge of the practicalities of building by talking to experienced building craftsmen in the counties in which he worked and gaining from them what he considered the most valuable information of all.[35] 'It has only been by constantly keeping my eyes open, talking freely whenever possible with all kinds of workmen, and reasoning out the knowledge gained that I have had any professional peace of mind for the last forty years,' he told Alfred Powell in 1894.[36] By 1888, he found that it had become almost impossible to find workmen experienced in local ways because the railway network, in making various materials, such as Welsh slate, widely and cheaply available, had

sounded the death knell for local character.[37] Webb informed Hale White that 'Our architecture, now, might be said to be designed by steam-carriage, which has almost completely killed local ingenuity.'[38]

In Webb's opinion, the builders having been restricted to working with local materials had led to an astonishing variety in the medieval architecture of the different districts of England. As well as for its greater simplicity, he preferred English Gothic architecture to that of France for its greater local variety, which in his view had come from the ingenuity evoked by the fact that its builders had to make do with less easily worked materials than the abundant freestone of France.[39] 'It is astonishing how much the material itself modifies architecture: even in this little England, one county differs from another – even in contemporaneous buildings, by the material used by necessity of circumstance,' he told Hale White in 1888.[40] 'I believe,' he continued, 'some decent building might be done now if architects had to make the best of extremely limited resources in material.'

Webb was not the first nineteenth-century architect to use local materials. At the beginning of his writing career, Ruskin drew attention to the beauty of simple cottages in his papers on 'The Poetry of Architecture' (1837–38) and decreed that local materials would 'always render the building the most beautiful, because the most appropriate'.[41] Pugin, all of whose important writings Webb would have read, recommended the use of local materials and used them himself – as did Butterfield, Street, and a few other architects, including Joseph Clarke, Oxford Diocesan architect for schools in the 1850s.[42] Despite Pugin having shown that architecture was a matter of construction, appropriate expression, and materials as well as of style, the latter remained an overriding factor with all these architects – even with Edward Buckton Lamb (1806–69), an idiosyncratic designer who used local materials with great verve and imagination and allowed them to influence the character of his churches, farmhouses, and cottages.[43] Their use of local materials was not backed by the same intensity of study that Webb devoted to traditional buildings in every district in which he worked or toured.

Despite his respect for local materials, Webb never allowed himself to become hidebound by them. In 1883, he roughcast the whole of Hill House (Greatham, Hartlepool; see chapter 11), for example, to stop wind-driven rain from penetrating the walls on the extremely exposed site and, for improved visual effect, he crow-stepped the gable that linked the entrance porch with the stable, though neither roughcast nor crow steps were traditional to the area.

The national vernacular and the 'Idea'

As well as reflecting the character of the surrounding landscape and the variety of local traditional buildings, Webb wished his larger buildings to have national character. To achieve this, he took inspiration from national building types; that is, from the national vernacular. On his tours of the 1850s, he had studied castles and Tudor, Elizabethan, and Jacobean great houses as well as Gothic churches; in the early 1860s, about twenty years before Shaw looked to the period for inspiration, Webb widened the field to include English Baroque buildings, some of which were brought to his attention by Warington Taylor, who greatly admired the large houses of that period.[44] As a result of his investigations, Webb concluded that

> at all times in England, when there was an art worth considering, by its characteristic qualities it acclimatised its gains from other countries and held its own in all reasonable equality. For instance, I know of no scholarly example of the monumental renaissance to equal St. Paul's of Wren. To my seeing there came a sea change almost instantly on landing, to any fresh fashion adopted from elsewhere.[45]

In his opinion, the native traditions reinforced by the 'revival of imagination' which had occurred in England in the fifteenth century had made 'our almost unique "perpendicular" [Gothic] [...] particularly interesting and inimitable'.[46] Native traditions had been strong enough to retain an overall English character in the buildings of the Elizabethan and Jacobean periods despite the use of some Classical elements, notably ornament. The inventive power of the English Baroque architects, and the freedom with which they used the Classical idiom, had been strong enough to retain national character despite their complete adoption of it. The buildings of these periods, being of English character (with the exception of the Palladio-influenced edifices of Inigo Jones (1573–1652) and his followers) were considered by Webb to be legitimate sources of inspiration for new designs. He took the view that from about the time of the accession of George I in 1714, architecture in England had ceased to be an art worth considering, due to the introduction, by a small number of architects and patrons, of the Palladian revival, in which there was no trace of a sea change.[47] To Webb, it was alien, developed for a foreign way of life with a different culture and dissimilar conditions, and was founded on an attempt to revive the debased Roman version of Hellenic architecture. The imposition of the Palladian style upon England was anathema to Webb, to whom a 'priesthood' dictating what is good in art was 'one of the worst heresies ever propounded'.[48] Webb used the term 'Renaissance' for Palladian buildings in England, to him a derogatory term signifying the start of the fall of Western art, the time when art ceased to 'carry the "people" with it; for it was the beginning of an aristocracy in all the arts'.[49] In his opinion, instead of 'absorbing new blood', Renaissance art had gone 'back, not to simplicity but to the complication and meaningless expression of the past paganism [...] without belief in it, and which could but result in affectation of belief'.[50]

It is important to understand that Webb's approach was not an insular one. He hoped that architects in other countries would reflect and celebrate their own heritage of distinctive vernacular architecture. When George Howard asked him to design a villa in Italy in 1875, Webb advised him to employ an Italian architect, and to incorporate as much of the existing old building as possible, and pay particular attention to the buildings of the locality.[51]

From about 1868, Webb often allowed the region in which the site lay, and the size of the proposed house, to suggest what he termed the 'Idea': a basic guide to overall form as well as arrangement, and a particularly helpful one in the case of a complex country house. In his biography, Lethaby indicated that the Idea was part of Webb's theory of design, but he did not explain its precise nature.[52] However, study of Webb's houses has shown that the Idea was a national building type, such as an Elizabethan great house or a Border pele, or even a specific building within a type, such as Compton Wynyates, the Early Tudor fortified house which influenced Standen (West Sussex, 1891; see chapter 7). Webb recorded discussions with clients only as brief notes in his site books, so it is not known whether he told them of the Idea; the probability is that he refrained from doing so in order to avoid being pestered for a pastiche.

This was not the first time in English architecture that building types from the past had inspired new buildings. Some Elizabethans built castles, for example, though the need for them was long past, including Robert Cecil who rebuilt a house at Snape, North Yorkshire, in the form of a corner-towered quadrangular castle, probably inspired by Bolton Castle (1377) in the same county. The difference between the use earlier architects made of such inspirations and that of Webb was that where his predecessors made the new building as much like older examples as possible, he borrowed only the essence and did not allow it to influence his detailing. Webb's Idea for Rounton Grange was a quadrangular castle, probably Bolton, some twenty-five miles away, but his house had no battlements; and nor did Four Gables (Cumbria, 1876; see chapter 11), although the Idea for it was clearly and aptly a Border pele. The Idea for the first design (1877) for Clouds was a combination of a medieval and an Elizabethan courtyard house, but the windows in habitable rooms were vertical sashes, not mullioned-and-transomed casements (see chapter 7).[53] Some of Webb's finest houses were those with the strongest Ideas but the source of inspiration is seldom immediately obvious to an observer. As with the local vernacular, he did not permit the Idea to become a handicap: if common sense so suggested, he would change it. His Idea for the first design for Rounton Grange (see chapter 7), for instance, was also a pele but, after the required amount of accommodation was increased, he changed it to the more appropriate quadrangular castle.

The influence of the English Baroque architects, notably of Vanbrugh

The usefulness of a governing Idea may have occurred to Webb through studying the buildings of the great English Baroque architects, in which designing within the Classical idiom, however freely, had curbed excessive originality. A hint of formality was evident in Webb's work from the beginning in the order and rhythm of some parts of Red House, in which Webb had not allowed Ruskinian changefulness (the 'perpetual variety' of every feature of a building)[54] to get out of hand, doubtless because of his training in the Classical idiom by Billing, who might have first drawn English Baroque buildings to his attention. Webb's explanation of his design for number 1 Palace Green, London, shows that he was familiar with the work of Wren and his peers by 1867

(see chapter 5). He was particularly impressed by the work of Vanbrugh, the influence of which is evident in his preliminary scheme for number 19 Lincoln's Inn Fields (see chapter 12), and of which he made a special study in the 1870s, probably on becoming involved in the designing of the Firm's stained glass for the chapel of Castle Howard in 1872.[55] Vanbrugh's work had been ignored by the Gothic revivalists despite the fact that it had influenced the development of Picturesque theory after first Robert Adam, then Sir Joshua Reynolds and Uvedale Price, had recognized that many of its characteristics fitted the new category of beauty, and despite Robert Kerr's praise in *The Gentleman's House* (1864) of Vanbrugh's 'remarkable vigour of design'.[56] The barbaric element, which Webb admired greatly, as will be demonstrated, was very evident in Vanbrugh's buildings, in which castle elements were often successfully combined with the Classical idiom and which have the vigour and gusto of the English castles and Elizabethan houses that both he and Webb admired.[57] They had a stimulating effect on Webb, their influence being most immediately obvious in the Bell Brothers Clarence Offices (Port Clarence, near Stockton-on-Tees, 1874 (demolished); see chapter 12). Though Webb disliked its 'discomfort and stateliness',[58] Castle Howard had qualities which he – like Adam, Reynolds, and Price – greatly admired: namely 'movement' (bold projections and recessions, and a varied skyline), and contrasts of light and shadow, and of texture. It also exhibited the contrasts of big and small, of bold geometrical shapes, and of horizontal, vertical, and diagonal lines and planes that Webb prized. Vanbrugh's buildings were often bold exercises in geometry which confirmed his claim that form and proportion, not ornament, were the important factors in architecture: a claim of which Webb might have been unaware but with which he was in accord.[59] His barrel-vaulted passages and extensive employment of round arches in interiors can also be traced to the influence of Vanbrugh, whose planning of country houses had an important influence on Webb's large buildings, including his liking for a central hall rising through a building to a roof lantern and his use of an east-west cross-passage (as will be shown in chapter 7).

English Baroque architects often used corner fireplaces to allow several flues to be grouped into one stack. Webb, who had quickly abandoned the use of external chimneys against a roof slope on finding that in windy conditions they caused fireplaces to smoke, adopted his predecessors' device in order to give chimneys their due importance in the composition of a house.[60] He employed it on a small scale in Sandroyd, Surrey (1860; see chapter 5) and Arisaig House, Inverness-shire (1863; see chapter 7), then extremely effectively in his new entrance of 1866 at Washington Hall, Tyne and Wear (see chapter 9). Subsequently his noble chimneys, which were vital compositional elements as well as essential practical ones, were frequently achieved in this way. His use of powerful stacks to anchor buildings to the ground and, as at Red House and Standen, as a pivot at the junction between the parts of large buildings, preceded by many years their employment by Frank Lloyd Wright for the same purpose in his Prairie houses.[61] Webb's chimneys are excellent examples of the quality of building workmanship that he achieved. He was particularly proud of his kitchen chimneys. 'In my own buildings, the kitchen chimney always struck me as having the finest touch of genius in it!' he told Sidney Barnsley, no doubt with tongue slightly in cheek.[62]

Blinkered by bias, Morris found Wren's St Paul's Cathedral 'the very type […] of pride and tyranny, of all that crushes out the love of art in simple people', and simply could not admit that anything about English Baroque architecture was good.[63] In contrast, in Webb's opinion, though St Paul's was regrettably an essay in style not 'living art', Wren's ingenuity and imagination had made it the finest example of the 'monumental Renaissance' style.[64] The more he studied the building, the more he esteemed it; in his last year in London, Webb spent many hours there, when, as George Jack recalled, 'he lost all thought of "style" […] but enjoyed the romantic abandon of Wren's compositions when compared to the pedantic stuff which goes by the same style name', and felt the 'profoundest admiration and sympathy' for 'Wren's abrupt changes, his spontaneous introduction of inventions of his own and for all [his] creative experiments'.[65]

In a letter of 1881 published in the *Builder*, Webb explained more about his admiration for the buildings of this period. He praised the then unknown designer of Ashburnham House (1662) in London for adapting the Classical forms rather than merely adopting them in what had become the 'fashion of the day'; for achieving to an even higher degree than Wren and his followers a 'richness and invention' combined with 'simplicity and directness' and a freedom from that 'vice of stateliness which so cursed the Renaissance art of Europe'; for attaining 'admirable proportion' and an 'appearance of space and dignity' yet with a 'homeliness of effect'; and for retaining in the detailing a 'touch of the naturalness and invention of an earlier style' – that is, of medieval architecture.[66]

Webb never embraced the Classical idiom. He merely allowed something of its formality – its relative formality, that is, compared to the freedom and irregularity of Gothic Revival buildings – to infuse his work. To avoid recognizable style motifs, and because he believed that only a genius, such as he did not class himself, could successfully adapt alien elements, as well as because he was against importing foreign elements on principle,[67] he did not use the Orders even when extending a Classical building, except in an apparently unique instance on the common-room fireplace at Warrens House, Hampshire (1897; see chapter 9) in a graceful compliment to John Nash, who designed the original building. In extensions to eighteenth-century houses, Webb achieved an appropriately Classical air by freely adapting the less overt features of the idiom, for example the arches with emphasized keystones of Exning House, Suffolk (1894; see chapter 9). Some of Webb's details that at first glance seem to have Classical inspirations were derived from medieval precedents. Round arches and circular windows were as much English Romanesque as Classical, for instance, and segmental arches appeared occasionally in English Gothic buildings.

The consistently good proportions of his buildings stemmed from an innate sense that was fostered by Billing and Street, and by Webb's study of medieval buildings and observation of the proportions employed by Vanbrugh and his peers. One of Webb's major aims was to make each of his buildings a 'consistent whole' but, as study of his work shows, by this he did not mean a building in which every detail was interrelated through specific mathematical ratios or multiples of a chosen module, according to Classical theory.[68] Achieving good proportions, for Webb, depended on countless studies of what had been achieved on earlier buildings, not on rules. As scholastic theory allowed, disbelief in absolute laws does not preclude the use of guidelines towards good proportion, such as the use of certain height-to-width ratios that countless observers had found to be pleasing; or of such theories as Ruskin's that a principal item with several smaller, less important ones, or one storey of greater height than the others, gives a more satisfactory appearance than when all are of equal value or size.[69] Factors such as these were what Webb had in mind, not immutable laws.[70]

The influence of Billing, Hutchinson, Street, and Butterfield

John Billing would certainly have introduced his pupil Webb to the architecture, furniture and fittings, and writings of Pugin, whose influence was then at its peak. Fortunately, Billing taught Webb to design in the Classical idiom as well as the Gothic styles, thus fostering the open-minded approach that allowed Webb to appreciate what was good in English Baroque architecture. Billing gave him a sound training in the practicalities of building, and ensured that he gained valuable experience in the office and on site of working on buildings of many types, sizes, and periods. From Billing's assistant Hutchinson, Webb learnt the value of the 'distributed middle term', that is of diagonals as dynamic contrasts to horizontals and verticals, and of greys and other soft colours as contrasts to black and white and bright colours, an appreciation that was increased by Webb's close scrutiny of Bewick's engravings.[71] With his liking for the gable, a traditional English element until the end of the seventeenth century, Webb was able to make full use of diagonal lines.

More credit is due to Street than to Billing for Webb's expert handling of composition, proportion, rhythm, and repetition, an absolutely essential skill that was evident in Red House, his first building. Webb regretted Street's devotion to the Gothic Revival, his participation in so-called restorations, and his use and encouragement of the use of foreign elements in buildings in England; but he spoke the truth in an informal sense in describing himself as Street's pupil. As well as introducing him to various decorative crafts, Street taught Webb to handle a building as an assemblage of hollow volumes of contrasting shapes and levels of light, and to use some repetition and rhythm as counters to over-irregularity. He brought to his assistant's attention the value of long rooflines and unbroken sweeps of walling, and the vital importance of designing all details oneself as a major aid to unity and consistent

high quality. In turn, the employer apparently learnt from the assistant, doubtless initially through debating design matters with him, and subsequently from the ideals and ideas expressed in the younger man's buildings, in which he took an interest. Street's turn away from assertive, muscular, foreign-inspired designs towards a gentler, more English manner in the 1860s and his growing respect for Wren's work were probably largely a result of Webb's influence.[72]

William Butterfield, whose work displayed a bold combination of common sense and invention, was the only architect whose work Webb admired almost unreservedly when he set up in practice in 1859 (as explained more fully in chapter 2, with regard to Red House). Butterfield's influence is most apparent in Webb's early work, including the furniture, but it also appears in the later buildings: in bedrooms lit by hipped or gabled dormers; in segmental arches, sashes and casements in the same building; in windows with lintels hidden under the eaves and polygonal bay windows under gables; in internal chimneys instead of the external ones called for by Pugin; in chimneys with brick dentils at the top; in string courses and, albeit less often, in arches with herringbone brickwork tympana. The major differences in approach between Butterfield and Webb are that unlike the younger architect, Butterfield remained faithful to the Gothic Revival and paid little heed to reflecting the building forms that had once been traditional in the particular district.

Architectural ornament

The major attraction to Webb of Butterfield's and Street's parsonages and small schools was their lack of ornament. At the same time as he rejected all revivals of past styles, Webb, being unlike most of his peers in rejecting Ruskin's contention that ornament is an essential element of architecture, decided to avoid the use of carved ornament almost completely. Webb found the ornament of his day deplorable on two counts. Firstly, instead of being used as 'enrichment of the essential construction' as Pugin had urged in his *True Principles of Pointed or Christian Architecture* (1841), all too often it was being used to conceal poor structural work.[73] In 1883, expressing a long-held view, Webb told his client William Thomas Tate that 'if all ornament were omitted in modern houses they would be much less offensive', but that 'unfortunately ill understood and therefore bad ornament is much cheaper than good construction'.[74] Secondly, because commercialism had atrophied the craftsmen's creative powers, contemporary ornament was lifeless: it had 'no sign of inspiration in it, no reward for the labour, which is always visible in a real work of art'.[75] Webb saw the ideal architect of the future as an upper foreman, skilled in one building craft and knowledgeable about the rest, in which the craftsmen, with creative abilities revived, would follow the architect's overall scheme but execute work such as mouldings and ornament to their own design. 'Till our born craftsmen are stirred to the depths to make their own designs in the different crafts, there will be none done of lasting value,' he told Constance Astley.[76] Had craftsmen of medieval calibre been available, however, Webb would still have restricted ornament to a minimum because of his liking for simplicity. 'Whatever you do, cut out, cut out!' he urged his assistant George Jack, who recalled how Webb repeatedly simplified his own schemes and who remembered how one scheme in particular, probably that for the rebuilding of Rougham Hall, Norfolk (c. 1870–72; see chapter 7), remained 'wonderfully elaborate and interesting' because the commission was withdrawn at an early stage.[77]

Influenced by Street's example, Webb resolved to design every part of a building himself in order to achieve his aim of making each building a consistent whole. Thereby, he demonstrated his rejection of Ruskin's contention that a piece of work of poor quality but made to a craftsman's own design was preferable to one slavishly executed to the design of another person. In repetitive mouldings such as cornices, Webb occasionally permitted slight variations, to give pleasure in the execution and limit the chance of lifelessness. For example, he allowed James Forsyth, who had worked for many distinguished architects including Shaw, to 'avoid slavish copying' of his drawing of the carving for a memorial cabinet, but he insisted on the general disposition of the sprays and leaves being as he had shown.[78] In another instance, once convinced of his outstanding ability, Webb permitted John Pearson to design as well as execute the floral ornament on some of the light-sconces for the drawing room at Standen, but insisted on the overall lines of his own drawing being followed.[79] Usually, Webb's drawings had to be followed meticulously. He told Lowthian Bell, for example, that it would be better to leave the rough block on the porch of Rounton Grange as it was than

to have the family emblem carved on it without guidance of his detailed design.[80]

Webb's drawings for ornament were excellent. George Jack, a talented woodcarver, found from experience that they were so good as to be 'rather an embarrassment to the carver'.[81] Webb always bore in mind the method by which the material would be worked and the tools that would be used, and he made the designs simple partly so as not to overtax the workman's limited abilities. He encouraged good workmanship by making informed critical comments and by showing appreciation, thus giving the building craftsman increased pride and pleasure in his work, and fostering his ability to judge its quality.

Most of Webb's houses had no carved ornament on the exterior or the interior. Although he was an expert designer of heraldic emblems, Webb was 'very much averse to ostentation' in their use, and seldom permitted them on an exterior, and, as with all forms of ornament, limited them in interiors, where he was 'dead against' using even a pattern unless it was 'really beautiful'.[82] Clouds, his largest building, had a considerable amount, however; executed during the 1880s when the Arts and Crafts movement was gathering force, it had a wide influence upon the work of the architects of the movement. Most of it was based, as Ruskin had urged, on natural forms. Webb believed that really good ornament resulted from 'some beautiful piece of nature' having so impressed a designer that by representing it in conventionalized form, he had been able to express and pass on 'some of the keen delight' he had felt.[83] Webb's assertion that the ground of a carved frieze should form a 'mosaic-like pattern effective at a distance' shows that he also appreciated the abstract qualities of ornament.[84] Webb obeyed Pugin's demand that two-dimensional ornament be obviously flat, with no suggestion of shadows, and because he accepted Ruskin's contention that machine-produced ornament was worthless because it carried no sign of a human mind and hand, he had all his designs for ornament carried out by hand.

The barbaric element, and multiplication of detail

Ruskin had discerned in the Gothic art of northern Europe a fresh, vigorous quality that he termed 'savageness'.[85] Webb, who valued this quality for its simplicity and directness, told Lethaby in 1903 that after years of considering the 'essentials' of the great architectures of the world he had concluded that regardless of geographical location they all 'had in some stage of them the "Gothic" element – that is, the barbaric; which led the builders to express themselves – and probably when at their best – in direct effectiveness, before consciousness of attractive detail'.[86] He had seen it in the so-called archaic early Greek architecture, in the early rock-cut temples of India, and in the 'earlyish Byzantine work, where the barbaric element again set architecture on its legs'. It was 'not barbarous', he continued, but was the 'beginning of throwing off fetters on the impulse of imagination', and was '*not* licentious as the satiety of the unrestrained is but rather the shyness of simplicity in growth'. He believed that the barbaric element in early Byzantine buildings had rescued architecture from the 'debased Greek art of the Romans' and led to developments that made Byzantine architecture the mother of all later Western art, and he sought to retain the same element in his own buildings.[87]

The barbaric element for Webb was bound up with what Pugin had termed the '*multiplying principle*': the increase in the number of details on a building in proportion to an increase in size, in contrast to the increase in scale of details on large classical-style structures.[88] Webb felt that such a 'multiplication and disposition of parts' was essential also in smaller buildings, which lacked the impact of magnitude, if the 'heavy-browed "wonder"' of the 'strength-giving' barbaric element were to be evoked.[89] Clouds illustrates Webb's multiplication of detail on a large country house, and number 19 Lincoln's Inn Fields, London (1868; see chapter 12) demonstrates his use of it to give a narrow building in a city the necessary visual strength appropriate for the business premises of successful solicitors.

Detail for Webb was the 'sign manual of instinct and imagination, applied only when called for by the object', and he never lost his belief in its importance; but he was continually exercised about the danger of excess, as he explained to Lethaby in 1903:

> The question to me, then, has been: how far can detail (ornament, structural or otherwise) be carried without losing the massive, direct, and simple qualities of the 'barbaric' saving element of breadth? I take it the answer would be that you may overlay simplicity with some gain, and without loss if the addition be not too mechanical — the work of slaves.[90]

Webb's wish to retain the barbaric element and his search for reality and simplicity fought constantly with his prolific invention.

The barbaric quality is certainly evident in Red House, Sandroyd, and number 1 (14) Holland Park Road, London (see chapter 5). As the 1860s advanced, multiplication of detail began to replace the slightly raw-boned effect of these first buildings, which Webb had begun to find too plain. He was probably influenced to a degree by the 1863 report in the *Builder* in which the 'degree of rudeness' of the internal finishes of his Worship Street shops and dwellings in London (see chapter 11) was deplored.[91] Furthermore, believing that to prevent architecture from stagnating architects should make careful but inventive experiments in the combining of building components and materials, and the use of the latter in new ways, he had come to accept that to reject improvements developed by earlier experimenters was to indulge in archaism, a practice he abhorred.[92]

Although Webb went back to the basics of good building, he was willing to learn from how it had been done successfully in the past. On the exteriors of his buildings, he abandoned the Gothic revivalist precept that all mouldings should be within the wall thickness. He began to model the wall planes with pilaster-strips, window surrounds, and corbelled string courses, in a manner inspired by late-sixteenth- and seventeenth-century English houses, and to soften the junction between wall and eaves by a simple cornice, always designing each detail afresh and contrasting the modelled areas with stretches of plain wall. Regarding them as archaic, Webb did not use exaggeratedly rough random-stone walls or thatched roofs, as a number of his disciples were to do.[93] He loved old stone-mullioned windows but rarely employed the type because, as has already been mentioned with regard to Red House (see chapter 2), he considered that vertically sliding sash windows were a functional improvement on casements. Except in one or two small cottages, he used vertical sashes for all living rooms, kitchens, and bedrooms, and reserved casements for such areas as passages, cloakrooms, and larders. He also used sashes in his many experiments with bay windows, which had been a traditional feature in England since the fourteenth century; at least one appeared in almost all his houses.

The over-plain to Webb was as reprehensibly ostentatious and attention-seeking as the over-ornamented, whether inside or on the exterior of a building. After the early 1860s, he used detail to create a sophisticated background that skilfully avoided the boredom of the plain and the surfeit of over-elaboration. The exposed timber lintels, brick arches, and notched wainscot cresting of Red House were superseded by architraves, plastered arches, and moulded cresting, sometimes with simple dentils. Timber beams in large houses were encased in plaster but he exposed the flanges of iron girders in the major rooms of his first country house, at Arisaig; in later buildings, they were usually plaster-covered except in some bedroom ceilings.[94] Hooded fireplaces in stone or brick gave way to the timber surrounds with the tiled jambs, bracketed mantels, and panelled overmantels that became characteristic of his work. He abandoned open grates in the mid-1860s in favour of the more efficient enclosed grates; if they wished, clients could choose from those made to his design by Longden & Co., some of which incorporated convected hot air.[95]

Reality versus picturesque appeal

Webb's understanding of simplicity and the barbaric element did not involve the plain, the barbarous, or the primitive, as his multiplication of detail demonstrates. His determination to retain the barbaric element, his liking for simplicity, and the emphasis he placed on reality prevented the increase of detail from turning the fundamentally practical basis of his work into a primarily pictorial approach. Since the days when he had hoped to become a painter, the real had always had great appeal. Webb believed that the ability to make 'picturesque sketches' was a 'fatal gift' to an architect, one that led to facile designs concerned with effects instead of structural realities.[96] He ignored the fashion for emphasized pictorial effects in architectural drawings. When studying and sketching an old building, he concentrated not on its picturesque effects but on the structure, on the way it had been put together and how well the details served their practical roles. Like those of Butterfield, his drawings for new buildings are simply information sheets from which to build, containing an exceptional amount of detail, including small explanatory sketches of timber joints and details of such matters as how to set out one of his characteristic interior flattened arches.[97]

Historical allusions, symbols, analogies, syntheses, and organic wholes

Except in his rare ornament, the deliberate use of historical allusions and symbols of any kind had no place in Webb's search for reality in architecture. Both he and Morris were bored by the current use of symbolism, as May Morris recorded.[98] To Webb, prominent roofs, chimneys, and porches were essentials of architecture, not mere symbols of shelter and warmth. Identifying his sources of inspiration, whilst fascinating, is not necessary in order to understand his buildings, for neither as a whole nor in their details do they contain hidden messages or morals. On rare occasions, believing that all ornament was necessarily representative, he did allow a client to persuade him to include a symbol in interior ornament. The chimneypiece carving of a bird returning to its nest, which indicates the important place of Clouds in the life of the Wyndham family (see chapter 7), is an example.

Webb disapproved of the making of analogies and seeking of syntheses between the various arts, whereby each was thought to gain in power, which was becoming increasingly popular as the nineteenth century advanced.[99] For him, a fine building such as the church of Tintern Abbey was a 'master-piece of the art of building [...] not at all like a poem, nor a symphony of music, nor a forest avenue', though just as 'stirring, mysterious and comprehensive'.[100] A work of architecture was sufficient in itself. Descriptive analogies, even between one type and another, lessened rather than increased the power of a building, and people who thought a 'dignified plain old church was like a barn' were 'mentally eyeless' to Webb, who accepted each type of building as being beautiful in its own right.[101] Despite his paying equal attention to what he termed its 'art' and 'science' sides, he believed that architecture was the mother of all the arts and the most important of them all.

One of the popular analogies made in the nineteenth century was that between architecture and natural organisms, which was in line with Wordsworth's ideas on the unity of all things, living and inanimate. The concept of an organic architecture suited the revivalists' hopes of creating a developed Gothic style, and they used the term an 'organic whole' to indicate a building developed to suit needs and conditions.[102] In a lecture of 1891, Morris contended that the architecture of the future must be organic; and, as one organic style can only spring from another, it must therefore be a developed form of Gothic.[103] Webb's buildings – being designed according to needs and conditions rather than fashion, to respond well to the effects of time, and to blend harmoniously into the surrounding landscape by being built of local materials, sometimes taken from the site itself – were arguably as organic as architecture can be. Not surprisingly in view of his dislike of analogies, Webb ignored this one, and used only the term 'consistent whole', by which he meant a building in which every detail and the whole were interrelated in character and scale.[104] This was not through lack of imagination and sensitivity but because for him architecture, the supreme art, was a product of man's intellect and invention, and to suggest even metaphorically that it was a natural organism lessened rather than enhanced both it and man's achievement. He used the terms 'living art' and 'living architecture' to indicate the opposite of the dead art of revivalism but, significantly, on the rare occasions he used an analogy when referring to actual buildings it was with other human achievements such as books and ships.[105] This explains the apparent contradiction in his practice of blending buildings into their sites, and mitigating some of the brash newness of their walls with climbing plants, whilst insisting that their major lines were not obscured.

Garden design

Webb's aim was to make his houses and gardens blend into their surroundings unobtrusively from a distance whilst at close quarters being clearly the products of the minds and hands of men. Bearing in mind the need to provide outdoor shelter for plants and humans, whilst studying the possibilities of the site in detail he sought the best position for the various elements of the gardens as well as for the house, and he allowed existing trees as well as the topography of the site to influence his choices. He provided easy access to the gardens from the building, often from the drawing room and dining room via porches, and ensured that there were plenty of sheltered sitting places outside, including summerhouses, and wall recesses warmed if possible by the kitchen range behind the wall. He expressed to the client his strong views on the garden that ought to surround the house, and insisted on designing any architectural features himself to avoid any conflict of material or character with that of the building. At Rounton Grange (for this and the other country-house gardens mentioned, see chapter 7), his anger was so great on finding that his wishes on the matter had been ignored that the owner Lowthian Bell good-humouredly had

the garden redone, with the main block rising unencumbered from greensward on the south front like the castles Webb loved, against a surrounding background of mature trees, and having a clear view of the parkland and the hills beyond it.[106] Roses and small shrubs occupied rectangular plots, enclosed by low walls and hedges to form outdoor rooms, along the east side of the main block and service wing, and a long, wide border, divided into flowerbeds by lawned paths, fronted the range of glasshouses and palm house containing Bell's special plants. Further away from the house, a small serpentine lake was created and, the site being flat, the earth from the excavation and stone from the same quarry as for the house were formed into a rock garden backed by trees. The high-walled kitchen garden, beyond the glasshouse range, would have been laid out in Webb's normal way by being divided by paths into four equal-sized plots for ease of crop rotation, with a well at the centre, around which a low circular wall would have made a convenient seat.

The amended Rounton layout was typical of Webb's country-house gardens. All existing mature trees were retained, and architectural features such as covered ways, archways, timber bridges, timber-framed pergolas, and simple wooden summerhouses, or two-storey 'view houses' as at Joldwynds and Standen, were kept near the house, and rectangular plots backed by a high wall, often with a seating recess like the rose garden at Smeaton Manor, and further enclosed with low walls or hedges, and fences or rose-covered oak trellises. Paved terraces often ran along the south fronts of the houses but none had a formal stone balustrade – just simple white-painted palings (even at the largest house, Clouds), or natural oak fencing. Plants in the sheltering porch, or in a conservatory designed as an integral part of the house, joined the well-tended climbing plants on exterior walls in visually linking the building with the garden. Further away from the house, greensward, shrubs, and trees gradually merged into the landscape beyond the grounds, at Standen through the use of a ha-ha across the end of the lawn. All the possibilities of the sites were utilized, and clay-pits and stone quarries were made into major garden elements – into a lake at Smeaton Manor and a rock garden at Standen, for example. In every case, the final result was a 'consistent whole', with the house and its immediate garden a work of art but one in complete harmony with the surrounding parkland and countryside.

Webb exerted a greater influence than his clients on the layout of their gardens, and in some cases on the planting, too, but unfortunately for historians he issued his instructions verbally (except for the architectural elements, of course). Apparently, he made only one layout drawing, an unsolicited one for Clouds, which is missing. An experienced gardener and plants-man, familiar with the varying conditions required by plants and trees, he could talk knowledgably with head gardeners and clients – often the client's wife – on site, probably whilst making and handing over small sketches to explain his wishes or suggestions.

Webb's exploitation of the possibilities of the site and careful positioning of the house within it, his enclosed flower gardens, his architectural elements in the same materials as the building itself, lessening in number and importance as the boundary was neared, and his use of plants to link house and garden, had a wide influence on Arts and Crafts gardens in Britain. His ideas were developed further by some of his followers, notably by the collaborators Sir Edwin Landseer Lutyens (1869–1944) and Gertrude Jekyll (1843–1932), who admired Webb's work greatly and knew some of it well, including his extensions to Great Tangley Manor and the architectural elements in the gardens surrounding it (described in chapter 9).[107]

Truthful expression of purpose, and external expression of the plan

Pugin had found in medieval Gothic architecture, but not in Classical edifices, three major truths: the truthful expression of the purpose of the building; the truthful expression of the structural method that had been employed; and the truthful use of materials. His aim in his own work, based on these, was for 'reality in design, material, and construction'.[108] The great test of architectural beauty for Pugin was the 'fitness of the design to the purpose for which it is intended'.[109] Sharing Pugin's search for reality, for Webb too it was extremely important that each of his buildings should have an appropriate appearance for its function, outside and inside. When he suggested the name for Four Gables, he informed Rosalind Howard that he would consider himself to have failed in his duty as an architect if it were thought necessary to include the word 'house' (she concurred but his wishes on this point were not always followed).[110] In Lethaby's words, Webb's 'houses embody houseness; they are homes' that incorporate 'heart, honesty, and humanity'.[111]

Webb's refusal to consider the appearance of a building until he had arrived at a convenient plan shows that he shared Pugin's contentions that such a plan was of primary importance and that the elevations should depend upon the plan and not vice versa.[112] Webb revealed the purpose of a building in its general appearance but he did not deliberately express the internal arrangement on the exterior, except perhaps in Red House and to a decreasing extent in the next two or three houses. His concern was more for the comfort and convenience of those who were to live or work in the building than to express freedom from the restraints of the Classical idiom, or to achieve Ruskinian changefulness. After the mid-1860s, if his major rooms were identifiable externally by their windows, it was not in a deliberate expression of the plan, as is sometimes thought, but because of his use of tall sash windows in all habitable rooms. Rounton Grange is an example. The four corner turrets bear no relation to the ground-floor plan; one houses the cloakroom and butler's room, another the library, and the remaining two are incorporated into the drawing room and dining room respectively, but the windows of all four are alike. This also demonstrates the lack of hierarchy in Webb's approach. He would happily use the same material or a similar moulding in a country house or a cowshed, as long as it looked right for the purpose of the building. He used pantiles, for long afterwards considered by most architects as suitable only for outbuildings, on the Rounton roofs and, above the main entrance, ogee-arched windows reminiscent of the one he had employed in 1864 in the gable of the steading at Arisaig House.

Truthful expression of construction

Webb's observance of Pugin's and Ruskin's demands that the structure of a building should be expressed truthfully, without any suggestion of a method being used other than the actual one, was modified by his common sense, and by his belief that technological innovations which improved on older methods should be adopted so long as their use would not make a building unsightly or out of harmony with its surroundings. In a practice of which Ruskin disapproved but which he did not ban, Webb often used brick for the inner leaf of a stone wall to save his client's purse, for instance at Rounton Grange. He employed iron – and sometimes steel in the 1890s – for lintels and, in large houses including Arisaig, as beams that freed the upper floors from the constraints of the ground-floor plan. Where it would spoil the appearance of a room if it were left exposed, Webb cased metal beams in plaster – a legitimate coating – but never enclosed them completely in wood as this could falsely suggest timber beams. This was in line with Ruskin's thinking but in Rounton Grange and possibly other large houses, and in the Bell Brothers Offices in Middlesbrough (designed 1881–83; see chapter 12), for the sake of an appearance of stability, Webb committed what Ruskin would have considered major deceits. He gave each of two rooms in one of the four corner pavilions of the grange a 'dummy beam' to prevent any unease arising in an observer who may have noticed the structural beams in the similar rooms in the other turrets.[113] Needing to admit the maximum amount of light into the ground-floor front rooms of Bell Brothers Offices, he used a wide but shallow bay window formed of three sashes on each side of the central entrance; to avoid giving the impression that the upper wall was carried by these expanses of glass, Webb set each behind a round arch but made it of sufficiently slender proportions as to make it clear to an observer that a concealed iron or steel lintel must be taking the load.[114] Butterfield, too, occasionally used structural elements for purely visual purposes.[115]

Truthful use of materials

Not surprisingly in view of his search for reality in his work, Webb adhered strictly to Pugin's and Ruskin's demands for the truthful expression of materials. He never used one material to imitate another. Wood veneers and marbled or grained paint are never to be found in his buildings or his furniture. He used certain coatings, however, including plaster, paint, hardwood strips, tiles, and occasionally thin marble panels and tile mosaics, because in his view they were truthfully expressed so long as they looked 'like *applied* decoration' and not as if they 'carried the house'.[116] He regarded roughcast as an honest coating material, and used it to weatherproof extremely exposed walls; but he abhorred stucco that was lined to look like masonry.

It is impossible to exaggerate the importance of materials in Webb's approach to the design of new buildings. 'All materials should settle the fitting design for their use,' Webb told Hale White – a comment that shows he concurred with Pugin on this matter.[117] To make sure he would know how to

do this, Webb had painstakingly gathered an unsurpassed knowledge of the products of brickyards and stone quarries in many districts; of the effects produced on the various types of stone by different hand-tools; and of the most suitable and durable profiles for mouldings in brick, stone, or timber. As a result of this knowledge, coupled with what George Jack described as an instinct for the right use of materials, each of Webb's details – every one of which had a purpose, as Pugin had decreed – had a shape and finish that suited the chosen material and its method of being worked, as well as the position and purpose of the item.[118] Study of his details, on exteriors in particular, reveals that his ingenuity equalled that of the builders of old whom he admired so greatly.

Webb's exploitation of the colour and texture of materials

By the 1850s, interest in architectural polychromy had become popular with the architects of the Gothic Revival through the writings of Owen Jones, Ruskin, and Street.[119] Colour had seldom been of interest or importance since the Palladian revival. In High Victorian Gothic churches, the process by which the wall was built was expressed in bands of colour – inside as well as outside in some – and marbles of different colours formed brightly patterned inlays in interiors. Butterfield was the foremost colourist. 'If my own work bears no resemblance to yours it is because I could not do good work like yours and therefore I do not try,' Webb told him in 1869.[120] Webb had used the colour and texture of materials to replace style motifs and ornament from the beginning, and by the late 1860s his work had veered further away from that of Butterfield. In number 1 Palace Green, number 19 Lincoln's Inn Fields, and Church Hill House (later Trevor Hall), East Barnet (1868; see chapter 7), Webb had introduced a more subtle and sensitive use of colour, against which Butterfield's polychromy sometimes appears strident.

Believing them to be to architecture what rhythm is to poetry, Webb studied the colours and textures of building materials with the concentration of a painter. He disposed them carefully about a building, shading the different materials together and balancing and contrasting light and dark with a consummate skill that was partly innate and developed further through his observation of the generally soft colours of the English landscape and his study of Thomas Bewick's use of mid-tones in engravings.[121] Webb reflected the wider choice of available materials in his buildings in the south of England; in the north and in Scotland few materials had been available locally before the coming of the railways, so in these regions he used a single wall material, relying for subtle colour effects on richly hued stone or hand-made bricks. George Jack recalled that Webb always specified seconds of the latter because of the greater variety of colour and surface, and ensured that plenty of dark headers were employed; and that he always used lime mortar, never cement.[122] Webb, who appears to have been the architect who reintroduced it for London buildings, had the exterior woodwork painted white, in town and countryside, as an aid to liveliness.[123]

Such was the importance of colour in Webb's buildings that they lost much of their effect in monochrome illustrations. This had no inhibiting effect on Webb because, following the 1863 criticism in the *Builder* of his Worship Street terrace, he had resolved never to publish or exhibit his work.[124] Some of his houses may seem a little disappointing when first encountered in such illustrations, in contrast to the immediate charm of Shaw's picturesque partly timber-framed country houses, for instance. In actuality, however, Webb's exteriors, in which colour and texture have great importance, are extremely pleasing. They increase in appeal as the onlooker becomes more familiar with them and observes how well the ingenious and inventive details serve their practical and aesthetic purposes, and how the material has influenced their design; for instance, how the profiles of mouldings are varied to suit the local stone.

Webb handled textures – to which he had been attracted through sketching, and by the drawings of Harding, the paintings of Boyce, and Ruskin's writing – as skilfully and sensitively as he did colour. Except where smoothness was necessary for practical purposes, he allowed the marks made by the particular hand-tools of a district to express the way the stone had been worked. Interesting texture at a distance was achieved by modelling the wall planes with simple items such as pilaster-strips, string courses, and cornices. In districts where the method had once been traditional, he sometimes used cut and rubbed bricks – on the wing he added to Cranmer Hall, Norfolk (1864–66; see chapter 9), for instance – but more often he created decorative vertical or horizontal bands using the bricks as simple blocks, and reserved complicated profiles for stone, which had to be finished by hand in any case. Standen, a masterly and innovative amalgam of stone, brick, tile-hanging, weatherboarding, and roughcast, with extremely subtle colouring and varied textures, is an excellent example, in both overall effect and in details, of Webb's fitting and sensitive, 'delicate tender' use of materials in inventive ways.

Whilst not accepting Harding's view that buildings are at their most beautiful in decay and Ruskin's that they reach full beauty only after surviving the battering of several centuries, Webb admired weathered materials for their intrinsic not associational beauty, and ancient surfaces as proof of authenticity against the falsehoods of neo-Gothic imitations.[125] He certainly believed that buildings should be designed with a view to their long-term appearance, to the inevitable changes that would be wrought by time and weather. With forethought and care, these changes could be for the better; and if buildings weathered well, they would remain in harmony with nearby traditional buildings (for which durability had been an economic necessity) and thus would be more likely to please future generations as well as costing less to maintain. To ensure long-term good and pleasing appearance, Webb eschewed ephemeral fashions and based his designs on his extensive knowledge of the effects of weather, moss, and lichen on materials, walls, and roofs of all aspects, and on buildings of every type, size, and age. In a slightly changed position or aspect, or when combined with new materials, reused materials would have created an unreal effect; so Webb seldom used them, and for this reason he advised John C Ramsden (1835–1910) against reusing roof tiles as weather-tiles at Willinghurst, Surrey (1886; see chapter 7).[126] To age materials artificially would have gone against reality, been untrue to time so to speak, and consequently Webb never permitted it – even when it meant that a replaced item, such as a replaced finial on Rounton Grange, would look slightly obtrusive for some years.[127]

As a result of their locality rather than of personal preference, roughly twice as many Webb buildings were of brick as were of stone or stone and brick combined. He was not the first architect to use red brick (as was pointed out regarding Red House in chapter 2), but it is understandable that some in the Pre-Raphaelite circle should have believed him so. It might have been one of the group – perhaps Dante

Gabriel Rossetti, a dab hand with a limerick – who added the last couplet to the verse circulating in London at the time:

> With reason is Caesar Augustus renowned
> For of marble he left what of brick he had found.
> But our Mr. Nash we must own is a master,
> For he found us of brick and he left us of plaster.
> Now Webb has succeeded in trumping the trick –
> For he found us of plaster and left us of brick.[128]

However, though not revolutionary in material, Red House and Sandroyd, and to a greater degree the studio-houses of the 1860s (number 1 Holland Park Road, number 1 Palace Green, and West House, Chelsea (1868; see chapter 5), greatly increased the popularity of red brick through their role in the development of the 'Queen Anne' manner.

In replacing style motifs with the colours and textures of well-crafted materials, and rarely countenancing applied ornament, Webb had given the work of the ordinary building workman a much greater importance by making first-rate workmanship in good materials essential. Webb achieved this quality through his vast knowledge of the qualities and capabilities of materials and the processes by which they could be worked; by his careful selecting of contractors, provision of good supervision, and insistence on the replacement of poor work and materials; and by his encouragement of the workmen through showing interest in their work and praising it when well done. 'Workman' was a term of respect to Webb; he seldom used 'craftsman', presumably because of his belief that the craftsmen of his day produced poor-quality work, albeit largely through no fault of their own. In 1861, the prospectus of the new Firm had been headed 'Morris, Marshall, Faulkner & Co., Fine Art Workmen'.

Webb's use of new technology

Webb's railings were all of traditional wrought iron, but he kept an eye on the possibilities of cast iron. Going against Ruskin's precept that metal should not be used in this way,[129] he supported an external balcony at West House on a length of cast-iron gas pipe, for example, and used slender cast-iron columns as mullions between the sashes of the two large Bell Brothers Offices windows. His abandoned design of the early 1870s for an engine house at Atherston Colliery in Lancashire (see chapter 12) included large cast-iron columns as well as iron roof trusses; notes on the drawings show that he understood the strains

and stresses involved.[130] Webb normally calculated the sizes of structural members himself, doubtless helped by technical books.

Possibly encouraged by his ironmaster clients and personal friends Lowthian and Hugh Bell, he sometimes replaced king-posts in trusses with one-inch iron king-bolts, and he used similar rods either as the uprights or in addition to them in latticed girders employed as purlins – in the stable block at Joldwynds, for example, or as the ridge-pieces of massive roofs, as at Rounton Grange.[131] In Smeaton Manor, North Yorkshire (1876; see chapter 7) and possibly other large houses, he used the rods, suspended from the roof and concealed in partition walls, to reduce vibration in floors and possibly also to reduce the size of beams in the ground-floor ceiling.[132] His use of the rods to reinforce the timber uprights and to reduce vibration appears to have been extremely unusual at the time.[133]

Given a willing client, a house constructed entirely of glass and iron would have been feasible and could have been adequately heated in Webb's day, but such a building would not have reflected old local buildings. He did employ iron-framed glass in conservatories and passage roofs, but used arches of brick or stone to make them part of the consistent whole, examples being the ambulatory and palm house at Rounton Grange and the conservatory at Standen.[134] His vertical sashes were always timber-framed, but he occasionally set casements in iron. The abolition of the duty on glass in 1845 and of the window tax in 1851 had stimulated the development and popularity of large sheets of glass. Webb used them in roof lights and conservatory roofs, but not in windows, because there they gave a false and disturbing impression of open space, which was avoided by the employment of small panes that also captured the sparkle of light reflected from their slightly varying planes.

Webb used concrete for foundations and some lintels but he did not share Shaw's interest in developing concrete building blocks and tiles, presumably because in his view this material would not weather pleasingly or be in harmony with traditional ones.[135] In 1890–91, he built a pair of octagonal iron-reinforced concrete vaults for the picture gallery in his extension to number 23 Second Avenue, Hove and designed an unexecuted iron and concrete saucer-dome for Standen (see chapters 9 and 7 respectively); but he never designed a complete structure in reinforced concrete, though they became practicable in the 1880s.[136] 'Reinforced concrete ought to do a lot for us,' Shaw opined to Lethaby; in contrast, when George Jack suggested to Webb that there might be a future in this construction, Webb replied, 'Perhaps so, but, Jack, it's not architecture.'[137] Webb could never have respected structures poured into a mould as he did those built course upon course by human hands.

He kept himself up-to-date on all technical developments, from the qualities of new cements to the Bowerbarffing of water pipes and the chemical action of soft water on lead pipes. In his opinion, most of his fellow architects had little knowledge of any of the practicalities of building and were reluctant to expose the fact or to lessen their own prestige by approaching experts in particular fields. Webb willingly consulted engineers on matters of water supply, drainage, and heating. He attended geology lectures to learn more about subsoils and, once convinced its primary purpose was not to improve its members' status or hide their ignorance, he joined the Sanitary Institute to keep abreast of developments in sanitation and drainage.[138]

He advised against gas lighting because of its damaging effects on interiors, but welcomed electric lighting, and designed delicate fittings to suit its character. He refused to have a telephone or typewriter in his office because of their disruptive effect. Webb was not against machines in general, only those which had unfortunate effects on the landscape or townscape and on craftsmanship, or which turned factory workers into slaves. He welcomed such machines as water-pumps because they saved irksome human labour, but was always angered by finding machines in a builder's yard where, in his opinion, they supplanted handwork and thereby led to carelessness, unwillingness to take pains, and ultimately to bad workmanship.[139]

Architecture: a product of individual genius, or of experience and effort?

The Romantic movement's understanding of art as the expression of the artist's spirit, a matter of individual genius unfettered by restraints, carried a grave danger that art might become solely a vehicle for indulgent and exhibitionist self-expression on the part of a genius – whether painter, sculptor, or architect. In Webb's opinion, good art of all types depended to great extent on the painstaking effort of a trained and experienced artist, not a flash of inspiration and invention on the part of a genius. 'All good work has been produced by strenuous effort in the past, now we are expected to do it as easily (as Morris said) as not answering our letters,' he told Lethaby, who believed that taking pains was the secret of Webb's success in his work; and he warned of the 'great danger' that students, including Lethaby's, might 'look on art as a trick to be learnt or found out', whereas satisfactory work could 'only come of hard pounding'.[140] Everyone has a degree of creative power, but geniuses possess most of all, and with strenuous effort can produce great work even in decadent times, when the stimulus of sharing the faith and hopes of a community is lacking. At such times, they often were 'flames of light to the world', but at others they had 'helped on corruption' – Michelangelo, in the consciousness of style and lack of simplicity in his later work, being an example.[141] However, Webb's belief that objects could be beautiful in themselves to all those with a 'natural aptitude for seeing into the best of things, though possibly without the power to master the subtleties of motive and execution' that an experienced architect or painter would have, makes it clear that he did accept that the associationist understanding of beauty as being dependent on the thoughts evoked in the mind of the observer by the object was true to an extent.[142] His thinking on this matter thus combined three different theories of art: as the expression of the individual; as the expression of the unconscious folk spirit; and as the product of the artist's expertise and experience.

Webb and the Neo-Baroque and Neo-Georgian styles

Webb's increased employment of symmetry, coupled with his use of vertical sashes and his reflection of local buildings from the late seventeenth and early eighteenth centuries, led and still leads some observers to assume that he either had espoused English Classicism or was willing to design in the Gothic or the Georgian style according to the whims of his clients (for more on this subject, in connection with Smeaton Manor, Exning House, and Warrens House, see chapters 8 and 9). That Webb's approach had not changed is demonstrated by the advice he gave in 1888 to a would-be client, Frederick A White, which lost him the valuable commission to design number 170 Queen's Gate, London. Webb was in need of jobs but nevertheless, as White recorded, he expounded at length his views on the relations between architect and client and insisted that White should reflect on the fact that Webb was 'very despotic, that he would never make a concession he might think unwise to economy, nor please his client at the expense of his conscience'.[143] White, who probably had shown Webb his sketches of the eighteenth-century type of house he required, decided to interview Shaw before making a decision. Presumably having signified his willingness to abide by White's sketches, Shaw got the job and designed the Neo-Georgian house accordingly.[144] Ironically, it had been Webb's West House, designed to reflect but not to copy the neighbouring houses of the early-eighteenth-century Cheyne Walk, which had led White to appreciate such buildings.[145]

Differences and similarities in the design approach of Webb and Shaw

Shaw's early work was influenced widely by Webb, whom in later years he considered was a 'very able man indeed, but with a strong liking for the ugly'.[146] Shaw probably had in mind the muscular manner known as 'Go', favoured by Lamb and a few other eccentric Gothic revivalists, which was regarded as a deliberate attempt to shock through ugliness.[147] In fact, Webb neither liked nor sought muscular ugliness. A 'delicate tender' quality had been discerned in his work of the late 1860s by Warington Taylor, who had in mind Ruskin's assertion that medieval Gothic architecture looked as if built by strong men yet had 'some exquisite tenderness which seems always to be the sign manual of the broad vision'.[148] Drawing Webb's work to the attention of his friend E R Robson, Taylor averred that the Gothic revivalists were seizing 'all that is huge [and] coarse in French Gothic', whereas 'everything English' was characteristically 'essentially small, and of a homely farmhouse kind of poetry', and that only Webb was aiming for a desirable and similar 'English softness'.[149] Lethaby thought that the term 'rustic delicacy', used by Webb to describe a certain cottage, 'illuminated the sort of things he cared for'.[150]

A fundamental difference in approach was that where Shaw saw control of invention as leading to the ugly, Webb believed that its indulgence led to unreality. Unlike Webb, Shaw was happy to add picturesque details; but he did exercise some control – Lethaby recalled that Shaw's favourite maxim was

'keep it quiet'.[151] In some of Shaw's large country houses, the major rooms are expressed as individual projections modelled by wide bay windows and inglenooks. This increased the picturesque appearance and the cost of his country houses, sometimes in the case of the latter to the detriment of the interiors through shortage of funds. Webb, on the other hand, conscientiously studied every detail of his buildings which, as Brandon-Jones points out, gave his work a strong 'feeling of reality and solidity that contrasted with the scenic effects of his rivals'.[152] Webb would never have left it to the builder to decide the position of an essential practical item such as a flue, as Shaw is known to have done.

Shaw was not in sympathy with Webb's searching for simplicity, his rejection of all past styles, his emphasis on the use of local materials and traditional local forms, or his fitting of the building into the site. Shaw considered it his duty to design beautiful buildings in any style he or his client desired. He and W E Nesfield created the Old English style as an inventive domestic Gothic for houses in the country, based chiefly on elements from the medieval manor houses of Kent and Sussex, which could be freely combined into an infinite variety of exuberant, romantic compositions. Shaw's application of the style in other parts of Britain without regard to local architectural traditions gave some of his houses – including Cragside, Northumberland (from 1869) – a slightly alien air. Allowing his country houses to dominate the landscape increased this effect. In contrast, Webb's careful fitting of a house into the site helped to ensure that it would be in harmony with its surroundings. Until the 1880s, Shaw used the so-called 'Queen Anne' style for his urban buildings, whereas Webb applied the same design approach to buildings in town or countryside.

Despite the great admiration he had for Pugin, Shaw did not always follow his call for truthful expression of construction. He used false timber framing at Cragside in the 1870s, for example. This can be equated with Webb's inessential beams at Rounton Grange, but whereas Shaw was aiming to deceive, Webb was merely seeking to reassure. Both men accepted Pugin's contentions that a convenient plan should be arrived at before the design of the exterior was considered, that the appearance of a building should be appropriate for its use, and that it should be of an appropriate national character, derived from using only traditional English buildings – or Welsh or Scottish, as the case might be – as sources of inspiration.[153] They each carried out inventive experiments in using traditional materials in new ways, and employed new technology when it improved on older methods; and they relied on a selected and experienced contractor and his workmen, who could be trusted to produce a sound structure under supervision.

In his first years in practice, Shaw played a part in the revival of the decorative crafts under the influence of Ruskin; but in later years he considered that all the critic's writing was 'fallacious'.[154] Ironically, however, he frequently allowed trusted assistants, pupils, and craftsmen to design the ornament for his buildings, the craftsmen thereby fulfilling the Ruskinian ideal of the Arts and Crafts movement – in contrast to most of the architects of the movement who, as already pointed out, followed Webb in designing everything themselves to ensure a unified whole.

By 1882, Shaw was deploring the fact that, whereas 'old work was real', his and that of most contemporaries was 'not real, but only like real', and he had decided that, since 1851, architects had been wrong to try to revive Gothic because it had proved to be 'quite unsuited to the present day'.[155] In the early 1880s, doubtless influenced to some degree by the fact that several of his students and assistants – including their mentor Lethaby – had recently turned to Webb for a more serious approach with strong ideals, Shaw began to design in a more consistent, thoughtful manner. This new approach still exhibited plenty of invention but also paid some attention to local character, and was based on the Palladian buildings of Inigo Jones, and the work of the English Baroque architects.[156]

Shaw's influence on the Arts and Crafts architects and their work

Shaw did not regard himself as belonging to the Arts and Crafts movement, but he is usually associated with it.[157] The movement began to take formal shape in Shaw's office in 1884 when the St George's Art Society, founded earlier by his pupils, amalgamated with the Committee of Fifteen, which consisted mainly of decorative artists and craftsmen, to form the Art Workers' Guild (AWG). As mentioned in chapter 3, the guild became the leading forum and meeting place of the movement, and similar guilds

or societies were soon established in many large towns. Shaw took a fatherly interest in the activities of the AWG but he never became a member. Seeing the architect as an isolated designer of masterpieces, he did not share the members' aims of reuniting architecture and the decorative crafts and improving the status of craftsmen on Ruskinian lines. Shaw's deliberate creation with Nesfield of the Old English style, and the intentional part he played in developing the 'Queen Anne' style, went against the important Arts and Crafts principle – which had come from Webb – of avoiding all style.

However, Shaw's Old English buildings certainly influenced the early works of many young British Arts and Crafts architects, including Baillie Scott and Lutyens.[158] The Old English houses and Shaw's 'Queen Anne' work influenced Arts and Crafts architects in continental Europe, and in America and Australia, where the 'Queen Anne' style was associated almost exclusively with Shaw. It is arguable whether or not the 'Queen Anne' style is part of the Arts and Crafts movement. As it encouraged the use of well-designed carved ornament, and as in many towns it was in harmony with the then prevalent houses of the late seventeenth and eighteenth centuries, 'Queen Anne' can be regarded as the urban Arts and Crafts manner. The houses designed by Shaw and others for Bedford Park, in a restrained version of the style, influenced the design of houses in the garden suburbs and cities that were certainly a part of the movement, and those of the early housing estates of local authorities.[159] Shaw's churches further encouraged the adoption of a calm, lighter, more English neo-Gothic for ecclesiastical buildings, including some Arts and Crafts churches. Importantly, he gave his pupils an excellent training, with some practical design work and invaluable experience on site as clerks of works. When they left his office, he handed them a commission with which to set up practice. Several of them became Arts and Crafts architects of distinction, including Ernest Newton (1856–1922), Lethaby, Edward Schroeder Prior (1852–1932), Sidney Barnsley, Sir Mervyn Macartney, and Robert Weir Schultz (1861–1951).[160]

Webb's influence on Arts and Crafts architects and their work

In the interests of historians, Webb's philosophy of architectural design must be given a name, though he would have judged any name to be undesirable and pretentious. The 'vernacular style', which it has been called, is a misnomer, whilst 'vernacular approach' disregards the importance to it of the more individually significant buildings – as does 'regionalism', which ignores, as Webb did not, the differences within a region.[161] The most apposite term is the 'national vernacular approach', which covers Webb's reflection of both the humble local vernacular and the more eminent buildings that form the national vernacular.

When the Arts and Crafts movement was taking shape in the 1880s, country-house commissions had become rare because of a sharp fall in land values in the previous decade. Webb had already demonstrated that designing the new category of rural dwelling, the 'small house in the country', was a worthy activity for architects, and that vernacular buildings of the humble type deserved attention and were appropriate sources of inspiration. Clouds, and number 19 Lincoln's Inn Fields and Bell Brothers Offices, proved respectively that the approach could be applied successfully to a large edifice and to urban office buildings. Webb's approach, which placed equal importance on the art and science sides of architecture, offered firm principles and practical guidelines on design, within which great variety was possible through the reflection of local character, and which granted ample design freedom to the individual, albeit with some self-abnegation. The combination of principle, guidance, and freedom was attractive to young architects seeking a serious philosophy of design and wishing to escape from the tyranny of style revivals. Most of the Arts and Crafts architects adopted Webb's national vernacular approach in whole or in part, amending it here and there to suit their own thinking and inclination. Some of them had learnt of it not directly from Webb but through his followers, that is via what George Jack termed Webb's 'most potent quality of silent influence'.[162] For instance, Webb never joined the AWG, despite being begged to do so, because he feared that it might further increase the gap between design and making, but several architects, including Halsey Ralph Ricardo (1854–1928) and James Marjoribanks MacLaren (1843–90), came under his influence through their own membership of the guild.[163]

At the time and since, some architects and commentators have believed that Morris exerted the chief influence on Arts and Crafts architecture. Morris, however, offered only general ideals, not practical suggestions for the actual design of new buildings. The only guide he offered for new architecture, it will be remembered, was that the 'form as well as the spirit, must be Gothic'.[164]

Webb's decision to return architecture to good building without thought of styles, new or revived, had a wide influence on Arts and Crafts architects, and made their work as much a revolt against style revivals as it was a reaction against commercialism and machine production. His contention that ornament is not an essential of architecture, and his proving of it in his buildings, had a similarly wide influence. Such ornament as he did employ – notably that of Clouds, executed during the 1880s when the movement was taking shape – showed that good, lively decorative art was possible under current conditions if the architect and craftsman co-operated closely, despite his avowed belief that this would only be achieved when craftsmen with revived creative powers could be trusted to design the work well. The Arts and Crafts architects shared Webb's belief but many of them followed his paradoxical example and themselves designed the ornament for their buildings, chiefly to ensure a unified whole but also because they enjoyed doing so, and thereby followed one ideal of the movement whilst going against another.

Most of Webb's closest followers met him in connection with the Society for the Protection of Ancient Buildings, through which Webb and Morris made the sympathetic repair of old buildings, instead of their so-called 'restoration' or replacement, a part of Arts and Crafts practice. Through the SPAB (as explained in more detail in chapter 8), Webb held an informal school of practical building, many of the unofficial pupils of which gained experience on site through his auspices. Most of them became prominent Arts and Crafts architects, including Prior and Webb's close friends Lethaby, Ernest Gimson, Detmar Blow, Alfred Powell, Charles Canning Winmill, Sidney and Ernest Barnsley, and Hugh Thackeray Turner.[165] Webb's admirers, including Lutyens, inspected and studied his buildings, particularly those in London and the surrounding counties. Christopher Hussey records that Lutyens attributed to Webb the inspiration for much of his own early work, and that he admired Webb's logic, knowledge of proportion, mastery of materials, and fertile invention, and set out to emulate him.[166] Lethaby, taught by Webb that 'architecture should mean solid realities, not paper promises, names, dreams', and Prior, whose design philosophy was very similar to Webb's, passed on the older architect's approach to their students at the Central School of Arts and Crafts and at Cambridge, respectively.[167] Voysey never credited Webb with having had any influence on himself or Arts and Crafts architecture in general but he must have known of his design approach through his own close friends, Mackmurdo and Lethaby. Voysey was not in sympathy with Webb's wish to reflect the local vernacular or to avoid creating a personal style, but he would have learnt a 'great deal from Webb's considered, rational interpretation of the vernacular' as Voysey's biographer Wendy Hitchmough says; and as John Brandon-Jones, who knew the man, points out, Voysey's notion of the ideal architect was fulfilled by Webb in his refusal to compromise his principles to suit a client's demands.[168]

Through his buildings and (as explained in chapter 3) his work for the Morris firm, Webb influenced British architecture, fittings, and furniture well into the first decades of the twentieth century. Largely under his influence, the Arts and Crafts architects created some of the most pleasing, successful, and influential buildings ever produced in Britain. In escaping from consciousness of style, Webb the pioneer had to exercise great control over his inventive powers. His disciples were able to follow his path with a less serious step, with the result that, at first glance, their buildings sometimes seem more attractive externally than do Webb's. Closer study, however, almost always reveals that his are the more interesting buildings, and often shows that he was exploring a particular notion long before the younger architects did so.

Webb's smaller houses and cottages, and his prototype 'Queen Anne' buildings in London, influenced – like Shaw's – the houses of the garden suburbs and Letchworth, and through them, local authority estate housing in the early decades of the twentieth century. Through some of his followers, notably Winmill, Webb's approach influenced the schools, the fire stations and other small municipal buildings, and the housing schemes, designed by the architects of the London County Council, which also affected local authority estates. Through his disciples, and illustration and commendation of his and their work in Muthesius's important *Das englische Haus* (1904–05) and the journals *Country Life*, the *Studio*, the *Hobby Horse*, and similar ones abroad, and via the architects – including Frank Lloyd Wright, for instance, a close friend of Ashbee – who travelled to Britain to see the buildings, Webb's approach influenced Arts and Crafts architecture in North America and in Europe, including the National Romantic buildings of Sweden.

Webb's influence on Modern movement architecture

Largely because of his abandonment of style revivals and exterior ornament, the emphasis he placed on function, simplicity, and common sense, and his truthful expression of materials and structure, propagandists of the architecture of the twentieth-century Modern movement saw Webb as one of its important pioneers.[169] Red House certainly had considerable influence. However, the movement's deliberate avoidance of all links with the past, its eventual creation of a new style for the machine age, and its extolling of industrialized building and ignoring of local materials and building forms, had no part in Webb's thinking. He should not be regarded as an intentional pioneer, except perhaps of a minority of the movement's architects who eschewed the new style and reflected local traditions to a degree. The International style of the movement, which matured in the late 1920s, was, as its name clearly indicates, the very antithesis of Webb's national vernacular approach, which sought to retain and celebrate national and local architectural differences.

Webb's guidelines: a summary of his national vernacular approach

Webb's approach, which placed equal importance on the art and science sides of architecture, could not be used with success unless it was founded on a mass of information on everything to do with good building – from planning, design, construction, sanitation, and ventilation, to decoration – and just as significantly on the characteristics and capabilities of materials, on how they had been used traditionally in many districts, and on the effects on them of tools, processes, time, and weather. Much of this knowledge could only be gained on site, and in builders' yards, joiners' shops, timber and brickyards, and quarries, and from listening to experienced craftsmen. Good building – based on common sense, simplicity, and directness – was the aim, and all revivals of past styles and attempts to create a new style for the day had to be avoided. Good composition, pleasing proportions, 'movement', contrasts of controlled irregularity with symmetry and rhythm, and contrasts of size, light and shadow, and of large and small elements, with the colours and textures of traditional materials, replaced styles and their motifs. Interiors were to be an assemblage of hollow volumes of varying shapes and sizes with contrasts of light levels; and should be of the same character as the exterior, forming a quiet background, free from ostentatious or attention-seeking designs. Ornament was to be limited strictly or avoided. If it were employed, for example in large buildings, it must be only on essential elements of the structure, such as openings. Inspiration for it was to come from the natural world.

A convenient plan that would fulfil the needs of those who were to live and work in the building was of first importance; until it had been achieved, the appearance of the building was not to be considered. Once his clients had accepted the plan, the architect should demand autonomy of design. In order to protect the landscape or townscape, no preconceived notions of the likely appearance of the new building should be held. An open-minded approach was to be taken, and obtrusive, ostentatious, or self-advertising designs avoided. It was important to study the likely effects of the building upon the surroundings, and to exploit the possibilities of the site by allowing its character to influence that of the building, and its topography to assist in making the work unobtrusive. Local vernacular architecture was to be reflected in the building but inventive experiments were to be made in the use and combination of traditional forms and local materials in order to avoid stagnation and to add to the building tradition. The appearance of the building must be appropriate for its function, externally and internally. Long-term good appearance was to be sought, therefore ephemeral fashions were to be avoided. Out of town, climbing plants could be used to mitigate any aggressive newness of house walls. The garden should be designed to merge gradually into the surrounding landscape.

Inspirations for the design of the building and its details were to be taken from the local and the national vernacular. Retention of a fresh, vigorous 'barbaric element' was desirable but had to be carefully balanced with 'multiplication of detail'. Reality – not picturesqueness, historical allusions, or symbols – was the goal, though symbols were acceptable in ornament. Each detail had to have a purpose, and to be designed to suit that purpose and the chosen material. Painstaking effort was called for in the designing of every detail to suit the chosen material, its position, and its purpose – and in making it, whether on the exterior or inside the building, a part of a consistent whole.

Handwork was vital because it carried the mark of the human sprit and hand, and because machines encouraged careless workmanship. Every part of a building was to be designed with the capabilities of the workmen in mind, with lifeless work being avoided by making repetitive work interesting and by praising good workmanship. Keeping abreast of new technology was important but new devices and new materials should be adopted only if they improved on traditional counterparts and would not be out of harmony with existing buildings. The construction should not be deliberately disguised, and all materials should be used truthfully, with no material imitating a more costly one. The increased emphasis placed by Webb's approach on the building crafts made first-class materials and workmanship essential.

Lethaby rightly considered that Webb's buildings were 'among the fine achievements of Victorian intellectual effort'.[170] Webb's national vernacular approach enabled him to escape from style revivals – a considerable achievement in an age devoted to them and to the categorizing of all things, in the case of architecture chiefly by the ornament that he largely avoided. With his approach, he produced pleasing, vigorous, up-to-date buildings that were convenient and comfortable in which to live and work, had beautiful interiors, were of widely varying appearance yet had both national and local character and were always in harmony with the surroundings in town or countryside. They added to the national and local building traditions and had links with the past without copying from it. As he himself said about Morris and the decorative arts, Webb had been able to assimilate all his architectural knowledge as a 'foundation for his work and [to] proceed with *real* originality' and 'thus avoid the fatal step of imitation'.[171] Not the least of his achievements is that Webb developed an approach to design that could be applied with good results and advantage to the environment at any time in the countryside, villages, towns, and cities of any country with a heritage of traditional architecture.

Chapter 7

THE COUNTRY HOUSES

Philip Webb completed the designs for ten country houses, of which nine were constructed. He made sketch designs for an eleventh, the proposed replacement of Rougham Hall, Norfolk, c. 1870–72, but the project was abandoned. Five of the executed houses were the administrative centres of large estates: Arisaig House (1863), Rounton Grange (1871–72), Smeaton Manor (1876), Clouds (1877–80), and Willinghurst (1886). Church Hill House (1868) was the home of a philanthropist who ran a charitable agricultural school for boys on a specially purchased forty-acre farm. The remainder, Joldwynds (1870–71), Standen (1891), and Hurlands (1897), were larger-than-usual examples of the new category of middle-class dwelling, termed the 'small house in the country' and made possible by the increasing prosperity of the professional and business classes and by the extensive railway network.[1]

Arisaig House, Arisaig, Inverness-shire, Scotland

Webb designed his first country house, Arisaig House, in 1863 for Francis Dukinfield Palmer Astley, a fellow member of then recently defunct Hogarth Club, who owned land and collieries, and was the grandson of the distinguished portrait painter John Astley. Francis Astley had an ancestral country house in Cheshire and another in Inverness-shire on the north-west coast of Scotland, on the outskirts of the village of Arisaig, where he spent much of the year with his family. He was an enlightened landowner. After purchasing the Arisaig estate in 1848, he had paid the crofters to renovate the old church, and to build a school and better cottages for themselves.[2] The existing house, a costly early-nineteenth-century mansion, by James Gillespie Graham (1776–1855) in the Gothick taste, was in a dark, damp situation, taking no advantage of the wonderful scenery, in which hills backed by mountains surround a sea-loch from which Prince Charles Edward had landed in 1745.[3] Astley, believing that the insalubrious position

of the house had led to his wife contracting tuberculosis, decided to build a new one on a better site. The London architects Stevens and Robinson designed a new house, with many Dutch gables and an unsuitably ecclesiastical spire, and a ground-floor suite for the invalid; but by the time they presented their finished drawing, dated 1863, Mrs Astley had died.[4] Later in 1863, having rejected their scheme but not the idea of rebuilding, Astley commissioned a design from Webb, who had not yet tackled a large house. The construction of the house, by a group of contractors under the control of Webb's clerk of works, was finished within twelve months – a truly remarkable achievement considering that the local stone had been difficult to work, that many materials had to come by sea, that Webb had had problems in getting his wishes understood by local Gaelic-speaking workers and by the stonemasons from Glasgow, and that the masons were no longer familiar with the once traditional methods of the district, and bitterly resented having to build sample walls repeatedly to meet the satisfaction of an architect and clerk of works who were Sassenachs.[5] The finished house was a testament to Webb's ability to handle both the difficult local stone and hostile workmen. He first saw the site in early spring 1863, after which he made several visits to the works, each lasting eight or ten days, during which he spent many hours on site.[6] It took him a long time to reach Arisaig village, to which the road from the nearest town, Fort William, was merely a rough track and at which passenger steamers called only rarely.

In contrast to the rejected scheme, in which the house stood starkly on an excavated plateau, Webb skilfully exploited the possibilities of the site to achieve an unobtrusive and sheltered building, yet one with fine prospects. He tucked the house into the side of the hill on a shelf of rock, with the well-orientated major rooms facing beautiful views south to the sea over a deep terrace with flowerbeds, and to the east, across the valley to the hills above steep

Opposite Arisaig House, Arisaig, Inverness-shire, Scotland (1863, constructed 1863–64): the south front, c. 1880 (Private Collection)

terraced gardens. He placed the bothy for bachelor gardeners, designed in 1864, in the north-east corner of the gardens. The drive continued beyond the north entrance court, which was protected by two service wings, one cutting into the hillside, then passed the gardeners' bothy to carry on to the farmstead in the valley, north of the house. The bothy, in the same materials as the house, was connected to the potting shed by an open porch and wet-weather workplace, with a lean-to roof supported on bracketed posts. This was the first of Webb's many covered ways. Another example fronted the two dwellings which he created in 1864 for the factor and coachman from the ruined farmhouse (now Borrodale Farmhouse), in which he retained the old spiral staircase and harled and whitewashed walls, both of which are traditional Scottish features. The farm buildings and stables, also by Webb, had similar walls, and they and the farmhouse were roofed in the same pleasing grey slates as the country house itself. The most striking

feature of the farmstead was the great roof of the huge steading, larger than the great medieval tithe barns, and swooping low towards the ground. John Brandon-Jones pointed out that it is of cathedral scale, and that these buildings have several features that were to become characteristic of Voysey's work, which they predate by over thirty years.[7] A small detached chapel was designed by Webb in 1866 but never built.[8] It would have had deep buttresses, a stubby tower with an attractive low spire in stone, and a partly inset porch leading to a vestibule under the tower, with a glazed screen opening into a combined nave and chancel lit by twin-light windows with simple bar tracery.

To enable the new mansion, Arisaig House, to fit on the flat shelf of the site, the kitchen and servants' hall were placed in the basement; the interconnecting major rooms, all with access to the gardens, were grouped round a large two-storey central hall; and the bachelors' bedrooms and Astley's billiard-room suite (billiard room, bedroom and WC)

Below Arisaig House: the entrance (north) front (collection of the late Miss M J Becher. Miss Becher's papers, drawings and photographs relating to Arisaig House are now in the RIBA Library Collection)

were placed on the second floor. The screens passage on the west side of the living hall gave access from the entrance lobby to the study, making the latter a useful business room, and led past the schoolroom – unusually positioned on the ground floor – and the 'lady's room', a sitting room for whichever female relation had become the chatelaine, who might also have been the governess. The first-floor gallery of the hall restricted the number of passages required to reach the twelve bedrooms and five dressing rooms on that floor. There were twelve more on the second floor, such a large number being necessary because, like the architect, all guests had to stay for several days. Heating was by open fires and partial central heating, and though, not uncommonly for the time, there was only one bathroom, WCs were plentiful.

Current notions of propriety and the perceived need at the time for a separate service room for every purpose meant that Victorian country house plans were extremely complex. Even in his first house of the type, Webb handled the complexities very well, and produced a generally convenient plan. It had two disadvantages, however. The steep site meant that the kitchen and servants' hall were above ground on the east side of the building, conveniently placed under the dining room, but with a very long passage, roofed with glass bricks, from the kitchen, along the base of the north front, to the minor offices and kitchen yard. The second disadvantage was that there

was a danger of cooking odours reaching the dining room through open windows or up the food-lift shaft. On the positive side, however, the servants had the same view as that of family and guests on the floor above, a rare facility at the time. A service drive reached the yard, unseen from the house, from the un-metalled road to the village.

Webb used two types of local stone. For random-rubble walling in the local manner, he used a blue-grey granite with pinkish and purple highlights, quarried on the estate and too hard to be cut to shape; and for the dressings and some areas of walling, a dark brown basalt termed whinstone, some of which came from the demolished old house and the rest from outcrops on the estate.[9] By 1863, Webb was using local materials whenever possible and he was beginning to reflect the local vernacular in his work but, for about forty miles around Arisaig in all directions, the only buildings were the small heather-thatched cottages of the crofters, and a few medieval castles and nineteenth-century Scottish Baronial-style edifices. Arisaig House was not designed in any recognized style, and had no Baronial features. Instead, Webb made it an unassuming affair of walls, gables, roofs, and plain chimneys, firmly braced against the hill on the eastern side by a buttressed and battered plinth. He fitted it so carefully into the landscape that it would only be

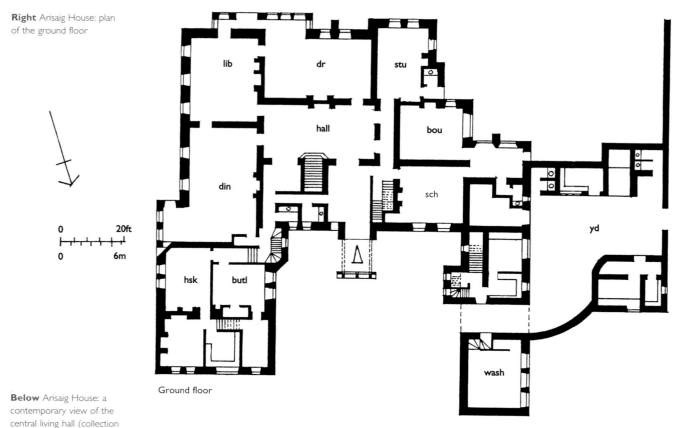

0   20ft

0   6m

lib   dr   stu

hall   bou

din   sch

yd

hsk   butl

wash

Ground floor

Below Arisaig House: a contemporary view of the central living hall (collection of the late Miss M J Becher)

seen at a distance, mainly from the sea, once the newly planted trees had matured. To make the building less dominant at closer quarters, he broke up the mass by using several roofs rather than a single massive one, as he was to do with his subsequent country houses. He used recessions and projections, gabled at different heights, on the south walls of Arisaig House for the same purpose.

The main part of the house had three parallel ridge roofs running east to west, flanked by two others running north to south. The many elements of the roofs, projections and recessions, and gabled dormers of differing heights, created some restlessness on the south front but the repeated window shapes counteracted this. The calmer eastern side had a quiet rhythm akin to that of Webb's later country houses.

The articulated roofs and gables, the local stone, and the grey roof slates (shipped from the Ballachulish quarry on Loch Leven) reflected the rugged hills and rocky terrain. The building appeared, as it proved to be, strong enough to withstand the often extreme weather. The forms resembled those of some of Butterfield's stone vicarages but, by employing vigorous modelling,

Webb adapted them and transferred them to a building of larger size with success and without using Gothic details. Even the two pointed-arch windows of the staircases on the north front, which constituted the only deliberate expression of the plan on the exterior, lacked medieval mouldings. Other rooms had vertical sliding sashes, with straight or segmental heads and, in some cases, relieving arches. Sensibly in such a wet coastal climate, painted woodwork was kept to a minimum except on the bell-turret and the partly glazed carriage-porch.[10]

The dark lobby opened into a high, well-lit central hall, which had a fireplace with a large stone hood and a first-floor gallery with, on the north side, an arcade of narrow pointed arches over three wider ones below. The brackets supporting the gallery were based on those which supported the roof timbers in Webb's Architectural Association design for a town church (1858; see chapter 12).[11] The gallery balustrade was vertically boarded, with pierced quatrefoils, and the steeply sloping painted roof had exposed iron beams, gilded zigzag patterning on the roof timbers, and figures of Webb's design in the panels.

Drama in the other major rooms was provided by the magnificent views, which were hidden on the approach to the house. In the dining room, drawing room, library, and study, beyond pointed stone arches supporting the upper walls, were bay windows with window seats and coved, white-painted ceilings of matchboarding, a common local material. In a truthful expression of structure, and a demonstration of Webb's willingness to adopt good technological innovations, the major ground-floor rooms had flitch-beams made up of iron girders with timber joists bolted to each side, the bolts and bottom flange being exposed, and the unplastered whole simply being painted white. In the dining room and drawing room, which had deep wallpapered friezes, Webb introduced the influential white-painted wainscot which was to appear in many of his later houses.[12]

Below Arisaig House: the drawing room in 1882, with Miss Gertrude Astley seated (collection of the late Miss M J Becher)

Above Arisaig House: the bothy for unmarried gardeners (1864)

Above right Arisaig House: Borrodale Farm, the entrance archways to the steading (1864)

Webb's wish to achieve what he later termed a consistent whole is apparent in this early house, of which he designed every detail himself, including the bookcases, benches and tables in the library and study, and all practical elements, including the beautiful pot on the laundry chimney. It was to become Webb's habit to use one or two worthy

items from demolished buildings in the replacements. In this house, the drawing-room fireplace surround, into which he inserted one of his Queen Square-pattern grates, came from the old mansion.[13]

Webb's disparaging statement about his early work being of his Gothic days applies somewhat more justly to Arisaig House than to Red House as,

Right Arisaig House: Borrodale Farm (1864), the two semi-detached farmhouses

though he avoided Gothic detail entirely on the exterior and generally inside the buildings, the central hall was the most overtly Gothic of all his domestic apartments. The inspiration for it possibly came from the central great hall of Wollaton Hall, Nottinghamshire (from 1550), by Robert Smythson (c. 1535–1614), combined with Webb's own halls at Red House and Sandroyd, where he had shown that even on a small scale, stair-halls could usefully supplement the major rooms.[14] It is likely that Astley favoured a central hall, as the Stevens and Robinson scheme had a central circulation hall, though it was not a sitting area. Indeed, Astley apparently had considerable influence on the plan as a whole: Webb placed his dining room, library, and drawing room in the same positions and with the same orientations as those of Stevens and Robinson's design, which suggests that this disposition, and the central halls of both schemes, might have been suggested by the client. However, Webb's central hall – galleried on all four sides, with a large hooded fireplace on the long west wall, and lit by windows in the gables of its high roof and a large window on the landing of the main staircase off its north side – was not only a circulation area but also a sitting room, as the early photograph shows. Most of the earlier revivals of the great hall had been intended for large-scale entertaining, of the tenantry in particular. Webb's hall at Arisaig was an early example of the great hall designed as a major sitting room, a living hall, which

had been introduced in 1850 at Mentmore Towers by Paxton & Stokes.[15] The living hall was a useful everyday room in which family and guests could mingle at any time, whereas the other major rooms were divided by the propriety of the time into male and female zones. The advantages of this freedom of use rapidly endeared living halls to clients; and also to architects, including Shaw and Nesfield, who adopted them soon after Webb had done so, because such a room presented an opportunity to create a large dramatic space. Living halls remained popular until well after the turn of the century, although from the 1890s single-storey ones, like those of Webb's Willinghurst, Standen, and Hurlands, were preferred.

Arisaig House was a praiseworthy first country house, particularly as Webb had had no experience in the designing and building of such large houses whilst with Billing or with Street. As with Red House, there was no main elevation. All the fronts were given equal attention, a matter by no means customary at the time. It was to become characteristic of all Webb's houses in the country, whether large or small. The remoteness and difficulty of reaching Arisaig House means that few architects would have seen it in the 1860s and 1870s, but it would have been known through Webb's drawings to those who had been members of the Hogarth Club with Astley, including the 'non-artistic' member Major (later Colonel) William James Gillum, the retired army officer and philanthropist, who commissioned Webb's second and smaller country house in 1868.

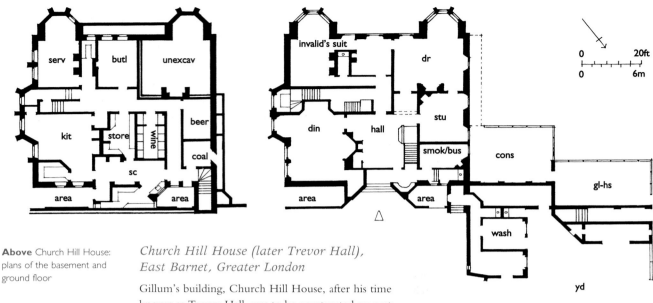

serv | butl | unexcav

kit | store | wine | beer

sc | coal

area | area

invalid's suit | dr

din | hall | stu

smok/bus | cons

area | area

wash | gl-hs

yd

0   20ft
0   6m

Church Hill House (later Trevor Hall), East Barnet, Greater London

Gillum's building, Church Hill House, after his time known as Trevor Hall, was to be constructed on part of the forty-acre estate which he had bought in 1860, at Church Barnet in Hertfordshire, some nine miles from London (now East Barnet, Greater London), and on which he had established the Farm School for Boys to train destitute boys in agricultural skills, with whose buildings Webb would become involved later in the 1860s and in the 1870s (see chapter 12).[16] Before the country house commission, Webb had

designed for Gillum the Worship Street of dwellings, workshops, and shops (1861, see chapter 11), and some furniture and a gardener's cottage (all 1860) for the Moated House, Gillum's residence in Tottenham.[17] Church Hill House was built between October 1868 and 1870 by Sharpington and Cole, and the stable block and lodge were erected in 1869 by direct labour under the clerk of works for the house.

Webb placed the subsidiary buildings of the complex near the road but set the house well back from it, facing south-west over fields towards the farm school and the village church.[18] For the sake of compactness, he made the house a square block, with second-floor bedrooms in the attics and major offices in the basement; the last was above ground, however, on the south-east front where the kitchen and servants' hall were placed. A low range of minor domestic offices, with a large conservatory backing on to the garden side, sheltered the entrance court.

A two-storey galleried living hall, almost central, was indirectly lit by a glazed screen at the rear of the partly inset porch and directly from the window in the gable over the porch into which the gallery extended. The drawing room, and Gillum's ground-floor bedroom and dressing-room suite (a necessity as he had lost a leg during the siege of Sebastopol),

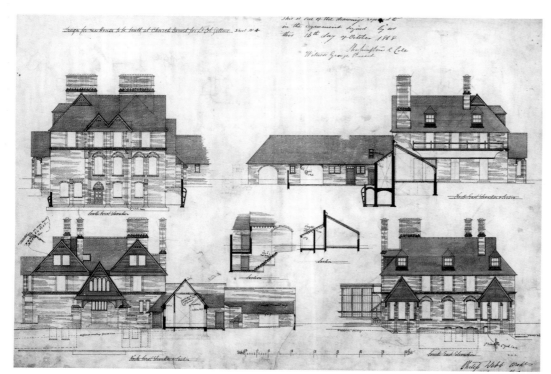

Left Church Hill House: Webb's elevations drawing of 1868 (Victoria & Albert Museum/ V&A Images)

occupied the south-east front. The closet of the suite, vented by a chimney flue as was to become Webb's custom in country houses, predated twentieth-century centrally positioned services by many decades.[19] A small room with direct access from the porch and an adjacent earth closet (EC) served as a smoking and business room. The dining room and the drawing room, appropriately facing south-east and south-west respectively, were roughly the same size but, by using recesses and bay windows, Webb achieved the difference in shape that was considered desirable at the time. A twin-gabled buttressed projection on the south-east elevation rose through three storeys and had two identical windows on each upper level. The two on the ground floor served the dining room and a serving closet, clearly demonstrating Webb's eschewing of both architectural hierarchy and the exterior expression of the plan. The serving closet was positioned most awkwardly on the basement stairs; the scullery, too, was inconveniently placed; and the butler, who had no view from his pantry of the approach to the house, had a tortuous route to the front door. These faults, which are not typical of Webb, and the domestic offices being in the basement, suggest that this house was designed unusually rapidly and with an urgent need to save money; this is likely, as Gillum financed the farm school unaided until 1875.

The house, in which Webb made further experiments with bay windows and repeated gables, had strongly modelled, basically symmetrical elevations on three of its four sides, with much emphasis on diagonal lines, particularly on the north-east entrance front, where the white weatherboarded porch gable was flanked at a higher level by red tile-hung gables. Red-brick walls, red wall and roof tiles, white weatherboarding, dentilated bargeboards, and hipped dormers, reflected the local vernacular and the availability of a wider choice of materials in the south of England, and the difference between the climate of Arisaig and that of Church Barnet. In the drier, warmer south of England there was no need to limit external woodwork, so Webb panelled Gillum's porch and the extended walls which concealed the basement areas, and, chiefly for visual purposes, gave the north-west front a balcony, with turned balusters above a deep, plain plaster cove which concealed the supports.[20] After similar balconies and tile-hung gables had become features of the so-called 'Queen Anne' style in the 1870s, Webb rarely used them, but throughout his career he occasionally used bold plaster cornices in the southern counties. The finely pleated tops of the Church Hill House chimneys had been introduced in 1864 on his Washington Hall extension (see chapter 9). He set the sash windows of the south-west front of Gillum's house in recessed pointed arches on the ground floor; on the first floor, above a bold brick string-sill, he flanked the windows with simple brick pilasters and hid the lintels in the eaves. These details, with segmental arches replacing the pointed ones, and the tilted and tiled eaves running across the base of the entrance-front gables – a feature with which Shaw also was experimenting in the late 1860s[21] – were to reappear in several of Webb's later houses. First-floor lintels in the eaves became characteristic of his work. The interior had Morris & Co. wallpapers, many paintings by members of the Pre-Raphaelite circle, and Webb's furniture from the Moated House, which included a round table, a piano, and many dining-room and bedroom pieces.[22]

The stable block, in the same brick and tiles as the house, had an unusually commodious six-roomed cottage at each side of its round-arch entrance, for the coachman and gardener respectively.[23] The four-bedroom lodge, also in the same materials, had identical gables on each side and a cruciform ridge with a central chimney, an arrangement that Webb was to repeat on a larger scale at Four Gables (1876). One corner was cut away to form a porch; the roof above it was supported on an oak post, with finely moulded capital, similar to those that supported the gallery in the hall of the main building.[24]

Church Hill House was in many ways one of Webb's most pleasing designs, as Pevsner pointed out.[25] It would have been known, like Arisaig House, to Webb's Hogarth Club friends, several of whom probably visited Gillum there. Later in the century, it

was certainly known to Webb's contemporary Mackmurdo, and it would have been one of the buildings sought out by Webb's young admirers in the Arts and Crafts movement, including Charles Winmill, who took photographs of the house for Webb.[26]

The three symmetrical elevations of Church Hill House, and the suggestion of Classical influence in its almost villa-like plan, resulted from Webb's increasing interest in English Baroque buildings.[27] Webb recognized that symmetry had been a characteristic of English country houses throughout the sixteenth and seventeenth centuries, and also, as Street had pointed out in 1853,[28] of many medieval buildings in England. From around 1868, several years before Shaw became interested in the subject, Webb habitually employed symmetry to reinforce the order and rhythm displayed in his earliest buildings.

House of Airlie, near Kirriemuir, Angus, Scotland

Frustratingly, there is a missing link in the evidence as to how Webb's interest in English Baroque buildings and Vanbrugh's planning in particular affected the plan of his third executed country house. The link was his abandoned scheme of 1868–69 for the rebuilding of Airlie Castle in Scotland for Lord Airlie, the brother-in-law of George Howard. To Webb's bitter disappointment and distress, the client abandoned the project, his pocket having proved not deep enough to support the construction of so large a house as the one he and his wife had requested (there is more about this affair in chapter 9, in connection with Cortachy Castle). Webb destroyed

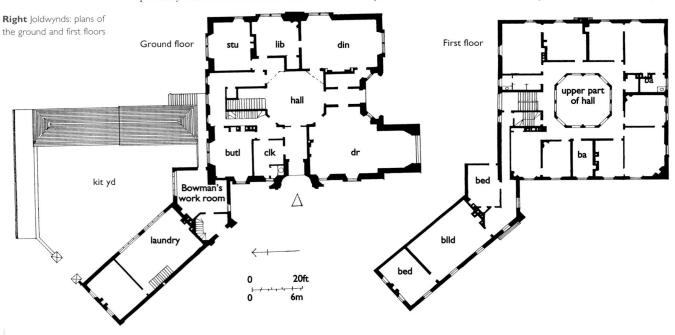

Right Joldwynds: plans of the ground and first floors

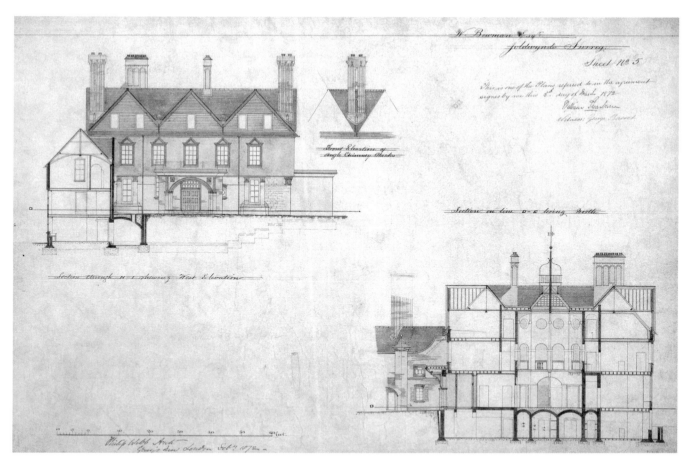

all the drawings, as was his habit in such cases, and so nothing is known of the intended plan or appearance of this mansion that would almost certainly have been the second largest of his country houses had it been carried out, as the estimated cost was £50,000.[29]

Joldwynds, Holmbury St Mary, Surrey

Joldwynds, in Surrey, Webb's third executed country house, was commissioned in 1870 by William Bowman (1816–92), a distinguished eye surgeon and ophthalmic research scientist, who was created a baronet in 1884. Bowman, a patron of Watts, had a country house in Holmbury St Mary, a village from which, owing to the recent extension of the railway to Shere and Gomshall four miles away, it was possible for professional men to commute daily to London.[30] Webb, who had undertaken a small job for Bowman two years previously, visited the existing house at the end of 1869 with a view to making alterations. However, as it was a poor-quality eighteenth-century building with an astonishingly

ugly, polychromatic brick addition of 1860, he undoubtedly would have advised rebuilding, which Bowman decided to do.[31] The new house was designed between 1870 and 1871, and built by William Shearburn of Shere between 1872 and 1874; the coach-house and entrance gates were erected in 1875 by direct labour organized by the clerk of works for the house.[32] A pyramid-roofed stair turret and a large library were designed by Webb in 1888 and constructed between 1891 and 1893, the library having a barrel vault in concrete and iron, an example of the architect's willingness to use new technology. At the same time, he inserted steelwork to halt the spreading of the billiard-room roof caused by a slight outward bowing of one wall.[33] This was an extremely rare instance of a structural defect developing in Webb's work.

As usual, Webb made use of the possibilities of the well-wooded site, which was sheltered to the west but had fine views to the south and north. In plan, the coach-house, the walled garden with an orchid-house, and the main block of the house were three squares,

Above Joldwynds, Holmbury St Mary, Surrey (1870–71, constructed 1872–74, demolished 1930): Webb's drawing of 1872 for the west elevation and section looking north (Victoria & Albert Museum/ V&A Images)

stepped transversely down the slope. The drive passed the coach-house, then ran between the orchid-house garden and an angled wing to the main entrance on the west front, and continued south towards the small belvedere, the View House that was also by Webb, in the garden, behind which it swept round and up to the coach-house again. The wing sheltered the entrance, and contained the billiard room over the laundry, and Bowman's workroom in the junction with the north-west corner of the main block.

By 1871, Webb's national vernacular approach was fully developed. The Idea that loosely governed Joldwynds appears to have been the fusion of a symmetrical, three-storey English manor house, triple-gabled on at least two fronts, fairly common in the sixteenth century, with an adapted Classical villa plan, constructed in the traditional building materials of Surrey. Webb emphasized two axes which, starting respectively at the main and garden entrances, met at right angles in an octagonal central living hall. No photographs of the finished interiors have been discovered, but Webb's drawings and a photograph taken for him during construction, show that this hall had a central octagonal space rising through three storeys to the pyramidal roof lantern; there were wide segmental arches on the ground floor, and a continuous round-arch arcade at first-floor level, above each arch of which was a circular opening to light the second-floor gallery.[34] It must have been one of the boldest and most striking Victorian interior spaces, the dramatic effect being increased by a huge circular window, lighting the main staircase, in the north wall of the house. The arcade resembled those by Vanbrugh in the halls of Blenheim, Oxfordshire (1705–25) and Seaton Delaval, Northumberland (1720–28). The house was furnished and decorated with Morris products.

Webb tucked the house into the hillside, and again used basement offices which, because of the slope, were largely above ground. The prospects and orientation of the rooms were good, and their arrangement round the hall was convenient, apart from food having to be carried across the hall from a serving passage. Variation in size and shape between the dining room and drawing room was again achieved by recesses and a bay window, the latter being a deep projection which spoilt the symmetry on paper but was not obtrusive in reality, because it was concealed from the drive by a bank of mature trees and shrubs, and a new wall. Bedrooms were on two floors with access from the galleries.

Right Joldwynds: the south front and the billiard-room wing (from a photograph in Webb's collection)

Externally, the house was decidedly English in character, with four symmetrical elevations, identical in their upper parts, each with triple gables. Four handsome brick chimneys, standing turret-like at forty-five degrees above the corners of the sixty-six-foot-square major block, joined a massive stack, with nine flues, on the billiard-room wing in providing important vertical accents in a composition of strong diagonals and horizontals. In the detailing, Webb experimented with repeated circles, semicircles, triangles, and squares. At the centre of the main roof, the lantern of the hall was surmounted by a wind-vane supported by a delicate cage of curving wrought iron. The roof tiles were of red clay, and the brick walls were faced on the basement and ground floor in stone ranging in colour from buff to grey with pleasing iron staining, and on the first floor with scalloped red clay tiles. The gables, weatherboarded in unpainted oak, bore no relation to the plan; some bedrooms on the second floor had to have angled walls to retain the regularity of the fenestration. Tiled eaves ran continuously round the main block below the triple gables, protecting the windows below from rain and midday summer sun, modelling the elevations, and forming a strong horizontal element. By setting some windows in recessed brick panels, Webb inventively reversed the Elizabethan and English Baroque tradition of brick walls with stone dressings. First-floor sashes had lintels and relieving arches hidden behind wooden triangular hood-moulds that formed a stop to the tiling. The balconies on the roof of the bay window to the drawing room and above the entrance porch were primarily visual elements, not intended for use except as fire escapes, as the wide spacing of the balusters indicates. The billiard-room wing was brick at first-floor level on the drive side, and timber-framed, with brick-nogging, on the kitchen-yard front.

The View House had a stone archway reminiscent of Vanbrugh's work, and white weatherboarded upper walls, with a viewing room above in which the two windows wrapped the corners of the building. In 1898, Voysey would improve upon Webb's interesting corner windows by taking the glazing right across the projecting staircase bay at Broadleys, Cumbria.[35] The U-shaped stable block, of dateless appearance, was clad in weatherboarding on the first floor, some of it painted white, and contained two pleasant dwellings of the room-and-a-passage plan, with the corridor in the

eaves, that were to become characteristic of Webb's flats for coachmen and gardeners. The steep slope of the site was used to gain basement workrooms off one of the orchid-houses. For the basement and ground-floor walls, Webb used both brick and the same randomly sized and attractively coloured stone of the house, carefully merging the two in places.

Joldwynds was very influential in the 1880s and 1890s. It, and the house built nearby at the same time by the painter Henry Tanworth Wells, attracted other people to the area. Street built himself a house in the village almost immediately, and during the next two decades, Shaw, Basil Champneys, Edwin Lutyens, and Voysey designed houses there for clients, and all of them, clients and architects, would have seen Webb's house.[36] Shaw's square, triple-gabled Chigwell Hall, Essex (1875–76) certainly shows the influence of Joldwynds.[37] Webb's young admirers sought out his houses including Joldwynds. Ernest Gimson recalled the enthusiasm of these pilgrimages in a letter to May Morris of 1915; Hugh Stannus of the Architectural Association led several of them, visiting Joldwynds on at least one occasion when Winmill, and probably Leonard Stokes (1858–1925) and Edward John May (1853–1941), were with him.[38] After their visits, similar prominent gables, the sensitive blending of brick and stone, and gardens with attractive walls and borders of shrubs and herbaceous plants, began to appear in their own houses – notably in several by Lutyens, including Homewood, Hertfordshire (1901), which has triple weatherboarded gables on the entrance front.[39]

Right Rounton Grange: plans of the ground and first floors

First floor

ironing

nurseries

blld ba bou

Lowthian Bell's room/bus

roof lt

palm house

gl-hs

aviary and plunge bath

amb   amb

wash   sc   hsk   din   dr

kit yd   kit   hall

dairy   serv butl   stu

0   20ft
0   6m

Ground floor

Rounton Grange, East Rounton, North Yorkshire

The renowned iron-master, scientist, and art collector Isaac Lowthian Bell, for whom the architect had enlarged Washington Hall in the 1860s (see chapter 9), commissioned Webb's fourth country house, Rounton Grange in North Yorkshire. In 1870, Bell asked Webb to improve the domestic offices, at a cost of around £800, of the country house on the estate at East Rounton that he had purchased in 1865.[40] By October the following year Webb's plan for doing this, and an alternative scheme for the rebuilding of the entire house, were being considered; persuaded by his son Hugh and by an improvement in the price of iron, Bell chose the replacement.[41] Bell's daughter Mary (Maisie) told her family's friend George Howard on 31 October 1872 of the arrival of the plans for the new house from Webb, and that they all found them very interesting and, as far as they could judge, quite charming, and she added that they were all longing for the time when they would be living in it.[42] Aided by a bill of quantities, construction by direct labour under a clerk of works took place between 1873 and 1876. The total cost, including that of the ancillary coach-house and farm buildings, the nearby Home Farm with

Right Rounton Grange, East Rounton, North Riding of Yorkshire (North Yorkshire) (1871–1872, constructed 1873–76, demolished 1951–1954): the entrance (west) front, before Webb inserted the upper-servants' dining room in the kitchen court archway (from a photograph, pre-1887, in Webb's collection)

extensive farm buildings, and a terrace of dwellings for the farm manager and farm workers (see chapter 11), and possibly East Rounton School (see chapter 12), was £32,880, a massive advance on the £800 Bell had first envisaged spending.[43]

Mature trees surrounded the flat site apart from one gap through which the Cleveland Hills were visible. A tree-lined drive led to the old lodge, where it bifurcated, one arm continuing to the coach-house (1875–76), a square brick and pantiled building with a long roof lantern over a central yard, and a typical, spacious three-bedroom first-floor flat for the coachman over the strikingly unusual archway.[44] The other arm curved east to the house, which occupied the position of its predecessor, and had the same orientation as Joldwynds: entrance on the west front, domestic offices to the north, and major rooms facing east and south.

The Idea behind Webb's first scheme for Rounton Grange was a Border pele on a large scale, suggested no doubt by the need for a tall house from which the hills could be seen above the surrounding trees. It consisted of a tower, with twin gables on at least one side, topped by a belvedere, and a lower wing of domestic offices, like the barmkin of a pele, on the north side; the kitchens occupied the low, ground floor of the tower, which had the major rooms round a central hall on the first floor.[45] The final design retained the tower-with-barmkin form, but combined it with a more appropriate source of inspiration for such a large house: a castle of the corner-towered quadrangular type that had been popular in the north of England in the late fourteenth century. Webb had probably been inspired by two in particular, both of c. 1378 – Lumley Castle in County Durham that Vanbrugh had re-fenestrated with large vertical sashes (from 1722), and Bolton Castle in North Yorkshire.[46] Webb dispensed with the central courtyard, however, and made his castle a solid, five-storey tower with four-storey corner turrets, and with major rooms on the ground floor as befitted a house for clients nearing their sixties. The use on the drawings of the term 'pavillions' [sic] for the turrets shows that Webb also had in mind Elizabethan houses, such as Wollaton. The barmkin of the pele scheme became two-storey ranges surrounding a rectangular kitchen courtyard on the north side of the tower. As well as the domestic offices, they contained a billiard room approached through a double-arch opening from the half-landing

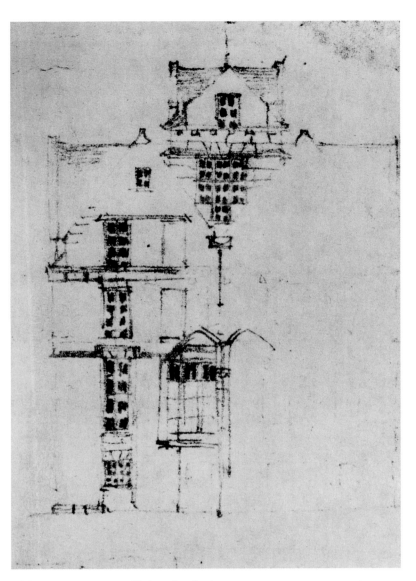

Above Rounton Grange: Webb's sketch of the pele scheme (Private Collection)

of the main staircase, Bell's 'own' or business room accessed by the same route and by a newel stair off the western kitchen court archway, the nursery suite for the Bells' grandchildren in the east wing and, in the attics, the servants' dormitories, which were divided into cubicles.[47]

Probably influenced by Vanbrugh's halls at Castle Howard, North Yorkshire (1699), Blenheim, and Seaton Delaval, Webb adapted the villa plan by extending the upper part of the living hall through to the entrance on the west front where it received direct lighting, being set back between the pavilions at first-floor level. In a similar arrangement to that of Church Hill House, the lower hall received light through a glazed screen in the porch and glazed doors

in the flanking lobby. Irregular rooms were once more set within symmetrical elevations. The two axes of Joldwynds were repeated, again extending from the main and garden entrances to meet at right angles in the centre of the hall; but to reduce draughts, the one from the main entrance was cranked through the lobby. With inestimable benefit to servants, at Rounton Webb abandoned forever the basement kitchens of his earlier country houses, in two of which, however, they were largely above ground because of the steeply sloping sites.

The pavilions reflected the plan only on the upper floors, where on the south front they housed large bedrooms with closets for WCs, ventilated by flues.[48] On the ground floor of the entrance front,

the cloakroom and butler's room shared the left turret room, whilst the library (termed the study on early drawings) occupied that on the right, again demonstrating Webb's disregard for hierarchy and for the expression of the plan on the exterior. Opening off the living hall, the dining room had an apsidal east end formed by a bay window with buttress-mullions, and the long drawing room had a similar bay at the centre of the south front, as well as east windows.[49] Between the pyramid-roofed pavilions, with outstanding views from its end windows in the gables, a picture gallery extended the full north-to-south width of the tower on the fourth floor.

To cater for Bell's horticultural hobby, a tile-roofed ambulatory with continuous glazing ran from the bay window of the dining room along the east front through the garden porch in the base of the clock tower, along the east wall of the lower block, where it had a glass roof and a brick arcade, to a range of glasshouses set at right angles to the north end of the house.[50] At the centre of the range, and linked to the ambulatory by Webb's strikingly simple glass-and-iron conservatory, was a most attractive palm house, also by Webb, with side and rear walls, piers, a round arch in brick, and an unusual pyramid roof of glass, supported by delicate, curving wrought-iron trusses and surmounted by a louvred lantern. Behind the conservatory were an aviary and a small heated swimming pool, termed the plunge bath; both had glass roofs, and were separated by an engine house and potting sheds, and all were primarily for Bell's use.[51] (The gardens are covered in chapter 6.)

The plinthless tower block seemed to rise out of the ground rather than sit upon it. It had pyramid-roofed pavilions and six tall, handsome major chimneys with beautifully worked stone pleating, each flue being subtly bellied or 'cambered' as Webb put it, and a wind-vane supported by a graceful

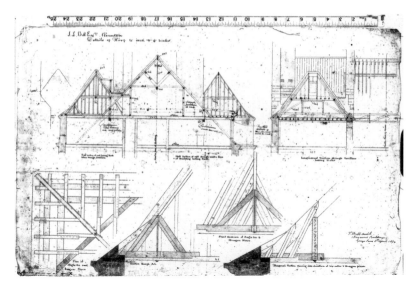

Above Rounton Grange: Webb's drawing of roof details (1874), showing his use of iron rods in the construction (Private Collection)

wrought-iron stay. The chimneys were necessarily huge as they carried flues from the numerous fireplaces and vent shafts from all the major rooms, the closets, and the drainage system. Four were placed symmetrically at the inner junctions of the pyramids with the central ridged roof; the other two were

Left Rounton Grange: the entrance porch, west front (from a photograph, pre-1887, in Webb's collection)

L-shaped, and defined the tower block above the northern part of the house. Apart from some cheerful red brick-nogged timber framing in the kitchen courtyard, the mansion was built of ochre-coloured sandstone from Bell's Scarth Nick quarry in the nearby hills, smoothly finished and randomly coursed. Like the local farmsteads, it was roofed with red clay pantiles, which at the time and for long afterwards were considered unfit for all except the outbuildings of a gentleman's house. The roofs were edged at the eaves with thin slates, not the heavy stone slabs traditionally used in North Yorkshire for the purpose, to ensure that all the rainwater ran from the boldly curved pantiles into the gutters. The broad areas of plain ashlar walling, the segmental and triangular hood-moulds, and the proportions of the vertical sash windows, gave the building a Classical air; but Webb ignored the rule of void over void, and many of his details, notably those of the porch, the hall windows above it, and the oriel of Bell's 'own room' or

business room, supported on a stone column, were free adaptations of medieval elements.[52] The lines of the pavilion roofs were echoed on a smaller scale by the triangular hood-moulds and the tops of the buttresses of the porch and bay windows. These and the other details were as inventive yet restrained, as well suited to the sandstone and the purpose of the item, and as pleasing and admirably worked as those of the several beautiful Early English Gothic abbeys of the county, with which the architect was familiar.

Webb employed up-to-date technology in Rounton Grange, as was his habit so long as it improved on older methods. The outer walls were of stone, with brick inner leaves, ventilated cavities, and stoneware ties through and across which rainwater could not penetrate. Lintels were of rolled iron, cased in wood and plastered, as were many of the ceiling beams, including those that were flitch beams of iron girders and timber, though some were encased in hardwood. Many iron hangers and one-inch tie-rods

Below Rounton Grange: the east front in 1915, after the replacement of the glass roof of the ambulatory in 1905 or 1906 by George Jack (© University of Newcastle upon Tyne)

were used in the roof trusses. The long ridge of the central roof of the tower block was supported on a continuous latticed girder of advanced design, with one-inch-diameter iron rods as vertical members, and iron straps reinforcing the joints where the inclined timber braces met the horizontal timber members. In turn supported by timber queen-strut trusses, it was a larger version of the lattice beams Webb had employed in the roof of the Joldwynds stable block. Plate glass was used in the large skylight of the billiard room. The house was partly centrally heated by hot water, piped from a boiler in the basement, with cast-iron coils (radiators), chiefly on the ground floor and in passages. The living hall and ambulatory had under-floor heating pipes in ducts. The major ground-floor rooms had fireplaces with grates designed by Webb from which convected warm air emerged through a grille above the fire. A small cupboard behind the one in the hall kept wine to hand at the right temperature. Wind direction was registered in this room on a dial, on the underside of the gallery, which was connected by rods to the elegant roof vane. Upper floors were soundproofed by a two-inch layer of lime mortar, and throughout the house electric bells, powered by wet-cell batteries, were installed for the summoning of servants, but the house was too early by just a few years to have electric lighting when first built. It had two types of piped water: drinking water pumped by steam engine from the river, and 'soft' water from tanks on the roof and from the large underground storage tanks, which were chiefly intended for use against fire. A goods lift serviced all floors except the upper two but the house had no passenger lift; electric lifts were not available until the mid-1880s, and the flat terrain of the immediate district was not conducive to the use of hydraulic power.[53] The WC closets in the pavilion bedrooms were enlarged to take baths, probably during construction.

The interior, which was comfortable rather than grand or luxurious, was furnished and decorated almost entirely with Morris & Co. products, many of them designed by Webb, enhanced by Bell's collections of blue-and-white china, and paintings of recent date. In the living hall, Webb did not continue his experiments with monumental arcades but set the gallery above a deeply coved oak-boarded cornice, and gave it an oak balustrade with turned balusters, thus making the room more informal than the central hall of Joldwynds. The oak wainscot in this room and elsewhere contained many panels that had been removed from Newcastle

upon Tyne Cathedral; all of it was untreated except for being washed annually with beer.[54] The Hoptonwood stone overmantel of the fireplace bore, in raised gilded letters, a text from Proverbs 13 about the value of a good wife. As in number 1 Palace Green

Above Rounton Grange: the kitchen court in 1915, looking south, with a twentieth-century first-floor addition above the kitchen at the southern end. (© University of Newcastle upon Tyne)

Left Rounton Grange: the Palm House and greenhouses; in the background, at right angles to the greenhouse range, is part of the ambulatory, with the original glass roof (from a photograph, pre-1887, in Webb's collection)

(see chapter 5), the primary staircase served only the first floor. Both the family staircases at Rounton had large oak balls on some of the newels, one of them being termed 'Uncle Charlie's Head' after a bald relation. They were typical of the way Webb occasionally exaggerated the size of such items, a practice that would be adopted later by Lutyens. The secondary family staircase was an open newel stair from the first floor upwards. A handsome octagonal newel, of a form that would become characteristic of Webb's stair posts, supported winders in one corner, and was echoed on subsequent floors, the posts rising one above the other from floor to ceiling.

The decorations and furnishings of the comfortably dignified rather than grand drawing room of Rounton Grange are described in chapter 3, including Morris's carpet, frieze, and ceiling. Morris painted the floriated ceiling himself, and the rather similar ceiling of the dining room, which was in bright colours on a parchment-coloured ground. The frieze, also mentioned earlier, which was based on Chaucer's poem *Romaunt of the Rose*, with figures by Burne-Jones, decorative details by Morris, and fauna by Webb, was designed in the mid-1870s for

this room. With emblematic figures of the Miseries and Beauties of Love facing each other across the room and, on the west wall between them, the Pilgrim in the Garden of Idleness seeing himself led by Love and by Danger, it took Lady Bell and her daughter Florence over eight years to embroider.[55] The handsome oak sideboard on the west wall, designed by Webb in 1877, and the oak serving table in the stone arched recess on the east wall, were adequately robust yet had a certain delicacy that was characteristic of all his furniture except the early pieces for Morris. The trellised back panels of the sideboard presaged those of Webb's staircase balustrades of the early 1880s, and preceded Mackintosh's exploitation of simple grids by about twenty years. The carved spiral fluting and reeding on its legs matched that on the legs of the fine serving table, and was very similar to the carving on the newels of the main staircase that Webb had inserted into Cranmer Hall in c. 1864 (see chapter 9).[56]

Rounton Grange, which in the 1980s was described as a beautiful house by the many people who remembered it, was well-known, though not published until 1911.[57] Many of Bell's fellow

Right Rounton Grange: the dining-room recess, with a side-table by Webb (from a photograph, pre-1887, in Webb's collection)

industrialists in Middlesbrough built heavy neo-Gothic or French chateau-inspired edifices outside the town. In contrast, despite its great height, Rounton Grange, a few miles further away, was an unostentatious but dignified building, with a strong, vigorous beauty suited to North Yorkshire, and a form and restrained inventive details that reflected the architectural heritage of the area.

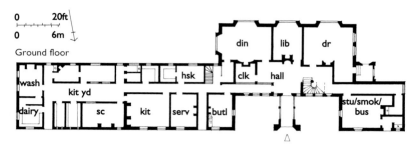

Above Smeaton Manor:
plan of the ground floor

Below Smeaton Manor,
Great Smeaton, North
Riding of Yorkshire (North
Yorkshire) (1876, constructed
1877–79): the south front,
from the lake, 1950 (Owen
Wicksteed; now in a Private
Collection)

Smeaton Manor, Great Smeaton, North Yorkshire

Webb's fifth executed country house, Smeaton Manor, was designed in 1876 for Ada Phoebe Godman (1850–1900), a daughter of Lowthian Bell, and her husband Major Arthur Fitzpatrick Godman (1842–1930), the fifth son of a wealthy Surrey landowner, who had retired from the army in the early 1870s after suffering a riding accident. In 1874, in anticipation of his marriage two years later, Godman had bought land at Great Smeaton, North Yorkshire, a village near the main line to London and only some seven miles by road from Rounton Grange, then under construction. His purpose was to build a country house with the necessary stables

and farm buildings in which to establish a horse-breeding business.[58] Ada Bell had known Webb since at the latest 1864, when he altered Washington Grange for her father, and she had lived for some time in Red Barns at Redcar, which Webb had designed in 1868 for her brother Hugh (see chapters 9 and 11 respectively). Undoubtedly she would have suggested that Webb should be commissioned, but by 1876 Godman, too, would have become familiar with his work for the Bells. It is clear from Ada's diaries that they greatly admired it, and that they shared his love of the countryside, horses, and old buildings.[59] The house, and the stables and farm buildings designed in 1877, were constructed by J W and M Mackenzie of Darlington, and were completed by the summer of 1879.[60] The Godmans were delighted with their new home but, to Ada's great distress, financial problems, caused in part by Godman having invested in the Bell firm not long before a serious slump in the iron trade, led them to have to retrench by living in Dresden for part of the 1880s, and in the 1890s the house, but not the stables, had to be let. It did not become the family home again until 1923, long after Ada's death in 1900, and the project that Webb had referred to as the 'possible extension of the West wing' never came to pass.[61]

The chosen site was a wide meadow, sloping southwards to the highway, with open farmland beyond, and sheltering mature woodland to the west and north. The general arrangement of a long house, with domestic offices to the east and stables to the west of a south-facing major block and north entrance court, resembled that of Vanbrugh's palatial Castle Howard, which Webb knew, having been closely involved with the design and insertion of the Firm's windows in the chapel in the early 1870s.[62] Against the convention of the time, the Smeaton drive passed the domestic offices at close quarters before reaching a north entrance court, where a long porch met the carriages; the drive then continued to the stables and farmstead, slightly north-west of the house, which were also served by a lane from the road.

Webb's Idea at Smeaton was clearly and appropriately based on the late-seventeenth-century brick-built English manor houses, of which many had the H-plan of medieval origin.[63] This plan, out of favour since the English Baroque period, was unpopular with Gothic revivalists because it was not conducive to irregularity, and its symmetry was associated with inconvenience. Webb's ingenious

plan combined the double-pile and cross-passage arrangement, used by Vanbrugh on a grand scale at Castle Howard, with an amended H-plan. Possibly influenced by Vanbrugh's small house King's Weston, Gloucestershire (c. 1710–14), Webb pulled back the side wings to allow the major rooms to project southwards, where they captured the sun from early morning in the dining room to late evening in the drawing room; unlike Vanbrugh in this instance, he used the wings to create a sheltered north entrance court.[64] The west wing contained a smoking-cum-business room and extended less far to the west than the corresponding service wing extended eastwards.

Webb's use of cross-passages preceded Shaw's at Bryanston, Dorset (1889–94) by over a decade; the plan of the family block of Shaw's Alderbrook, Surrey (1879) bears a strong resemblance to that of Smeaton Manor.[65] On the ground floor, the Smeaton cross-passage, at right angles to the entrance axis, extended through the entire house, apart from the minor domestic offices, from the eastern extremity at the kitchen yard to the furthermost western wall, cranking only in the hall to accommodate the main staircase which served solely the first floor, as in Rounton Grange. The cross-passages on the upper floors had windows at each end. The first-floor

Above Smeaton Manor: the main part of the south front of the family block; the central chimney was removed and the remaining pair were reduced in height in the twentieth-century

passage bent in a U-shape to pass through the main family block between the south-facing bedrooms and, to the north, Godman's dressing room, a bathroom, a WC, and the main stairs. Fulfilling the demands of propriety – by ensuring that there was no access to spinsters' and maids' bedrooms from the east-wing bedrooms for bachelor guests – prevented the passage from running the full length of the building on the second, attic, floor. In the main family block, the cross-passage divided the children's rooms to the south from the nursery-staff bedrooms, a housemaid's closet, and the children's bathroom, to the north. The proprieties were observed further by making the bedrooms of the manservant and butler accessible only by a stair from the latter's pantry. An unusual feature of the plan at the time was that the stairs to the nurseries were adjacent to the principal bedroom.

All the buildings were of brick with pantiled

roofs, stone being used only for some copings in the kitchen yard. Godman's estate, unlike Lowthian Bell's, did not include a stone quarry and, although not far from Rounton Grange, it was in a district where clay was plentiful and brick had long been the traditional local material. The bricks for the house were made on site, probably for economy, although the concept of creating the building from the clay on which it would stand would undoubtedly have appealed to Webb. However, because many thousands of unfired bricks were washed away during a storm, he never repeated the experiment.

The main family block had a large hipped roof, from the top of which rose three massive slab-like chimneys, with corbelled tops and strings, in a similar manner to the four of Winslow Hall, Buckinghamshire (1700).[66] Webb had placed all the fireplaces and vent shafts of the major rooms against the central spine wall that, in effect, thus continued above the roof, though the central stack was set slightly south of the flanking pair. Each of the side wings had two gabled roofs, one parallel to the south front, the other at right angles to it, and a crisply pleated chimney. Highly unusually, iron rods passed down through the inner walls from the beams of the main roof, their purpose apparently being to lessen vibration in the bedroom and attic floors.[67] On the south front, the central part of the major block had an interesting ground-floor arcade of five segmental arches, under a pantiled lean-to roof, three of them housing twinned sashes under herringbone brickwork tympana, and two being blank seating recesses. In the Church Hill House manner, the five single sashes on the first floor had lintels concealed by the eaves and plain brick pilasters, around which a simply moulded white plaster cornice broke to form capitals. The pilasters and cornice details were repeated on all the elevations of the main block.

The long porch on the north front had panelled double doors inset beneath a wide segmental arch, flanked by angled buttresses with crenellated tops and roofed in pantiles. The porch was curtailed slightly during construction, when groups of triple casements on the long walls replaced the continuous glazing shown on the contract drawing. Also during construction, a nursery bathroom and small kitchen replaced the second-floor box room in the centre of the north front. To accommodate them, Webb added a large gabled dormer, flanked by single-flue chimneys, set at forty-five degrees, and separated by

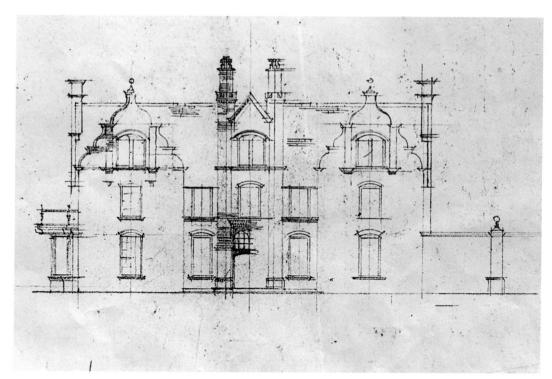

Left Rougham Hall, Norfolk:
Webb's sketch design for a
new country house, c.
1870–72, unexecuted
(Private Collection)

a window, with a triangular hood-mould that echoed
the small gable of the porch roof below. These details
resembled, in a less elaborate form, those of Webb's
sketch of a symmetrical H-plan main block, with a
pair of Dutch gables on two elevations, for one of
his unexecuted country house designs, the proposed
Rougham Hall, Norfolk of c. 1870–72.[68] On the
north front of Smeaton Manor, a small flat-topped
lead-covered structure between the roofs of the
central block and west wing permitted access from one
to the other.[69] Webb had used this strange-looking
device at Rounton to gain access from the picture
gallery to a pavilion roof. His Gothic training and
experience led him to accept readily what to adherents
of the Classical styles would have been a solecism.

The interior was much lighter in effect than that
of Rounton Grange, partly because there was no oak
wainscot or heavily decorated ceilings. All the
woodwork, except the principal staircase, was
painted white or a pale colour. The single-storey hall,
here more a circulation area than a living hall, had
so many doors and windows that it was wallpapered,
not panelled. The lower part of the striking and
unusual staircase consisted of winding steps, partly
supported on several strong newel posts that rose
from the floor and alternated with turned balusters.
At the foot was an octagonal post, like those of the

secondary staircase at Rounton, which Webb termed
a 'stair-storey' post. Designed after the contract was
signed, and jokingly reputed to have almost caused
the death of several family members, the Smeaton
staircase was replaced in the 1950s by an open-well
stair similar to that on Webb's contract drawings but
with a wrought-iron balustrade.

Morris & Co. decorated the whole or most of
the house between 1880 and 1885.[70] The
wallpapers, fabrics, and carpets of the firm were
accompanied chiefly by simple country furniture
bought at local farm sales. The dining-room
fireplace had embroidered panels, illustrating the
wild birds and animals that frequented the garden,
designed in 1885 by the Godmans' friend Thomas
M Rooke (1842–1942), Burne-Jones's studio
assistant, and worked by Ada Godman.[71] Wall
hangings were the chief feature of the delightful
drawing room. They took Mrs Godman fifteen and
a half years to embroider in blue, brown, green,
and pink wool on ivory linen, to the *Artichoke*
pattern designed for the room by Morris in 1877.[72]
Plain light-coloured curtains were chosen to
emphasize the hangings. As was usual in Webb's
houses, at his request the curtains were hung
simply, without pelmets, to avoid obscuring the
architrave of the windows. The simple band of

Above Smeaton Manor: the drawing-room fireplace in 1950, with the hinged mirrors removed from the two niches (Owen Wicksteed; now in a Private Collection)

Right Smeaton Manor: a detail of the *Artichoke* wall-hangings, embroidered for the drawing room by Ada Godman to the design made for her in August 1877 by William Morris (from a photograph by the author of a portion of the wall-hanging in a Private Collection)

ornament under the mantel of Webb's fireplace was a foretaste of his more intricate fretwork at Clouds.

Access to the garden was provided from the long leg of the drawing room through a glazed west door leading, not into the conservatory of the contract plan, but into a smaller brick porch with round recessed brick arches and a pantiled butterfly-shaped roof. The porch opened into Mrs Godman's flower garden, immediately west of the house. On the south front of the house, a lawn ran unencumbered down to two lakes formed in the pits from which the clay for the bricks had been taken. East of the lawn were rose, alpine, and wild gardens. Probably at the suggestion of Webb, who had installed trelliswork on the terrace walls of Arisaig House, herringbone-patterned wood trellises were fixed to all the walls of the main block except the entrance front, and to the exterior and interior walls of the garden porch.[73] All Webb's garden walls were handsome, including those of Smeaton Manor, which were in the same materials as the house, and had brick dentils, and pantile copings with galleting under the ridge tiles in the traditional local manner. He provided a most attractive arched and wainscoted arbour for Mrs Godman, in the north wall of her special garden.[74] West of her garden was the walled kitchen garden that had a central well, and was overlooked by the south range of the stable block, which had a pyramid-roofed cottage at each end, for the groom and the gardener respectively, with a dormitory for the bachelor farmhands between them. A tower over the idiosyncratic archway to the stable yard was added during construction to house a clock given by Lowthian Bell.[75]

Although not expressed externally as such, Smeaton effectively consisted of three basic parts: family rooms to the west; major services, servants' rooms, and offices in the centre; and minor offices around a kitchen yard at the east end. This tripartite long-house arrangement, with east-to-west cross-passages dividing major rooms to the south from minor ones and those in which direct sunlight was undesirable, to the north, proved to be convenient. Webb used it as a starting point for the planning of all his later country houses, except for Clouds, which had unusual requirements. Doing this was a matter of common sense as it saved a great deal of time in juggling with the multitude of rooms then found desirable in a country house. He saw no point in seeking novelty just for its own sake. He had not

ceased to design each building afresh or to exploit the possibilities of the specific site, however. The long-house could be adapted to fit the topography of most sites by being raised or lowered in height, or being angled – if necessary at right angles – at either or both junctions between the three parts. This adaptability, with the fact that within it the sizes and arrangement of rooms were not standardized, allowed Webb to approach each commission with an open mind as to the detailed plan and the appearance of the building. As will be shown in connection with Standen, the cross-passage sometimes lost its clarity as a scheme developed, a fact that has misled some investigators into thinking that Webb always started with a very irregular arrangement. Long vistas, deliberate contrasts of light and relatively dark areas, and the sudden opening out where they met the main staircase, gave his cross-passages considerable spatial drama.

Smeaton Manor was a gracious and welcoming house of almost dateless English character.[76] It was an extremely influential building. The beautiful, light-filled major rooms influenced those of many Arts and Crafts houses by Webb's followers. Other architects also found inspiration in more specific features of the house, such as the unusual porch which clearly had an impact on the design of the entrance archway of number 8 Addison Road, Kensington (1906–07) by Halsey Ricardo, an acknowledged admirer of Webb's

work.[77] As with West House, however, careless observation of Smeaton Manor led some architects to believe that Webb had fully embraced the Classical idiom, and therefore much of its influence was towards the adoption of the neo-Georgian style, which it predated by several years.[78] Such an influence must have saddened Webb, who believed that reviving past styles limited invention and ingenuity. Closer inspection would have shown that though the central block of Smeaton was symmetrical, Webb ignored the Classical rule of window over window, and the only motifs which could be loosely categorized as being of that style were the small brickwork pediments above and upon the porch.

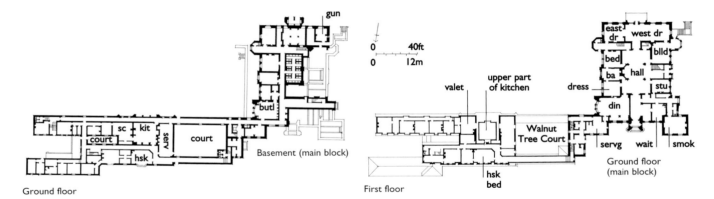

gun

butl

Basement (main block)

0   40ft
0   12m

sc   kit

court

court

serv

hsk

Ground floor

valet   upper part of kitchen   dress

Walnut Tree Court

First floor   hsk bed

east dr   west dr

blld

bed

ba   hall

stu

din

servg   wait   smok

Ground floor (main block)

Above Clouds: plans, showing the basement and ground floor of the main block, and the ground and first floors of the service wing

Clouds, East Knoyle, Wiltshire

In late December 1876, Webb received what by then had become a rare type of commission, a country seat for an aristocrat. Clouds House, or Clouds as it soon became known, was to be designed as a comfortable family home and, in the words of John Brandon-Jones, also as:

> a setting for house parties in the days when the government of England depended to a great extent upon arrangements made at these elaborately informal meetings where Cabinet decisions were anticipated and society weddings arranged.[79]

It would be Webb's sixth, and largest, most costly country house. In 1874, through the Firm, Webb had designed a chimneypiece with side cupboard for the London house of the Honourable Percy Wyndham, younger son of the first Lord Leconfield of Petworth, who had also consulted him the same year about making alterations to Wilbury House (now Wilbury Park) in Wiltshire, which Wyndham had leased and hoped to buy.[80] This having proved impossible, towards the end of 1876 he purchased the Clouds Estate in the same county and asked Webb to design a new house. Wyndham was an irascible but respected character who, amongst other eccentricities, gargled into his finger-bowl at dinner. He shared Webb's keen sense of duty, respect for hard work, and love of rescuing old buildings. In 1877, Wyndham became a founder member of the SPAB. Having left the army in 1856 after contracting malaria in the Crimea, in

Right Clouds, East Knoyle, Wiltshire (1877–80, constructed 1881–86): the south front (from a photograph in Webb's collection)

1860 he had become the MP for West Cumberland, a district he was to represent for twenty-five years, and had married the vivacious Madeline Caroline Campbell (1835–1920), an intelligent and talented amateur artist with a fine sense of colour, who, in 1872, co-founded the Royal School of Needlework.[81] The Wyndhams were friends of the Howard family – George Howard's father was the MP for East Cumberland – and so they knew number 1 Palace Green and, through their friendship with and patronage of Prinsep and Watts, they would know of if not have seen two more of Webb's studio-houses.

In December 1876, at their request, Webb showed the Wyndhams drawings of some of his earlier houses, and had his Statement of Business Arrangements accepted; at the end of the following January, he sent them a rough plan, intended merely to help them decide the size and position of rooms because, as he explained, until he had 'spent some hours in particular examination of the site and surroundings', he could not determine the position of the building or its final plan.[82] Already, and as it proved rightly, Webb feared that the strict budget of £75,000 for the house and stables would not cover the accommodation requested by these clients, who habitually dispensed boundless hospitality on a grand scale to their countless friends from the fields of politics, art, literature, theatre, and music. He produced an improved, slightly smaller plan in August 1877, which, after a further minor reduction, was accepted by Wyndham, who had inspected Rounton Grange earlier in the summer, doubtless at Webb's suggestion.[83]

The Wyndhams wished to employ a provincial builder but Webb, having scrupulously pointed out that the cost would be twenty to twenty-five per cent higher, persuaded them to seek an estimate from the first-rate London firm, George Smith and Co., because it had the necessary experience, expertise, and workmen to do the work to his high standard and, importantly, had had experience in the handling and setting of iron girders, and in working with the local stone.[84] The estimate, based on a bill of quantities, of May 1879 was too high, and by November that year Webb had produced a new design, in which, for economy, the central courtyard of the first scheme was replaced by a two-storey hall such as he had earlier cautioned his clients against having because of the cost and difficulty of heating such a large space.[85] The Wyndhams had ignored his warning that the number

and size of rooms must also be reduced, and so again the estimate exceeded the budget. Webb then suggested trying a smaller house, by another architect should they so wish; after reducing the size of the house a little, however, a revised price was accepted in June 1881.[86] At this point, legal problems made it impossible for Smith and Co. to do the work unless Webb would agree to the purchasing of a small building firm and Smiths doing the work under its name. He rejected the idea out of hand, and it was decided that, after all, a provincial builder must found. Webb investigated the work and business affairs of a

small number of firms, and obtained tenders from a few of them; on his advice Wyndham accepted that of Albert Estcourt of Gloucester, who had done work for the late William Burges at Cardiff Castle and had been recommended to Webb by Burges's erstwhile chief assistant, and by the architect Ewan Christian (1814–95).[87] The house and stables were constructed at a good speed between 1881 and 1886, entirely to Webb's satisfaction apart from a few items that had had to be redone. Albert Estcourt worked for Webb again, at Forthampton Court in 1889, and Exning House in 1895 (see chapter 9).

The Wyndhams moved into Clouds in September 1885, and the house rapidly became a favourite meeting place of the Wyndhams' extended family and friends. Their generous hospitality came to an abrupt if temporary halt in the early hours of 6 January 1889, when the main block was almost completely gutted by a fire started by a lighted candle left in a cupboard by a maid. Ironically, the central hall, initially opposed by Webb, funnelled and intensified the flames.[88] The Wyndhams immediately decided to reinstate Clouds exactly as it had been; in demonstrating so conclusively that his house had fulfilled all their practical and aesthetic needs, they paid Webb the greatest possible compliment. Only a few very minor changes were made during the reinstatement, which was completed by Estcourt in 1891.

In 1876, on his first visit to the fine well-established park, with many mature trees, of the Clouds Estate, Webb had decided to build the new house on the site of the existing modest late-eighteenth-century house, at the head of a narrow valley backed by moorland and sheltered by trees to east and west but with fine views southwards over the park and Blackmore Vale.[89] At an early date, he resolved to use a long wing of domestic offices at right angles to the main block of the house, allowing it to overlap the latter only sufficiently for communication. Almost detached in this way, it could be of simpler treatment and cheaper materials than the main block, thus reducing costs considerably, and it would shelter an east garden; most importantly, however, it would ensure greater privacy for the many politicians amongst both the family and its guests. The main block was aligned almost due north to south, with the range of offices, at a lower level because of the fall of the ground, joined to its north-east corner at right angles by the necessary water tower. East of the service wing, beyond a long greenhouse, was the

head gardener's house, converted by Webb from an old pair of thatched cottages.

The position of the house on the site, with the entrance on a north front sheltered by the rising ground, and the relationship of the office wing to the principal block, the locations of many of the rooms, and the general character of the elevations, were the same in both the central courtyard or Yew Court scheme, and the executed design.[90] The room-and-a-passage arrangement of the rooms in the principal block still pertained on the second floor, where a directly lit passage encircled the roof of the two-storey hall, and on the first floor where the hall gallery

Above Clouds: the west front (detail): Webb's segmental-arched doorway was replaced with the architrave and pediment shown here, from a much older building, in the twentieth century

Opposite Clouds: the south front

Left Compton Wynyates, Warwickshire (early sixteenth century) (from a photograph in Webb's collection, probably taken by William Weir)

provided the means of access. The perimeter of the hall formed the circulation area on the ground floor but traffic of servants therein was reduced by their being able to approach from the basement up strategically placed staircases. Webb used two axes that met at right angles in the precise centre of the hall. The entrance axis ran north to south through the block, from the central porch on the north front, through the hall and drawing room, to the balcony on the south front (because of the steep slope of the site, the basement was above ground on the south and east sides of the block). The second, the west-to-east axis, extended from the garden door in the centre of the west front through the hall to the centre of its important fireplace. The south front was occupied by the main and east drawing rooms which, with double doors between them, could become effectively a single room over seventy-six feet long for grand occasions. The dining room was on the east front, with Percy Wyndham's private suite between it and the east drawing room, overlooking the east gardens and conveniently positioned next to the serving room that was housed in one of the two corner pavilions on the north front. The distance between the dining room and major drawing room created a long and impressive 'dinner route' through the central hall, a facility considered highly desirable at the time. The west front housed the billiard-room – which had access to the garden and, most unusually, a door to the drawing room – and the main staircase and the study. The smoking room in the north-west pavilion, and the study, could be used for business, there being an adjacent waiting room and WC.

Clouds was a development of Rounton Grange as regards the central hall and the corner pavilions of the plan, and in external appearance, with greater multiplication of detail as befitted its larger size, and a greater variety of building materials because of its location in the south of England. The Idea for the first design apparently came from a combination of a medieval fortified house – probably specifically Compton Wynyates in Warwickshire, photographs of which Webb had in his collection – and an Elizabethan central courtyard house, articulated by polygonal bay windows.[91] The courtyard was abandoned in the final design in favour of a central hall as found in some Elizabethan houses and several by Vanbrugh, but some influences remained constant. The influence of Compton Wynyates was revealed in the tower and the parapet; in the warm red-tile roofs

and prominent gables; in the brick diapering of the top of the central feature on the east front; and in the arched porch and its flanking corner buttresses, which had an expansive welcoming air. Two polygonal turrets, one on the west and the second on the east front, echo the medieval garderobe turret in function – on all floors they housed WCs – but were more Elizabethan in shape and size. The greater symmetry, the regularity of fenestration, and the multiple gables on all fronts, reflected some Elizabethan houses, and Webb's own Joldwynds. The influence of Vanbrugh was also revealed in the polygonal turrets, and in the pavilions, and the central projection on the east front.

The principal block was unified by the symmetry about the centre of each front; by windows of similar type and shape being used throughout; by the repetition of gables an all elevations; and by the parapet, or in some places just its mouldings, being taken all round the building. The major chimneys, plain slabs of red brick mostly of equal height, were disposed in an orderly way, with some slender, polygonal single-flue stacks as contrasts. The walls were of greensand, the local sandstone, with stone from the paler-coloured beds being reserved for dressings, the parapet, and the patternwork in some tympana. Webb used alternating bands of stone and red brick to shade the colour of the walls into that of the red roofs in the lower walls and mullions of the south front, and the upper parts of the tower, which was surmounted by a small bell turret and wind-vane. The upper parts of the gables were boarded in oak. The roof tiles and most of the bricks were made locally to match those of the demolished house, the front door of which was reused on the luggage entrance.[92] Windows in the habitable rooms were tall sashes, similar in detail to those of the 1877 design; in circulation areas, they were single, or mullioned and in some cases also transomed, casements. The large balcony on the south front had one of Webb's attractive wrought-iron balustrades, and retractable canvas canopies.

The interior of the principal block revealed the influence of Vanbrugh in the barrel-vaulted passages and many round arches. The general character of the fixtures and fittings was the same as in all Webb's houses, except that there was more carved woodwork and more decorative plasterwork because of the greater size of the major rooms. His drawings for ornament carry detailed notes instructing the woodcarvers and plaster-modellers precisely how to do the work, and telling them to make the depicted items, usually leaves, sharp, and the gouging deep, in items far from the eye. Most of the fireplaces were by Webb, though some antique Italian ones, bought with his approval, were used in major rooms, within his panelled surrounds. The house was centrally heated and gas lighting was installed except in the main reception rooms where the Wyndhams preferred the softer effects of candlelight. In the opinion of Wilfrid Scawen Blunt, a frequent visitor, the main bedrooms, with fitted cupboards, washbasins with hot and cold running water, and easy access to bathrooms, were 'perfect in form, decoration, and above all in comfort and convenience'.[93]

Madeline Wyndham and Webb had similar tastes, so the decoration was of a much lighter character

Left Clouds: the central living hall (from a photograph in Webb's collection)

than that of Rounton, with a preponderance of plain walls, most of them white. Other rooms were distempered in pale tints to match the fabrics. Throughout the house, small areas of intense colour, often blue, were provided by Morris & Co. carpets and cushions, and pieces of old and new fabrics bought by Madeline, and embroideries worked by the chatelaine and her daughters, as well as by Wyndham's collection of paintings. The nurseries and a few other rooms had Morris wallpapers. Shutters having been provided in all rooms, not all the windows were curtained. The furniture consisted chiefly of English pieces from the late eighteenth century, on the purchase of some of which Webb had been consulted, with new ones in similar styles.

The great hall was a living hall, in use constantly for conversation, playing games, and attending musical and theatrical performances. In the early

Right Clouds: the main staircase (detail of the first-floor screen)

1900s, in his influential *Das englische Haus*, Hermann Muthesius rightly described the hall as being 'admirable for its spaciousness, monumentality and entirely original design.[94] Four slender piers, with capitals of a combined Gothic and Classical air carved to Webb's foliage design, carried two transverse round arches and divided the hall into three bays, each lit by a large square roof-lantern, beautifully designed and worked in teak. Two aisles were created by timber arches, supported on shafts flanking the piers; the former were of the characteristic flattened form that Webb had introduced in his early cabinets, and used subsequently, on a small or large scale, for most arches that were not load-bearing. Above the arches, the galleries were panelled in oak below the leaded casements that Webb used to prevent servants hearing conversations in the hall below, and which admitted ample light from the lanterns. Hard cement, moulded with geometric panels, formed a most unusual dado in the gallery passages. The central bay was the chief sitting area, defined at floor level by a large Morris & Co. carpet in deep pink, blues, greens, and white. On the east side of it, the aisle was broken by a huge hooded fireplace from which screens extended at forty-five degrees to meet two of the piers, creating a sophisticated inglenook and screening the doors of Wyndham's bedroom and bathroom. Webb ordered that the plasterwork cornice was to be 'modelled boldly' because it was about twenty-eight feet from the view point; the design was based on his sketches of artichokes in the New Place garden.[95] At his own risk, Morris designed *The Forest* tapestry (mentioned in chapter 3), with animals and birds by Webb, to hang under the casements of the south gallery; after he decided that its proportions were unsuitable, the Wyndhams commissioned from his firm *The Orchard* tapestry, designed by John Dearle, for this position.[96]

The main staircase, off the hall opposite the fireplace, was of untreated oak. It had a band of foliage carving under the trellised balustrade, open-box type newels with central posts and carved ball finials, and an unusual screen, with a considerable amount of carved work, and twin segmental arches separated by a narrower straight-headed opening containing turned balusters. The large and striking staircase window consisted of two storeys of mullioned and latticed lights arranged as three-between-two, in the front of which the inner leaf of the wall formed a beautiful two-tier screen, largely

of stone. Two pairs of stone pillars supported, on the lower level, a central segmental arch flanked by two pointed arches, and on the upper one, a lower segmental arch between two round arches.

The ceilings of the two drawing rooms had geometrical panels derived from English Baroque plasterwork but highly personal in treatment, without visible beams. Elsewhere, however, beams encased in plaster were evident, a small number being false ones included for visual balance, as in Rounton Grange.[97] The major drawing room was entered from the hall through a short vestibule with a coffered barrel vault, and had a welcoming and comfortable air, despite its great size. It had a plasterwork frieze, of Webb's design based on the crown imperial lily, and a panelled ceiling in low relief, consisting of a band of large hexagonal panels down the centre, each with a short central pendant, surrounded by half-hexagons and small square panels. The band of ornament on each of the hexagons had a deliberately lace-like effect, as did the foliate fretwork panels surmounting Webb's white-painted bookcases on the end walls.[98] The hood of the fireplace bore a carved foliage design, adapted from that on an Indian pot, in which Webb incorporated a beautifully depicted bird returning to its nest as a symbol of the central importance of Clouds to the Wyndham family.[99] Morris designed his longest carpet for the room, with large arabesques on a blue ground. Plain white curtains increased its effect. The east drawing room that has sometimes been termed the library, though not by the Wyndhams, had a much simpler ceiling of shallow square coffers.[100] The plaster

from a distance and from the major block, the red of its walls and tiled roofs echoing that in the banding and roofs of the principal block. The large square kitchen had dormer windows and, at the apex of its high pyramidal roof, a two-tier lantern, reminiscent of that of the fourteenth-century abbot's kitchen of Glastonbury Abbey, but ventilated by up-to-the-minute apparatus in the upper part. The servants' hall, thirty-nine feet long, in which thirty could be seated at once around Webb's two-part table and benches, looked onto a pleasant private court containing an old tree. This Walnut Tree Court was enclosed to north and south by long barrel-vaulted passages that provided, through the tower, the only internal access from the wing to the family block. The south passage, along which food was taken from the kitchen, led to the basement of the block, from which the ground floor was served via secondary staircases and the food was taken up to the serving room by an hydraulic lift. The upper of the two north passages led to the serving room, which was well equipped with food-warming apparatus, and the dining room on the ground floor and, up the tower, to the first floor.

Allowing the service wing to overlap the main block sufficiently only for communication, and placing the Walnut Tree Court and servants' hall between the tower and the kitchen, meant that the servants had to walk great distances, and up and down many steps. This was not through lack of care for their welfare on Webb's or the clients' behalf, however. Privacy was imperative in the main block. Also, in such a large mansion where meals were cooked daily for over forty people and often many more, it was necessary to protect the major rooms from the odours and noises that emanated from the kitchen and sculleries. The servants' lot was mitigated by having storage rooms and hot and cold piped water on every floor, and by the hydraulic food and luggage lifts in the tower. Overall, arrangements for their ease and convenience, to which both Webb and Madeline Wyndham had paid great attention, were well above the norm (even the 'odd man' had a bath of his own).

Webb and Mrs Wyndham were not as much in accord about the gardens as they were about the house (see chapter 13). Ultimately, Madeline and Harry Brown, the head gardener who came to Clouds from Wilbury with the family, designed the planting schemes. Webb insisted on there being only lawn sweeping away from the south front of the main block,

frieze had geometrical panels, and the plaster cornice was ornamented with flowers and foliage. White-painted bookshelves by Webb lined the walls; two matching freestanding ones created an intimate area in front of the fireplace, which had a carved architrave and a diamond-panelled overmantel.

The dining room had a sash-windowed recess on the north wall, probably in lieu of the breakfast room dropped from the second design, created by two round arches and a central pillar. The east wall was occupied by a large bay window, with three sashes set within a wide round arch. The oak wainscot had a narrow band of carved foliage near the top, and the fireproof ceiling had an unusual shallow segmental vault down the centre, interrupted at intervals by encased beams. The vertical and near-vertical surfaces of the ceiling carried plasterwork ornament of Webb's design with deeply recessed grounds to give a lace-like effect.

The brick service wing was vigorously articulated on its south front to make it unobtrusive when seen

with a simple white-painted oak fence, similar to the one he had used near the main entrance of Rounton Grange, between it and the park. He allowed a red-paved terrace, for dancing on in summer, to be laid between the house and greensward, but permitted no planting along it. He designed the two loggias, the twin-arched one under the balcony and the one with three arches on the south wall of the offices, and also a 'little garden house' in the south wall of the gardens, and the handsome brick walls of the kitchen garden which lay west of the house in his chosen position.[101] Although his detailed but unsolicited design for their layout was not accepted, he insisted on the gardens being east of the block, fronting the office wing, and on the retention of the old farmyard enclosed by chalk-block thatched walls in front of the gardener's cottage that terminated them. A garden devoted to spring-flowering plants was created within these old walls. Webb would have approved of the general character of the planting in the east gardens, which he had probably influenced as usual after all, where rectangular

beds overflowing with flowers and shrubs were surrounded with grass, and enclosed by yew hedges.[102]

Clouds soon became renowned. From the late 1880s to the First World War, it was a favourite meeting place of the Souls, the group of cultured aristocrats of which Madeline and several of her family were prominent members.[103] It was spoken of as the house of the age, and Wyndham told Webb

Above Clouds: the plasterwork frieze in the west drawing room, a design by Webb based on the crown imperial lily

of an American architect seeking out the house because he had heard that it was the masterpiece of modern English domestic architecture.[104] Shaw admired Clouds, according to his son, and so did Lethaby, who found, as other contemporary and later observers have done, that it took a little time to appreciate fully what he described as Webb's combination of 'houseness, modernism, tradition, invention, science, and poetry'.[105] Clouds, the largest of Webb's executed designs, was probably the only nineteenth-century house of its size in which every detail, whether inside or out, important or insignificant, was designed by one man, in what later became known as 'total design'.[106] This mansion could never have made Webb's fortune because his percentage-of-the-cost fee did not even approach paying him for all the hours he had worked. Clouds increased his renown and his influence but many potential clients, thinking he would have become too grand to take on lesser work, sadly went elsewhere.

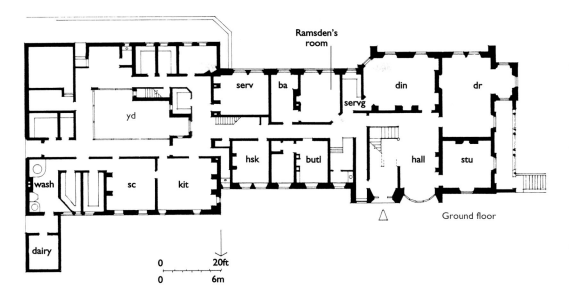

Ramsden's room

serv · ba · servg · din · dr

yd

hsk · butl · hall · stu

wash · sc · kit

dairy

0 ——— 20ft
0 ——— 6m

Ground floor

Left Willinghurst: plan of the ground floor

Opposite above Clouds: the east drawing room in 1904 (Country Life)

Opposite below Clouds: the dining room (from a photograph in Webb's collection)

Willinghurst, Shamley Green, Surrey

Webb's seventh country house, Willinghurst, near Shamley Green in Surrey, was commissioned by John Charles Francis Ramsden, a retired Royal Artillery officer who, early in 1886, asked him to design a country house for his Sparelands estate on the wooded south slope of Winterfold Heath. Joldwynds and Coneyhurst were only a few miles away, and would probably have been known to Ramsden and his wife Emma, who would have heard of Webb through Ramsden's cousin Lord Muncaster, a close friend of the Wyndhams, though they did not visit Clouds until after commissioning the architect.[107] The unbridled ambitions and indecision of the Ramsdens caused Webb to produce four schemes and countless amendments, and twice to urge them to appoint another architect, before the fifth design, of July 1886, was accepted, and even that one had to be amended more than once (see chapter 13). The house and the stable block (designed in 1888) were erected between 1887 and 1889 by Mitchell Brothers of Shalford, who also built the two identical lodges and a gardener's cottage, which bear the dates 1897, 1898, and 1900, respectively.[108]

In the early summer of 1888, Webb kept an eye on the progress of Willinghurst, the remedial work at Joldwynds, and the enlargement of Great Tangley Manor (see chapter 9) whilst recuperating from a severe attack of rheumatism on a farm near Cranleigh. Still unable to draw, he allowed his chief assistant George Jack to design a few details for the house. When Mrs

Ramsden rejected Jack's designs for bedroom fireplaces, Webb promised him that he would tell her what she would be losing 'in the way of "prentice" work', a pretty compliment referring to the superb ornamental work of the fifteenth-century apprentice at Rosslyn Chapel whose skill was greater than his master's; as another consolation, he told Jack to 'play high jinks' in turning the recesses in a bedroom into 'love cupboards, for visitors to peep in when they go to bed, and find the most lovely store of French stories, not otherwise obtainable in the house'.[109]

Webb placed Willinghurst on a plateau halfway up the hillside, with a north entrance court between it and the stables.[110] A long U-shaped drive with a lodge at each end climbed up from the road, passed through the north entrance court, then veered round the kitchen garden east of the house to join the road again. The house, another long-house, ran east to west across the slope. Low ranges of domestic offices surrounded a kitchen yard at the east end. A narrower three-storey, twin-gabled central section contained, on the ground floor, the butler's and housekeeper's rooms and Ramsden's bedroom and bathroom, made necessary by a war wound. The main entrance and major family rooms occupied a slightly wider west block.

In the same arrangement as Rounton Grange, the dining room, drawing room, and study, with magnificent views to the south, south and west, and west respectively, were grouped round a single-storey living hall. On the two main floors, the cross-

Right Willinghurst, Shamley Green, Surrey (1886, constructed 1887–89): the south front, before demolition of the central part (from a photograph in Webb's collection)

Below Willinghurst: the main entrance on the (north) front of the family block

passage began at the eastern extremity of the central section but ended short of the west wall of the major block. Contrast in shape between the drawing room and dining room was achieved by using a deep bay window to make the former L-shaped, and by making the latter D-shaped by cutting off the south-east corner, a device which also gave spectacular south-eastern views to the dining room and the major bedroom. A glazed passage along the exposed west front protected and shaded the drawing room and study, and provided garden access.[111]

The house was built of red brick, with some carefully positioned blue-grey headers, and faced on the lower north and south walls of the west block with a warm cream stone quarried on the estate, and on the first floor with red tiles except over the entrance. The large, twin gables of the central block – the northern pair tile-hung, the southern pair weatherboarded – added dynamic lines, and contrasted in shape with the hipped roofs of the west block. They also helped the chimneys and buttresses of the south front to visually anchor the building to the steep hillside. The recessed arch of the main entrance had Webb's reinterpretation of a Tudor hood-mould above it: a panel of diapered red and blue headers, with a projecting border of red headers. The arch was combined, under a coved plaster cornice similar to that of the west-front bay window, with the leaded casements of the luggage entrance and the bow window of the living hall. Despite the exposure of the site, these cornices, and similar ones at Standen, have survived for over a century without deterioration. Two attractively shaped stone corbels flanked the hall window and supported the cornice, the mouldings of which demonstrated Webb's penchant for contrasting large and small items of the same shape. The minuscule dentils of the fascia echoed the small timber and large brick dentils of the main string on the north front. The leaded casements of the large landing window looked fine from the interior but less attractive from the exterior. This, with the slight sense of unease induced by the lack of any link between the entrance bay and bow-window bay at the roof level, probably reflected Webb's frustration at repeatedly having to redesign this part of the building to please his awkward clients.[112]

On the south front, a first-floor balcony with a simple white-painted balustrade linked the three parts of the long-house visually. It also shaded Ramsden's bedroom and bathroom from the midday sun in summer; doubtless partly for the same purpose, Webb added louvred wooden shutters, not initially envisaged, to the exposed south and west fronts

Below Willinghurst: from the south-west

during construction.[113] To combat wind-driven rain, he filled the cavities between the outer and inner leaves with well-packed cement. With the probably sole exception of Rounton Grange, this seems to have become his custom.

Webb certainly fulfilled his aim of making the panelled living hall a 'pleasant place to sit in'.[114] Approached through a low-ceilinged inset porch, in which sections of the panelling ingeniously formed protective night shutters for the double doors, the hall had a fairly plain fireplace and a window-seat in the wide bow, which was set beyond a tall three-centred arch and, in a rare instance of Webb permitting such items in a house, had armorial stained glass in some of its lights. A beautiful staircase rose from one of Webb's fine polygonal oak stair posts, with open-box type oak newels, and white latticed balustrade panels, a little more elaborate than the grid panels of Clouds and more pleasing than the latter on the incline. The pattern of the panels was repeated in a simpler form on a shallow frieze in the drawing room, which had a fine chimneypiece, with sharply cut foliage on the architrave and more detailed but lower-relief carving on three painted pine panels between it and the mantel shelf, the central one bearing a pelican as a symbol of devoted motherhood (though no offspring are shown), doubtless requested by Mrs Ramsden.[115] The dining-room fireplace had a carved architrave and latticed panels in fretwork below the mantel shelf; the grate, with a 'scoured iron' plate-warming rack above the fire, was made to Webb's design by Thomas Elsley. Webb used similar but not identical racks on the dining-room fireplaces of Forthampton Court, Standen, and Exning House; these attractive features were probably put to use at breakfast when, in the late nineteenth century, the family customarily served itself.

The echoing of details, such as dentils, on different items and at differing scales on the exterior, and the similar repetition of exterior details in the interior, helped towards the consistent whole for which Webb always aimed. At Willinghurst, the dentils of the exterior reappear inside the house on cornices and fireplaces, and on a long many-paned ceiling light, lit from above by nine roof lights, in the cross-passage on the first floor of the main block. This most pleasing element is a revealing contrast to the sometimes rather unpleasant open light-shafts by Shaw who, more concerned with the detailing of his exteriors, occasionally failed to pay meticulous attention to all those of the interior. Nothing is known of the original decoration of Willinghurst. However, the Ramsdens are known to have admired Clouds, so probably a great deal of white and light-coloured paint, and at least some Morris & Co. products, would have been involved.[116]

The attractive subsidiary buildings were constructed of the same bricks and tiles as the house, and had similar details. An old timber-framed, tile-hung cottage, with its integrity retained, was incorporated as the coachman's dwelling with the stable block, which had a most pleasing pyramid-roofed archway. The influence of this element can be seen in numerous later Arts and Crafts houses. A structural detail in the coach-house range demonstrated Webb's inventive use of timber. As vertical posts could have been damaged by coaches, he supported the eaves of the entrance wall of this range in an unusual way – on

Below Willinghurst: the box-newel of the main staircase

Above Willinghurst: the living hall

Below Willinghurst: a detail of the drawing-room fireplace, showing the symbolic pelican carved to Webb's design

twin struts that were inclined from the centre of the coach-house floor to the eaves, and fastened, one on either side, to the posts separating the coach bays.

The interesting two-storey cottage for the gardener, at the south-east corner of the kitchen garden, had a wide gable; below it, the left-hand corner of the building formed an open porch with the entrance to the dwelling set at forty-five degrees to the gable. On the centre line of the latter, a relieving arch in brick over a three-light window on the ground floor carried the date 1900 between simple sprays of leaves in plasterwork. Webb had already used similar pargetting on the gables of the two small single-storey lodges, which bore Ramsden's initials and the respective dates, 1897 and 1899.

Despite the slightly unsatisfactory entrance part of the north front, and the apparent lack of a strong Idea governing the design as a whole, Willinghurst was an interesting and attractive house, especially in the interior. The early troubles were not due to Webb having misinterpreted his clients' needs and wishes, as the similarity of the final scheme to the sketch plan made on his first visit to the site demonstrates. Though at times it seemed that the

Ramsdens would never be satisfied, ultimately they must have been, as besides the delicate and unobtrusive lead-roofed open summerhouse to George Jack's design they added in 1906,[117] they made no further additions – not even the smoking room Webb designed in 1896. Disgusted by finding the hillside near Coneyhurst 'blasted by a beast of a large new house', Webb found with great relief that his 'simple and unostentatious' Willinghurst had 'all the advantages of sufficient view' without being an 'eyesore to all the country round'.[118] This had been difficult to achieve, as his liking for reticence was in conflict with the Ramsdens' liking for show. The clients, and the existence of the old cottage, influenced the choice of the actual site; Webb would probably have preferred to build lower down the hillside in a much less prominent position. He managed to persuade them to accept the breaking-up of the mass of the building and to allow the use of both gables and hips and of a variety of wall materials, which made it less obvious from a distance. As a result, however, the south front was less unified than those of his other country houses, though by no means disastrously so.

Left Willinghurst: the stable-yard archway, designed in 1888

Right Standen, near East Grinstead, West Sussex (1891, constructed 1892–94): the south front from a high level, showing how Webb tucked the house into the hillside to prevent it from dominating the landscape, whilst ensuring that there would be fine vistas from the major rooms

Standen, East Grinstead, West Sussex

Webb must have been relieved to find that the clients for whom he designed Standen were entirely in sympathy with all his aims. James Samuel Beale (1840–1912) and his wife Margaret (1847–1936) were both from prominent, cultured families in

Birmingham. A wealthy man, Beale had charge of the London branch of the family firm of solicitors, Beale & Co., and he and his wife lived at number 32 Holland Park. In 1890, he bought a small estate of three farms near East Grinstead, West Sussex, a town easily accessible from London by rail. The estate offered ample scope for his interest in horses and shooting and his wife's love of gardening, and lay in beautiful, undulating countryside overlooking the Medway valley and the Ashdown Forest. Beale intended to build on the estate a house in which to entertain, to spend weekends and holidays, and to live in permanently after he retired. As the couple had seven children, a large extended family and many friends, however, it was to be a full-scale country house. The Beales were familiar with Webb's work for Alexander Ionides at number 1 Holland Park (see chapter 3), through whom it is believed they met the architect, and they would have known Upwood Gorse, Surrey (see chapter 11), the home of another friend, John Tomes, and perhaps Joldwynds too, as Beale's brother was one of Bowman's physicians. In March 1891, Beale commissioned Webb to design

Right Standen: plan of the ground floor

Ground floor

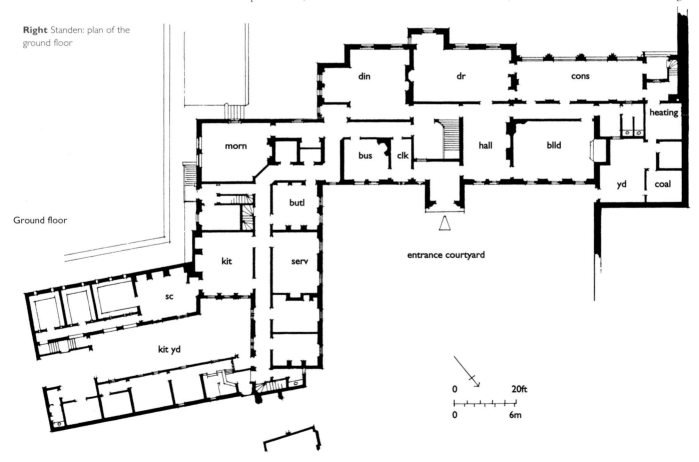

entrance courtyard

0   20ft

0   6m

the house, knowing that, despite the required size, he would provide an unpretentious building such as he and his wife were seeking because, in the opinion of their granddaughter, Elizabeth Motley their puritan ancestry forbade extravagance.[119]

Webb's first plan, of May to June 1891, established the basic layout and orientation but, as his drawings show, it underwent several reductions and changes before the final design of September that year. Peter Peters of Horsham constructed the house and stables between 1892 and 1894. Charles Rice of East Grinstead executed Webb's last works at Standen: a pair of three-bedroom semi-detached dwellings known as Standen Cottages in 1896 and, in 1898, a bay-window addition to the living hall, a second seating recess in the billiard room, and a garden shelter.[120]

In the earliest drawings, the plan of the house is based on Webb's long-house arrangement with a straight east-to-west cross-passage. Soon, however, the topography of the land and the Beales' wish to have a 'wind-mill pump' which necessitated a water tower in the house, led Webb to return to the medieval fortified house Compton Wynyates for the Idea.[121] He angled the long-house plan at the junctions between the three parts, and used rising ground and his stables to the

north, a rock outcrop to the west, and the main block and the central portion (the east wing) of the house to enclose a north entrance court, roughly equivalent to the central court of Compton Wynyates. A link, containing the entrance archway to the court, connected the north end of the east wing to the fifteenth-century tile-hung Hollybush farmhouse, onto which Webb's stables backed, and from which the new house took its name until 1894. The minor domestic office range projected eastwards at the north end of the east wing, carefully angled so as not to obstruct the view from the morning room.[122] These components of the group, with an old barn to the north, loosely enclosed an outer court that was named Goose Green after the intruder-deterring geese that grazed upon it.

The approach to Standen was by a lane from the north. At the point where it passed Webb's attractive cottages, which were in the same materials as the house and were expressed as a whole rather than as two dwellings, the visitor was afforded a first glimpse of the tower of the house.[123] The lane then swung east, to pass the stables and the old granary and enter Goose Green, then south and west to the entrance court. This route, like the approach to Arisaig House, evoked an agreeable sense of mystery and expectation, intensified by all parts of the house never being in

Below Standen: Hollybush Farmhouse (from 1450), with the northernmost end of the new house on the left, seen from Goose Green

Above Standen: the archway from Goose Green into the entrance court

Opposite Standen: the south front of the main block, showing the bay-window of the drawing room, the extended roof of which gives shade in midsummer

two floors only. This scheme was judged to be too costly as it was, and consequent reductions obscured the similarity to Smeaton and the clarity of the ground-floor passage, which was finally chopped in two in 1898 when a section of it became a second seating recess in the billiard room. The central library on the south front was omitted, the staircase was transferred from beside the porch to behind it, the dining room was turned on its axis, the living hall was reduced in size and changed in shape, and the billiard room was pulled back into the block. The conservatory was retained.

Webb exploited the qualities of the many traditional building materials available in the district: red hand-made roof- and wall-tiles; hand-made red Keymer bricks, and pink to grey Horsham stock bricks, with dark stretchers used to form subdued stripes; creamy-yellow stone from the outcrop next to the house, dressed like that of an old wall in East Grinstead; grey Portland stone; and leadwork, brown to silver oak boarding, off-white roughcast, and white-painted woodwork.[126] All of these were combined and carefully disposed into a subtly coloured, richly textured tapestry. He also employed a considerable quantity of iron: as rods in roof trusses; as components of flitch-beams; as huge beams supporting the hip of the east wing; as joists surrounded with concrete in the fireproof floors of the kitchen, first-floor cross-passage, and water-tank room; and as the light framework of the conservatory roof, which was based on that of his central lantern in the Bell Brothers Offices, Middlesbrough (designed 1881 to 1883; see chapter 12).[127]

Webb articulated the building with hips, gables, and tall, judiciously placed plain stacks. The tower, which acted as a pivot between the principal block and the east wing, was an important element in the composition from all viewpoints, with a unifying and anchoring role. A higher tower would have helped the composition of the house seen from the south-east but would have been too high on the south front. Clearly, Webb was aware of this problem as, following Vanbrugh's habit, though possibly unknowingly, he stipulated that the final height of the tower was to be decided by his own eye as work progressed.[128] The tower slightly resembled that of Compton Wynyates but it had a useful belvedere instead of crenellations and was roughcast because of the exposure of the upper walls.[129] The notion of placing the strongroom in its base was felicitous.

view at once.[124] Beale had intended the house to be built on a prominent site already levelled for the purpose by George B Simpson, a London landscape gardener he had commissioned to design the grounds before he asked Webb to design the building. With reluctance, Beale allowed the architect to place the house a little to the east and further into the shoulder of the hill, where it would be less dominating, and where it could be made even more unobtrusive through integration with some of the worthy old buildings. After the house was completed, Beale readily conceded that Webb had been right.[125]

Webb's early drawings show that the plan of the principal block was to have been similar to that of Smeaton. It had a central porch in a north entrance court created by flanking wings (the western wing containing a billiard room not a business room), and three major rooms in a projecting south front, a conservatory in the same position as that proposed for Smeaton, and a cross-passage, lit at each end, on

Right Standen: the main entrance porch

Opposite Standen: the east wall of the dining room and the major bedroom

On the north front – the principal block actually faced slightly east of north – the porch, aptly described by Lawrence Weaver as debonair and welcoming, had a striking red-brick arch similar in form to the stone arches on the exterior of the thirteenth-century great hall at Penshurst Place, Kent.[130] The entrance bay was in stone, in the tradition of those of large, red-brick Elizabethan and Jacobean houses. The tall arched recesses flanking the landing window were developed from the niches on Webb's hall fireplace at Forthampton Court (see chapter 9). The intended central symmetry about the porch was broken during construction when a five-light window was substituted for the twin sashes of the hall. So, when he was asked in 1898 to create more space in the hall for a grand piano, and the larger than expected daily tea-parties, Webb suggested the addition of a bay window, rightly believing that Beale would reject his preferred solution of throwing together the hall and billiard room.[131] Webb made the new window polygonal to catch light reflected from the walls of the court and thereby add a lively appearance, and used a small side window to catch the evening sun.[132] To avoid conflict with the gabled porch, he gave the bay window a flat roof, with a parapet. The enlargement would not have been necessary had Webb's earlier design for square, larger hall been accepted. Interestingly, the square hall was to have had a bold ceiling of polygonal coffers round an iron and concrete saucer-dome, in a development of the vaulting of the picture gallery he built in Hove for the Beales' friend Constantine Ionides (see chapter 9),

Right Standen: the south front, including the conservatory and the garden-house

and very like the one Lutyens would design a decade
later for Marsh Court, Hampshire.[133]

On the south front, a handsome arcade, of five
recessed round brick arches on stone piers, made the
conservatory and garden-house integral parts of the
consistent whole. The garden-house, a more pleasing
version of the View House at Joldwynds, was
envisaged from an early stage, chiefly as a definite
stop to the elevation, as is shown by Webb's being
able to promise the use of its upper room to young

Helen Beale in exchange for a sixpenny piece.[134] A
row of five small projecting gables on the roof
repeated the rhythm of the arcade, and protected the
major bedrooms below from the hot summer sun so
much disliked by Victorians. The bay window in the
drawing room, an all-weather alternative to the
canvas-roofed balcony at Clouds, had deep sheltering
eaves which also shaded the adjacent windows for
much of the day. Visiting the completed house,
Webb was gratified to note that even on a blazing

summer day it was 'delightfully cool'.[135] The idiosyncratic corbel-cum-capital, without a shaft, which supported the arches of the twin sashes on the east walls of the dining room, joined the red-brick architraves of these windows, which are in a stone wall, in being examples of what Ricardo found at Standen in 1900, and aptly described as the 'waywardness of detail' that prevented Webb's respect for tradition from becoming a constriction.[136]

The sequence of varying ambiences of the approach continued inside the building, where they depended more on contrasts of natural lighting and prospects than changes in geometry. Shady rooms looked out onto the sunlit entrance court, contrasting with the relatively dark passage and the brightly lit south-facing rooms with open aspects. Twin round arches pierced the loadbearing wall at the foot and head of the staircase, which had pierced oak balusters inspired by those of mid-seventeenth-century vernacular houses, and a flat handrail such as Webb often employed in the 1890s. The bay window in the green-panelled dining room was fitted with oak sideboards as a breakfast alcove, similar to the smaller one he had added to Nether Hall in 1874 (see chapter 9). The fireplace in this room had a Hoptonwood stone surround, a panelled overmantel with a band of fretwork, a plate rack, and a scoured iron inner surround embossed with a simple curvilinear design. Like several others in the house, the coved chimneybreast expands to support the hearth above, a feature reintroduced from Red House, though there they were angled or corbelled. The stone surround of the drawing-room fireplace had copper jambs embossed to Webb's design with a more elaborate, floral pattern as befitted the softer

Below Standen: the living hall, with the bay window added by Webb in 1898 to accommodate the grand piano

metal. He customarily used wide jambs, usually tiled, to achieve the more pleasing proportions of the earlier open-grate fireplaces whilst using the more efficient enclosed grates.

The house had electric lighting, generated by a donkey engine. Webb designed the wall lights for the drawing room, in which the bulb, and delicate glass shade he judged appropriate for this relatively new ethereal light source, were suspended by the cable from a metal bracket, the fixings to the wall being concealed by copper sconces. Webb permitted the experienced craftsman John Pearson to 'vary the flower and leafage' of the sconces of these fittings, but only on the general lines that he provided.[137] Throughout Standen, most of the wallpapers and fabrics, chosen with Webb's help, and the rugs, carpets, and other furnishings, and designs for some of the embroideries, came from Morris & Co.[138]

Right Standen: the breakfast alcove in the dining room, with fitted sideboards and shelves designed by Webb

The gardens were a composite of Webb's and Simpson's layouts and Mrs Beale's liking for colourful rather than old-fashioned plants, but the architect managed to prevent Simpson's liking for strictly formal flowerbeds from giving the house an inappropriate setting.[139] As usual, Webb countenanced flower and shrub gardens east of the house, here beyond a sunken garden with a central mulberry tree at the south-east corner, and insisted on having an expanse of lawn to the south of the principal block. He ran a wide terrace along the south front, bounded by a low wall backed by oak trelliswork of his design, on which old roses would be grown, and used a ha-ha to merge the lawn into the surrounding meadows with no visual interruption. A path along the north-western edge of the lawn led to his charming garden shelter: a seat under a red-tiled hipped roof supported on oak posts. The stone quarry, as Webb undoubtedly would have envisaged, formed an ideal rock garden near the house, with a pool, and a planting scheme of low-growing shrubs rather than alpines.

As their granddaughter Elizabeth Motley recorded, the Beale family found Standen delightful and wonderfully comfortable; loving it as it was, they made few changes to the house, which ran smoothly

Left Standen: the diningroom fireplace, showing the plate-warming rack and the fender, which also are by Webb

and luxuriously, but also unpretentiously.[140] Standen was a highly influential building, designed and constructed when young architects were already taking great interest in Webb's approach to design, and in his buildings. It was brought to public

Left Standen: the fireplace wall of the drawing room

Right Standen: an electric-light fitting, designed for the drawing room by Webb and made by John Pearson, who was allowed a little freedom of design when working the back-plate

Below Standen: the conservatory, with roof construction based on the glass roof over the main staircase of Bell Brothers Offices, Middlesbrough, which was designed by Webb, probably in 1889 or 1890

attention in 1900 when Ricardo used it as an example of an ideal country house in a paper in the *Magazine of Art*, and again in 1910 by Weaver, who shared Ricardo's opinion, in his study of Standen in *Country Life*.[141]

Elements adopted or adapted from those of Standen appeared in many houses by Webb's admirers. Lutyens, for example, used a coved chimney breast like that of the dining room in his common room at Goddards (1899) but with unplastered brickwork, and he based the courtyard archway of Orchards (1899) on that of Standen.[142] Webb's use of embossed and fretted metalwork, and fretted timber, increased the popularity of these crafts and influenced many designs, for instance a pair of firedogs of c. 1905 by Ernest Gimson.[143] Some thirty years after Webb designed

them, several of the fireplaces and the morning-room bookshelves from Standen were cited and illustrated as excellent examples in the influential book, *The House and its Equipment*, edited by Weaver.[144]

The incorporation of the old farmhouse in a prominent position on Goose Green, and the small gables on the south front of the new house, have led some observers to assume mistakenly that Webb intended Standen to appear as if built over centuries, as Devey might have done, or that he was trying to disguise it as a cottage or over-large farm, or that he took his inspirations for it from small cottages. As explained earlier (in chapter 6), Webb never aimed for a false suggestion of age, and he based his Idea on a building or building type from the national vernacular of similar size to the proposed building. He studied buildings of all sizes in the specific district to see how the local materials had been used, and how well or otherwise they had weathered, not in order to copy cottage details. The row of small gables reflected those found on several large Elizabethan and Jacobean houses, perhaps specifically the five added in c. 1603 to c. 1608 to Knole in Kent. At Clouds, Willinghurst, and Standen, Webb linked a subsidiary part of the house to an old structure, of the worthy type that he could never bear to demolish, to help the new building to merge into its surroundings, and to mitigate any effect of brash newness. In all three cases, he carefully preserved the visual and structural identity of the ancient structure, making it obviously an old dwelling linked to a new house, not an early part of a greatly enlarged building.

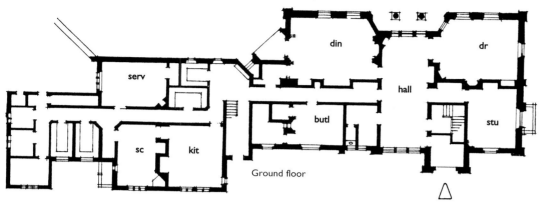
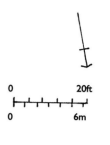

Ground floor

0   20ft

0   6m

Hurlands, Puttenham, Surrey

Webb's last country house, Hurlands, near Puttenham in Surrey, was commissioned in January 1897 by Miss Agneta Henrietta Cocks, of whom little is known, except that she had connections with the London banking firm Cocks, Biddulph & Co., and was a friend of Mary Ewart, for whom Webb had designed a smaller house, Coneyhurst, in 1883 (see chapter 11). Miss Cocks did not purchase the land near Puttenham, just a few miles from Coneyhurst, until Webb had inspected and approved it. She accepted Webb's initial design for the house,

presented in late February, subject only to some small reductions, and on condition that a successful well could be sunk and that the estimate of William and George King of Abinger Hammer, the firm that had built Coneyhurst, was within her means.[145] All went well, and by July 1899 Miss Cocks had moved into the house; the stable block, for which the contract was signed in February 1899, was built by Charles Rice, the constructor of the Standen Cottages, possibly because Kings were too busy to do so.

Hurlands was another three-part long-house, stretching almost due east–west across the site,

Left Hurlands, near Puttenham, Surrey (1897, constructed 1897–99): the entrance (north) front

overlooking pleasant open farmland to south and west, and backed by gently rising, well-wooded ground.[146] The drive approached from the north-west, then turned east to run between a pyramid-roofed well-house and the house to the U-shaped stable block. The latter, open on its eastern side and in the same materials as the house, plus some oak weatherboarding, contained a flat for the coachman over the coach-house, and a cottage for the gardener in the south range. As at Willinghurst, the cottage sheltered the south garden, aided here by a high wall connecting the stable block to the house.[147]

The Idea for Hurlands was apparently a combination of Webb's long-house, containing an east-west cross-passage, with a Classical villa, complete with a *distyle in antis* portico on the garden front, and one pavilion, the stable block, connected by a blind colonnade. The large living hall extended through the main block from north to south, flanked at the southern end by the D-shaped dining room and similar drawing room. The south front of the major block was symmetrical but the positioning of the porch and half-landing above it being off-centre, in the Willinghurst and Standen manner, prevented this on the entrance front. On the ground floor, the cross-passage was angled round the back stairs and ended in the study, but on the first floor it extended through the block and part of the service wing from east to west, and had windows at each end.[148] A change in the notions of propriety is revealed by Miss Cocks's insistence that the WC door be moved into the hall from its discreet position in the passage.[149] Another change was evinced by the smaller area needed by 1897 for offices in a country house that was within reach of local dairy, laundry, and butchery services that had become widely available. This reduction in size led to some merging of the central and eastern parts of Webb's long-house arrangement.

Hurlands was roofed in red tiles and built of many-hued but predominantly bright-red bricks,

Below Hurlands: the south front of the main block, from the garden

faced on the ground floor on the south and west fronts of the main block with inset panels of random rubble Bargate stone. The stone was finished like the old garden walls of Great Tangley Manor, a building some ten miles away that Webb had enlarged (see chapter 9). The brick arches of the colonnade were also filled with this stone. The upper walls were roughcast, primarily because of their exposure, as Webb told his friend Alfred Powell; between the stone panels and the roughcast was a deep, projecting cement-rendered string, painted off-white and tiled on top, which protected the ground-floor windows from rainwater.[150] The projecting south front, under a hipped roof, had three almost semicircular brick arches and two polygonal columns and capitals in Portland stone, which created an inset porch and supported a central balcony that had seven timber posts, one being central against the Classical tradition, with pendant wooden arches between them. Brackets from the posts supported the flat, leaded roof of the balcony, which protected it from too much midsummer sunlight. Louvred shutters with the same purpose flanked the windows of the south and west fronts. The garden porch off the dining room was intended to have Tuscan columns and a lead-covered dome but during construction the dome was changed to a tiled roof.[151] This is a typical example of Webb's habitual simplifying of his designs. The western part of the north front was in effect an adaptation in different materials of the triple gables of the ancient timber-framed Great Tangley Manor. The flanking gables had roughcast upper walls; the projecting central gable was in brick, with a recessed entrance arch and a decorative brick sill to the five-light landing window. A lingering result of Webb's Gothic revival training is revealed by his refusal to allow the symmetry of this part of the elevation to dictate the use of a smaller hall window than was desirable within the room.

As in all Webb's houses, large or small, the major rooms of Hurlands were well lit and comfortable, with a pleasing elegance that was not in the slightest way grand. Characteristic round and segmental arches over doorways and niches, and attractive fitted cupboards, some of them glass-fronted, abounded. The hall had a plain segmental barrel vault in plaster, rising from a bold corbelled and plastered brick cornice, and a French window to the inset porch. The main staircase, with a plain balustrade and flat oak handrail, and a glazed screen to the cross-passage,

had at its head a simple oak screen which repeated the pendant timber arches of the balcony. Webb kept in mind Miss Cocks's large pieces of furniture when designing the house, and he ensured that her old brass fenders would fit his polished Hoptonwood stone fireplaces, which were set within panelled surrounds as usual, in the dining room and drawing room.[152] Judging by contemporary photographs of the Hurlands hall and the Coneyhurst drawing room, Agneta Cocks and Mary Ewart shared a liking for plain walls in light shades, plain fitted carpets, thin translucent summer curtains, antique furniture of the simpler type, and good paintings and ceramics.

Despite some disunity between the south and

Above Hurlands: the living hall, in Miss Cocks's time (© V Moores)

Below Hurlands: the dining room, in Miss Cocks's time (© V Moores)

north fronts, which cannot be seen together however, and a lack of rhythm at the eastern end of the latter, Hurlands was an attractive and unusual house. Though the exterior lacked some of the charm of that of Standen, which stemmed largely from the exploiting of possibilities offered by its greater size and more interesting site, Hurlands showed that Webb had retained his inventive powers to the end of his career. Furthermore, the Site Book for the house shows that his interest in the science side of architecture, in matters connected with drains, septic tanks, grease traps, limes, mortars, and timber shrinkage, and in climbing eighty feet down the well to check its construction, was as keen as ever.[153]

Hurlands increased the popularity of roughcast and, within a year or two of it having been designed, some of Webb's admirers were also using domed or tile-roofed porches with Tuscan columns. Ernest Newton, for instance, used roughcast on the upper walls of Steep Hill, Jersey (1899–1900), taking ground-floor arches up into it, much as Webb's arches broke into the string at Hurlands, and he employed Tuscan columns and a half-dome on the porch; and in 1899, Lutyens, who had used them previously only for a pergola, employed Tuscan columns in the fountain court of Overstrand Hall, Norfolk, and in the tile-roofed garden pavilions of the Pleasaunce, also in Overstrand.[154] The red-brick, recessed-arch entrance of Hurlands joined the earlier ones on some of his smaller houses (see chapter 11) in being adopted for many local authority and speculative housing estates, as well as for individual residences, in England until after the Second World War.

Conclusion

Webb's clients found their new country houses deeply satisfying, a fact that is an indication of his skill, not least in producing a convenient plan. Few of them made changes to the buildings, and those who did, made only minor ones. The country houses became widely known, without any effort on Webb's part, because the owners entertained large circles of friends in their homes, and his architect friends knew them through his drawings. Also, from the mid-1880s onwards, the houses and their gardens were visited and studied by many young Arts and Crafts architects, who had turned to Webb in their search for an inspiring approach to architectural design, an approach that was firmly based on practicality but had strong ideals and clearly defined

aims and guidelines, without any of the restrictions of a revival of a past style.

After 1914, the history of Webb's country houses became in general an unhappy one, chiefly through the deaths of heirs in the two world wars, the increasing difficulty in obtaining servants, and the rise in their wages and in the cost of maintaining large buildings. Arisaig House, after being gutted by fire in 1935, was almost completely rebuilt on a smaller scale to a design by Ian B M Hamilton; having been an hotel for some years, it is now a private residence. The death at Dunkirk in 1940 of the male heir (Godman's grandson, whose own father had predeceased him) led to the sale of Smeaton Manor a few years later; a subsequent owner reduced its size and removed some Webb fittings, but it has again become a loved and respected family home. Percy Wyndham, his son, and his son's heir, all died within a three-year span, the last being killed in action in 1914; three sets of death duties, and the bequest of several annuities, forced the sale of most of the Clouds estate, and eventually of the house itself in 1936. The domestic offices became dwellings. Tragically, the tower was demolished; the rooms on the north front including the dining room, with the turrets on the east and west fronts, were sliced off the main block; and Webb's handsome gables were replaced with small dormers. The truncated building, once the house of the age, has had a useful institutional role for many decades, as a home for unwanted babies, then a school for maladjusted boys and, today, as a treatment centre for people who have become dependent on alcohol and drugs. The central part of Willinghurst was demolished in the second half of the twentieth century, when the principal part and the offices became separate houses. Hurlands became a Surrey County Council children's home in 1960, with a small cottage for the matron replacing Webb's garden porch at the western end. In the late 1970s, after the removal of some Webb fittings, the house was sensitively converted into three dwellings.

Three of the country houses were completely destroyed. After small houses had been built in the grounds, Church Hill House was demolished. Rounton Grange, for which obtaining servants had long been a problem, was dismantled between 1951 and 1954 after loss of capital during the First World War, and two recent close sets of death duties met by selling land, had made its upkeep untenable. Joldwynds was demolished in 1930 simply because

Wilfrid Greene (later Lord Greene), the new owner, fancied an International-style house by Oliver Hill (1887–1968). Hill's house failed to please Greene so he sold it, ironically after building a small traditional house in the grounds. Both Webb's Joldwynds and Hill's replacement have an important place in the history of architecture, the first as a fine Arts and Crafts house, a celebration and inventive development of English architectural character, which fitted unobtrusively into its surroundings and was built of local materials; the second, as a good International-style house of the Modern movement, a pristine white sculpture, with no national or local connotations, standing out crisply against the landscape.

Fortunately, the sadly truncated Clouds, constructed when the Arts and Crafts movement was beginning to gather momentum, retains a great deal of the very fine architectural ornament, the high quality of which is attributable to Webb's great talent and to his complete understanding of the qualities of the materials and the ways they could be worked. It demonstrates conclusively that he believed a limited amount of ornament had an important role in large buildings, despite the great importance he placed on simplicity. This refutes the belief, widely held in the twentieth century, that he repudiated all architectural ornament. In its original form, Clouds as a whole proved that, contrary to the belief of some critics, Webb's approach – the Arts and Crafts approach – could be applied successfully to buildings of its scale and importance.

By the greatest good fortune, Standen, a most beautiful and important country house by Philip Webb, the architect who had the most influence on Arts and Crafts architecture, has survived intact, with all its fittings. It was generously bequeathed to the nation by the Beales' unmarried daughter Helen, who died in 1972, and with further help from Arthur and Helen Grogan, the National Trust was able to accept the house.[155] Today, Standen is open regularly to the public, so all who wish can see at first hand that Webb did indeed achieve his aim of creating houses that, whilst clearly of their own time, would be in harmony with their surroundings and look well for many decades. Standen demonstrates that he did this, not by copying a style from the past, but by concentrating on good building, the possibilities of the specific site, the creative use of traditional local building materials and the sensitive exploitation of their colours and textures, and the inventive reflection of traditional national and local architectural forms.

Webb's open-minded national vernacular approach produced great differences in external appearance according to the location of the country houses but all were appropriately designed, and all demonstrated his excellent handling of composition, proportion, scale, 'movement', and contrast, and of elements that had been used and reinterpreted in Britain by many generations. It is clear from Webb's sketches that, after absorbing the brief and becoming familiar with the district, he conceived the overall layout and the particular Idea that loosely governed the form of each country house whilst on site, and that he worked out a convenient plan that fulfilled the needs of the particular client, family, and servants who were to live and work in the building, before deciding on the external appearance of the house. His country houses were designed as a building in which to live, not as a picturesque or startlingly unusual edifice to be admired from without. Each house and all its details were carefully designed for the purpose, both functional and visual, and for the chosen materials, and in such a way as to form a consistent whole, inside and out, in which everything about a building and its surroundings had been conceived by the architect, and all the furniture, wallpapers, and fabrics had been designed, or failing this, approved by him. His beautiful, almost dateless interiors were interesting and comfortable settings for daily life, never grandiose or overwhelming.

Webb was deeply concerned with the art side of architecture but his drawings, and the instructions written on them, show that he was just as concerned with its science side: with making everything work well, with using new technology so long as it improved on older methods, and with providing up-to-date services. He was as keen to design a moulding so that it would throw off rainwater well, as to design a handsome entrance, for example, or to achieve perfect ventilation in kitchens and major rooms, as to provide a fine staircase. Christopher Hussey was certainly unjust, in the case of Philip Webb, and of his disciples, when in writing about Hill's Joldwynds in 1934, he asserted that before the Modern movement no architect had designed houses from 'basic human requirements', or with 'applied scientific thought', and that before this movement, all architects had put external appearance before internal convenience.[156]

Chapter 8

THE SOCIETY FOR THE PROTECTION OF ANCIENT BUILDINGS

May Morris recorded that in 1877, 'Webb, with William Morris, founded the Society for the Protection of Ancient Buildings'.[1] Ultimately, however, Morris became the figurehead of the society, the first institution to be dedicated to the preserving of the architectural heritage, and consequently he has usually been given sole credit for its foundation. This has led to Webb's importance not always having been fully appreciated. Philip Webb was the society's chief guide on matters of policy, and its foremost consultant on the repair of old structures. Furthermore, Webb introduced the practical methods of making old buildings sound without damaging their historical authenticity that ensured the lasting success of the Society for the Protection of Ancient Buildings (the SPAB) and which, with Webb's use of them in his own work, made the sympathetic repair and enlargement of old houses rather than their replacement an important aspect of the Arts and Crafts movement.

By the mid-nineteenth century, a large number of ancient English churches had suffered more damage from 'restoration' than they had from centuries of time, weather, or neglect. The reformers in the Anglican Church – the Tractarians of the Oxford movement, and the members of the Cambridge Camden Society that became the Ecclesiological Society in 1845 – were intent on introducing the splendour and ritual of the medieval Church into Anglican worship. Initially they, and the Gothic revival architects who became involved with Anglican churches, advocated the late-thirteenth- and early-fourteenth-century Middle Pointed Gothic (Decorated Gothic) style as the ideal choice for new churches. During the 1850s, the more severe but arguably more beautiful First Pointed Gothic (Early English Gothic) style became the ideal for new edifices. Ancient churches were enlarged and refurbished in one or other of these favoured styles, any earlier and later medieval work being removed and replaced in the approved manner. In some cases,

a church was enlarged in the style of its earliest part. This process of returning a building to what the Ecclesiologists believed it might or should have been originally, and to an arbitrary period, was known as 'restoration', and many eminent architects were involved in it. Inside and outside, worn medieval features were re-carved to what was thought to have been their original condition. Windows were replaced in the chosen style, fittings and memorials of the Perpendicular era and later were removed from interiors, and medieval plaster was scraped from walls.

The antiquarians, viewing medieval buildings as valuable archaeological records, had long been urging the preservation of old buildings, and were against such 'restorations'. In *Contrasts* (1836), Pugin castigates the restoration, or 'improvement' as it was termed at the time, of several cathedrals – including that of Salisbury Cathedral, 'conducted by James Wyatt, of execrable memory', during which the bell tower and two chapels were demolished, and medieval screens and tombs were removed.[2] He contends that though some recent restorations are accurate as to moulding and detail, and show that the 'mechanical part of Gothic architecture is pretty well understood', they contain nothing of 'the soul which appears in all the former work'. Without the latter and without a full understanding of the principles on which medieval architecture was based, 'all that is done will be a tame and heartless copy, true as far as the mechanism of the style goes, but utterly wanting in that sentiment and feeling that distinguishes ancient design'.[3] In 1849, Ruskin vigorously attacked restoration in *The Seven Lamps of Architecture*, and urged that the preservation of ancient buildings should be considered a primary duty. He, too, believed that true restoration was impossible because the spirit behind the hand and eye of the medieval craftsman could not be summoned up to guide the nineteenth-century craftsmen. Therefore, to Ruskin restoration meant 'the most total destruction which a building can suffer: [...] a destruction accompanied

Left St Alban's Abbey, Hertfordshire: before 'restoration' in the nineteenth century (Richard Dennis)

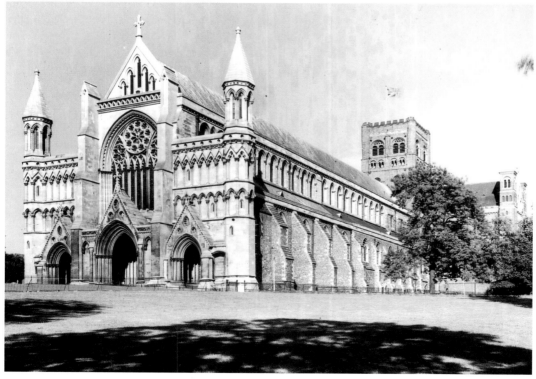

Left St Alban's Abbey, after 'restoration': an example of the partial transformation of a building through the substitution of neo-Gothic features for the genuine medieval elements (Reproduced by permission of English Heritage. NMR)

with false description of the thing destroyed'.[4] He contended that much of the value of an ancient building lay in its untouched surfaces, not only because of their weathered beauty but because they were emotive living evidence of the craftsmen who had worked them. Copying or re-carving medieval work could never be truthful because the original finish had lain in the half-inch that time had erased. Ruskin's 1854 treatise *The Opening of the Crystal Palace* is chiefly a diatribe against restorations and a call for the establishing of an association devoted to the protection of ancient monuments. He proposed that such an association should have scouts in all the important towns, whose first duty would be to list all the ancient buildings in the district, and then to report any changes with which they were threatened. From funds provided by members, the association would buy monuments that came onto the market, or would help the owners of them to maintain such buildings, and it would work actively to prevent 'unwise restoration, and unnecessary destruction'.[5] Ruskin's words alerted some of his readers to the damage being wrought in the name of restoration, but his call for an association to fight against the practice went unanswered until 1877.

Webb's antipathy was first evoked in 1852 or 1853 (as mentioned in chapter 1) – soon after his apprenticeship ended and apparently before he read *Seven Lamps*, when he witnessed the unnecessary heightening of the spire during the restoration of St Mary's Church in Oxford.[6] Morris had been drawn to the disastrous effects of restorations when he read *Seven Lamps* at Oxford. However, neither of them appears to have actively opposed restorations until the 1870s. In the mid- to late 1850s, Webb could not afford to alienate Street, who undertook several restorations during these years. Webb must have been deeply disturbed by being involved in these, and very thankful indeed that his employer did all the design work himself. By the early 1870s, concern about restorations had begun to increase, and in 1874 events occurred which would undoubtedly have encouraged Webb and Morris to join the fight. In *Seven Lamps*, Ruskin had castigated the architects who undertook restorations for securing for themselves a steady income for several years by recommending restoration, rather than repair, to the church authorities. On these grounds, he refused to accept the RIBA Gold Medal in 1874, the year a parliamentary Survey showed that since 1855

spending on restoration had been greater than on new churches. The Survey led Frederick George Stephens, a member of the original Pre-Raphaelite Brotherhood and at the time the art editor and critic for the *Athenæum*, to campaign against the restorers in the journal.[7] Morris and Webb signed a petition, written by Basil Champneys in 1874, against the demolition and replacement of the tower of the parish church of Hampstead; encouragingly, the proposal was abandoned in 1876.

The sight of Burford Church in Oxfordshire under restoration by Street in the summer of 1876 stimulated Morris into drafting a letter suggesting the founding of a protection society (G G Scott junior and Basil Champneys organised a successful protest against the threatened violation of this church). He did nothing more until 1877, when Tewkesbury Abbey was threatened with a similar fate at the hands of Sir George Gilbert Scott. On 5 March, Morris wrote to the editor of the *Athenæum*, suggesting the immediate founding of a society that would protest against restorations and encourage respect for old buildings. His letter was published on 10 March, and the inaugural meeting of the SPAB, to which Morris had invited interested parties, was held on the 22 March 1877 in the showroom of Morris & Co., in Queen Square.[8] Ten people attended; others who agreed with the purpose of the meeting sent apologies for their absence. Not surprisingly, most if not all these founding members, amongst whom were Boyce and Faulkner, and those who joined soon afterwards, came from the Pre-Raphaelite circle and were friends or clients of Morris and Webb, or acquaintances of their friends. Morris became the honorary secretary and temporary treasurer of 'Anti-Scrape' – the popular nickname he coined for the society – and a sub-group of Webb, George Wardle, and Morris was appointed to draw up the manifesto of the SPAB.

The phrasing of the manifesto is Morris's, clearly influenced by Ruskin's earlier words, but it is equally apparent that Webb had a hand in its content. As their letters over the years demonstrate, Morris was in the habit of consulting Webb on many matters, particularly those that were of great importance to them both. Morris, with his extreme distaste for the Classical styles, would probably have preferred not to include such buildings amongst those which the SPAB would seek to protect. William De Morgan, a committee member of the society, recorded that at the first public meeting, on 21 June 1878, when Morris had to read out a letter from Thomas Carlyle in which Wren's City churches were extolled, his chagrin was evident in his voice.[9] With his more open-minded approach, Webb ensured from the start that the society had a broad base, with the entire secular and ecclesiastical architectural heritage coming under its umbrella.

The manifesto noted that during the previous fifty years ancient buildings had become the subject of enthusiastic historical studies, and that if restorations were to continue, there would be no unspoilt ones for the next generation to study. Before the introduction of the revivals of past styles, architecture had been the art of the people; succeeding generations had built in the manner of their day, with the result that an ancient structure became a living record of its long history. After restoration, which necessarily involves destruction, an old building was a feeble and lifeless forgery. On behalf of the as yet unspoilt buildings, the manifesto ended with an eloquent plea for help:

> It is for all these buildings, therefore, of all times and styles, that we plead, and call upon those who have to deal with them, to put Protection in the place of Restoration, to stave off decay by daily care, to prop a perilous wall or mend a leaky roof by such means as are obviously meant for support or covering, and show no pretence of other art, and otherwise to resist all tampering with either the fabric or ornament of the building as it stands; if it has become inconvenient for its present use, to raise another building rather than alter or enlarge the old one; in fine, to treat our ancient buildings as monuments of a bygone art, created by bygone manners, that modern art cannot meddle with without destroying.[10]

A protection society had at last been established, on the lines Ruskin had advocated twenty-three years earlier. It continues to thrive today, and its original manifesto has never been superseded.

There is a paradox in the manifesto, however. Ancient buildings are extolled as living historical documents, on which each generation has left its own record, and the restorers are castigated for stopping this history at some arbitrary date; yet, if the new society's proposals were carried out to the letter, the history would be halted abruptly. No nineteenth-century pages would be added and the proposed ban on the introduction of new statues and monuments in ancient churches, as called for by Ruskin in *The*

Opening of the Crystal Palace, if carried out would have a similar result to that of the removal, by the restorers, of memorials of unacceptable date.[11] The paradox arose because Webb and Morris believed that the enlargements, building elements, and memorials added by the restorers to medieval churches in Gothic styles were shams, unreal and untrue, and utterly unfit to stand beside the genuine work of medieval craftsmen who, enthused by a shared religious faith and a feeling for art that no longer existed, had been so much more creative and skilled than nineteenth-century craftsmen. Morris was so concerned about this that, although he must have realised the adverse effect this prohibition would have on his business, he announced in April 1877 that Morris & Co. would no longer supply its stained-glass windows for installation in restored or improved medieval churches, except those already containing one or more of his windows. In 1900, Webb refused to support the proposal to set up a memorial to Ruskin because he could not countenance the introduction of '(as certainly it must be) incongruous modern work, whether of statues, monuments, stained glass, or useless ecclesiastical trifles' into Westminster Abbey; such a memorial would be inappropriate for the man who had 'shown the way with unequalled literary force how ancient buildings should be guarded from mutilation and unseemly addition'.[12]

In the event, however, as the SPAB made any essential additions in an understated, simple manner, without aping the old details, a new page was added to many of the buildings it repaired. It is a page which reveals a concern for conservation, if nothing of contemporary design, and is a historical record, albeit often an unseen one, of the extreme sensitivity, care, and skill with which the work was carried out. Despite its overriding concern for old structures and for historical authenticity, the society was not reactionary, contrary to what was sometimes believed. Its aim was, as it remains, to save ancient buildings for the benefit of future generations, not to copy them or their details in any new work.

There were only three architects on the first committee: Webb, George Aitchison and John James Stevenson. This is not surprising as so many well-known Gothic revivalists were undertaking restorations – including Street, who ambivalently demolished structures that postdated the Decorated Gothic period although, in the *Ecclesiologist* in 1857, he had denounced the French and Italian practice of destroying, re-carving, or copying medieval sculptures.[13] There was no attraction at all for the restorers in joining a society which, if it were successful, would curtail their incomes severely. Morris's castigation of architects in his *Athenæum* letter as being, with very few exceptions, hopeless because bound by interest, habit, and ignorance, would certainly not have encouraged any architect to join. Several members of the committee were artists, mostly painters of whom some had made old weathered buildings the subject of their work. They included George Boyce, who was a very active member. Fortunately for the status of the SPAB, its early members included several important public figures, notably Ruskin and Carlyle, who sat on the committee. By 1879 the committee, now with ninety members, included seven MPs, from both the Liberal and Conservative parties. One of them, Sir John Lubbock, was responsible for the passing of the 1882 Ancient Monuments Act, the first legislative measure to protect old buildings by providing for their public ownership.[14] However, the SPAB did not promulgate public ownership, and it was not and never has been a political organization. Its members have always come from a broad spectrum of society, covering all shades of political belief.

In March 1878, Morris raised the possibility of the SPAB acting to save buildings under threat in other countries. The committee appointed its first foreign corresponding secretary, Charles Fairfax Murray, who lived in Florence and with whom Webb had stayed during his winter in Italy. Murray was urged to persuade the Italians to establish a building protection society. A permanent Foreign Subcommittee was formed on 28 March 1879 at Morris's suggestion, and during the following months the society's manifesto was printed in French and Italian. By 1880, the society had helped to establish the Societé des Amis des Monuments Parisiens, and in 1881 it worked effectively in Egypt with the Comité de l'Art Arabe. A group modelled on the SPAB was established in Belgium after the journal *L'Emulation* promoted its ideals. There was an international conference in Paris in 1890 on the protection of art and buildings, in which the society took part and at which its aims were promulgated. In Germany, the SPAB ideals were promoted by the architect Hermann Muthesius, author of the influential study, *Das englische Haus* (1904–05). Philip

Webb had a direct influence himself on the development of good conservation practice in Italy through his close friendship with the Italian architect and important conservationist Giacomo Boni, whom he had met during his winter in Italy.[15]

In 1877, the SPAB began to amass a detailed record of every unspoilt church in the country, but soon this proved too time-consuming and costly. Instead, each member was asked to complete building report forms, such as had long been used by antiquarians, on the edifices in their own district. Seven hundred and forty-nine such reports on un-restored churches were returned in the first year. By October 1878, the SPAB had established a system for tackling cases of proposals for restoration. An experienced committee member would examine a building under threat, and then prepare a detailed structural report. Next, a letter of inquiry would be sent, with a copy of the manifesto, to those responsible for the maintenance of the building; after which negotiations would take place, aimed at securing protection instead of restoration. If this approach failed, a threat of going to the press sometimes had the desired effect. By 1882, Anti-Scrape was undertaking around one hundred and fifty cases annually; eight years later the figure had reached almost three hundred.

By autumn 1878, it had already become inadvisable to allow Morris to undertake casework because, with his quick temper, intolerance, and habit of naming the culprits' names, he was alienating the very people the SPAB hoped to influence. He resigned as honorary secretary in November the following year, and a paid secretary was engaged to work as instructed by the committee. In the 1880s, when Morris was deeply involved in active politics, his role in the society's affairs diminished, though he lectured for the society, attended its annual general meetings, and signed annual reports and letters of protest on request, but many of these were now prepared by the committee. Webb, who had always been in charge of all matters of repair, assumed control of SPAB policy as well – a situation accepted by Morris when he returned to the fold in 1890. Believing that he himself could not write or speak well on the subjects nearest his heart, Webb was happy to leave lecturing on behalf of the SPAB to Morris, who became the society's figurehead. The SPAB lectures, with others on art and politics, made Morris a public figure, and subsequently to his receiving more than his fair share of credit for the society's achievements.[16]

Letters written on behalf of the SPAB by Webb show that the architect had a calm, reasonable manner, and always listened to an opponent's point of view. He explained the society's case firmly but with patience and restraint, and frequently to positive effect. He gave countless hours to the cause without monetary reward, many of them spent in report writing.[17] By letter and in person he tried, usually successfully, to persuade anyone whom he thought had influence to join the society.[18] Many of his friends and at least thirteen of his clients joined and, at his urging, involved their own friends and acquaintances in the SPAB. They kept an eye open in the field and the press for buildings in danger, and reported these cases to it, usually through Webb. As he seldom missed a committee meeting, there was no delay in action being taken in the society's name against threatened sacrileges. Webb's recruits responded promptly to his requests for information, and willingly lent their names in support of protests. In spite of a long-held distaste for societies and committees, Webb served on the SPAB committee from its foundation until his death almost fourteen-and-a-half years after he retired from his practice and left London in January 1901, which indicates the depth of his feelings about so-called restorations and their perpetrators.

The deliberate despoilment of any ancient building caused Webb to suffer anguish akin to that of losing a relation or close friend. As Lethaby noted, loyalty to ancient buildings became 'part of Webb's central soul – his religion'.[19] Webb found it monstrous that a small group was taking away the 'birthright of beauty' of the people without so much as a 'by your leave'.[20] The anger and distress evoked in him by the restorers is evident in many letters to his friends. They refer to the 'quick-salving "eminents"', with whom he classed Viollet-le-Duc, the renowned French Gothic revivalist and restorer; and abound in such terms and phrases as 'the proposal is – of course, brutal and stupid, as usual in such cases'; 'tampered with by a former restless and reckless parson'; 'damned by witless fiddling'; and 'ravished, sicklied over with a pale cast of idolatry'.[21] Webb's bitterness is obvious in a request for the help of Hale White and his friends in the fight to save Dunblane Cathedral: 'The heritors are about to preserve this wonderfully beautiful piece of the scarce remains of Mediaeval Scotland, by

spending £25,000 on it'; the authorities were prepared to spend this then huge sum, far higher than the cost of conservative repair, on chiefly unnecessary work when 'they would not spend 25d on preserving a starving family.'[22] On another occasion he told William Weir (1865–1950) of his despair brought on by some botched repairs, and of the hopelessness of trying to drive into 'wooden and parsonic heads' the fact that old buildings deserved the 'application of the best of intelligence, and not of shiftlessness lazily employed'.[23] In 1899, he told his friend George Wardle, a fellow member of the SPAB committee, that contemporary architects' lack of knowledge about building, of 'love and sincere appreciation' of it, and of an aptitude for meeting unforeseen difficulties, and their dependence on a clerk of works and an expensive builder telling them what to do, had resulted in 'most of our cathedrals being ruined', but that there was an 'even worse evil: the rascal clergy will have their architects make a recognizable splash'.[24]

Inevitably, the society sometimes failed to achieve its aim, as on the occasion when it called for rescue work to be undertaken at Kirkstall Abbey near Leeds. After the authorities refused to undertake repairs, Webb commented caustically in a letter to Hale White that 'nether gilded ease would nor grovelling labour could listen to us'.[25] The failure of the battle to save the west front of Peterborough Cathedral from restoration by the architect John Loughborough Pearson (1817–97) was a bitter pill. In December 1896, George Bernard Shaw asked Webb, who had been forewarned of the threat to the building, to protest against the project because he believed Webb's voice would be heard – which shows that by this date Webb, too, had become something of a public figure through the SPAB. However, Webb preferred to help Shaw to write the powerful protest that was published in the *Saturday Review* on 2 January 1897; obviously at Webb's insistence, it appeared above the meaningless initials 'D S M' in order to prevent Pearson and fellow restorers from accusing Webb and the other architects of the SPAB of self-advertisement.[26] After listing the problems, the letter continued in what are obviously Webb's words, and exemplify his approach:

> The foundations can be carried down to the rock by under-pinning; the inclination of two feet does not matter in the least with a wall seven feet thick; and the disintegrated core can be removed bit by bit, and replaced with sound bonded work, without touching or

Opposite St. Mary's
Church, East Knoyle,
Wiltshire: the tower,
repaired by Detmar Blow
under Webb's direction
between 1892 and 1893

disturbing one grain of dust on the priceless Front which is the glory of the edifice.

Despite a vigorous SPAB campaign, supported by the Society of Antiquaries, the restorers unfortunately won the day.

In the 1880s, the SPAB began to take an active role in the repair of old buildings, under Webb's guidance. Morris, not being an architect, had no experience in such work, whereas Webb had developed ways of repairing old structures with minimal damage to the ancient surfaces – including the one described in the Peterborough letter – in his own practice. These became the methods of the SPAB. Viewing the demolition of an old building as being preferable to its being turned into a sham, with all vestiges of the hand and mind of its original craftsmen obliterated, Webb had always taken a conservative approach to the repair of an ancient structure, in his words 'sustaining it without injury to its historical interest'.[27] After executing what he thought would be unobtrusive repairs to St Dunstan's Church, Hunsdon, Hertfordshire in 1871 to 1872, he had been 'dissatisfied with the amount of change', and had at once determined to be 'even more radically conservative in future'.[28] In 1875, he explained to his client George Howard that his first aim when working on Naworth Castle in Cumbria was to do his work in such a way that the next architect to be 'turned on to Naworth' could 'sweep it all away', and no injury would 'have been done to the fabric by the former Arch-e-brute'.[29]

The cases carried out for the SPAB under Webb's control or with his involvement are fine exemplars of what could be achieved using his methods of minimal, largely invisible repair. Two examples are the tower of St Mary's, East Knoyle, repaired between 1892 and 1893, and Lake House, Wilsford, repaired in 1898 – both in Wiltshire, and for both of which Detmar Blow was the architect on site.[30] The Perpendicular Gothic tower at East Knoyle, the first example, was in such an unstable state that demolition was proposed. Fortunately Webb's largest house, Clouds, lay in the parish, and its owner, the Honourable Percy Wyndham, MP, was a committee member of the SPAB. By dint of promising to pay half the cost of repair, Wyndham persuaded the incumbent to delay demolition until Webb had examined the tower. Eventually, it was repaired for about half the estimated cost of demolition and rebuilding. Ill-considered alterations had caused the

tower to crack, and bell-ringing had widened the fissures and loosened the rubble core. Webb prevented further movement of the nave arch with an iron rod. Then he strengthened the walls of the tower by removing small sections of the inside face, supporting the wall above with temporary wooden posts, and rebuilding the core using Portland cement mortar and hard local bricks, masonry, and concrete. Particularly weak spots were stiffened with regular bands of Staffordshire blue paving bricks. Blow termed this method a 'Webb sandwich'. Cracks in the outer face were patched and bonded into the wall. Decayed parts of the bell cage were made good by inserting new wood between the outer surfaces of the timbers and bolting all together. To cope with stresses from bell-ringing, new beams were fitted at a lower level to take some of the weight of the bells, which was transferred to them by diagonal wooden bracing installed under the old beams. Webb decided that the bells should be rung from a lower level. He designed and installed a simple ringing floor under the tower vault, reached by a ladder, to limit the use of the stair turret and noise from the bells, and to keep the tower floor free for other use as he had done in his own Brampton Church (1874–75; see chapter 12).

The second example, Lake House, was a beautiful Elizabethan manor house, with walls chequered in stone and flint, owned by J W Lovibond. Lack of proper drainage at the base of the walls had allowed the chalk beneath the house to soak up the water. This rose up through the walls, causing the outer face to part from the core in places, and major cracking to occur in walls, mullions, and transoms, and decay to take place in the large bonding timbers and lintels. Blow was put in charge of the remedial work, with Webb as the enthusiastic and inspiring consultant. The sandwich system was applied to the walls, leaving the outer face untouched apart from filling the open joints from the inside, and mending external fissures by inserting a hard tile or slate, flush with the face of the wall and bonded to it, set in sand and cement. Cracked mullions were repaired similarly, and broken transoms were secured with copper cramps, or with copper dowels set below the surface and bedded in hot sulphur, the hole then being filled with cement and sand. Weakened timber lintels on the inside of the walls were saved by inserting concrete lintels above them, plastered where not hidden behind the old wainscot. Timber beams were repaired from above without disturbing

the original plasterwork. When all was finished, Lake House was in a perfectly sound and stable condition, with its original surfaces unchanged.

The SPAB refunded the modest expenses of those working on its cases, but the costs of repair and the professional fees of the architect were the responsibility of the owners of the building or the institution responsible for its maintenance. Webb waived the fee and expenses for his work on the East Knoyle tower and, judging by his account book, for all his SPAB jobs. He was involved with the repair of at least eight churches, and with the Guildhall, Exeter, as well as Lake House. He worked for the society tirelessly, with infinite patience and painstaking care, and without monetary reward for over twenty-six years, thereby setting a fine example for the younger SPAB architects.

Webb always stressed the fact that major structural problems, including the chief one of unstable walls, could usually be avoided through regular maintenance – by replacing broken roof tiles, keeping gutters and drains clear, and underpinning weak walls – and by not making any alteration, however small and seemingly insignificant, without determining that doing so would have no adverse effects on the structure. If original items such as mullions, jambs, finials, or facing stones were beyond repair, Webb would replace them either with courses of thin clay tiles or with a frankly new piece, sympathetic in form and material to the old item but not a copy of it. Such replacements can look obtrusive, as Ruskin had admitted in *The Opening of the Crystal Palace*, but still he had contended that replaced items should not imitate the original.[31] Webb agreed with Ruskin on this matter, and refused to allow copying, or false weathering.

Webb and Shaw contended, in their letter of protest against the Peterborough Cathedral restoration, that Pearson, a typical architect of the day, could 'knock down a genuine medieval building and substitute for it a sham one — no man more efficiently', but he could not '*preserve* a building,

Below Lake House, Wilsford, Wiltshire (c. 1578): in 1899, after repair by Webb, with Detmar Blow as the architect on site, in 1898 (RIBA Library Photographs Collection)

because that work cannot be done on drawing-boards or imitated from medieval "styles", nor can several such jobs be undertaken and carried out simultaneously'. With 'twenty important works demanding his attention in the year', they continued, Pearson necessarily had to design and then delegate whereas a preserving architect could neither design nor delegate because he could never tell in advance how his work ought to progress, and he had to be on site constantly to 'choose at almost every step between what to renew and what to let alone, as well as how to get round unforeseen difficulties and solve all sorts of petty engineering and building problems'.[32] After expressing himself in similar terms about contemporary architects' abilities, Webb told Wardle in the previously mentioned letter of 1899 that 'the fatal ignorance of what to do' which forced them to depend on the limited knowledge of a 'regulation clerk of works' and of an expensive builder, had led to 'most of our cathedrals being ruined'.[33] He had long since found it necessary in his own practice to have one or other of his experienced assistants employed as the site architect, supervising the work at all times, whenever an ancient building was involved. This became the normal SPAB procedure: an older architect directed the work, whilst a younger one, used to working on site and knowledgeable about all the building trades, acted as site architect. Webb himself trained three architects, who later controlled repair work done under the supervision of the SPAB, in his conservative methods of sensitive repair: William Weir (1865–1950) and George Jack on his own private commissions, and Blow at East Knoyle.

Weir was Webb's assistant in his private practice from 1888 to 1897. He acted as the site architect for Webb's extensive enlargement of Exning House, Suffolk, from 1895 to 1896. After leaving Webb in 1899, Weir worked full-time for the SPAB until his death, becoming its leading architect and the most significant practitioner and developer of Webb's methods. He made over a thousand surveys and reports on old churches, and supervised the repair of many of them. Under Webb's direction he repaired two churches in Wales – the Church of St Brewis and St Athan (Eglwys Brewis), Glamorgan, and the Church of St Margaret Marlos (Eglwys Cummin), Carmarthenshire – from 1899 to 1902, and one in Norfolk – All Saints', Wilby – from 1901 to 1902.[34] To Webb's designs, a kneeling desk and an altar rail

were made for the former, and roof timbers and chancel furnishings for the latter. After Webb had been consulted, Weir also repaired All Saints', Sutton on Trent, Nottinghamshire, from 1902 to 1903.

George Jack joined Webb as a qualified architect in 1882, and took over his practice in 1901. From 1884, as Webb's chief assistant, he spent whole days on site during the critical stages of all work involving old structures. He joined the SPAB in 1891, and served on the committee from 1892. He supervised repairs, designed and made church fittings, and acted as site architect for Weir, at Rievaulx Abbey, North Yorkshire, from 1908 to 1909, for example.

Blow served his apprenticeship with Wilson and Aldwinckle from c. 1885 to 1889, and toured in France on an Architectural Association scholarship from June to December 1888, during which he prepared drawings of old buildings for Ruskin. He finished this work the following year. In 1890, when he joined the SPAB, he was still undecided about what course his career should take, whether to continue drawing for Ruskin and become his secretary or to practise as an architect. He sought advice from Webb, who soon convinced him that real architecture was based on good building not fine drawings, and that he ought to become involved with the realities of building work and building materials. In 1891, he introduced Blow to Hugh Fairfax-Cholmeley, who commissioned Blow to design a small house, Mill Hill, Brandsby, in North Yorkshire, where Blow gained practical experience working with the masons on the stables.[35] Whilst this house was still under construction, Webb involved Blow in the repair of the church tower at East Knoyle. On Webb's advice, Blow then served an apprenticeship with a builder in Newcastle upon Tyne, apparently as a stonemason.[36] Subsequently, as well as designing new houses, he repaired several churches and country houses for the SPAB, working with his own band of experienced craftsmen – including Lake House (on which he worked again in 1912, reinstating it after a disastrous fire) and, from 1899, the medieval Haddon Hall, Derbyshire. From 1900 to 1901, Blow was involved with the SPAB in an ultimately abandoned proposal, on which Webb's advice was sought, to re-erect two recently fallen stones of a trilithon at Stonehenge in Wiltshire.[37]

In the late 1880s and 1890s, and the early years of the twentieth century, several other young architects, as well as those of Webb's generation, joined the SPAB. Most of the former were, or became, his followers, and he became their helpful friend as well as their mentor. They included Gimson, Ernest and Sidney Barnsley, Powell, and Winmill; Francis W Troup (1859–1941), a committee member for thirty-five years; Hugh Thackeray Turner, the secretary of the society for many years and latterly chairman of the committee; Albert R Powys (1881–1936), who greatly increased the society's reputation as a practical and expert body and was its secretary from 1911 until his death in 1936; and Lethaby, who was appointed Surveyor of Westminster Abbey in 1906. All these men, with George Jack and Blow, were prominent Arts & Crafts architects, and the SPAB – with Webb at its centre – became a major meeting place for them. From Webb, whose knowledge on the subjects was unsurpassed, they learnt not only how to make sensitive long-lasting repairs to old buildings but also a great deal about the less glamorous aspects of architecture, which were ignored by many architects of the day: for instance, how to achieve efficient drains, chimneys, and ventilation; how various materials would weather according to their position on a building; which mortars to use with different types of brick and stone; and the best mix for lining flues. Importantly, they learned from Webb that by exploiting the characteristics and capabilities of materials, and the traditional ways in which they had been used locally, new buildings could be in harmony with the old ones of any neighbourhood, without copying them. They absorbed these matters whilst supervising SPAB work and on Thursdays, when the committee meetings in Buckingham Street were followed by supper and talk with Webb at Gatti's Italian restaurant in the Strand. There and during their visits to his chambers, Webb discussed his own buildings and his approach to architectural design, and made constructive comments about their schemes.[38]

The SPAB had become Webb's informal, unofficial training ground – in Lethaby's words, a 'real school of practical building – architecture with all the whims which we usually call design left out', and a 'school of rational builders'.[39] In their work for the SPAB and in their own architecture, and with great importance in Lethaby's case through his writing and his teaching at the Central School of Arts and Crafts of which he was Principal,[40] Webb's disciples carried his approach to the repair of ancient structures and to the design of new buildings well

into the twentieth century. They passed on to the next generations of architects Webb's concept of architecture as a matter of good building not of design, style revival, or flamboyant self-expression. Philip Webb never had an articled pupil but through his unofficial SPAB school of practical construction, and through his buildings, he had an astonishingly wide influence on the theory and work of the British Arts and Crafts architects and, largely through them and their work, on the architecture of the Arts and Crafts movement in Europe and North America.

In 1903, *Notes on the Repair of Ancient Buildings* issued by the Society for the Protection of Ancient Buildings was published by the society; based on Webb's aims and methods, it is thought to have been written by Thackeray Turner.[41] However, it is inconceivable that Webb, still an active member, would countenance such a publication without having some say in its contents. Having by then retired from practice, he would have had ample time to help Turner to write the notes; the belief that he did so is supported by the omission of the name of an author.[42] In 1929, Albert Powys wrote a handbook for the SPAB, *Repair of Ancient Buildings*, based on the earlier one and on notes he made whilst working on SPAB jobs, under Weir and under Walter Cave respectively, in 1902 and 1904; Unfortunately he did not credit Webb as the instigator of the society's approach or its methods of repair, and therefore, although Powys carried the SPAB message into the 1930s, the full extent of Webb's role in ensuring the initial and long-term success of the society was forgotten, and it is not yet appreciated widely.[43]

At the beginning of the twenty-first century, when, sadly, protection is needed as much as ever, largely due to endless proposals for inappropriate alterations and additions, the SPAB continues to grow in membership and influence. It is the premier building conservation society, with its aims and ideals accepted in many countries, and an unrivalled knowledge about how to extend the life of an old structure. The SPAB runs courses and publishes booklets on all aspects of the repair of old buildings, and it demonstrates how to do so in a conservative manner. It upholds and promotes Webb's and Morris's aims and ideals through its work, through its William Morris Craft Fellowships for craftsmen and Lethaby Scholarships for young architects, and through its annual Philip Webb Award, in memory of the architect, for the best church repair programme based on his principles. The SPAB is consulted by Central Government on new planning bylaws and historic building matters, and by all the local authorities on planning applications to demolish or alter listed buildings and on dangerous structures. Church authorities, local societies, and the National Trust, and many private owners of old buildings large and small seek and benefit from its advice. The society played a great part in keeping craftsmanship alive during the second half of the twentieth century, when so many architects lost all interest in the traditional building crafts and materials. For over a hundred and twenty years, it has been instrumental in saving hundreds of old buildings from harsh restoration and neglect, and in protecting the immediate environment of many of them from unsympathetic change. The work of the SPAB has made the architectural heritage of Britain far richer today than it would otherwise have been. As the man who did so much more than any other to ensure the success of the Society for the Protection Ancient Buildings, by establishing its principles of repair, devoting countless hours to its affairs, and introducing the actual methods of repair it applied, Philip Webb is one of the most important figures in the history and practice of building conservation.

Chapter 9

ALTERATIONS AND ENLARGEMENTS

Philip Webb bore in mind the character of the original building and that of local vernacular architecture when designing enlargements, and used the same wall and roof materials in order to integrate the new work with the old and to ensure its being in harmony with nearby older buildings. He designed the additions in his own manner, however, not in the style of the existing structure, and carefully avoided any false suggestion of age. On undertaking an enlargement of an old dwelling, he considered it his first duty to advise 'as to the best way of supporting, repairing and adding to the accommodation of the house with as little injury as possible to its character'.[1] He refused to be hurried with such work, and believed it was essential to be dictatorial on matters to do with the welfare of the ancient building. 'I will do what I think right and as little badly as possible'

and 'will mind your objurgations no more than the braying of your peacock,' he told George Howard when designing work for Naworth Castle.[2] Webb adhered to these self-imposed principles throughout his career from when he undertook his first enlargements in 1864, and he made them a major part of the policy of the SPAB.

The SPAB and the building conservation organisations set up in its train have usually regarded all the additions made to a building in the past as part of its history and therefore sacrosanct. Webb took this approach in all cases with which the SPAB was involved. In his own work, however, he had no compunction in removing additions of eighteenth- or nineteenth-century date if they were out of character, or badly designed or built; or if by doing so a worthy old structure could be saved when their

Below Cranmer Hall, Sculthorpe, Norfolk: the original house of 1721, with Webb's drawing-room wing of 1864– c. 1866 on the left, and the remnants of his clock tower behind it

retention might cause the loss of the entire building through unmanageable maintenance costs. In these cases, he did not return the building or a part of it to what it might have been or he thought it should have been when first built, as was the way of the so-called restorers. He simply gave his work a similar character to that of the old structure without copying its style or that of any other period. When he judged an old building to be unworthy of repair, or beyond it, he demolished it but reused all sound materials and installed any well-designed items, such doorways or fireplaces, in the new building as mementoes. For the major alteration and rehabilitation of a large building such as Forthampton Court (of which an account is given in this chapter), his fee was seven-and-a-half per cent of the cost of the work on the ancient part and five per cent of that of new blocks and stables.

Cranmer Hall, Sculthorpe, Norfolk

Webb received the commission for his first important enlargement scheme early in 1864, when Sir Willoughby Jones (1820–84), a cousin by marriage of his client Astley, asked him to alter and enlarge Cranmer Hall (1721), near Sculthorpe in Norfolk.[3] Between then and late 1866 or early 1867, Webb added a wing and a clock tower; inserted a new main staircase in the existing building; improved the offices; and rebuilt the stables as a red-brick and pantiled block with a striking round-arched entrance, diagonally braced double doors, and two long, horizontal windows, each one composed of several identical casements.[4]

Webb's single-storey wing extends south-west from the house, reflecting its character in the material and detailing of the red brick walls. The part nearest the original building contains the drawing room, and remains almost unchanged externally. The six sash windows of the room, on the south-east garden front, are grouped in pairs and set between four brick pilasters; the two gauged brick arches with fine joints above each pair are linked visually by an integral rubbed hood-mould. The pilasters, the entablature, the four plinths above it and the three pedimented gables that rise from them, all have rubbed brick mouldings. Until replaced by small plain windows in the late twentieth century, each gable contained an architraved niche.[5] This inventive elevation has a distinctly Classical air, demonstrating that even at this early date Webb willingly took inspiration for new

designs from seventeenth-century English buildings where this was appropriate. Rubbed and gauged brickwork was important in Norfolk, and in England generally, during the seventeenth and early eighteenth centuries. Webb's employment of it at Cranmer Hall is an early instance of a revival of interest in the use of this once traditional method. He never used it so extensively again, probably because it became a characteristic of the so-called 'Queen Anne' manner of which he was unintentionally a pioneer but which he repudiated when it became a fashionable style, used regardless of local character.

The drawing room had a high plaster barrel vault ornamented with birds and arabesques in relief – probably Webb's first exercise in moulded plaster ornament – and a single pillar in front of a recess. The vault was removed in 1929, when bland neo-Georgian items replaced all his fittings in this room.[6] His main staircase in oak remains, however, with

Above Cranmer Hall: a detail of the south-east front of Webb's drawing-room wing (1864–c. 1866); this is an early example of the use in the nineteenth century of rubbed and gauged brickwork

Above Cranmer Hall: the main staircase inserted by Webb, with the first of his many floor-to-ceiling newels, in this case bearing carved spiral ornament

turned balusters and the first of what were to be his many characteristic newel posts, inspired by Elizabethan examples, which rise from floor to ceiling on each flight, one above the other, and bear spiral carving similar to his later serving table for Rounton Grange (as mentioned in chapter 7).

Right Cranmer Hall: the stable archway, showing one of the massive double doors

Washington Hall, Washington, Tyne & Wear

Also in 1864, Webb was commissioned by Lowthian Bell to enlarge Washington Hall, County Durham (now Tyne and Wear), a red-brick house designed for Bell in 1854 by the Newcastle architect Alfred Burkin Higham (1821–62) in the 'Jacobethan' style. If Bell had not met Webb already through the painters in the Pre-Raphaelite circle, of whom he was a patron like several other middle-class entrepreneurs of the Newcastle area, he probably went to him on the recommendation of Ruskin, who had stayed at Washington Hall in 1863.[7] Webb increased the size of the conservatory on the east side of the house and added a Turkish-bath suite, study, and first-floor bedrooms to the north-east corner of the building, the most notable features being a striking stone-capped chimney in finely fluted brickwork, lead-gabled dormers with bold horizontal roll-joints, and a long horizontal window, composed of identical square lights, in the lean-to bath suite (now demolished).[8]

In 1866, Bell asked Webb to provide further accommodation, at the south-west corner of the house, comprising a new entrance hall, a dining room, two first-floor bedrooms, and a second-floor flat that was probably for his son Hugh and his bride, who married in 1867. In both extensions, Webb kept to the same rooflines as the original building, and used the same bricks, grey Welsh slates, and stone for the dressings. On the south front in 1866, he repeated Higham's diaper pattern in dark headers and his first-floor casement windows but used a buttress to indicate the start of the new work, as well as to avoid an unpleasant junction of old and new brickwork, and gave the new dining room a large mullioned and transomed window, not a bay window like Higham's. Designed about two years after his Cranmer wing, the inset porch on the west front, with a moulded pointed arch in stone and a stone-ribbed brick vault, was one of the most overtly Gothic of Webb's main entrances. The two large fluted chimneys set at right angles to one another about a lead-gabled dormer on the west front are noteworthy items. The first of Webb's influential fitted sideboards – with a main shelf supported on turned posts, bracketed display shelves, and a coved top – was installed in the dining room; it was removed in the twentieth century.[9] In 1866 or early 1867, Webb replaced the spire of Higham's tower with a suitably domestic upper stage in which he exploited the decorative possibilities of plain bricks.[10] It has a gabled roof surmounted by one of his characteristic small bell turrets, and originally housed a clock with a diamond-shaped face by the architect. Ultimately, Webb felt that it had not been possible to be 'quite successful in adding to the house' but Bell was delighted with the work and subsequently commissioned him to design Rounton Grange, and several buildings for his iron-founding firm (see chapter 12).[11]

Above Washington Hall: the upper stage of the tower added by Webb in 1866 or early 1867 to replace Higham's spire and accommodate the clock presented by Bell's workmen (from a photograph by the author)

Left Washington Hall, Washington, County Durham (Tyne and Wear): the entrance and dining room, with bedrooms and a second-floor flat above, added by Webb in 1866 to the house of 1864 by A B Higham; the ground-floor window was inserted in the twentieth century (from a photograph by the author)

Cortachy Castle, near Kirriemuir, Angus, Scotland

Webb made alterations and additions to three ancient British castles: Cortachy in Scotland, and Berkeley and Naworth in England. He inspected Cortachy Castle, near Kirriemuir in the Tayside region of Scotland, in 1868 for David Ogilvy, the Earl of Airlie, and his wife Blanche, a sister of Rosalind Howard, with a view to repairing the roof of an ancient turret, extending the library into the turret, and refitting the room.[12] As previously mentioned (in chapter 7), during his visit, Webb was asked to consider the feasibility of building a new country house on the site of the old family seat, Airlie Castle, destroyed by the Campbells in 1640, and an alternative one of improving and enlarging its substitute Cortachy – an ancient rectangular tower to which a wing, stair tower, and porch, all in the Castellated Gothic style, had been added in the early nineteenth century.[13] Webb decided that there was 'nothing worth saving at Cortachy except the original block' which 'should in no way be seriously altered', and therefore that the nineteenth-century wing should be replaced.[14] He produced designs for both schemes between 1868 and 1869, after warning Airlie that the costs would inevitably be high. Failing to heed the warning, Lord Airlie was astounded by the estimate of £50,000 for the Airlie scheme, which he could not afford; without indicating a maximum cost, he asked Webb to produce a second scheme for enlarging Cortachy. As a result of Airlie's reticence, and of Webb being misled by the grand ideas of Lady Airlie – who was envious of the greater financial resources of Rosalind and George Howard and of their about-to-be-constructed Webb house in London, number 1 Palace Green – the second Cortachy scheme produced an estimate over £11,000 above the £25,000 that Airlie could manage. Finally disclosing this limit, he asked the architect to reduce the design. Having spent many months on designing, preparing drawings, and procuring the estimates, Webb was deeply disappointed, and had to opine that the castle could not be enlarged successfully for the figure. Lord Airlie withdrew the commission, to Webb's distress, and paid him £600 for the three schemes and estimates, and for the originally proposed repair and alteration work at Cortachy, which had been carried out.[15] Lady Airlie was pleased with the library but she added to Webb's distress, after his second scheme for enlarging Cortachy – over which she had enthused – had had

to be abandoned, by putting it about that she disliked it.[16] This treatment by the Airlies accounts for the painstaking care that Webb subsequently took to avoid commissions from would-be clients who did not appreciate his work, or were not conversant with it and therefore would be unable to judge the finished effect from the drawings; and, after a little more experience with difficult clients, led to his decision that all would-be clients must sign his statement of business arrangements before he would accept their jobs (see chapter 13).

Naworth Castle, Brampton, Cumberland

Naworth Castle, near Brampton in Cumbria, licensed to crenellate in 1335, had an irregular quadrangle, surrounded by ranges and towers, chiefly of fourteenth- and fifteenth-century date. Anthony Salvin's sympathetic reinstatement of the building after a disastrous fire of 1844 and the construction of his Morpeth Tower were finished in time for the castle to become the country home of George and Rosalind Howard when they married in 1864. Webb's first visit to Naworth, in 1868, was made simply as a friend but, having failed to persuade Howard to commission a local man, he became involved professionally with the castle from 1873 to 1879, for the last two of these years as the official architect to the Naworth Estate.[17] In 1874, Webb designed a clock-face, which with its works was installed the following year in a gable overlooking the courtyard.[18] Between 1874 and 1879, he converted the Moat or Bote House – an ancient detached building jutting into the dry moat – into a studio for Howard, without injuring the ancient fabric in any way. Instead of inserting new windows, for example, he put lights into the renewed roof and filled a redundant doorway with latticed glazing.

Webb created a delightful a private retreat, the 'Bower', for Rosalind Howard in the top of Salvin's tower between 1877 and 1878, by inserting a floor supported chiefly on two iron girders that also carried the chimney for his characteristic fireplace; he rebuilt the roof at a higher level, and inserted windows and an oak staircase that rose from the room below, and had a trellised balustrade and one of his handsome 'stair-storey' posts.[19] In 1877, he designed bookcases for one of the drawing rooms, made the following year by the estate joiners, and five more for the large two-storey room that was or became the library. At the castle in September that year, the Howards discussed with Webb their hopes of fitting the library on two levels, and Webb made a perspective sketch showing how he might do this.[20] Extremely busy with the Clouds project at this time, he was slow to produce drawings for other jobs; probably because of this and the Howards' vacillation about where best to house their many books, nothing was done until July 1878, when the estate joiners were ordered to make just one of the five bookcases designed earlier. Whilst inspecting the condition of the castle and the site of a proposed new wing on 8 September 1879, Webb found that a doorway had been cut in the old walls without his knowledge. He expressed his disgust to George Howard, allowed his own anger to cool for a few days, then informed him by letter that he considered the matter to be an insult to his experience and judgement, and wrote of his great disappointment on finding that Howard, who he thought had understood and shared his often repeated wish to keep the ancient fabric sacrosanct, had allowed 'forever irreparable' work to be done 'without so much as "by your leave"!'.[21] In the letter, he recommends Charles J Ferguson of Carlisle as his successor.

Ferguson duly added the new wing (later demolished) and, in 1881, carried out the refitting of the library on the lines of Webb's scheme but with at the least some of his own details. Two galleries, each approached via a narrow newel stair, were installed along the end walls, and the upper part of the long wall above the fireplace was brought forward at first-floor level over coving to allow access behind it from one gallery to the other. Ferguson's chimneypiece of

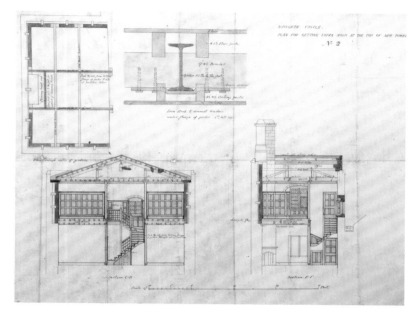

1885 houses *Flodden Field*, a relief designed and painted by Burne-Jones (who paid Webb £30 for designing the frame and drawing the horses), and modelled in plaster by Sir Edgar Boehm.[22] The huge Morris & Co. tapestry that hung on the upper part of this wall is no longer in the castle. Webb's friendship with the Howards survived; he continued to advise on all matters to do with their London house, and to design family memorials on request.

Berkeley Castle, Gloucestershire

Between 1874 and 1877, Webb was involved with Berkeley Castle in Gloucestershire, the seat of Lord Fitzhardinge, probably initially through the Firm and its successor, Morris & Co., which redecorated several rooms in 'flatted' white paint under his direction. In the fourteenth-century great hall, the estate workmen made and installed wainscot and bench seats to Webb's designs; and with his guidance, a Morris craftsman painted the later fireplace 'gold on a dark ground' to 'soften' its incongruous parts.[23] Surprisingly, in view of Webb's insistence on all details being worked according to his drawings, he allowed the bench ends that had been carved without such guidance to remain, because their 'simplicity', he told Lady Fitzhardinge, 'was more suitable than any addition that I could make'.[24] Another instance of his disliking elaboration is that after the setting up of a trial light for the re-glazing of the great hall windows with existing armorial shields set in quarries and borders of his design, he found it 'not quite

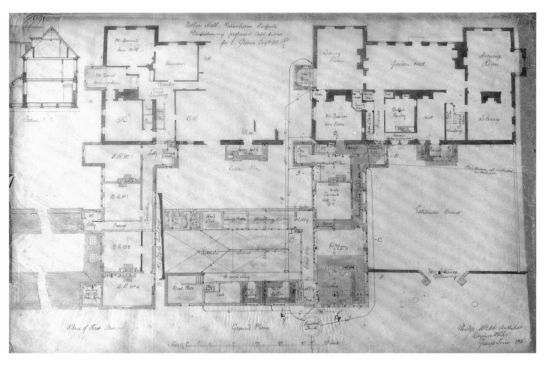

satisfactory' and, with Morris's concurrence, advised that the shields should be set in plain glass instead.[25] Webb's letters to the Fitzhardinges and their estate manager contain strongly worded calls for the setting aside of well-seasoned oak and suitable stone for use in future repair work, and for the removal of gas lighting from the hall before it could damage the medieval timber roof.

Nether Hall, Pakenham, Suffolk

In 1874, Edward Greene (1815–91), an MP and brewer, wished to further his interest in horses and innovative agricultural practices. After consulting Webb as to its suitability, he purchased the Nether Hall estate – for which the architect would later design a farmstead (see chapter 11) – in Pakenham, Suffolk, and asked him to enlarge the hall, a timber-framed house probably of sixteenth-century date that had apparently been encased in brick early in the following century and given sash windows in the eighteenth century.[26] Webb made no major changes to the interior of the building, apart from forming a new main entrance on the north front which allowed the large central entrance hall on the south front to become a major reception room – the Garden Hall – and converting what was probably a kitchen in the north-east corner of the house into a business room.[27] He built a two-storey wing of domestic offices and

bedrooms, with a water tower and a kitchen yard with minor offices on its eastern side.[28] The wing sheltered the new north entrance court and was in red brick like the house, as too was Webb's bold and pleasing round-arched porch. Originally, the house had four parallel gabled roofs, running north to south; Webb protected the remaining north gables

and the gable of his porch with weatherboarding. He reflected the detailing of the fine sixteenth- and seventeenth-century brick houses of Norfolk in the heavily corbelled cornices of the rebuilt and heightened chimneys and the water tower, and in the pinnacle-topped and angled buttresses, and gables surmounted by single-flue chimneys, of the projections that he added to the drawing room and library on the west front.[29] He made no changes to the south front, on which the four original gables had been replaced by a single roof; it was re-fenestrated after Greene's death by an unidentified architect.[30]

Many of Webb's fittings remain, including numerous fireplaces, most of them with Morris, Marshall, Faulkner & Co. tiles. In the library, he inserted into the existing chimneypiece a tall and narrow closed grate flanked by two curving panels of blue-and-white tiles, including his own raven, rabbit, and cockerel patterns. His drawing-room fireplace has a typical overmantel and a Queen Square-type grate with turned iron and brass posts. In the dining room, he installed oak wainscoting and a fireplace with a bracketed mantelpiece in oak, and added a small but deep projection for a breakfast table, the forerunner of the larger breakfast recess at Standen. Developed from those he had designed for number 26 Queen Square (the Morrises' first house in London) and for Washington Hall, the fine fitted sideboard has a serpentine main shelf on turned supports, a square-panelled back fronted by three display shelves with brackets and Webb's idiosyncratic depressed or flattened arches, and a deeply coved, boarded canopy, carried by two polygonal posts, which returns at the sides over the flanking doorways.[31] Apart from the egg-and-dart moulding on the cornice, a rare instance of Webb using a Classical motif, the sideboard demonstrates conclusively that his work in this field was not crude or unnecessarily heavy as has occasionally been suggested.

Rushmore Lodge, Tollard Royal, Wiltshire

Between 1882 and 1885, Webb designed various items and a gatehouse for Rushmore Lodge, an undistinguished house of 1760 at Tollard Royal in Wiltshire, at the request of Lieutenant-General Augustus Henry Lane Fox Pitt-Rivers (1827–1900), the celebrated archaeologist, whose wife was a sister of Rosalind Howard. The impressive gatehouse scheme of 1885, which was not executed, incorporates a pair of three-bedroom lodges with polygonal stair-turrets, and a striking entrance front of a triumphant martial air appropriate for the client. It has an arcade of five round arches, the central one being three times as wide and one-and-a-half times the height of the flanking ones, with a low springing point and alternately emphasized voussoirs, under a tall, partly balustraded parapet. Unfortunately Pitt-Rivers' desires exceeded his means, so this handsome design and the proposed enlargement of the mansion

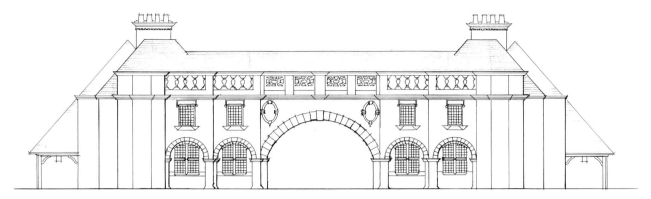

were abandoned in favour of wrought-iron gates hanging from pyramid-topped stone gateposts, and a few minor alterations to the house.[32]

Number 23 Second Avenue, Hove, East Sussex

Webb undertook alterations and enlargements for several members of the Kensington coterie of wealthy Greeks, whom he liked whilst not sharing their taste for elaborate and costly embellishments. Much of this work lay in interior decoration, mostly undertaken by the Firm and later by Morris & Co., under Webb's direction, but he altered and considerably enlarged Fairfield Lodge in Addison Road, Kensington (demolished in the 1960s) from 1871 to 1878 for, successively, Mrs Euphrosyne Cassavetti and her son Alexander, Prinsep's solicitor. The most architecturally interesting additions were done for two of Mrs Cassavetti's nephews; both of 1889, the enlargements were the smoking room for Alexander A Ionides at number 1 Holland Park, Kensington (described in chapter 3), and a picture gallery commissioned by his brother Constantine Alexander Ionides, a stockbroker and art collector for whom Webb had altered and extended the speculatively built number 8 Holland Villas Road, Kensington, in the 1870s.[33] The gallery was added between 1890 and 1891 to number 23 Second Avenue (now subdivided into flats) in Hove, East Sussex. An elongated octagon, thirty-seven feet by eighteen feet, the gallery has two shallow octagonal iron-reinforced concrete vaults supported in part by an arch spanning the centre of the room and stabilized by a large external buttress. Each of the domes is faced with the good-quality fir used as centring and left in position, and has a large octagonal central roof lantern.[34] It is particularly fortunate that the gallery has survived as it shows that despite the primary importance he

placed on traditional materials, Webb did not ignore technological developments.

Great Tangley Manor, Wonersh, Surrey

In the late 1880s and the 1890s, Webb undertook four larger, more influential enlargements: those of Great Tangley Manor in Surrey, Forthampton Court in Gloucestershire, Exning House in Suffolk, and Warrens House in Hampshire. Wickham Flower (d. 1904), a solicitor and connoisseur, had employed Morris & Co. to decorate Swan House, his London home designed in 1875 by Shaw, and had been a committee member of the SPAB since 1877. In 1884, he bought Great Tangley Manor, a dilapidated moated house of reputedly Anglo-Saxon origin (now two dwellings) in Wonersh near Guildford. Webb repaired and enlarged it for Flower and his wife in two stages, designed in 1885 and 1893 respectively, and in 1891 he added a stable block and a pair of semi-detached cottages, with roughcast upper walls, for the coachman and the gardener.[35] The first enlargement included a service range (now demolished) at the rear of the house, and a new entrance hall, with bedroom above, at the western end of the timber-framed, triple-gabled

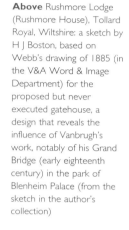

Above Great Tangley Manor, near Guildford, Surrey: the entrance (south) front, with the old house of 1582 at the centre, flanked on the left by Webb's entrance block of 1885–87 and to the right by his library addition of 1893–94; the half-timbering on the left-hand addition was added in the twentieth century

front of 1582. To preserve the integrity of the Elizabethan frontage, Webb played down the entrance addition by putting the bedroom within a tiled hip roof, and bringing the latter down over a loggia (that was enclosed by a later owner), which was divided into a porch and a veranda by a wall of the old courtyard that fronted the Elizabethan part of the house. He designed the necessary bridge over the moat as a roofed structure that continued as a covered way to the new porch, sheltered on one side by the old court wall. With its timber framing and red roof tiles, this element was intended to link the old house visually to the grounds surrounding the moat. His clients, however, preferred a simple pathway. Webb told them he had designed the covered way as much for aesthetic as for practical reasons – 'to help the surroundings of the house rather than detract from them' – but that if they preferred not to incur its cost, he would reconsider his scheme without it.[36] Fortunately, as it is one of Webb's most beautiful and influential garden features, they capitulated. The matching tile-roofed open screen, with which he filled a gap in the south wall of the court to retain the sense of enclosure within it but which gave intriguing glimpses of the Elizabethan front from beyond the moat, was removed in the late 1940s.[37]

The 1893 addition, at the eastern end of the 1582 front, contained a library, new stair-hall, and first-floor bedrooms. The oak beams, wainscot, bookshelves, and fitted cupboards, and the bold, good-looking stone fireplaces – that of the library revealing Vanbrugh's influence – were impressive features of the interior.[38] On the exterior, the ground-floor walls were constructed in the same local Bargate rubble stone as the old court walls after Webb had shown the foreman exactly how to bed the stones

and the ashlar quoins, and how to point them.[39] To make it unobtrusive, the first-floor wall was roughcast not timbered like most of the ancient upper walls, and a dominant roof was avoided through the use of two parallel ridge roofs, with gables facing east. The windows, apart from one that echoed the oval shape of embrasures in the old court walls, were oak mullioned and transomed casements, not Webb's customary sashes. Having increased the size of the house for the second time with reluctance, he informed the Flowers that any further enlargement would seriously damage the character of the original building; he was proved right in the late 1890s when chief assistant George Jack, given the private job at Webb's suggestion, added a music room and bedrooms to the western end.[40]

Flower's major reason for buying the old manor house, which had only an old orchard and a vegetable plot, had been the opportunity it offered to create gardens several acres in extent. As soon as he took possession, he and his gardener Whiteman began clearing the overgrown moat and laying out the grounds, aided by eighteen labourers. In September 1885, after seeing the results of their work so far, Webb told Boyce that 'something must be done' to remove all or some of the 'miserable handiwork' of the 'pleasure garden maker' (to which man he referred is not clear); in late November, he reported that 'the garden arrangements are being made somewhat more decent in appearance'.[41] He particularly disliked the layout of the garden in the old court that fronted the house, in which shrubs and trees were dotted around haphazardly, with a single bush in a raised bed surrounded by brickwork as a focal point; the offending items were replaced as he wished by a lawn with herbaceous borders and a

central mulberry tree. Old photographs reveal his hand in the abundant climbing plants clothing the new walls of the house and covered way, and those of the old court, and in the layout of two other gardens, each enclosed by hedges – one of lawn and flower borders to the west of his covered way within the moated area, and the second, east of the moat, of a medieval type like that of Red House.[42] Even so, in 1888 he still found the grounds too 'spick and span', and Morris and Boyce, agreeing, annoyed Flower and his wife by telling them so. Having failed to appreciate their sensitivity about their surname, Webb too had irritated them by playing on it in the design of a sundial but, having not really approved of such an item, he was pleased when they removed it – even though, unbeknown to them, he had paid Louis Cassella for making the dial.[43]

In 1894, Webb installed a second bridge to link the central gardens with those east of the moat. Less important than the one leading to the house, it is not roofed; planks are carried high above the water on a massive beam supported at each end by a trestle and a strut, with a handrail on one side.[44] The design of the pergola, further away from the house, suggests that it too was by Webb; made of poles not sawn timbers, it had a projection, with seats, midway along its length leading to a landing stage.[45] Despite their occasional disagreements about the gardens, the Flowers were pleased with Webb's work, and Mrs Flower's letter of appreciation led to a close friendship with the architect.

Above Great Tangley Manor: the covered bridge and covered way, leading over the moat to Webb's entrance addition (1885–87)

Left Great Tangley Manor: the library, from a photograph of 1895 by Bedford Lemere (Private Collection)

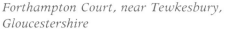

Ground floor

Forthampton Court, near Tewkesbury, Gloucestershire

Forthampton Court, near the banks of the Severn in Gloucestershire, had been the country house of the abbots of Tewkesbury until the mid-eighteenth century, when it became the seat of the Yorke family. When John Reginald Yorke (1836–1912), an erstwhile MP, inherited it in 1889 it was damp, dilapidated, unpleasantly smelly, and hopelessly inconvenient, but with the great hall, chapel, and most of the oak roofs surviving relatively intact from the medieval period. Soon after 1788, Anthony Keck had re-fronted the central south-west wall of the U-shaped entrance court on the south-west side of the house, giving it a Tuscan door-case and a pediment with a Diocletian window, and adding parapets to the flanking wings. An arcade was constructed along the base of Keck's front in 1860, probably by Richard Armstrong.[46] On inheriting the property, John Yorke immediately decided to demolish the house and build a new one. He inspected Clouds, having heard that it was one of the best of the recent English houses, and was introduced to Webb by Percy Wyndham, a contemporary of his at Eton. Yorke asked Webb to design the house but, within ten days of inspecting the old building, the architect submitted a report recommending its rehabilitation and explaining how he believed it could be made into a more convenient

and acceptable home without any loss of character, quality, and interest.[47] Yorke accepted his advice, and Webb's schemes for altering the old house (1889), and adding a laundry block, menservants' quarters, additional domestic offices, a billiard room, and new stables (the last two were designed in 1891), were carried out between 1889 and 1892. Having been converted to the cause by Webb, Yorke became a member of the SPAB committee in 1891.

Webb first thought to remedy the primary fault of the old house – the smallness and inconvenience of the major rooms – by building a new wing in the centre of the entrance court, parallel to the flanking ranges. Such an addition would have blocked in the valuable south-west-facing hall and the bedrooms above it, however, and the creation of a new entrance on the north front would have damaged

unspoilt medieval fabric. So he decided that the entrance court should continue to serve its purpose, but with the arcade and Keck's pediment and parapets removed because they detracted from the

medieval character of the building. He built generously wide passages at basement, ground-floor, and first-floor level along the north-west wall of the south-west wing, thereby improving the insulation of that wing, which was the coldest part of the house. The passages – the upper one having a timber-framed and brick-nogged wall – terminated in a roughcast, three-storey tower-like form containing a spacious inset porch and, on each upper floor, one large bedroom. In the hall, the existing main entrance was replaced by a wide and deep bay window which, with further enlargement by the removal of internal walls at its north-west end, turned the room into a useful living hall. At the western end of the ensuing space, behind an attractive vertically boarded screen, Webb installed a new main staircase which was lit from a newly formed light well. He was then able to extend the dining room into the previous stair hall. The library and bedroom above, and the main bedroom, were enlarged by adding two twin-gabled and partly timber-framed projections on the south-east front.[48]

A floor had been inserted in the great hall, the upper part of which, open to the fine medieval roof, was the existing drawing room. Webb retained this, rather than returning the hall to its original proportions, as the latter would not have been as conducive to comfort, and the butler's and housekeeper's rooms and servants' hall in the lower part were conveniently placed. He installed oak wainscoting in the drawing room and gave it a small oriel window and an adjacent service stair in a new turret in a corner of the entrance court.[49] The domestic offices and servants' quarters were brought up to the standard of the day by adding a triple-gabled, roughcast storey to the old laundry block; enlarging the windows in the existing kitchen; and building a T-plan block of offices served by a covered way that enclosed a court and gave access to the new billiard room at the north-eastern extremity of the house.[50]

Important remaining interior features by Webb include: the hall chimney-piece with a Latin inscription recording the rehabilitation of the building; the library shelving and English fossil marble fireplace, with the Yorke insignia in a small jewel-like panel carved by George Jack to Webb's design, and gilded by Kate Faulkner; the dining-room fireplace with a plate-warming rack below an embossed copper plate; and an unusually large

revolving bookcase designed for the drawing room and made by the contractors.[51] Most striking of all is Webb's beautiful oak main staircase, with turned balusters and finely shaped posts, some of them mushrooming boldly against the ceiling of the upper landing, from which there is a dramatic view of the ancient chapel through a latticed screen.

Above Forthampton Court: the lower part of the main staircase

Opposite Forthampton Court: the upper part of Webb's main staircase

Left Forthampton Court: a detail of the library over-mantel, designed by Webb, with delicate panels in fretwork, and a small heraldic panel carved by George Jack and gilded by Kate Faulkner

Above Exning House, Exning, near Newmarket, Suffolk: the entrance (west) front, showing the original house by Andrews Jelfe (1734) and Webb's new block (1894, constructed 1895–96)

Exning House, Exning, near Newmarket, Suffolk

Captain Edward William David Baird (1864–1956) purchased the Exning House estate near Newmarket in Suffolk in 1891 to further his interest in horse racing. In 1894, on Yorke's recommendation, he asked Webb to enlarge the house, which Andrews Jelfe had designed in 1734.[52] Webb made as few changes as possible to both the exterior and the interior, having persuaded Baird to demolish rather

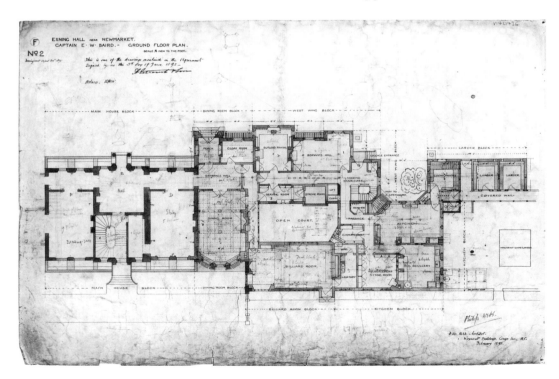

Right Exning House: Webb's plan of the ground floor, dated 1895 and signed as part of the contract (RIBA Library Photographs Collection)

than alter the rooms that had been added to its north side, and to build a new two-storey family block roughly the size of the original house but of only two storeys, and a three-storey block of domestic offices and servants' rooms.[53] Webb's designs were executed between 1895 and 1896. The family block included a new main entrance and hall, a dining room, a billiard room and, and on the first floor, a children's suite on the west front and Mrs Baird's on the eastern side. He placed the block at the northern end of Jelfe's building and unified the two by using the same red brick for the walls and stone, in an inventive design inspired by Elizabethan and English Baroque

Right Exning House: Webb's bay window to the dining room and main bedroom (east front)

Opposite Exning House: the east front, showing Webb's additions on the right and the old house on the left

Above Exning House: a detail, showing Webb's use of glass blocks in a corridor ceiling

Above, right Exning House: the billiard-room ingle-nook, with an old fireplace re-used by Webb

Right Exning House: the dining-room fireplace

houses. Webb skilfully achieved a classical-style air without use of the Orders, the main entrance bay on the west front and the two-storey bay window on the east elevation – which are chiefly in stone to avoid an unpleasant junction between old and new brickwork – being particularly commendable. The rendered, colour-washed upper walls of the restrained block of domestic offices reflect the Suffolk tradition.

There are several interesting Webb features in the interior, including plaster barrel vaults and a staircase balustrade of avant-garde design in iron, with paired square-section verticals, every third one having eight interlocking circles one above the other below a single larger one under the plain handrail. The striking Hopton Wood limestone chimneypiece in the dining room has a bold round arch, with an elongated keystone, within which the fireplace is surrounded by geometrical inlay in the light and dark shades of the stone. The billiard room, now considerably changed, had a large window overlooking the garden to which it had access, and a lower area with a coffered barrel vault, which survives, at one end that served as the smoking room, with a reused fireplace in a Webb surround.

Warrens House, Bramshaw, Hampshire

Warrens House in Bramshaw, Hampshire, was an unusual building apparently comprised of two villas of similar appearance, the first and larger one to the north designed by John Nash (1752–1835) in 1804, and the second one by an unidentified architect some time later. The villas were linked to present a unified front to the garden, facing a little south of east, by what must have been a conservatory or garden room, apparently the work of Nash.[54] George Edward Briscoe Eyre (1840–1922), of the printing firm Eyre and Spottiswode, who played a major part in the early history of New Forest conservation, inherited the house from a bachelor uncle and, finding it too small for a family home, had it enlarged extensively between early 1897 and October 1899 by Webb, whom he might have known since the 1860s when the Firm installed their stained glass in St Michael's Church, Lyndhurst.

When enlarging and improving the convenience of Nether Hall and Exning House, Webb had been able to apply his rational tripartite arrangement, in a cranked form at the first and longitudinally at the second. The great length of Warrens House, however, as with the jumble of ancient structures at Forthampton Court, made compromise inevitable. He converted the link into the desired common room, and placed most of the required domestic offices and bedrooms in a new three-storey block of the same height as the villas, on the western side of the house, avoiding cutting into the villa roofs so that if a future owner desired it could be removed in the future without trace. His new main entrance, on the same side of the house as the previous one but in a more central position, was in the north-west corner of the new wing. It had a deep inset porch and passage like Forthampton Court but with a round-arched doorway set at forty-five degrees under a bold stone canopy supported by consoles. Webb retained the old kitchen, and added a floor of menservants'

Below Warrens House, Bramshaw, Hampshire: the garden (east) front, showing the two villas (with that of John Nash on the right), the link that Webb converted into the common room between 1897 and 1899, and his central chimney (the glazing in the common-room windows was replaced in the late twentieth century, without the radiating bars in the fanlights)

bedrooms to the existing scullery wing, under a triple-gabled roof surmounted by a cupola, and linked it to his new wing with a single-storey range. The inclusion in the servants' quarters of a large so-called 'occasional room' and a study for the menservants is an interesting indication of late-nineteenth-century social developments.

The only external changes Webb made to the garden front were to take the bay window of Nash's villa up to the cornice like that of the other villa (a structural fault having developed in the original wall), and to add a new roof surmounted by a central chimney stack of two flues with a partly open arch between them, in the manner of Sir John Soane (1753–1837). Each stone of the existing parapet was numbered, carefully stored, and finally replaced exactly as before.[55] Webb used similar windows, cream bricks, and grey slates to those of the villas, apart from the red-brick lower and roughcast upper walls fronting the kitchen yard. To create the common room in the link, he inserted double doors between it and Nash's dining room, a new western wall to support the fireplace and chimney – making the room a little narrower – and a plaster barrel vault

that was partly supported by a central longitudinal lattice girder. This vault, unlike that of Cranmer Hall, is plain, its simplicity contrasting effectively with the finely detailed plasterwork frieze of strapwork and foliage ornament in deep relief. Webb's curved, high-backed bench seats, in oak like the wainscot and derived from his curved screens in the living hall at Clouds, form a sophisticated inglenook and conceal the two service doors.[56] The chimneypiece has a curved panel of blue-and-white Persian tiles behind two marble columns, which have beautifully detailed Ionic capitals with volutes at forty-five degrees that were modelled to his design by Laurence Turner and are linked by an entablature worked by the Hopton Wood Stone Co. in its own material. This use of a Classical Order, apparently for the first and only time, was perhaps a graceful compliment to Nash. The fireplace, coupled with the English strapwork of the frieze, shows that the Idea for the common room came from barrel-vaulted Elizabethan long galleries but Webb certainly did not reflect the typical crudeness of their Classical motifs. In the twentieth century, his connection with Warrens was forgotten, his block was demolished after further social changes

Right Warrens House: Webb's common room, with curved settles flanking the chimneypiece, for which, in an apparently unique instance, he employed a Classical Order

had made it redundant, and it became an Eyre family legend, which would have delighted him, that 'Mr Webb' had been the master-plasterer. Fortunately, his fine common room survived intact apart from two skylights, and now serves as the dining room.[57]

Conclusion

The enlargement work includes some of Webb's finest interior fittings and ornament, and was as well known to his architect-admirers – particularly those who were SPAB members – as were his houses. Lutyens first saw Webb's out-of-town work, which deeply impressed him, in 1891 when taken to Great Tangley Manor by Gertrude Jekyll, who had known it when it was a farmhouse. In 1898 and 1905, the manor house was illustrated and favourably described and discussed in three articles in *Country Life*, of one of which Jekyll is believed to be the author; Muthesius also praised it as a 'very attractive work' and included two illustrations of the library in his important *Das englische Haus* (1904, 1905).[58] The influence of the library and the bedroom above it, and of his main staircase at Forthampton and common-room ornament at Warrens, is evident in the work of many Arts and Crafts architects, notably in that of Lutyens, and of Gimson, the brothers Ernest and Sidney Barnsley, and others of the so-called Cotswold school.[59] Webb's skilful use of the old court walls, the covered way, and the small hedged enclosure within the moated area to merge the house into its surroundings and to create a pleasing sense of mystery and anticipation, and his use of abundant freely growing flowering plants contained within formal walls and hedges, had a similarly wide effect on Arts and Crafts gardens, most of which had at least one timber-framed feature in his manner.

By the late 1890s, some architects believed that Webb had adopted the neo-Georgian style, and in the late twentieth century one or two critics suggested that Webb worked gradually towards a complete adoption of the Classical idiom in the 1890s. Smeaton Manor, which when seen briefly from a short distance away can seem to resemble an eighteenth-century house, and his last two major enlargements, at Exning and Warrens, which by coincidence were both classical-style buildings, undoubtedly fuelled these misunderstandings. The Cranmer wing, however, demonstrates that Webb took inspiration for new designs from seventeenth-century and early-eighteenth-century English buildings, where he

considered it appropriate, in his early years in practice. His work at Warrens, Exning, and number 23 Second Avenue, Hove, refutes any assertion that his creative power had diminished in his last decade in practice. The family block at Exning House is a particularly fine example of his inventiveness. Clearly a domestic building, it nevertheless joins St Martin's Church, Brampton (1874–78), and the Bell Brothers Offices (1881–91) in Middlesbrough (see chapter 12) in giving an indication of the many vigorous, dignified but unpretentious large public buildings that Webb might have produced had he not been so averse to working for committee clients.

Left Warrens House: a detail of the plasterwork frieze in the common room

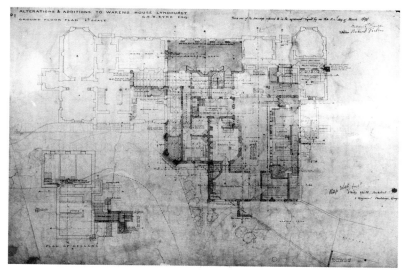

Below Warrens House: Webb's plan of the ground floor, showing all his additions, signed in March 1898 as part of the contract from a photograph by the author of the original drawing (Society for the Protection of Ancient Buildings)

Chapter 10

WEBB THE SOCIALIST

In 1883 Philip Webb and William Morris, hitherto staunch Radical Liberals, became active Socialists or, as Morris preferred to put it, Communists.[1] Webb's change of allegiance stemmed from the beliefs about art and society that also lay at the root of his architectural philosophy. Whilst the majority of British people probably regarded industrialism as progress, Webb followed those thinkers, such as Thomas Carlyle and William Cobbett (1763–1835), who feared that the spiritual qualities of mankind would be destroyed by a materialistic society in which men were regarded solely as a commodity, as labour. Aware that economic and working conditions affect the spiritual and imaginative qualities of life, the critics believed that the feudalism and *noblesse oblige* of the Middle Ages had given each man his own place in harmony with his fellows and with nature. In their own day, workmen were beginning to be seen as machines, and the wealthy were growing richer whilst the poor were becoming dispossessed.

Pugin adopted Cobbett's device of contrasting beautiful medieval Gothic edifices with utilitarian buildings of nineteenth-century institutions to great effect in *Contrasts* (1836). By attributing the excellence of medieval architecture to the religious enthusiasm and faith shared by its builders and their community, in *Contrasts* and in *The True Principles of Pointed or Christian Architecture* (1841),[2] Pugin showed that architecture is not just a matter of style, but also expresses the qualities of the society which builds it. From this it followed, as Webb saw, that there could be little or no hope of great architecture springing from an unsatisfactory society. As previously explained (in chapter 6), Webb was also strongly influenced by Ruskin's contentions that the glory of medieval Gothic architecture stemmed from its expression of the free, creative spirit of the craftsmen and their pleasure in the work; that this spirit and enjoyment had been impaired by commercialism having forced craftsmen to work slavishly to the designs of others; and that, in the nineteenth century,

the creative spirit of craftsmen and their ability to judge the quality of their work were being threatened with extinction under the new system of machine work and divided labour.

These various influences, coupled with his reading of Goethe, who saw medieval Gothic as a quality rather than a style, and his own extensive knowledge of Gothic buildings, led Webb to conclude that medieval art was a folk tradition, an unconscious natural development welling up from deep sources, a 'kind of happy sing-song of labour and unconscious feeling'.[3] His initial reaction to industrialism as a threat to the English landscape, villages, and ancient buildings he loved, had become a conviction that the entire commerce-driven society of his day was evil. He believed that in the medieval community, with its shared faith, hopes, and beliefs, the 'daily life of the craftsman was a positive incentive to imaginative creation'; whereas in the nineteenth century, the 'art-workman' had been made even 'more of a mere mechanic' than in the Renaissance, the time when Gothic art had begun to decline as it ceased to 'express the deeper feelings of the people' and simplicity started to be replaced by artificiality, as 'artists began to be supported by the upper classes and to pander to the luxury of the time'.[4] After studying Byzantine architecture, long before he went to Italy, he became convinced that the only hope of a similar 'new life spring' to that which had occurred in the Byzantine era, and culminated in the great Gothic buildings, lay in the 'submerging of commerce' and the 'general purification of England from luxury'.[5]

Experience had strengthened this belief. In order to avoid poor and careless craftsmanship in his buildings, Webb had found it essential to avoid those builders who, in their profit seeking, allowed the use of machines in their workshops. He had observed how some of his painter friends started with high ideals but succumbed to commercialism. 'The painters do mainly wear financial spectacles, I am afraid,' he told Boyce, 'and nature gets denaturalized through those lenses.'[6] In the course of his work, he had found that though most of his own clients pursued enlightened and useful lives, this was far from universal amongst the well-to-do. He had concluded that the factory system, 'hugger-mugger breeding', and the 'herding of labouring men like herrings in a barrel' had created a 'class of rich people [...] whose greed could grasp more than "the dreams of avarice" had forecast'; in 'fat ignorance of those who earned for them their means of waste', they frittered away time and money on non-essential fripperies that had often been made under miserable conditions.[7] Such idleness and needless spending was deeply offensive to Webb, who saw work as a duty and believed that man's purpose was to use his intellect to improve life for his fellows, and whose personal taste for a simple, uncluttered home had been reinforced by Ruskin's tenet of the need to do without all objects that were not the product of 'healthy and ennobling labour'.[8] London's terrible slums, compacted by railway building and swollen by Irish immigrants, would have heightened Webb's awareness of the growing contrast between rich and poor, and he must have often thought about how the thoughtlessly squandered money of the wealthy could have enabled hundreds of the impoverished to live as well as he did himself. Believing that in general the land-owning or 'gentle' class understood the needs of their workers and ruled their estates accordingly and with justness, Webb reserved his contempt for the 'vulgar' class, the 'great majority of the fairly well-to-do', a 'bad bred lot' whose sole aim was a life of ease earned for them by others, an 'ill-gotten race' that 'must die out, for no good can come of them'.[9]

For Webb, the need for social change was inextricably bound up with the hope of a revival of art – a revival in which art would again be part of everyday life for all people, and through which the feeling for and appreciation of art and nature that had been crushed out of existence in working men and their families under the existing system, would be reawakened. Cromwell's Commonwealth would have been entirely good for England, Webb averred, but for its 'horror of anything beautiful', which had had devastating effects at the time and had left a lingering legacy of contempt for art.[10] Until Webb was about fifty, there was little hope of achieving his aims of reviving art by freeing craftsmen to work as

they wished, and of rescuing the English landscape from industrial desecration through a complete change of social organization, so he pursued a quiet personal crusade for the improvement of architecture and the decorative arts. Although he knew many of the Christian Socialists who had founded the Working Men's College in 1854, and who also had accepted Ruskin's contentions about the relationship between art and work,[11] Webb looked to the Radical Liberals for some amelioration of the lot of those less fortunate than himself. He kept abreast of political affairs through his reading, and through fellow Liberals and those of his clients who were or hoped to become members of Parliament, with whom he aired his views uninhibitedly.[12] On one occasion, he sent a message to William Ewart Gladstone (1809–98), then Leader of the Opposition, demanding greater seriousness in the House of Commons instead of unproductive laughter.[13] By 1879, however, when he assured the newly elected George Howard that his duties as a Member of Parliament would not interfere with Howard's 'proper work as a painter', Webb was losing faith in the Liberal Party.[14]

The first realization that social change might be achieved through working-class efforts, rather than those of the middle classes, probably came to Webb and Morris through their involvement with the Eastern Question Association, of which Gladstone was a figurehead and Morris was the treasurer. The association was formed in 1876 during the Balkan crisis of 1875 to 1878, after revelations of the atrocities committed by Turkish mercenaries against Christian Bulgarians, to promote resistance to the alliance made with Turkey by the Prime Minister, Benjamin Disraeli (1804–81).[15] The need for such a body receded in 1878, but in working for it Morris and Webb had been involved for the first time with political agitation, and with a working-class organization, the Labour Representation League. In the early 1880s, both Webb and Morris began to see a real hope for a revival of art and eventually of great architecture, as well as a better life for the working classes, in the revolution that British Socialists believed to be imminent. They joined the Democratic Federation (founded in 1881) in 1883, a year before it openly espoused socialism and changed its name to the Socialist Democratic Federation.[16]

Morris made the first move but, contrary to what so many writers on Morris have assumed, Webb did not follow suit simply through loyalty to his friend. Indeed, with his distaste for joining institutions, he would not have become a member at all had he not felt extremely strongly about its major aims. Morris himself proclaimed that Webb was 'the man who taught me Socialism', and there is no reason to doubt this.[17] Webb had been thinking on socialist lines for a long time, since his early years in London at the latest. He used to joke in Morris's presence about having brought him up by hand, and he was far from being a mere follower.[18] May Morris, who considered Webb a genius, described him as her father's 'complement, not only in architecture, but in each of the many-sided activities of his life', whilst Rossetti considered Webb to be one of the leaders of the Pre-Raphaelite circle.[19] Certainly, Webb would have contributed at least an equal share of ideas to the debates that he and Morris enjoyed frequently on all subjects. Their letters to one another confirm that this was so. Before they met, and in both cases largely as a result of reading Ruskin, each had determined to do something for art, a resolve that was subsequently strengthened by their shared enthusiasm.[20]

Webb had first become aware of the worst effects of large-scale industries in 1854 at Wolverhampton. In the 1860s and 1870s, he had become personally involved with it in and around Middlesbrough when he designed buildings for Lowthian Bell's ironworks (see chapter 12). He was familiar with the appalling conditions in which industrial labourers and their families had to work and live, and of the despoilment of the landscape by heavy industry. Webb's strong reactions to all this would have stirred the repugnance of Morris to these effects, which apparently he did not encounter directly until after 1883.

Webb became a pacifist long before Morris did; in the early 1860s he had refused to join the Volunteers with Morris, Rossetti, and Burne-Jones.[21] Webb abhorred war, which he attributed to greed, and always fervently hoped that international disputes would be settled peacefully. He told George Howard of his hopes that 'cutting and carving of carcasses' would be avoided in France in 1877, and that the 'Boer nut' would be 'cracked without more bullets' in 1880.[22] Webb was an anti-imperialist, as well as a pacifist. This was demonstrated before 1883 when he expressed his belief that Britain deserved to be taught a lesson by being beaten in the war that had broken out with Afghanistan in 1878; a later indication,

amongst many others in his letters, is the extreme disgust with which he viewed the displays of jingoism occurring after the relief of Ladysmith in 1900.[23]

Webb personified Morris's idea of a good man, and he also showed him by example that a life based on creative work and fellowship, with just a few possessions all of the highest quality and none made by slavish labour, could be happy and satisfying. This was the way of life that Morris — who had two homes, several servants, a collection of rare and costly medieval manuscripts, and a commercial business with its necessary accumulation of capital — would put before the masses as an ideal.

Already out of step with their generation in openly disapproving of two important phenomena of the times — industrialism and imperialism — Webb and Morris turned their backs on their own class in 1883 in order to campaign for a revolution that they hoped would destroy its commercialism. During the next eight years, and to a lesser extent a further five, they gave all the time they could spare to the cause, facing loss of livelihood if their political activity led patrons to desert them, and risking and doubtless receiving castigation and scorn from many of their fellows. Morris gave generous financial support to the cause. Webb donated every penny he could spare of his meagre resources, ultimately leaving himself insufficient to buy a cottage for his retirement. He also gave a lot of help to individual socialists, displaying, according to his executor Emery Walker, a 'boundless generosity in helping lame dogs over stiles, including similar services to some pretended lame dogs'.[24]

Whilst not imagining the Middle Ages to have been perfect, Webb and Morris believed that in the fourteenth century the craft guilds had achieved for their members a life of creative work and fellowship near to their own ideal.[25] This was what they sought from socialism: not a life of ease after the sharing out of wealth but the universal abnegation of the accumulation of wealth. Their ideal depended upon their beliefs that mankind was inherently righteous, that the creative faculty was innate in all people, that under favourable conditions it would revive, and that most people would then find creative work enjoyable and satisfying. In the first case, apparently ignoring Darwin's theory of natural selection, Webb believed that man was 'endowed with exceptional faculties beyond the brute beast', and that 'nature' had not stopped at the gorilla but had made man, the 'worst-

and-best animal', who could 'set things straight and make them plain'.[26] In the second case, he contended that 'no-one is wholly without art imagination' and that 'the having it, or not having it, is only a matter of degree'; and as for the third, he maintained that: 'Living art — after all is said — is but a representation of right living.'[27] Webb's conception of what right living might be under socialism coincided with that described by Morris in 1890 in *News from Nowhere*.[28] In view of the closeness of their ideals and aims by the early 1880s, it is inconceivable that Morris's utopia was not coloured by Webb's thinking. Writing of an England a century after a successful communist revolution, Morris envisages a country of healthy, helpful, and hospitable people, living as they choose (alone, in single families or small groups), in beautiful houses set in gardens amidst the fields, or in villages or small, well-wooded towns. All the people would be made happy and contented by their pleasurable labour, whether creative or administrative and chosen at will. Their minds would be refreshed by agreeable physical labour such as gardening, and all the unpleasant but necessary tasks would be shared, and eased by machines. All would live and work in peace, surrounded by and in harmony with the world of nature, and with art. There would be no private property, therefore no commercialism, no heavy industries, no pollution, no money, no greed or theft, no police or prisons, and no central government (the chief purpose of governments being the protection of property, in Webb's opinion). As each small community would reach its own decisions, there would be no need for large-scale local government and therefore no bureaucracy, no large institutions, and no formal system of education. The hateful 'boy farms', such as those to which they themselves had been banished, would be no more. Patently owing much to Ruskin, apart from the complete equality, this utopia would have perfectly suited Morris and Webb, who attached the highest importance to the freedom of the individual and, as Morris put it, had 'an Englishman's wholesome horror of government, interference and centralization'.[29] Their dream was very unlike the stolid, repressive, and bureaucratic Communist states that would be established in the next century, in which the individual would be subservient to the state.

The following note by Webb, of a topic for discussion, indicates why he believed it right to seek to overthrow the Government by revolution:

> Supposing that the various forms of authority had succeeded in giving a fairly satisfactory life to the masses, there might be some excuse for endeavouring to continue them; but as they have evidently and miserably failed, the masses are bound as honest men to displace authority which has proved itself incapable.[30]

However, though Morris apparently accepted that the revolution was likely to be a bloody one,[31] and Webb's zeal for the cause was no less than his, it is difficult to believe that such a compassionate pacifist as Webb would promulgate a violent uprising in which men might be killed and ancient buildings destroyed. In fact, there are strong indications that he never believed that the revolution would take this form. He urged his communist comrades to have sympathy for the police, for instance.[32] Also, though he accepted the view of Karl Marx (1818–83) that history was to a large extent an unrolling of a partially written scroll,[33] Webb rejected his contention that the middle and working classes would unite to overthrow the governmental powers of the aristocracy, after which the masses would seize all power. He was convinced that the bourgeoisie as a whole would never help the working classes, and thus that nothing could be accomplished until socialism was understood and desired by the masses; he saw the role of enlightened middle-class socialists like himself as not to lead but to educate.[34] In the early 1880s, it was apparent that socialism was far from being widely understood, and that the period of education would be a long one; a lengthy delay offered hope that the social revolution could be achieved without bloodshed through the withdrawal of labour. All this being so, Webb felt able to jocularly tell his aristocratic friend Rosalind Howard that he was putting aside his 'blood-thirsty knife' to write to her.[35]

Before his winter in Italy of 1884 to 1885, during which he kept in touch with Morris and other socialist friends by letter and fretted daily because he was not helping them 'in their efforts for the mass of mankind', Webb's political activities are obscure, but he gave at least one lecture, entitled 'The Source of Capital', to the Horton branch of the federation, probably in 1883.[36] As he never lectured for the SPAB, despite feeling so passionately about the importance of its work, this indicates the strength of his political convictions. On his return to England in 1885, he joined the Socialist League, which Morris and others had founded after seceding from the Socialist Democratic Federation because they disagreed with proposals to make the latter an orthodox political party.[37] Morris and Webb regarded such a move, and the seeking of reforms through parliamentary measures, as an acceptance of some of the capitalist policies they abhorred. By 1886, Webb had succeeded an inefficient Morris as treasurer of the Socialist League, and had become a member of its council and its ways and means committee, and was writing occasional articles for its journal, the *Commonweal*; on occasions he acted as chairman of the Bloomsbury branch for which he was also treasurer, and for which he gave and arranged lectures.[38] Webb's Saturdays, and Monday and Thursday evenings, were devoted to League business, and remaining evenings to branch affairs, until his almost fatal attack of rheumatic fever in October 1887, after which he abandoned lecturing, writing, and branch matters.[39] He continued to serve as League treasurer and he increased his financial support, however, and frequently stood bail for members in trouble with the law; 'the League required as much bailing as a leaky boat!', he recalled.[40]

In 1888, after the secession of those members wishing to seek reforms through Parliament, the anarchist faction, some members of which advocated armed insurrection, gradually gained control of the Socialist League. This led Morris and the Hammersmith branch to leave in November 1890 in order to found an independent body, the Hammersmith Socialist Society, with the aim of preserving and promulgating the principles of socialism.[41] Webb, who had some sympathies with the anarchists (as the quoted passage about displacing the authorities shows) tried to stay on, thus conclusively demonstrating his independence of thought and action.[42] However, he was ostracized and forced to resign as the treasurer and as a member because of his closeness to Morris; he joined the new society in January 1891, and from then until his illness in the winter of 1893 to 1894 regularly attended its meetings.[43] The Independent Labour Party was founded in 1893 but neither he nor Morris became members, because its standpoint was parliamentarian.

Morris died in 1896 and, already severely curtailed by ill health, Webb's political activity came to end after he was one of the speakers at the final meeting of the Hammersmith Socialist Society on 6 January 1897; but he remained a socialist, albeit an extremely pessimistic one.[44] Urging patience in 1884, and recognizing that they had to deal with what men had become under commercialism, Webb had warned Morris that a major hindrance to socialist success would be the 'want of no man wanting to get anything out of it for himself', to which he had added:

> I think that the best of us English, if we were without money, could be 'got at': we, even we, who are well off could not be sure of ourselves if the pinch came to us. The English cannot live on a little—when food fails them, spirit fails also.[45]

In the event, the working classes opted for material reward, and reforms and political power achieved slowly through Parliament, in preference to the ideal life sought for them by Morris and Webb that might have been attained through revolution and subsequent radical social and economic changes.

It is sometimes wondered why, as an architect who was also a socialist, Webb did not design public buildings or working-class housing. In the first place, he was a Liberal for the first twenty-four years of his time in his own practice, well over half the total number. Many competitions were held for the design of public buildings during those years but, because of the way he both chose to and felt bound to work, he had no time to spare to prepare such speculative schemes. Furthermore, the notion of producing the sort of self-advertising designs that often succeeded in winning competitions was contrary to his philosophy. In 1864, having been invited to compete for the commission to design the Bradford Wool Exchange, he produced a design but did not finish the drawings, presumably having recognized these factors.[46] When in late 1864 or early 1865 he was approached by Lowthian Bell, on behalf of a subcommittee of directors, about becoming the assessor for the competition to design the Middlesbrough Exchange, he apparently refused to do so, though he was short of work at the time. His decisions about each of the exchange buildings would have been influenced by the deep antipathy he already felt for the commercialism they would epitomise. From 1866 to 1867, when he was involved with the designing of a new street for the Corporation of Newcastle upon Tyne, and from 1874 to 1878, during the designing and erection of St Martin's Church for the Brampton Church Building Committee, a great deal of his time and effort was wasted and he became extremely averse to committees. (These projects are covered in chapter 12.)

Local authority housing only began to appear towards the end of his career but, in any case, such a confirmed individualist as Webb could never have accepted being a permanent employee of a committee, especially after his experiences at Newcastle and Brampton. In 1861, his third major commission had been to design the terrace of combined dwellings, workshops, and shops in Worship Street, London, for Major Gillum (see chapter 11). Unfortunately, a similar philanthropic commission never came Webb's way again but, though around half his clients were extremely wealthy, the others were of modest means and, for the rich, he designed many commodious and well-equipped cottages for their estate workers with as much care as for the country mansions. Early in his career, he chose to become a self-styled 'house architect': to design buildings that would fulfil the general human needs, with each house suiting the way of life and requirements of the specific family and its staff.

Webb himself was convinced that his change of political allegiance in 1883 had not affected his architecture at the time or later. 'Though, as a real Socialist, I have some ideas on the "Theory of Life" [...] I do not think these "ideas" are detrimental to my considered way of making mortar,' he averred in 1899.[47] His philosophy of architectural design had been fully mature for over fifteen years by the time he became a socialist, and it did not change. His one design with a political intent, sketched in 1886, was a satirical joke: a grandiloquent Jubilee monument for Trafalgar Square, to be built at a cost of £15 million, the 'Capital to be raised by Limited liability company paying dividends, as best representing the religion of Vic²⁵ [sic] reign'.[48]

Webb's buildings and his approach to architectural design influenced the buildings of the London School Board, through its architect Edward Robson who had been kept informed of Webb's thinking in the 1860s and been urged to study his work by Warington Taylor.[49] The London schools influenced the design of others throughout England. Webb's younger followers, some of whom were socialists, carried his design philosophy into the London County Council housing department, and applied it to the houses in the garden suburbs and new towns, which in turn influenced the housing schemes of provincial local authorities.

Although in the event the parliamentarians had won the day, the efforts of Webb and Morris to bring about social change did have some success. They were the first creative artists to join the socialist movement and to attempt to help formulate its policy.[50] They succeeded in making the concepts that work should be rewarding in a spiritual sense, and that art and fellowship are essential to a full life, part of late-nineteenth-century British socialist theory. From there it passed into the twentieth-century philosophy of both the Communist and Labour Parties in Britain, and led Clement Atlee (1883–1967) to maintain that Morris meant more to the Labour Party than Marx.[51] Morris's role in this achievement was the greater. Webb was prevented by ill health and his meagre financial resources from leaving his work for days at a time to lecture around the country, as Morris was able to do. Furthermore, he knew that he was not as good a writer or speaker as his colleague, and that he would find the public exposure extremely distasteful. Significantly, he later referred to these years as his 'trying times of socialistic display'.[52] However, Webb's contribution was not nearly as insignificant as has sometimes been supposed. At the very least, he was a pillar of strength for the Socialist League during the vital period 1883 to 1888. He had taken an active role on its council and he had rescued its finances from the troubled waters into which Morris had cast them. He promulgated the ideas and ideals of the League amongst his wide acquaintance, and he gave Morris invaluable encouragement and support in his efforts in this field. Importantly, Webb had helped Morris to form his views on art and society, and had contributed to them, and in the early years of their active socialist endeavour, he had exercised a vital curb on Morris's impetuosity.

By 1910, Webb had found, as he told Hale White, that despite the 'detested contest in declamation either by lies or honest speech', he preferred the 'rule by Parliament of tongues, and seeming waste of words, to the rule of blood and thunder'.[53] In his late years, Webb had become 'neither an optimist or a pessimist but one in the middle', as he told Lethaby, when pondering whether or not the social and political changes that had occurred represented progress. 'The world is so wonderfully adjusted, I should not like to take it upon me to alter anything,' Webb continued, and added: 'it has a wonderful self-righting power like a ship.'[54]

Chapter 11

THE SMALLER HOUSES

Philip Webb designed many more small houses and cottages than he did country houses. During the 1860s, starting with his studio-houses, he developed his own approach to architectural design, with which he produced innovative but unassuming houses based on common sense, simplicity, and good building. Those built out of town were early examples of a new category – the small house in the country, which, ironically, had been made feasible by the railway system he disliked and the commercial or industrial profits of which he disapproved. His small houses in the country would today be regarded as large dwellings. They and the cottages, lodges, and coachmen's flats (see chapter 7 for the latter two types), were planned and detailed with the same care as his large country houses, and had many of the same attributes, including generously sized well-lit rooms, well-made fittings, and ample storage facilities. His houses of near date often have similarities of plan and detail; these did not stem from a lack of effort, however, but from his habit of making several experiments with a particular inspiration or detail. The smaller houses in the country and the cottages demonstrate Webb's sympathetic understanding of the varying needs of those who were to live or work in his buildings. The first to be considered are his three terraces of workers' dwellings, of which one is a very early scheme. These are followed by a pair of semi-detached cottages designed in 1899 at the end of Webb's career, built by Jane Morris as a memorial to her late husband William. These are investigated out of their chronological order because two documents written about them, by Webb, help to explain his thinking about the planning of small houses and his study and reflection of local vernacular buildings; these factors remained constant from the time his philosophy reached its full development in the 1860s. The twelve executed commissions for houses for middle-class occupiers, chiefly the clients themselves, then follow chronologically.

Workers' Terraces

The first of Webb's three terrace schemes was designed for his friend Major William James Gillum, for whom he had already built a small cottage for a gardener in Tottenham.[1] Gillum owned six dilapidated houses, with eight miserable cottages behind them, in the London district of Shoreditch – in 1861 an insalubrious area of mixed dwellings and trades. In 1851, the property had housed a hundred and two people, probably at a density of one room to each family.[2] Partly from necessity but chiefly as a benevolent experiment, Gillum decided to demolish the buildings and replace them with a terrace of six houses for independent artisans and their families: numbers 91 to 101 Worship Street, built between 1861 and 1863, each with a shop and workshop. Webb must have been delighted to receive the commission in 1861 as he was in need of work and also because the terrace would enable six families to experience a life in which creative handicraft would be fully integrated.[3] His pleasure would have been mitigated somewhat, however, by the fact that about 60% of the inhabitants of the demolished cottages would be forced to leave for slums elsewhere as the necessary economic rent of the new houses would be £75 a year against £20 for the existing houses.[4] The unusual philanthropic experiment was an economic and a social success for Gillum and for the fortunate among his tenants. The buildings have remained in tenancy for almost a hundred and forty years, until relatively recently chiefly by craftsmen and their families, as originally envisaged. The workshops have not survived and changes have been made to the interiors but the street front remains almost as Webb designed it.

The three-storey houses had generous living accommodation (WC, four bedrooms including two in the attics, sitting room, kitchen and scullery) plus a cellar store, a ground-floor shop, a back yard with a second WC, and a workshop over an open-fronted work-shed. Number 91 was wider than the others

because of a coach-way through to its yard; it had a smaller shop but also an office, more bedrooms, and enclosed ground-floor workshops, including a forge. On the street front, the projecting shop windows were made as wide as possible by having a single entrance to serve both house and shop in each case. They form a tiled lean-to that, like the main roof, is continuous along the terrace apart from the upward projections of the dividing walls that were decreed by the building regulations.[5] The oak-framed windows had canvas sun-blinds and wooden night shutters. The iron grilles above the windows and to the cellars below them are an early instance of Webb's penchant for using simple grids in metal or wood. Except at number 91, a deep porch with an angled wall that directs customers inside flanks the shop window. The upper wall of the terrace is supported on the ground floor by wide segmental arches behind the shop windows.

The houses are roofed in what were termed common flat tiles, and have walls of yellow London stock bricks, with a number of stone dressings. Three stone bands form horizontal lines interrupted only by

the handsome rainwater heads and the downpipes, with further horizontal emphasis being contributed by the regular second-floor sashes, the lead-covered parapet, and the cornice in which appears Webb's first use of brick dentils (timber eaves were forbidden by the building regulations).[6] Each unit has a wide pointed relieving arch on the first floor, containing twin sashes of which the segmental arches spring from a shaped stone at the top of the central mullion. Webb used this idiosyncratic detail again, for instance at Standen in 1891, but there the relieving arch is segmental too. The chimneys, with tall plain pots (not the shaped stone tops shown on Webb's drawings) and the large French-influenced dormers similar to that of Red House provide vertical accents which, with the porches and pointed relieving arches, express each dwelling individually within a unified whole.

The workshops at the rear were framed in oak, with brick-nogged panels, and had long strips of casement windows that predated by three decades those which Voysey and Frank Lloyd Wright (1869–1959) were to make one of their trademarks.

Above Numbers 91–101 Worship Street, Shoreditch, London (1861, constructed 1861–63): the street (south) front on which Webb's early liking for simple grids in metal or wood is demonstrated; the drinking fountain is in the foreground on the right

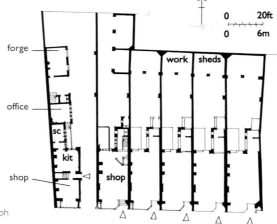

Below left Numbers
91–101 Worship Street:
rear view of two of the
houses (from a photograph
in Webb's collection,
copied by the author)

Below right Terrace of
farm-workers' cottages, East
Rounton, North Riding of
Yorkshire (North Yorkshire)
(completed 1875): part of
the south front of the terrace

The drinking fountain that forms a stop at the eastern end of the terrace has a finely moulded capital above a polygonal column, a combination that would appear in many of Webb's buildings, the majority being in timber. The fountain is of Red Peterhead granite 'rubbed perfectly smooth but not polished' according

to Webb's command; the design of the upper part was simplified considerably during execution, and the finial was modelled in wet clay and modified by the architect before carving commenced.[7]

The Worship Street terrace was criticised in 1863 in the *Builder* by an anonymous observer who thought that 'the degree of rudeness in the fittings' might make the properties difficult to let at an economic rent; in fact, they were similar to those of Red House and Sandroyd, and they were no hindrance, three dwellings being tenanted by the end of that year, and all by 1864.[8] The success of Gillum's Worship Street philanthropic venture probably lay behind George Howard's asking Webb in 1874 to design a terrace of dwellings for artisans and their families, to be built in Brampton, Cumbria. He produced three preliminary sketch designs, in one of which a gable to the street expresses each house individually, but the proposal was abandoned. The third of Webb's terrace commissions, a string of five dwellings for farm workers, the larger one at the east end being for the farm manager, was designed and built some time between 1872 and 1876 for the ironmaster and landowner Lowthian Bell on his Rounton Grange estate in the village of East Rounton, North Yorkshire.[9] The plan of the smaller cottages is interesting chiefly for the provision of a third bedroom in the roof, as such generous accommodation was unusual in agricultural cottages at the time. The exterior of the terrace is very pleasing. Some of the local farmsteads were of stone and some of red brick; the terrace and the farm

buildings behind it reflected the latter whilst Rounton Grange itself, designed by Webb a couple of years earlier (see chapter 7), was built in stone, but both the mansion, now demolished, and the terrace had red pantile roofs. Warm, cheerful, and attractive, on the ground floor the cottages have sash windows with herringbone tympana under segmental arches, reminiscent of Red House, with above them a bold string of angled bricks, paired first-floor sashes with lintels in the eaves, and a dormer window. Around 1868, doubtless inspired by Butterfield's use of them, the use of lintels hidden in the eaves had become a Webb custom – a highly influential one.

Morris Memorial Cottages, Kelmscott, Oxfordshire

In 1899, thirty-eight years after designing the Worship Street terrace, Webb designed the two Morris Memorial Cottages, which were built between 1902 and 1903 in Kelmscott, Oxfordshire, for Jane Morris. The cottages, with his letter to Jane Morris explaining the thinking behind the design, are particularly interesting because they illustrate the great care that Webb always took to understand the way of life of those who would inhabit his buildings and to ensure that his work would enhance their lives. They also demonstrate that he paid great attention to making the small cottages as well built and durable, and as much in harmony with the surroundings, as his country houses.

Webb was intimately familiar with Kelmscott Manor, the country home of the Morrises where he had often stayed, and with the vernacular architecture of Kelmscott village and the surrounding district; but nevertheless he inspected the site again before starting work. His first drawings were sent to Jane Morris with the explanatory letter.[10] He wrote that he had positioned the cottages at the north end of the field, bordering the village street, because there the old boundary wall would fix the width of the plot, and in itself would help to assimilate the cottages with the village. He had not expressed them individually, feeling that the 'broader in effect the 2 cottages could be made the less of upstart in character would be the result', but he had made them identical apart from being handed, and had set them under 'two simple gabled roofs crossing each other', with one of the wider gables facing the road. This arrangement had the added advantage of being economical. He had placed the entrances at opposite ends of the block to

best 'keep the peace of the place', and sited the wells in the front gardens to avoid contamination from the earth closets (ECs) at the rear.

To give the families 'breathing space', he had provided each cottage with a single living room – the 'keeping room'– instead of a small one and the 'usual little <u>waste</u> room' or parlour, and had made the dwellings large enough to allow three bedrooms upstairs. He believed that the keeping rooms should face the road but to admit sunlight he had given them an east and west window respectively, set in a recess for a 'work table'. Each cottage had a larder and a washhouse off the hall, and a yard with sheds and a covered way in which the mother 'could do a good deal of wet work out of doors', and safely air 'her pots and pans as well as her children'. He suggested that if an indication of the memorial role of the dwellings were desired, it should be placed between the upper windows in the north gable, and take the form of a 'rudimentary tree and a couple of birds, to signify to those who cared '"the town of the tree"' from a poem by Morris.[11] Later, Webb made a beautiful design of Morris sitting under an oak tree, which was carved in stone by George Jack, and placed on the central gable of the cottages, facing the road.

By May 1900, the working drawings for the cottages had been completed and a price had been requested from a builder, Joseph Bowley of Lechlade.[12] Webb wrote detailed instructions in a notebook for George Jack, who was to direct the construction.[13] Jack was to explain to Bowley the quality of work required, and to make a thorough inspection of the site and the quarries from which the various types of

Right Morris Memorial
Cottages: the *Morris in the
Home Mead* plaque,
designed by Webb, carved
by George Jack, and set
between the first-floor
windows on the gable facing
the village street (© Helen
Elletson, William Morris
Society)

Below Number 19 Park Hill
(Wensum Lodge),
Carshalton, Surrey (1867–68,
constructed 1868): the
south front, from the road

stone would be taken for the rough yard walls, the
ashlar walls of the cottages, the paving slabs, and the
roofing slates, and to note the tools used for finishing
the stone. Webb ordered that plain ashlar 'should be
axed, and only shaped work should be chizelled [sic]'.
Examples of the ashlar finish he required were to be

sought amongst old local buildings and shown to
Bowley, to whom Jack must explain precisely how
the stones in the various parts of the walls and
chimneys were to be laid. Jack was to explain that
the stones and the bricks of the inner leaf were to be
particularly well-bedded in lime mortar to prevent
the escape of the 'Blue Lias lime concrete' that would
fill the cavity to waterproof the walls because of the
porosity of the local limestone. He must tell the
builder that the grouting was to be done in the old
local manner, which left little of the porous stone
exposed. Bowley's joiners' shop and timber stocks
were to be inspected, together with the sources,
characteristics, and quality of the proposed bricks,
limes, cement, and damp-proof course materials.
Samples of these materials were to be brought to
Webb, and old buildings in which they had been
used were to be sought. 'All local materials fit for
their purpose, if good, would be preferred,' he stated.

Through careful design, observation, and
investigation, and insistence on exactly the type and
quality of finishes he had specified, Webb had
succeeded yet again in making his building an
entirely satisfactory addition to its surroundings. The
cottages reflected and were in harmony with nearby
older dwellings without copying them; were of an
attractive appearance that would weather well; and
were not pretentious or self-advertising. Morris would
surely have been delighted with these commemorative
cottages, which are a testament to his own belief in
the value of craftsmanship, and to the design
philosophy and expertise of his old friend Webb.
Small semi-detached cottages, designed by Webb in
1891 and 1896 respectively, were also built at Great
Tangley Manor where they are a handed pair, each
with a gable on the entrance front and with brick,
roughcast, and weatherboarded walls; and at Standen,
where they are expressed individually in the same
stone, brick, and weatherboarding as the main house.[14]

Number 19 Park Hill, Carshalton, Surrey

Number 19 Park Hill, Carshalton, Surrey (later known
as Wensum Lodge, now in Greater London), designed
between 1867 and 1868, was the first of Webb's smaller
houses other than the studio-houses to be designed for
a client's own use. The client was William Hale White
– a civil servant and, under the pseudonym Mark
Rutherford, a journalist and author who had strong
views on the sanctity of home life, and who believed
that a house should impart a sense of comfort and

express something of the life of the specific family.[15] Having moved his family from several unsatisfactory houses already, he was annoyed by Ruskin's assertion of 1865 in the *Daily Telegraph* that people were happy with their speculatively built 'blotches'; White wrote to the editor, recounting his search for a good house, describing the discomforts of the best he could find at an affordable rent, and asking whether Ruskin could say if it were possible to build a 'solid and plain' house near London 'fit for a human being to live in?'.[16] Correspondence between White and Ruskin followed, and in October 1867 Ruskin recommended Webb to White as an architect who would give 'perfectly sound and noble work for absolutely just price'.[17] The following year this resulted in the construction of what proved to be an entirely satisfactory house, with which White was delighted, and in the architect and client forming a close friendship that would last until White's death in 1913.[18] In 1896, rooms were built over the scullery range but apart from this and the throwing together of the hall and parlour, the building is essentially unchanged and remains a private dwelling.

Hale White's house is particularly interesting for the light it throws on the extent to which Webb allowed his clients' practical needs and desires to influence his buildings. White's obsessions with privacy and adequate heating and against noise and draughts exercised considerable influence on the plan. The drawing room was placed at the rear of the house to ensure even greater privacy than that afforded by the site itself, which rises steeply from the road. Internal walls are of nine-inch brickwork to reduce sound transmission, ground-floor windows originally had stout external shutters, and there are no chilly second-floor bedrooms. An entrance porch and a lobby reduce draughts, and three doors, the hall, and the rear lobby originally separated the kitchen from the dining room to reduce noise. White suffered from claustrophobia, so the four bedrooms are exceptionally well lit, with extra light being reflected from the sloping ceilings. For maximum warmth, fireplaces are on internal walls, and have or had convected warm air grates. Heat from the fires in the bedrooms was supplemented by warmed air from the hall fire, which rose through a well in the passage floor. Rainwater was collected in a tank in the yard from which it was pumped to the scullery, and also in a cistern in the roof to serve the upstairs WC which, with the linen cupboard, is warmed by the kitchen flue.

At present, because of the ubiquitous early- to mid-twentieth-century semi-detached dwellings, the twin gables of White's attractive house suggest that it is two cottages; but this would not have seemed so in the 1860s and 1870s. The bricks, the tiles hanging on the upper walls, and the roof tiles were to have been red; presumably to cut costs, stock bricks varying from yellow to grey, and grey roofing slates, were used instead. However, the red tile-hanging gave the building a warm, welcoming, and cheerful appearance that was enlivened by white window frames and shutters. The interior was decorated with Morris, Marshall, Faulkner & Company products.

Upwood Gorse, Caterham, Surrey

In 1868, John Tomes (1815–1895), one of the earliest eminent dental surgeons, commissioned Webb's second smaller individual house, Upwood Gorse, which was built in the countryside near Caterham, Surrey. Completed in 1869, and possibly intended for use only at weekends initially, it was designed with Tomes's eventual retirement in mind.[19] Webb placed the house on the plateau of the exposed site, from

Below Upwood Gorse, Caterham, Surrey (1868): the north-east and south-east fronts, showing on the former the extension added by Webb in 1888 to the study and main bedroom

Right Upwood Gorse:
plan of the ground floor

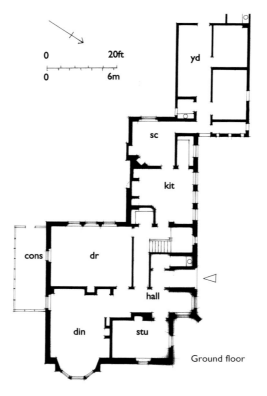

Far Right Upwood Gorse:
the entrance front, after the
Webb additions of c. 1873
and of 1876 (from a
photograph in Webb's
collection)

Ground floor

which the land falls rapidly to the south and west, and
sheltered it from the north and east with an L-shaped
stable and coach-house block. The latter contained
one of his characteristic first-floor flats for the
coachmen or grooms, with generous sunlit rooms off
a north passage. Webb extended the house later but

originally it consisted of a four-bedroom two-storey
family block with, on its south-west side, a single-
storey range of domestic offices that had a small yard
and lesser offices off the north-west corner.[20] This
long arrangement protected the sunlit sloping area,
on which and around the house Webb and Tomes
created a garden; with the additional aid of judiciously
positioned walls, hedges, and shrubs, it had sheltered
parts whatever the wind direction.

The red-brick main block, tile-hung above the
ground floor, has a dominant, red-tiled pyramid roof,
with small hipped dormers slightly resembling ears and
bold plain stacks rising above it. The hipped roof of
the stair tower originally finished just below the main
eaves but was raised in 1876 when Webb extended the
porch with an almost flat lead-roofed canopy on white
posts, and added two floors above the enlarged offices.
The original porch, with a brick barrel vault, was the
first of Webb's many wide round-arch main entrances.
Whilst the house was being built or during the 1876
enlargement, the glazed garden porch off the dining
and drawing rooms on the plan, was changed by Webb
into a wider and longer room with a long horizontal
band of windows and a tiled roof over a coved match-
boarded ceiling like that of the bay window in the
drawing room of Arisaig House (1863).[21] In 1888, he
extended the study and main bedroom above it north-
eastwards and added to the drawing room a wide bay
window, containing a half-glazed china cupboard and
a seat over a concealed radiator. Nothing is known
about the original interior decoration.

As with all Webb's houses set in gardens, as soon
as the first part of it had been completed, climbing
plants and shrubs were placed along the frontages to
soften the walls and merge the building with the
garden. Such an effect was particularly desirable for

Right Upwood Gorse: the
entrance porch on the
north-west front, with the
outer part added by Webb
in 1876

Upwood Gorse, an unpretentious but strikingly red and, in its first stage, gaunt building. Tomes was pleased with his new home, and spent the almost twenty years of his retirement there, entertaining his friends and conducting the campaign to improve dentistry for which he was knighted in 1886. In the 1960s, the coachman's flat and coach-house were combined into a single dwelling and the main house was subdivided sensitively; at present it forms three dwellings with most of Webb's fittings remaining.

Red Barns, Coatham, Redcar, North Riding of Yorkshire

Later in 1868, Webb designed an equally unassuming house, Red Barns, for Thomas Hugh Bell, the son of Isaac Lowthian Bell. Before joining the family firm, Hugh had received a sound science-based education in several countries.[22] In 1867 he married Mary Shields, who according to a family friend shared Hugh's 'zeal for liberalization and progress' and 'taste for art and literature', and they began married life in the second-floor suite that Webb had added to Bell's parents' home, Washington Hall (see chapter 9).[23] In the hope that sea air would improve his wife's poor health, Hugh Bell asked Webb in 1868 to design a house to be built on a two-acre site near the sea at Coatham, a small fishing village near

Left Red Barns: the south front, showing Webb's additions of 1881 (the large chimney has been removed from the hip roof of the schoolroom block)

Redcar in the North Riding of Yorkshire (now Redcar & Cleveland Borough) which was in the first stages of being developed as a dormitory for Middlesbrough.[24] Sadly, Mary did not revive as had been hoped, and she died in the new house in 1871 after the birth of her son Maurice, leaving Bell with two children, the first being Gertrude (1868–1926), who became a famous traveller, archaeologist, and government servant. In 1876, Hugh married his second wife Florence née Olliffe (1851–1930), by whom he soon had three more children; a schoolroom wing became necessary.[25] Designed by Webb in 1881 and built the following year, it was connected by a two-storey laundry to the stable

Left Red Barns, Coatham, Redcar, North Riding of Yorkshire (Redcar and Cleveland; 1868, completed by mid–1870): the entrance (north) front, showing the additions Webb made on this side of the house in 1881

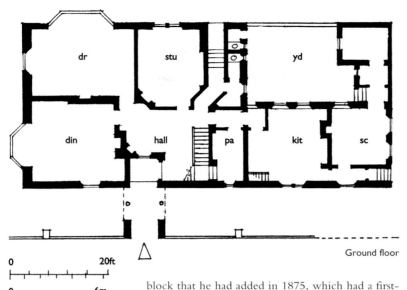

dr | stu | yd

din | hall | pa | kit | sc

Ground floor

0   20ft

0   6m

Above Red Barns: plan of the ground floor

Below Red Barns: as first built, from the south-east (© University of Newcastle upon tyne)

building, including the parts added by the school on the site of the stables.

The site Bell leased had open countryside to the south, with views of the Cleveland Hills. The railway formed the southern boundary; Bell was able to board the train near his house for daily travel to the firm's offices in Middlesbrough and for frequent business trips to London. Webb placed the house along the long northern boundary flanking the new road, Kirkleatham Street, to create as large a garden as possible and shelter it from the frequent northeasterly gales, and to leave room to the west for the later stables. He extended a covered way from the inset porch to the road to give the family and their guests some protection on arriving at and departing from the house. The ground-floor plan was similar to that of Upwood Gorse, but with a two-storey stair-hall and better use made of southerly aspects. The six bedrooms on the first floor were served by a long east-west passage that was a precursor of the longitudinal cross-passages of Webb's later country houses. The children's block of 1881 had a basement playroom beneath a schoolroom and a play-passage with access to the hall and to the garden.

Red Barns is less gaunt and more attractive than is Upwood Gorse but is still surprisingly unpretentious for the home of a third-generation industrialist, its appeal like that of Red House depending upon its materials, proportions, and basic forms. The main entrance in the porch, with a common ledged, braced, and battened door, is much less imposing than the Georgian doorways of many of the farmhouses of the district. A deep angled-brick string in the same multihued local bricks (Webb had specified seconds which vary from bright red to dark purples and browns) provides the only decorative element, and it too has a functional role as the windowsill. Exterior woodwork is kept to the absolute minimum because of the exposure of the site. The roofs are covered in red-clay pantiles, the material that had replaced thatch in the district long before the 1860s. These tiles are too robustly profiled to have been entirely successful on the small pyramid-roofed dormers of the attic bedrooms; thereafter, Webb seldom used them on such elements.

Trellises for climbing plants were fixed to the east and south walls, presaging those added to Smeaton Manor in the late 1870s (see chapter 7). Webb created a sheltered exterior seating recess with a rear wall warmed by the kitchen range for Florence Bell,

block that he had added in 1875, which had a first-floor flat for the groom and gardener. Also in 1881, Webb added a dressing room and bathroom off the major bedroom, and on the street front, a small hall for the servants with a bedroom above it. In 1897, he enlarged the bay window in the drawing room. For part of the twentieth century, Red Barns housed the headmaster and the boarding pupils of Sir William Turner's School, Redcar, during which period several changes and additions were made to the service quarters. Fortunately, the family quarters, used as the headmaster's residence, remain much as Webb had designed them apart from the removal by a subsequent purchaser of many of his fittings in the 1980s. The present owners live in the family quarters and run a private hotel in the western part of the

as he had done for Tomes's wife at Upwood Gorse. The later Red Barns additions are in the same materials as the original work, apart from some timber framing on the west wall of the stables (demolished) but new window and wall details clearly express the children's wing as an addition. Webb did not attempt to express the plan of it, however. The play-passage began in the new block, where it had a large window identical to that of the schoolroom, and continued as a single-storey tile-roofed element, with a row of small casements.

The staircase and gallery balustrades are simply boarded in oak, like Red House but with plain newel posts. The oak flooring inlaid with ebony strips in the dining room is more sophisticated. This room had a half-glazed corner cupboard and a sideboard by Webb, whilst the drawing room had a glass-fronted wall-mounted bookcase and a convected warm air grate, designed by Webb and made by Longden, in a characteristic surround; these and the study and major bedrooms were curtained and papered with Morris & Co.'s products, the paint colours being chosen by William Morris to match the papers.[26] The drawing room had blue silk damask in the Oak pattern on the walls, the blue *Peacock and Dragon* woollen material for curtains and upholstery, and the hand-knotted Hammersmith *Redcar carpet*, with an ivory background and a foliage pattern mostly in blues, designed for the room by Morris, c. 1879–81.[27]

Red Barns is obviously a dwelling but as is suggested by its name – one of the earliest of the soon-to-become-fashionable farm-associated names – it reflects the farm buildings of the district more than the farmhouses.[28] Charming, unassuming, and almost dateless, it is the antithesis of the imposing, highly ornamented Gothic and Italianate villas, perched above basement kitchens, envisaged by the landowner and illustrated on the advertisements for the sites.[29] Like Upwood Gorse, Red Barns reflected the taste of its owner more than his status.[30] Both these buildings are much plainer than houses in the so-called 'Queen Anne' style, the initial development of which Webb had unintentionally set in motion in the 1860s with his studio-houses and which, after input from other architects, became deliberately picturesque and highly popular, particularly in seaside resorts such as Redcar (see chapter 5).

Oast House, Hayes Common, Kent

Oast House, Webb's next small house in the country, was designed for an aristocratic client, albeit a far

Left Red Barns: the drawing room in 1905, with Florence Bell reading (© University of Newcastle upon Tyne)

from typical one. Lord Sackville Cecil (1847–98), a younger son of Robert Cecil, the second Marquess of Salisbury, had trained as a railway and a telegraph engineer after taking his degree at Cambridge.[31] In 1872, he asked Webb to design a house to replace two old cottages in an orchard that had been enclosed in 1773 from the surrounding Hayes Common in Kent (now in Greater London).[32] Cecil might have been expecting to get on well with Webb, with whom he had in common a great capacity for conscientious work and sympathy for those in difficulties. However, during construction in 1873, a problem arose, probably as a result of Cecil attempting to direct the building work himself, which certainly Webb would have taken as an insult to his experience and skill. Charles Vinall took over

Below Red Barns: a detail of the *Redcar* carpet designed by William Morris in c. 1879–1881 for the drawing room (Collection of Mr Thomas Hugh Bell, on loan to the Society of Antiquaries of London at Kelmscott Manor)

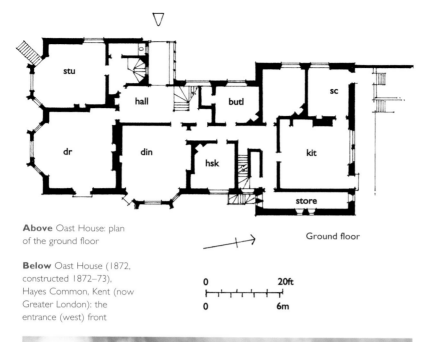

Above Oast House: plan of the ground floor

Below Oast House (1872, constructed 1872–73), Hayes Common, Kent (now Greater London): the entrance (west) front

Ground floor

0   20ft

0   6m

the supervising of construction; Webb refused to accept any fee, and returned the client's cheque.[33] Ultimately, Cecil must have been satisfied with his new home as he lived in it for the remainder of his life without making changes. Oast House, still almost as first built externally, remains an unusual, extremely attractive single residence, and the stables are a house under separate ownership.

Webb positioned Oast House so as to preserve as many of the old fruit trees as possible and to create large gardens to the east and south. The minor offices are at the north end near the road, at a lower level than the main block because of the rising ground. The groom's cottage in the eastern end of the stable block, south-east of the house, doubled as a lodge (now a dwelling in separate ownership). The main block contains the usual major rooms for a house of its size – dining room, drawing room, and study – and a brick-vaulted basement laboratory for Cecil's electrical and mechanical experiments, served by an adjacent spiral stair and a WC. Access to the garden is provided from the laboratory, study, and dining room.

In general, the exterior reflects the prominent hipped roofs topped by a massive chimney of the fifteenth-century Wealden timber-framed houses; but the west front, with two gables and off-centre porch, echoes those of medieval manor houses in stone. A symmetrical effect is created on the east front by four dominant gabled dormers and four brick chimneys with corbelled tops. The red-tiled roof sweeps down in a cat-slide to cover the bay window of the dining room and the long pantry at the northern end. On the south front, the roof covered a balcony (subsequently altered and glazed) which served two of the major bedrooms and was an early result of the interest in healthy living that was then developing.

In Oast House, Webb celebrated the wide variety of locally available materials. The walls, with their subtle blending of colour and texture that contrasts well with the red roof, are of local squared ragstone rubble, roughly finished except for the quoins, with dressings and some patches of walling in red brick. The two gables of the west front, and the gabled dormers on the eastern side, have characteristic Webb bargeboards with small dentils, and white-painted boarding in the upper parts. The main porch has pleasingly robust oak framing, with open trelliswork panels above a long seat on the north side, and an almost flat lead-covered roof. The L-shaped lesser offices are roofed in red pantiles, edged at the eaves

with small tiles. On the side of these domestic offices that faces the kitchen yard is one of Webb's characteristic covered ways with bracketed wooden posts, whilst the wall flanking the drive has no openings and is faced with tarred weatherboarding, a traditional material for farm buildings in Kent. The coach-house has the same roof tiles as the main block, and similarly detailed chimneys, but has walls of London stock bricks.

Nether Hall Farm, Thurston, Suffolk

Webb's next small house, Nether Hall Farm in Thurston, Suffolk, was designed in 1875 and completed by early 1876 for the brewer and agriculturist Edward Greene, MP, for whom the architect's enlargement of his country house Nether Hall in Pakenham was then in progress (see chapter 9). Greene had served on the Committee for Artisans' and Labourers' Dwellings in 1866 and held advanced views on the importance of providing good accommodation for employees. He asked Webb to design a house and farm buildings for the use of Matthew Witt, a man of considerable local standing, who managed Greene's five hundred acres and thirty-four agricultural workers. Webb referred to the buildings as Nether Hall Farm but later they ceased to form part of the Nether Hall estate and became known as Manor Farm; this change and the location in the parish of Thurston not Pakenham led to the Webb connection being forgotten until the author identified the building in 1990. With great good fortune, this fine example of Webb's smaller houses, now listed Grade II★, had suffered little change apart from the loss of the ground-floor fireplaces. New owners, appreciating its quality, had recently had it sympathetically refurbished by an architect and a designer, each of whom had recognized it as a fine

house of the Arts and Crafts period.[34] The original farm buildings remain in reasonably good condition. To avoid confusion with the present Nether Hall Farm, which is in close proximity to the hall, Webb's farmhouse is referred to below by its present name.

Webb used as the initial Idea for Manor Farm the form and double-pile plan of the late-seventeenth- and early-eighteenth-century farmhouses of East Anglia. This type is common also in north-east Yorkshire but he had not reflected it in Red Barns, a fact that shows how much his interest in symmetry had increased in the early 1870s. An inset porch leads into a central hall, flanked on one side by the drawing room and farm office and on the other by the dining room and kitchen, with a cloakroom and WC under the half landing. The low L-shaped wing at the rear, with a characteristic covered way, contains the minor domestic offices and partly encloses a kitchen yard.

Like those that inspired it, the south-facing, red-brick house has a hipped roof and five windows about a central entrance; but only the ground floor has vertical sash windows, and the usual pillared or pedimented entrance is replaced by an inset porch with a wide round and recessed arch, rising not from vertical supports but from the robust imposts Webb preferred, in this case in rubbed brick, the traditional method of shaping bricks that he had been one of the nineteenth-century architects to revive when he used it extensively on the new wing of Cranmer Hall, Norfolk in 1864 (see chapter 9). It echoes the slightly more elaborate arch with rubbed brick mouldings on

Left Oast House: from the south-east

Below Nether Hall Farm, Thurston, Suffolk: plan of the ground floor

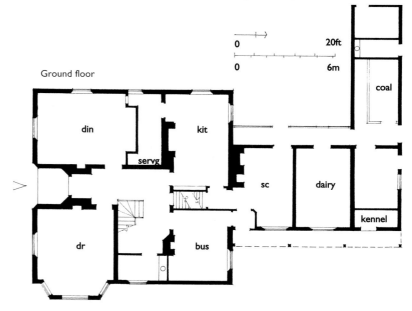

Right Nether Hall Farm (Manor Farm), Thurston, Suffolk (1875, constructed 1875–76): the entrance (south) front (the dormer between the chimneys is possibly a replacement)

Far right Nether Hall Farm: from the north-east

the porch that Webb was adding to Nether Hall. The two niches housing wooden seats in the Manor Farm porch have half domes in rubbed and gauged brick. Each sash window has a round relieving arch with a herringbone brickwork tympanum; these are similar but not identical to those of the East Rounton farm terrace and were repeated in a slightly different form at Smeaton Manor a few months later. A corbelled, dentilated, and tile-topped brick string-sill, appropriately for East Anglia being even bolder than the one on the East Rounton terrace, circles the building above the arches. The first-floor casement windows have lintels in the eaves and partly canted ceilings, which make the height of this floor unusually low on the elevations. Four large chimneys,

Right Nether Hall Farm: the entrance porch

with tops similar to those Webb was adding to Nether Hall, crown the red-clay pantile roof, which has flat tiles at the eaves. It is broken by two pantiled dormers extending east and west respectively like those of Upwood Gorse. The bay window on the east elevation was added either as construction progressed or in the early twentieth century by another architect at the time when the ground-floor sashes appear to have been replaced.[35] The timber balustrade round the central lead flat is a late-twentieth-century addition.

The interior of Manor Farm is characteristic, with generously sized, gracious, and well-lit rooms; a large half landing and a plain staircase balustrade with knobbed newels as in several of Webb's small houses, each one slightly different; and bedroom fireplaces with tiled jambs and bracketed mantel shelves. Roof timbers are exposed in the major bedrooms, and the one-inch iron rods that strengthen the corners of the hips. Iron rods, which by the mid-1870s had become characteristic of Webb's roof construction, also appear in the agricultural buildings at Manor Farm – a group of a similar character (apart from having some locally traditional weatherboarding) to the red-brick, pantile-roofed farm buildings he designed at about the same time for Lowthian Bell at East Rounton. Both groups are of pleasing appearance, and have proved to be practical and durable throughout many decades, despite the changes in agricultural practice.

Numbers 2 & 4 Redington Road, Hampstead, London

Webb used the same Idea as for Manor Farm for his next small houses, a pair of semi-detached dwellings, numbers 2 and 4 Redington Road, Hampstead, designed and built in 1876 for William Chisolm (brother-in-law of Hale White), who retained one for his own use.[36] The houses stand above the road on the north side and are most attractive and welcoming in appearance, and commodious and convenient inside. They have suffered little change, especially number two, and at present are still single private dwellings.

The plan of each house resembles that of Manor Farm, with a dining room, drawing room, study, and kitchen in the four corner positions; a central hall with a cloakroom and WC under the half landing; four major bedrooms and a bathroom on the first floor; and in the attics, two further bedrooms, a second bathroom, and a tank room and store room. The building regulations required the dividing wall to project on the elevations and above the roof, which decreed their expression as two units albeit under a shared single hipped roof. These identical but handed, south-facing houses are built of London stock bricks, with tile-hanging on the first floor in the same small red tiles as cover the roof, and finely moulded brick tops to the tall chimneys. Unusually for a Webb building, the walls have a plinth, with an angled top without a drip like the stone plinths of seventeenth-century yeomen's houses. Commodious inset porches with recessed round arches on corbelled and rubbed brick imposts replace the ornamented central doorway of the Queen Anne houses, as at Manor Farm. The porches are flanked by bay windows: twin-sashed, flat-roofed rectangular ones for the dining rooms, canted ones with four sashes for the drawing rooms. The brick mullions with corbelled tops have a pilaster-like effect. A narrow plaster cornice breaks round the simple brick pilasters that flank the first-floor sashes to give a good stop to the tiling, a detail that Webb used later the same year for Smeaton Manor. The bedroom windows on the entrance front have louvred external shutters. The stair windows, on the side elevations, have arched upper panes similar to those of Oast House. The single-storey office ranges at the rear are in the same brick as the main block but have pantiled roofs edged in small tiles, again like Oast House.

Four Gables, near Brampton, Cumberland

In September 1875, George Howard, on behalf of the trustees of the Earl of Carlisle, asked Webb to design a house – Four Gables – for John Grey, the agent of the Naworth Estate, which he did early the following year.[37] After the clerk of works to the estate, Thomas Warwick, had submitted what Webb considered a 'most extravagant price' for the house alone, without the stables, competitive tenders for the separate trades

were requested by advertisement.[38] Grey feared that individual contractors would not 'pull well together', but Webb accepted prices from some of them, inserting contractual clauses that required all trades not to hinder one another and to submit weekly to him daily records of work done, materials used, and all extras.[39] Warwick caused trouble and delays in early 1877 by permitting work to begin on the walls before

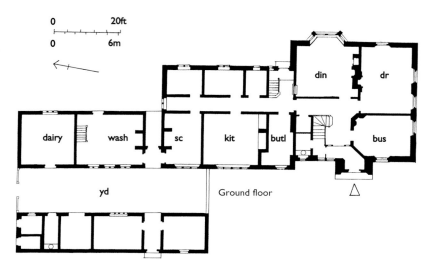

0   20ft

0   6m

din

dr

dairy   wash   sc   kit   butl   bus

yd   Ground floor

Above Four Gables: plan of the ground floor

Below Four Gables: the entrance (west) front of the tower and part of the kitchen wing

Webb had inspected the foundation trenches, and by passing inferior bricks and allowing the damp-proof course to be laid in a careless manner. Suspected of doing this to bring the cost nearer his own figure, he was dismissed from his post and the construction of the house was supervised by his replacement, William Marshall.[40] Few changes have been made to the house, which was named by Webb after the most prominent features and has been a privately owned, well-maintained residence for many decades.

Four Gables is similar in size to Manor Farm but of very different appearance, as befits its location in what was then Cumberland (now Cumbria). Each of these handsome houses has an appropriately commanding and dignified presence for the status

and role of the tenants. The site chosen for the agent's house is in high, open Border country near Naworth Castle. It presented Webb with a more appropriate opportunity to use as the initial Idea a pele, the distinctive defensive building of the Border region, such as had inspired his early design for Rounton Grange (see chapter 7). Four Gables, which is built entirely in the attractive local red sandstone and roofed with the green slates of the region, consists of a square, three-storey tower containing the drawing room, dining room, and study on the ground floor, and two floors of bedrooms, the upper ones partly in the roof, with a bathroom on the first floor. The domestic offices and servants' quarters occupy a lower wing stretching northwards, which corresponds to the barmkin of a pele; a stable block lies further north still. To retain the symmetry of the elevation, the porch is placed in the centre of the west front, creating a staggered entrance, off which is a cloakroom and WC conveniently near the agent's study-cum-business room.

Four Gables exemplifies Webb's free and inventive adaptation of an Idea. A pele has only two gables, for example, and no bay window such as the one in the dining room which gives views over the fine gardens surrounding the house. The four dominant gables, three of them identical, edge the cruciform roof of the tower block, which is surmounted at the centre by a massive rectangular chimney. A string course runs round the tower across each wall beneath the gable and the windows in it, echoing the rectangular hood-moulds of the latter, with square modillions like inverted crenellations under it at each end, which typify Webb's 'faith in the elementary', as Pevsner points out.[41] The deeply projecting spouts above them, functional in heavy rain, are pele features. The handsome round arch of the porch, springing from kneelers (corbels), is derived from that of a niche in the courtyard of the nearby castle. Webb's Gothic Revival training and his liking for symmetry led to three awkward pig's ears: the ceiling of the inner part of the porch had to rise sharply to avoid obstructing the window; the floor of the half landing crosses another window; and a bedroom wall had to be angled to allow the central window over the porch to light the landing.

Webb was not disturbed to find that through 'want of aesthetics' the new agent, Christopher Stephenson, disliked the house; if he wished, the architect wrote, he could '"grain" it from top to bottom – at his own expense'.[42] Ultimately, the two were on good terms and, after consulting Webb, Stephenson chose wallpapers from Morris & Co., then the architect inspected and approved his choices. Assuming that most of the woodwork would be painted white, Webb advised that it should match a 'clean piece of parchment of medium colour', except in the sitting room and bedrooms where it should be 'painted "bastard flat"' because that would keep its colour and not turn yellow; if a positive colour were to be used in any room, Webb pointed out that the service provided by Morris's manager, of sending a board painted to suit the paper, would save 'great trouble and expense in getting the right colour'.[43]

The Vicar's House, Brampton, Cumberland

In 1877, undoubtedly at George Howard's prompting, the trustees commissioned another small house, the Vicar's House, from Webb, who by then had become the official architect to the Naworth Estate.[44] The house, designed as a vicarage to be rented from the estate by the incumbent, was built near St Martin's, the parish church of Brampton then under construction to Webb's design (see chapter 12). Having served as the vicarage for only a few years, the

building was sold and became a private dwelling under the name Green Lane House; at present, almost unchanged externally and altered as little as possible internally, it serves as a residential home for the elderly.

Perhaps to the annoyance of the wife of the Reverend Henry Whitehead – whom Webb termed the 'Sally Brass of Brampton' after the domineering woman in Dickens's *The Old Curiosity Shop* who delighted in aggravating people – Webb took his Idea for the Vicar's House not from a defensive tower but from the farmhouses of the area, and provided the

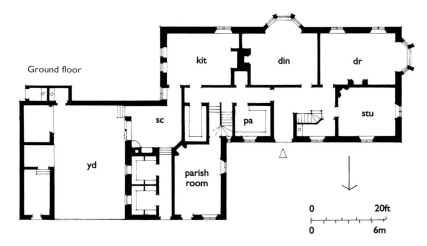

Above The Vicar's House: plan of the ground floor

Below The Vicar's House (Green Lane House), Brampton, Cumberland (Cumbria) 1877, constructed 1877–79): the south front

Above The Vicar's House: from the north-west (from a photograph by the author)

requested accommodation in an appropriately unpretentious and welcoming building for the shepherd of a human flock.[45] Webb adopted the cat-slide roof found on local farms for his church, Four Gables (on the rear of the kitchen wing), and the vicar's house, on the latter employing it on the entrance front and inserting in it a long horizontal dormer to light the staircase and first-floor passage. The front is basically symmetrical but he did not hesitate to partly lose this by placing the parish room projection in the most convenient but asymmetrical position. Although this house lacks the harsh muscularity of some of Street's and of Butterfield's vicarages, it can look a trifle severe in monochrome photographs. In reality, however, the red sandstone and green slates being given full play, the Vicar's House, long and low like the farmhouses, is a most pleasing and interesting building, with a two-storey bay window of unusual design roughly in the centre of the south front.

New Place, Welwyn, Hertfordshire

In the same year, 1877, Webb began designing a house, New Place, for his brother Henry (Harry) Speakman Webb (c. 1827–1911), who had a general practice in Welwyn, Hertfordshire, where he had lived with their two unmarried sisters since 1864.[46] The final drawings were prepared in December 1878, and the house was built between 1879 and 1880 by a local builder, William Lawrence of Datchworth.

The L-shaped house consists of a long gabled wing running east to west and containing the dining room and study at the eastern end, the stair hall and surgery in the centre, and the kitchen at the western end. The drawing room occupies a shorter, wider

and gabled wing, with a slightly lower roof, extending southwards at right angles from the dining-room end of the longer wing. Dr Webb saw many of his patients in their homes, so his surgery was chiefly an office and a dispensary from which their servants collected medicines. For greater security, the approach to it was through the kitchen yard that was overseen by his domestic staff. The house had a piped gas supply but no bathroom and no WCs. Drainage from WCs was not yet completely safe and Webb disliked cesspools because they made it 'impossible at times to avoid a bad smell'; properly managed ECs were free from odours and provided a supply of good manure that was much appreciated by keen amateur gardeners, such as his brother and himself.[47]

New Place is a compact, well-balanced, and pleasing composition of gables, roofs, tall plain chimneys with hipped and tiled tops and tall red pots, and bay windows. The twin buttresses on the short-wing gable are derived from those of a medieval example seen and sketched by Webb in 1857 at Lindisfarne Priory in Northumberland.[48] The flues from scullery and kitchen fireplaces, on the west gable, and that of the bedroom over the kitchen curve together under tiled shoulders to emerge in a central stack. Apart from a limited amount of white woodwork and white plaster cornices, the building is red, like Red House and Red Barns. It is decidedly English and domestic in character but the composition and the textures give the house something of the pleasing and vigorous barbaric element that Webb had found and admired in the small Byzantine churches he had studied in books.

Inside New Place, Webb created contrasts of space such as were seldom if ever seen in small houses at the time, by forming an enfilade that runs east to west through the full length of the building from the entrance porch, through the central hall, and into the bay window of the dining room. Access to the south garden is provided partway along it, opposite a fitted bench seat in a recess. An unusual staircase, a prototype of the one he was to design for Coneyhurst a few years later (described later in this chapter), adds interest in the hall. Webb had intended to use a newel stair similar to that of Smeaton Manor but instead decided on one surrounding a square open well, with some of its oak newel posts extending from floor to ceiling. The dining room contained a fine oak organ case which was illustrated in 1910 by Charles H B Quennell, who averred that the 'simple

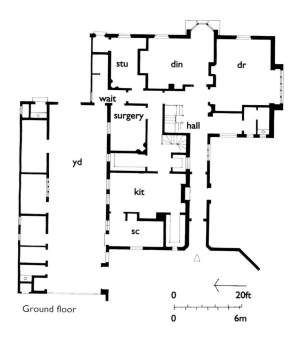

Ground floor

0   20ft

0   6m

Far left New Place: plan of the ground floor

Left New Place, Welwyn, Hertfordshire (1877–78, constructed 1879–80): the entrance porch and the north gable

lines of its panelled framing, combined with the delicacy of the moulded architrave surrounding the upper grilles' created a 'very charming whole', the charm coming from its austerity.[49] Hardwood items throughout the house, which was furnished with a mixture of the Firm's products and old family pieces, were left natural but most of the woodwork was painted white – such as the ceilings, friezes, passages, and back staircase – or in pale colours to match the wallpapers that were chiefly by Morris & Co. This was not surprising as New Place was Webb's home too on alternate weekends, where the cook and the housemaid, both resident, ensured that he had a comfortable break from architectural work, a

Left New Place: view from the south-west (the flat-roof bay-window was added in 1923)

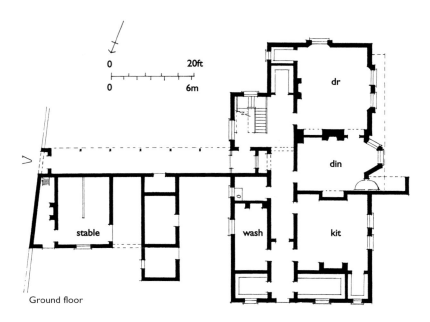

0   20ft

0   6m

dr

din

kit

wash

stable

Ground floor

Above Hill House: plan of the ground floor

Below Hill House (Briarmead), Greatham, Hartlepool (1883): the entrance (east) front from the road at the time the rehabilitation of the building was nearing completion in the early 1980s
(© Hartlepool Borough Council)

coachman drove him about if he so desired, and he could do pleasurable tasks in the garden, and have enjoyable discussions with the gardener about plants, or sketch them.[50] After the Webbs left, the erstwhile cloakroom was incorporated into the drawing room in 1923 and a bay window facing west was added to the room; in the 1970s neo-Georgian houses were built in the grounds; and in the 1980s, the house was divided into two dwellings without exterior change. Many of Philip Webb's fittings remain, but sadly not the oak organ case, which was admired greatly by Lawrence Weaver, who was reminded by it of 'how much modern furniture design' owed to Webb.[51]

Hill House, Greatham, Hartlepool

In 1883, Webb designed Hill House (now Briarmead) in the village of Greatham, near Hartlepool, for William Thomas Tate (1843–1921), who was an accountant with the National Provincial Bank in Hartlepool and a trustee of the local Athenaeum.[52] Presumably Webb had been recommended to Tate, their friend and fellow Freemason, by Lowthian Bell, an MP for the town from 1875 to 1880, or by his son Hugh. The working drawings were prepared by a local architect, who supervised the erection of the building; therefore, as was his custom in such cases, Webb did not accept a fee. Subsequent owners of the house were unaware of his involvement.[53] In 1981, after finding a memorandum in Webb's hand in his address book stating that Tate of Hill House was 'the man for whom I designed a cottage about 1884', and searching the village on foot, the author identified Briarmead as Webb's Hill House of 1883. It has since been listed Grade II and conservatively repaired and refurbished as a private house.[54]

The commanding but extremely exposed site on the brow of a hill faces west over open countryside towards the Cleveland Hills. The fine prospect and the frequency of bitter winds off the North Sea determined the arrangement and the plan of the house. The main wing, containing the major rooms and three attic rooms, is positioned along the top of the site close to and parallel with the east boundary, creating as sheltered a west-facing garden as possible. A short east wing, extending roughly from the middle of the major one and connected by a wall to the small stable block, defines a kitchen yard to the north and shelters the garden to the south and the main entrance, from which a covered way extends to the roadside. On the west front, a short loggia conceals the terrace from view from the kitchen window, and shelters it and the French window of the dining room, which has an additional solid door for protection during westerly gales. On both the ground and the first floor, cross-passages separate non-habitable rooms on the cold eastern side of the house from the drawing room, dining room, kitchen, and bedrooms, on the west front. The drawing room, with direct access to the dining room to avoid the chilly hall, is in the south-west corner where it receives both south and west sunlight, and the main bedroom lies over the kitchen for maximum warmth.

Compact and well balanced from all angles and anchored to the ground by gables and large chimneys, this handsome and interesting house looks and has proved to be resistant to the fiercest gales. For protection, the roof is as simple as possible, exterior woodwork is kept to a minimum, and all the red-brick walls and chimneys are roughcast to prevent penetration by wind-driven rain, although this is not a traditional local method. The gables of the house are the dominant elements, and have stone water tabling (copings) and kneelers (corbels) in the local manner but the roadside gable of the stable is crow-stepped in the manner common in eastern Scotland not north-eastern England. Colourwashed the parchment shade Webb termed white, the roughcast contrasts well with the boldly profiled local red clay pantiles of the roofs, giving the house a pleasingly textured and exceptionally unified appearance.[55] The windows of habitable rooms are chiefly vertical sashes, those in the drawing room and dining room being grouped into two bay windows under a continuous lean-to roof like the one Webb had introduced at the Briary, Isle of Wight, in 1872 (see chapter 5). Other windows are of the horizontally sliding sash type known as Yorkshire slides, some of them being much taller than normal.[56] Tate followed Webb's advice to avoid ornament on the exterior – and indeed also in the interior, which has characteristic Webb fittings, including fireplaces with bracketed mantelpieces and grates by Longden to Webb's design, and a staircase with a freestanding bottom flight and a balustrade with square balusters and knobbed newels.[57]

Coneyhurst, Ewhurst, Surrey

The penultimate and ultimate small houses designed for a client's own use by Webb were each for a woman. The first, Coneyhurst (now Coneyhurst-on-the-Hill; Webb had no connection with the nearby house presently named Coneyhurst) was for Miss Mary Anne Ewart (d. 1909), the granddaughter of a successful Liverpool merchant and daughter of William Ewart, a Liberal MP, who was a relation of William Ewart Gladstone, prime minister. Mary Ewart, a founder member of the SPAB, was a friend of Gertrude Jekyll and of Webb and his sisters; an active and generous supporter of better education for women, she established and for many years managed a fund that enabled young women without means to train as teachers.[58] In 1883, Miss Ewart asked Webb, with whom she shared an interest in plants and gardening, to design a five-bedroom house, to be built near Ewhurst in Surrey; the house, a cottage for

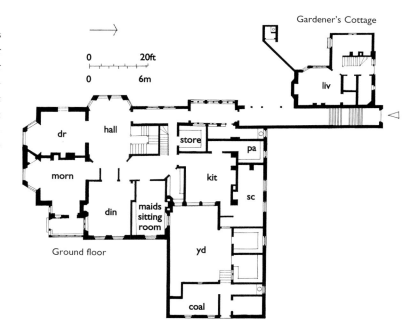

the gardener, and a small stable block were constructed between 1884 and 1886.

The layout was governed by the site, which slopes steeply from south to north and a little less so from west to east on the southern escarpment of the Hurt Wood, and by Webb's wish to make a unified and well-balanced composition of the house, gardener's cottage, and stables.[59] The stable and integral

Above Coneyhurst: plan of the ground floor

Below Coneyhurst (Coneyhurst-on-the-Hill), Ewhurst, Surrey (1883, constructed 1884–86): the south front, from the garden

Below Coneyhurst: the
drawing room, in Miss
Ewart's time (Private
Collection)

coachman's dwelling lie to the east of the house at a
higher level near the road, where originally the
cottage also served as a lodge. Developing the
entrance arrangements of New Place and Hill House,
Webb made the main porch a part of the gardener's
cottage and linked it to the house by a long entrance
passage, with a lean-to roof, running against the
kitchen wing. The entire site, except for a private
terrace on the south front, was overlooked from one
or other of the cottages, to give Miss Ewart security.
The plan is rather similar to that of New Place, with
the dining room replacing the surgery, a morning
room of equal size to the drawing room instead of a
study, and a much larger hall. It is an octagonal,
galleried living hall with the main staircase off one
side, and is lit directly by, unusually for Webb, a two-

storey bay window the full width of the room. Miss
Ewart was a keen amateur painter who liked to
entertain on a considerable scale. Webb gave her a
large studio on the second floor and, by installing
double doors between the living hall and the dining
room and also the drawing room, he provided a
usefully adaptable and at its maximum an
exceptionally large entertaining area for a relatively
small house.

There is nothing specifically feminine about the
architecture of Coneyhurst. The house and gardener's
cottage have red-brick walls, clad on most of the first
floor with the same red tiles as covered the roof. The
combined stable and coachman's cottage is linked to
the house visually by having the same roof tiles and
by white weatherboarded walls which echo the
boarding in most of the gables of the main house.[60] To
make the house unobtrusive, the roof is subdivided
into a dominant and stabilizing central ridge, gabled
at each end and running east to west across the
hillside, and two lower roofs at right angles, to north
and south respectively, each having twin ridges. The
ridges on the south front terminate in gables above
the two-storey bay-window projection that buttresses
the house against the hill. The brick-pillared balcony
of Miss Ewart's bedroom stems from the increasing
contemporary preoccupation with healthy living. A
less attractive feature is the plaster cove on the west
wall of the inner porch; a similar cove is successful
over the void of the New Place porch but the
Coneyhurst cornice gives the false impression that
the passage wall below it is a later infil.[61] Miss Ewart
created beautiful gardens around the house, almost
certainly with Webb's advice, and perhaps because
they delighted him, she managed to persuade this
reticent architect, in a unique instance, to inscribe
his name on a brick in the outer porch.[62]

The interior offered even more dramatic spatial
contrasts than those of New Place. The outer porch
began as a dark burrow before becoming cloistral at
its lower level where it was open to the west lawn;
the enfilade then widened a little in the inner porch,
then narrowed again in the lobby before opening into
the unusually large and well-lit living hall.[63] The
staircase, with a freestanding upper flight, white
latticed balustrade panels, and full-height oak newels,
forms a dynamic hollow sculpture. At the upper level,
the deep gallery on the western side originally
accommodated the audience when theatricals were
performed below in the hall. The interior decoration

was unusually restrained for the date. The paintwork and ceilings were white or light-coloured, as had long been customary in Webb's houses, and pale distemper or very small-patterned Morris wallpapers formed an unobtrusive background to the client's collection of watercolour paintings. A plain carpet was fitted throughout the ground floor and on the staircase, and was relieved here and there by oriental rugs.[64]

In the late twentieth century, the main block of Coneyhurst was carefully divided into two houses, with minimal change to the exterior and interior, and the gardener's cottage and stable block each became a dwelling under separate ownership.

Goldenfields, Liphook, Hampshire

It was probably Gertrude Jekyll, a friend of Mary Ewart and a venerator of Webb's work, who recommended him to her own acquaintance Mrs Mary Anne Robb (1829–1912), for whom Webb designed his final individual small house, Goldenfields in Liphook, Hampshire, between 1890 and 1891. The widow of naval officer Captain John Robb and the granddaughter of Matthew Boulton, the celebrated eighteenth-century engineer and industrialist, Mrs Robb had been fascinated by plants since her childhood at Tew Park in Oxfordshire, where her father had created fine gardens. She became an amateur horticulturist and gardener of some renown, with many friends in the horticultural world including William Robinson (1838–1935) and E A Bowles (1865–1954). Mary Robb lived mainly in London but had purchased land at Liphook in 1869, and had added more later, a large part of which she had turned into beautiful gardens; judging by her notice 'Beware of the Lycopodium', which kept out the local boys, she had good sense of humour.[65] In 1890, intending to live at Liphook most of the time, she asked Webb to design a cottage for her gardener, and a large house for her own use to be built on the site of the existing Chiltley Farm; Webb prepared a preliminary plan for the house but, presumably finding the estimated cost of £3,300 too high, Mrs Robb had the cottage built for herself instead, and it was completed in 1892.[66]

Webb had enlarged the cottage scheme by adding two rooms, one above the other, at its south-west corner, and a long two-storey room extending eastwards parallel to the road, with a gallery, partly in the roof and lit by dormers, such as his client had

requested for the proposed large house.[67] At the northern end of this room he had placed a clock tower, horizontally boarded in oak and set at forty-five degrees, with a loggia on the garden side and topped by a small open belvedere overlooking the grounds.[68] Mrs Robb had requested two loggias, one at first-floor level, so Webb provided a deep, covered balcony with timber posts and balustrade off her bedroom (the room beneath was extended under it many years later, and the balustrade was probably replaced). As the site is well above sea level and considerably exposed, most of the upper walls of the red-brick house received protective claddings, variously of roughcast or weather-tiles or oak boarding.

Despite the increase in size, with its articulated red-clay tiled roofs Goldenfields retained the unpretentious, cheerful character of the original design. The interior, apart perhaps from the two-storey room, had a similar warm and modest ambience, not inappropriately for Mrs Robb, who undoubtedly considered gardening her major role. Seen from the garden – which had several architectural features including archways, low walls, and lych-gates by Webb – the attractive clock tower with the lean-to roof of the loggia at its base strongly resembles the fourteenth-century detached bell-house of St Mary's Church, Pembridge in Herefordshire, which Webb studied in 1890, taking detailed measurements of the timber framework of the oak-boarded upper part.[69] Mary Robb proudly recorded Webb's and her own involvement with the building on a simple plaque in a porch that had been added for her by the architect Owen Little, who in

Above Goldenfields: the clock tower

1905 enlarged the house in a sympathetic manner, and was similarly acknowledged.[70] The building was divided in 1951; later it underwent further subdivision and alteration, and houses were constructed on most of the garden.

Conclusion

In the 1880s and 1890s, just at the right time, when commissions for large country houses had become extremely rare through the decreased income from land, Webb's small individual houses in the country demonstrated that buildings of this new middle-class category were worthy of an architect's attention. His reflection and inventive use of local building traditions showed that vernacular architecture, as well as being living history, could be a valuable source of inspiration for new, avant-garde houses. Architects and articled pupils visited his small houses whilst they were under construction or soon after completion, for example on tours of new buildings organised by the Architectural Association. Although Webb's connection with Manor Farm, Hill House, and Goldenfields, had been forgotten by the mid-twentieth century, and though most of his small houses were not published until very late in his career if at all, during his lifetime they were as well known and influential as his country houses. Henry-Russell Hitchcock notes the similarity between Webb's Upwood Gorse and the Shingle style of America but concludes that this was a coincidence.[71] However, the house was known to many of Webb's followers and there was considerable interchange between them and architects in America, so it probably did influence the American style. The importance that Webb placed on the reflection of local vernacular buildings would certainly have crossed the Atlantic in time to influence the interest in farmhouses and barns that developed in the United States in the 1880s.[72]

Influences from Webb's small houses in the country can be clearly discerned in many British houses by his near contemporaries and by the younger Arts and Crafts architects. He used rows of contiguous casements as early as 1861 in the workshops of numbers 91–101 Worship Street, and in 1875 at Upwood Gorse in the garden porch and the service wing, in the long dormer of the Vicar's House in 1877, and in the play-passage of Red Barns in 1881. Similar windows became characteristic of Voysey's houses; indeed his large bay window at The Cottage, Bishop's Itchington (1888), is almost identical to the Upwood Gorse garden porch. The four large dormers of Voysey's Walnut Tree Farm, Herefordshire (1890), strongly suggest an acquaintance with Oast House, as does his use of a cat-slide roof at Moorcrag, Cumbria (1898), to cover ground-floor projections in order to increase the effect of simplicity and repose. Oast House probably also influenced the corbelled stacks of Lutyens's Fulbrook, Surrey (1897), and possibly the gabled dormers of the Nathan G Moore House, Illinois, USA (1895), by Frank Lloyd Wright, who was kept informed by Ashbee of new houses in Britain, some of which Wright saw for himself. The houses in Redington Road, Hampstead, are quieter but no less inventive and pleasing than the 'Queen Anne'-style buildings erected nearby, and would have been known to the many architects working in Hampstead at the time and later. Webb's Manor Farm appears to have influenced Manor Farm, Frognal, Hampstead (1879–80), designed by Basil Champneys, who is known to have greatly admired Webb's work.[73] Webb's inset round-arched porches became popular with Arts and Crafts architects, including Voysey, and the recessed round arches in brick of Manor Farm, Thurston, and the Redington Road houses, appeared in countless speculative suburban detached and semi-detached houses until well after the Second World War.

Coneyhurst in particular was visited during construction by Webb's young followers. At this innovative house, as John Brandon-Jones pointed out, they 'learnt to respect Webb for the freshness and common sense of his approach to building'.[74] Influences from Coneyhurst can be found in several turn-of-the-century houses. The bracketed gables and the extended wall planes on the wall at the northern end of the house appear to have inspired or influenced the similar features that became trademarks of Voysey, who battered the wall extensions and treated them as buttresses, for instance at his New Place, Surrey (1897). Lutyens used a coved plaster cornice on the entrance archway at the Salutation, Kent (1911); the courses of horizontal tiling such as Webb used on the gardener's cottage at Coneyhurst were adopted by Lutyens for several of his houses, including Tigbourne Court, Surrey (1899). By the 1890s, two-storey living halls had become unfashionable for large country houses but that of Coneyhurst influenced their popularity in small houses in the country, such as Voysey's Norney, Surrey (1897), and Baillie Scott's Blackwell,

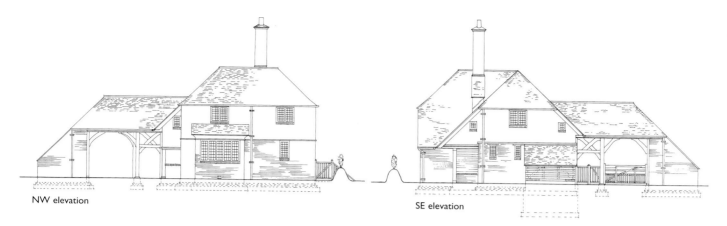

NW elevation

SE elevation

Cumbria (1898). Staircases winding round an open well with floor-to-ceiling newels were used by many architects, including Voysey at Broadleys, Lutyens at Littlecroft, Surrey (1899), and Mackintosh, who also made a feature of lattice and latticed patterns in fittings and furniture, at his Hill House, Helensburgh (1902). Baillie Scott followed Webb in seeking more adaptability and spaciousness in small houses through the use of folding doors and removable partitions, for example in his own Red House, Isle of Man (1892–93). Webb's enfilades at New Place and Coneyhurst might have influenced Lloyd Wright, who used the feature in several of his houses, whilst Voysey, at Brooke End, Warwickshire (1909), and Ricardo, at number 8 Addison Road, London (1905–07), adopted Webb's roadside-to-entrance covered ways of Red Barns and Hill House.[75]

The freshness, simplicity, and unity of Webb's Hill House must have been striking in the 1880s and early 1890s. Webb's admirers would have known of the house from his drawings and some of them would have seen the actual building, as it was easily accessible from the rapidly expanding town of Middlesbrough where many London architects were undertaking commissions. Almost certainly Webb's house influenced the roughcast houses that Voysey began to design a few years later and that became the latter's trademark and, through Voysey's buildings, those that Baillie Scott was designing a decade later.[76] Although the main source of inspiration would have been the harled buildings of their native Scotland, Webb's Hill House also had an influence on the work of Robert Lorimer (1864–1929), James MacLaren, and Mackintosh, judging by its similarity to several of their houses.[77] Lorimer set up practice in 1892 after working in London for Webb's friend Bodley; MacLaren joined the Art Workers' Guild in 1886 and was certainly influenced by Webb's number 19 Lincoln's Inn Fields (see chapter 12); and Mackintosh was introduced to the ideas and ideals of Webb and the Arts and Crafts movement in the early 1890s by Francis Newbery, who was a member of the SPAB and had been a member of the William Morris circle before leaving the South Kensington Schools in London to become Director of the Glasgow School of Art.

Webb's young followers were able to take full advantage of his thinking and his innovative, experimental buildings, and to apply his design philosophy in a less serious and earnest manner because he, the pioneer, had escaped from the morass of style revivals by returning to the fundamentals of good building and ignoring the concept of choice of style. As a result, their buildings sometimes seem more immediately attractive than Webb's, but his are usually the more interesting in the long term. His smaller houses, whether terrace or estate cottages or small houses in the country, for a century or more have been greatly appreciated by successive owners and tenants as homes of pleasing appearance inside and out, comfortable and convenient in which to live, and extremely durable. Clearly, Webb had the necessary empathy, as well as professional knowledge and experience, to satisfy fundamental human needs.

Above Goldenfields, Liphook, Hampshire (1890–91, constructed 1891–92): sketch elevations by H V Kirk, based on Webb's unfinished drawing, in the RIBA Drawings Collection, for the original cottage (from the sketches in the author's collection)

Chapter 12

THE NON-DOMESTIC WORK

Not surprisingly in the case of a man who was proud to term himself a house architect, Philip Webb's body of non-domestic work was small. It includes memorials and tombs (too numerous for all to be described here), a village school and a village hall, a handful of industrial buildings, a row of shops (unexecuted), three blocks of offices, and three churches and two chapels of which one of each was erected, and an unfinished and unsolicited design for a cathedral.[1]

Memorials

Webb was always saddened when designing memorials, particularly if friends or their families were involved, but to please the bereaved he did so with patience, sympathy, and understanding as well as his customary attention to detail. Each memorial demonstrates his careful choice of the most suitable local materials and the skill with which he brought out their particular qualities. A comparison of the actual gravestones with his designs for them reveals that the various masons obeyed his command that the drawings and the instructions written thereon were to be followed exactly.[2] He usually designed the letters afresh for memorial inscriptions, in a modern not a medieval manner, displaying great skill in the designing and the arranging of the letters on the plate or stone. His letters for memorial plates were softly rounded to facilitate the making of the wax model, to which he made final adjustments before it was cast in brass or bronze, usually by Longdens of Sheffield, the firm which made most of his fire-grates. Two fine examples are the simple brass plate of 1873 in memory of the Reverend I Dodgson in the church of Lanercost Priory, Cumbria, and the larger, more elaborate bronze plate of 1895, topped with a band of fretted ornament, to Lady Henrietta Maria Stanley (mother-in-law to both George Howard and Lowthian Bell's daughter Maisie) in Nether Alderley church, Cheshire.[3] The first plate fulfils Webb's belief that memorial inscriptions should be 'as simple and direct as possible'; the second shows that not all his clients shared his view.[4]

Webb's lettering for gravestones was more angular because it was to be cut straight into the stone, not modelled in a softer material and then cast in metal. Three fine examples, seemingly carved by the same mason who worked on Rounton Grange nearby, were designed for the Bell family and lie in the East Rounton churchyard, North Yorkshire. Two of them mark the graves of Sir Lowthian Bell's grandchildren, Kate the daughter of Lyulph Stanley and his wife Maisie (1884), and Philip Hugh the son of Walter and Florence Johnson (1886). The flat Stanley memorial bears the three-year old child's sobriquet 'Kitty', and a pot of lilies in relief as a symbol of her purity and innocence; the coped gravestone of the infant Philip carries a simple cross formed by arrises and outlined by flower heads. The third tombstone, designed in 1887, marks the grave of Sir Lowthian Bell and his wife Margaret, who predeceased him.[5] It is a prime example of Webb's fine heraldic designs and of the expert craftsmanship of the mason. Another recumbent cross stretches the length of the stone, in this case with foliage forming the ends of the arms and the top of the post, with the two Bell escutcheons on beds of vines and oak leaves flanking the stepped base. Quotations relating to children lie to the left and right of the cross, each one in a panel, whilst the names and dates of the deceased are on the sloping plinth. The entire memorial is made from one piece of stone.

In 1856, Webb designed a much simpler tombstone for William Morris, his close comrade of many decades. According to Sydney Cockerell, it was inspired by an ancient stone in the churchyard of St George's Church, Kelmscott, Oxfordshire, where Morris was buried, but to those who are familiar with Morris's love of Iceland and its sagas as Webb certainly was, it calls to mind the Vikings' turf-roofed halls with well-defined ridges.[6] The coped slab, worked by Laurence Turner, is supported on

Above St Lawrence's Church, East Rounton, North Yorkshire: the tombstone of Sir Lowthian and Lady Bell, designed by Webb in 1887

stone blocks and each of the two long sides of the 'roof' is divided by a thin branch with two oak leaves at the top, creating four compartments in which were carved Morris's names and dates in slightly informal lettering designed by Webb, and in due course those of Jane Morris and their daughters Jenny and May. Webb told Cockerell by letter that Jane was 'pleased to be content' with the tombstone; he continued:

> You could hardly guess how much the doing of the silly-simple thing has exercised me; for I do not like setting up memorials even to strong men, as the stone is too apt to perpetuate the weakness of the doer as well as the strength of the done-by.[7]

Webb need not have worried; none of his memorials displays any sign of weakness on the designer's part.

His most interesting and unusual memorial cross was designed for the Astley sisters Gertrude, Constance, and Beatrice, in memory of their parents, Francis Dukinfield Palmer Astley and his wife Gertrude Emma (1827–62), and their brother Francis Dukinfield Astley (1853–80) who had drowned accidentally in a Canadian river and from whom Gertrude had inherited the Arisaig estate on the coast of north-west Scotland.[8] The sisters first thought of building as a memorial Webb's chapel designed for their father in 1866 for erection at Arisaig House (see chapter 7). As renovation and redecoration was to be undertaken on Arisaig House, Webb made the long and difficult journey to it in July 1881, which necessitated a stay of a week just at the time he was trying to settle the contract for Clouds. During the visit, the chapel proposal was abandoned because the increased prices of materials and lack of skilled workmen in Arisaig familiar with Webb's exacting standards had made the cost too high; instead, the sisters decided to erect a memorial cross on Francis's grave in the village churchyard to Webb's design.[9] Despite the difficulty of extracting pieces of the local

Right St Mary's Church,
Nether Alderley, Cheshire:
the memorial plate to Lady
Henrietta Maria Stanley
(mother of Rosalind
Howard); Webb designed
the entire plate including the
letters and numbers in 1895
(from a photograph by the
author)

whinstone of a suitable size, Webb insisted that in the 'rude little churchyard with its ancient ruins standing by, the native stone would look more congruous than any imported stone'.[10] Carved by a Scottish mason, the cross was erected under the supervision of the clerk of works for the renovations to the house.[11] Webb had plaster models of the leaves on the 'horns' of the cross made in London to ensure that they would be 'done properly'.[12] When the Astleys changed the wording of the two bronze inscription plates, in wry good humour Webb patiently produced the necessary new designs for recasting by Longdens.

Gertrude Astley insisted upon having a tall cross so, as he explained, he made his design 'as different as possible to a, so-called, Runic Cross or a village cross', in part to 'mark it as much as might be (considering its height) as a private memorial', and he placed the inscription high up on the polygonal shaft, under the cross head, to mark it as a personal monument and where it would also be 'out of the way of injury'.[13] The shaft broadens to house the plates, which are set in protective raised stone frames – one at the front, the other on the back of the memorial. The cross head has four identical arms linked by a circular moulding, with the four horns at the base, each one bearing carved ornament of a different design.

The memorial is much larger than Webb wished, though he managed to reduce the height from the ten feet Gertrude Astley first proposed. It is a bold,

Right The Astley memorial
cross, in St Mary's
Churchyard, Arisaig,
Inverness-shire, Scotland,
designed by Webb between
1881 and 1882

most unusual, and extremely effective design. Webb's use of the local stone, coupled with his avoidance of the appearance of a public memorial and the position being near the further boundary looking out to sea, ensured that the large memorial would be in harmony with its surroundings. It looks as well after over a century as it did when first erected, thanks to his understanding of how the stone would weather in the exposed conditions and his designing it accordingly.

Between 1887 and 1890, for Boyce Allen of Sydney, Australia, Webb designed a mausoleum that would have been built in a cemetery had it gone ahead. The drawing shows a small pitch-roofed building on a larger podium with a vault beneath that would have accommodated twelve coffins.[14] Each gable of the pleasing stone-walled and -roofed structure has fairly elaborate wrought-iron double gates, segmental headed within a wider pointed arch. The side walls have three blind arches under small gabled roofs, the outer arches bearing the inscription plates and the central ones housing an ornamentally carved stone panel.

Webb designed three larger memorials – the Morris cottages at Kelmscott (discussed in chapter 11), a church (discussed later in this chapter under 'Ecclesiastical buildings'), and a clock tower intended to be built in Ledbury, Herefordshire, in memory of the poet Elizabeth Barrett Browning (1806–61) – of which the last two were not built.[15] Webb was asked to design the tower in 1890, possibly by the local MP Michael Biddulph. He inspected and advised on the various suggested sites, measured parts of the buildings thereon, studied the rest of those surrounding the Market Place (which comprised a mosaic of timber-framed, stone, red-brick, and stuccoed structures), and inspected the many types of local stone, before producing two designs in 1891 and 1892 respectively. After the scheme had been extended to include a memorial institute, Webb apparently withdrew from the commission in 1892 because he could not countenance the pulling down of a worthy seventeenth-century timber-framed house to create a large enough site.[16]

The Barrett Browning Memorial Institute and Clock Tower were erected soon afterwards to the designs of the architect Brightwen Binyon, who chose timber-framing for the upper stage of his rock-faced tower as well as for the conjoined institute, to the detriment of the flamboyant timber-framed seventeenth-century Market House and the other timber structures – as is pointed out by Pevsner, who finds Binyon's building terrible.[17] Webb had sensibly chosen stone to prevent his proposed tower from detracting from the Market House and made it as much unlike a church tower as possible, with buttress-free random rubble walls and simple rectangular windows. An upper stage in ashlar with segmental-arched, small-paned windows would have been surmounted by two polygonal stages, the first an open belvedere and the second a latticed belfry for the clock bell, and a stubby lead-covered pyramid.

School buildings and a village hall

Webb was involved with buildings for three schools, the first being the National School at Heathfield in East Sussex, which replaced an earlier school of an unusual circular plan erected in 1819 under the auspices of the National Society for Promoting the Education of the Poor in the Principles of the Established Church (the National Society).[18] A larger building being necessary by 1861, the school managers commissioned a design from John W Billing, who was currently restoring All Saints' Church in the village.[19] After the early, unexpected death of Billing, his erstwhile instructor and employer in Reading, Webb offered to arrange and supervise the erection of the building gratuitously, as Billing had intended to do.[20] Doubtless to reduce the cost, Webb

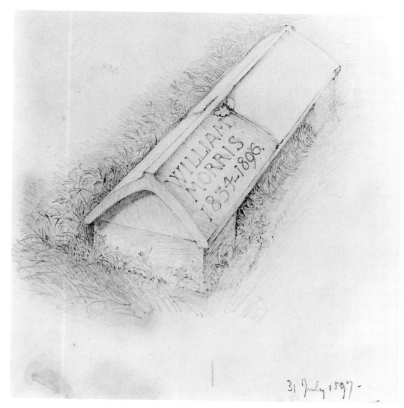

31 July 1897 –

Above One of Webb's drawings (this one is dated 1897), for the tombstone of William Morris, which is in St George's Churchyard, Kelmscott (William Morris Gallery, London)

simplified the elevations and chimneys of the red-brick, slate-roofed building by reducing the number of stone dressings, and he improved the shape of the pointed-arch windows in the gables and substituted small panes for Billing's large panes, before the school was built in 1864 by the local builders Piper and Harmer.[21] At present, the building serves as the All Saints' and St Richard's Church of England Primary School; minor alterations have been made at various times and extensions have been built at the rear.[22]

In 1875, Webb was asked by Lowthian Bell to design a Board School to serve East Rounton and the nearby larger village of West Rounton, North Yorkshire. It was to be paid for by Bell, who had also provided the site in East Rounton, where Rounton Grange was reaching completion. Bell, a Member of Parliament at the time, would have been stimulated by the Education Act of 1870, which established the elements of a universal primary school system and the setting up of local school boards. The plans received the necessary approval of the Education Department in London by 9 June 1876.[23] The school opened in July 1877 and closed in June 1967; during the intervening years, several members of the Bell family, deeply interested in education, visited it

Above East Rounton School, North Riding of Yorkshire (North Yorkshire) (1875–76; now a private house): from a rare archival photograph (in the author's collection), which does not show the tall chimney bearing the school bell under a pitch roof canopy

frequently.[24] The building was converted into a house in the late 1960s, with an inserted first floor, altered windows, added dormers, and the loss of the bellcote.

The East Rounton school was smaller than that at Heathfield, the highest number of pupils at any one time being only sixty-nine. Webb's plan closely resembled that of Billing, which had been based on the guidelines of the National Society.[25] The long gable-roofed schoolroom, shorter but wider than that of Heathfield, was similarly placed at the rear of the building, parallel to the road; like Billing's school, it was fronted at the centre by a smaller classroom for the infants, with a western gable facing the road and flanked by porches – one for the boys, the other for the girls and infants. In contrast to the narrow ones of Heathfield, the porches were almost square and were entered from the north and south respectively, not from the west. The playgrounds for both the schools were large, with small blocks of earth closets positioned well away from the main building.[26]

The two major rooms are emphasized as separate units at East Rounton, but Webb appears to have done this not so much to express the plan as to be able to have on the classroom an east gable to carry the chimney and the wooden canopy for the bell. In the unpretentious, friendly building with small-paned windows, Webb incorporated his reinterpretations of local building traditions, including water-tabling (gable copings) rising from kneelers (corbel stones) on the gables, and a major roof descending as a cat-slide – a feature of some local farmhouses – on the west side to cover the porches. (The Heathfield porches were covered by the classroom cat-slide.) The red bricks of the walls were originally left exposed but were

roughcast against wind-driven rain before the 1950s.[27]

The three main gables had tall windows with brick hood moulds following the lines of the gable coping to take rainwater away from the windows. Victorian schools are often assumed to have had high sills to prevent pupils from being distracted by events outside. In fact, low sills were believed to produce an uncomfortable direct glare from the pupils' desks. Webb explained, with regard to a new schoolroom he was designing in 1875 for Major Gillum's Boys' Farm School, that it was 'absolutely necessary for the proper lighting and ventilation of the school' that the top of gable windows should be at high level in order to obtain a 'diffused light – not a direct light', that is from light reflected by the inclined planes of the under side of the roof, thereby 'doing away with all shadows'.[28] Former pupils remember East Rounton School as being light and airy inside but say they would have liked lower sills.

In 1860, the year before Webb designed the Worship Street shops and dwellings for him (see chapter 11), Major Gillum had become a member of the management committee of the Industrial Home for Destitute Boys in Euston Road, London, which had been founded by his wife's brother George W Bell and another, unrelated, George Bell.[29] In the same year, Gillum established a supplementary Farm School for Boys (usually referred to as the Boys' Farm School or Boys' Farm Home and in Webb's papers as the 'Boys' Home') on a forty-acre farm, Church Farm, which he had bought for the purpose at East Barnet, Greater London (then in Hertfordshire). It is possible that Webb extended the old farmhouse on the site for the boys' use in 1860 or 1861 at the time he was designing and supervising the construction of the cottage for the gardener on Gillum's estate in Tottenham (see chapter 7).[30] From 1867 to 1868, the New Buildings were built to Webb's design near the old farmhouse.[31] They contained living quarters on two floors and the attics of a relatively large block with a twin pitched and gabled roof, and a kitchen, dairy, and cow-house in a lean-to below the gables of the north-east front. Webb added a new dairy in 1874, and the following year he converted his cow-house into a large schoolroom by raising it in height and inserting tall windows and two chimneys. He also added dining rooms and a new kitchen.[32] A contemporary perspective sketch of the school shows the original farmhouse just south of the church, with the New Buildings aligned to the north-west on its left.[33]

Economy was of importance as Gillum was funding the school himself. Consequently, Webb's buildings were simple and lacked mouldings and carved ornament. The major portion of the New Buildings had his characteristic relieving arches over windows and typical brick strings below the chimney tops. The twin gables were each weather-tiled around three single-light windows, in a similar manner to the gables of Church Hill House (see chapter 7), designed by Webb for Gillum in 1868 and built to the north-west of the school buildings. The new schoolroom had a range of small-paned six-light windows closely resembling the later, single windows in the East Rounton school gables; the interior was open to the roof timbers, and had a gill stove at each end.[34] Webb's New Buildings remain, and at present again form part of a school, for children who are excluded from regular state education.[35]

In 1891, Webb designed a village hall for Arisaig, consisting of a public room, a classroom, and a porch, the cost of which, including his fee, was paid for by Constance Astley (the Miss Astley, her elder sister having married) who was continuing the benevolent practice of her father (see chapter 7). The building, named the Astley Hall, cost £445 9s 8d and was constructed in 1892 and 1893 by the local joiner, Alexander McVarish, who arranged for and superintended other craftsmen as necessary. The final cost to Constance Astley was around £851 1s 2d, which included the surrounding fence and gates and probably all the fittings and furnishings.[36] In 1910,

George Jack, who earlier had taken over Webb's practice, added a club room and a hip-roofed porch in the angle between it and the original part, at Constance Astley's expense.[37] It was probably at this time that the central hall was enlarged by removing the wall and chimney between it and the classroom and moving the stage into the latter.

Webb decided that the building should be a three-cell structure under a single roof. Placed parallel to the road on the southern side, it was about seventy-one feet long by twenty-three feet wide, and comprised a central hall almost forty-four feet long, with a so-called classroom and a so-called porch of equal length at the west and east end respectively. The porch, at the more sheltered eastern end, effectively formed an additional room and, after Jack's porch was built, served as such (it is now the community office). A random rubble plinth – of stone dug nearby and roughly dressed, over the whole of which mortar was trowelled and then cut back over the stone faces – supported a timber-framed, weatherboarded building with a hip roof covered with Ballachulish slates like those of Arisaig House. To conserve heat, only small roof lights were installed on the northern side of the building, the leaded windows in wrought-iron frames designed specially by the architect being restricted to the warmer south and west fronts. The roof was supported on unusual trusses, which had crossed spars rising above the double collars from the purlins, and a half-inch-diameter iron rod suspended from the ridge piece and extending into a post that rose from

Below Boys' Farm School, East Barnet, Hertfordshire (Greater London): the New Buildings (1867–68) by Webb, with his later alterations and additions, from a photograph taken around 1930 (© Barnet Museum)

double tie-beams at eaves level to the crossing joint of the spars. Inclined struts rose from posts attached to the vertical wall frame members to reinforce the junction of the spars, purlins, and collars. Diagonal bracing strengthened the walls, which were boarded in deal in the interior. The doors throughout were framed, braced, and boarded. The stone plinth rose high enough to form a timber-encased seat along the inside of the outer walls. All the exposed timber was left unpainted and unstained. The hall was heated by a Gurney stove, the classroom by an open fire.

Webb's fee for this commission was a mere £20, but every detail of the building was drawn or sketched and described in the specification.[38] To cope with the frequent gales from the sea, Webb reinforced the joints of the timber framing with iron straps, bolts, and large nails, and used tenterhooks as well as galvanized nails to prevent the slates from lifting. Tarring the rebates of the timber frames and the outer surface of the weatherboarding kept out the all-too-prevalent rain. Webb insisted on having the chimneys within the building to avoid inefficiency in high winds which, with the common-sense wish to avoid heat loss, explains why he had abandoned external chimneys almost completely by the early 1870s. As for his houses, he provided extra ventilation for the village hall via vent shafts in the chimneys. Interestingly, whilst the vent-shaft chimneypot was a working one, those on the two flues had a purely aesthetic role, the flues exiting below the capping to prevent smoke from blowing down into the building; birds were kept out by iron grilles. The floors were of concrete to keep out damp and the rats that were then a problem in the village, probably having come ashore from boats. Webb had reservations about the seasoning of local timber; his specification included a clause that, should any difficulty be found in getting the foreign timber specified, he was to be informed as to what timber was available that was 'sound and good' and had been 'proved by use in the place to be trustworthy and lasting'.[39]

A notable point about the village hall is that Webb planned it 'on a system' which he refused to 'throw out' by reducing the porch to lengthen the hall; instead, he insisted on adding an extra bay to the hall.[40] The contrasts of the textures and colours of the materials – the rough stone plinth, the dark brown boarding, the chunky green-grey slates, and the white-painted leaded windows – ensured that his unpretentious but extremely pleasing building fitted harmoniously into the village scene.

The building, now listed Category B by Historic Scotland, still serves its original purpose but, between late 1999 and 2002, Webb's part was re-clad inside and out after his frame, which was generally sound, had been conservatively repaired; George Jack's wing, which was unsafe, was rebuilt, a new club room was added on the north side of the hall, and an up-to-date kitchen and lavatories were inserted in the rebuilt wing, at a total cost of £475,000.[41]

Industrial buildings

It may seem hard to believe that Philip Webb designed three buildings for an ironworks, when his life and thinking had been so much influenced by his reaction against heavy industries because of the drastic effects they were having on the landscape and on the people who worked in or lived near them. He was totally loyal to his friends and hated to refuse

Below Arisaig Village Hall (the Astley Hall), Arisaig, Inverness-shire, Scotland (1891, constructed 1892–93): the south front

their requests for help, and he was abidingly grateful to those who had also been his early clients. At the time when Lowthian Bell asked him to design the first of the ironworks buildings in 1867, Webb might also have been embarrassed by having refused to assess the competition designs for the Middlesbrough Exchange and by having withdrawn from the commission to design a new street in Newcastle, in both of which Bell had involved him (both are discussed later in this chapter). It is likely too that, despite his weeks in Wolverhampton, Webb had not yet seen ironworks at close quarters when he complied with Bell's request that he should design a clock tower for the Clarence Works, which Bell and his brothers had established at Port Clarence, Stockton-on-Tees, on the north bank of the river.[42] Anxious not to make it an expensive tower but wishing to 'avoid making it ridiculous', Bell had sent Webb two designs made by the firm's draughtsmen, 'one with coins [sic] of stone and the other white brick corners and crossbars and redbrick panelling' and, with apologies for bothering him with 'such a trumpery affair', had asked Webb for a sketch of a tower of suitable appearance.[43] It was not Webb's custom to design without having inspected the site and its surroundings, or to have his work circumscribed by schemes prepared by others, but he complied, thereby making it impossible to refuse when Bell requested help with further industrial buildings.[44] No other London architect of renown was commissioned to design industrial buildings for the north-east of England in the nineteenth century.

Strict timing was involved in the blast-furnace process, so it was essential that the men working the furnaces could see a clock. The tower was sited facing south across the river, fairly near the 1845 bank of massive cylindrical blast furnaces and even closer to where the New Side bank, already envisaged, would be erected in the 1870s. Square in plan, the tower was built of red brick but, despite Bell's instructions, Webb added a few stone dressings to give it some distinction. They included a low plinth, a string, a cornice above several courses of corbelled brickwork, and the architrave of the entrance – in which he inventively combined a Classical pediment hood mould with a Gothic joggled arch – and those of the tall rectangular cross windows (a type he used only rarely). Above the cornice, a gallery provided access for cleaning the clock-faces, and had a white-painted wrought-iron balustrade with tall cast-iron corner

posts connected by cast-iron brackets to a turret with characteristic diamond-shaped clock-faces on three of its sides. Suspended from each of the brackets was a bell – probably a symbol of Bell Brothers, the name of the firm, rather than being functional.[45] The turret and its slightly curved pyramid roof were covered in lead, with diagonal roll joints. The tower held a hydraulic machine for weighing the pig iron from the furnaces. The notion of having relatively delicate ironwork on an ironworks tower seems highly inappropriate but it echoed the open ironwork of the Armstrong hydraulic hoists that were to be erected between the new furnaces, to the summits of which they would carry the raw materials. Arguably, however, an upper stage in boldly modelled brickwork such as the one Webb added to Washington Hall for Lowthian Bell a little later (see chapter 9) would have given it more visual strength. Inevitably when seen from some points after the huge

Below Arisaig Village Hall: the interior of the main hall, showing Webb's timber-framed construction (the scissor trusses are hidden by the boarding), in which paired tie beams clasp the braces; during construction in 1892–93, vertical posts appear to have been substituted for the iron rods shown on Webb's drawing

New Side furnaces were installed, the tower seemed dwarfed by them; but seen from the river and the rival works on the opposite bank, it certainly did not look ridiculous.

In 1873, Lowthian Bell asked Webb to design the elevations of a blowing-engine house, again based on a drawing showing the necessary parts and dimensions of the building, and prepared by the works draughtsmen.[46] Doubtless mollified by Bell's having decided in 1871 to rebuild rather than just

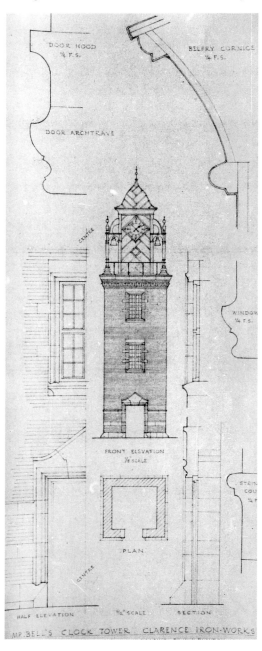

improve Rounton Grange, Webb obliged. By this time, he had become familiar with the sight of the massed ironworks on the banks of the Tees through travelling by train from Middlesbrough to Redcar in connection with Red Barns, the house he designed for Bell's son Hugh in 1868 (see chapter 11). It was a sight that always made him nauseous.

The blowing-engine house comprised a single-storey block, facing north and containing various pumps with, at the left-hand side of the entrance in the gable, a square pyramid-roofed turret containing a hydraulic accumulator that required no windows and presumably was connected to the Armstrong hoists. The entrance was a wide, round, recessed arch of the type Webb used on several buildings in the mid-1870s. Behind the block, at right angles to it and as high as the turret, another range, roofed overall by a huge water tank, contained the blowing engines. A round-arch arcade with tall pilasters articulated the walls of the engine house, with above it a cornice of smaller round arches springing from corbels and topped by several corbelled courses of bricks similar to those of the cornices on the turret and the earlier clock tower. The arcade and cornice stiffened the walls of the engine house to support the great weight of the water and tank, and helped to make a necessary utility into a quite impressive building.[47] The vertical blowing engines required windows on two levels to facilitate their servicing; each pair of the two rows of narrow windows in the arcade had a circular opening between them vertically. On the north side, the blast mains conveying compressed air from the engines to the furnaces passed into the entrance block through the circular openings, whilst those on the south front contained the ventilators that supplied air to the engines.

Increased business had created the need for larger offices in the Clarence Works by 1874, when Webb was asked to design them.[48] Undoubtedly, for a building of such size and importance, Webb would have insisted on inspecting the site and its surroundings in detail and on not being bound by any scheme by the draughtsmen. The Clarence Offices (sometimes termed the Works Offices) were built by the firm's craftsmen and labourers from early 1876 to 1878; there was a slump in the iron trade at the time, so it was an undertaking that combined a show of faith, philanthropy, and common sense, as it kept the trained craftsmen in employment and discouraged them from seeking jobs elsewhere.[49]

The office building was sited much nearer the

river than the clock tower and blast furnaces, with no large structures between it and the water over which it faced south towards the firm's competitors on the south bank. It was a centralized symmetrical building, square in plan, with a central hall containing the staircase and serving as the reception area, and approached through wide passages from the centres of the south and north fronts.[50] The hall was drawn up through the building into a square central tower, from the four large windows of which it received ample lighting. The wages and time offices, a strong room, a kitchen, a refreshment room, the cloakrooms, and rooms for supplies and stores, surrounded the hall on the ground floor; the more prestigious offices – including those of the secretary, the directors, various managers, and the chief engineer – and the drawing office were grouped round it on the first floor.[51]

The Clarence Offices had load-bearing walls of red brick with only a few stone dressings. Four pyramid roofs, covered in slate that would be washed clean by rain, surrounded the gabled tower, which had four chimneys set diagonally at the corners and a cross-pitched roof. Lattice-girders, four feet six inches deep, of wood (possibly with some vertical iron rods) and encased in plaster, supported the inner edges of the pyramid roofs from the centre points of the outer walls to the tower walls, beneath wide valley gutters that gave access to the exterior of the tower for maintenance and window-cleaning.[52] The ground floor walls were plain, relieved only by tall sash windows, with small panes and segmental arches but no architraves, and on the south front by the wide recessed brick arch of the main entrance, above which were three small arched windows. The first-floor wall on the east, south and west fronts, and in the centre of the north front, was arcaded above a vigorous corbelled and dentilated string-sill. The segmental arches, most of them housing tall sashes, sprang from idiosyncratic stone imposts placed well below the brick and stone capitals of the brick pilasters. On each side of the tower, above the segmental hood mould of the large three-light segmental-arch window, a projecting moulding followed the line of the cross-pitch roof below a parapet that rose to a point in the centre and was flanked by open arches that braced the tall chimneys against high winds. The angled chimneys were plain apart from a stone string, which had projections at the corners near the top, probably to act as fixings for ropes or ladders. Little is known about

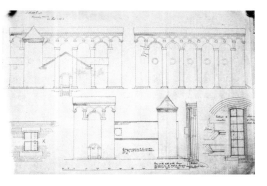

the internal finishes of the building but a photograph of the central hall, showing plastered walls, moulded skirtings, and dado rails, indicates that they would have been similar to those of the Bell Brothers Offices in Middlesbrough (described later in this chapter).[53] The cantilevered staircase had stone steps of triangular section giving a smooth, unbroken surface beneath the treads, and a plain balustrade in wrought iron.

Webb relied for visual effect on the geometry of the building which, with the diagonal lines of the roofs, contrasted well with the giant cylinders of the blast furnaces. A square, symmetrical building, with all elevations of equal importance, it was right for a site on which it could be seen from all directions. The tower pinned the large but relatively low building to the site and provided contrasting vertical lines. It imparted distinction, as did the prominent arcading which echoed that of the blowing-engine house and had the same wall-strengthening purpose. The arcading evokes thoughts of the civic structures of the Roman Empire that Webb possibly had in mind when designing the building, though the greatest influence clearly came from Vanbrugh; he too had experimented with pyramids, had pulled a central hall up into a lantern turret in several buildings, and had designed turrets with diagonal piers – for Blenheim Palace, for instance.[54] Webb's tower at the centre of four pyramid roofs, however, was probably unique. The inspiration apparently came from two schemes for Rounton Grange, the early scheme of a tall tower with a lantern turret amid cross-pitched roofs and the executed design with four pyramids around a long, pitched roof (see chapter 7).[55] It might have been in part a reflection of the new home of the managing director but Webb's views on symbolism make this unlikely.

According to the people who worked there, Webb had provided excellent working conditions.[56] This is not surprising, as the Bells were considerate employers and their skilful architect had the

Above Bell Brothers Clarence Works: the Works Offices (1876–78): a perspective view taken just before the demolition of the building in 1970 (© John K Harrison)

employees' welfare at heart, too. The Clarence Offices building fulfilled the visual role equally as well as the functional one. As seen from the works of competitors on the south bank of the river and by businessmen approaching from Middlesbrough by ferry, it was impressive, dignified, and unusual, without being grandiose or attention-seeking, as befitted the well-established Bell Brothers firm.

The clock tower and blowing-engine house were demolished in the 1930s when the ironworks closed. The Clarence Offices survived, with just a few minor alterations, to serve as the pay office for all Bell Brothers' other works on Teesside. It continued as such after being amalgamated with Dorman, Long, & Co. until late 1970 when, regrettably, it was demolished during the clearing of the riverbank area.[57]

Webb's only other industrial structures, a winding-engine house and large chimney for Atherston Colliery in Lancashire, were designed in 1871 or early 1872 for Herbert Fletcher (d. 1895) of Bolton, a colliery proprietor who was active in local and county affairs.[58] It is probable that Webb had been recommended by Lowthian Bell or Francis D P Astley, who were involved with coal mines, or by Ruskin, of whom Fletcher was an admirer. It is not known why the scheme was abandoned but (for reasons explained in chapter 13) Webb refused to accept his fee and demanded the return of his drawings.[59]

The chief points of interest of the Atherston scheme are that it shows Webb was willing to design an iron-framed industrial building, and that he understood the mechanics involved in the structural use of wrought, cast, and rolled iron. As well as a

handsome red-brick polygonal chimney with a stone gallery near the top, his drawings depict a slate-roofed rectangular block, containing the winding-engine house and the so-called 'stage' for the unloading of coal from the wagons, with a smaller block at right angles for the boilers. The engine and boiler houses are of brick with stone dressings, but the stage is a framed structure. Open on the ground floor, it is of iron to first-floor level, with cast-iron polygonal columns and braces giving an arched effect; and in timber, with some strengthening vertical iron rods, from there to the eaves. The weatherboarded upper walls have sets of double doors through which the coal would pass after being graded. The upper floor had to be strong enough to carry the coal. Webb's annotations explain the construction: 'common joists' rest on girders that are 'supported by double tension rods bolted through shoes resting on [the] iron columns'; two 'binders' run longitudinally between the girders, resting on saddles and being 'trussed with single tension rods' that run across the building under the binders. An iron brace springs from each column to the girder, its purpose being to 'resist the lateral thrust', not to carry any weight.[60] The roof trusses are of iron, a scissor type with vertical members in the long block, and with king posts and braces in fan formation in the boiler house.

Two opinions expressed by Webb to his client are also enlightening. The first is that to look stable 'chimneys and iron columns should not appear to be planted on the ground but in it'; to this end, the iron columns have no bases. The second, which demonstrates Webb's interest in civil engineering and explains the white paint on the Bell Brothers' clock tower, is that for the iron 'any paint used should be black or white', and preferably the latter because 'cast iron work on a large scale never looks so well as when painted white—witness Brunel's works'.[61]

Commercial and professional premises

In 1864, Webb was one of the architects invited by the organisers to compete for the commission to design the Bradford Wool Exchange. There were two different factions amongst the directors on the Exchange Committee, as a result of which the competition was mishandled, leading to bitter debate in the press.[62] Most of the committee members were in favour of employing some local architect and of having a Classical building to match most of the nineteenth-century public buildings in Bradford; on the opposing side were three prominent leaders of the town who, as admirers of Ruskin, were determined to have a Gothic building. The first architects to be invited to compete, all with practices in the north of England and all devotees of the classical styles, were Lockwood and Mawson (Bradford), Paul & Ayliffe (Bradford), Milnes & France (Bradford), W and G Audsley (Liverpool), and Cuthbert Broderick (1822–1905, of Leeds). Alfred Harris, the Secretary of the Exchange Committee and one of the three in opposition, soon procured invitations for Burges, Street, Waterhouse, Shaw, and Webb. Another of the opposers, John Aldam Heaton, the furniture and fabric manufacturer who eventually became associated loosely with Shaw in London, already knew Shaw, Burges, and Rossetti, and almost certainly Webb. Lockwood and Mawson, who in 1851 had designed St George's Hall in Bradford and were based in the town, had an obvious advantage. In May 1864, Ruskin gave a lecture in Bradford at the instigation of Heaton, who asked him to advise the townsfolk on the most appropriate style for their new exchange. After castigating them for not caring sufficiently about the matter and for regarding style as a matter of fashion and not as the expression of morality, Ruskin advocated Gothic as the better style for all buildings.[63] Probably as a result, all the submitted designs were Gothic.

The competitors had little time to prepare their schemes, as the submission date was 1 April 1864, which gave the local architects a further advantage. Scott, Street, and Waterhouse withdrew; and Broderick and Webb failed to complete in time, possibly deliberately in Webb's case, as he would have been disgusted by the various machinations. Most of the directors, aware of the identity of all the supposedly incognito designers, voted for Lockwood and Mawson.

The site for the Wool Exchange was a restricted triangle of ground in the town centre. The executed winning design is in what Lockwood regarded as being freely interpreted Venetian Gothic, with a large square-plan, spire-topped tower with pinnacles, in the apex of the triangle.[64] The exchange hall itself is not visible from outside; on one front, it is concealed by a screen wall for the sake of a regular elevation.

In Shaw's many-gabled design, the exchange hall is again in the centre of the building, lit by eight clerestory bay windows.[65] There is a massive tower of alien appearance in the apex of the site. Many of the small windows are rectangular but most larger ones have pointed arches. Webb's exchange hall is in the centre of the building but he expresses it on the exterior by reducing the height of the shops and offices directly in front of it, and by marking it with a large two-stage timber-framed roof lantern, which lights the hall along with the twin sashes under pointed arches (with ornamented tympana) in a row of three identical gables. Both he and Shaw chose randomly coursed rubble for the walls, a considerable area being absolutely plain in both schemes. Webb's tower, far smaller than Shaw's so as not to dominate the surrounding buildings, has large diamond-shaped clock-faces beneath an open belfry in timber topped by a smaller leaded cone than that of the lantern. Webb reflects the existing surrounding buildings by using vertical sashes for most of his windows, albeit under pointed or flat hood moulds. Over the wide, flat windows of the shops, he expresses on the exterior the pointed arches that support the upper walls and which in his Worship Street shops of 1861 are hidden by the projecting shop window itself and are segmental (see chapter 11). Shaw, too, uses pointed arches over some of the shops but over a projecting bay window akin to Webb's at Worship Street.

Instead of designing a grand, imposing edifice to mark and celebrate the position of the town as the successful centre of the woollen trade, such as the directors and the burghers sought, Webb chose to express reality: that the Bradford Exchange was to be an impressive exchange hall set amid shops and offices occupied by proprietors with different needs. His design would have produced a building much more in harmony with neighbouring structures than was the executed design or than Shaw's would have been, but it would not have found favour with the directors.

In 1864, being by then an admirer of Webb's work and probably having seen his drawings for the Wool Exchange, Lowthian Bell tried to secure for the architect the commission to design the Middlesbrough Exchange (see chapter 10). As a director of the newly established Middlesbrough Exchange Co. Ltd, Bell proposed at the first committee meeting of the directors in August 1864 that 'one Architect of repute and standing' be asked to design the exchange and supervise its construction.[66] His proposal was rejected in favour of the holding of an open competition, and a subcommittee was elected to organise it. Bell, who was not member of the subcommittee, subsequently suggested to it by letter that an independent assessor for the competition should be appointed, and he proposed that this be Webb.[67] In January 1865, his letter having been read to it, the subcommittee resolved that Bell be asked to obtain the 'information as to the fee demanded by Mr. Webb'.[68] From the phrasing of the request, it seems that Webb had already signified to Bell his willingness to take on the job. However, unless he had proposed too high a fee, which is unlikely, his final decision must have been to have nothing to do with a building that would be representative of the commercial system of which he so heartily disapproved. Ultimately, Waterhouse was appointed to examine the designs and estimates of the competitors and, through no fault of his, the competition became a controversial and unethical affair.[69]

Having failed in his attempt to secure for Webb the commission to design the Middlesbrough Exchange, Lowthian Bell tried to do the same with a proposed new street in Newcastle upon Tyne. Newcastle Corporation had obtained an Act of Parliament in 1866 permitting the creation of the street, which would link the Central Railway Station more directly with Grainger Street in the centre of the town. The subcommittee for the St John's Lane Improvement, meeting on 15 December 1866 to discuss how best to obtain a good design and plan, agreed that one architect be appointed 'without competition', and that Alderman Bell, Vice-Chairman of the Finance Committee and a former mayor, be asked to 'make a preliminary enquiry of Mr. Webbe' [sic].[70] Bell, delighted with Webb's enlargement of Washington Hall and probably having seen the Worship Street shops, obviously had extolled his protégé's capability and suitability for the job.

As a result, Webb made a site inspection in December 1866, and by 24 January 1867 he had submitted his report and drawings to the subcommittee, which on that day passed them on to the Borough Engineer and the Town Surveyor for their written comments. These were ready the following day, when the subcommittee decided to send them to Webb with a copy of the 'New Streets Regulations' that were applicable to the project, and to request that Bell invite Webb to meet the committee in order to discuss the officers' reports. Webb did so on 5 March 1867, when certain amendments to his line for the proposed street were accepted, and he agreed to send a new plan to the committee before making his elevations. However, on 28 March 1867 the committee accepted a letter

Below The Bradford Wool Exchange Competition: one of Webb's unfinished elevation drawings of 1864 (RIBA Library Photographs Collection)

from Webb in which he withdrew from the engagement, and consequently it was decided to open up the invitation for proposals for the street to other architects, with a premium of one hundred guineas for the best one. Several plans were submitted but none was approved and, after seemingly endless argument, a revised plan by Lamb, the Town Surveyor, was accepted, with specific modifications.[71]

The minutes of the subcommittee meetings and of the full Newcastle Council do not record why Webb withdrew, and his letter is missing. However, by March 1867 he was deeply involved in finishing the design for number 1 Palace Green, the mansion-cum-studio-house for George Howard (see chapter 5), and would have had no time to waste on the preparation of more drawings and reports, or on repeated journeys to Newcastle. He would have foreseen that these were likely to result from the many differences of opinion of the councillors and officials about the precise line of the proposed street, and from his own strong recommendation that each building in the street be designed individually.[72] On his first site visit, he had listed various factors about the project with the clear intention of putting them in his report (also missing), most of them being on this point. In the event, probably not through Webb's recommendation but because the sites were not taken up as quickly as had been envisaged, the buildings were built piecemeal to suit each lessee. The lack of an overall scheme such as he had envisaged resulted in conspicuous disunity.

Webb's list throws considerable light on his approach to the design of an urban terrace.[73] He noted that it would be inadvisable to use the same plan for all the sites (which were to be let for shops and houses), that the size of the sites should be variable, and that each building ought to be designed individually according to the needs of the specific lessee. 'No architect has the right to throw away the advantages of <u>special use</u> of any building,' he wrote, adding that a 'great amount of variety may be obtained without incongruity or even loss of unity'. 'The mere wishes of the several tenants […] would enable the archt [sic]—tho' keeping in mind the street as a whole to give great individuality of expression to each house or each series of houses,' reads another note. Varying the size and elevation details of each unit would avoid the 'uncomfortable appearance of a <u>stepped</u>- -uniformity' on the rising ground of the new street, and the extra cost of each

design could be added to the purchase price of the particular unit. 'In designing a street of a number of houses, an architect has not the advantage to be obtained in designing a larger public building with uses of the same well & clearly defined,' he wrote; if some larger units were available, one might be taken for such a use and thus enable the architect to 'obtain a much greater effect'.

Webb's elevation drawing of part of the proposed street shows that he had in mind frontages of a similar dignified and well-controlled appearance to those of his scheme for the Bradford Exchange, in which the use of plain walls and sash windows were unifying elements. In the Newcastle scheme, the same purpose is also served by the horizontal lines of first-floor balconies and of the parapets, the latter being broken by gables only where the level changes between some of the units. Gothic details are not so evident as in the Bradford scheme. Gone are the boarded doors and medieval-type hinges, and the only pointed arches are the two upper arches over the entrances to the back lane and adjacent passageway. The shop windows are bows, highly unusual in 1867, beneath round arches supported on freestanding octagonal columns and containing the mezzanine windows as in his Bradford design. The use of round rather than pointed arches to prevent the wide windows on the ground floor of commercial buildings from giving an appearance of instability was still rare over a decade later.

Webb's unifying elements and the rhythm of the repeated sashes resulted in a calm frontage that would have been more in harmony with the classical-style façades of Grainger Street (1835–39) at the top end of the new street and that of the Central Station (1846–50) at the bottom end (both by John Dobson (1787–1865)) than are the hotchpotch of designs that were erected. Lowthian Bell must have admired Webb's elevation as it foreshadows some parts of the exterior of Rounton Grange, designed four years later.

In 1868, Leonard Rowe Valpy (d. 1883), a wealthy London solicitor, gave Webb his chance to design a prestigious urban building, albeit not a public one and not on a large site. Valpy, a patron of the Pre-Raphaelite circle, would have known Webb for some time, perhaps having been introduced to him by his own client Ruskin. Valpy commissioned Webb to design an office block to replace a seventeenth-century house, number 19 Lincoln's Inn Fields, London.[74] The Fields had been developed in the mid-seventeenth century when long terraces of houses were built round a large rectangular open space; some rebuilding had taken place during the following century, and by 1868 several houses were being used as offices. In August, Webb measured the existing four-storey brick house, situated in the northern terrace facing south over the square; the contract was signed early in 1869 by Charles Aldin, a London builder, and the building was in use by 1871.[75] It is used as offices still but the interior was gutted and redone in 1975, permission to do so being conditional on the retention and preservation of the entrance front (some minor parts of the wrought-iron balustrades had been removed previously). Most unfortunately, however, the fine spiral staircase and the important chimney turret above it were removed when a lift was installed.

The new structure consisted of two blocks facing in opposite directions and separated by a light well that had a connecting flat-roofed link of three floors on its western side. The south block, fronting the square and of five storeys and an attic floor, contained the major offices and the housekeeper's commodious high-level quarters, and was very tall in proportion to its width of just under twenty-four feet. A circular stairwell rose through the centre of the block from the basement to the attics, closely surrounded by all the fireplaces, flues, and vent shafts, and on the first three floors by the cloakrooms and WCs, which took secondary lighting from the well and were vented via the chimneys. The two-storey north block edged the back street from which it had no access, the service entrance being into the basement (which covered the whole site) via a customary London area below the entrance front of the south block.

Several designs were made for the main front: a preliminary scheme with two bold round arches on the ground floor (a choice of detailing was given); the executed design; and a slightly later one almost entirely in brickwork.[76] The elevation shown at a larger scale on the preliminary drawing has the arches, with emphasized keystones, carried on a central detached column and flanked to the right and left of the front by pilasters. The column projects to support balconies, with wrought-iron balustrades, at the level of the cornice of the entablature; between them an oriel, supported by the central column, rises through two storeys, with oval windows or niches on the first floor, small arched windows on the second, and a flat roof with another iron balustrade. All this stonework would have been expensive. The elements are treated with great freedom and the elevation has a markedly English Baroque appearance long before the interest in a Neo-Baroque style developed. Undoubtedly, Webb would have simplified the detailing before erection but this front would still have been expensive, which probably explains why Valpy rejected it, and why he did likewise for a time with the second scheme before he and his architect decided that the location required a more sophisticated frontage than that of the third, all-brick design.

The executed three-bay frontage is much less emphasized and less costly at street level but has more important detailing at a high level. The outer bays are in brick; the wider central one is occupied by a stone-faced bay window, four storeys high and roofed by a stone balcony that spans the front and has a wrought-iron balustrade. The balcony is supported on bold stone corbels, and on two polygonal attached columns that rise from ground level at the angles of the bay window. The windows are small-paned vertical sashes, those in the brickwork being mainly under segmental arches, and the paired lights in the stone central bay having flat arches, some of which have joggled voussoirs. A three-light window under a wide

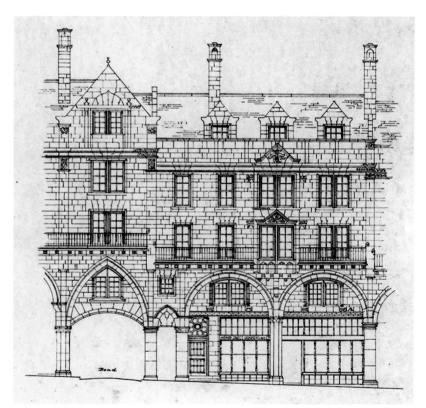

Below Design for a New Street in Newcastle upon Tyne (late 1866–68, unexecuted): part of the street front of the terrace, from one of Webb's drawings of 1867 (Victoria & Albert Museum/ V&A Images)

segmental arch occupies the brick gable, flanked by buttresses and with Webb's characteristic upturned crenellations beneath the sill. Originally, four huge chimneys rose from the grey slat roof, strikingly banded in stone and brick and linked by low-level open arches, to form a turret set at forty-five degrees around the pyramid roof lantern. On the back street elevation, brick pilasters of the pantiled rear block create panels, housing twinned sashes with segmental relieving arches on the ground floor, and with lintels in the eaves on the first floor.

Webb provided Valpy with an office block of radical and convenient plan, with an avant-garde, possibly even unique at the time, central circulation and service core that reduced passages to a minimum, admitted light, and provided readily accessible, well-ventilated cloakrooms and WCs. He placed the doorway and hall to one side rather than retain the symmetry of the front by using a central entrance, because on such a narrow site the latter would have created flanking rooms of inadequate width. The striking main staircase spiralled dramatically up the smooth walls of the well from the basement to the attics, and the semicircular secondary staircase in the link provided further impressive geometry.

The entrance front was as radical as the plan. Webb's use of multiplication of detail, using mouldings not carved ornament, to give the narrow building an appropriate importance and dignity for its role as the premises of successful London solicitors is worthy of investigation. The older houses in the terrace are reflected in the materials and the fenestration, but by breaking the existing parapet line with a gable-to-the-street in the medieval tradition, Webb demonstrates that this is an individually designed building. Gracefully curved upturns at the base of the gable link it smoothly to the adjoining buildings.[77] The gable is the major distinguishing feature between Webb's front and that of 1812 by Soane at number 13 in the same terrace, which is an imaginative interpretation of the Classical idiom, with a horizontal roof-line. Each of the frontages have stone-fronted projecting elements and are symmetrical apart from having off-centre doorways. Whilst Webb expresses his entrance honestly with a functional canopy, Soane retains apparent symmetry by recessing the door under an arch like those of the adjacent windows.[78]

Webb's central stone bay, doubtless inspired by the multi-storey central porches of several Elizabethan

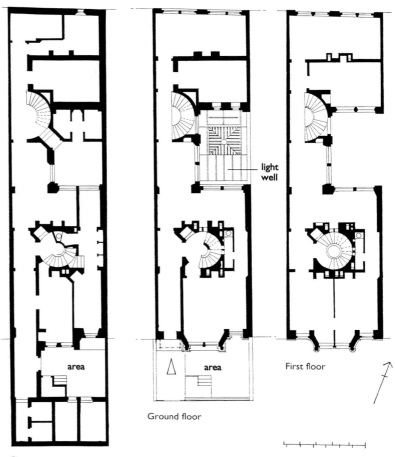

Basement

Ground floor

light well

First floor

and Jacobean country houses, adds colour contrast and, as the stone could be worked more finely than the rubbed bricks, sophistication.[79] The two polygonal columns, stemming from the polygonal buttresses of some large Tudor houses, are divided by the string-sills into sections, thus avoiding an over-attenuated look and calling to mind the superimposed Orders of the early-seventeenth-century porches. The pediment hood moulds join the canopy in repeating the diagonals of the gable at a smaller scale, whilst the columns strengthen the angles of the bay actually and visually, and carry the eye up to the balcony.

The earlier balconies in the terraces round the square were on the first floor. Webb's unusual fourth-floor balcony adds vigour, movement, and contrasts of light and shade, forming a strong horizontal line on a frontage of overall verticality and, when seen from below, acting as a cornice. It also allowed the housekeeper to take fresh air and enjoy the fine view. The balustrade demonstrates Webb's understanding of the way wrought iron is forged. The verticals branch

Right Number 19 Lincoln's
Inn Fields, London (1868,
constructed 1869–70): the
front (south) elevation; the
chimneys were removed in
1975 (from a photograph in
Webb's collection)

into upturned fleurs-de-lis under the handrail; and scrolled brackets, which remain, helped to support the slender arches that once framed the view.[80] In 1871, Waterhouse followed suit with high-level balconies, wrought-iron balustrades, and a large gable-to-the-street, when he designed the office block replacement for the adjacent houses (numbers 17 and 18).

The balcony, and the group of chimneys that undoubtedly was influenced by Vanbrugh's turrets, provide the high-level interest Webb considered desirable on a building that would be seen across a large open space. He also follows Vanbrugh, Wren, and their peers in gathering all the flues into massive chimneys for a striking effect. The eye is prepared for the bold banding of the stacks by the brick and stone quoins that visually stitch the bay window to the brick wall.

Several further points could be made about the façade but sufficient have been made to indicate how Webb used his wide knowledge of English architecture as a source of inspiration for inventive experiments in design, always aiming for truthful expression and an overall national character, without any intention of creating a Progressive Eclectic style. This is what George Warington Taylor had in mind when expressing his hope that number 19 Lincoln's Inn Fields would have 'its right moral effect on future generations'.[81] At the time it was built, there was no

building in London like it. The plan was never published and therefore did not have the influence it deserved. The fine entrance front affected the design of Shaw's London houses and it soon joined his and Webb's other metropolitan buildings in largely determining the character and elements of the so-called 'Queen Anne' manner (of which Webb heartily disapproved once it became a fashionable style).[82] He appears to have been the first nineteenth-century architect to use, in London, stone and brick banding derived from English Baroque buildings such as Wren's St Benet's Church, Paul's Wharf (1677–83).[83] It was soon being adopted by other architects, including Bodley, Shaw, MacLaren, and John Francis Bentley (1839–1902), and its popularity lasted for several decades.[84]

Around the turn of the century, Professor Pite at the Royal Academy, the tutors of the Architectural Association, and Lethaby, Ricardo, and George Jack at the Central School, and a little later Prior at Cambridge, were encouraging their students to study Webb's buildings.[85] In 1900, Pite rightly opined that number 19 Lincoln's Inn Fields, some thirty years after being erected, still marked a 'position in direct beautiful expression of artistic design and of reliance upon and mastery in the spirit of building craft [...] ahead of and beyond any subsequent similar work'.[86]

In 1881, when the Secretary of Bell Brothers, Hugh Bell, asked him to design a new main office block on the site of the firm's existing offices at number 7 Zetland Road in Middlesbrough, the centre of the local iron trade, Webb received his chance to demonstrate something of what he had had in mind at Newcastle for a prestigious urban building – albeit not a public edifice – that would be larger than number 19 Lincoln's Inn Fields. Webb sent a tracing of his first plan to Hugh Bell in November 1881; after making some suggested changes, he dispatched a rearranged plan in January 1882, and by early in 1883 his design had been accepted. The project was put aside after a sharp fall in trade but a rise in 1888 led the directors, all of them members of the family, to decide to build the office block. The £6,440 estimate (excluding the electric lighting, the iron and concrete floors, and several other items) of a local builder, John Johnson, was accepted. The contract was signed in June 1889, construction under the clerk of works H Luscombe began in July, and the building was completed early in 1891.[87]

The original offices were created in nineteenth-century houses occupying an almost square mid-terrace plot in the centre of Middlesbrough, facing north across Zetland Road to the railway station, the forecourt of which was almost a storey higher than the mean ground level of the site. Webb's plans of 1883 became those of the 1889 contract. His building covers the entire site. The basement originally housed the cloakrooms, various service and store rooms, a private entrance and lobby for the family members of the firm (from which a newel stair rose to all floors), and a room for the batteries, dynamo, and gas stove that provided electricity for lamps, bells, and the telegraphic apparatus. The main entrance, within an inset porch at the centre of the north front, leads into a two-storey central hall, from which an arm extends to the eastern perimeter of the building and contains the main staircase. Flanking the entrance on the left was the Bells' private room, which had a private office and WC off its small lobby and, to the right, a 'special' office approached through the clerks' office.[88] The board room and an office for a senior executive overlooked Brunswick Street. On the first floor were the office of the chairman and managing director Lowthian Bell, with its own waiting room and WC; four further offices; two waiting rooms; and the telegraph room.[89] On the second or attic floor, two offices overlooked Zetland Road, with lumber rooms behind them, and the remainder was covered with low roofs but offered space for further accommodation.

The load-bearing brick walls are of exposed red-brown vitrified bricks up to sill level on the ground floors, above which they are faced in stone on the ground and first floors of the Zetland Street front, apart from the roughcast gables on the attic floor, which are whitewashed. The chimneys and the Brunswick Street front above basement height are also roughcast and whitewashed to unify the building. Red clay pantiles cover the roofs. The basement has an iron and concrete vault; the fireproof upper floors are of concrete and steel; paired iron girders support the wall over the three great arches on the ground floor of the entrance front; and reinforced concrete lintels made on site span the narrower openings.[90]

The basement, half above ground level, has windows with iron grilles on both fronts. Above it on the ground floor of the entrance front are what Webb termed the 'three great arches'; the central one spans the recessed porch, each outer arch

encompasses a bow window of three lights separated by cast-iron colonnettes.[91] The porch has windows in its canted side walls, and panelled double outer doors and inner half-glazed swing doors in oak. Five of the seven sashes on the first floor are set behind a colonnade; at each end of it, a narrower sash is in line with the columns, with the cornice of the colonnade extending over it. An undulating parapet wall combines the three second-floor dormer windows, each with twinned sashes, into a single unit that rises to an apex, originally crowned by a finial, over each dormer. Small rectangular openings in the parapet give access to the gutters and roofs behind it.

To reduce costs, on the Brunswick Street front the two superimposed colonnades of the 1883 drawing were replaced on the ground floor by a simpler arcade of flat pilasters and round arches containing segmental-headed sashes and, over a dentilated string-sill on the first floor, by a row of segmental arches rising from bold imposts below an equally bold cornice with cast-iron modillions filled with concrete. This cornice was removed in the twentieth century. The timber window frames were painted dark green with, as on

Below Number 19 Lincoln's Inn Fields: the entrance front (detail)

Above Number 19 Lincoln's Inn Fields: the entrance front, with that of the adjacent building (Numbers 17 and 18) by Alfred Waterhouse (1871).

Webb's major concern when designing the office block, as he explained to Hugh Bell in the letter of 10 November 1881 that accompanied the tracing of his first plan, was how to fit in the required rooms 'with regard to gaining as much light as possible under the circumstances'.[92] Direct lighting was possible on only two sides, on one of which light would be restricted by the high forecourt of the railway station. He explains that he has 'tried to get as much sun as possible into the heart of the block from the south'. This he proposes to do by means of windows on the Brunswick Street front, a glass roof over the central hall and staircase, and clerestory windows in the upper hall looking over a lower part of the building at the back (the last had to be abandoned when the required number of offices necessitated a first floor over the whole site). On the north front, he proposes having two large bow windows on the ground floor, and three on the first floor on which the major offices would be placed, undoubtedly for the best light, with the main entrance at the centre of the ground floor 'for instant communication'.

All the rooms in the building are well lit, and even on a dark day in winter the two-storey hall and the waiting rooms off it are astonishingly bright. The barrel-vaulted entrance lobby, and the central hall and staircase, provide interesting contrasts of relative shade and bright top-light. The glass roof of the hall has a framework of delicate wrought iron, a development of Webb's pyramid roof on the palm house at Rounton Grange; the design was used again for the conservatory at Standen. Another striking feature of the interior is Webb's repeated use of a square grid or trellis throughout the ground and first floor. Grids first appear in the leaded glass of the fanlight over the entrance and are repeated in the hall on two levels in the wide-arched and leaded internal windows, in the small circular internal windows over the staircase, and in the cast-iron panels of the balustrade on the staircase, the gallery, and the bridge that crosses over the staircase dramatically on the first floor. They are also found in the leaded glazing of the screens that create the waiting rooms overlooking the staircase and in others acting as dividers within offices; in the radiator casings; in some half-glazed cupboard doors; and in the small hardwood cubes on the treads of the staircase, landings, and bridge. Webb's liking for this simple pattern, which he had used first in many of the

the entrance front, white sashes. Almost all the materials came from Yorkshire: sandstone from the Scarth Nick quarry on Lowthian Bell's estate (with the same bedding, jointing, tooling, and pointing as used for Rounton Grange); bricks from nearby Linthorpe; steel from Middlesbrough; York stone for hearths, corbels, copings, and pad-stones; and stone from Pateley Bridge for the fireplaces. The few items from further afield include Hoptonwood stone from Derbyshire for the columns (the bases and capitals are in sandstone), and Westmorland green slates for the edging of roofs at the eaves. Iron came from the Clarence Works over the river in what was then part of County Durham.

windows of Red House, might indicate a Japanese influence but probably stemmed from what Pevsner terms Webb's 'faith in the elementary'.[93]

The interior fittings of the spacious rooms, for example the half-glazed cupboards in Lowthian Bells' room that unfortunately have been removed, were little different from those of Webb's houses. The fireplaces have his characteristic bracketed mantels and panelled overmantels. The oak wainscoted boardroom had a cupboard and bookcase, and the first-floor general office had a handsome double-sided oak desk some twenty-five feet long, with a raised central shelf and a continuous top supported at intervals by integral chests of drawers. Webb also designed a large, robust oak seat, with a slatted back and wooden balls at the ends of the arms, for the hall.[94] Hugh Bell took an interest in every detail of the new block and ensured that it was equipped with up-to-date technology and the latest office amenities, including an ingenious signalling system of his own design whereby he received ample warning of the impending arrival in the station of any train he wished to catch.[95] A passenger lift was purchased but never installed, probably because it would have obstructed the space and light in the hall. Judging from several reports of senior and less exalted staff, the well-lit and well-ventilated building itself – which had sound-proofed floors and, at Webb's insistence, ample cloakroom facilities and WCs – and the office accommodation it provided were found to be excellent.[96] This, and the appropriate appearance of the entrance front, ensured that the building continued to serve its purpose as the head offices of iron-trade firms for some eighty years. In the entrance front, Webb achieved 'a great amount of variety […] without incongruity or even loss of dignity' such as he had hoped might be possible in the new street in Newcastle. The superbly crafted main elevation – unusual and interesting without being flamboyant, and suitably impressive without being grandiose – expressed the high status of Bell Brothers, a pioneering firm of national and international renown.

Webb soon abandoned his first idea of having two tiers of great arches, presumably on discovering that his customary sashes would admit enough light to the first floor. The use of sashes reduces the proportion of window to wall, thereby increasing the visual stability of the front. Placing the bows behind the great arches has a similar effect, and the slenderness of the arches makes it clear that concealed beams must be carrying the upper wall. All the main elements of the Zetland Road front appear on Webb's drawings of 1883, which were completed before his winter in Italy of 1884–85. Some observers have suggested that the office block was influenced by the Byzantine and Italian Renaissance buildings he saw there but, in view of his comment to Boyce in 1885 about being thankful that no-one would be able to say that anything good about Clouds had come from his having seen Italy, any major influence is unlikely.[97] The boldly projecting cornice supported by modillions, which replaced the 1883 entablature bearing pediment mouldings, is more likely to have come from the practical need for a platform from which to clean the gable windows and maintain the roof than from a wish to reflect an Italian palazzo.

The great arches encompassing what Webb termed 'bows' but are actually shallow canted bay windows are clearly a development of the ground-floor windows in his Bradford and Newcastle schemes and the dining-room window at Clouds. Executed before 1883, the wall immediately above the Clouds window had a short arcade of segmental arches with plain pilasters that presaged Webb's colonnade over round arches at Middlesbrough.[98] Using a colonnade above the necessarily wide arches of the ground floor of the office block meant that he could relate his building to the adjacent houses by using similar vertical sashes, and by continuing the eaves line of the houses with his cornice. In the 1883 and 1889 drawings, the colonnade finishes idiosyncratically at each end with a space not a column, as did the arcade on the Clarence Offices. The colonnade provides vigorous modelling, which is particularly valuable on a street front chiefly seen in sharp perspective. By raising the basement and recessing the entrance, Webb was able to gain an additional contrast in depth and an impressive flight of steps. He reunified the front by returning to the three-bay arrangement of the ground floor on the attic floor, and relating the latter to the first floor with stone window surrounds and buttresses.

The curving line of the Zetland Road parapet was derived from the gable at number 19 Lincoln's Inn Fields. All the carved ornament – two small panels flanking the entrance, the beautiful foliate panels on three sides of each finial (all different), the unusual scrolled top of the parapet buttresses, and the admirable narrow band of stylized leaves and flowers

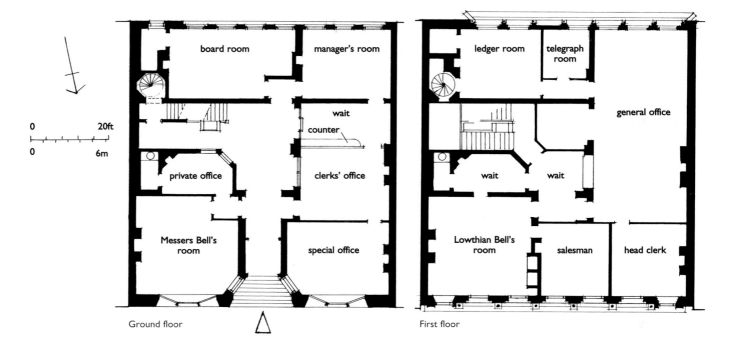

board room

manager's room

wait

counter

private office

clerks' office

Messers Bell's room

special office

0   20ft

0   6m

Ground floor

ledger room

telegraph room

general office

wait   **wait**

Lowthian Bell's room

salesman

head clerk

First floor

Above Bell Brothers Offices, Middlesbrough: plans of the ground and first floors

Opposite Bell Brothers Offices (Webb House), Number 7 Zetland Road, Middlesbrough (designed 1881–83, constructed 1889–91): the entrance (north) front, Zetland Road

round the top of each capital – was English in character. The form of the capitals, however, does resemble that of some Byzantine examples but without the typical basket motif. Apart from the new cornice and the simplification of some details, the only other changes made in 1889 were to have the ground and first floors entirely in stone not brick with stone dressings, and to substitute a plain roughcast finish for the dentilated brickwork of the gabled parapet and small gilded copper spheres for the large stone balls on the finials.

Evidently, the Bell Brothers Offices were not published during Webb's lifetime but his drawings would have been seen and discussed by his disciples in London, and the freedom of his use of architectural elements regardless of derivation would have encouraged the adoption of a similarly experimental approach. In this, he was a pioneer of the Edwardian Free style. His use of round arches over wide ground-floor windows increased their popularity; they appear in many early-twentieth-century commercial and civic buildings. His use of roughcast on a prestigious urban office block, as well as for Hill House, Greatham in 1883 (see chapter 11), largely explains its popularity with Arts and Crafts architects, notably Voysey. Perhaps Webb's celebration of the simple grid in the Bell Brothers Offices led Mackintosh to follow suit, notably in his own roughcast Hill House in Helensburgh

(1902–04).[99] Voysey's interiors of the Essex and Suffolk Equitable Insurance Society's Office in Capel House, New Bond Street, London (1906), have round-arch interior windows and screens with square panes similar to those of number 7 Zetland Road.[100] George Jack was so impressed by the Zetland Road front that, in 1918 and 1919 when designing a proposed extension to the offices that would replace the adjacent houses, he could think of nothing better than to repeat Webb's front in every detail (the rebuilding never took place).[101]

The building itself has undergone significant alterations since its construction, but fortunately most of Webb's work remains, apart from the upper cornice on the Brunswick Street front, the finials on the entrance front, and some interior fittings.[102] In 1906, George Jack created further offices on the second or attic floor, thereby adding another storey to the rear, and altered the tops of Webb's chimneys. The building served as the headquarters of successive iron or steel firms until 1977, when the British Steel Corporation moved into a new local headquarters building in Redcar, which had been built because of an application made a few years earlier for permission to demolish number 7 Zetland Road and the neo-Gothic bank by Waterhouse at the end of the same terrace as they lay on the route of a proposed major bypass. The applications were rejected after a public inquiry was held in 1974.[103] In 1977, the building was sound but

Right Bell Brothers Offices: the upper part of the main staircase

Below Bell Brothers Offices: the entrance hall, in which Webb demonstrated his liking for simple grids (from a photograph in Webb's collection)

some six years of neglect and vandalism followed, leaving it in extremely bad condition. Purchased for the nominal sum of £1 by Middlesbrough Council, on its behalf in the 1980s the exterior was restored and extensive dry rot was eradicated from the interior at a cost of around £100,000, after which it was converted into a hostel and workshops for people with special needs, for another £300,000 (and named Webb House in honour of the architect). After further repair and conversion in 2001 costing £350,000, it is currently split into nine self-contained flats and a bed-sitting room, for people in some need of care.[104] The proposed dual-carriageway road was constructed on a slightly changed line, since when traffic has passed the Grade II★ listed building at an elevated height within a few metres of the Brunswick Street front.

Pevsner considered the Bell Brothers office block to be 'the most valuable building in the town', and John Brandon-Jones, in his important testimony read out at the public inquiry, affirmed that it was 'one

the most interesting and important nineteenth-century buildings surviving in Britain'.[105] The then Secretary of State Geoffrey Rippon and his inspector, the architect V Leslie Nash, judged it to be of sufficient importance to require the costly realigning of a proposed major road. The building is important as a major work by Webb and also because it is representative of the history of the rapid development of Middlesbrough from a town with a population of c. 7,500 in 1852 to 75,000 in 1891, which was due almost entirely to the local iron industry in the expansion of which Lowthian and Hugh Bell and Bell Brothers had a major role.

Left Bell Brothers Offices: a waiting room on the first floor (from a photograph in Webb's collection)

Below Bell Brothers Offices: the Bells' office on the ground floor (from a photograph in Webb's collection)

Ecclesiastical buildings

The opinions of two reviewers of Webb's design for the interior of a town church exhibited in the Royal Academy exhibition of 1858 have been covered already (in chapter 1). All that need be said in addition is that the church was a narrow one without aisles, with a chancel narrower than the nave, flanked by a vestry to the south and an organ chamber to the north, and with a panelled and painted nave ceiling supported on pointed arches with brick and stone spandrels.[106]

Webb's first commissioned ecclesiastical building was the ultimately unexecuted chapel for Arisaig House, designed for Francis Astley in 1866 (see chapter 7). In the early 1870s, efforts were made to have the Holy Trinity church in Washington, County Durham (now Tyne and Wear) rebuilt. George Gilbert Scott (junior) evidently produced a design, and Webb agreed to comply with his request that whilst at Washington Hall he, Webb, would inspect the trenches for the foundations of the new church once they had been dug; Webb also promised to urge Lowthian Bell to use any influence he might have on Scott's behalf.[107] The project was abandoned, however, and Webb prepared a rough sketch design for the church himself, perhaps at Bell's suggestion or possibly for his own amusement; as no mention of his involvement is made in the records of the parochial meetings, this too came to nothing.[108]

In c. 1868, Adam Steinmetz Kennard of Great Stanhope Street, London, about whom little is known except that he apparently was wealthy, asked Webb to design a church to replace the existing St Bartholomew's parish church in the small village of Thurstaston in Cheshire. In view of subsequent events, the new church was probably intended to be a memorial to his wife's father, who had died in 1865. Webb prepared several preliminary schemes, one of them taken to working-drawing stage, the first being for a new building on the site of the existing church and the final one on an adjacent plot of land.[109] A full set of drawings was ready and apparently agreed by 1871 but for an unknown reason this project too was abandoned in 1872. In 1887 a new church in the Early English style, on the same site but designed by John Loughborough Pearson, was consecrated; it had been funded in Joseph Hegan's memory by his two daughters, one of them Kennard's wife who died before the work was finished.[110]

Despite not having been executed, Webb's design for the Thurstaston church is important, firstly on its own merits and secondly because it influenced his design for the Brampton church, which was erected (and is covered at the end of this chapter). The Thurstaston design reveals a three-bay nave with a plain walled area at the western end for the font; a chancel as wide as the nave; and a spacious north aisle, which has its own entrance and small porch and at the eastern end opens into an organ chamber. On the south side of the building are a projecting porch near the western end and a vestry with its own entrance and a doorway to the chancel. A tower with a stone spire rises above the eastern bay of the nave and is supported on two massive square-plan piers set diagonally, with integral moulded shafts on the corners, and by the south wall, which has pilasters backed by large buttresses and moulded to match the piers. Four identical pointed arches link the piers and pilasters, the eastern one forming the chancel arch. The central arch of the north arcade is of the same design but the western one is a narrower and lower pointed arch within a rectangular frame. The aisle has three transverse arches which, in the two easternmost bays, are partly supported on the north wall, which again has pilasters matching the piers and backed by buttresses.

Most of the walls of the church are of randomly coursed ashlar, with some irregular panels of random rubble, all in the local red sandstone. The fairly steeply pitched slated roof is the same height on the nave and the chancel, and the northern slope of the nave roof extends to cover the aisle. Except on the chancel, all the walls have parapets, which are neither pierced nor crenellated. All the buttresses are

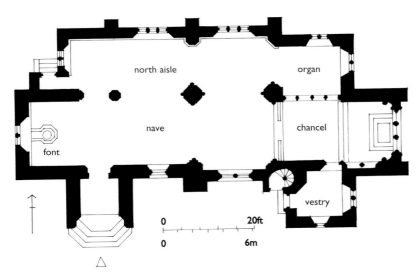

Below Thurstaston Church design: plan

north aisle

organ

nave

chancel

font

vestry

0   20ft

0   6m

functional, and are gabled, with no offsets except on the tower. At the point where the tower decreases slightly in width, the buttresses become smaller and diagonal. At the parapet, they have gabled offsets above which they become functional pinnacles that help flying buttresses and the wall buttresses to support the tall spire, and have gabled tops surmounted by a spirelet topped with a small copper ball. The two-tier spire lights face the cardinal points, and are flanked by miniature buttresses and divided horizontally by a band of minuscule crenellations. The three-light nave windows in the north wall are rectangular, as are many of the small ones throughout the building; the others have pointed arches. Most of the lights have ogee heads, some of them with cusps.

The interior of the church has plain plastered walls with stone dressings, and a pointed barrel vault in timber over most of the nave, but a flat ceiling under the tower and in the chancel, which has a coved cornice. The east end is enriched by the open mullion-and-transom screen to the organ chamber, and by a moulded arch that spans the chancel three feet in front of the east wall; the latter curves at each end to meet the pilasters of the arch.

Webb's design for the Thurstaston church, although not antiquarian, is undoubtedly Gothic. Nothing else would have been acceptable to the Anglican authorities at the time. However, within this constraint he exercised considerable freedom. Despite his great admiration for Early English architecture, he did not design in that style. He designed each item afresh, taking inspiration from whichever Gothic period had produced items of the right shape and character for the purpose and the position in the building of the particular item. He treated Gothic motifs in as cavalier and inventive a manner as he was to do the Classical ones in Middlesbrough a decade later. The pinnacles joined to the spire by flying buttresses and horizontal ties were to appear next, suitably amended for making in cast iron, in the Clarence Offices, thereby revealing Webb's disdain for architectural hierarchy. By growing out of the buttresses at parapet height, the pinnacles, set at an angle, overcame the uncomfortable effect that is sometimes evoked by a polygonal spire rising from a square tower. The influence of Street can be seen in the spire lights, which are slightly reminiscent of those in his competition scheme for Lille Cathedral, on the drawings for which Webb had worked in 1856.[111] Webb's own idiosyncratic detail,

in which the apexes of the gables of the pitch roofs on the porch and the vestry appear as tiny pediments above the parapets, would be realized in an amended form on the porch that he added to Nether Hall in 1874 and on later buildings.

Webb's handsome, well-composed design for the Thurstaston church was entirely appropriate for a parish church in a small country village, and its additional role as a memorial would have been marked, albeit without deliberate symbolism, by the restrained enrichment at the base of the beautiful spire. It is a matter of regret that the scheme was never executed.

Two more of his church designs were never built. The first was prepared in August 1881 at the request of Morris's eldest sister Emma, the wife of Joseph Oldham, vicar of Clay Cross, Derbyshire. From her letter, Webb gathered that Mrs Oldham and her husband required a design and an estimate for a small church, exhibiting some degree of dignity, which they could show to the parishioners and explain what money would be necessary.[112] Webb designed for them a long, narrow building in brick, with a simple round-arched porch and an east window of three cusped lights. The existing parish church, St Bartholomew's, was built in 1851 and had a vestry of 1858 by Street, so Webb's scheme was for a mission church to be built elsewhere in the parish. His letter to Mrs Oldham, which accompanied the drawings and estimate, is the last record of the project amongst his papers.

The second scheme, of 1886, was an unsolicited one, probably inspired by the conditions for the first Liverpool Cathedral competition of 1884. It is unfinished but the two sheets of drawings, comprising a half-plan with major dimensions and small sketches of every important item, show a well-considered, practical design that is capable of being constructed. The main feature is the circular central space, almost ninety feet in diameter and covered by an inventive Gothic vault. The Idea from which Webb developed a new design entirely suitable for an English cathedral, was undoubtedly Brunelleschi's great dome in Florence, which he admired so deeply and had studied so thoroughly in Italy, coupled with another object of his respect, Wren's St Paul's in London. It is a pity Webb never had the chance to

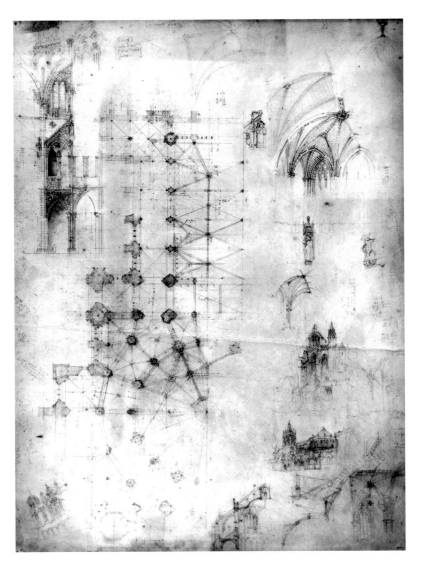

young middle-class women as Anglican deaconesses; once trained, each deaconess was attached permanently to one of the poorer London parishes, to become part of its daily life and to help the parishioners in many practical ways including ministering to the sick. By 1896, the institution had moved from its first quarters into number 85, a large eighteenth-century house. A local firm, John Garrett and Son, built the chapel, which was a separate entity linked by passages to the house. Work began immediately after the contract was signed in August 1896 and was completed in the summer of 1897, a few months later than envisaged because of bad winter weather. As the work progressed, Mrs Gilmore asked Webb to design an altar, a credence table, a lectern, a piscina, an altar cloth, and a silver altar cross (the last two of these are mentioned in chapter 3); he complied with her request in 1897.[114] Stained glass by Morris & Co. was inserted in the five-light south window in 1911 (with figures by Burne-Jones), and the three circular windows in the chapel between 1911 and 1913.[115] The house and the chapel are listed separately as Grade II. In 1970 the house (now Gilmore House) was converted into accommodation for married students from overseas and their families, and an accommodation block was built within a very few feet of the north front of the chapel. Under new ownership and after further conversion and conservation work in 2002, the house became a mixed hostel for a wider variety of tenants, with the chapel and its Morris & Co. windows fortunately remaining unchanged.[116]

The main front of the chapel faces north and is tucked into an angle of the old house, with the original kitchen to its west and dining room to the south, to which it is connected by ground-and first-floor passages in a narrow flat-roofed link along the western end. The basement, partly above ground level, originally contained two small courts, one open and the other covered, a cellar, a large scullery, a heating chamber, and a staircase to the first floor. The chapel, a little over forty-seven feet long by twenty-three feet wide externally, with a recess for the harmonium in a projection on the south side, occupied the whole of the first floor.

The building has yellow stock brick walls, and a pantile roof, hipped at the eastern end and gabled at the end nearest the house, and is edged at the eaves with plain tiles. The main north front has an arcade of three semicircular brick arches and flat pilasters,

build on this scale for, in the words of John Brandon-Jones, 'he was probably the only man of his generation who could have rivalled the work of his friend Bentley at Westminster'.[113]

Webb was more fortunate with his penultimate and his final ecclesiastical commissions, both of which were executed. The final, smaller one is considered first. In 1896, Morris's third oldest sister Isabella (b. 1842), the widow of naval officer Arthur Hamilton Gilmore, asked Webb to design a chapel, to be built at her expense for the Rochester Diocesan Deaconess Institution at number 85 (now 113) Clapham Common North Side, London, of which she was Head Deaconess. Mrs Gilmore, who had had experience in working with the poor, founded the institution in 1887 as a centre for the training of

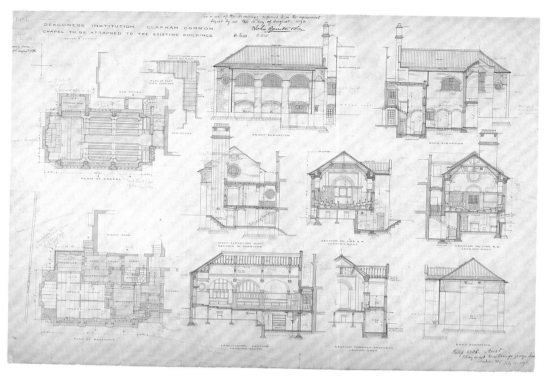

containing wide five-light windows with stone sills on the first floor. The wall above the arches and its coved cornice is roughcast, continuing on the west wall to meet the massive chimney that is plain apart from a projecting string. There are no windows on the east wall. On the south front, at the rear of the chapel, a six-light rectangular window under a round arch with a roughcast tympanum lights the harmonium projection, and there is one five-light window like those on the north front. There are four circular windows, one in the passage link and three in the chapel (one in the west gable, the others near the altar on the north and south walls). All the windows have leaded lights.

The chapel is not divided into a nave and chancel. It is a single space, apart from the harmonium recess, which has a simple open timber screen. Instead of being on the exterior as is customary, the buttresses on the north and south walls project on the inside of the wall, where they carry the roof trusses and serve as the projecting pilasters of two round-arched internal wall arcades. The unusual roof trusses have both king-posts and inclined queen-struts, and curved braces under the tie-beam with, immediately above and parallel to them, straight struts extending to the purlins. Further curved braces extend from the bases of the king-posts and queen-struts to the purlins and to the longitudinal beam that supports the flat part of the ceiling. The roof is open below the collar, purlins, and straight struts, the four spaces between the exposed members of each truss being filled with timber trellises. Banks of tiered bench seats with vertically boarded backs face each other in the collegiate manner. The walls are wainscoted up to door-head height, above which they were originally painted white. The east wall has a tall, round recessed arch springing from the cornice of the wainscot. The cornice continues across the arched recess to form a flat canopy over the altar. Stone steps lead up to the beautiful altar of English

Right The Rochester Diocesan Deaconess Institution Chapel: the silver cross, designed by Webb in 1897 to hang behind the altar, and made by Robert Catterson-Smith (Victoria & Albert Museum/ V&A Images)

crown surmounting the vertical arm, the symbol of the Lamb at its base, and a central circular boss bearing 'IHS'. The reading desk of the simple oak lectern is supported by three robust posts of rectangular cross-section, the only ornament being the notching of small struts arranged in diaper fashion between the two posts nearer the reader. The altar and lectern (made by John Garrett and Son), the cross, and the super-frontal embroidered to Webb's design by May Morris (described in chapter 3) are in the Victoria and Albert Museum.[117]

Webb's impressive but unpretentious chapel was achieved at moderate cost through the ingenious and effective use of simple elements. It has nothing Gothic about it whatsoever, which is indicative of the client's as well as of Webb's open-mindedness. The building is in harmony with the eighteenth-century house, the only items that marked its use, and then in a subtle way, being the large leaded windows. The chapel is certainly a consistent whole. All the fittings and furnishings were designed by the architect; the external round-arched arcade is repeated inside the chapel, and leaded glazing is used throughout, its grid pattern being repeated in the panels of the roof trusses, the low screens in front of the two banks of seating, and the tiles of the floor. The Morris & Co. stained glass, though a later addition, is in character with the building.

oak, which has fifteen fretted front panels and was covered by the altar cloth worked by May Morris to Webb's design (see chapter 3). His fine silver cross, excellently crafted by Robert Catterson-Smith, used to hang on the wall behind the altar. The cross is of wood encased in repoussé patterned silver, with a

Right The Rochester Diocesan Deaconess Institution Chapel: the interior in 1972 (© London Metropolitan Archives)

The chapel seems almost to have been forgotten in the late twentieth century but Webb's admirers in London would have known it a century earlier. His avoidance of Gothic and his use of buttresses on the interior undoubtedly would have encouraged the ecclesiastical experiments of Prior and Lethaby. Prior used internal buttresses to support transverse arches in St Andrew's Church, Roker, Sunderland (1904–07), where his use of wide, mullioned windows with no stained glass also suggests an influence from the chapel.[118] The exteriors of two buildings of 1902 by Voysey – the Carnegie Library and Museum, Limerick, Ireland, and the Sanderson & Sons Factory, Chiswick, London – suggest that he too was influenced by the chapel.[119]

Webb had received his penultimate and most important ecclesiastical commission, for St Martin's Church, Brampton, Cumberland (now in Cumbria), in 1874 – two decades before the deaconesses' chapel – at the instigation of George Howard, who was encouraged and supported by his wife Rosalind and his father Charles Howard. At the time, the Howards were full of enthusiasm for Webb's work as a result of their delighted satisfaction with number 1 Palace Green, and they would have known how disappointed he was about the Thurstaston project. The existing late-eighteenth-century parish church at Brampton was of poor quality, badly in need of repair, and had no free pews for the poorer townsfolk.[120] In August 1873, a year before the parish authorities decided to replace the existing church, George Howard had apparently asked Webb to advise him about the feasibility of doing so; Webb inspected the old church and its site in February 1874, and made up his mind 'as to the character of church for a new one to suit that site'.[121] In April 1874, the Trustees of the Naworth Estate, in charge because of the dementia of the eighth Earl of Carlisle, appointed the Reverend Henry Whitehead (1825–96) as vicar of Brampton on the recommendation of George Howard, who would have known that as an opponent of appropriated pews, he would almost certainly support the replacement of the church.[122] Whitehead took up his post in April, and the scheme began to move ahead rapidly. A committee was set up to look into and report on the state of the existing church; at a public meeting on 14 September at which Charles, George, and Rosalind Howard were present, Whitehead explained why a new church was needed, and the

committee, of which he was chairman, resolved to build one.[123] A considerable amount of money had already been promised; including £500 from Charles Howard, and £2,000 from the Trustees of the Naworth Estate, who made it conditional on their approving the choice of architect and made it clear that they favoured Webb.

On 29 September, on being approached by George Howard, Webb promised to advance the ideas he had earlier in the year sufficiently to be able to give Howard an estimate of its cost.[124] Webb met the committee – which had asked him to inspect and report on some alternative sites, on the likely cost of a new church, and on the proposal in general – on the 22 October, and examined the sites with some of its members. In his report, submitted on 4 November, he recommended the site of the existing church for a number of reasons: it was near the centre of the small market town; the parish already owned it; it fronted the high road to Carlisle; and the new building would protect the existing graveyard. He assumed that the committee would wish the new building to be 'well and substantially built, and in such proportions as would suit the situation, and with the character, necessarily, visibly to express its office', and opined that £6,845 including the architect's fee would provide a church to hold five hundred people.[125] He suggested that the building should occupy the northern part of the site from boundary to boundary and consist of a nave, a chancel, two aisles, and a west tower, with a vestry in the north-east corner and a porch in the north-west corner. He

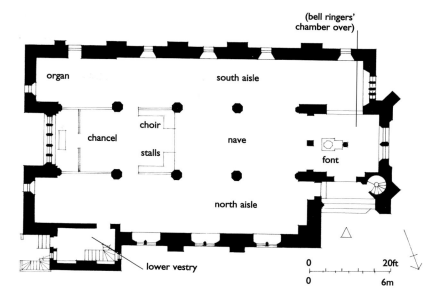

Above St Martin's Church, Brampton, Cumberland: plan

proposed walls of local red sandstone, partly rubble, partly coursed, and a roof of stone-flags (the thick green slates of the district). He also suggested that the upper stage of the tower could be modified during the construction period to suit the amount of funds that might be in hand. The committee decided to go ahead but asked him to reduce his estimate to £6,000 maximum; Webb promised to bear this in mind and to produce the necessary drawings by the end of February 1875. He sent his completed drawings in early March but the estimated cost was £6,070 without the belfry. After some talk of requesting a new design, the committee resolved to proceed but to postpone the building of the tower and porch.[126] Delay having been caused by the first tenders being too high, the estimate of £5,678 6s 3d from Beaty Brothers of Carlisle was accepted, the contract was signed in February 1877, and the church was constructed under the supervision of the clerk of works J Morland between then and September 1878; the final cost, including extras, a smaller porch, and a tower with a temporary belfry stage and roof, was in the region of £7,335, excluding Webb's fee.[127]

During the building period, work on the first-floor vestry had to be halted after the owner-occupier of the house to the east of the church complained through his solicitor that it impinged upon his lights. In 1875, Webb had already advised the committee against moving the vestry to the south aisle, on the grounds that the position of the vestry had 'considerably regulated the disposition of parts of the whole of the north side' and that the 'displacement of one part wd. affect the whole'.[128] His great annoyance on finding similar suggestions being repeated provoked Webb into unwonted vulgarity. He retorted to George Howard that the complainant must be imagining that the disrobing Whitehead would be 'shewing [sic] his backside' out of the vestry window to the complainant's wife for hours on end, and that the woman 'would not mind if he did', though he, Webb, could hardly tell the solicitor so.[129] The complainant eventually settled for £50 in compensation.

In 1884, some problems with damp having emerged, Webb inspected the church and made a detailed report as to the various causes and the necessary remedial work, which was carried out according to his instructions.[130] The following year, his extreme annoyance on either learning of a new scheme for lighting the church by gas or discovering that such a scheme had been carried out provoked an angry letter to the agent of the Naworth Estate in which he explained that

> the newly devised plan of gas lighting, in connection with the forms of the architecture is a mistake, fatal to this scheme of decoration; will certainly be injurious to the stone work and walls; and is in character too childish for a serious building.[131]

He then vowed never to advise on any matter to do with the church in the future. Fortunately, his temper had cooled by the time he was consulted about tiling the sanctuary floor in 1891, when he recommended red marble instead of ceramic tiles.[132]

In 1896, Mrs Whitehead, with whom he had differed in the past about the Vicar's House (see chapter 11), offered £500 towards the completion of the tower if it were done in memory of her late husband. Nothing much was done about it until after Webb had retired. Great debate ensued, during which two Carlisle architects were approached, one being Ferguson, who repaid Webb's kindness in recommending him as architect to the Naworth Estate by strongly urging the completion of the tower according to the original design. Finally, in 1904, the committee accepted Webb's suggestion that the tower be completed by George Jack as the supervising architect, to the design that he, Webb, had prepared for his own satisfaction in 1878 on realizing that the original scheme, with an octagonal

Below St Martin's Church, Brampton, Cumberland (Cumbria) (1874–75, constructed 1877–78): the south front, showing the tower, with the upper stage designed by Webb in 1878 and 1904

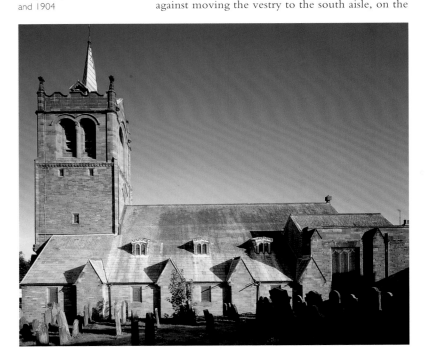

belfry and stone spire, would be too costly.[133] Webb gratuitously modified the design, Jack produced the working drawings from Webb's sketches, and the tower was completed by John Laing and Son of Carlisle in 1906.[134] The cost was around £1,817 excluding Jack's fee, making the total cost of the church in the region of £8,813. George Howard contributed £600 towards the tower; he, his family, and their guests had paid almost half the cost of the entire building.[135]

Eventually, Morris & Co. stained glass was installed as individual memorials in all the external windows except those of the ringers' chamber, the upper vestry and staircase, and the small dormers. A small terracotta relief portraying St Martin was commissioned for the porch by Mrs Whitehead in 1906 as another memorial to her husband; in 1908, the oak font cover in her memory was made by the Keswick School of Industrial Art, an appropriately Arts and Crafts institution; and in 1928, the Morris & Co. arrangement of a specially woven curtain hanging below a gesso panel of wheat and vines was replaced by an oak reredos of sympathetic design, incorporating the panel, by Hicks and Charlewood of Newcastle.[136] After the First World War a memorial chapel was created in the former lower vestry. Webb's wish to retain the character and unity of his building was respected by the parishioners throughout the twentieth century. The church is in excellent condition at present and is widely appreciated by the townsfolk as well as by architectural historians and devotees of Morris & Co. stained glass.

The final building, with the exception of the upper stage of the tower and the porch, differs not at all from Webb's succinct description in his 1874 report, and from his 1875 drawings chiefly only in some of the details. These include the two less unusual buttresses that were substituted for the more costly but intriguing ones that were to have stood independently of the north wall for over half their height before being connected to it by the flying buttress that formed their upper parts. The nave and chancel share a continuous ridge roof that sweeps down in a cat-slide – inspired by the traditional Cumbrian farmhouse element and Webb's own roof on the steading at Arisaig (see chapter 7) – to cover the south aisle, and is met at right angles by the three identical pitched, gabled, and crenellated roofs of the north aisle. These gables might have been inspired by

the three on Pugin's Convent of the Sisters of Mercy, Liverpool (1841–43) but it is more likely that they resulted from Webb's wish to get light into the nave through high aisle windows rather than a traditional clerestory, as the necessary height of the aisle vaults would prohibit the use of a cat-slide.[137] Each gable contains a tall pointed-arch window and is crenellated (this motif appears again on different scales in the porch parapet, the corbels of the hanging buttresses on the middle stage of the tower, the small dormers over the south aisle and, upside down, on a string course on the tower). The north front also has a small gabled projection near the eastern end, containing the heating chamber in the basement and the staircase to the upper vestry; it was to have been balanced by a gable on the porch but the latter, intended to reach the road, was simplified and curtailed in length during construction to reduce costs.[138]

The symmetrical east front has a large east window under the central gable, in a recess formed by the aisles, which project a few feet beyond the chancel and are raised in height and gabled; respectively, they house the upper vestry and the upper part of the organ. The east window has five foiled lancets with reticulated tracery. The lower tracery lights are blind because the masonry at this point helps to support the chancel ceiling; the three uppermost lights were intended to light the chancel roof by means of glass or louvers, but are now

Left St Martin's Church: from the north-west

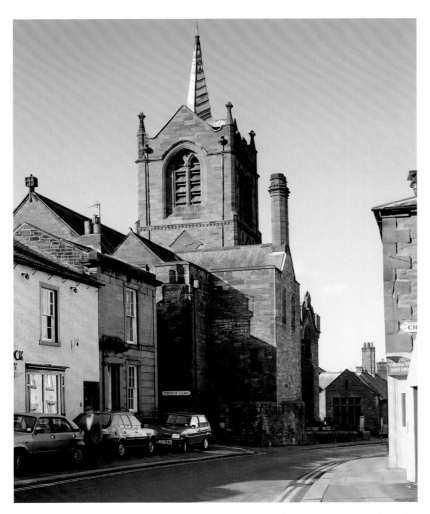

Above St Martin's Church: from the north-east, showing the constricted site

north front of number 1 Palace Green, containing twin rectangular windows in the base of the tower, and a pair of foiled lancets in the ringers' chamber.[140] The temporary pitch roof with weatherboarded gables was replaced by an ashlar belfry with paired openings under segmental hood moulds on the north and south sides, and twin lancets with a quatrefoil in the tracery of a pointed arch in the east and west gables. A clock was installed, with lozenge-shaped faces on all but the south side; to save expense, Webb repeated his design for the Naworth Castle clock (see chapter 9). The form but not the details of the topmost part of the tower was obviously inspired by the peles of the Borders district. A ridge roof connects the gables and has at the centre a slender lead-covered spirelet surmounted by an even slimmer metal cross; at the base of the spirelet, two dormers with doors to the tower peer over the north and south parapets, echoing the idiosyncratic miniature pediment on the porch arch. The parapets on the north and south sides of the tower are somewhat similar, on a much smaller scale, to that of the Bell Brothers Office in Middlesbrough.

The church is entered via the porch and the base of the tower, which serves as an inner lobby and as the baptistery.[141] On passing through one of the twin arches into the west end of the nave, the predominant and striking impression is one of openness, of surprising spaciousness for an Anglican church designed in the 1870s. Webb's intention had been to provide a nave that was 'spacious and large in scale – open and broad', not long and narrow as was usual at the time; in getting away with this as well as with many other matters, Webb was helped by Henry Whitehead, whose Broad Church views allowed wide limits to orthodoxy. Webb's plan, as Penn points out, made the church easily adaptable to congregations of widely differing sizes.[142] The nave and chancel are of equal width, and the aisles are exceptionally wide – the northern one being the same width as the nave – and are open to the nave through the tall, wide arches of the four-bay arcades (which have admirable crisply moulded capitals). Unusually for the date, there is no transverse arch or screen between the nave and chancel, there are no high screens between the chancel and the aisles, and the choir stalls, with innovative reading desks at their western ends, are in the easternmost of the three nave bays rather than in the chancel, with backs kept low so that they do not restrict the flow of space. The

boarded.[139] The south front, beyond which is the rising ground of the graveyard, has four massive, plain buttresses with gables and slated roofs backing onto the base of the cat-slide, above which are three small lead-covered dormers, of which two were added by Webb at the suggestion of Harvey Goodwin, the Bishop of Carlisle. The profile of the kneelers, which project to the side rather than forward in the traditional manner, is continued as a cornice between the buttresses above each of three small rectangular windows. The aisle is also lit by a large circular window in its western wall alongside the tower and, towards the eastern end, by a large three-light window that illuminates the organ.

The walls of the tower incline almost imperceptibly towards the top to give an impression of greater height, and on all but the south side they bear characteristic lozenge-shaped clock-faces. The west wall has a tall pointed arch similar to that on the

open backs of the long bench seats that Webb designed for the congregation serve the same purpose. Highly unusually, there is no pulpit but a moveable lectern was provided.[143] In the eastern end of the aisle, the upper vestry, with a panelled white wall and a boarded white ceiling below it, seems at first glance to be suspended within the eastern bay of the north aisle, with space flowing into the lower vestry beneath it (now the memorial chapel). In fact, it is supported on robust beams, with Webb's characteristic many-centred timber arches beneath them.

From the baptistery, the sense of open space is increased by the continuous white-painted, chiefly horizontal timber ceiling of the nave and chancel. The eye is carried along to the large east window, set within its own arch, by the lines of the bottom members of the longitudinal lattice-girders, which serve as purlins, and the connecting ties of the king-post trusses.[144] The bottoms of the iron rods, including those acting as king-posts, are also exposed. Above each column are what Webb termed 'wood-vaulted spurs'; decidedly idiosyncratic, they are built round the struts that strengthen the trusses.[145]

The chief sources of light in the nave are the three twenty-feet-high windows in the north gables, light from which is also reflected by the white-painted pointed barrel-vaulted ceilings, which were possibly inspired by the stone vaults in the north aisle of Fountains Abbey, a building Webb knew well.[146] The south aisle is adequately lit at low level by the small rectangular windows and circular window, and the three small dormers admit shafts of sunlight that contrast with the diffused northern light. The timber ceiling of the south aisle, also white, begins as a deep cove above a narrow cornice, rises vertically in front of a third longitudinal latticed girder, and is then canted up to the top of the arcade wall. White-painted tie-beams extend from the base of the girder to corbels just above the capitals of the arcade. The walls, plastered flush with the red sandstone dressings, are whitewashed, which possibly reveals the influence of some of Pugin's and Butterfield's rural churches.[147] The pervading whiteness helps to unify the building and make it a consistent whole. It also adds to the sense of free space and ample but gentle light, and is a great contrast to the dark stone walls of most Victorian churches – for example, of Bodley's St Martin's-on-the-Hill, Scarborough.[148] At the western end, the nave gains secondary lighting from the west window of the tower through a

Left St Martin's Church: the nave from the baptistery

delightful glazed screen, the stone mullions of which seem to grow organically from the mouldings of the twin arches below it. Space flows from the nave into the baptistery, around a characteristic polygonal timber post and Webb's beautiful stone font – an octagonal bowl on an octagonal base, of no recognized style – and into the end of the south aisle.

Webb's well-considered colour scheme of general whiteness contrasting with the red sandstone and carefully positioned patches of rich colours depended on the introduction of stained glass made by Morris & Co. – the only firm, he told the committee in 1877, on which he could rely 'for such work being in accordance with the design of the church and of sufficient artistic excellence'.[149] He also informed the committee in 1877 that 'it would be best to consider any part of the ornamental glazing of the windows with regard to the whole', and he

Right St Martin's Church: the nave looking east

explained to one would-be donor that he particularly wished to 'avoid the use of harsh crude design and inharmonious colouring, the ugliness of which spoil most of the churches in which they are placed'.[150] Parishioners were encouraged to donate windows by the committee's ban on new memorial tablets inside the church and by Whitehead's vetoes on all cheaper glass by rival firms. The windows were not planned as an integrated set but, since the subjects exhibit, in Penn's words, a 'non-doctrinal, liberal Christianity, with a total absence of representations of the great moments in salvation history', this might indicate the influence of Whitehead the Broad Churchman, George Howard the Unitarian, and Webb the agnostic.[151] Webb's close association with Morris & Co., and his early experience in the art, ensured that the design and colouring of each window suited the character of the building and the position of the specific window in it.[152] Some were required to admit light through almost clear quarries, for instance in the south aisle, whilst in others jewel-like colour was more important. The east window is the prime example of the latter. It was commissioned by George Howard in memory of his father Charles, who died in 1879, and designed by Burne-Jones; it cost £677, of which Webb contributed ten guineas.[153] There are fourteen Morris & Co. windows in all. This church, designed by the renowned architect member of the Pre-Raphaelite circle, and with glass by one of its most famous painters and its most well-known designer, would have had a ceiling painted by a minor artist of the group had George Howard taken up Webb's suggestion – thought at first to be a joke – that he should paint the main ceiling once it had dried out and settled.[154] St Martin's is indeed a consistent whole, an excellent example of the design unity that would become a major principle of the Arts and Crafts movement in the next decade.

Webb, of course, did not design the exterior in any particular Gothic style, or as if it had evolved through centuries. He aimed for something new yet with the links to the past that he considered inevitable and which, in an Anglican church of the 1870s, were effectively mandatory. He provided the committee with a building that was sufficiently Gothic in character to visibly 'express its office', but one in which invention was as important and as evident as respect for the past, with a plan and many items that were unorthodox and innovative. Webb noticed that the people of Brampton were not

Above St Martin's Church: the north aisle

anxious to express any pleasure in their new parish church, but he believed that the town had gained a public building 'which to say the least of it' was 'certainly a great addition to its appearance'.[155]

The effort Webb put into the Thurstaston design was not entirely wasted. As he had no actual church for the Brampton committee to inspect, he presented it with copies of some of his Thurstaston drawings. The quality of design displayed would undoubtedly have encouraged the committee to put their new church in Webb's hands. Although the Thurstaston scheme was for a village church and Brampton is a market town, there are some similarities between the designs; both have a nave and chancel of equal height, random rubble walls with areas of ashlar, a wide north aisle, bold plain buttresses with gabled tops, and a stone spire.

The influence of St Martin's, Brampton appeared in several churches by Arts and Crafts architects, with whom white-painted walls plastered flush with the stone dressings became popular. Mackintosh's Queen's Cross Church, Glasgow (1897–99), for

example, has such walls, as well as a random rubble exterior with two tall gables to the street, a tower with battered walls, and a pointed timber barrel vault in the nave.[156] Prior too used the device of inclined walls in St Andrew's, Roker but to suggest greater massiveness in the nave walls rather than extra height, and he used canted north and south walls to make the chancel seem longer than it is.[157] St Andrew's also has random rubble walls, and fittings influenced by

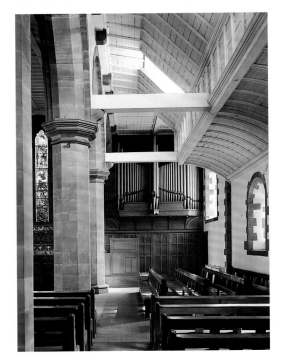

Webb's at Brampton and by his domestic furniture.[158] Prior was able to display an even greater faith in the elementary than Webb had done at Brampton because, by the beginning of the twentieth century, some authorities in the Anglican Church – including those involved with St Andrew's – had begun to accept a Gothic flavour rather than a medieval appearance in new churches. By using transverse reinforced concrete arches and creating side passages through the internal buttresses that formed their bases, Prior achieved a single space more completely than Webb was able to do, or than Bodley managed in St Augustine's, Pendlebury (1874), from which Prior's passages might have been derived.[159]

Webb's difficulties with the Church Building Committee, added to his experience with Newcastle Council, led to his not accepting another committee-client commission until the one for the Ledbury tower in 1890, and never again thereafter His output of non-domestic work was small but innovative, interesting, and influential. The larger buildings in this category demonstrated that his approach to architectural design could work as successfully for commercial buildings and churches as it did for houses. It seems a pity that he did not design more in these fields. However, in order to do so in addition to the houses, he would have had to change his way of working, of designing every detail of each building himself with painstaking care, the method that contributed in no small measure to the unity and originality of his architecture.

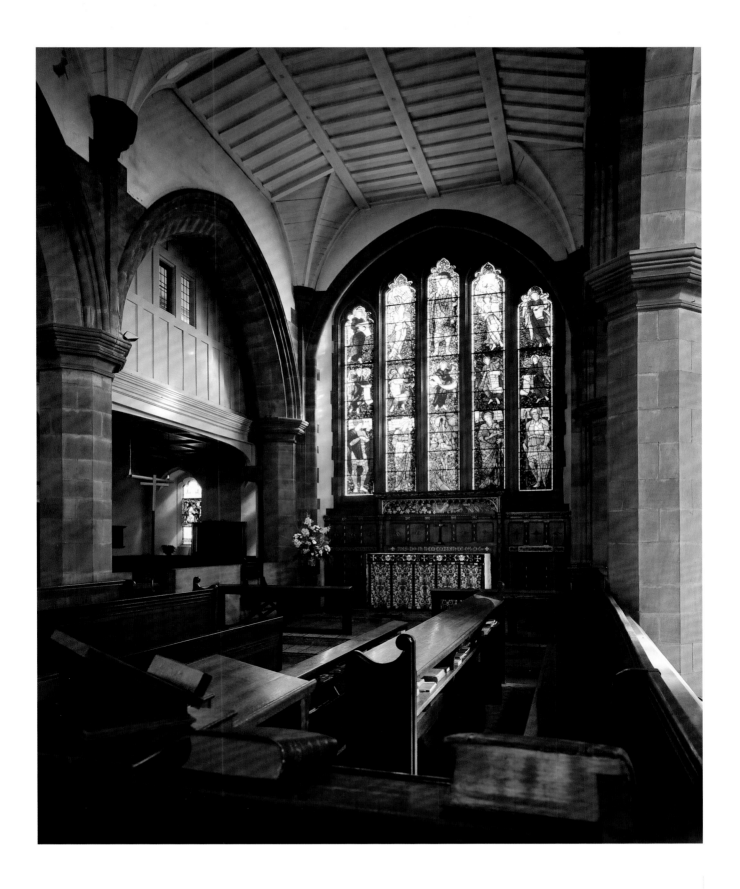

Chapter 13

WEBB AND HIS CLIENTS AND CONTRACTORS

Philip Webb's national vernacular approach imposed demands upon his clients. They had to accept his contention that good architecture depended on simple good building, not on the revival of any past style. This meant the abandoning of preconceived notions of the style or appearance of their proposed building, and of any expectation of an elaborate or strikingly different edifice, even of one in a recognizably Webb style, with which to display their own and their architect's taste and status. A willingness to pay for first-class materials, construction, and craftsmanship was required, and a liking for simplicity and lasting value instead of for the showy, meretricious ornament and ephemeral fashions of their commercial age. Not only had they to trust Webb to fulfil their practical needs but, because he believed that his creative powers, reinforced by training and experience, gave him the sole right to determine all design matters, they also had to be courageous enough to allow him to do so. Most clients of the day would not have accepted these rigorous demands. Fortunately, a sufficient number to allow Webb to work as he wished did accept them.

Most of his clients came from the members and friends of the Pre-Raphaelite circle and its patrons, not because of a deliberate attempt on Webb's part to be the architect for an artistic elite but as a result of his refusal to seek publicity and his insistence on designing every detail of each building himself. When Percy Wyndham accused him of avoiding likely clients, Webb – probably having the Airlies in mind (see chapter 9) – replied that it was merely a matter of his not wishing to lay himself out to work for people who 'did not in any degree want' what he 'could honestly do for them'.[1] Refusing a commission in 1874 because of pressure of existing work, he explained to the prospective client:

> Also, to avoid any possibility of misunderstanding I will say that for some time past, I have decided not to undertake to build for anyone who is not conversant with my work and able to judge of what would be the finished effect of that which I should agree to carry out.[2]

Avoiding misunderstanding was important for his peace of mind but, though he was too proud to admit it, just as crucial was the fact that working as he wished meant he could not afford to produce scheme after scheme, amendment after amendment, in an attempt to satisfy an unappreciative client, when the fee he received would be the same however long it took. Webb's apparent exclusiveness was a matter of reticence on the one hand and common sense on the other.

In the second half of the nineteenth century there can have been few English architects whose clients were not art collectors at least in a minor way. By the 1860s artists no longer worked chiefly to commission but for a wide, appreciative public. They painted what and how they wished, and displayed their work in London, almost all of it for sale, in well-attended exhibitions, including those of the short-lived Hogarth Club, and in their own studios. Art had become more respectable as well as more commercial, and at these exhibitions and the Sunday afternoon gatherings in Little Holland House, the home Thoby Prinsep and his wife shared with G F Watts, and in the homes of several wealthy Greeks, notably the Ionides family, the Pre-Raphaelites and other artists mingled as equals with their eminent patrons. The result, as shown in contemporary letters, diaries, and memoirs, was a new phenomenon which made several painters wealthy: an extensive, loose network of poets, writers, musicians, actors, scientists, diplomatists, politicians, industrialists, men of medicine, and so forth, most of them from the middle classes and all with an interest in art.[3] Almost all Webb's clients belonged to it, and bought paintings by several artists not just from the Pre-Raphaelite group.

To view Webb as an art-architect whose work was sought partly as an addition to his clients' art collections and partly as a demonstration of the artistic taste of the specific client, carries the danger of his primary message – that good architecture is good building – being missed. It also exaggerates the importance of art in the lives of the majority of his clients. Indeed they were educated, cultured people who viewed those lacking an interest in the arts as philistines, and they certainly liked paintings and desired beautiful rooms, such as those Webb provided, in which to hang them; but art was not the pivot of their lives (except for the artist-clients, of course). Detailed study of them and their correspondence with Webb shows that they understood his message and admired his work, and believed that he would give them a building of good and appropriate appearance; and also that they went to him because he was an expert in the practical side of architecture, who would fulfil their prime requirement of a sound, durable, and convenient building suited to their individual requirements. All were good judges of quality, who liked value for their money, and they found, as they expected, that Webb fulfilled practical as well as aesthetic needs. Had this not been so, his clients would not have returned to him for later work, as so many of them did.

Webb's clients were enlightened and progressive people. They had liberal views regardless of their political affinities, a sound respect for reason and common sense, an unshakeable belief in the virtue of work, and a conviction that it was their duty to remedy some of the evils in contemporary life. The artists crusaded for the unity of the fine and decorative arts, and for more art in everyday life. Many of the men improved the lot of their fellow men through their professions, and those who were employers, on a country estate or in industry, ameliorated the welfare of their workmen and their families. In their free time, they tackled community matters with gusto and dedication, spending far more time on this voluntary work than on their art collections. They became involved in national or local politics, served on local or county councils and as Justices of the Peace, and helped to establish and support hospitals, schools, colleges, universities, concert halls, libraries, and art galleries. Major Gillum, for example, in just two years – 1860 and 1861 – became a manager of the Industrial Home for Destitute Boys in Euston Road, London, established the Boys' Farm School, and commissioned Webb to design his philanthropic terrace of dwellings, shops, and workshops in Worship Street, London. Lowthian Bell gave Washington Hall to Miss Emma Watson as a home for destitute boys, and was a founder and financial supporter of the Newcastle College of Science which became Armstrong College of Durham

University; he was a councillor, then an alderman of Newcastle, twice being mayor and, as chairman of the Finance Committee, being responsible for many improvements including the lengthening of the quay. Bell was Deputy Lieutenant and Sheriff of County Durham, a Justice of the Peace in Durham, Newcastle, and the North Riding of Yorkshire, and a Liberal MP for Hartlepool; in all these places he was deeply involved in educational affairs. His son Hugh also took a great interest in the welfare of their firm's workers, and served as a Justice of the Peace. He was instrumental in achieving an adequate supply of safe water for the rapidly expanding population of Middlesbrough, of which town he was thrice mayor. He was an alderman and Lord Lieutenant of the North Riding, Deputy Lieutenant and High Sheriff of County Durham, a member of the Senate of Durham University, Chairman of the Council of Armstrong College (now the University of Newcastle), and a member of the board of the Imperial College of Science and Technology, London.

The women, whether wives of clients – several of whom probably had some influence on the choice of architect – or clients in their own right, were prevented from undertaking any form of remunerative work by the conventions of their day, apart from Jane Morris who embroidered for the Firm. However, as well as supervising the running of their homes, doing some light gardening, and devoting hours to creative work such as jewellery making, photography and, in particular, embroidery, they too devoted much time and energy to community projects, particularly education. Again using the Bell family as an example, Lowthian's daughter Ada Godman served on the committee of Northallerton hospital, helped to establish the district nursing service in the North Riding of Yorkshire, and nursed sick women herself in her village, where she taught singing voluntarily at the school and, to the annoyance of the vicar, set up a coffee house for tramps at the reading room she had organized. She often sang at concerts for local charities in Darlington and Middlesbrough. Hugh Bell's second wife, Florence, who was created a Dame of the British Empire in recognition of her social work, also took part in charity concerts, and was a playwright, a composer, and an author of books of various types. She founded the People's Winter Garden (1907) in Middlesbrough, and devoted much time and effort to the welfare of Bell Brothers' workmen and their families, and instigated and directed a pioneering detailed survey of all aspects of the life and work of all the district's ironworkers and their families. Her account of the survey, *At the Works* (1907), is a classic in its field.

As almost all the clients either knew Webb or went to him through recommendation, most would have been familiar with at least one of his buildings already. Where this was not the case, Webb made sure that they inspected one of his buildings so that he could be sure they knew the general character of his work before he accepted the commission. At the outset, he informed all intending clients that he would be the sole arbiter on design, and he refused to indicate what the character of the proposed building might be. Clearly, any client who did commission Webb could not have hoped for a building in a specific historical style. In many cases, their education was not such as to have induced a taste for the classical styles, and by the 1860s neo-Gothic was no longer popular for houses, interiors in this style having being found unpleasantly heavy. Those of them who wished to move to the country – as much to escape from polluted urban air, to which in a few cases their own works contributed, as to realize dreams of a rural idyll – would not have approached Webb had they wished for a romantic overgrown cottage. Webb's clients, the men and the women, were individualists to whom Webb's unusual buildings, of which no two were alike, would appeal.

Certain other factors also predisposed them towards finding his designs pleasing. The first was that the English landscape painters, notably Cotman, whose paintings had been popular since the beginning of the century, had opened the eyes of their own patrons and students to the beauty of the forms and materials, colours and textures, of vernacular buildings. Many of their students were women – to be a good amateur watercolourist was a desirable female accomplishment – just at the time when women were beginning to have far more say in the appearance of their new houses both outside and inside than hitherto. Upper- and middle-class girls studied under these artists, or worked from their instruction books. George Howard's mother, for example, was a pupil of De Wint, and his aunts of Cotman, and Spencer Stanhope's mother studied under Gainsborough. Many of Webb's male clients collected the English watercolourists' landscapes, and

appreciation of these would encourage a sympathetic reception of Webb's belief that he had a duty to protect the landscape from obtrusive buildings. The mid-century turn away from the grand and imposing in architecture, noted in 1864 by Kerr in *The Gentleman's House*, which probably was partly inspired by fear of working-class unrest, would have encouraged acceptance of Webb's unimposing, vernacular-influenced houses.[4]

Not the least important predisposing factor was the influence of Ruskin, whose three important early works – *Modern Painters, Seven Lamps*, and *Stones of Venice* – were so astonishingly widely read that it can safely be assumed that all Webb's clients had either done so, or were familiar with the author's main points. Many of them knew Ruskin, a member of the Hogarth Club, who alerted readers to the beauty of architecture, even if like Webb they did not accept all his contentions on the matter, and who instilled or developed in many of them a liking for lasting goodness and relative simplicity in contrast to the often ostentatious, sometimes badly built edifices of the day. For instance, it was probably Ruskin's influence on his cosmopolitan admirers and friends Hugh Bell and his wife Florence, which made them content, long after they could have afforded a much larger establishment, to live in their simple house by Webb, Red Barns – a house so small that, even after enlargement by the architect, their many eminent friends from the London literary, musical, theatrical, and art worlds often had to be accommodated in nearby houses. Ruskin's castigation of the so-called restoration of old churches probably ingnited the interest of some of Webb's clients in the protection of ancient buildings, including Hugh Bell, who in 1871 sought Webb's help in preventing the demolition of the house of Raphael's father in Urbino.[5] As previously mentioned (in chapter 8), at least thirteen of Webb's clients became members of the Society for the Protection of Ancient Buildings, and they in turn persuaded many of their friends to do likewise. However, despite Ruskin's great persuasive power, those of his readers who commissioned Webb rejected the writer's demand that new buildings should be in the Gothic style.

The clients for whom Webb designed a significant building (most of which were constructed), or for whom he greatly altered and enlarged an existing one, numbered forty-five. These comprised six painters; three industrialists and seven or eight landowners (one of them might merely have been wealthy) from the aristocracy and gentry class, some of whom were also Members of Parliament; five military and three medical men; four London solicitors, one of them a Greek; a further two wealthy Greeks, respectively a stockbroker and a diplomatist; a railway and telegraph engineer; a printer; a civil servant-cum-author, and a business manager; a bank accountant; a church building committee; a town council; and seven women who commissioned work in their own right. The engineer and two of the artists were also aristocrats, two of whose families owned collieries, as did one of the landowners and one industrialist.

The painters, the first five having been Webb's friends since the mid-1850s, were: William Morris; Spencer Stanhope (second son of wealthy Yorkshire aristocrat John Spencer Stanhope and his wife Lady Elizabeth, daughter of the Earl of Leicester); George Price Boyce; Valentine Cameron Prinsep; George Frederic Watts; and George Howard, later the ninth Earl of Carlisle, who joined the Pre-Raphaelite circle in the 1860s. Lowthian Bell and his son Hugh were Webb's most important industrialist clients; Lowthian, who was created baronet in 1885, probably went to Webb on Ruskin's recommendation, or on that of Boyce, a mutual friend. The third industrialist was Edward Greene, a successful brewer, agricultural innovator and Conservative MP, who possibly met Webb through George Howard's father, a fellow MP, or through fellow East-Anglian Sir Willoughby Jones, the first aristocratic and second landowner client. Jones would have known of Webb through his own cousin, the wife of Francis D P Astley, Webb's first land- and colliery-owning client and a member of the Hogarth Club. The other aristocrats were George Howard's brother-in-law the Earl of Airlie, for whom Webb designed a scheme for the enlargement of his country seat (1868–69, not executed); the Honourable Percy Wyndham, Conservative MP, younger son of the first Lord Leconfield (of Petworth), cousin by marriage of Spencer Stanhope and friend and patron of Burne-Jones; and Lord Fitzhardinge of whose first meeting with Webb nothing is known. The same is true of Adam Steinmetz Kennard, a wealthy man and possibly a landowner. The two remaining landowners were Charles North, who was probably introduced by Willoughby Jones, and the Conservative MP John Reginald Yorke, who was introduced by Wyndham

after having inspected Clouds on hearing that it was one of the best modern houses in England.[6]

The military men, all retired officers who owned or bought country estates, were: Major, later Colonel, William Gillum, philanthropist and amateur painter, member of the Hogarth Club, and pupil of Ford Madox Brown; Major Arthur F Godman, Lowthian Bell's son-in-law; Lieutenant-General Augustus Henry Lane Fox Pitt-Rivers (1827–1900), the archaeologist and ethnographer, on whose behalf his brother-in-law George Howard first approached Webb; Captain John C F Ramsden, who probably heard of Webb through the Wyndhams; and Captain Edward W D Baird, who was introduced by Yorke.[7] The men of medicine were, first, Sir John Tomes, Queen Victoria's dental surgeon, who probably met Webb through the second, Sir William Bowman, Tomes's colleague at King's College Hospital and consultant ophthalmologist to the Queen, and to Watts and Rossetti of whom Bowman was an early patron; and, third, Webb's brother, Dr Harry Speakman Webb.

The solicitors were Leonard Rowe Valpy, who acted for Ruskin and was a patron of Rossetti and Boyce; Alexander Cassavetti, whose mother was a Webb client and patron of Burne-Jones; Wickham Flower, a wealthy antiquarian, collector, member of the SPAB and friend of Boyce; and James S Beale, a friend of the brothers Constantine and Alexander A Ionides, respectively the stockbroker and diplomatist clients who were patrons and friends of Rossetti and Burne-Jones. The railway and telegraph engineer was Lord Sackville Cecil, a younger son of the second Marquess of Salisbury by his second wife; and the printer was George Eyre, of Eyre and Spottiswoode, printers to the Queen. It is not known how Cecil and Eyre met Webb. The civil servant and author was William Hale White, who wrote under the name Mark Rutherford and went to Webb on Ruskin's recommendation, and whose brother-in-law William Chisolm was the business manager client. William Thomas Tate, the bank accountant, was a friend of the Bells. The committee-clients were Newcastle Council, at the instigation of Alderman Lowthian Bell, and the Brampton Church Committee, which commissioned Webb to design St Martin's Church after the Trustees of the Naworth Estate, guided by George Howard and his father, made it clear that the size of the estate contribution depended upon Webb being the architect.

The women clients were: Mrs Euphrosyne Cassavetti, mother of Alexander, and a member of the Ionides family; the daughter of a Liverpool merchant, Miss Mary Anne Ewart, who was a friend of Webb; Miss Agneta Henrietta Cocks, a friend of Mary Ewart; Mrs Mary Anne Robb, to whom the architect was probably recommended by Gertrude Jekyll, an admirer of his work, who also was a friend of Miss Ewart; Miss Constance Astley, daughter of Francis D P Astley; and William Morris's wife Jane and his sister Mrs Isabella Gilmore, principal of the Rochester Diocesan Deaconess Institution.

In all, these forty-three clients commissioned: six studio-houses; ten country houses (nine were executed) and ten smaller houses; a pair of semi-detached houses and a pair of memorial cottages; two churches and two chapels (one of each was executed); a terrace of offices in Newcastle (not executed) and two office buildings (in London and Middlesbrough respectively); three terraces of dwellings (two were built); four farms, a village school, and a village hall; buildings for an iron-works (a clock tower, a blowing-engine house, and works offices); numerous estate buildings including lodges, gardeners' cottages and hostels for other estate workers; repairs and additions to two ancient castles; and thirteen enlargements (several of which were later extended further by Webb). He also undertook minor jobs for other clients, including investigating the soundness of buildings which they were thinking of purchasing, reporting on the likely effects of alterations proposed by neighbours, repairing structures, making minor alterations, and designing drinking fountains, fittings, furniture, and many memorials. His complete list of architectural works numbers far fewer buildings than those of most of his peers – Shaw, for instance, designed over two hundred buildings – because of Webb's insistence on painstakingly designing and supervising every detail of each building himself.

Webb's unfortunate experience of working for committee-clients has been mentioned already (see chapters 10 and 12). His relationships with individual or married-couple clients, whether near his own age or not, were far more felicitous. Where there had been no previous acquaintance, the relationship began fairly formally but almost invariably friendship had been struck by the time the building was finished. Webb believed that all people were equal, and treated his clients accordingly, regardless of their wealth or status. As Lethaby recorded, Webb's relationship with all his clients was that of a man who was going to give more than he received, and would do so only on his own terms. He rarely had a serious disagreement with a client. When he did, it was because his professional expertise had been questioned or slighted, or because the client had interfered on site, perhaps by having it levelled, as Beale did at Standen, or by taking on men without Webb's prior agreement. To avoid confusion, he always directed that all instructions were to be given to the builder by himself. In 1872, to save Watts' shallow pocket, Webb had the painter's studio-house, the Briary, constructed by the London builder Tyerman, who had built West House and Sandroyd and usually could be trusted to do the work well without constant supervision by a clerk of works. An annoyed local builder said the work was not properly done; after examining it, Webb found, that this was not the case, and the accusation was withdrawn. Unfortunately, Watts took up residence before the roof was finished and, finding the house damp, he wrote angrily to Webb impugning his professional integrity, got the local builder to investigate the problem, and brought in local tradesmen. Equally angry, Webb requested the London architect C G Vinall to examine the building; as a result of Vinall's report and under his supervision, Tyerman finished the house, including the remedial work necessitated by the efforts of the local workmen. Webb refused to take any part of his due fee. In so doing, he incurred financial difficulties because he had done likewise the previous year in connection with Oast House, where it is likely that Lord Sackville Cecil had interfered on site when trying to emulate his own father's habit of personally supervising all building work at Hatfield House.[8]

In 1872, when Herbert Fletcher, colliery owner and philanthropist, decided not to go ahead with Webb's design for an engine house and large chimney at Atherston Colliery in Lancashire, he sent the architect a smaller amount than was due with the comment that Webb had not done enough to justify more. Webb burnt the cheque, and did so again with the second one, even though it was accompanied by an apology, Fletcher having remembered belatedly that Webb had visited the site.[9] Tardy payers usually responded to a reminder, sent after two months, that Webb's account was due for payment. Lord Fitzhardinge, however, failed to pay even after a reminder in which Webb explained that it would be a convenience to him to receive the money; Webb reminded him again, ending with the following comment: 'If this present letter is not acknowledged, I shall suppose that your Lordship is unwilling to pay me for my work, and shall not again press the matter upon your attention'.[10] The bill was paid immediately. In 1875, W A Cardwell (son-in-law of Sir Benjamin Brodie for whom Webb had done minor work at Brockham Warren, Surrey in 1872) refused to pay for an abandoned house design for which the working drawings had been prepared; bitterly upset by having to claim his just dues, Webb took the matter to court, unsuccessfully in the event.[11]

Almost all his clients, however, treated Webb as an experienced professional gentleman, without a hint of patronage or condescension. By the 1860s, architects in general had achieved this status, of course, but it does seem that Webb formed a close friendship with more of his clients than was common. An example of the respect he received is that in her diaries Ada Godman referred to her architect as 'Mr. Webb', though she had known him for years and was his friend, but referred to William Morris, with whom she was well acquainted, merely as 'Morris', as if he were a mere shopkeeper, despite his renown as a poet and designer.[12] Letters show that clients who became close friends invited Webb to their homes more often than he accepted, valued his opinion on matters other than architecture, and exchanged frank opinions with him on highly personal matters. His letters to George and Rosalind Howard, for instance, begin in 1867 on the usual fairly formal if friendly business footing; but by 1870 Webb was indulging his dry humour, with much poking of fun at his own expense. He joked about architects being the 'enemies of mankind', and confessed that though they should know best on building matters, sometimes, as he knew from personal experience, they only pretended to do so.[13] In a single letter of 1872 to Rosalind Howard, he advised her always to be absolutely honest because this 'became' her; asked if she found it as difficult to be sure of what she disbelieved as of what she believed, and suggested she excuse herself for not promulgating her agnosticism by saying that she did not wish to lead others into the same uncertainty; sympathized with her attempts to teach her son that 'injuring live things is not beautiful' when 'the love of injury is deeply ingrained in humanity'; and admitted that he had a 'strong natural bent' for shooting animals, one which

he had learned to regard with disgust.[14] In 1877 he headed a letter to the Howards with a sketch of himself, nude but for a fool's cap, being tempted back into their Eden, Naworth Castle, by George's arm dangling money bags and Rosalind's waving hearts symbolizing loving friendship.[15]

Some clients, including the Howards, became sufficiently intimate with Webb to tease him about his deepest ideals. One evening in 1878, after he, Morris, and the artist Walter Crane had dined at Lady Stanley's, they were entertained by a performance of Florence Bell's *The Votaries of Art*. This operetta, performed three years before the first production of the Gilbert and Sullivan opera *Patience* on the same theme, satirized the Aesthetic movement that had developed from the attempts to improve design with which Morris and Webb were so deeply involved through Morris & Co. Lyulph Stanley reported to his sister Rosalind Howard that it was performed by members of the Stanley, Bell, and Olliffe families, wearing gowns of 'artistic coloured Bolton sheeting fashioned like Crane's Bluebeard pictures &c' and accompanied on the piano by Florence, and that 'the artists enjoyed it very much'.[16] When Webb became a dedicated and active socialist in 1883, his major clients, the Bells, Howards, and Wyndhams, were not in the least perturbed. Henceforth they seized every chance to pull his leg about it, with great good humour on all parts.[17]

Before accepting a commission, Webb first considered whether or not it was in a client's best interests to go ahead with the proposal. In the case of a suburban house, or when he suspected that a client's means were very limited, he advised them to think again before deciding to build. He told Mrs Lucy Orrinsmith (a sister of Charles and Kate Faulkner), for instance, that it was never worthwhile to build for oneself unless the house was to be 'better planned and better built' than those of an 'ordinary type'. He then warned her that building a house with a 'careful arrangement of plan & proportion' and constructed in a 'sound and workmanlike way, with the most simple of good materials', would cost more in labour 'from the mere departure from routine'; and that it would not be 'so easily let or sold for its cost value as one of an ordinary type'.[18] When her brother Frank Faulkner involved Webb in a project to build a house for letting, Webb explained that generally 'the better the house, the poorer the investment'; and that a house built 'with some attention to the scientific parts of its construction &c' might not fetch its cost price if sold, particularly if it was 'fairly good' as to the 'art part of the matter', because the 'popular idea' was for 'much show at little cost', whereas the art value depended upon considerations which had 'no market value'.[19]

Once a client decided to proceed, Webb reported on the feasibility of the proposal after noting the accommodation required and investigating the site and, in the case of enlargements and alterations, the existing building in more detail. He considered the suitability and possibilities of the site, ensured that all boundary matters were firmly settled, and where necessary ascertained that a well sunk thereon would produce an adequate supply of pure water and that cesspool drainage would be practicable. At this point, before beginning to design the building, Webb required the client to sign his 'Statement of Business Arrangements' which he had drawn up after the unfortunate Cardwell affair, because he could not afford to waste time on designs for which he might not be paid, or money on abortive court cases. In his letter to Wyndham of 28 December 1876, he expressed his willingness to accept the commission to design Clouds and superintend its construction subject to Wyndham's acceptance of these business arrangements. Webb explained:

> That all drawings, whether of works done or only proposed, shd. be my property (This not to exclude my providing you with all the necessary plans &c for your future use after the work was done)—That my payment shd. be at the rate of 5 per cent on the cost of all the works done under my direction, & further payment of travelling expenses for myself and assistants—That if plans in whole and in detail are prepared by me ready to be laid before contractors and the works shd. not be carried out, 2 per cent on my estimated cost of the execution of the works be paid to me—That if only preliminary sketches and plans be made 1 per cent on my estimated cost be paid me for the same—I must ask you to excuse these particulars, as it has been found that such care & explanation between client and Architect before any work has been entered upon, tends very much to the avoidance of any disputes or awkwardness afterwards.[20]

Common sense had prevailed again. The only settlement of account problems in future would be that occasionally a client, despite clear warnings by the architect, would fail to appreciate fully how much unforeseen contingencies and their own requested extras were likely to add to the builder's final account.

The Statement having been signed, Webb produced a rough plan, based on his first visit to the site, to force the client and, where applicable, the client's wife, to make decisions on the sizes and relative positions of rooms. Whilst they did this, he began his painstaking investigation of every detail of the site, of local building forms, of the use of local materials in old buildings nearby, of the characteristics of these materials and of the effects on them of time, weather, lichen, and local hand tools. He inspected all the brick and tile yards and quarries in the district, checked that brick-makers and quarrymen could maintain an adequate supply of material, and had small samples of sands and cements sent to his office for testing. In the case of a large site, he had a detailed survey made which included the type, location, and diameter of every tree so that he could position the building in such a way that none had to be felled.

Some clients asked for a larger building than their pocket could support. Once this became apparent, Webb repeatedly reduced and amended his scheme, or started afresh with a new one, with great patience and good humour. A scheme favoured by Mary Ewart, for example, could not be cut down without being spoiled, so Webb offered to start afresh though he would then have been the loser. His offer was not accepted, and when the selected builder's estimate proved even higher than expected (partly because of the number and quality of the built-in cupboards), Webb reminded Mary Ewart that it did not include the cost of a garden or his own fee. He offered to reduce the scheme after all, and to delay sending his account.[21]

There were limits to his patience, however. When Ramsden – who had already asked for seven more rooms at no extra cost after the design of Willinghurst had been agreed – requested major changes after the plan had been pegged out on the site and many drawings had been prepared, Webb mildly pointed out how the size of the house had grown despite his own attempts to keep it in bounds, and offered to start from scratch again should Ramsden not prefer to go to another architect. In return Ramsden proposed even more radical changes, provoking the following angry response:

> I can safely say that I have never before taken so much time & trouble in sifting the arrangements of a house

before the definite plans were proceeded with, as I have in this of yours. I do not in any way complain of this, indeed I congratulated myself in thinking that whatever time & trouble had been bestowed upon the plans before the final drawings were made, so much time would be saved in the long run. [...] I feel very doubtful whether your confidence in me as an Architect is such as to make it reasonable for me to undertake fresh plans for you; for, from several criticisms on my character of design made verbally here & some note in your letters with regard to my having run into expensive roofing for insufficient cause, make me hesitate in any way to lead you to repose further confidence in my experience and ability as an Architect. [...] I would seriously urge upon you whether it would not be better that the proposed re-disposition of the arrangements of the house were undertaken for you by some other architect.[22]

However, Ramsden and his wife, probably the only clients who did indeed value the cachet of the architect's name more than his actual work, were determined to have a house by Webb.

Such antagonism was rare, in spite of Webb's insistence on design autonomy. He suffered surprisingly little interference on aesthetic matters. When clients did make suggestions, he listened courteously before explaining why his own design was preferable; if this failed to persuade them, he pointed out the extra cost of their ideas, which usually settled the matter. At Wyndham's request, for instance, he designed some 'medieval' buttresses but explained that his own earlier design would cast less shade and would look right for a garden wall whereas the others would look as if they should be supporting a roof. Wyndham capitulated.[23] Very occasionally Webb did adopt a client's suggestion, such as the oriel windows proposed by Madeline Wyndham for the 1879 design for Clouds,[24] and he readily consented to arrange a room to accommodate some beautiful, recently purchased old wainscot. Very rarely he gave way on a matter he did not consider vital; for example, though he believed that to look right a 'wall should be attached to something more than a gate alone', he granted Godman's wish to have walls not fences flanking the entrance gates of Smeaton Manor.[25]

Webb sometimes enlisted the aid of his assistant or the clerk of works in persuading a stubborn client that a particular feature was not only a practical element but also vital to the successful appearance of a building. An example is the beautiful covered way across the moat to Webb's new entrance at Tangley Manor. When Wickham Flower and his wife thought of removing it from the design, Webb persuaded them to leave it in by telling them that he, his chief assistant George Jack, and George Wardle the manager of Morris & Co. (who had been in charge of the Firm's decoration of the Flowers' London house) all agreed that it 'would help the surroundings of the house rather than detract from them'.[26] Just occasionally, a client's unfortunate idea would sting him into a harsh riposte. For instance, a conservatory proposed by Mrs Ramsden so appalled him that, as he informed George Jack, he 'sat upon the idea flat, without mercy, & likened the thing to a Brixton villa'.[27] Pitt-Rivers produced a heraldic design and would not accept Webb's opinion that it would be too obtrusive if placed above a fireplace; so Webb refused to supervise the making of the plaster model and the carving of the marble.[28]

When he judged it necessary, Webb insisted on having his way on a practical matter, even if it meant going against an apparently expert opinion on the part of the client. At Smeaton Manor, for instance, knowing himself to be an expert on the welfare of horses and designing of stables, he insisted that his conclusion as to the right amount of space in the hay-loft was the right one, not Godman's – though the latter was a retired cavalry officer.[29] On most practical matters, however, Webb consulted the client fully. In every case, conscious that it was not he who was to live in the house, he took great care to ensure that the client understood and was happy with the plan, giving detailed explanations of his reasoning on such matters as the best aspects and prospects for the various rooms, and the desirability of using the service quarters to screen the garden. Even after construction was well advanced he willingly made minor adjustments, to the position of an internal door for example, at the client's suggestion if doing so would improve convenience.

Although he designed all the fittings for his buildings, Webb did consider the client's views. He tried to make all the rooms of his houses beautiful, not through elaborate fittings and ornament, but in essence, through their proportions, shapes, and natural lighting. On producing a plan for their consideration, he urged clients to consider it not just 'with regard to aspect, size, & communication' but 'more particularly as to the individual beauty & convenience of each room'.[30] Despite their liking for relative simplicity, even Webb's clients expected somewhat richer finishes in their own rooms than in those of their servants but, by ensuring that all parts were equally well-crafted and by avoiding luxurious or showy materials and details, he played down the difference between the rooms of family and staff. He rejected a plan suggested by Pitt-Rivers because amongst other deficiencies its long corridor would have been a dark and weary way for the servants.[31] As George Jack recalled, if a client objected to commodious kitchens and offices, Webb would offer to cut down the size of the drawing room.[32] In fact, most of his clients were anxious to provide good working and living conditions for their servants. At Hurlands, for instance, Miss Agneta Cocks herself asked Webb to enlarge the maids' sitting room.[33] Long before he became active in politics, Webb's servants' quarters were well above the average in quality. That this was so at Clouds became apparent to the Wyndhams when the disastrous fire caused them to live in the servants' quarters during the reinstatement of the main block; they found themselves as comfortable as in their own rooms, and jokingly attributed this to Webb's being a socialist.[34]

When deciding whether or not to accept a design, Webb's clients were not helped by finished elevation drawings or by elaborate perspectives with picturesque backgrounds such as Shaw produced. Webb often made preliminary sketches at one sixteenth of an inch to one foot scale, for Standen for instance. More rarely he made unfinished perspective drawings, for the early Clouds schemes and for Thurstaston Church, for example. He often made explanatory sketches whilst explaining matters, or placed tracings of alternative designs over earlier drawings for comparison. When satisfied that the proposed design would fulfil his client's needs, he made eight inch to one foot scale finished drawings in sufficient detail to form the basis of a bill of quantities and the contractors' estimates; these became the contract drawings once the scheme had been accepted. When Ramsden tried to soothe Webb by describing his drawings as beautiful, Webb rightly replied that they were 'only plain straightforward "working" drawings, made without the waste of useless labour on them whatever'.[35] As he designed each building, Webb made rough working drawings to ensure that the scheme was what he termed practicable and workmanlike, and to help the quantity surveyor (whom Webb advised to charge one per cent of the estimated cost if the project was

abandoned and two per cent if it was built). Webb then prepared the 'Specification' and 'Conditions', which he and the contractor usually signed before work began on site. During the construction period, Webb made working drawings to the appropriate scale, including many full-size details.

Whilst all this was taking place, Webb would have been investigating possible builders: inspecting their previously completed buildings, seeking references from architects for whom they had worked, and visiting their yards to inspect timber stocks, to see whether too much reliance was placed on machines, and to watch their craftsmen at work. Rather than employing labour directly or seeking competitive tenders, Webb preferred to negotiate a price, based on a bill of quantities, with an approved local builder, preferably one whose work was well known to him. Rounton Grange was built by direct labour in the early 1870s, probably at Lowthian Bell's request; the stonemasons' repeated demands for higher wages, the extra responsibility placed on the clerk of works, and the difficulty of arriving at a just figure for his own fee, turned Webb against this method.[36] As for competitive tendering, he explained to Mary Ewart that though it was a real advantage to employ a good, responsible local builder, it always resulted in higher prices than if the work were put to tender; but that with tenders 'if the work is taken at a lower price than a paying one [for the builder] the loss must come out of the building, however careful the Arch. may be in watching the work', and that accepting a higher tender would not automatically ensure good work.[37] As previously explained (in chapter 7), because of the great size of Clouds and the consequently unusually large amount of interior ornament and joinery, Webb advised the Wyndhams that however good a country builder might be, such a firm would be unable to compete with Smiths, the large London firm he favoured, in 'fineness of material & perfection of execution of Joiners' work'.[38] However, against his expectations, after Smiths had had to withdraw for legal reasons, he managed to find a provincial builder capable of constructing the mansion to his high standards.

Once the method had been decided, Webb summoned the chosen builder, or the representatives of the carefully selected contractors who were to submit prices, to his office, where he explained his design in detail. He then directed them to inspect the site, and, if unfamiliar with his work, to see examples of it to ensure that they fully appreciated the high standard he required, before preparing their price.[39] If the job was large enough to warrant one, Webb appointed a clerk of works, who was paid, according to his ability and experience, between £3 and £4 a week by the client but worked to the architect's instructions. Webb preferred to have a clerk who had worked for him before and knew his standard, in particular the Yorkshireman John Hardy, who was clerk of works for Smeaton Manor, Willinghurst, Forthampton Court, and Standen. If Hardy were unavailable, Webb sought recommendations from fellow architects. For some of his houses or major enlargements, his assistants acted as part-time clerks of works, their wages paid half by Webb and half by the client. William Weir acted in this capacity at Exning House. Where no clerk of works was employed, the builder's foreman supervised the work, supplemented by visits from the architect or his assistant at important points in the construction, for instance at Warrens House, where George Jack was the assistant architect concerned.

The participation of the client or clients did not cease when construction began. Webb encouraged them to meet him on site, though he insisted on making his detailed inspection with only the clerk of works and the builder or builder's foreman. During the site visits, Webb usually managed to disguise his feelings when clients irritated or appalled him by making suggestions, even with Mrs Ramsden, probably the most troublesome of them all, of whom in letters to George Jack he used the terms 'dragon', 'she-confusion', 'auld cat', and 'auld betch'. On one visit, as Webb told Jack, he asked Mrs Ramsden's acquaintance Lady Spencer of Althorpe, whether she did not think that 'good architects must have the best of tempers to undergo whimsical clients'; agreeing, Lady Spencer added 'and they so ignorant too'; and 'so old and incapable of mending', finished Webb.[40] On such occasions he took snuff in great quantities. When Standen was completed, as a token of their gratitude the Beales gave him a silver snuff box inscribed 'When clients talk damned nonsense I take a pinch of snuff'.[41]

Webb's Site Books show that he visited the site at all crucial stages in the work, such as the laying of foundations and placing of floor joists and roof timbers, which worked out at roughly once a month. Accompanied by the builder, he decided the best place for the latter's plant and materials, and made final adjustments to the position of the building after it had been pegged out. If stone was used, he decided from which bed in the quarry it should come, and instructed his clerk of works to visit the quarry regularly to ensure that the right stone was being delivered. Sample walls were built and rebuilt until the result satisfied Webb, who told the clerk of works to allow the masons to do only 'plain work' until they had got 'their hand in'.[42]

During construction, working drawings for every part and detail of the building, numbering several hundred for large buildings, were produced as necessary at scales of one sixteenth of an inch, half an inch, and one inch to one foot. Believing that few workmen could use materials with the simplicity and directness of their medieval counterparts, Webb indicated the size and position of every stone and, in all but the most straightforward walling, every brick. Full-size drawings were made of all details, however insignificant, even of the chimney pots, in order to avoid ready-made ones of fanciful and bad design. Webb's scale drawings were finished by his assistants, who then traced them for the builder.

As he had no time to spend on training a pupil from scratch, Webb never took an articled pupil. He expected a new assistant to be of 'fair education' and already to have 'laid the foundation of his knowledge of the building arts in a practical way in a good businesslike office'; to be 'anxious to extend his knowledge and give the use of his head and hands in an energetic way to the practical work'; and to have a 'natural turn for construction' and a willingness to 'master the difficulties which occur in adapting construction to art matters in various kinds of buildings'.[43] Having proven his competence, an assistant was given considerable responsibility for the construction of buildings, and sole responsibility for making measured drawings of existing buildings, and if the job involved only repair work, was occasionally allowed to handle it himself. However, assistants were not permitted to design anything. This rule was broken only once. During the few months in 1888 when rheumatism made it impossible for Webb to draw, he permitted George Jack, his chief assistant and a qualified architect who had managed the practice so capably during his employer's illness and convalescence in Italy, to design a few items such as bedroom fireplaces for Willinghurst; however, they had to be approved by Webb, who valued Jack's opinion on aesthetic matters whilst openly deploring his tendency towards the 'architecturalooral'.[44]

Webb's assistants made site visits between his own, when they helped the contractor to peg out the building, for instance, and were allowed to demand the replacement of poor materials. Webb made all the decisions on matters of design, and gave any instructions for the pulling down of bad work. In the case of Clouds, one of his assistants worked full-time in the quantity surveyor's office to facilitate the preparation of the bill of quantities. Webb handled any worrying affairs such as cracked walls himself, and personally inspected and approved all such items as boilers, cooking stoves, parquet floor, and light fittings. He made the detailed records of work done and of the accounts of the clerk of works and the builder, and he prepared the interim payment certificates for contractor and tradesman.

Webb usually had excellent relationships with his builders and their workmen, and in most cases construction progressed smoothly and was well done. If a contractor failed to ensure that the work was done in a sound and workmanlike way, he received one of the architect's 'stiff' letters. Webb instructed Tyerman, the builder of Boyce's West House, to be present on site the next working day to receive instructions to demolish work not done according to the drawings, and added that 'unless the works proceed in a better way than they have done', work would be stopped.[45] The work improved immediately. On the rare occasions when Webb judged that a mistake or failure to spot substandard materials was the fault of himself or his clerk of works, he paid for it to be put right. To perfect the water supply at Clouds, for instance, he paid for an additional cistern, even though at £70 it threatened him with bankruptcy, whereas it would have been a paltry sum to Wyndham, who was paying around £80,000 for the house.[46]

Webb treated all the workmen on his sites with consideration and respect unless they proved unworthy of it, encouraging them by giving praise wherever it was due, and delighting them by ensuring that they received a suitable gratuity from the client when the roof timbers were in place. When difficulties did arise, he dealt with them firmly and justly. When at Willinghurst they were caused by a clash of temperament between the clerk of works and the foreman, he rebuked each man privately. The foreman was asked to respect the clerk's judgement and experience, as Webb himself did, and to work peaceably with him for Webb's sake as the architect

bearing 'heavy responsibility', and was reminded that it was Webb's personal rule and pleasure to work to the utmost of his ability 'in a perfectly friendly way with all classes of working men'; the clerk of works was requested to help Webb for the sake of the client by narrowing the cause of the differences.[47]

Before handing over a new building to a client, Webb made a minute examination of every detail, and ensured that all services were working efficiently. In the case of the vast Clouds, he stayed with the Wyndhams during their first two days in the house to explain its arrangements to them and their servants.[48] Finally, twelve months after work was completed, he made a last detailed inspection before releasing the certificates authorizing final payments, and submitting his own account.

In the case of houses, this was seldom the end of his involvement as almost every client consulted him about the furnishing and decorating of their new or newly enlarged home. As he recommended that until two to three years after completion only a coat of distemper be applied to the walls, furnishing the house came first. In general, except for the artists and furniture collectors such as Wyndham, his male clients evinced less interest in this than they had taken in the planning, design, construction, and finishes of the house, though a few commissioned Webb to design large pieces, such as Lowthian Bell's sideboard for Rounton Grange.[49] Some of them, including Eyre, asked his advice as to which furniture from their present house was suitable for the new one, and Webb always gave his opinion with forthright honesty.[50] At clients' request, notably Wyndham's, he sought suitable paintings, furniture, fireplaces, old tiles and ancient wainscot, and purchased them, often at auctions; but eventually he had to stop doing this because increasingly he was being left with items on his hands.[51] Occasionally he produced ornamental designs for a piece of furniture, such as the piano decorated by Kate Faulkner for Alexander Ionides, but when Pitt-Rivers asked him to do this for a hall table, Webb refused on the grounds that the article was 'rather worthless'.[52]

In the case of a married couple, according to the convention of the time the man appeared as the client in all records but it is clear from Webb's letters that their wives were just as much his clients as their spouses. They played an equal part in determining the sizes, relative positions, and fittings of rooms and, with his help, took a greater part in deciding the

number of cupboards, larders, sinks, cooking stoves, and suchlike, and in the furnishing of the house. Webb consulted them on all these matters. When Mrs Beale wished to take a huge wardrobe to her new house, he readily agreed to the omission of a fitted cupboard of his own design so that it could be accommodated.[53] Almost all the men except the artists left the decoration of their homes entirely to their wives, who sought Webb's help in choosing carpets,

fabrics, wallpapers and paints. He accompanied them to showrooms, to that of Morris & Co. in particular, though with his customary fairness he also recommended well-designed products by other establishments. Should they prefer to choose in his office, or in their homes, he would arrange for samples of fabric and paper to be sent there, with boards painted to match the colours of the backgrounds of suitable papers.[54] Webb was always

Above Philip Webb (centre) with Sir William Bowman on the scaffolding at Joldwynds in 1891, when the library addition was under construction (a detail from the photograph in Webb's collection)

paid for specially commissioned designs for furniture and decorative items but, because he failed to request it, he seldom, perhaps never, was recompensed for time spent advising about decoration and furnishing.

An experienced gardener and knowledgeable about plants, Webb had strong views about the gardens around his houses. Most of his clients accepted his advice about the position of the kitchen garden, which was always decided well before the house was complete so that the same builder could construct its walls. Many also consulted him on the design of the pleasure gardens, in which the women usually took more interest than their husbands. Madeline Wyndham, having bowed to Webb's liking for the south front of his houses to be unencumbered with flowerbeds and shrubberies, proposed not to adhere to the unsolicited design he had prepared for the garden on the east front. After acknowledging that she was free to do as she wished, Webb tried to persuade her to reconsider:

> With regard to the East Garden, I should naturally have an opinion, as the whole surroundings of the house have been under my consideration for some years, and as I have had experience of many failures happening from want of careful attention to all circumstances I arranged my plan with such knowledge and taste as I had. It was a pretty piece of ground and required delicate handling and doubtless you saw this in your dealing with it.

He continued his letter with a plea for the abandonment of two further proposals he feared might be disastrous, the first being an alternative use for a pleasant sitting place he had thoughtfully provided:

> Would it not be well to defer fitting up the little garden house [...] till things are more settled? It should be a handy neat and tidy place and wd. be very convenient. I say this because of the rather wild suggestion to turn it into a dirt hole of a mushroom house. The kitchen garden would be the place for such things where proper heat will be supplied.

The second concerned the precipitate buying and positioning of a large greenhouse:

> As to makers of glass houses, they are legion. There is Weekes of Chelsea, Smith of Ipswich +c but care would have to be used in dealing with them or you will be fitted with work at great cost & which would ruin the appearance of the most lovely place in England. [...] Of course it wd. not do to put the green house on the East side of [the] gardener's house as it wd. be in full view of all who come up to Clouds. I dare say you have noticed the pretty look of that corner as you pass the stables towards the house?[55]

He mitigated these strictures somewhat by providing the names of suppliers of various types of plants and trees, and giving his blessing to whatever Mrs Wyndham decided to do within the kitchen garden.

Despite his above description of Clouds, Webb was rarely completely satisfied with the appearance of his buildings. He explained to Percy Wyndham in 1886, on thanking him for his cheque, that:

> The money was a convenience to me; but your pleasant expression of complete satisfaction with the house at Clouds was very cheering, and will continue to be a help in my work when a sense of hopelessness at times creeps upon one, that all one's efforts to make modern architecture in some way genuine seem to be futile.[56]

In Webb's view his buildings never fulfilled his potential. In 1884, he explained to Boyce, who was depressed about his own painting, that:

> 'tis some years past now that I gave up all hope in my own work and was sad in the extreme for some time and, indeed, great sadness has possession of me in whiles even now, but I ceased to be troubled with my disappointment at finding I was not what I at times thought I was, and barring the times when my soul is in the pit, I am merrier mostly now than I ever used to be for, I have not yet ceased to believe that I have within me what I shall certainly never be able to bring out.[57]

In the same letter, he advised Boyce to take consolation as he did himself from the 'exquisite beauty of the natural world' and in 'glorious appreciation of all that noble souls have conceived'. In after years he never regretted that a scheme had been aborted. 'If my best efforts were <u>not</u> carried out (they were always the best) it was all the better,' he explained to George Jack, 'as they would remain in my mind as darlings, without the risk of proof.'[58] The proof of his design for Rounton Grange, for instance, when he visited it soon after completion, disappointed him so much that, as he told Boyce, he 'longed to be a stonebreaker rather than a setter-up of stones'.[59] However, he would doubtless have become more satisfied with it after a while, when its light yellow masonry and terracotta pantiles had mellowed a little and, as he told Jack he expected to be with Coneyhurst, when climbing plants had veiled the new walls.[60] He found that some houses improved on acquaintance, including Willinghurst, where he thought this was partly due to the trouble he and George Jack had taken in fitting the house into the site.[61]

Nevertheless, he remained convinced that his ideas about good appearance were right, and he continued to enjoy his work, whilst regretting that just occasionally a partial lack of sympathy with his aims on the part of clients prevented them from enjoying the results. 'I find it very general that so soon as I have walled a man in, he walls me out of his esteem,' Webb wryly told George Howard in 1875.[62] However, Webb knew that this was a huge exaggeration. Perhaps during the design stage a small number did fail to sympathize completely with his aims, particularly as to what constituted simplicity; but ultimately all his clients – even the most exacting Mrs Ramsden, and Agneta Cocks, whom he termed 'the petticoated burr' – were well pleased with their new buildings or extensions. They told Webb of their satisfaction, usually in muted tones in view of his extreme dislike of praise. He was consoled by the fact that, with the sole exception of a few members of the Church Building Committee at Brampton who did not approve of his new church, his clients liked his buildings more than he did. As he told the Godmans, when in addition to his fee he received a 'thoughtfully kind letter of thanks' it made him feel almost overpaid.[63]

It is not surprising that they were pleased. In every case, Webb fulfilled Ruskin's recommendation of him to Hale White as an architect who would provide 'perfectly sound and noble work for absolutely just price'.[64] Except when clients themselves called for changes which exceeded it, he did this within the agreed budget and almost always by the date appointed for completion. His clients recommended Webb to their friends but, as he could handle only two or three jobs at one time because of the way he chose to work, some commissions had to be turned down, especially during the years 1877 to 1886 and 1889 to 1892 when he was so deeply involved with the design, construction, and reinstatement of Clouds. Though the fame of this house reached North America and Germany, the droves of would-be clients forecast by Wyndham did not materialize, because admirers, including the 'Souls' – the cultured upper-class group of friends for whom the house became a focal point – assumed that so renowned an architect was too busy or too important to undertake anything less than another Clouds. Instead, they went to Webb's disciples. Ironically, the house that brought Webb to the height of his fame and influence, both within and outside his profession, almost ruined him. In his last few years in practice he more or less had to take what came his way. Fortunately, enough commissions did materialize to make it unnecessary for him to sink his pride and seek work.

Chapter 14

THE LAST YEARS

'My coat feels thinner [...] one would think I had lost a buttress,' Philip Webb told Lethaby after William Morris died in October 1896.[1] This comment has led to a supposition that Webb gave up his practice four years later solely because he missed the stimulus of his old comrade. Certainly, he felt the loss of Morris deeply, and that of Faulkner who died in 1892, of Boyce whose death occurred in 1897, and of Burne-Jones and Kate Faulkner, who both died in 1898. 'I do not mope over the repeated losses of beloved intimates,' he told Hale White in 1899, 'but feel the want of the steadfast rock of assurance their bodily presence afforded me.'[2] Physically no longer strong, he had begun to find his work extremely tiring, and had become aware that he urgently needed 'to get more fresh air and muscular exercise', he wrote; for two years, he had felt that time had told upon him 'both bodily and spiritually', and that unless he moved 'into a freer air, with more freedom of life', he would collapse unnecessarily quickly. There was an even more pressing reason for retiring from practice, however, as he had indicated in a slightly earlier letter to White. After thanking White, who had advised him to die in harness, for thinking about him, Webb continued:

> I rejoice in the friendliness [...] but you could not realize that it would be impossible for me "to go on till I drop" —for certain it is, if I neglected the signs, that I should shortly drop, having come to the end of my professional tether. I have been losing money over the last 3 of my pieces of work, and the rent and other costs of living in London are eating me up—mind body and estate. I believe I can live in a cheap country for 10 years on £150 a year; and my only risk is, that perhaps I may live too long under stimulus of free air and freedom from anxiety.[3]

By 'a cheap country', Webb meant anywhere in the British countryside where the cost of living was low. After Clouds, the 'house of the age', was completed, he had received very few commissions (as mentioned in chapter 7 and 14), apparently because the people who would have liked a new Webb house failed to approach him, thinking mistakenly that he would be too busy with other large country houses, or would have become too important to consider anything smaller. Although he was still at the peak of his renown at the end of the century, Webb simply could not have afforded to stay in business, even had his health and strength been perfect.

On the 28 September 1899, after thirty-five years in residence, he gave preliminary notice of his intention to leave Raymond Buildings.[4] His meagre savings would not stretch to building a cottage, so he set about finding an existing one at a low rent. He asked all his remaining friends if they knew of such a place. He investigated the possibilities in South Wales during a visit to examine two churches, Eglwys Cummin and Eglwys Brewis, for the SPAB, but though he found the countryside beautiful he also discovered that his hope of the district being 'free from "posters", and the nineteenth-century craze for decoration with waste paper', was unfounded in the populous districts, and that no cottage was to be had amongst the lonely hills where the peace and bracing air would have suited his needs.[5] After visiting friends in the Cotswolds, in a district that would probably have been beneficial for his rheumatism, he decided that was where he would like to live. He explained the reasons to Hale White in May 1899:

> I have been to a beautiful place on the Cotswolds, 6 miles out of Cirencester – "Pinbury" to wit, which has loveliness and other satisfactory things. It is just possible harbourage might be found for me there, but that is very doubtful – 600 feet or so above the sea, on limestone earth; with a string of Duntisbournes – villages, and hamlets, as neighbours; [...] Much out of the ways of this world upon wheels, and within ¾ of a mile of 3 friends who have settled there these last five years, and are living – family like, in 3 contiguous houses in a kind of tribal way, and would be good-naturedly human if I should get to be there.[6]

The friends were Ernest Gimson and Sidney

Barnsley, who had spent much time with Webb when their chambers were next door to his in London, and Ernest Barnsley. With Webb's help and encouragement, they had established craft workshops and architectural practices in the area but though they searched widely, nothing suitable was found at a rent within Webb's means.

In April 1900, Webb's old client and friend Sir Lowthian Bell offered him a recently purchased small country house in North Yorkshire, Arncliffe Hall (1753–54), designed by John Carr (1723–1807). Feeling that he was still in Webb's debt, Bell implored the architect to let him pay him a professional fee for his advice, which would involve no drawing, merely giving his opinion. Refusing the generous offers, Webb jokingly suggested that his old client, out of the kindness of his heart, was trying to encompass his 'moral destruction'.[7] Hale White, having tried but failed to find Webb a place near his own home in Kent and longing to have him near enough for frequent visits, kindly offered to buy half an acre at Uckfield or Buxted, or some untouched agricultural village, on which Webb could build a cottage at White's expense, which, he added tactfully, would be an investment for himself.[8] Webb, of course, was too proud and too independent to accept either of these offers, and so the search continued.

Wilfrid Scawen Blunt, the poet and from 1883 to 1894 the unfaithful lover of Jane Morris, learnt of the dilemma when Webb visited him in May 1900 with Sydney Cockerell, who had become Blunt's secretary.[9] Blunt recorded in his diary that the 'worthy old fellow' Webb had been 'too honest to make his fortune' and talked of 'living in a £10 cottage', and that he, Blunt, would try to find him one.[10] Unselfishly, he offered to let Webb have Caxtons, an old house in Worth, West Sussex, which he had recently taken in hand for his own occasional use; Blunt's wife, Lady Anne, thought that having Webb living there would add a delightful new interest to their lives.[11] Cockerell told Webb of Blunt's offer, describing Caxtons as an old-fashioned cottage, without a bathroom or even a gasometer, but one that could be made very comfortable and was in a healthy position on a hill, near a Saxon church and Worth Forest; he added that Blunt would be proud if Webb would occupy it and roam over his portion of the woodlands, and that he, Cockerell, considered the name of the cottage a good omen for a friend of the Kelmscott Press.[12] The establishing of this press had been Morris's last business venture.

Webb visited Caxtons on 30 June 1900 with Cockerell and Lethaby, when he found the sixteenth-century yeoman's house to be a larger one than he had envisaged for his last years. However, it was most attractive, unpretentious and unspoilt, partly brick, partly timber-framed and weatherboarded, with a red tiled roof, in pleasing surroundings. He hesitated to accept the tenancy, however, because Blunt's initial wish to retain the use of a lower and an upper room for his own occasional use led him to fear that Blunt did not understand that Webb would be at Caxtons constantly; also, Webb was worried about the cost of making the cottage fit for his permanent residence and, of course, of being under an obligation. He explained to Cockerell that he had had 'too much to do with born aristocrats of a really kindly turn of mind – even generous – not to know they cannot understand the restricted ways of a poor lower-middle-class man', and that therefore he probably ought to try to find 'another kind of landlord and the freedom of action so necessary' for his own simple life.[13] In his next letter, he told Cockerell of his concern that to make Caxtons ready for Blunt would cost only around £20, whereas around £150 would be needed to make the house suitable for his own permanent use. He continued:

> Hence the tangle in my mind. Nearness to London; obligation to Blunt; spending of his or my money, (the latter preferable but not possible, as the funds go down like the bucket in the well. [sic]). Last but not least, I could not spare a bedroom, and so W B would be kicked out of his own house, as it were.[14]

Webb made a second inspection of Caxtons on 27 July, when he was shown round by Blunt's agent Caffin and his stud groom Holman, with whom he shared a picnic of sandwiches, ginger beer and whisky, before making detailed notes of the plus and minus points of the building. He reported to Sidney Barnsley that the 'little house, little garden, and little orchard' were all to the good, as were the facts that he could be in by the end of the coming October and have an undisturbed tenancy until death at a rent of £15 a year, and that Blunt would spend £150 on repairs.[15] The drawbacks he mentioned were: the nearness to London; the height above sea level of only 340 feet; the fact that Blunt's forester had committed suicide in the cart-shed not long ago, though this did not really disturb Webb; that he would be required to receive his landlord as a guest for an occasional night or so, when Blunt needed to visit his Worth stud; and that Webb himself was only half-hearted about the house because his other, larger half still preferred the Cotswolds. On his way home

Webb was dismayed to see squadrons of hateful new villas being built a mile away at Three Bridges, but he concluded that the railway line would protect Worth from similar excrescences, unless Blunt were to forsake love of his land for easy money.

Matters were becoming desperate, and as nothing was forthcoming in the Cotswolds, in early August 1900 he accepted the tenancy of Blunt's house, which he felt would be his home until 'tripping-up time'.[16] This proved to be the case and, in spite of his misgivings, he would spend fourteen peaceful, contented and, in general, very happy years at Worth. Caxtons had three first-floor bedrooms, stretching east to west, and three large rooms beneath them: a kitchen at the east end, a central living room known locally as the keeping-room, and a parlour at the west end. At the rear of the building were a saddle-room, larder, large earth closet, and a deep well with good water. At the front was a narrow flower garden between the house and the road and, at the back, an orchard, with a field beyond, in which grazed Arab horses from Blunt's nearby Crabbett Park estate.

Caxtons had to be prepared for Webb's use, after suffering several years of neglect. Making it warmer in winter to ameliorate Webb's rheumatism took priority. The floor and roof tiles were re-laid; the oak weatherboarding to the first floor was renewed, as were the rear door and porch, which opened into the kitchen, and the fireplaces in the keeping-room, parlour, and east and west bedrooms; and in the kitchen the old open fire with its separate copper and corner bread-oven was replaced with a plain and functional Longden cooking range.[17] Beginning in September, the work was done chiefly by Blunt's estate workmen, following drawings prepared by Webb, who made thirteen supervisory visits, some of them with his chief assistant and friend George Jack, to whom he gave his practice on leaving London.[18] Completion of the work was delayed by the dilatory Irish foreman but, by 16 December 1900, Cockerell could point out to Webb that he would get a new house and a new century at the same time.[19]

Before he left London, Webb sold all the books he could bear to lose, and he also sold to Birmingham Art Gallery the copy by Fairfax Murray of Carpaccio's St George that he had commissioned when in Italy, and for £100 to Lawrence Hodgson, a customer of Morris & Co., his animal drawings for the 'Forest' tapestry.[20] The resulting funds allowed him to retain most of his independence after all, by paying for the repair of Caxtons himself. He could not bring himself to sell anything that had been given to him, however. He returned his two landscape studies by Burne-Jones to the painter's family, gave away his Madox Brown drawing and more by other artists, and presented to Cockerell a Rossetti sketch of a sofa and the Rossetti watercolour painting *The Meeting of Dante and Beatrice in Paradise*, which he had accepted from Boyce on the condition that it would become the property of whichever of them lived longer.[21] In 1902, after pondering about their disposal for a couple of years, Webb donated to Trinity College, Cambridge, his Kelmscott Press books, which he had accepted from Morris only after Morris told him that he printed them chiefly for Webb and a few others, and which he considered were 'too valuable, either to be sold for a profit, or locked from the attention of students in the arts'.[22] These gifts proved to be singularly altruistic, as Webb's fear that he might live too long would be confirmed, and his hope of managing on £150 a year would be shown to be out by over £50 a year; his retirement lasted a little over fourteen years, for the last few of which he would have been almost destitute had it not been for the surreptitious topping-up of his bank account by kind friends.[23] His current account stood at only £180 in June 1901; in the summer of 1903 he had to sell £200 worth of Consols; and by 1906 his savings were down to £1,219. The following year he had to borrow from his brother Harry and, despite a payment by his nephew in 1909 of £547 10s 6d (which was probably Webb's share of the proceeds from the sale of the Oxford property that he and his siblings had inherited, and which hitherto had given him £4 a year), by summer 1910 his account stood at only £624, which appears to have been his entire resources.[24] In contrast, Morris spent £1,900 during his last year on two medieval manuscripts, and died worth £55,069.[25]

Webb moved from London on 4 January 1901, a week before his seventieth birthday, helped by George Jack and Cockerell, after they spent a final evening together in his chambers, drinking the last of his cellar.[26] As he was leaving, Lethaby told him he should have for epithet 'He fought the good fight'. 'And received a black eye,' Webb replied; 'Let us hope providence will temper the shorn lamb to the prevailing winds.'[27] He had been easily depressed and irritated by his work during his last couple of years in practice, and had found his last year in London a 'quiet time of somewhat sad reflection'; he was exhausted by the move, and deeply moved by his enforced withdrawal from so many of his beloved friends.[28] However, as he and his friends had hoped, his health and spirits soon revived under the stimulus of beautiful countryside, fresh air, and a regular routine of physical work and walking. After only three weeks, Blunt was able to inform Cockerell that Webb had settled into Caxtons well; and by June, Webb could assure Sidney Barnsley that the routine of his new life had been established, in a 'pleasant place' which answered almost all his needs, and was 'singularly beautiful though not quite in the way the more poetical district of the Cotswolds' had appealed to him.[29] He went on to tell Barnsley there was so much physical work to do – chopping wood, drawing water, rescuing the garden and orchard from neglect and damage by the builders – that he was busier than when in practice, and that the designing of a bookplate for Cockerell and Emery Walker, who had recently established a printing firm, could only be done on Sundays. Webb told Cockerell that he rose early, and drew water from the well, swept the paths and opened the shutters, before washing and dressing properly in time for breakfast, feeling 'both sane, and hungry', after which he busied himself with wood-cutting and other household and garden chores until he took dinner at one o'clock.[30] 'Time goes faster than a "motor",' he told Sidney Barnsley a year later, 'but happily without the noise and stink.'[31] His housekeeper recorded later that Webb spent hours at the back door shooting rats with great skill, and that he picked the fruit in the orchard, gave daffodils to the village children, bought the best of clothes for a local crippled boy, and insisted on carollers singing properly before he would give them cakes and money (this led some local children to think him a crotchety old man).[32]

The housekeeper, Margaret Dickinson, who had been found for him by his old friend Mrs Wickham Flower, was more in need of a refuge from an unsatisfactory husband and of a good home for her offspring than of a high wage.[33] Not having lived with children since his childhood, and being so used to his own 'solitary companionship' that it had grown upon his 'shoulders like a comfortable old coat', Webb had probably been concerned about sharing his home with Alice and Reginald but, as he told Cockerell in 1901, they proved to be 'no nuisance' and he minded 'their chatter no more than that of a magpie, or a clock's ticking'.[34] He helped with their lessons, taught them about flowers and about birds from his Bewick book, and instructed Reggie how to draw.[35] It is apparent from his letters to their mother, which almost invariably end with an affectionate message for the children, that Webb had quickly become very fond of them.[36]

Mrs Dickinson fully understood the need to avoid extravagance. Webb's letters to her when away from Caxtons himself show that he was deeply concerned that she and the children might economize on food to the detriment of their health, and that she might over-tax herself on cleaning the house. With his customary thoughtfulness, Webb got Holman to find a 'dependable man' to help her should he, Webb, become bedridden, and habitually he took his annual holiday at his brother Harry's home in August so that Mrs Dickinson could take one herself with her children at her parents' home during the school holiday.[37] This concern for her and the children's welfare is a revealing contrast to

Morris's keeping up a young maidservant until the early hours just to mend his fire whilst he and his comrades debated their socialist ideas for the improvement of the life of her class.[38]

The kitchen was Mrs Dickinson's domain, and the parlour was Webb's private retreat.[39] They had separate staircases to their bedrooms but ate together with the children in the keeping-room, and lived in complete harmony and in friendship despite the housekeeper's lack of a good sense of humour and her love for such things as a 'newspaper murder-drama' and the 'miserable shanty-shops of Three Bridges', because, as Webb told Cockerell, his housekeeper was 'the essence of an industrious woman' and an excellent cook.[40]

Although he had made a clean break from architectural work, apart from his efforts for the SPAB, Webb hoped to supplement his shallow funds by designing commissioned items other than buildings in the few leisure hours left after doing the daily chores. At first all went well, and he spent a few months of his free time designing the mace for the recently founded University of Birmingham. It was made of wood sheathed in silver, enamelled in part, to Webb's drawings of January to April 1902, by Messrs W H Haseler of Birmingham. At Webb's request the work was supervised by Robert Catterson-Smith, a member of the Art Workers' Guild and later the principal of the Birmingham Central School of Art, who executed some of the silverwork himself (he had already made the altar cross for Mrs Gilmore to Webb's design (see chapter 12)). Webb was still disturbed by the separation of designer and maker but every effort was made to interpret his design faithfully and sympathetically. In 1903, the mace was illustrated and criticized favourably in the *Studio*.[41]

In 1901 and 1902, Webb directed the repairing of Eglwys Cummin for the SPAB, the work being supervised by William Weir, with Webb himself designing a new roof truss and some chancel furnishings.[42] During this period he also designed several bookplates, including the one for Cockerell and Walker, and another for J R Holliday of Birmingham; with the fees for these, Webb built a woodshed to ease his outside work in bad weather.[43] He made a small design of a peacock for Madeline Wyndham with which he supplied an outline sketch of the bird to help her with the enamelling of the design.[44] In 1902 he designed the relief panel, *Morris in the Home Mead*, for the front wall of his Memorial cottages at Kelmscott (1899–1900); George Jack, who supervised the construction of the cottages, carved the panel.[45]

On being asked by James Beale in 1902 to alter the arrangement of some of the bedrooms at Standen to suit his reduced household, Webb adhered to his resolve of leaving architecture to the younger men; his recommendation that George Jack should be appointed instead was accepted.[46] In 1905, however, George Howard (who had become Earl of Carlisle in 1889) having made it a condition of his contribution to the cost that the architect for the upper part of the tower of Webb's St Martin's Church in Brampton should be Webb himself, the old architect amended his original design without charge but he insisted on Jack supervising the construction (for more on this, see chapter 12).[47]

By the time he had lived at Caxtons for a year, Webb had fully regained his normal cheerful spirits and good health; but in November 1902 he had a bout of rheumatic lumbago so severe that his friends feared for his life, and he had to spend much of the next twelve months in bed, nursed devotedly by Mrs Dickinson.[48] Sadly, the onset of this illness signified the end of his hopes of improving his finances a little, as he was never again able to draw and could sketch only rarely, although in other respects he eventually made a good recovery. Lowthian Bell asked him to sell him one of his drawings to hang at Rounton Grange, at whatever price Webb chose; there is no evidence that Webb complied, and it is highly likely that instead it was at this time, in an altruistic gesture of sincere admiration and friendship, that he gave Bell almost all the several hundred drawings from which the house had been built.[49]

Apart from the chronic rheumatism that prevented him from designing artefacts and drawing the birds and animals of the district as he had hoped to do, and minor troubles from time to time with his hearing, sight, and failing memory as the years advanced, Webb enjoyed generally good health until his last few months. In 1908, after his 'man-help' suffered a stroke, he was able to resume all the physical tasks, though they limited his hitherto daily walks to Sundays. As late as June 1913, when Webb was eighty-one, Blunt reported to Cockerell that the old man was in 'perfect health of mind and body, able to discuss politics and all things else in excellent spirits'.[50] Though political activity had been abandoned, Webb retained his interest in this

field; but it was less important to him than his interest in art, and in the theory and practice, by others, of architecture, past and present, on a large scale and in detail, as his letters reveal. Lying in bed ill in 1902, for example, stimulated him into urging Cockerell to tell architects always to 'keep the windows on the south side low' when designing bedrooms, so as to 'get plenty of sunshine without too much heat and glare'.[51] Other instances include his request to Cockerell in 1904 to send him some sand from the desert to test whether or not it would make good mortar; his letters to Lethaby of 1904 about the dangers of importing foreign architectural styles; and his calling upon Lethaby, the director of the Central School of Arts and Crafts, to press upon his students the importance of mastering the possibilities of each site.[52]

Having inspected them, Webb told Lethaby that most of the significant early-twentieth-century buildings in London were 'incumbrances of the ground'; he felt 'beaten down' by their 'hopelessness in the way of invention', he wrote, and longed for 'some quite serious and substantially simple public buildings being set up in place of the usual unintelligent masses of Portland stone which have been done lately, and are still doing under Government ignorance'.[53] In 1908, he was infuriated by the lack of plans in the

Above Caxtons: the entrance front

published drawings for the new County Hall, Westminster, designed by Ralph Knott (1879–1929) in that year. 'The plan, the plan, the plan, and all the <u>plan</u> is all one's help for making out what the effect of such a building would be on the excellent site,' he told Lethaby, and went on to say that the design 'might do if the planning were good' and to hope that the detailing would not be of the 'commonplace' type to which 'architects in these days are given'.[54] In this instance, of course, he was using 'commonplace' to mean undistinguished and unimaginative. In 1912, after Charles Winmill, the second-in-command of the London County Council architects in the fire-service department – who, some time after becoming a keen disciple of Webb upon seeing Joldwynds in 1888, had been introduced to his idol by William Weir – sent the plans of County Hall to Caxtons, he was summoned there to explain the scheme in detail.[55] However, the turn-of-the-century building Webb admired most was Westminster Cathedral (1895–1903). The designer of the building, John Bentley, had tried vainly to get him to agree to finish this building should he, Bentley, be unable to do so. Writing to Lethaby in 1905 after a visit to the cathedral, Webb said he was sharply touched by being unable to tell Bentley that the 'doubling of the spaces between his width of domed bays' was a triumph, one that constituted the 'making of the inside effect' of the building, the 'great skeleton' of which would not be spoilt even if the surface decoration were to prove inferior.[56]

Webb was greatly disturbed to find the twentieth century carrying on the nineteenth century's 'brutalising of the simplicity of original settlements'.[57] The recuperative time he spent in digs near the home of Lady Burne-Jones – who looked after his welfare untiringly – at Rottingdean in Sussex in 1903 was marred by the discovery that the 'leprosy of modern vulgar ostentation' was gradually eating away the town's grace.[58] Yet, although he was disappointed with early-twentieth-century buildings, Webb continued to hope for an eventual improvement, which he believed could be achieved only by abandoning the copying of past, and foreign, styles and by returning instead to an emphasis on structure not style, and to 'simple but excellent building' – in other words, to the creed that had governed his own architecture.[59]

Needless demolitions and savage restorations continued to cause Webb deep distress, reinforcing his belief in the importance of the work of the Society for the Protection of Ancient Buildings, on which he continued to advise. He served on the committee of the society throughout his retirement. He still enjoyed studying old churches, and sketching them when this was possible, alone or with a friend such as Hale White, with whom he visited Etchingham church, East Sussex, in 1909.[60] Webb corresponded with Lowthian Bell about the latter's rebuilding of a monk's cell, and enlargement of the manor house at the Carthusian abbey of Mount Grace, North Yorkshire, and he kept in touch with Giacomo Boni, the Italian building conservator who had come under his influence years before, and who visited him at Caxtons in 1907.[61] Webb delighted in receiving, and studying through his magnifying glass, the many postcards of old buildings which his friends habitually sent him when travelling in Britain or abroad.

He remained uninterested in his own professional renown, and showed no particular gratification when Cockerell told him of the interest students were taking in his work – of an admiring Henry Goodhart-Rendell, for instance, who collected photographs of Webb's buildings and spent time gazing at the front of 19 Lincoln's Inn Fields, as Cockerell himself had done.[62] After Clouds and Tangley Manor had received belated publicity in 1904 and 1905 through articles in *Country Life*, by Blunt and Gertrude Jekyll respectively, the architect commented sarcastically to Cockerell that if only he had hung on to practice, 'orders for more by the dozen' would have been sent to him.[63]

Although designing was impossible, and London concerts had been replaced by his musical box and rare performances by amateurs, such as Mrs Hale White on her pianoforte and Cockerell's friend Walter Cobbett on his violin, many other activities ensured that Webb's leisure hours at Caxtons were full and happy.[64] Occasionally he was able to sketch as well as to observe the trees, plants, animals, and people near his house. Letters, whether written to him or passed on by friends, brought the same delight as ever, and though he still disliked the activity, he too wrote interesting letters, wide-ranging in their subject matter. His chief happiness came from the countryside, the 'divine gift of personal friendships', and books that were 'filled with hopes and loving-kindness', he explained to Hale White.[65]

On his feet again after his long illness, he told Cockerell in 1904 that though 'shanks's mare' was 'not so elastic' as an Arabian one, still the beauty of the countryside had lifted him 'above the poverty of grumbling'.[66] Webb had previously lived in the countryside only during his weekends at Welwyn but he fitted easily into his new life because he was a countryman at heart. The peace and simplicity of his new life at Caxtons both suited and contented him. When fit enough, he delighted in doing the necessary physical work. He revelled in the countryside's changing moods, however bad the weather, and found perennial entertainment and fascination in every aspect of the farming year, and in watching Blunt's horses. Apple blossom transported him with joy in May, and cloud formations were a constant source of delight and wonder, especially on evenings when the sun went down 'with fiery dogs on his haunches'.[67] Mercifully his eyesight remained good enough to the end of his life to prevent books from failing in their 'mission to bless'; he exchanged them with friends, particularly Hale White and Cockerell, and debated in person and by correspondence the content of works of fact and fiction, including several by Tolstoy, Scott's *The Fair Maid of Perth*, Carlyle's *Frederick the Great*, Bunyan's *The Holy War*, and Lethaby's *Greek Buildings*.[68]

Webb made new friends of all types at Worth, though there were more 'carriage folk' amongst his neighbours than suited his inclination; 'aristocrats and their imitators much abound', he grumbled, 'along with "bags" of 14 hundred! pheasants at a day's murder'.[69] The entertaining of the friends he had known for many years, whatever their age, gave him the greatest pleasure of all. He informed Hale White that even the great delight he got from walking alone in the forest came second best to the company of a 'fitting companion'.[70] After Burne-Jones died, Cockerell told Thomas Rooke, the painter's erstwhile assistant, that they must cherish Webb, 'the only one of those great heroes that remains to us'.[71] Cockerell, who venerated Webb and had found that he was 'absolutely modest, like all really great persons; learned withal, well read, witty, generous, and unselfish', did indeed cherish the old man.[72] As well as sending frequent letters, and daily postcards when away, he made the hour-long journey from London to Caxtons roughly every fortnight. He often took along other friends such as Emery Walker, in spite of Webb's expressed hope that friends would call on him singly to spin out the pleasure, and he kept others, including Lethaby, up to the mark with their attentions. Rooke, for whom Webb was the last of the 'assembly of the Goodliest Knights (as Malory

Left and below The ceremonial mace of Birmingham University, designed by Webb in 1902 for Alice Beale, the sister-in-law of James Beale of Standen, who presented it to the newly-founded institution (University of Birmingham Collections)

Above Webb's pipe, tobacco jar, and snuff boxes (Private Collection)

Shirley, later Earl Ferrers, who was Winmill's friend and an admirer of Webb, called at Caxtons fairly frequently.[76] So, too, did Blunt, who found Webb's conversation 'delightful'; he developed a sincere affection and admiration for the old architect, whose opinion he sought on his own writing and poetry, and debated with him on many matters, including Tolstoy's social theories.[77] At times, Webb had so many callers that he could not get on with his gardening and repair work. One day, Jack and Weir arrived unexpectedly as he was fixing weatherboards. 'Go home, who asked you two villains to come here?' Webb asked, before descending the ladder to give them a good tea.[78] Fortunately his housekeeper could cope with any such influx. In a single week, for instance, Walker brought Jane Morris to see Caxtons, and Weir called to see Webb on a later day, as subsequently did Mrs Flower, who wrote often and called occasionally on the old architect; as Webb told Cockerell, '"Missa Dick" had to skip about in that week; but she did it womanfully – without turning a hair'.[79]

Webb remained in contact with his dear old friends Jane Morris and Georgiana Burne-Jones to the end, and stayed at least twice with the latter at Rottingdean. Other old clients, including Percy Wyndham and John Yorke, often called on him, sometimes with their families. May Morris's account of a typical day at Caxtons shows that it was not merely a matter of duty; it gave pleasure to the visitor as well as to Webb. First, there was the walk to Caxtons from station, where he always met expected friends; then a stroll in the forest and a spell of watching and discussing the Arab horses. This was followed by the 'beautiful hospitality, the sweet homeliness of the spread table, the touching insistence that one should eat heartily of some simple dainty'; and, finally, by long talks in Webb's inner sanctum.[80]

As well as his annual holidays with Harry at Winchester, Webb visited Hale White and other friends, and made several day-trips to London every year, sometimes spending the day alone but often meeting Lethaby, or George Jack who, Webb gratefully acknowledged, was 'good and helpful over the roughs of time, always'.[81] A typical day with Jack would begin at a watchmaker's or shoemaker's, then, after luncheon and an inspection of any new buildings in progress, end in a pilgrimage to St Paul's Cathedral. As the years passed, Jack noticed sadly that Webb had to reduce his beloved snuff from two boxes a week to one and then to none, and had to

says) that ever was', and who visited him often, told the old architect how often Burne-Jones had eulogized him and talked with affection of their friendship; and how he and the other SPAB committee members hoped to have Webb, to the end of their need, to help and guide them, so that they might 'bring up a younger generation' to carry on Webb's work.[73] Several other SPAB members visited Webb regularly, including William Weir, and Charles Winmill, who had often taken tea in Webb's chambers with Lethaby and, during the last year in London, had walked with Webb almost every evening. In 1901, Winmill asked him to be the best man at his wedding; refusing, Webb opined that 'in these days of bad architects a man of such quality is not easily found'.[74] During Webb's last two years, Winmill travelled to Worth on his motorcycle; the first time, knowing his host's hatred of noisy machines on wheels, he hid the vehicle, but to his surprise Webb was intrigued, and made him ride up and down outside Caxtons, explaining how it worked.[75] Walter

turn to a ready-made shop on finding bespoke boots beyond his means; however, he observed happily that the old man's boyish delight on a boat trip on the Thames, and his enjoyment of Wren's inventiveness and creative experiments, never diminished.[82]

Webb was interested to the end in everything that came his way. At the age of eighty, for instance, he began to study the stars with the aid of astronomical maps and articles in the *Daily News*.[83] National and world affairs were a continuing fascination but, apart from the deaths of friends and his sometimes faulty memory, they also brought the only real clouds to his horizon. He was as horrified and depressed by the continuing trouble with the Boers and the awful carnage of the First World War as he had been, in his younger days, by the Crimean and Franco-Prussian Wars, and the threatened invasion by France. Inevitably, he was grieved by the deaths of his siblings (the seven who had survived into the 1880s were a loving, close-knit family) and of his friends. His sister Caroline died in 1909, followed two years later by their brother Harry, for whom she had continued to housekeep after he retired to Winchester in 1900; they had kept in constant touch with Philip by letter. In 1907, on hearing of the death of George Bodley – whom in 1869 he had helped by keeping an eye on the last stages of construction and decoration of a small group of houses in Malvern whilst Bodley was ill – Webb told Lethaby that the architect had been a 'man of some taste and discrimination' whose companionship he had enjoyed until 'it died away' as Bodley began to undertake church restorations.[84] On hearing of Shaw's death in 1912, in a letter to Lethaby, Webb wrote, 'I had thought that the old and trustworthy friend, Norman Shaw, would have held on as long as myself, but no.'[85] 'And he had done good and serious work,' he added.

Long blessed with a phenomenal memory, Webb was naturally disturbed when it began to fail but for many years its lapses were only occasional, and he accepted them philosophically. After a trip to London in 1908, he told Cockerell that 'an everlasting attack of old age is appreciably whittling my wits away' and that, after brightening up under the influence of Cockerell, Walker, and Signor Branca (a waiter at Gatti's), his 'terribly defaulting memory' had met him at the gate of Caxtons 'like the ghost of old age', and subsequently had nearly driven him to 'tears of vexation' during a long spell of writing.[86] In 1910,

though not nearly so depressed by old age as Hale White, Webb sympathized with his friend's blunderings in dealing with tradesmen and his bank book blunders with which he, too, had been beset through memory failure, but wrote that he had been able to laugh at his 'ridiculous position as a grown man!', however, and that the countryside, the forest, and the stars had brought him solace.[87]

Towards the end of 1914, Mrs Dickinson expressed her concern about Webb's seriously defaulting memory to Hale White and Lethaby, and asked the latter to come to Caxtons, for what proved to be the last time he saw Webb. The old architect had not recognized him at first, Lethaby reported to Cockerell, but eventually he had 'seemed nearly his recent self' and, as usual, had insisted on walking part way to the station with him.[88] Webb's memory was obviously stimulated by talking to friends, and reminiscing with them about old times, but he had a fall at Christmas, after which he could not sleep, and talked and laughed continuously. He longed to go home to Oxford, the town which had meant so much in his life, so Walker tried to take him there but they had to turn back.[89] The old man slowly weakened, and he died on 17 April 1915. Cockerell, devoted friend to the very last, described Webb's last hours in his diary:

> Reached Caxtons … and found dear Webb still alive but unconscious. Mrs Dickinson … and a very kind and helpful male nurse were with him. He had been in much the same state since 5 a.m. yesterday. […] At 6.30 P. W. died peacefully, his breathing becoming weaker till it ceased. It was the first time I had been actually present at a death (when Morris died I was in the next room) and I found it, at any rate in the case of an old man, a natural event attended with no horror.[90]

He felt there was little cause to grieve as Webb had lived eighty-four happy and contented years, and had lived them 'manfully and finished his work'.

Webb's many friends were deeply saddened by the news but found consolation in their remembrances of him. Mrs Flower kept thinking of Webb's wonderful life and even more wonderful personality, and about how happy she was to have known him; and Georgiana Burne-Jones gave thanks that 'his noble spirit' had 'passed out of the baffling clouds that obscured it' during his last months.[91] Lethaby, 'weak and sore', told May Morris that Webb had been 'truly heroic', the 'strongest man' he had ever known, whose vision he had at times believed 'would save England'.[92]

In the Cotswolds, Gimson and the Barnsley brothers remembered their fascination with Webb and his work during their London days, and recalled his 'many kindnesses and a ready helpfulness' when they lived near him in Gray's Inn, and the enthusiasm of their 'pilgrimages to his houses'.[93] Winmill, who had told his young daughter many times that anything he knew of architecture was due to Philip Webb, was so distressed on hearing of his old mentor's death that he was temporarily overcome, and knelt sobbing beside her bed.[94]

On 20 April 1915 Webb's body was cremated at Golder's Green in north London. In July, his remains became part of the English landscape that he had loved so intensely, when Cockerell, accompanied by Emery Walker and fellow printer St John Hornby, scattered his ashes within an ancient camp on the windswept wholesome down above the White Horse at Uffington in Berkshire now in Oxfordshire, a spot dear to Webb and his old companion Morris.[95] In 1902, he had expressed his feelings to Cockerell about a biographical memorial:

> So far as any <u>written</u> memorial of me is concerned, I don't care two crossed straws, and there may be fifty written for all I care, and each signed by the President of the Royal Academy and R.I.B.A. Of course, any brief thing that Lethaby might wish to write, no hurt to my feeling could come from such, save that he has a tendency to give overdue value to a way-worn modern's strivings.[96]

With Cockerell's enthusiastic encouragement, Lethaby did write a biography, far from brief, which has been and remains of inestimable help to all students of Webb and his work. It was published in the *Builder* in 1925 as a series of papers, 'Philip Webb and his Work', and in book form in 1935 after Lethaby's death.[97]

After Webb died, faithful Mrs Dickinson, who considered her years at Caxtons to have been the happiest of her life, returned to service with Mrs Flower.[98] Webb left his meagre estate of £1,643 2s 2d to his sisters, Sarah and Caroline; but only the former, the last of the eleven siblings, had survived him.[99] Webb's executor Emery Walker had stopped him from burning his papers when he retired, and Webb had allowed George Jack and Winmill to take some of them away; after his death Jack and Winmill gave two hundred and nineteen of his drawings to the RIBA and others to the Victoria and Albert Museum, and Walker allowed the authorities of the two institutions to select what they wished from the remainder. Walker retained the note and letter books, and the remaining drawings, which he bequeathed to his daughter Dorothy, who gave over three hundred of the drawings to the RIBA, and the remainder with many of Webb's other papers to one of the architect's greatest admirers, the architect, John Brandon-Jones (these are now in a private collection).[100]

At the news of Webb's death, obituary notices and memorial articles appeared in *The Times*, and in most British journals with an interest in architecture. In a letter published in the *RIBA Journal*, Arthur Keen (1861–1938) drew attention to Webb's 'unusual ability for clear, original thought', his 'mastery of composition', 'fine instinct for proportion and right scale', and 'good understanding of colour'.[101] In *Country Life*, Sir Edwin Lutyens praised Webb, amongst other points, for having had the courage to refuse work that was 'incompatible with his ideals'; for not degrading 'labour by forcing it to adopt unworthy methods and bad materials'; and for the 'keen sense and knowledge of proportion', the mastery of the 'right use of material', and fertile invention which had given his work a 'quality of surprise' and an 'enduring charm' that was the 'apotheosis of construction rather than the mask of architecture'.[102] He recalled how he had come to recognise the 'freshness and originality' in Webb's work as the product of the 'eternal youth of genius' conjoined with 'another attribute of genius—thoroughness'. Every detail, no matter how small or trivial, had been 'carefully and equally thought out and fitted to meet its special requirements, designed 'to fit its purpose'. By studying Webb's buildings, drawings, and specifications, architectural students would better equip themselves to 'attain to his ideal', and to 'endue all members of the building trades [...] with dignity and honour'.

At a General Meeting of the RIBA – the association Webb had steadfastly refused to join – members paid him tributes, which were published in the *Journal*. Edward Guy Dawber (1861–1938) spoke of Webb as a pioneer who had left a great mark on English architecture. Philip Norman (1842–1931) said he had known no man 'more absolutely determined to do his duty'; he recalled Webb's 'profound conscientiousness' and 'unerring sense of proportion', and said that he was a 'man of great gifts' who had set them all a 'noble example'. Halsey Ricardo expressed his belief that the 'vitality and life' in its every part was the main characteristic of Webb's work, which he lauded for being full of ideas and suggestions for development and further invention; these attributes, stemming from Webb's knowledge and application of building materials, had made his work inspiring, unlike most buildings of their own day. 'What higher praise,' Ricardo asked, 'can we give to a man's work than that besides being distinguished it is fruitful?' Professor Lethaby stated his belief that Webb had been a great force and a great man, a 'great building architect and a great decorative architect', who had anticipated by two to three decades what the 'Arts and Crafts people tried to do', and who had 'set the pattern for what became the ambition in building in the latter end of the nineteenth century'.[103]

In his appreciation of Webb in the *Architectural Review*, George Jack wrote that Webb had in him a 'most potent quality of silent influence', one which 'removed "architecture" from the architect's office to the builder's yard and the craftsman's workshop',

and one which held many younger architects 'under its spell without knowing it, as was proved by their work afterwards'.[104] In the *RIBA Journal*, he expressed his belief that Webb's greatest faculty had been his knowledge of 'all kinds of building materials, and the inventive skill he displayed in their use'; when he first studied his work, Jack had concluded, as he still believed, that 'of all the architectural genius of the nineteenth century, Webb's was the most vital and the most inspiring'.[105]

In accordance with his expressed wish, no monument was set up to Philip Webb but he has many fine memorials including, of course, his buildings and the venerable edifices he rescued or helped to rescue. The finest of all, however, are the thriving and influential Society for the Protection of Ancient Buildings, and his own national vernacular approach, an approach that could be applied at any time in any country with a heritage of traditional architecture, to produce good buildings, clearly of their own day yet always in harmony with their surroundings.

Below A sketch of Philip Webb in the kitchen at Caxtons, by Thomas M Rooke (Private Collection)

KEY TO THE PLANS

amb	ambulatory
area	open area
ba	bathroom
bed	bedroom
blld	billiard-room
bou	boudoir (Lady's Room at Arisaig House)
bus	business room
butl	butler's room
clk	cloakroom
coal	coal store
cons	conservatory
din	dining room
dr	drawing room
dress	dressing room
gdn-hs	garden-house
gl-hs	glass-house
hall	living-hall
hay	hay loft
hsk	housekeeper's room
kit	kitchen
kit yd	kitchen yard
lib	library
liv	living-room
maids	maidservants' bedrooms
men serv	menservants bedrooms
models	models' changing room
morn	morning room
pa	pantry/larder
roof lt	roof light
sc	scullery
sch	school room
serv	servants' hall
servg	serving room/area
smok	smoking room
smok/bus	smoking cum business room
stu	study
stu/bus	study cum business room
unexcav	unexcavated
wait	waiting room
wash	wash-house/laundry
yd	yard

CATALOGUE OF ARCHITECTURAL WORKS

KEY

c: client
t: type of building
d: date designed
e: date constructed
b: builder
cw: clerk of works
ct: cost (where a relevant Certificate Book of Works in Progress survives, the cost is based on figures therein; the cost of most of the buildings has been calculated from the amount of Webb's fee as recorded in his Account Book)
ds: location of Webb's drawings
sw: subsequent work by Webb
pu: present use of the building
The omission of any of the above categories in entries in the Catalogue of Works signifies that the author's exhaustive searches have yielded no information on those subjects for the building in question.

AB: Webb's Account Book
BAL/RIBADC: British Architectural Library/Royal Institute of British Architects Drawings Collection
BL: British Library
CB: Webb's Certificate Books of Works in Progress
HP: Howard Papers, University of Durham
LB: Webb's Letter Books
NT: The National Trust
NYCRO: North Yorkshire County Record Office
PC: a private collection
RO: record office
SB: Webb's Site Notebook
SPAB: The Society for the Protection of Ancient Buildings
V&A, W&I: Victoria & Albert Museum, Word & Image Department

Literary references are given in the chapter notes.

The figure given for the cost of a building does not include the salary of a clerk of works or the amount of Webb's fee.

Work on buildings in connection with the SPAB is not listed (see chapter 8).

It should be noted that although the names of the wives of Webb's clients are not included in his accounts and most letters, the women exercised considerable influence on the plan, the fittings, and the decoration and furnishing of the houses.

ARCHITECTURAL WORKS

1.   Red House, Bexleyheath, Kent (now Greater London)
c: William Morris, painter (at the time of designing)
t: studio-house in the country
d: 1858–59
e: 1859–60
b: William Kent of Bermondsey
ct: £4,000 (Webb did not receive a fee)
ds: V&A, W&I; BAL/RIBADC
sw: 1864, additional wing and alterations to create an attached dwelling for Burne-Jones and his family (not executed)
pu: Red House became a National Trust property, regularly open to the public, in 2003.

2.   Sandroyd (later Benfleet Hall), Fairmile, Cobham, Surrey
c: John Roddam Spencer Stanhope, painter
t: studio-house in the country
d: 1860
e: 1860–61
b: George Wood
ct: £1,858 (AB)
ds: V&A, W&I; PC
sw: 1864, enlargement of the domestic offices (ct: £310 (AB));1870, enlargement of the main block (ct: £400 (AB))
pu: flats and 2 cottage wings, created from the house (most Webb fittings removed); stables, a dwelling under separate ownership.

3.   Cottage at the Moated House, Tottenham, London
c: Major William James Gillum (later Col.), ex-army officer, philanthropist
t: cottage for gardener
d: 1860
e: completed before April 1861
ds: V&A, W&I; SPAB
pu: demolished c. 1966.

4.   Numbers 91–101 Worship Street, Shoreditch, London
c: Major William James Gillum, ex-army officer, philanthropist

t: terrace of 6 dwellings, each with a shop and a workshop, for craftsmen and their families (replacement for 6 dilapidated houses and 8 miserable cottages)
d: 1861
e: 1861–63
b: Edward Robinson & James W Browne
ct: £2,786 (AB) including the cost of the cottage for the Moated House (above)
ds: BAL/RIBADC; SPAB; PC
pu: offices, with interiors changed to meet regulations; workshops demolished.

5.   Enlargement of a house at Hatfield, Hertfordshire
c: Dr Charles Drage, GP
t: new wing containing additional domestic offices, bedrooms, stables (with hay and straw loft above), coach-house, and surgery
d: c. 1861–65 (presumably unexecuted: no fee in AB)
ds: V&A, W&I.

6.   Arisaig House, Arisaig, Inverness-shire, Scotland
c: Francis Dukinfield Palmer Astley, landowner and colliery owner
t: country house
d: 1863, house; 1864, gardeners' bothy, Borrodale Farmhouse (2 dwellings created from ruined farmhouse, for coachman and factor), farm buildings and stables; 1866, chapel (not executed)
e: 1863–64, house; 1864–66, bothy, farmhouse, stables and farm buildings
b: a group of Scottish contractors for the separate trades under English cw; main contractor: James Connell of Glasgow, masons
cw: John Smith
ct: £12,181 (AB)
ds: BAL/RIBADC; V&A, W&I; PC; drawings studied whilst in the collection of the late Miss M J Becher are now in the BAL/RIBADC
sw: 1882–83, improvements to drainage system, some redecoration (ct: £1,400 (AB))
pu: private house, after a period as an hotel (rebuilt in 1930s after a fire: smaller but with some Webb work remaining including the basement); bothy now a holiday cottage; farmhouse (private house) and buildings remain but major part of latter re-roofed (unfortunately not in slate) after another fire.

7.   Number 1 (14) Holland Park Road, Kensington, London
c: Valentine Cameron Prinsep, painter
t: studio-house
d: 1864
e: 1865
b: Jackson & Shaw of Westminster
ct: £3,108 (AB)
ds: BAL/RIBADC
sw: 1876–77, enlargement of studio and increase of accommodation (b: Ashby Brothers of Shoreditch; ct: £730 (Ashby's tender); ds: BAL/RIBADC); 1892–93, further alteration and extensive enlargement (b: C W Bovis of St Marylebone; £8,908 19s 9d (CB); ds: BAL/RIBADC))
pu: in flats (converted 1948; most of Webb's fittings removed).

8.   The National School (now All Saints' and St Richard's Church of England Primary School), Heathfield, East Sussex
c: the school managers
t: replacement of existing, circular-plan National School of 1819
d: 1861, by John W Billing of 12 Abingdon Street, Westminster, London (with whom Webb had served his articles in Reading)
e: 1864 to Billing's design with gratuitous small modifications and supervision by Webb
b: local builders Piper and Harmer

ds: East Sussex RO, Billing's drawings; Webb's, if made, are missing

pu: Heathfield Church of England School (much enlarged at rear).

9. Hendred College, Berkshire
c: a Mr Galland; the trustees of the college
t: unknown; re-arrangements
d&e: c. 1864–65; c. 1875–76
ct: £390 (AB); £320 (AB)

10. Bradford Wool Exchange Competition
t: competition for the design of the Wool Exchange, Bradford
d: 1864
ds: unfinished, not submitted: BAL/RIBADC
Webb was one of 10 architects invited to compete.

11. Number 16 Cheyne Walk, Chelsea, London
c: Dante Gabriel Rossetti, painter
t: studio addition to existing house
d&e: c. 1864
sw: 1871, Webb improved the studio's natural lighting
pu: private residence.

12. Cranmer Hall, Sculthorpe, Norfolk
c: Sir Willoughby Jones, landowner
t: enlargement and improvement of country house (1721): new single-storey drawing-room wing, clock tower, main staircase, dining-room fittings, and stables; improvement of domestic offices
d: 1864–c. 1866
e: 1864–late 1866 or early 1867
ct: £6,720 (AB)
ds: most are missing; BAL/RIBADC (dining-room fireplace and drawing-room ceiling c. 1865, only); Art Workers' Guild (1 drawing for a ceiling panel)
pu: private house; Webb's main staircase and wing remains but the drawing-room barrel vault and fireplace were removed by Jones's son in 1929; 1990s, stables converted to a house (separate ownership).

13. Washington Hall (later Dame Margaret Hall), Washington, Tyne & Wear
c: Isaac Lowthian Bell (created baronet 1885), MP, industrialist, iron-master, and landowner
t: Additions to house of 1864 by Alfred Burdakin Higham of Newcastle upon Tyne
d: 1864, rear extension; 1866, new entrance, dining room, bedrooms, and second-floor flat enlargement, and replacement of spire on tower with clock stage.
e: 1864–c. early 1867
ds: BAL/RIBADC; NYCRO
ct: £6,952 (AB)
pu: nursing home; some changes with loss of some fittings, the conservatory, and the Turkish bath suite; Webb's clock was later installed in the Smeaton Manor stables.

14. Bonnington's, near Hunsdon, Ware, Hertfordshire
c: Salisbury Baxendale
t: estate cottage
d&e: c. 1866
ct: £320 (AB)
ds: PC
This design is very similar to that of the gardener's cottage at the Moated House, Tottenham (above).

15. A new street formed from St John's Lane, Newcastle upon Tyne
c: Newcastle Council
d: late 1866 to March 1867
ds: V&A, W&I
Webb withdrew from the commission. A competition was then held but ultimately the street was laid out to the Town Surveyor's plan.

16. Buildings for the Boys' Farm School, East Barnet, Hertfordshire (now Greater London)
c: Lt.-Col. Major William James Gillum, ex-army officer, philanthropist
t: buildings for a farm school for boys
d: 1867–68, detached block of living quarters for boys, with kitchen, dairy, and cow house in long lean-to, known as New Buildings; 1874, new dairy; 1875, cow house converted into schoolroom, new dining room and kitchen
e: 1867–68; 1874; 1875
b: New Buildings: J. H. Morgan of Kilburn; 1874 and 1875 works: probably Morgan or William Bradley of Cockfosters (who built later works designed by C G Vinall)
ct: £810, New Buildings; £1,460 for the 1874 and 1875 work
ds: missing
pu: New Buildings houses a school for children excluded from regular state education, administered by the public school Mill Hill.
Webb might have altered the existing farmhouse for use by the school in the early 1860s (AB).

17. Number 1 Palace Green, Kensington, London
c: The Hon. George James Howard, painter (later ninth Earl of Carlisle)
t: town mansion-cum-studio-house for Howard and his wife, and his father, the Hon. Charles Howard, MP
d: 1867–68
e: 1868–70; 1873–74, large schoolroom on 3rd floor with servant's bedroom above
b: Richard Ashby & Sons, Bishopsgate, London; 1873–74 work: Ashby Brothers (the name changed after the death of Richard Ashby)
ct: £10,702 (AB)
ds: BAL/RIBADC; V&A, W&I; SPAB; PC
sw: c. 1881–96: improvements to drainage system, moving of some internal walls, re-plastering of drawing-room ceiling, redecoration (ds: HP)
pu: private flats
In 1957, after Webb's fittings had been removed, the building was converted into flats by the Crown Commissioners, with the insertion of a small number of windows.

18. Buildings for Bell Brothers Clarence Iron Works, Port Clarence, Stockton-on-Tees
c: Isaac Lowthian Bell (created baronet 1885), MP, industrialist and iron-master, for Bell Brothers
t: clock tower, blowing-engine house, and works offices
d: 1867, clock tower; 1873, blowing-engine house; 1874, Clarence Offices
e: clock tower possibly early 1870s; 1873–74, blowing-engine house; 1876–78, Clarence Offices
b: Bell Brothers' craftsmen and labourers
ct: clock tower, c. £340 (AB); engine house, unknown; Clarence Offices, £3,955 12s 7d including furniture (Bell Bros. Records; Webb based his fee on costs of only £1,700 (AB))
ds: clock tower: PC; engine house: PC, V&A, W&I (1 drawing for engine-house chimney); Clarence Offices: missing (a measured plan and front elevation, 1970, by and in collection of J K Harrison)
pu: demolished: 1930s, clock tower and blowing-engine house; 1970, Clarence Offices.

19. Number 19 Park Hill (later Wensum Lodge), Carshalton, Surrey
c: William Hale White, civil servant and author 'Mark Rutherford'
t: small house in the country
d: 1867–68
e: 1868
ct: c. £800 (the client's stipulated figure; Webb took no fee)
ds: V&A, W&I

pu: detached private house
In 1896 when rooms were built over the scullery range for a later owner, the staircase was probably moved to give access to them, and then or later, the hall and parlour were thrown together; in the twentieth century the house was divided into 2 flats, and subsequently returned by John Brandon-Jones to a single house.

20. Upwood Gorse, Caterham, Surrey
c: John Tomes, dental surgeon (knighted 1886)
t: small house in the country
d: 1868
e: 1868–69
b: Morris Regis
ct: £3,320 (AB)
ds: BAL/RIBADC; SPAB
sw: c. 1873, a north range of domestic offices; 1875–76, entrance porch extended, domestic offices enlarged and 2 floors added above, garden porch rebuilt as garden room (e: 1876, b: C E Scrivener of Caterham Valley, ct: £880); 1888–89, study and main bedroom above extended, bay window added to drawing room (ct: £614); 1894, gardener's cottage (e: c. 1895, ct: £280) (all costs: AB)
pu: 3 attached houses (house), 2 detached houses (coach-house and flat, gardener's cottage).

21. Church Hill House (later Trevor Hall), East Barnet, Hertfordshire (now Greater London)
c: Col. William James Gillum, ex-army officer, philanthropist
t: country house
d: 1868, house; 1869, stable block with cottages for coachman and gardener, a gate lodge
e: 1868–70
b: Sharpington and Cole; stable block and lodge: by direct labour under cw
cw: Robert Baker
ct: £10,494 14s 4d for house, stables with cottages, and lodge
ds: V&A, W&I
pu: before demolition c. 1960, house had been divided into flats with most Webb fittings removed; lodge and much-altered stable cottages survive.

22. West House, Glebe Place, Chelsea, London
c: George Price Boyce, painter
t: studio-house
d: 1868
e: 1869–70
b: John Tyerman of Walworth Road, London
ct: £2,448 (AB)
ds: V&A, W&I; BAL/RIBADC (small sketch plan)
sw: 1876, a dressing room over an open, brick-vaulted passage (b: Tyerman; ct: £500 (AB), ds: V&A, W&I)
pu: private house (extended northwards and various changes made to the interior after Boyce's death).

23. Number 19 Lincoln's Inn Fields, London
c: Leonard Rowe Valpy, solicitor
t: professional offices
d: 1868
e: 1869–70
b: Charles Aldin
ct: £5,827 (AB)
ds: BAL/RIBADC
pu: offices (interior stripped and refitted in 1975, chimney turret removed).

24. Red Barns, Coatham, Redcar, North Riding of Yorkshire (now Redcar & Cleveland Borough)
c: Thomas Hugh Bell, industrialist
t: small house in an expanding hamlet near Redcar
d: 1868, house; 1875, stables with flat for groom and gardener
e: finished by mid-1870; 1875 stables
ct: house: £1,550; stables: £560 (AB)
ds: missing for original house apart from small ground plan in BAL/RIBADC

sw: 1881 (b: Thomas Davison Ridley of Middlesbrough; ct: £2,320 (AB)): dressing room and bathroom, small servants' hall and laundry; and schoolroom block (e: 1882); 1897: enlargement of bay window in drawing room (b: Ridley; ct: £280 (AB); ds for the subsequent work: BAL/RIBADC; NYCRO; Teesside Archives)

pu: original family quarters (almost unchanged apart from removal of some Webb fittings in 1980s by previous owner) as the home of the proprietors of the hotel and public house that occupies the schoolroom block and the twentieth-century additions made on the site of the stables when Red Barns was the home of the headmaster and boarding pupils of Sir William Turner's School.

25. Cortachy Castle, near Kirriemuir, Angus, Scotland
c: David Ogilvy, seventh Earl of Airlie, landowner
t: repair, alteration, and enlargement of castle
d: 1868–69: the repair of a turret and extending of adjacent library into its top storey; new library fittings, and 2 schemes for adding a new wing and improving the castle
e: 1868–69, turret/library work (1869, both new wing schemes were rejected and Lord Airlie withdrew the commission)
ct: cost of turret and library work unknown; Webb's estimates of cost of new wing: between £15,000 and £20,000, 1st scheme and £36,240, 2nd scheme
ds: turret sketches, SB 1865–77; new wing drawings presumably destroyed by Webb
pu: country seat of the Earl of Airlie; Webb's library fittings were replaced in 1949
Webb received £600 from Lord Airlie in 1869 to cover the design and execution of the turret/library work, the two schemes for a new wing, and the abandoned scheme for a new country house on the site of Airlie Castle (see next entry).

26. House of Airlie, near Kirriemuir, Angus, Scotland
c: David Ogilvy, seventh Earl of Airlie, landowner
t: country house on site of ruined Airlie Castle
d: 1868–69; project abandoned 1869
ct: Webb's estimate £50,000
After working drawings and a bill of quantities had been prepared, the project was abandoned, the estimated cost being too high (no maximum figure had been indicated). The usual fee of 2% of the estimated cost for a scheme abandoned at this stage would have been £1,250 but Webb received only £600 for this and all the designed and executed work for Cortachy Castle. Apparently, no documents survive in the Airlie Archives connecting Webb with work for Airlie or Cortachy Castle.

27. Toft Hall, Bexton, Cheshire
c: Rafe Oswald Leycester, landowner
t: alterations and improvements of domestic offices and servants' quarters
d: 1868
e: 1868 or 1869
cw: William Lever of Fulham
ct: £1,420 (AB)
pu: converted to offices
Leycester's wife was a niece of Mrs William Cowper, through whose husband Morris, Marshall, Faulkner & Co. had obtained the commission to decorate part of St James's Palace in 1866.

28. Thurstaston Church, Thurstaston, Cheshire
c: Adam Steinmetz Kennard, a wealthy client
t: church to replace the existing parish church of St Bartholomew
d: 1868–71 (unexecuted)
ct: estimated £5,826 (AB)
ds: BAL/RIBADC; V&A; W&I; HP; PC
Scheme abandoned 1872, reason unknown: present church by J L Pearson consecrated 1887.

29. Number 77 Park Street, Mayfair, London
c: Dr E Dowson, probably a GP
t: alterations and additions (including a dining room) to existing house
d: c. 1867–72
e: 1868–1873
b: William Shearburn of Dorking
ct: £1,700 (AB)
pu: demolished.

30. Lancaster Lodge (later number 78 Honiton Street), Kensington, London
c: Robert Braithwaite Martineau, painter
t: studio
d: 1869
e: 1869 at corner between Honiton Street and Gloucester Walk
pu: Lancaster Lodge and studio demolished.

31. Beaumont Lodge, Shepherd's Bush, Hammersmith, London
c: Edward John Poynter, painter
t: conversion of stables to garden studio, and minor alterations to house, including panelled recess in dining room
d: 1869
e: c. 1869–70
b: 'Mr Dunn' of Brewer Street
ds: BAL/RIBADC
pu: demolished late 1890s to make way for railway sheds
Walter Crane took over Poynter's lease of this property and his studio.

32. Number 6 Cheyne Walk, Chelsea, London
c: Rafe Oswald Leycester, landowner
t: alteration and refurbishment
d: c. 1869–70
e: 1871–72
ct: £1,680 (AB)
sw: 1887, Webb was consulted about the adverse effects that a proposed house next door might have on number 6
pu: residential, subdivided.

33. Number 8 Holland Villas Road, Kensington, London
c: Constantine Alexander Ionides, stockbroker
t: addition to rear of existing house (morning room with schoolroom above)
d&e: 1870
b: Richard Ashby & Sons, Bishopsgate, London
ct: £923 8s 2d (AB)
ds: V&A, W&I
sw: 1879–1881, further alteration and enlargement (b: W H Holland; ct: £980 (AB))
pu: the house has been converted into flats.

34. Lockleys, Welwyn, Hertfordshire
c: George Dering
t: picture gallery and conservatory
d: 1870
ct: £4,500 (Webb's estimate)
For an unknown reason, Webb received no fee for this design, which presumably was not executed.

35. Joldwynds, Holmbury St Mary, Surrey
c: William Bowman (created baronet 1884), consultant ophthalmologist and landowner
t: country house (replacement of poor quality 18th-century house with ugly 1860 addition)
d: 1870–71, house; 1875, coach-house with flats for coachman and gardener, and entrance gates; precise date unknown, View House (two-storey summerhouse)
e: 1872–74, house; 1875, coach-house and entrance gates
b: William Shearburn of Shere; coach-house and gates by direct labour under Robert Baker
cw: Robert Baker

ct: £14,110 (AB), house, coach-house, entrance gates and View House
ds: BAL/RIBADC; V&A, W&I
sw: 1888 (e: 1891–93) library extension, insertion of steelwork to stop spreading of billiard-room roof, design of fitted cupboard for the View House serving room (b: William & George King of Abinger Hammer; ct: c. £3,292 (CB))
pu: house, and probably orchid- and glasshouses, demolished 1930; coach-house and View House are almost unchanged
The International-style replacement by Oliver Hill is a private house.

36. St Andrew's Church, Cobham, Surrey
c: Revd Gerard Banks
d&e: 1870–71; 1871–72
t: new lych gate; new ceiling to south aisle roof and new churchyard gates
ct: £315 (AB); £420 (AB)

37. Rougham Hall, Norfolk
c: Charles North, landowner
t: country house
e: scheme abandoned because of lack of funds for the education of the client's children
d: c. 1870–72
ds: unfinished sketch drawings, PC.

38. St Dunstan's Church, Hunsdon, Hertfordshire
c: Salisbury Baxendale
t: conservative repair
e: 1870–72
ct: £514 10s 0d (AB)
When Baxendale asked Webb to alter this church in 1878, the architect refused and sent him details of the recently founded SPAB.

39. Rounton Grange, East Rounton, North Riding of Yorkshire (now North Yorkshire)
c: Isaac Lowthian Bell (created baronet 1885), MP, industrialist, iron-master, and landowner
t: country house and associated buildings
d: 1871–72, house; 1875, fowl house; 1875–76, alteration of existing farm buildings and design of new coach-house (with coachman's flat) incorporating some of them; c. 1872–75, Home Farm (farm buildings and a terrace of dwellings for farm workers, including larger one for farm manager)
e: early 1873 to late summer 1876, house; 1875, fowl house; 1875–76, Home Farm (terrace completed 1875); 1876, coach-house
b: direct labour under cw
cw: John Graham who, having failed to give satisfaction, was replaced by W Taylor in early 1875
ct: £32,000 (AB) for all the buildings
ds: NYCRO; BAL/RIBADC; SPAB; PC
sw: 1896, creation of upper servants' dining room in western archway of kitchen court (ct: £980; ds: BAL/RIBADC); in 1898, Webb made a thorough investigation of the condition of the entire building (SB)
pu: house, dismantled and demolished 1951 to 1954; coach-house (poor condition), as stonemason's workshop and flat; Home Farm still in use, with 2 of the terrace cottages made into 1 dwelling.
For George Jack's additions and alterations, and his estate and village buildings, see chapter 7, note 44

40. Atherston Colliery, Lancashire
c: Herbert Fletcher, colliery owner
t: winding-engine house, boiler house, and large chimney
d: 1871 or early 1872 (unexecuted)
ds: V&A, W&I.

41. Fairfield Lodge, Number 6 Addison Road, Holland Park, London
c: Mrs Euphrosyne Cassavetti, a member of the wealthy Ionides family
d&e: c. 1871–72
t: alterations and additions, including studio, to speculatively built house
ct: £3,000 (AB)
sw: 1876–78 for Alexander Cassavetti, the solicitor son of Euphrosyne: alteration, enlargement, and new stables (ct: £6,930 (AB); b: Ashby Brothers of Shoreditch)
pu: demolished late 1960s.

42. Pusey House, Pusey, Faringdon, Berkshire
c: Mr and Mrs S B Bouverie Pusey
t: alterations to country house
d&e: 1872
ct: £2,000 (AB)
sw: in 1877, Webb was approached regarding the alteration and extension of the stables but this does not appear to have gone ahead
pu: private residence.

43. The Briary, Freshwater, Isle of Wight
c: George Frederic Watts, painter
t: studio-house in the country
d: 1872
e: 1872–73
b: John Tyerman of Walworth Road, London
ct: unknown (Webb refused to accept a fee)
ds: BAL/RIBADC
pu: destroyed by fire 1934; rebuilt to a different design (private house).

44. Oast House, Hayes Common, Kent (now Greater London)
c: Lord Sackville Cecil (a younger son of the second Marquess of Salisbury), railway and telegraph engineer
t: small house in the country
d: 1872
e: 1872–73
ct: £4,361 13s 4d (based on Webb's return to Cecil of a £218 1s 8d cheque)
ds: most are missing; contemporary site plan showing house and stables; and ground and first-floor plans (after those by John Brandon-Jones based on Webb's drawings): PC
pu: private house in good condition, some changes internally including removal of wall between hall and dining room; few changes externally except for enclosure of first-floor balcony; stables: now a private house in separate ownership.

45. Brockham Warren, Tadworth, Surrey
c: Sir Benjamin Collins Brodie, surgeon to Queen Victoria
t: alterations to Regency country house and extension of conservatory
d: 1872
e: c. 1873–74
ct: almost £3,320 (Webb to Brodie, 18 July 1874, LB 1; the fee also covers small work on 'The Beeches Inn' for Brodie)
ds: BAL/RIBADC
pu: divided into 4 houses (Webb's conservatory demolished; his French doors with associated columns and the fireplace in the dining room remain).

46. Proposed house at Bexton, Cheshire
c: Rafe Oswald Leycester, landowner
t: detached house with five bedrooms and nurseries
d: 1873 (unexecuted)
ds: V&A, W&I
ct: estimated cost not known (Webb did not receive a fee)
An unexecuted design for a long, five-bedroom house, partly timber-framed in the Cheshire tradition, with the minor domestic offices creating an overall L-shape, and with an arrangement of the main rooms, including the first-floor nurseries and billiard room, similar to that of the much larger Rounton Grange (above).

47. Naworth Castle, Brampton, Cumberland (now Cumbria)
c: The Hon. George Howard and the Trustees of the Naworth Estate
t: alteration of and additions to the castle, Howard's country residence
d;: 1873–79
e: 1873–79. Webb's major works were the conversion of the ancient Moat (or Bote) House into a studio (1874–79) for George Howard, and a new room (1877–78) for Rosalind Howard in the top of the Morpeth Tower; he also designed and installed staircases and fireplaces, and bookcases for a small drawing room, and designed fittings for the library
b: the tower room was executed by separate contractors including Beaty Brothers of Carlisle (masonry); panelling, library fittings, and other woodwork was done by estate workmen under the estate clerk of works Thomas Warwick and his successor (in 1877) William Marshall
ct: tower room: £473 7s 6d plus cost of joinery
ds: BAL/RIBADC; PC
pu: family home of the Hon. Philip Howard and his family, and as a select private function venue; Moat House as a garage.
Webb was the official architect to the Naworth Estate from 1877 until his resignation in 1879. Charles Ferguson, architect, of Carlisle, installed fittings in the library in 1881, apparently adhering to Webb's overall design and arrangement but changing details, including those of the fireplace. Most of Webb's fittings remain.

48. Nether Hall, Pakenham, Suffolk
c: Edward Greene, MP, brewer and landowner
t: alteration and enlargement of country house of c. 16th-century origins (timber framed, later encased in brick)
d: 1874
e: 1874–75
b: Alfred Andrews
ct: £2,540 (AB)
ds: PC (ground floor plan)
sw: see Nether Hall Farm, Thurston (1876) below
pu: private residence; Webb's wing and most of his fittings remain.

49. Berkeley Castle, Gloucestershire
c: Lord Fitzhardinge, landowner
t: minor alterations and installations, some decoration, some re-glazing by Morris & Co. under Webb's direction
d&e: 1874–75 under William Cuthbert, estate carpenter
ct: £960 (AB)
pu: country seat; some Webb fittings removed.
Webb's involvement continued until 1877 through decoration works by Morris & Co..

50. St Martin's Church, Brampton, Cumberland (now Cumbria)
c: Church Building Committee at instigation of the Hon. George Howard
t: replacement for existing dilapidated parish church
d: 1874–75
e: 1877–78, with temporary roof to tower
b: Beaty Brothers of Carlisle
cw: J Morland
ct: c. £6,996 without belfry stage of tower (HP)
ds: BAL/RIBADC; Cumbria R.O, Carlisle; SPAB
sw: 1884, inspection and report on remedial work; 1891, advice on tiling the sanctuary floor; 1904, Webb modified his 1878 design for the belfry; from this design and various Webb notes and sketches, George Jack produced working drawings, and the belfry was executed, 1905–06, under Jack's supervision (b: John Laing and Sons of Carlisle; ct: c. £1,817; ds: BAL/RIBADC; SPAB)
pu: parish church (with 14 stained-glass windows by Morris & Co.).

51. Terrace of dwellings for artisans and their families, Brampton, Cumberland (now Cumbria)
c: The Hon. George Howard and the Trustees of the Naworth Estate
d: 3 schemes of 1874, 1875, and 1876 respectively (unexecuted)
ds: HP; PC
Webb ordered the clerk of works to the estate to seek tenders; it is not known whether he did so or why the scheme was abandoned.

52. Number 12 Orme Square, Bayswater, London
c: Edward Dannreuther, musician
t: addition of studio (a music room in which Dannreuther taught and held chamber concerts) to existing house
d&e: c. 1874–77 (started soon after the Dannreuthers moved in (1873); concerts held in studio from 1877–93)
b: Ashby Brothers of Shoreditch
pu: house and studio destroyed by bomb, 1940.
The ceiling of the studio having proved faulty, for which Webb blamed himself in part, it was redone in 1876, the cost being shared by architect and client. Dannreuther's wife Chariclea was the sister of Alexander A Ionides for whom Webb enlarged number 1 Holland Park.

53. House in Eastbourne, East Sussex
c: W A Cardwell, son-in-law of Webb's client Sir Benjamin Brodie (of Brockham Warren)
t: house
d: 1875 (unexecuted)
Cardwell refused to pay for the design and working drawings; Webb took him to court, unsuccessfully.

54. Nether Hall Farm (later Manor Farm), Thurston, Suffolk
c: Edward Greene, MP, brewer and landowner
t: house for Matthew Witt, estate manager, with farm buildings
d: 1875
e: 1875–76
b: probably Alfred Andrews
ct: £1,800 (AB)
pu: private house and farm.

55. Board School, East Rounton, Northallerton, North Riding of Yorkshire (now North Yorkshire)
c: Isaac Lowthian Bell (created baronet 1885), MP, industrialist, iron-master, and landowner
t: new Board School for East and West Rounton villages
d: 1875–76
e: 1876–77
ct: £880 (that is, if a £44 fee was for the school not an estate building)
ds: NYCRO
pu: private house, converted late 1960s.

56. Numbers 2 & 4 Redington Road, Hampstead, London
c: William Chisolm, a business manager (husband of Hale White's sister Mary)
t: a pair of semi-detached houses, one of them for the client, the other for a relation of his or of his wife
d&e: 1876
b: Ashby Brothers of Shoreditch
pu: private houses (number 2, with Webb's fittings, essentially unchanged apart from additional bathroom, bedroom, and new dormer, created in attics).

57. Smeaton Manor, Great Smeaton, North Riding of Yorkshire (now North Yorkshire)
c: Major Arthur Fitzpatrick Godman, ex-army officer, landowner, horse-breeder
t: country house; stable block for horse-breeding, farm buildings
d: 1876, house; 1877, stables and farm buildings
e: 1877 to early 1879
b: J W & M Mackenzie of Darlington
cw: John Hardy
ct: £12,601 12s 10d (Webb's account sent to Godman (PC))
ds: V&A, W&I; stable block: PC
pu: private house (some alteration, demolition of part of the service quarters, removal of some Webb fittings by a previous owner)
Webb designed 2 cottages at about the same time as the house (unexecuted, drawings missing).

58. Four Gables, near Brampton, Cumberland (now Cumbria)
c: The Hon. George Howard on behalf of the Trustees of the Naworth Estate
t: house and stable for John Grey, agent to the estate
d: 1876, house; 1879, stables
e: 1877–79
cw: Thomas Warwick, clerk of works for the Naworth Estate, succeeded by William Marshall
b: estate carpenters, separate contractors for other trades, under cw (major contractor: Sproat Brothers of Talkin, masons)
ct: £3,698 7s 3d; stables c. £500 (HP)
ds: 2 PCs
pu: private house; stables a private house in separate ownership.

59. The Vicar's House (later Green Lane House), Brampton, Cumberland (now Cumbria)
c: The Hon. George Howard and Trustees of the Naworth Estate
t: house, with large parish room, for rental by Revd Henry Whitehead, vicar
d: 1877, house; 1879, stables
e: 1877–79, house; 1880, stables
b: Beaty Bros of Carlisle
cw: William Marshall, cw to Naworth Estate
ct: c. £2,400 (HP)
ds: V&A, W&I; PC
pu: residential home for the elderly; outbuilding and stable converted into further accommodation and a bungalow.

60. New Place, Welwyn, Hertfordshire
c: Dr Henry Speakman Webb, GP
t: detached house with surgery
d: 1877–78
e: 1879–80
b: William Lawrence of Datchworth
ct: £2,403 agreed with the builder (probably not including stables and cottage)
ds: BAL/RIBADC; V&A, W&I; PC
pu: house as 2 dwellings (divided in the 1980s by blocking 3 passages; no external changes); coachman's cottage as a house in separate ownership.
In 1923 the drawing room was extended into the cloakroom and given a west-facing bay window; 7 houses were built in grounds in the1970s.

61. Clouds, East Knoyle, Wiltshire
c: The Hon. Percy Scawen Wyndham, MP, landowner
t: country house (Webb's largest)
d: 1877, 1ˢᵗ design (Yew Court scheme); 1879, 2ⁿᵈ design; 1879–80, final design (amended 2ⁿᵈ scheme); 1884, water tower (sited to the west of the house)
e: 1881–86 (occupied September 1885)
b: Albert Estcourt of Gloucester
cw: James Simmonds of Blandford

ct: £81,413 (AB)
ds: BAL/RIBADC; V&A, W&I; SPAB; PC
sw: 1889–91, reinstatement after major fire of 6 Jan 1889 (b: Estcourt; cw: Simmonds; ct: £20,580 (AB))
pu: house (under lease) since 1983, as an alcohol and drug dependency treatment centre set up by Col. Stephen Scammell who lived in the house converted in the 1940s from part of the stable block, a portion of which is used for horses at livery; remainder of domestic offices as dwellings; since 1836, gardener's house (converted by Webb from old thatched cottages) has been a dwelling under separate ownership.
Detmar Blow turned the second-floor nurseries into a library (1911–12). In 1937, after Clouds had been sold, architect Charles Biddulph Pinchard demolished the rooms on the north front of the main block (including the dining room), the tower and part of the service range, and two turrets on the west front, and turned the second floor into attic space by removing Webb's windows and gables, in order to make Clouds a more manageable size; the length of the central hall was reduced also. Whilst Clouds was a Church of England Children's Society nursery for unwanted babies (1944–64), rooms were created again on the second floor, with flat-roofed dormer windows. From 1965–83, Clouds was a school for maladjusted boys.

62. Number 1 Holland Park, Kensington, London
c: Alexander Alexander Ionides, diplomatist
t: enlargement and refitting of speculatively built stucco villa of 1864 (staircase extension at rear with inset porch; mosaic pavement on first-floor landing; refitting of dining room)
d: 1879
e: 1879–83
b: possibly W H Holland of Holland Park
cw: supervised by architect C G Vinall
ct: total cost including the later works below: £3,019 (AB)
ds: missing apart from design for iron gate to 1879 porch (BAL/RIBADC) and the design for the mosaic pavement (V&A, W&I)
sw: 1888, exercise room in garden (unexecuted); d: 1889 and e: 1889–90, waiting room or smoking room off main landing, with loggia below (b: Carey & Co. of Holland Park, the firm which apparently took over W H Holland in 1888; ds: BAL/RIBADC)
pu: bomb-damaged in Second World War; demolished by LCC in 1953 by which date all Webb and Jeckyll fittings had been removed
The room over the loggia was referred to variously in the nineteenth century as the waiting-room, smoking-room, Marble Room, Marble Hall, and gallery for antiquities. In the 1870s, for A A Ionides, Thomas Jeckyll had added a sitting room with billiard room above to this house.

63. A Proposed Mission Church for Clay Cross, Derbyshire
c: Revd Oldham and his wife Emma, sister of William Morris
t: small mission church
d: 1881 (unexecuted)
ds: V&A, W&I (E.157–1916, dated August 1881)
Webb prepared a design and estimate for these clients to show to the Church authorities and their parishioners as an example of what could be built for a certain sum.

64. Bell Brothers' Offices (now Webb House), number 7 Zetland Road, Middlesbrough
c: Thomas Hugh Bell, industrialist, for Bell Brothers
t: Main offices of Bell Brothers, a major iron-founding firm
d: 1881–83; project shelved 1884, revived 1888
e: 1889–91, with minor amendments
b: John Johnson of Middlesbrough
cw: H Luscombe
ct : £9,218 8s 3d (CB)

ds: BAL/RIBA; Corus (formerly British Steel Co); SPAB; Teesside Archives
pu: 9 self-contained flats, 1 bedsit, for people in some need of care
George Jack added further offices on the second floor in 1906; his design, 1918–19, for doubling the size of the building was not executed (Corus).

65. Rushmore Lodge (later Rushmore House), Tollard Royal, Wiltshire
c: Lt.-Gen. Augustus Henry Lane Fox Pitt-Rivers, ex-army officer, landowner, archaeologist, and ethnographer
t.: interior alteration of 1760 country house, some new fireplaces and fittings
d: 1882; 1885, gatehouse with 2 lodges (not executed; instead, wrought-iron gates and pyramid-topped gateposts (all by Webb) were erected)
e: 1882–83
b: A H Green of Blandford
ct: £1,264 (AB)
ds: BAL/RIBADC; V&A, W&I
pu: Sandroyd School (by coincidence the school moved here in 1940 from the pseudonymous studio-house Webb had designed for Spencer Stanhope in 1860).

66. Hill House (later Briarmead), Greatham, Hartlepool
c: William Thomas Tate, bank accountant
t: detached house
d&e: 1883
b: unidentified local builder supervised by architect James Barry of Hartlepool who apparently made the working drawings
pu: private house
In 1901 W H Linton designed the back porch with pyramid roof and a detached range consisting of a second stable and cottage (now a house in separate ownership). The house was carefully and sympathetically renovated in 1981.

67. Coneyhurst (now Coneyhurst-on-the-Hill), Ewhurst, Surrey
c: Miss Mary Anne Ewart, a friend of Webb and his sisters
t: small house in the country
d: 1883; 1885, gardener's cottage; 1886, stables
e: 1884–86
b: William & George King of Abinger Hammer
ct: £7,125 (AB)
ds: BAL/RIBADC; V&A, W&I
sw: survey of crack, 1893
pu: 5 homes: 3 in the house; the gardener's cottage now detached; stables converted into a house.
Miss Ewart persuaded Webb to sign his name on a brick built into the gardener's cottage (now partly obscured by double glazing).

68. A 'Pump House for Ayot Green', Hertfordshire
c: not identified
t: small timber-framed pump house (for drinking water) with tiled pyramidal roof, and slatted gates, erected on the village green at Ayot St Lawrence or Ayot St Peter
d&e: 1884
b: Lawrence & Son of Datchworth
ds: V&A, W&I.

69. Great Tangley Manor, Wonersh, Surrey
c: Wickham Flower, solicitor, antiquarian, and connoisseur
t: alteration and enlargement in 2 phases of moated manor house with 1582 frontage
d&e: phase 1 (1885–87): house (d.1885, e. 1885–86): new domestic offices range, entrance hall with bedroom above, and loggia; grounds: timber screen in garden wall, bridge over moat with covered way to entrance, rearrangement of gardens; stables: designed 1886 (unexecuted)

phase 2 (1891–94): stables (1891, 2nd design, e.
1891–92) including semi-detached cottages for
coachman and gardener; house (d. 1893, e.
1893–94): library with bedrooms above, and new
stair and new stair-hall; grounds (1894): 2nd bridge
over moat

b: house, William & George King of Abinger
Hammer; stables and cottages, Mitchell Brothers of
Shalford

ct: phase 1, £1,000 (AB); phase 2, £2,106 3s 6d
(CB), farm buildings and cottages; a little over
£1,825 0s 4d (CB), library extension and bridge

ds: BAL/RIBADC; V&A, W&I

pu: as 2 houses; the cottages, much altered, in separate
ownership.

70. Willinghurst, Shamley Green, Surrey
c: John Charles Francis Ramsden, ex-army officer,
landowner
t: country house
d: 1886; 1888, stables; 1896, smoking room
(unexecuted); 1897, 1898, two lodges; 1900,
gardener's cottage
e: 1887–89, house and stables; 1897 and 1898, lodges;
1900, gardener's cottage
b: Mitchell Brothers of Shalford
cw: John Hardy
ct: £12,905 10s 7d (CB)
ds: BAL/RIBADC; V&A, W&I; SPAB
pu: main house and stables as four detached houses
(central part of house and of stables demolished to
create them); one lodge and gardener's cottage
have been altered

In the early stages, Webb refers to the house as
'Lapscombe'; a summerhouse by George Jack was built
in 1906 near the house.

71. Sketch Design for a Cathedral (probably for Liverpool)
ds: two unfinished drawings, one dated 16 February
1886 (BAL/RIBADC) (unexecuted)

This, Webb's only scheme for a church of cathedral
scale, appears to have been inspired by the publication in
January 1886 of the results of the first competition for a
cathedral for Liverpool.

72. Number 42 Kensington Square, London
c: Sir William Bowman, ophthalmologist (Bowman's
daughter and her husband John Merriman were
living in this house)
t: garden walls and trellis-work
d&e: 1887
b: Francis Saunders of New Street, Dorset Square,
London
ct: £502 1s 1d (LB 1)

73. Felday House, Number 25 Young Street, Kensington, London
c: Sir William Bowman, ophthalmologist, for his
younger son Frederick and his wife
t: alteration, enlargement, refitting, and redecoration
of existing house (extended across full width at
rear, cellar lowered, roof raised and attic rooms
created)
d: 1887
e: 1887–88
b: Francis Saunders of New Street, Dorset Square,
London
ct: £3,165 6s 1d (CB)
ds: V&A, W&I
pu: demolished.

74. All Saints' Church, Datchworth, Hertfordshire
c: Revd H S H James
t: repairs and maintenance work
d: c. 1888–89
e: before late 1890
b: William Lawrence of Datchworth
ct: £280 (AB).

75. Number 37 Cavendish Square, Westminster, London
c: Charles Tomes, dental surgeon, son of Webb's client
Sir John Tomes (of Upwood Gorse)
t: alteration, repair, and decoration of existing house
and dental surgery
d: 1889
e: 1889–91
b: C W Bovis
ct: £510 6s 8d (AB)
pu: a public house.

76. Number 23 Second Avenue, Hove, East Sussex
c: Constantine Alexander Ionides, stockbroker
t: picture gallery extension
d: 1889
e: 1890–91
b: William and Thomas Garrett of Brighton
ct: £2,793 14s 7d (CB)
ds: BAL/RIBADC
pu: house now flats; gallery, a snooker room.

77. Forthampton Court, near Tewkesbury, Gloucestershire
c: John Reginald Yorke, MP, landowner
t: alteration, repair, and enlargement of basically
medieval house; new stables and billiard room
d: 1889–91, house, including a new laundry block,
menservants' quarters, and additional domestic
offices; 1891: billiard room and new stables
e: 1889–92
b: Albert Estcourt of Gloucester
cw: John Hardy
ct: £17,232 14s 5d (Webb's account in the Yorke
Archive)
ds: BAL/RIBADC; V&A, W&I; SPAB; PC; stable
drawings missing
pu: country seat, with some of Webb's work
demolished or altered but much remains including
the main staircase, library fittings and fireplace,
revolving bookcase made by Estcourt, billiard
room (now separated from house), and stables.

78. Proposed Mausoleum to be placed in a Cemetery
c: Boyce Allen of Sydney, New South Wales,
Australia
t: mausoleum
d: 1887–90 (unexecuted)
ds: V&A, W&I

Webb produced his first sketch design in 1887 and his
second and final design in 1890: a small pitch-roofed
stone building standing athwart a large, paved podium
above a larger chamber below ground, which has alcoves
for 12 coffins. Allen commissioned Webb in 1887 whilst
residing at 27 Queensbury Place, London, where he saw
the first sketch design, and received the final design in
1890 when staying at the Burlington Club, London. The
Allen mausoleum in Sydney was not built to Webb's
design.

79. Goldenfields, Liphook, Hampshire
c: Mrs Mary Anne Robb, an amateur horticulturalist
and plant collector
t: small house (originally intended as a cottage for a
gardener)
d: 1890–91
e: 1891–92
b: William & George King of Abinger Hammer
ct: £1,900 (CB)
ds: BAL/RIBADC
pu: 4 dwellings (house enlarged twice for Mrs Robb
by other architects; divided 1951; subdivided
further and houses built in the grounds, 1983).

80. Clock Tower Memorial to Elizabeth Barrett Browning, Ledbury, Herefordshire
c: Tower Committee
t: clock tower
d: 2 designs, of 1891 and 1892 respectively (each

unexecuted – Webb withdrew from the commission)
ds: BAL/RIBA; PC
ct: estimated £1,040 (AB)

In 1892, Webb apparently resigned from the
commission; a clock tower and institute was built soon
afterwards to the design of Brightwen Binyon.

81. Village Hall (now the Astley Hall), Arisaig, Inverness-shire, Scotland
c: Miss Constance Astley, daughter of Webb's client
F D P Astley (of Arisaig House)
t: village hall
d: 1891
e: 1892–93
b: local joiner Alexander McVarish, in control of
other craftsmen
ds: BAL/RIBADC (from the collection of the late
Miss M J Becher)
ct: £445 9s 8d (Constance Astley's papers, Collection
of the late Miss M J Becher, now in the
BAL/RIBADC)
pu: original purpose

In 1910, George Jack added a new porch, entrance, and
clubroom; between late 1999 and 2002, Webb's building
was repaired and refurbished, Jack's clubroom was rebuilt,
a new kitchen was created, and a new clubroom was
added at a cost of £475,000.

82. Standen, near East Grinstead, West Sussex
c: James S Beale, solicitor and landowner
t: country house
d: 1891; 1895–96, Standen Cottages (a pair, semi-
detached); 1898, additions: bay window to the hall,
second seating recess in the billiard room, and a
garden shelter
e: 1892–94, house and stables; 1896, Standen
Cottages; 1898, the above additions
b: house and stables, Peter Peters of Horsham;
cottages and 1898 work, Charles Rice of East
Grinstead
cw: John Hardy
ct: house: £16,774 9s 7d; Standen Cottages: £763;
1898 bay window, seating recess, and shelter: £418
17s 3d (all from CB)
ds: BAL/RIBADC; NT Standen Collection; SPAB;
sketches, PC
pu: a National Trust property, almost unchanged and
open regularly to the public

Standen became the property of the National Trust in
1972 at the bequest of the Beales' daughter, Miss Helen
Beale; acceptance of the legacy was made possible
through the generous aid of Arthur and Helen Grogan.

83. Number 1 Pembridge Place, Bayswater, London
c: Col. William James Gillum, ex-army officer,
philanthropist
t: creation of ground-floor suite and insertion of
fireplaces and fittings in existing house;
redecoration by Morris & Co.
d&e: 1894
b: Head & Son
ct: £1,780 (AB)
ds: chiefly missing; V&A, W&I (fireplaces and
sideboard)
pu: residential, subdivided.

84. Exning House, Exning, near Newmarket, Suffolk
c: Capt. Edward William David Baird (later
Brigadier-General), ex-army officer, landowner,
and racehorse owner
t: large-scale enlargement of country house by
Andrews Jelfe, 1734
d: 1894
e: 1895–96
b: Albert Estcourt of Gloucester
cw: William Weir (Webb's assistant; whilst he
supervised this job, his salary of £3 per week was
paid half by Webb and half by Baird)
ct: £15,198 2s 6d (CB)

ds: BAL/RIBADC; SPAB
pu: seven self-contained dwellings (converted recently); many Webb fittings remain)

Webb added a second family block and a block of domestic offices and servants' quarters, underpinned Jelfe's walls, and created bedrooms for menservants in his basement. In 1907, George Jack, adhering to the original drawings, reinstated part of Webb's service wing after a fire.

85. Morris Cottage, Much Hadham, Hertfordshire
c: Miss Henrietta Morris, sister of William Morris
t: conversion of 2 small cottages into one dwelling
d&e: 1895
b: Mr Thargood of Much Hadham
ct: unknown (Webb took no fee)
ds: BAL/RIBADC; V&A, W&I; SPAB (sketches); PC
pu: private house.

86. Medmenham Abbey, Buckinghamshire
c: Robert W Hudson
t: alteration and repair of country house of 1595 and Gothick hotel (possibly combining them into one house), new laundry, and cottages for coachman and gardener
d: 1895–96 (unexecuted)
ct: estimated cost c. £6,000 (AB)
pu: private house

The facts that Webb was paid as early as 1896, that his drawings are missing, and that the present neo-Gothic building is largely of 1898 by Romaine Walker, suggest that Webb's scheme was abandoned. In the 18th century, under the tenure of Sir Francis Dashwood, Medmenham Abbey was the headquarters of the Hell Fire Club.

87. Rochester Diocesan Deaconess Institution (now Gilmore House), Number 85 (now number 113) Clapham Common North Side, London
c: Mrs Isabella Gilmore, head deaconess and sister of William Morris
t: chapel
d: 1896
e: 1896–97
b: John Garrett & Son of Clapham
ct: £1,693 6s 9d (CB)
ds: V&A, W&I; BAL/RIBADC
pu: the chapel is almost unchanged; the Webb-designed altar, embroidered altar frontal, altar cross, and lectern, are in the V&A.

88. Hurlands, near Puttenham, Surrey
c: Miss Agneta Henrietta Cocks, a friend of Webb's client Mary Ewart (of Coneyhurst), country estate owner
t: country house
d: 1897; stables: late 1898 or early 1899
e: 1897–99; stables 1899
b: William & George King of Abinger Hammer; stables, Charles Rice of East Grinstead
ct: house: £6,916 16s 11d (CB); stables: £1,319 16s 1d (CB)
ds: BAL/RIBADC; SPAB
pu: 3 dwellings (incorporating a cottage built at the west end in the 1960s); stables as one house (converted after 1978).

89. Warrens House, Bramshaw, Hampshire
c: George Edward Briscoe Eyre, printer
t: enlargement and alteration of existing country house designed by John Nash and subsequently enlarged by an unidentified architect
d: 1897
e: 1898–99
b: Franklin & Son of Southampton
cw: none
ct: £8,8000 (AB)
ds: BAL/RIBADC; SPAB
pu: private residence; Webb's large block was demolished 1979 but his common room, and floor of menservants' bedrooms with cupola above added to the earlier scullery range, remain.

90. Morris Memorial Cottages, Kelmscott, near Lechlade, Oxfordshire
c: Jane Morris, widow of William Morris
t: pair of semi-detached cottages for farm workers and their families
d: 1899
e: 1902–03, supervised by George Jack
b: Joseph Bowley of Lechlade
ct: £987 19s 11d (CB)
ds: V&A, W&I; BL (Add MS 45344); PC (Webb's drawing for panel Morris in the Home Mead)
pu: dwellings.

91. Caxtons, Worth, West Sussex
c: Philip Webb, architect
t: repairs to existing cottage owned by Wilfrid Scawen Blunt for Webb's use
d: 1900
e: 1900 by Blunt's estate workmen under William Dench, carpenter, supervised by Webb (13 site visits)
ct: c. £150 (preliminary estimate in Webb to Sydney Carlyle Cockerell, 28 July 1900)
ds: BAL/RIBADC
pu: private house.

NOTES AND REFERENCES

Full details of the manuscripts, books, and papers, cited in the notes are given in the Bibliography and List of Sources.

List of Abbreviations

AA Jl	Journal of the Architectural Association
AB	Webb's Practice Account Book (private collection)
AddB	Webb's Address Book (private collection)
AJ	Architects' Journal
Antiquaries Jl	Journal of the Society of Antiquaries of London
AR	Architectural Review
Architectural History	Journal of the Society of Architectural Historians of Great Britain
B	Builder
BAL/RIBAAC	British Architectural Library, RIBA Archives Collection
BAL/RIBADC	British Architectural Library, RIBA Drawings Collection
Bank AB	Webb's Bank Account Book
BD	Building Design
BL	British Library
BN	Building News
CB	Webb's Certificate Book of Works in Progress (private collection)
CL	Country Life
DNB	Dictionary of National Biography
E	Ecclesiologist
Howard Papers	Howard of Naworth Papers, University of Durham
Kelmscott CB	Webb's Kelmscott Certificate Book, later used by George Jack (private collection)
LB 1 and LB 2	MS Letter Books in which Webb copied his business letters, 1874–1888
M&Co	Morris & Co.
MMF&Co	Morris, Marshall, Faulkner & Co.
MMF&Co AB	Webb's Morris, Marshall, Faulkner & Co. Account Book
NT	Collection of the National Trust
NYCRO	North Yorkshire County Record Office, Northallerton
OEB	Webb's Office Expenses notebook
RIBA	Royal Institute of British Architects
RIBA Jl	Journal of the Royal Institute of British Architects
RO	Record Office of specified county or town
SB	Webb's Site Books in which he wrote memoranda whilst making site visits
SPAB	Society for the Protection of Ancient Buildings
V&A	Victoria & Albert Museum
V&A, FT&F	Victoria & Albert Museum: Furniture, Textiles & Fashion Department
V&A, NAL	Victoria & Albert Museum: National Art Library
V&A, SMC&G	Victoria & Albert Museum: Sculpture, Metalwork, Ceramics & Glass Department
V&A, W&I	Victoria & Albert Museum: Word & Image Department
USA	Unites States of America

CHAPTER 1: THE EARLY YEARS

1. William Richard Lethaby, *Philip Webb and his Work* (Oxford: Oxford University Press, 1935); repr. edn and introduced by Godfrey Rubens, containing additional material written by Lethaby, London: Raven Oak Press, 1979, p. 7. Lethaby's invaluable biography first appeared in 1925 as a series of articles in the *Builder*; after Lethaby's death they were published unchanged by Oxford University Press as a book. The 1979 reprint edition incorporates a list of corrections and includes valuable additional material from Lethaby's MS of the additions he had intended to insert before the work appeared in book form, edited by Rubens (the draft is in the BAL/RIBAAC). Throughout these notes, references to the original edition are indicated by 'Lethaby (1935)', and those to the additional material written by Lethaby but added by Godfrey Rubens to the reprint edition are indicated by 'Lethaby (1979)'.
2. Webb to George Price Boyce, 29 August 1884, BL Add. MS 45354.
3. Lethaby (1935), pp. 127–8.
4. Lethaby (1935), p. 2, quoting from Forrer, VI, p. 400.
5. Lethaby (1935), p. 15; Lethaby (1979), p. 250.
6. Webb to Sydney Carlyle Cockerell, 20 November 1902, in *Friends of a Lifetime*, ed. by Meynell, p. 109.
7. Webb's copy of Harding's book is in a private collection.
8. Webb to Cockerell, 7 March 1904, in Meynell (ed.), *Friends of a Lifetime*, p. 114.
9. Northamptonshire Record Office kindly provided information about Aynho school. Nicholas Cooper in *Aynho, a Northamptonshire Village* gives further information. The building, considerably altered, is now a private house.
10. Lethaby (1935), p. 8.
11. Webb to Rosalind Howard, 7 September 1869, J22/64, Castle Howard Archives.
12. The quoted words come from Webb to William Hale White, n.d. [soon after 10 February 1899], MR 10/14, Central Library, Bedford; Webb reveals his

13. uncertainty in his letter to Rosalind Howard of 17 September 1872 (J22/64, Castle Howard Archives).
13. For Webb's hope of becoming a painter, see Lethaby (1979), p. 249. Webb never lost the longing; at the end of his career, he regretted that it was 'too late to attempt a Natural History' such as he would have liked to have undertaken (ibid., p. 250).
14. See Powell, pp. 9–10.
15. I am indebted to the late H Godwin Arnold for providing information on Billing, some of which appears in his booklet *Victorian Architecture in Reading*, and also to Sidney M Gold and his book *Biographical Dictionary of Architects at Reading*, pp. 12–13, of which the BAL/RIBAAC and the Reading Library have copies. Billing opened a second office, in London, in 1853, and by 1855 had left Reading for the metropolis.
16. Webb's No. 3 Specification Notebook (private collection).
17. AB; Lethaby (1935), pp. 9–10.
18. Webb to George Howard, 29 September 1874, J22/64, Castle Howard Archives.
19. Lethaby (1935), p. 12.
20. AB.
21. AB.
22. AB. His subscription, one guinea, was paid on 29 June 1856.
23. Arthur E Street, *A Memoir of George Edmund Street*, pp. 13, 283.
24. Lethaby (1935), p. 17.
25. The information on Street at this time is taken from Arthur Street's Memoir, and from Hitchcock, 'G. E. Street in the 1850s', pp. 145–71.
26. Lethaby (1935), p. 22.
27. In the early biographies of Morris, he is said to have gained a wide knowledge of English medieval churches whilst at Marlborough; Miele shows that this belief is not substantiated, and that most likely it was Guy who evoked his first real interest in them (see Miele's 'Introduction' in *William Morris on Architecture*, pp. 6–15). For Webb meeting Morris at Street's office, see Lethaby (1935), p. 13.
28. For information on Morris and Burne-Jones, in addition to many other helpful books listed in the bibliography, I found the following invaluable: Mackail, *The Life of William Morris* and Georgiana Burne-Jones, *Memorials of Edward Burne-Jones* (both of which contain first-hand information from friends of Morris and Burne-Jones); and MacCarthy, *William Morris: A Life for our Time*.
29. Lethaby (1935), pp. 18–19.
30. Webb to William Hale White, 1 March 1888, MR 10/5, Central Library, Bedford.
31. Ibid..
32. Mackail, II, p. 291; see also I, pp. 356–57.
33. Lethaby (1979), p. 250.
34. William Morris, 'Gothic Architecture', first delivered as a lecture to the Arts and Crafts Exhibition Society, 7 November 1889, in *William Morris on Architecture*, ed. and intro. by Miele (p. 156).
35. Webb to Hale White, 1 March 1888, MR 10/5, Central Library, Bedford.
36. Rooke, ed. by Lago, p. 184.
37. This magazine, produced by the Morris and Burne-Jones circle at Oxford and friends from Cambridge, was published monthly in 1856.
38. Lethaby (1935), p. 122.
39. In George Edmund Street, 'On the Future of Art in England', pp. 240.
40. Lethaby (1979), p. 248; Rooke, ed. by Lago, p. 186.
41. Webb to Hale White, 28 October 1899, MR 10/19, Central Library, Bedford.
42. Webb to Rossetti, 21 May 1866, Taylor to Webb letters, V&A, NAL, 86.SS.57.
43. LB 1: a reference and two letters to, and one from, Rosenthal, 1873, loose in the book, and Webb's letters about Burbridge, fols 7, 8, 10, 11, 1874; Bank AB.
44. See Mrs Boyce to Cockerell, 25 May 1915, kept with the Webb to Boyce Letters, BL Add. MS 45354; Lethaby (1935), p. 195.
45. From Cockerell's foreword, in the album of Taylor to Webb Letters, 12 November 1915, V&A, NAL, 86.SS.57.
46. Webb to D G Rossetti, 21 May 1866, V&A, NAL, 86.SS.57, fol. 11.
47. AB; Saint, p. 15.
48. 'The Architectural Exhibition, 1858', p. 46.
49. 'The Exhibition of the Royal Academy', p. 306.
50. 'The Architectural Room at the Royal Academy, 1858', p. 172.
51. Webb, 'Street, George Edmund (1824–81)', *DNB*, pp. 42–5.
52. Lethaby (1935), pp. 17–18. The words are Lethaby's but probably repeat those of Webb.
53. AB. In later years, he received about £4 annually from property owned jointly with his siblings, and occasionally he made enough profit to invest a very small sum.
54. *The Diaries of George Price Boyce*, ed. by Surtees, p. 26. The information about the club is taken chiefly from *Rules of the Hogarth Club and List of Membership*, and Cherry, 'The Hogarth Club'.
55. For near-contemporary accounts of this project see Prinsep, 'A Painter's Reminiscences'; Mackail, I, pp. 120–33; G Burne-Jones, I, pp. 158–68; William Holman Hunt, *The Story of the Painting of the Pictures on the Walls and the Decorations on the Ceiling of the old Debating Hall (Now the Library) in the years 1857–8–9*.
56. See MacCarthy, p. 141, for Jane Morris never having loved her husband.
57. G Burne-Jones, I, p. 196.
58. Mackail, I, p. 141.
59. The quotation and most of the information on the tour is from Lethaby (1935),

pp. 23–6 (p. 25).

60. The information in this paragraph is taken from Webb's Account Book.

61. John Henry Parker, *A glossary of Terms used in Grecian, Roman, Italian and Gothic Architecture* (1850). It has proved impossible to further identify the first two books. In later years Webb usually wore brown tweed (Lethaby (1935), p. 188).

CHAPTER 2: RED HOUSE, BEXLEYHEATH (1858–59)

1. For the site having been chosen to please Webb as well as Morris, see Burne-Jones, I, p. 196, and May Morris, *William Morris*, I, pp. 395–6.

2. Morris had a great passion for medieval architecture but in the late 1860s it was based on intuitive feeling rather than knowledge (see Miele's introduction in *William Morris on Architecture*).

3. William Morris to Andreas Scheu, 15 September 1883, in May Morris, *William Morris*, II, p. 10 (Scheu was an anarchist and a furniture designer). In this book about her father's achievements, May Morris states that he was 'helping the planning of house and garden to meet his own desires', which entirely supports the view that Webb was the chief designer of the house and the garden (I, p. 13). Rossetti told Ruskin's friend Charles Eliot Norton that although the house was built under Morris's immediate inspection, he believed that as a work of architecture it was more the work of Webb than that of Morris (D G Rossetti to Professor C E Norton, Cambridge, Massachusetts, 9 January 1862, in *Ruskin, Rossetti, and PreRaphaelitism: Papers 1854–1862*, ed. by William Rossetti, p. 268). Red House is discussed, for example, in Hollamby's Red House, in Girouard's 'Red House, Bexleyheath. Kent'; and in Peter Blundell Jones's *'Red House'*. In the last, five of Webb's contract drawings for the house (from the V&A, W&I) are reproduced in colour (pp. 40 (figs 14, 16, and 18) and 41 (figs 19 and 20)).

4. For such a palace having long been his dream, see Mackail, I, p. 142.

5. William Morris to Andreas Scheu, 15 September 1883, quoted in May Morris, *William Morris*, II, p. 10. Furniture made to commission was not uncommon at the time.

6. Mackail, I, p. 147. A table for Red House was made at the Industrial Home for Destitute Boys, Euston Road, London, one of the managers of which was Colonel W J Gillum, a member of the Hogarth Club and an early client of Webb.

7. Webb to William Kent, Builder, Bermondsey, 16 June 1859 (as copied by Webb in his Address Book, private collection).

8. See Mackail, I, pp. 163–6, and Burne-Jones, I, pp. 209–12.

9. Georgiana Burne-Jones writes of the difference made by motherhood (Burne-Jones, I, pp. 213 and 235–6).

10. Burne-Jones, I, p. 277. According to Burne-Jones, Webb's first scheme would have completely enclosed the well court, making the building quadrangular, but such a plan is not shown on the drawings. Possibly he was referring to an initial sketch plan, or perhaps the fourth wing was omitted as it was to be built at a later date. Webb's elevations and sections drawing from his first scheme for enlarging Red House, reproduced in this chapter, is number E.107–1916 (V&A, W&I); for more of his drawings for the proposed enlargement, from the same collection, see Blundell Jones (pp. 48–9, figs 36–42).

11. Burne-Jones, I, pp. 282–84. May Morris recalls the 'heart-break' of leaving Red House in *William Morris*, I, p. 72.

12. Burne-Jones, I, p. 196. There is no indication that enlarging it specifically for the Burne-Joneses was envisaged at this stage.

13. The studio is termed the study on Webb's plan but it is clear from Georgiana Burne-Jones's *Memorials* (1904) that it was referred to and used as the studio.

14. The unfinished panels are illustrated in colour in Ray Watkinson, 'Painting', in *William Morris*, ed. by Parry (p. 95, fig. 44).

15. Webb to Sydney Carlyle Cockerell, 28 May 1898, in *Friends of a Lifetime*, ed. by Meynell, p. 98.

16. Burne-Jones recorded that he designed tiles for the Red House fireplaces (Burne-Jones, I, p. 213) but the tiles in the dining-room jambs appear to be Dutch, except perhaps for those that are decorated with sunflowers (see Jennifer Jenkins Opie, 'Tiles and Tableware', in *William Morris*, ed. by Parry (p. 180)); an anonymous visitor to the house in 1863 described the dresser as being 'ornamented richly with painted decoration' (quoted in Vallance, p. 50).

17. Some of this glass remains in the house, and some is in the Fitzwilliam Museum (illustrated in Robinson and Wildman (p. 19, pl. 12)).

18. The Morrises took the grate from number 26 Queen Square (to which the family moved in 1865) to Kelmscott House (their final home in London), where it remains (see Morris, *Collected Works*, ed. by May Morris, vol. XXII, introduction, p. 366). Several of Webb's houses were to have grates of this pattern.

19. Jane Morris's panel (at present in Kelmscott Manor), and three partly completed panels worked by her sister Elizabeth Burden and later made into a screen (Castle Howard Collection) are illustrated in Parry, 'Textiles', in *William Morris*, ed. by Parry, (p. 227, fig. 91), and as catalogue exhibit M.7, p. 236).

20. Burne-Jones quoted in Burne-Jones, I, p. 209.

21. For the warship, see Mackail, I, p. 163.

22. At the time of writing, the settle is in situ but the painted doors were removed in 1865; two of them were mounted in a single ornate frame now in the National Gallery of Canada, Ontario (no. 6750).

23. See May Morris, *William Morris*, I, p. 13.

24. William Morris, 'The Story of an Unknown Church'.

25. Burne-Jones, I, p. 212.

26. See May Morris, *William Morris*, I, p. 395. The stable is illustrated in Weaver, chapter 2, 'The Red House, Upton, Kent', *Small Country Houses of Today* (p. 11, fig. 9).

27. Wendy Hitchmough devotes the second chapter, 'The First Arts and Crafts Garden', to the Red House garden in *Arts and Crafts Gardens*, pp. 28–39.

28. St Marie's Grange and the Bishop's House are illustrated by Alexandra Wedgwood, who emphasizes Pugin's pioneering use of red brick (p. 43), in 'Domestic Architecture', in *Pugin: a Gothic Passion*, ed. by Atterbury and Wainwright (pp. 42–61, figs 77–81, 88, and 89). This well-illustrated book covers all Pugin's many fields of work.

29. Examples are illustrated in, for example, Hitchcock, *Early Victorian Architecture in Britain*, and in Allibone, *Anthony Salvin*.

30. John Ruskin, 'The Poetry of Architecture; or the Architecture of the Nations of Europe in its Association with the National Character', a series of articles first published in John Julius Loudon's *Architectural Magazine* in 1837 and 1838 (in *Works of John Ruskin*, ed. by Cook and Wedderburn, pp. 1–185).

31. George Edmund Street, *Brick and Marble in the Middle Ages: Notes on a Tour in North Italy* (1855).

32. People who did know these buildings at the time Red House was built referred to them as being in the 'farmhouse' style (see, for example, BN, 12, 1865, p. 657); however, except for the fact that they lacked ornament, this was not very apt as, with their component parts carefully articulated to express the plan, they resembled few English farmhouses. Thompson notes that scarcely any of Butterfield's secular buildings were published, and suggests that, as admirers such as Webb had to seek them out, they perhaps valued them the more highly (Paul Thompson, *Butterfield*, pp. 355–6).

33. Chief amongst the other parsonage style users was William White (1825–1900); no indication has been found amongst Webb's papers as to whether or not he admired this architect's work.

34. Lethaby (1935), p. 67.

35. There are sketches of Butterfield's schools at Great Bookham and a 'house at Highgate' in a Webb sketchbook (private collection). Butterfield's Alvechurch and Baldersby buildings are the only contemporary structures mentioned in Webb's County Lists (private collection). Webb had no need to sketch Street's buildings, as he was familiar with them.

36. See Webb to Charles J Faulkner, 26 May 1873, in John Brandon-Jones, 'Letters of Philip Webb and his Contemporaries', p. 61. Thomas Graham Jackson designed the Examination Schools in 1876.

37. Webb to William Butterfield, 27 November 1869, and Butterfield's reply, 11 December 1869, in Brandon-Jones, 'Letters of Philip Webb and his Contemporaries', pp. 53–4.

38. Webb's sketch, from his notebook in a private collection, is reproduced in John Brandon-Jones, 'The Work of Philip Webb and Norman Shaw' (p. 40).

39. See Lethaby (1935), p. 132, and Ruskin, *Seven Lamps*, preface to 2nd edn, section 4.

40. G Jack, 'An Appreciation of Philip Webb', p. 3; Lethaby (1935), p. 136. Webb to C L Eastlake, 14 March 1870, in Brandon-Jones, 'Letters of Philip Webb and his Contemporaries', pp. 66 and 71 (fig. 4).

41. Butterfield's ground-floor plan of the Alvechurch rectory is reproduced in Thompson, *Butterfield*, p. 108, fig. 21, and by Peter Blundell Jones, who points out its similarity to Webb's plan, in 'Red House', p. 39, fig. 10. Pugin's use of a first-floor drawing room is pointed out in *William Morris and the Middle Ages*, ed. by Banham and Harris, p. 112. William White's plan for the Little Baddow vicarage is similar to that of Red House; designed in 1858, it too was probably influenced by the Alvechurch rectory (for White's plan see, for example, Stefan Muthesius, p. 80, fig. 47).

42. Pugin's perspective with ground-floor plan had been published in 1841 in one of Pugin's articles for the *Dublin Review*, and subsequently in the book based on them: *The Present State of Ecclesiastical Architecture in England*; it is reproduced in Wedgwood, 'Domestic Architecture', p. 51, fig. 89.

43. D G Rossetti to C E Norton, 9 January 1862, in *Ruskin, Rossetti, PreRaphaelitism*, ed. by William Rossetti, p. 268.

44. Red House apparently first appeared in print, with illustrations, in 1897 in Vallance, *William Morris*. It has been illustrated and discussed in countless books and journals since then.

45. Examples of notable Arts and Crafts houses with L-shaped room-and-passage plans include Lethaby's The Hurst (1893–4, demolished); C F A Voysey's Walnut Tree Farm (1890), Perrycroft (1893–4), Broadleys (1898), and the Homestead (1905–6); M H Baillie Scott's Blackwell (1898); and C R Mackintosh's Windy Hill (1900–01) and Hill House (1903–4).

46. John Brandon-Jones pointed out in 1955 that it was not in Red House but in his later work that Webb made his 'great personal contribution to the British building tradition' ('The Work of Philip Webb and Norman Shaw', p. 10).

47. Weaver, *Small Country Houses of Today*, pp. 5–12 (p. 5).

48. Hermann Muthesius, *The English House*, English edn, pp 17–18 (p. 17).

49. Alfred Horsfall, an editor of the *Studio*, owned the house in the 1920s. A later owner, the architect Dick Toms inserted a second kitchen and bathroom so that two families could inhabit the house, and the Hollambys became tenants of Toms and his wife in 1952; in 1957, the house was bought by architect Jean Macdonald

and her husband, from whom the Hollambys purchased it in 1964 (this information was kindly provided by Sonia Crutchlow, Chairman of the Red House [Bexleyheath] Trust).

CHAPTER 3: MORRIS, MARSHALL, FAULKNER & CO.

1. Mackail, I, p. 51. The essays by various experts, and the catalogue entries, in the prolifically illustrated *William Morris*, published to coincide with the exhibition 'William Morris 1834–1896', held at the V&A in 1996, and edited by the curator Linda Parry, is a valuable source of information about the work of the Firm and Webb's work for it. Other books in which artefacts designed by Webb for the Firm and for Morris & Co., and in most cases some interior fittings in his houses, are illustrated include, for example: Banham, MacDonald, and Porter, *Victorian Interior Design*; Jeremy Cooper, *Victorian and Edwardian Furniture and Interiors, From the Gothic Revival to Art Nouveau*; Hitchmough, *The Arts & Crafts Home*; Parry, *William Morris Textiles*.
2. The painter Arthur Hughes (1832–1915) was to have been the eighth partner but he withdrew before the prospectus was issued (Mackail, I, p. 152).
3. Morris to F B Guy, 19 April 1861 (quoted in full in Mackail, I, pp. 153–4).
4. For the founding of the Firm, its first financial arrangements, and the prospectus see, for example, Mackail, I, pp. 148–62.
5. For Pugin's involvement with the decorative arts and crafts, see the articles by various specialists in the different fields, which also included jewellery and book design, in *Pugin: a Gothic Passion*, ed. by Atterbury and Wainwright.
6. For Ruskin's views on craftsmen, the decorative arts, and architecture generally, see his *Seven Lamps*, and *The Stones of Venice*.
7. Quoted in Lethaby (1979), p. 251.
8. Between 1840 and 1876, 1,727 new Anglican churches were built and 7,144 old ones were rebuilt or extensively restored at a total cost of over £25 million (taken from Charles Harvey and Jon Press, 'The business career of *William Morris*', in *William Morris: Art and Kelmscott*, ed. by Parry, pp. 3–22 (pp. 7–8)).
9. According to Vallance, Bodley had promised commissions for stained glass before the Firm was established (see Vallance, p. 56). It is possible that the partners asked Bodley to join them in the Firm (see Martin Harrison, 'Church Decoration and Stained Glass', in *William Morris*, ed. by Parry, pp. 106–115 (p. 107)). Webb had long been a close friend of Bodley, whom he probably met at Street's office where Bodley (who had been George Gilbert Scott's first pupil) worked occasionally when Webb was chief assistant. In the 1860s, when they were thinking on similar lines on house design, Webb influenced Bodley's turn towards a more English neo-Gothic for his churches.
10. Rossetti taught at the Working Men's College; for Webb testing Campfield, see Vallance, pp. 64–5.
11. Between 1860 and 1861, Webb designed and built an estate cottage in the grounds of the Moated House, Tottenham, for Gillum; and in 1860, before the founding of the Firm, he designed several pieces of furniture for the main house (see Lethaby (1935), pp. 36–7).
12. Mackail, I, p. 154.
13. Burne-Jones, I, p. 142. Later, Lucy Orrinsmith (née Faulkner) wrote about domestic interior design.
14. Quoted in Lethaby (1935), p. 189. Lethaby describes and illustrates the piano (which he considered the 'most beautiful piece of modern ornamental work' he knew) that Kate decorated c. 1895 to Webb's designs in 'Philip Webb and his Work', *B*, pp. 672–3, figs 1–5. Sir Giles Gilbert Scott installed the reredos in the institution's new chapel in Wandsworth in 1930; Webb's drawing for it is in the V&A, W&I (E.1589–1916).
15. Webb's drawing is in the V&A, W&I (E. 158–1916). The reredos is illustrated in Cole, *Whitelands College: the Chapel*. Scott did not give the reredos the raking side light intended by Webb and by Morris (who designed the decidedly Gothic lettering along the top). The reredos is now flanked by stone pillars bearing angels and fronted by a much longer altar table than the original item.
16. For more on this subject, see Callen, *Women in the Arts and Crafts Movement, 1870–1914* – first published as *Angel in the Studio*.
17. MacCarthy, pp. 179–81 (this fine biography contains much about the Firm and its work). Several of Webb's exhibited pieces are described and illustrated by Frances Collard in 'Furniture', in *William Morris*, ed. by Parry, pp. 155–63; the catalogue pages contain further examples (pp. 164–179).
18. *Daisy* was the first paper to be published according to Mackail (I, pp. 160–61).
19. Much of the information in this paragraph is taken from Mackail, I, chapters 5 and 6; the scheme to enlarge Red House is covered in chapter 2 of the present volume.
20. Warington Taylor to E R Robson letters, 1863–c. 1867, Burne-Jones Papers, in the collection of the Fitzwilliam Museum.
21. Taylor to Webb, c. July 1869, quoted at length in Lethaby (1935), p. 57.
22. Taylor to Webb, on behalf of the Firm, 17 May 1867, V&A, NAL, 86.SS.57, fol. 61.
23. Both these letters are given in full in Lethaby (1935), (p. 55).
24. From Webb's account book with the Firm (MMF&Co AB), which is of great value to a researcher. John Brandon-Jones pointed out in 1955 that it was Webb who was responsible for all the architectural aspects of the Firm's work (John Brandon-Jones, 'The Work of Philip Webb and Norman Shaw', p. 10).
25. Webb to Morris, December 1873, in Brandon-Jones, 'Letters of Philip Webb and his Contemporaries', pp. 62–3. Meetings were held to discuss Webb's proposal

during 1874 (Lethaby (1935), p. 61).
26. There is an uncharacteristic tone of self-interest in Webb's letter; only concern for Morris could have led Webb to write the letter in such a way. An astute man, he would have foreseen that trouble might ensue from some of the partners. He believed that only public bodies should be permitted to lend at interest (Lethaby (1979), pp. 246–7).
27. See MMF&Co AB.
28. Rossetti left Kelmscott Manor finally in 1874 (see MacCarthy, pp. 335–6). When applied to the village, 'Kelmscott' sometimes has only one 't'; opinions differ as to which is correct; I have used two, whether referring to the village or the manor or Morris's London house.
29. Webb had known Merton College Chapel since a child, and he had included York Minster in his 1857 study tour of the north of England.
30. Sewter, I, p. 73; ibid., p. 25. Sewter states that Webb's pattern-work ceased to appear around 1874, but it should be noted that from 1869, pattern-work in new designs for windows was by Morris (see Harrison, 'Church Decoration and Stained Glass', p. 113). Interestingly, Sewter points out that Webb's 'cloud-wave' motif in the background of the west window (1864) in St Stephen's, Guernsey, in its 'emphatic linear animation and its pure strong colour', is Art Nouveau thirty years before the international establishment of the style (p. 73).
31. See MMF&Co AB. Webb's cartoon for *Adam naming the Animals* is reproduced in *William Morris*, ed. by Parry, p. 120, H.8 (V&A, W&I E.1289–1931)).
32. May Morris, *William Morris*, I, p. 18. Webb's outline drawings of animals possibly influenced those in C F A Voysey's wallpapers. For details of the Firm's work in this church see, for example, the two guide books by David Winpenny and the late Hal Langley respectively.
33. See MMF&Co AB. In these years, he mentions having coloured the arrangement drawings.
34. See Lethaby (1935), p. 38.
35. See MMF&Co AB. The chapel was extensively altered between 1870 and 1875. The MMF&Co windows were designed and made between 1872 and 1874. Webb was paid £20 for a preliminary drawing and the 'complete arrangement and full sized cartoon'. Webb designed the fine ass on which Mary and Jesus ride in the *Flight into Egypt* window, and other fauna. Burne-Jones drew the figures.
36. Webb to A H Powell, 19 December 1904, quoted in Lethaby (1935), pp. 61–2.
37. Nine of Burne-Jones's cartoons for the east window are in the Tullie House Museum and Art Gallery, Carlisle (1922.45.1–9); his cartoon for *The Pelican in her Piety* is in the William Morris Gallery, Walthamstow. For more on the Morris & Co. windows at Brampton, see Penn, *Brampton Church and its Windows*, in which four of Burne-Jones's cartoons are reproduced (the Pelican, the Good Shepherd, an angel and St George, pp. 59, 61, 64 and 67).
38. Webb told Lethaby that it was after inserting new windows in Oxford Cathedral (from 1871–8) that Morris decided they were not right for ancient churches, and that for this reason he refused to make a window for Westminster Abbey (Lethaby (1979), p. 245).
39. See MMF&Co AB.
40. See MMF&Co AB. The Brighton chancel and the nave ceiling of Jesus College Chapel, with Webb's panels (designed 1866), are illustrated in Harrison, 'Church Decoration and Stained Glass', p. 115, fig. 55 and p. 114, fig. 54. Webb designed many heraldic shields for the Firm's decoration of the Combination Room, Peterhouse College, Cambridge (MMF&Co AB). For Webb doing the heraldry, see Lethaby (1935), p. 38. Morris took over the designing of flat pattern from Webb in 1869 (see Harrison, 'Church Decoration and Stained Glass', p. 113).
41. This frontal (Collection of the Vicar and Church Wardens of the Parish of St Martin-on-the Hill) is illustrated in *William Morris*, ed. by Parry, pp. 238, M.12.
42. The super-frontal (V&A, W&I, T.379–1970) is illustrated in *William Morris*, ed. by Parry, p. 251, M.36.
43. See Webb's MMF&Co AB and, especially for the later work with which Webb does not appear to have been involved, Mitchell, 'William Morris at St. James's Palace'; for Cowper's friendship with Rossetti, see Surtees, *The Paintings and Drawings of Dante-Gabriel Rossetti*. The two ceilings were painted white in the twentieth century.
44. See MMF&Co AB; see Lethaby (1935), p. 44 for the inspiration for the frieze. Webb's watercolour drawing for the upper walls (V&A, W&I, E.5096–1960) is illustrated, with a Webb and a Morris drawing (V&A, W&I, E.1169–1940 and E.1170–1940) for the ceiling pattern (ultimately Morris's drawing was largely ignored) in *William Morris*, ed. by Parry, pp. 150–51, I.6, I.7a and I.7b. The Firm was approached initially by Henry Cole, Richard Redgrave, and Francis Fowkes, the designer of the new buildings (MacCarthy, p. 212). The directors, having almost withdrawn the commission, told Mackail c. 1899 that it had proved economical in the long term, only the ceiling having had to be repainted (Mackail, I, p. 182). Not all the colours of the recent repainting appear to repeat the original ones.
45. The Firm does not appear to have been directly involved in the decoration of this house though some wallpapers and fabrics were probably bought from it.
46. The upholstered seating, with the silk intact, is in a private collection. The *Rounton Grange* carpet (private collection) is illustrated in colour in *William Morris*, ed. by Parry, p. 282, M.107, where it is suggested that the carpet might have been designed for the dining room but, as it reflects the colours and design of the drawing-room ceiling and repeats the indigo blue of the walls and upholstery, this

seems unlikely.

47. Morris's words, as recorded by Lowthian Bell, and quoted in Lethaby (1935), pp. 94–5.

48. For the frieze (on panels, finished with the help of Walter Crane, and now in the Birmingham Museums and Art Gallery), see 'The Cupid and Psyche frieze by Sir Edward Burne-Jones at No. 1 Palace Green', *Studio*, 15, no. 67 (1899), pp. 3–13. There is a photograph of the drawing room in George Jack, 'An Appreciation of Philip Webb' (p. 3). See George Llewellyn Morris, 'On Philip Webb's Town Work', for more on the interiors and three sketches by E A Rickards (pp. 203, 205, and 207). Four Webb drawings for the drawing-room ceiling are in the V&A, W&I (E. 104–106–1945).

49. For more about this house, see Day, 'A Kensington Interior'; J Gleeson White, 'An Epoch-Making House'; G Ll Morris, 'On Philip Webb's Town Work'; and Crane, *Ideals in Art*, pp. 131 and 258–61. All Webb's fittings had been removed by 1953 when the house was demolished.

50. A garden house designed by Webb in 1888 was probably abandoned in favour of the 1889 smoking room above a loggia.

51. William Burges had exhibited such pieces in 1859, and had revived a medieval technique for painting on wood which Morris adopted for the work of the Firm (see Collard, 'Furniture', p. 156).

52. *BN* (9 August 1862), p. 99.

53. The King René's Honeymoon Cabinet is illustrated in *William Morris*, ed. by Parry, p. 170, J.13.

54. This wardrobe is illustrated in colour in Collard, 'Furniture', p. 157. Burne-Jones gave it to the Morrises as a wedding present.

55. The Backgammon Players' Cabinet is illustrated in Collard, 'Furniture', p. 157.

56. See Dresser, p. 81; or for his quoted criticism, and more information about the chair and the settle, see Dufty, 'Kelmscott: Exoticism and a Philip Webb Chair'; Dresser is quoted on p. 118.

57. Webb's chair and Rossetti's settle (missing), which also have a slightly Egyptian air, were designed before the Japanese exhibits in the exhibition aroused wide interest. Rossetti's drawing for the settle, and a 1900 photograph of it, is illustrated for example in *William Morris*, ed. by Parry, p. 171, J.14.

58. George Jack, born in the USA in 1855, was articled to Horatio K Bromhead in the early 1870s in Glasgow; he moved to London in 1875 where he worked for C G Vinall until he joined Webb (Vinall helped Webb occasionally by supervising jobs on which no clerk of works was employed or from which Webb had withdrawn).

59. For Webb's beautiful drawing for this ornamented cabinet, see Lever, p. 88, fig. 64. A sideboard by George Jack with tall posts inspired by the characteristic stair-storey posts of Webb's staircases is shown in Collard, 'Furniture', p. 163, fig. 78, and, in the catalogue pages, an inlaid cabinet by Jack is illustrated (p. 179, J.33).

60. Taylor to Robson, W Taylor to E R Robson, n.d. [1860s], Fitzwilliam Museum, xxiii (25).

61. Taylor's sketch of the chair, from his letter to Webb, is illustrated in *William Morris*, ed. by Parry, p. 156, fig. 68. Taylor also brought other items to Webb's attention, and he extolled the virtues of Queen Anne furniture (see Taylor to Webb Letters, V&A, NAL (86.SS.57)).

62. MMF&Co AB. Examples in many fields are illustrated in *William Morris*, ed. by Parry.

63. There are examples of these in several Webb fireplaces, notably at Nether Hall, Suffolk (see chapter 9).

64. See Webb's MMF&Co Account Book for thumbnail sketches of the various table glasses he designed for the Firm. In comparison, the enamelled glasses for Red House were more elaborate and less pleasing. For more on the Firm's tiles, see Richard and Hilary Myers, *William Morris Tiles*; Webb's tiles are illustrated on pp. 10, 34, 55, 65, 82–3, 103, and 120–21. For more on Webb's glass tableware, and further illustrations of it, see Opie, 'Tiles and Tableware', in *William Morris*, ed. by Parry, pp. 180–85 and the relevant catalogue pages.

65. Webb received £10 for designing the Llandaff altar cloth (MMF&Co AB); see May Morris, *William Morris*, I, p. 28, for Morris having designed many of the birds himself in the later years.

66. A detail, of the frieze showing the flock, is illustrated in *William Morris*, ed. by Parry, p. 240, M.15a. Sir Hugh Bell gave the frieze, which is badly faded, to the William Morris Gallery.

67. These drawings, which Webb sold with a small pencil drawing of a peacock to Lawrence Hodgson for £100 in December 1900 (receipt in BL Add. MS 52760) are now in a private collection; there are 25 sketches and drawings relating to this work in the BAL/RIBADC (WEBB [68]); the tapestry is in the V&A, FT&F (T.111–1926). Webb's *The Hare* is illustrated in *William Morris*, ed. by Parry, p. 233, fig. 99, and his *The Fox* and the tapestry itself on pp. 111, 114, and 115.

68. Crane is quoted on this by Isabelle Anscombe and Charlotte Gere in *Arts and Crafts in Britain and America*, p. 14; the Bedford Park estate, for which Shaw designed houses and other buildings, was a speculative venture by Jonathan Carr. Morris interiors became popular and influential chiefly by example and personal recommendations from satisfied clients, but they were illustrated in some late-nineteenth- and early-twentieth-century books. An example is W Shaw Sparrow's *Hints on House Furnishing*, which illustrates Morris & Co. interiors with fittings by or influenced by Webb (frontispiece, and pls. opposite pp. 106, 113, 177, 187, 218, and 283).

69. Sydney Cockerell explained to John Brandon-Jones (who told the author) that when Mackail was researching for his biography of Morris, Webb had agreed to help only on condition that his own name should be kept out of the record as much as possible.

70. Pite, p. 90.

71. Weaver, *Small Country Houses of Today*, pp. 5–18.

72. An example of the thriving state of handicrafts today is that within around ten miles of Thirsk, North Yorkshire, there are over a dozen cabinetmakers, all with thriving businesses. Many of them were trained in the local workshops of the late Robert Thompson (1876–1955), the renowned 'Mouseman' of Kilburn, where his great-grandsons now run the workshop, combining good cabinetmaking and sound training, and keeping machine use to a minimum.

CHAPTER 4: THE MIDDLE YEARS

1. AB; Lethaby (1935), p. 187; OEB 1885–95. Webb's landlord was Edwyn Jones of Fountain Court, Temple, London EC.

2. Lethaby (1935), p. 187. The information about the living-room office is from Webb's Account Book and his MMF&Co. Account Book. He bought two batches of wallpaper in the *Daisy* and the *Venetian* patterns, the latter probably for the living room.

3. Jack's share of the profits apparently varied according to the time he spent in charge during Webb's periods of ill health and convalescence. The information on finance and assistants is from Webb's Account Book. Bassett joined Webb in 1869. T C Yates worked for several years for Webb and was followed by Edmund Buckle (later the architect to the Diocese of Bath and Wells), and by William Weir, who gave occasional assistance after Bassett's departure and then worked full-time for Webb from 1889 to c. 1897.

4. For Wyndham, see Webb to Wyndham, 19 March 1878 and 12 August 1881, LB 1, fols 126 and 193.

5. See Saint, p. 193.

6. Webb to the Surveyor of Taxes, 11 November 1896 (Webb's copy in his AB).

7. Lethaby (1979), pp. 246–7; Bank AB.

8. Cockerell told this to John Brandon-Jones, who kindly passed it on to me.

9. Webb to Rossetti, 21 May 1866, mounted with the Taylor to Webb letters, V&A, NAL, 86.SS.57.

10. See two letters, Warington Taylor to Webb, n.d., V&A, NAL, 86.SS.57, fols 60 and 67. The first of these is a fragment of a hasty note in pencil.

11. Taylor to Webb, November 1868, V&A, NAL, 86.SS.57, fol. 88.

12. Webb to Hale White, 13 May 1899 and 22 January 1910, MR 10/15 and 10/34, Central Library, Bedford; see Winmill, p. 37.

13. Taylor to Webb, 26 July 1868 and Webb to Taylor, 27 July 1868, V&A, NAL, 86.SS.57, fols 77 and 79.

14. See Webb to Howard, 17 July 1877, J22/64, Castle Howard Archives.

15. Webb recorded in his address book the details of the medical people whom he involved in Kate's care. The Faulkner family lived in Bloomsbury, having moved there from Birmingham.

16. Burne-Jones to Rosalind Howard, n.d. [but 1882 or 1883], Castle Howard Archives, quoted by Caroline Dakers in *The Holland Park Circle*, p. 104.

17. See Webb to Hale White, 20 January 1905, MR 10/25, Central Library, Bedford, and Webb to Boyce, 20 June 1882, BL Add. MS 43534.

18. Quoted by Lethaby (1979), p. 240; Webb to Cockerell, 10 November 1902, in *Friends of a Lifetime*, ed. by Meynell, p. 110.

19. Some of Webb's sketches are in the BAL/RIBADC; others are in his surviving sketchbooks in private collections.

20. For Webb and his friends playing 'American bowls', see Burne-Jones, *Memorials*, I, p. 289.

21. Webb to Howard, 2 October 1872, J22/64, Castle Howard Archives. With Peter Barron (of London), Frank Speakman Webb (of Oxford) co-owned the Warwick Brewery, Warwick from 1866 until 1879; by 1881, he was living in Margate but in the Census he still listed his occupation as being a brewer (I am indebted to Peter Cormack for this information).

22. Webb to Howard, 25 April 1886, J22/64, Castle Howard Archives.

23. Webb to Howard, 13 September 1872, and Webb to Rosalind Howard, 11 March 1873, J22/64, Castle Howard Archives.

24. Lethaby recorded him saying this in July 1898, but Webb had always lived in this way (Lethaby (1979), p. 252).

25. See Lethaby (1935), pp. 175 and 187.

26. See Lethaby to Cockerell, 31 July 1915, in *Friends of a Lifetime*, ed. by Meynell, pp. 133–4, for Webb's suits and boots, and his AddB for his braces design; the information about the cigars and snuff came from Emery Walker and Sydney Cockerell to John Brandon-Jones, and thence to me.

27. Webb to Rosalind Howard, 10 December 1868, J22/64, Castle Howard Archives.

28. Dame Laurentia to Cockerell, 7 January 1920, in *Friends of a Lifetime*, ed. by Meynell, p. 259.

29. Webb to Boyce, 12 October 1881, BL Add. MS 45354.

30. The information in this paragraph is from: Webb to Boyce, 21 February 1881 and 11 September 1885, BL Add. MS 45354; Warington Taylor to Webb, n.d., V&A, NAL, 86.SS.57; and May Morris to Lethaby, in Lethaby (1979), pp. 267–8. Webb designed a music room for Dannreuther in the 1870s.

31. Webb to Hale White, 1 March 1888, MR 10/5, Central Library, Bedford.

32. Cockerell to Lethaby, 29 July, and Lethaby's reply, 31 July 1915, in *Friends of a Lifetime*, ed. by Meynell, pp. 132–4.
33. Webb's purchase of Ruskin's *Stones of Venice* is clearly recorded as having taken place on 3 December 1855 in an afterthought entry on the page headed '1856'.
34. See Lethaby (1979), pp. 251–3.
35. Webb to Hale White, 28 October 1899, MR 10/19, Central Library, Bedford.
36. Lethaby to Cockerell, 31 July 1915, in *Friends of a Lifetime*, ed. by Meynell, pp. 133–4.
37. Webb to Hale White, 22 January 1910, MR 10/11, Central Library, Bedford.
38. Mary (Maisie) Bell to Rosalind Howard [her sister-in-law-to-be], 19 August [c. 1874], Castle Howard Archives.
39. Webb to Hale White, 19 February 1888, MR 10/4, Central Library, Bedford.
40. Webb to Rosalind Howard, 19 August 1869, J22/64, Castle Howard Archives.
41. See, for example, Morris to Jane Morris, 14 December 1877 in the *Collected Letters of William Morris*, ed. by Kelvin, I, pp. 419–20.
42. Information in this paragraph is from: the AB; Webb's letters to Boyce, Howard, and George Jack; Lethaby (1935), pp. 47–8; and Lethaby (1979), p. 246.
43. Information about Webb's winter in Italy comes chiefly from Lethaby (1935), chapter 9, pp. 160–86, from Webb's letters to Boyce, George Jack, and Morris (in the BL), and from Webb's Italian sketch book (private collection).
44. Webb to Kate Faulkner, 24 January 1885, quoted in Lethaby (1935), p. 179.
45. Quoted from Webb to G Jack, no date indicated, in Lethaby (1935), p. 161.
46. Webb to Boyce, 5 January 1885 and 27 November 1884, BL Add. MS 43534.
47. Webb to Boyce, 27 November 1884, BL Add. MS 43534. Webb sketched details more often than whole buildings, of vernacular houses and as well as of grander structures.
48. Webb to Boyce, 27 November 1884, BL Add. MS 43534.
49. The comments about Fra Angelico and Mantegna are from Webb to Boyce, 5 January and 5 March 1885, BL Add. MS 43534; those about Michelangelo are from Webb to Hale White, 28 October 1899, MR 10/19, Central Library, Bedford, and Webb to Kate Faulkner, 24 January and 7 February 1885, quoted in Lethaby (1935), pp. 179–80 (p. 179) and pp.180–82 (p. 180).
50. Webb to Hale White, 28 October 1899, MR 10/19, Central Library, Bedford.
51. Webb to Kate Faulkner, 7 February 1885, quoted in Lethaby (1935), pp. 180–82 (p. 180).
52. Webb to Kate Faulkner, 24 January and 7 February 1885, quoted in Lethaby (1935), pp. 178–80 (p. 179) and pp. 180–182 (p. 180).
53. Webb to Boyce, 5 March 1885, BL Add. MS 43534.
54. Webb to Giacomo Boni [an Italian conservationist], 21 December 1884, quoted in Lethaby (1935), p. 167.
55. See Robert Macleod, *Style and Society*, pp. 46–7; Brandon-Jones, 'The work of Philip Webb and Norman Shaw', p. 18.
56. Webb to Boyce, 5 January 1885, BL Add. MS 43534.
57. Lethaby (1935), p. 135.
58. Webb to Boyce, 5 January 1885, BL Add. MS 43534.
59. Webb to Boyce, 4 May 1885, BL Add. MS 43534.
60. Webb to Hale White, 16 May 1899, MR 10/16, Central Library, Bedford.
61. The information about Webb's health is taken from his LB 2, AddB, Standen Certificate Book, his letters to Boyce and to Hale White, and from Lethaby (1935).
62. Webb to the Art Workers' Guild, 1892, quoted by Lethaby (1935), p. 124.
63. RIBA registration did not become compulsory until 1931.

CHAPTER 5: THE STUDIO-HOUSES, AND THE 'QUEEN ANNE' STYLE

1. For more on artists' houses in London see, for example, Walkley, *Artists' Houses in London*, for a full history in which three of Webb's studio-houses (for Prinsep, Boyce, and Watts) are discussed and illustrated; Dakers, *The Holland Park Circle*, for a history of artists' houses in Holland Park (including Prinsep's, George Howard's, and Watts') by Webb); G Ll Morris, 'Philip Webb's Town Work', for a contemporary description of Webb's houses; Girouard, 'The Victorian Artist at Home'.
2. See Stirling, *A Painter of Dreams*, p. 297, and Stirling, *The Letter-bag of Lady Elizabeth Spencer-Stanhope*, II, p. 259.
3. The passage area of Sandroyd was much less than that of Red House, where the passages were probably for exhibiting paintings. For the plan of Mentmore see, for example, Franklin (pp. 70 and 139). It has been suggested that the plan of Sandroyd was influenced by that of Waterhouse's Hinderton (1858) (see Hitchcock, *Architecture: Nineteenth and Twentieth Centuries*, 1977 repr. edn, pp. 358–9; and Stuart Allen Smith, 'Alfred Waterhouse: Civic Grandeur', in *Seven Victorian Architects*, ed. by Jane Fawcett, p. 106). In fact, the Sandroyd plan as built – single-room width in part, with the hall extending through the building and the staircase opposite the entrance – was similar to Hinderton only in its orientation and the position of the domestic offices. Webb's first, unexecuted, plan did resemble it and, as he is sure to have seen the Hinderton plan in the *Builder* (15 January 1859), it might have influenced him initially. His first plan differed from the second in having a smaller second floor served by the backstairs, a stair hall alongside the drawing room, and a small stable attached to the minor offices.
4. The north front of Alvechurch parsonage is illustrated, for example, in Thompson, *Butterfield*, p. 222, fig. 149.
5. See Rooke, ed. by Lago, p. 77.

6. Stanhope's Italian villa, which had walls stencilled by G F Bodley, is described in Stirling, *Life's Little Day*, pp. 145–6.
7. Quoted by Daphne Du Maurier in *The Young George Du Maurier*, p. 113.
8. Stephens, 'Artists' Homes – No. 8: Mr. Val. C. Prinsep's House, Kensington', p. 511 and pl. opposite p. 498. In 1863, after adverse criticism of his Worship Street shops, Webb had resolved never to publish or exhibit his work but presumably at Prinsep's request, he relaxed this rule and even provided the necessary information from which Maurice Adams produced the plans accompanying this paper.
9. Godwin, pp. 799–800. Aitchison's house (Leighton House, number 2 Holland Park Road) is illustrated in Girouard, 'The Victorian Artist at Home', p. 1278.
10. Butterfield's gable is illustrated, for example, in Thompson, *Butterfield*, p. 313, fig. 261.
11. See Stephens, p. 511. A photograph of the studio, taken in 1884, is reproduced in Cooper, *Victorian and Edwardian Furniture and Interiors*, p. 156, fig. 400.
12. This was also G Ll Morris's view ('Philip Webb's Town Work', p. 206). One of Aitchison's designs for the Arab Hall in Leighton House is illustrated in colour in Gere, p. 22, fig. 16.
13. Webb to Hale White, 30 March 1904, MR10/23, Central Library, Bedford.
14. See Dakers, *The Holland Park Circle*, pp. 83–4. For a biography of the Howard couple see Surtees, *The Artist and the Autocrat*.
15. The earliest reference to Webb in Rosalind Howard's Diaries, which have many gaps between entries, records her visit to 'Morris and Webb's furniture place in Queens Sq.' on 3 November 1866 (J23/102/12, Castle Howard Archives).
16. They saw Prinsep's house under construction and in 1866 after completion (Rosalind Howard's Diaries, Castle Howard Archives); the Howards were close friends of Hugh Bell and his siblings one of whom, Ada (later Mrs Arthur Godman), was courted by Rosalind's brother Lyulph Stanley, who eventually married her sister Mary (Maisie); see 'Death of F. D. P. Astley, Esq., Lord of the Manor of Dukinfield', *Ashton Reporter*, 28 March 1868, p. 5.
17. See *Northern Kensington*, ed. by Sheppard, pp. 185–7 (p. 185), in which there are six floor plans and six photographs of number 1 Palace Green. Webb's drawing for the south gable addition (BAL/RIBADC) is reproduced in Kirk, 'Philip Webb (1831–1915)', vol. 2, fig. 35.
18. Webb to Howard, 7 September 1867, J22/64, Castle Howard Archives.
19. Pennethorne to Charles Gore, 16 October 1867, quoted in *Northern Kensington*, ed. by Sheppard, p. 185; copy by Webb of the letter Pennethorne wrote to him, 16 October 1867, J22/65, Castle Howard Archives.
20. Copy by Webb of his letter to Pennethorne, 18 October 1867, J22/65, Castle Howard Archives.
21. For a long quotation from Salvin and Wyatt's report, see Surtees, *The Artist and the Autocrat*, pp. 52–3; Webb to Howard, 3 March 1868, J22/64, Castle Howard Archives. In this letter, Webb included the response he wished Howard to pass on to Gore verbatim; as the response makes no mention of Webb considering the construction and proportion of the building to be essentially Gothic whilst Howard's letter to Gore does, it seems that Howard must have added this himself (see *Northern Kensington*, ed. by Sheppard, p. 187).
22. George Howard to 'Sir' [Charles Gore], 23 March 1868, J22/65, Castle Howard Archives.
23. Webb to Howard, 3 March 1868, J22/64, Castle Howard Archives. Shaw was to use a rather similar brick parapet on part of Lowther Lodge, London (1871; illustrated, for example, in Saint, p. 140, fig. 118).
24. See T H Wyatt to 'Sir' [Webb], 28 March 1868, J22/65, Castle Howard Archives. Rosalind Howard recorded in her diary, 28 March 1868, that this letter was sent to Webb (J23/102/15, Castle Howard Archives).
25. See Webb to George Howard, 4 June 1868, and to Mr and Mrs Howard, 10 August 1868, J22/64, Castle Howard Archives.
26. See Webb to Howard, 23 May 1868, J22/64, Castle Howard Archives.
27. Number 180 Queen's Gate is illustrated in Saint, p. 235, fig. 175.
28. G Ll Morris, 'Philip Webb's Town Work', p. 204.
29. G Ll Morris, 'Philip Webb's Town Work', p. 204; there are three interior sketches of number 1 Palace Green in this article, pp. 203, 205, and 207. There is a photograph of the drawing room in George Jack, 'An Appreciation of Philip Webb', p. 3.
30. This information was provided by a descendant of the Bell family; the full story, including the subsequent division of the Howard estates, is told by Surtees in *The Artist and the Aristocrat*.
31. For Boyce having to move, see *The Diaries of George Price Boyce*, repr. edn ed. by Virginia Surtees, pp. 48 and 107 n. 8.
32. The landing is illustrated in Stamp and Goulancourt, p. 63, and the dining room in Swenarton, p. 37, fig. 2.3.
33. This window, not shown on the contract drawings, may have been built in two stages – the lower part during the initial construction, and the upper part at the same time as the extension, which has some similar details.
34. See Arthur E Street, 'George Price Boyce, R. W. S', in the *Old Water-Colour Society's Club Nineteenth Annual Volume*, ed. by Randall Davies (London: by the Society, 1941), p. 6.
35. For more on the dispute between Webb, the builder, and Watts, see chapter 13, and Dakers, *The Holland Park Circle*, pp. 150–52, and Webb to Watts, 8, 17, and 18 July 1874, LB 1, fols 1–5.
36. On 1 December 1871, Watts announced his intention of painting portraits to pay for the new house (Watts, I, p. 253).

37. For more on this dispute, see (as well as chapter 13 of the present volume) Dakers, *The Holland Park Circle*, pp. 150–52. Webb received no fees at all from any client in 1874 and 1875 (AB).

38. For this and life at the Briary, see Troubridge, pp. 19–26.

39. An elevation drawing for number 6 Melbury Road (demolished) is reproduced in Dakers, *The Holland Park Circle*, p. 154, fig. 70.

40. Waterhouse's plan is illustrated in Franklin, pp. 161–2. Only one drawing and a few preliminary sketches of Webb's drawings for the Briary have survived, and the only illustrations of the building found so far are a sketch by Malcolm Fraser in O'Connor (p. 261), and a photograph of the exterior by Julia Margaret Cameron (Collection of the National Portrait Gallery), reproduced in Ford, p. 13.

41. See O'Connor, p. 266.

42. See Troubridge, p. 298.

43. Pite, pp. 77–96 (pp. 89–90).

44. Lethaby recorded that number 1 Palace Green became a 'pattern-book of "features" for those who designed by compilation from cribs' (Lethaby (1935), p. 88). Lethaby's belief that Webb reintroduced rubbed brick dressings was mistaken (ibid., p. 88), as James Wild had used them in 1849 on his yellow-brick Northern Schools (London, demolished). However, Webb's extensive use of them in the wing he added to Cranmer Hall in 1864 was in advance of his peers, and highly influential (see chapter 9).

45. Girouard, *Sweetness and Light*, p. 1. Webb's pioneering role is covered in Girouard's comprehensive study of the style.

46. See Girouard, *Sweetness and Light*, chapters 2 and 3. In the 1860s, Bodley, Shaw, and Nesfield were in close touch. The 'Queen Anne' manner developed for the London Board Schools in the early 1870s by Champneys, Robson, and Stevenson revealed Webb's influence. For primary sources, see, for example, Robson, *School Architecture* (1874); Stevenson, *House Architecture* (1880); and Jackson, *Modern Gothic Architecture* (1873).

47. Saint points out that Nesfield was the best of them at fusing disparate elements into a coherent style (*Shaw*, p. 45). Saint illustrates Nesfield's Temperate House Lodge on p. 46, fig. 31.

48. St Martin's vicarage is illustrated in Girouard, *Sweetness and Light*, p. 34, fig. 26, and Cefn Bryntalch in Hall, pp. 60–61, figs 6–10. When Bodley was ill in 1869, Webb helped him by drawing the last few details and supervising the final stages of the construction of his houses at Malvern Link (see the correspondence between Webb and Bodley in Brandon-Jones, 'Letters of Philip Webb', pp. 63–5.) These houses are illustrated in Stamp and Goulancourt, pp. 66–7.

49. Comment by a Mr Cabot during a debate held by the Boston Chapter of the American Institute of Architects, 1877 (see '"Queen Anne" in America', *Architect* (USA) (24 March 1877), p. 202).

50. Webb to Percy Wyndham, 20 July 1886, LB 2, fols 59–61.

51. Webb to Hale White, November 1899, MR 10/20, Central Library, Bedford.

CHAPTER 6: WEBB'S APPROACH TO ARCHITECTURAL DESIGN AND ITS INFLUENCE

1. The term 'Progressive Eclecticism' was introduced in 1858 by Benjamin Webb, the Secretary of the Ecclesiological Society, and popularized by Beresford Hope, the president. For more on the situation at the time see, for example, Stefan Muthesius, *The High Victorian Movement*, and Crook, *The Dilemma of Style*.

2. Webb to Hale White, c. 10 February 1899, MR 10/14, Central Library, Bedford.

3. See Webb to Hale White, 29 October 1909, MR 10/33, Central Library, Bedford.

4. AB, 29 June 1856. Ruskin became friendly with Morris and Burne-Jones and, like Webb, often visited them in their rooms in number 17 Red Lion Square (see Lethaby (1935), pp. 28–9). Although the society had links with the Oxford Tractarian movement (which sought to renew Roman Catholic thinking and practice within the Church of England), its leaders were architectural historians not theologians, therefore it was not obsessed with ritual and belief. Ruskin and Webb were not attracted towards Roman Catholic practice.

5. Webb to Rosalind Howard, 25 July 1878, J22/64, Castle Howard Archives.

6. Lethaby (1935), p. 119.

7. From Webb's initialled MS in the SPAB Archive, pp. 20 and 11, of the thirteenth annual report (henceforth 'Thirteenth Annual Report') of the society (which was published as *Thirteenth Annual Meeting of the Society, Report of the Committee and Paper read thereat by Revd W. Cunningham DD, June 1890* (London: SPAB, 1890)); and from Webb to George Y Wardle, 9 May 1899 (SPAB Archive). See Swenarton, pp. 53–4, for his discussion of Webb's views on these matters.

8. Webb, 'Thirteenth Annual Report', p. 11, quoted by Swenarton, p. 54.

9. Lethaby (1935), p. 120.

10. E, xxiii, NS, 20 (1862), p. 229, quoted by Crook, *Dilemma of Style*, p.162.

11. For the history of 'Queen Anne' and its influence, see Girouard, *Sweetness and Light*.

12. Seddon's lecture is cited by Peter Collins in *Changing Ideals in Modern Architecture, 1750–1950* (London: Faber and Faber, 1965), 1971 paperback edn, p. 143.

13. See Webb to Percy Wyndham, 16 August 1886, LB 2, fol. 62; Lethaby (1935), p. 18; 'pleasant without pretences of style' is Lethaby's phrase.

14. Webb to Lethaby, 3 July 1904, in Lethaby (1935), p. 138; Webb told Lethaby that 'Common sense is our only ware' (ibid., p. 136).

15. Webb to Hale White, 20 January 1905, MR 10/24, Central Library, Bedford, and to Lethaby, 18 January 1905, in Lethaby (1979), p. 261. Webb preferred to use synonyms for beauty because he thought the quality itself could not be

16. defined, only its many manifestations, one of which was a well-laid-out drainage system (see Lethaby (1979), p. 251, and (1935), p. 123).

17. Webb to Lethaby, 14 April 1905 (Lethaby (1979), p. 262), and to Hale White, 13 May 1899, MR 10/15, Central Library, Bedford.

18. See Ruskin, *Seven Lamps*, preface to 2nd edn, section 4; Webb to Lethaby, in Lethaby (1935), p. 132. The chief interest of a building for Ruskin lay in 'venerable or beautiful, and otherwise unnecessary' features that were added to the utilitarian structural elements (this is pointed out and Ruskin's words are quoted by Michael W Brooks, p. 22). Ruskin saw beauty in vernacular cottages but did not consider them to be works of architecture.

19. Webb to William Morris, 17 June 1896, V&A, NAL, 86.TT.13, fol. 76, quoted by Peter Brandon in 'Philip Webb, the William Morris Circle, and Sussex', p. 10.

20. Webb to Lady Fitzhardinge, 25 July 1876, LB 1, fol. 41.

21. Lethaby (1935), p. 136.

22. G Jack to Lethaby, n.d., in Lethaby (1935), p. 36.

23. Lethaby (1935), p. 127.

24. See, for example, William Gilpin, in a quotation from his *Remarks on Forest Scenery* (1791) in *The Genius of the Place: The English Landscape Garden 1620–1820*, ed. by Hunt and Willis, 2nd edn, p. 339.

25. Webb to George Howard, 7 September 1867, J22/64, Castle Howard Archives; to Jane Morris, 12 November 1903, BL Add. MS 45343; and to G Jack, 17 and 27 May 1888 (private collection).

26. Webb to Boyce, 26 September 1883, BL Add. MS 45354.

27. See, for example, Webb's letter to George Howard, 1 October 1875, J22/64, Castle Howard Archives.

28. Webb to Lethaby, 21 December 1909, quoted in Lethaby (1935), p. 130.

29. Webb probably read the work of St Thomas Aquinas in 1869 at Warington Taylor's prompting (see Taylor to Webb, August 1869, V&A, NAL, 86.SS.57), but he would have discussed it years before with Burne-Jones, who was considered an authority on the subject when an undergraduate (see Taylor to E R Robson, Burne-Jones Papers, Fitzwilliam Museum [9 December 1865], xxii (22)).

30. For more on the scholastic theory see, for example, de Zurko, pp. 38–43.

31. Webb to Hale White, November 1899; Webb found Wordsworth's poetry consoling but was bored by his 'philosophizing', whereas he admired Scott wholeheartedly. Trevor Garnham discusses connections between Morris's, Webb's, and Romantic movement thinking in 'Crafts and the Revival of Architecture', in Jackson, *F. W. Troup*, pp. 86–8.

32. William Wordsworth's *A Guide through the District of the Lakes in the North of England ...* (1835) was the most popular guidebook for the area when Webb visited the Lakes in 1859; in view of his insatiable curiosity about the landscape, he is certain to have consulted it.

33. Quoted in Lethaby (1979), p. 251.

34. Brandon-Jones, 'The work of Philip Webb and 'Norman Shaw', p. 12. For Devey, see, for example, Allibone, *George Devey*. Webb and Devey had much in common, including living for their work, refusing publicity and uncongenial commissions, and avoiding professional institutions and the seeking of patronage.

35. No mention of Devey has been found in Webb's papers. Arthur E Street, whose wife was Boyce's niece, stated in the second version of his paper 'George Price Boyce, R.W.S.' that Boyce served his articles with 'Mr. Devey' but this could not have been so because Devey did not establish his practice until after Boyce had finished his training (p. 2). In fact, Boyce served his articles with Wyatt and Brandon (see *The Diaries of George Price Boyce*, repr. edn ed. by Surtees, p. viii). However, it is evident that Devey and Boyce, who died before the paper was written, were well acquainted.

36. See Lethaby (1935), p. 122. For Webb's use of traditional materials, see also Sheila Kirk, 'Philip Webb and traditional materials', in *Architecture 1900*, ed. by Burman, pp. 145–55.

37. Webb to A H Powell, 28 March 1894, quoted in Lethaby (1935), p. 123.

38. See Webb to Hale White, 1 March 1888, MR 10/59, Central Library, Bedford.

39. Webb to Hale White, 11 March 1888, MR 10/6, Central Library, Bedford.

40. See Webb to Lethaby, 14 April 1905, in Lethaby (1979), pp. 262–3, and Webb to Hale White, 1 March 1888, MR 10/5, Central Library, Bedford.

41. Webb to Hale White, 11 March 1888, MR 10/6, Central Library, Bedford.

42. Ruskin, 'The Poetry of Architecture', p. 47.

43. Webb read all the nineteenth-century writings on architecture that he could find, and he would certainly have discussed Pugin's theories with Street, a great admirer of the architect; Joseph Clarke recommended the use of local materials (in his *Schools and Schoolhouses: a series of Views, Plans, and details for Rural Parishes* (1852)), and used them himself. Webb would have known Clarke, and his book, as he was a diocesan colleague of Street. George Gilbert Scott recommended the use of local traditional styles for small buildings – but only if modified to make them suitably neo-Gothic – in his *Remarks on Secular and Domestic Architecture*, pp. 128 and 136.

44. See, for example, Crook, *The Dilemma of Style*, pp. 134–6. It is not known whether Webb admired Lamb's work, but there are affinities in their handling of local materials.

45. Information taken from Webb's county lists of buildings he had visited (private collection). In his letters to Webb, Warington Taylor reported on old houses he had found, and with one of them he enclosed a list, compiled from county handbooks, of buildings worth seeing (Taylor to Webb Letters, V&A 86.SS.57).

45. Webb to Lethaby, 3 July 1904, in Lethaby (1935), p. 138.
46. Webb to Lethaby, 1903, in Lethaby (1935), p. 133.
47. See Webb to Gertrude Astley, 21 October 1881 (LB 1, fol. 199), in which he makes it clear that in his view all buildings up to that date are 'ancient' – are living architecture, that is.
48. Webb to Hale White [c. 10 February 1899], MR 10/14, Central Library, Bedford.
49. Webb to Hale White, November 1899, MR 10/20, Central Library, Bedford.
50. Webb to Hale White, 28 October 1899, MR 10/19, Central Library, Bedford.
51. See Webb to George Howard, 6 February 1875, J22/64, Castle Howard Archives.
52. See Lethaby (1935), p. 141.
53. This drawing is reproduced in Caroline Dakers, Clouds, p. 58, fig. 29.
54. Ruskin, Stones of Venice, 2, chapter 6, para. xxvi.
55. John Brandon-Jones, in 'Philip Webb', in Victorian Architecture, ed. by Ferriday, pp. 249–65, points out that Webb had studied the work of Vanbrugh at the South Kensington Museum in Colen Campbell's Vitruvius Britannicus (1715–25), making sketches from it and copying the plan of King's Weston in his sketchbook (private collection).
56. For quotations from these admirers of Vanbrugh see, for example, Christopher Hussey, The Picturesque, pp. 188–90, 193, and 198; Hussey asserts that Adam's definition of 'movement' and his praise of Vanbrugh was the beginning of English picturesque architecture); Robert Kerr regretted the costliness and pretension of English Baroque architecture, and its inconvenient plans and wastefulness of space, but he praised Vanbrugh's 'remarkable vigour of design' (in his The Gentleman's House, 3rd edn, 1871, pp. 45–7).
57. Vanbrugh's liking for castles is obvious from the many features in his buildings derived from them; Downes suggests that Vanbrugh admired Elizabethan great houses for their dramatic massing, visual associations with castles, their 'manly beauty', rationalistic plans and elevations, and their Englishness, and points out that his buildings depend upon a similar movement, repetition of groups of windows, and varied skylines for their effect. (Downes, pp. 333 and 337.)
58. Webb to George Howard, 7 October 1875, J22/64, Castle Howard Archives.
59. See Vanbrugh to the Earl of Manchester, 9 September 1707 (quoted by Downes, p. 276).
60. For Webb's abandonment of such external chimneys, see Webb to Constance Astley, 1 April 1891, in the author's collection of photocopies of letters in the collection of the late Miss M J Becher). Corner fireplaces were probably first introduced by Inigo Jones in the Queen's House; Webb had seen the plan in Colen Campbell's Vitruvius Britannicus; see repr. introduced by John Harris, pl. 14).
61. Wright's Prairie houses (from 1901) are illustrated in, for example, Hitchcock, In the Nature of Materials.
62. Webb to Sidney Barnsley, 1 May 1904, in Lethaby (1979), pp. 259–60.
63. Morris, Collected Works, ed. by May Morris, XXII, p. 208.
64. Webb to Hale White, 28 October 1899, MR 10/19; Webb to Lethaby, 3 July 1904, in Lethaby (1935), p. 138.
65. G Jack, quoted in Lethaby (1935), p. 228. See Winmill, pp. 31–2, for Charles Winmill's many visits with Webb to St Paul's.
66. Webb, 'Ashburnham House', pp. 30–31. It is now known that John Webb (1611–72) designed this house. There is apparently no family connection between him and Philip Webb.
67. See Webb to Lethaby, 8 April 1904, in Lethaby (1935), pp. 139–40. Lethaby had suggested importing craftsmen from the East; Webb feared this would lead to the copying of alien strains rather than the reviving of craftsmanship as Lethaby hoped.
68. The extent to which Renaissance architects believed in and obeyed absolute laws of proportion is controversial but see, for example, Wittkower, Architectural Principles in the Age of Humanism.
69. Ruskin, Seven Lamps, chapter 4, paras xxvi and xxviii.
70. This is demonstrated by Webb's comment to Wyndham that the 'greater part of our 19th-century architecture is ruined in appearance for want of attention to knowledge of the laws of proportion' when the matter under discussion, a 'matter of taste', was Webb's insistence that a simple paling fence, too '"cottagy"' to his client, on the south front of Clouds would increase the apparent size of the house (Webb to Percy Wyndham, 17 July 1886, LB 2, fol. 58).
71. See Lethaby (1935), p. 10.
72. Street's Laverstoke parsonage, Hampshire (1858) is an example of his gentler, more English manner. Webb considered that the buildings Street designed in this way, based chiefly on 'English models', were his 'more characteristic work' (Webb, 'Street', DNB, p. 45). John Hutchinson and Paul Joyce draw attention to Street's frequent assimilation of ideas from his ex-pupils, and to the change to an English manner, in George Edmund Street in East Yorkshire, pp. 9 and 11. For the work of Street during Webb's time as his assistant, see Hitchcock, 'G. E. Street in the 1850s', pp. 145–71.
73. Augustus Welby Northmore Pugin, The True Principles of Pointed or Christian Architecture, repr. edn (1969), p.1.
74. Webb to W T Tate, 13 June 1883, LB 2, fol. 13.
75. Webb, 'Thirteenth Annual Report', p. 20, quoted by Swenarton, p. 53.
76. Webb to Constance Astley, 10 February 1904, BAL/RIBAAC, LeW/2/1, quoted by Swenarton, p. 56.
77. G Jack to Lethaby, n.d., quoted in Lethaby (1935), p. 137, n. 77. Mrs Pamela S North kindly informed me by letter, 19 June 1984, that the proposed rebuilding of the hall (c. 1870–72) was abandoned because of the cost of educating a large

family. Webb's sketch plans and elevations are in a private collection. The unexecuted house designed by Webb in 1873 for Rafe Leycester, intended to be built at Bexton in Cheshire, is another example (see the Catalogue of Architectural Works).
78. From notes on Webb's drawing WEBB [51] 1–4, (1), BAL/RIBADC, illustrated in Lever, p. 88.
79. Webb's drawing WEBB [42] 59, BAL/RIBADC. Pearson was one of the original members of C R Ashbee's Guild of Handicraft.
80. See Webb to I L Bell, 4 April 1877, LB 1, fol. 78.
81. G Jack, 'An Appreciation of Philip Webb', p. 4.
82. Webb to George Howard [c. October 1867], J22/64, Castle Howard Archives; Lethaby (1935), p. 135.
83. Lethaby (1935), p. 135.
84. Ibid..
85. Ruskin, Stones of Venice, 2, chapter 6, para. vii.
86. Webb to Lethaby, 1903, in Lethaby (1935), pp. 132–4.
87. Webb to Hale White, 11 March 1888 (MR 10/6), Central Library, Bedford.
88. Pugin, True Principles, pp. 53–4.
89. Webb to Lethaby, 17 September 1903, in Lethaby (1935), pp. 131–2 (p. 131).
90. Lethaby (1935), pp. 133 and 132.
91. B, 21, 1863, p. 620.
92. Lethaby recorded that Webb believed an architect should be 'properly an experimenter, developer, adapter – an inventor in building, not a supplier by rote of tired and stale grandeurs in the styles' (Lethaby's words, Lethaby (1935), p. 136).
93. In what was apparently his only use of the material, Webb replaced the exhausted thatch on the old cottages that he converted into a house for the Clouds head gardener. Examples of the use of thatch by his disciples include E S Prior's The Barn (Devon, 1895) and Ernest Gimson's Stoneywell Cottage (Leicestershire, 1898), which are discussed and illustrated in Stamp and Goulancourt, pp. 120–21 and 128–9, and A H Powell's Long Copse (Surrey, 1897), which is discussed in Gradidge, pp. 172–6.
94. For example, in 1868 he exposed a flange in the ceiling of the major bedroom at Red Barns (Coatham, Redcar).
95. For clients being able to select from his designs, see Webb to W Thomas Tate, 13 June 1883, LB 2, fol. 13.
96. Lethaby (1935), p. 137.
97. See, for example, a) the Clouds drawing (WEBB [24] 71, BAL/RIBADC) of a flattened arch, and b) the bridge at Great Tangley Manor (WEBB [43] 19, BAL/RIBADC) and Standen Cottages (WEBB [42] 75, BAL/RIBADC), reproduced in (a) Robert Macleod, Style and Society, fig. 3.4, and (b) Richardson, pp. 18 and 21, figs 9 and 13.
98. May Morris, William Morris, I, p. 36n.
99. See, for example, Hugh Honour, Romanticism (London: Allen Lane, 1979; repr. edn, Harmondsworth: Penguin, 1981), chapter 3.
100. Webb to Sidney Barnsley, 28 November 1900, in Lethaby (1979), p. 258.
101. Webb to Hale White, 5 January 1902, MR 10/21, Central Library, Bedford.
102. For the organic analogy see, for example, Germann, trans. by Gerald Onn, and Collins, chapter 4, pp. 149–58.
103. William Morris, 'Gothic Architecture', p. 156.
104. See Webb to George Howard, 3 March 1868, J22/64, Castle Howard Archives.
105. See, for example, Lethaby (1935), pp. 130 and 96.
106. See Lethaby (1935), p. 111.
107. For Lutyens's gardens see, for example, Weaver, Houses and Gardens by E. L. Lutyens and Brown, Gardens of a Golden Afternoon. Wendy Hitchmough discusses Webb's influence on gardens in Arts and Crafts Gardens, chapter five, pp. 70–88.
108. Pugin, B, 8 (1850), p. 134.
109. Pugin, True Principles, pp. 35-6
110. Webb to Rosalind Howard, 7 December 1878, J22/64, Castle Howard Archives. Webb suggested that the name be put on the house to ensure its acceptance; it was carved on a mounting-block near the entrance.
111. Lethaby (1935), p. 130.
112. See Pugin, True Principles, p. 52.
113. On his one of his working drawings of 1875 for Rounton Grange, Webb wrote: 'Note The S. W. & S. E. ROOMS [in the corner turrets or pavilions] to have a dummy beam to correspond with trusses in other pavilions' (ZFK MIC 2129/ 151-155, NYCRO). For Ruskin's contentions on structural and other architectural truths and deceits, see Seven Lamps, chapter 2: 'The Lamp of Truth'.
114. Webb's drawing (Zetland Road elevation and a vertical section) shows a lintel formed by two iron I-beams (contract drawing dated 28 June 1889, signed 29 June 1889 (WEBB [36] 4, BAL/RIBADC). As Dorman Long & Co. supplied steel joists for the building (AB), the lintels might be of steel not iron.
115. Thompson gives instances of his deceits in roofs, in William Butterfield, p. 170.
116. Webb to G Jack, 23 May 1888, private collection.
117. Webb to Hale White, 21 February 1902, MR 10/22, Central Library, Bedford. It is clear from this letter that Webb agreed with Pugin, who maintained in True Principles (p. 1) that 'designs should be adapted to the material in which they are executed'.
118. G Jack's recorded words, n.d., Lethaby (1935), p. 125; Pugin, True Principles, p. 1.
119. The important works were Owen Jones, The Grammar of Ornament (1856); Ruskin, Stones of Venice; and Street, Brick and Marble in the Middle Ages. For more

on the revivalists' use of polychromy, see, for example, Stefan Muthesius, *High Victorian Movement*, chapter 4, pp. 59–92.

120. Webb to Butterfield, 27 November 1869, in Brandon-Jones, 'Letters of Philip Webb', p. 54.

121. See Lethaby (1935), p. 10.

122. G Jack to Lethaby, n.d., quoted in Lethaby (1935), pp. 117–18 (p. 118).

123. Webb told Lethaby that the Firm had introduced white for window frames in London; as Webb handled all the Firm's architectural work, this means that he was responsible (see Lethaby (1935), p. 45).

124. See Webb to Charles L Eastlake, 14 March 1870, in Brandon-Jones, 'Letters of Philip Webb', pp. 66 and 71. Webb told Eastlake that to include his work in the latter's *A History of the Gothic Revival* (1872), in which he considered it would be out of place, would break his self-imposed rule never to make his work 'unnecessarily public'.

125. John Piper noted Harding's enthusiasm for beauty in decay in his *Buildings and Prospects*, p. 95 (cited by Donald Smith in 'The Work of Philip Webb', p. 16n); see Ruskin, *Seven Lamps*, chapter 6, para. xvi.

126. Webb to J C Ramsden, 6 June 1887, LB 2, fols 93–4.

127. On 25 July 1898, Webb reminded himself in his Site Book to instruct that the finial was not to be 'aged' (SB 1896–1900).

128. Quoted by Roberts in *The Radical Countess*, p. 36. The original verse, with slightly different wording, first appeared in *The Quarterly Review*, June 1826.

129. See Ruskin, *Seven Lamps*, paras. ix–xi. In brief, Ruskin contends that because observers are accustomed only to judging traditionally constructed buildings, iron should only be used for holding things together not as a support, whether that be a column or a beam; for him, the use of iron girders in place of wooden beams makes a building cease to be 'true architecture' (para. x).

130. Webb's Atherston Colliery drawings (V&A, W&I, E.110-113–1916) are undated but his letters in a private collection indicate an early 1870s date.

131. Webb appears to have first used iron-rod king-posts in his second extension to Washington Hall (1865) for iron-master Lowthian Bell.

132. The unusual floor-stiffening rods in Smeaton Manor (which was designed for Lowthian Bell's daughter and her husband) were found during alteration work in the 1980s, and kindly drawn to my attention by Clive Cruddas of Dennis Lister and Associates, Middlesbrough.

133. David T Yeomans kindly answered my queries and sent useful material relating to the use of iron in roofs in the nineteenth century.

134. He chose large glasshouses from the catalogues of horticultural engineers – in the case of Rounton Grange, from that of W G Smith & Co., Bury St Edmunds, Suffolk.

135. In the 1870s, Shaw collaborated with the builder W H Lascelles in the development of concrete building blocks faced to imitate weather-tiling and supported on a timber frame (Saint, pp. 165–71). They were used by a subsequent owner on an extension to Hale White's Webb house, number 19 Park Hill, Carshalton (1868).

136. The Standen ceiling appears on an early plan (collection of the National Trust, Standen). Lutyens's dining-room ceiling at Marsh Court (1901–04) — illustrated for example, in *Edwin Lutyens*, ed. by Dunster, p. 54, pl. 5 — resembles Webb's design for Standen, the drawing for which he would have seen For the early use of reinforced concrete construction see, for example, Hudson, pp. 54–6.

137. Shaw to Lethaby, 1910, in Lethaby (1935), p. 77; G Jack, 'An Appreciation of Philip Webb', p. 5. The date of Shaw's letter is mistakenly given as '1900'.

138. See Lethaby (1935), p. 83.

139. Disgusted by finding too many machines and much poor craftsmanship in the yard of Peter Peters, who built Standen, Webb resolved to write him a 'stiff letter' on the matter (5 April 1893, SB 1892–96).

140. Webb's recorded words, 11 August 1898 (Lethaby (1979), pp. 253–4); Lethaby (1935), p. 194; Webb's recorded words, n.d., Lethaby (1935), p. 126.

141. See Webb to Hale White, c. 10 February, 28 October, and November 1899, MR 10/14, /19, /20, Central Library, Bedford.

142. Webb to Hale White, November 1899, MR 10/20. Central Library, Bedford.

143. F A White to Lethaby, quoted in Lethaby (1935), pp. 115–16. White was a cement manufacturer and connoisseur of eighteenth-century furniture.

144. White's sketches are in the Royal Academy archive. For more, and an account of Shaw's building, see Saint, pp. 243–50.

145. See Lethaby (1935), p. 115.

146. For Webb's work being the 'starting point' for Shaw's town houses see Saint, p. 137; Shaw quoted in Lethaby (1935), p. 75.

147. The others were S S Teulon, F T Pilkington, E Bassett Keeling, Thomas Harris, and, arguably, Butterfield. For more on 'Go' or Modern Gothic see, for example, Crook, 'GO versus Gothic', in his *William Burges and the High Victorian Dream*, pp. 123–8, and his *Dilemma of Style*, pp. 133–48.

148. W Taylor to E R Robson [1860s], Fitzwilliam Museum, xxiii (25); Ruskin, *Stones of Venice*, 2, chapter 6, para. cxl.

149. W Taylor to E R Robson, Fitzwilliam Museum, xxiii (23). Girouard quotes from Taylor's letters in *Sweetness and Light*, pp. 15–16.

150. Lethaby (1935), p. 230.

151. Quoted in Lethaby (1935), p. 76.

152. Brandon-Jones, 'Philip Webb', p. 261.

153. See Pugin, *True Principles*, pp. 52, 35–6, and 46–8. Pugin pointed out that buildings designed for other climates were unsuitable for use in England, and that

154. Shaw's opinion ('Every word I believe to be fallacious, but I read it with pleasure and lay it down with regret.') is quoted in Saint, p. 321.

155. From Shaw to J D Sedding, 20 November 1882, in Saint, p. 219 (for long quotations from Shaw's two letters to Sedding on this matter, see ibid., pp. 217–19); from Lethaby's condensed account of a Shaw interview that was published c. 1902 under the title 'Mr. Norman Shaw's Lament over our Lack of Continuity'(Lethaby (1935), pp. 76–7 (p. 76)).

156. See Saint, pp. 319–20 for Shaw's pupils and assistants turning to Webb as 'master', and pp. 219–20 for Shaw beginning to take a more thoughtful approach.

157. See Saint, p. 320. Saint discusses Shaw and the Arts and Crafts movement on pp. 319–21.

158. See, for example, Scott's Red House, Isle of Man (1892–93) in Haigh, pp. 86–9, and Lutyens's Crooksbury House, Surrey (1890) in Weaver, *Houses and Gardens by E. L. Lutyens*, repr. edn (1981), p. xvi.

159. Baillie Scott, Richard Barry Parker (1867–1941), and Sir Raymond Unwin (1863–1940), for example, designed houses for Letchworth, the first Garden City (from 1903) and Hampstead Garden Suburb (from1905). For Bedford Park see, for example, Bolsterli, *The Early Community at Bedford Park*; for Letchworth and Hampstead Garden Suburb see, for example, Frank Jackson, *Sir Raymond Unwin*.

160. All these architects and many more are discussed and their work is illustrated in Davey, *Arts and Crafts Architecture*.

161. Webb would not have approved of the term 'English Domestic revival', with which some historians refer to Arts and Crafts houses. 'National Romanticism' could be applied to Webb's approach were it not so closely associated with some Scandinavian Arts and Crafts architecture; to Webb, however, the term itself would probably have smacked of picturesque concerns rather than reality.

162. G Jack, 'An Appreciation of Philip Webb', pp. 16–25. The influence of Webb can be seen in the illustrated work of many architects in books on Arts and Crafts architecture, for example in Davey, *Arts and Crafts Architecture*, and Hitchmough, *The Arts and Crafts Home*.

163. See Lethaby (1935), pp. 124–5. In a letter of 1892 to the AWG, quoted by Lethaby, Webb said that the prime reason he was declining the invitation to become a member was that he was not a craftsman and was too old to become one, and that he hoped the practitioners of the numerous crafts would 'be able to drop the misleading title of "designer"'.

164. Morris, 'Gothic Architecture', in *Morris on Architecture*, ed. by Miele, p. 156. For more on Webb influencing Morris rather than vice versa, see above in chapter 1, and in Kirk, 'William Morris, Philip Webb and Architecture', in *William Morris and Architecture*, ed. by Crawford and Cunningham, pp. 39–43.

165. For more on Webb's influence upon these architects, see chapter 8 of the present volume; and also see Drury, *Wandering Architects*, and Greensted, *Gimson and the Barnsleys*.

166. Hussey, *The Life of Sir Edwin Lutyens*, pp. 14 and 26. Hussey knew Lutyens well.

167. William Richard Lethaby, 'Ernest Gimson: London Days', in *Ernest Gimson*, ed. by Lethaby, pp. 2–4. For Lethaby's teaching work, see Godfrey Rubens, *William Richard Lethaby*. Prior was consulted by the SPAB about some of its cases but it is possible that he was not a member (information kindly supplied by Cecily Greenhill, Honorary Archivist, SPAB).

168. Hitchmough, *C F A Voysey*, p. 19; see John Brandon-Jones, 'C .F. A. Voysey: an introduction', in John Brandon-Jones and others, *C. F. A. Voysey*, p. 19.

169. See, for example, Pevsner, *Pioneers of the Modern Movement*.

170. Lethaby (1935), p. 88.

171. Webb on Morris, quoted in Lethaby (1935), p. 220.

CHAPTER 7: THE COUNTRY HOUSES

1. Webb's Coneyhurst (1883) is almost as large as Hurlands, so it could have been considered as a country house but, as its stable block was very small, it has been categorized as 'small house in the country', in line with Lawrence Weaver, who in 1922 added a chapter on Coneyhurst to the third edition of his *Small Houses in the Country*, (pp. 13–18).

2. Astley's obituary, *Ashton Reporter*, p. 5.

3. Graham's house, Clarisburgh Cottage, was a large building, erected around 1811 at a cost over £32,000, for which William Burn designed a large addition in 1819 (unexecuted).

4. Astley probably commissioned Stevens and Robinson, of number 10 Sackville Street, London, in 1861 or early in 1862 before his wife died. Two of their elevations and a plan, dated March 1863 (collection of the late Miss M J Becher, now in the BAL/RIBADC), are illustrated by Susan C Forster (who kindly lent me a copy of the unpublished thesis) in 'Philip Webb and the Astleys: A Re-evaluation of Webb's work at Arisaig' (figs 9, 13, and 14). Miss Becher's drawings, including several of Webb's for Arisaig House, are now in the BAL/RIBADC.

5. See G Jack, 'An Appreciation of Philip Webb', p. 4.

6. See Webb to Messrs Nathaniel Ramsay & Son, Quantity Surveyors, Glasgow, 5 January 1882, LB 1, fols 221–2. Webb found Nathaniel Ramsay helpful with his difficulties with workmen; he was involved at Arisaig again 1882, in connection with redecoration and the installation of a new drainage system designed by Webb

for Miss Gertrude Astley, who had inherited the house from her brother in 1880.

7. Brandon-Jones, 'Philip Webb', p. 252, and 'The Work of Philip Webb and Norman Shaw', p. 12.

8. The Astley sisters thought of building the chapel as a memorial to their parents and brother before deciding in 1882 to have a memorial cross by Webb instead (see chapter 12). Webb's drawings for the chapel are in the BAL/RIBADC.

9. See Webb to Constance Astley, 26 October 1880, LB 1, fols 171–3 (172). Ultimately, all but the kitchen wing (now Glen House) of the old house was demolished to provide stone. The basalt was unreliable, often fracturing whilst being worked.

10. A drawing of the porch, prepared by John Brandon-Jones from one by Webb, is illustrated in Lethaby (1979), fig. 19.

11. Webb's drawing for this church is in a private collection.

12. The photograph of the drawing room taken in 1882 shows that the wainscot was painted white when the house was first decorated (collection of the author). Webb implies in a letter that the original papers were by M&Co, which is possible as the firm was marketing them by the time the house had dried out (Webb to Gertrude Astley, 29 November 1882, LB 2, fols 1–2). In the redecoration of 1883, Webb had the woodwork of the second-floor bedrooms, for which the wallpapers had not been decided, painted the 'parchment colour white' that in his view was the only tint safe to use with paper of any colour (Webb to Gertrude Astley, 27 April 1883, LB 2, fols 9–10).

13. A photograph of this fireplace and grate *in situ* is reproduced in Forster, 'Philip Webb and the Astleys', fig. 10. Other reused items included the stone columns in the servants' hall, a stone fireplace in the kitchen, the corbels of the balcony, and internal doors.

14. The plan of Wollaton is illustrated, for example, in Girouard, *Robert Smythson & the Elizabethan Country House*, p. 98.

15. For the Mentmore living-hall (which, unlike Arisaig House, is not in a central position and has no galleries), see, for example, Franklin, pp. 66–74.

16. After being renamed, Church Hill House (well known to Webb's disciples) lapsed into obscurity until rediscovered in the early 1950s by Pevsner (see Pevsner, 'Colonel Gillum and the Pre-Raphaelites'). In 1858 and 1859, Gillum was taking lessons from Ford Madox Brown, and in 1860 or 1861 he was paying a monthly sum in advance for paintings to Rossetti, to whom he was introduced by Browning (see William Rossetti, *Some Reminiscences*, II, p. 314, and *Diaries of Boyce*, ed. by Surtees, p. 90 n.).

17. The gardener's cottage, a pyramid-roofed, whitewashed building, with shuttered casements and a central chimney, was demolished around 1966. Webb's drawing for the cottage (from the V&A, W&I) is illustrated in MacGregor, pp. 72–3, figs 7 and 8, and in Kirk, 'Philip Webb (1831–1915)', vol. 2, fig. 56.

18. On the contract drawing, the elevations are wrongly titled, a mistake apparently made by Webb's assistant, and presumably caused by the north point, roughly pencilled on the ground-floor plan, in which the west and east points are transposed. The entrance front, marked north-west on the elevation drawing, actually faced north-east, the dining-room front south-east, and the garden front south-west.

19. An EC is shown on the contract plan but as WCs are indicated on the drawings for the lodge and cottages, they might also have been installed in the house.

20. The panelling is not shown on the contract drawings, but appears on Webb's photograph of the house (private collection). The balcony was on the south-west side; it gave little protection to the French windows below it, and the bedroom windowsills were too high for easy access (illustrated in Pevsner, 'Colonel Gillum', fig. 32).

21. By the time Webb was placing greater emphasis on this feature at Joldwynds, his next country house, Shaw was replacing it with a timber beam, usually in a timber-framed gable.

22. An entry of 26 September 1860 in a Webb notebook (see Lethaby (1935), p. 37); the furniture was probably made by boys of the Home Industrial School, Euston Road, London, the management committee of which Gillum joined in 1860 (Pevsner, 'Colonel Gillum', p. 78). Two of the Gillum tables, one of them Japanese-influenced (now in the V&A), are illustrated, for example, in Pevsner, 'Art Furniture of the 1870s', AR, 101 (1952), repr. in Pevsner, *Studies in Art, Architecture and Design: Victorian and After* (p. 121, figs 6 and 7).

23. One of Webb's drawings (V&A, W&I) for the stable block is reproduced in Kirk, 'Philip Webb (1831–1915)', vol. 2, fig. 62. The block has been converted into two houses.

24. The lodge, now a private house, is illustrated in Kirk, 'Philip Webb (1831–1915)', vol. 2, fig. 61.

25. Pevsner, 'Colonel Gillum', p. 81.

26. For Mackmurdo, see Pevsner, 'Colonel Gillum', p. 81; John Brandon-Jones kindly provided the information about Winmill. Winmill's photographs are missing.

27. Webb studied all notable English buildings, and would have known Blenheim Palace in Oxfordshire and Vanbrugh's own house in Greenwich, and he studied Vanbrugh's work in Campbell's *Vitruvius Britannicus*.

28. George Edmund Street, *An Urgent Plea*, p. 14.

29. See Webb to George and Rosalind Howard, 10 August 1868, J22, Castle Howard Archives. In 1985, Mr David L Laird, factor to the Airlie Estate, brought to my attention the Cortachy drawings now lodged on loan in the National Archives of

Scotland (RHP 5167/1–13); most kindly, he searched through them but found no trace of Webb's involvement with Cortachy Castle and the House of Airlie, and he confirmed that there are no letters from Webb in the Airlie archives. Lord Airlie paid Webb £600 in 1869 (AB).

30. Having first met him professionally, Bowman had been a patron of Watts, who introduced him to the Pre-Raphaelite circle, since the early 1860s (Watts, I, p. 217).

31. In 1867 Bowman paid Webb £14 (AB); SB 1865–77, 11 November, 29 December 1869, fols 75–6. In 1870 Bowman paid Webb £110 10s 0d, presumably on account for the designing of Joldwynds or the new orchid-house.

32. Shearburn had refused to finish the alterations to the London house of Dr E Dowson (Webb to Shearburn, 1 and 11 February 1876, LB 1, fols 29–31 and 109–10).

33. See Webb to Bowman, 10 October 1887, LB 2, fols 99–100.

34. This photograph and several more of Joldwynds (and the house it replaced), taken for Webb during construction, are in a private collection. The two of them – a view from the south-west of the house under construction – are reproduced in Kirk, 'Philip Webb (1831–1915)', vol. 2, figs 64 and 66.

35. Voysey's window is illustrated, for example, in Hitchmough, *Voysey*, p. 96.

36. Holmdale (1873–80) was by Street; Hopedene (1873–74) by Shaw; Moxley (1888) by Basil Champneys; Pasturewood House (1893) by William Flockhart and Lutyens. Voysey converted a large barn into a house, and Waterhouse designed part of his brother's house, Feldemore (c. 1881). For these houses and the growth of Holmbury St Mary, see Bird, *Holmbury St Mary*.

37. Illustrated, for example, in Saint, pp. 126–7, figs 105–7.

38. Ernest Gimson to May Morris, 22 April 1915, BL Morris Papers 10, Add. Ms. 45347, fol. 118; Winmill recorded his visit to Joldwynds with the Architectural Association in a letter to Sir Sydney Cockerell (quoted in Winmill, p. 22). Stokes and May are known to have attended Stannus's excursions.

39. Other Lutyens examples include his sensitive blending of brick and stone at Tigbourne Court (1899), and his walled garden with a central pool, which resembled the Joldwynds orchid-house garden, at Deanery Garden (1901). These houses, and Homewood, are illustrated, for example, by *Weaver in Houses and Gardens by E. L. Lutyens*, pp. 42–6, 53–60, and 63–5.

40. Lowthian Bell to Webb, 1870 (private collection). No detailed description or illustration of the earlier house have been found but about sixty years ago it was remembered as a large brick building of poor quality (information from the late John Mawer, local historian). The ground area of this building, shown on one of Webb's plans in outline (ZFK MIC 2129/189, NYCRO), was similar to that of his replacement but it had fewer storeys. Judging by the many buttresses shown on the plan, it was probably in the Gothick style.

41. Hugh Bell to Webb, 17 October 1871 (private collection). The year's delay before construction began started was presumably caused by Bell having to sell all or part of his chemical works at Washington to pay for the new house.

42. Mary Bell to 'Mr. Howard', 31 October 1872, Castle Howard Archives. It is possible but unlikely that this Mr Howard was George's father, Charles.

43. These buildings, all designed before the end of 1876, and Rounton Grange, are discussed in Curry and Kirk, pp. 21–6. The cost, excluding Webb's fee, has been calculated from the latter (AB). In 1896 Webb created a dining room for upper servants in the western archway of the kitchen court, pulling the room forward. After Webb retired, George Jack added a large common room, designed 1905 to 1906 and built soon afterwards at the northern end of the north ambulatory, the glass roof of which he replaced with tiles and dormer windows. In the same decade, his small bell-turret was erected on the main roof, and he replaced the glazed south wall of the southern ambulatory with a stone one containing a garden door. He also designed and built the East Lodge (1908), a cottage for the head gardener, a pair of semi-detached cottages, and the Square (village hall with attached dwellings).

44. Webb referred to the coach-house as the 'stables'; he retained and altered some existing farm buildings and incorporated them in his coach-house, with a newly roofed central courtyard and a coachman's first-floor flat in the new south wing (ZFK MIC 2129/91–103, NYCRO). It is obvious from the detailing that he improved the west lodge but no drawings have been found; the central chimney, which (as shown in a photograph in the Gertrude Bell Archive, University of Newcastle upon Tyne) had a more elaborate top than at present, was clearly his, and probably also the pyramid roof. A 'fowl house' was built to his design in 1875.

45. Webb's undated roughly sketched plan and elevation (private collection) is reproduced in Kirk, 'Philip Webb (1831–1915)', vol. 2, fig. 72. He also sketched the rough outline of what it has been suggested were his first thoughts about the new house, but judging from the greater likeness to his final scheme, it is more likely to represent his first thoughts after the pele-based design was abandoned (SB 1865–77).

46. According to his County Lists of old buildings he had visited (private collection), Webb had seen these buildings, and castles of the same type at Langley, Northumberland, and Sheriff Hutton, North Yorkshire.

47. Some minor offices were to have been retained, but sometime after December 1872, possibly after building began, Webb redesigned the 'barmkin', increasing the area of first-floor family rooms (his original ground-floor plan appears in Lawrence Weaver's paper 'Rounton Grange, Yorkshire, A Seat of Sir Hugh Bell, Bart.', p. 911). The cubicles, all painted white, were preferable to shared rooms, and constituted better accommodation than that of many public schools at the time.

48. Wall ducts carried fresh air up from the cellars; stale air was taken up the chimneys, emerging just above the tiles or continuing to the top; bedroom fireplaces had similar fresh-air ducts.

49. The garden door in the drawing-room bay window, shown on the early plan, was omitted but sometime before 1896 Webb inserted double doors, which George Jack replaced later to a different design.

50. Webb added the clock tower, not shown on the early plans, after building had begun.

51. The plunge-bath, a small swimming pool of twenty-six feet six inches by fourteen feet, and from three feet to five feet deep, was constructed (drawing: ZFK MIC 2129/511–516, NYCRO); it was apparently filled in when Jack's common room (1905–06) was built east of the house at the northern end of the ambulatory.

52. The triangular hood-moulds were stone versions of the timber ones of Joldwynds, and the segmental ones were actually part of the joggled voussoirs; the oriel might have been inspired by that of Castle Acre Priory. The east windows of the drawing room were to have had ogee arches but after one had been constructed, it was decided to make them segmental (drawing, 20 May 1876, ZFK MIC 2095/521, NYCRO).

53. In the hilly terrain of Cragside (enlarged by R N Shaw in several stages between 1869 and 1884) in Northumberland, Lord Armstrong, a friend of Lowthian Bell, was able to generate electricity by hydraulic power and, using his engineering expertise, to install a passenger lift sometime between 1870 and 1880. Webb's convected warm-air grates were up-to-date, however; at Rounton he used them to heat the room in which they were fitted and, at Willinghurst, he used some to heat adjacent rooms.

54. Some panels from the demolished house were also reused; the late Mr George William Dale, who undertook the task, told me about the beer wash (21 April 1980).

55. *The Romance of the Rose* frieze, now faded, is in the William Morris Gallery, Walthamstow (F. 140), and there is one drawing for it at Wallington Hall, Northumberland. The pedestals for the figures, and several of the animals, are obviously Webb's work, a supposition supported by the entries (with no payment recorded) in his Morris & Co. Account Book (fols 65 and 67) for the 'Arrangement for Mr. Bell's Tapestry'. Lethaby recorded Webb's belief that there should be an object of special interest at a high level in the rooms of large houses (Lethaby (1935), p. 94).

56. Webb told Lowthian Bell by letter that he would design the sideboard [which is missing] (4 April 1877, LB 1, fols 78–9 (fol. 78)); Weaver records that Webb designed the table [presumably at about the same time as the sideboard] (Weaver, 'Rounton Grange', p. 911). Giles Ellwood, in 'Three Tables by Philip Webb', suggests that some late-seventeenth- or early-eighteenth-century Spanish tables were the source of inspiration for the form and the carved ornament of the Rounton table. Webb might indeed have seen such tables in the South Kensington Museum, but he disapproved of taking inspiration from a foreign source. There is a strong similarity but spiral carving had been used in England since the Middle Ages.

57. With one exception, all the people consulted about Rounton described it as having been beautiful. The following artists and architects stayed at Rounton Grange: the artists Boyce, H T Wells, E J Poynter, T M Rooke, A W Hunt, W B Richmond, Frank Bramley, Herbert Marshall, and George Howard; and the architects R J Johnson, A E Street, and A M Poynter (Rounton Grange Visitors Book, the collection of Sir John and Lady Bell). Apparently, Rounton was first illustrated, though not discussed, by Ernest Willmott in *English House Design*, figs 76 and 77.

58. I am most grateful to Mrs F H Towill (Polly Godman) for kindly providing this and further information about Smeaton Manor and her grandparents.

59. The Ada Godman Diaries are in a private collection.

60. Webb's four contract drawings, dated June 1877 (V&A, W&I) are illustrated in John Brandon-Jones, 'Notes on the Building of Smeaton Manor' in *Architectural History*, 1 (1958), pp. 31–58 (pp. 37–8). The letters from Webb to Godman in this paper demonstrate Webb's keen attention to such matters as the services, garden walls, and animal welfare, as well as to those of the house and its fixtures and fittings.

61. Whilst the house was being built, the Godmans lived in their Queen Anne house (East House) in Great Smeaton. Webb's letter to Godman of 15 August 1878 mentions the future extension of the wing (Brandon-Jones, 'Notes on the Building of Smeaton Manor', pp. 33–4).

62. See MMF&Co AB.

63. That Webb conceived this Idea at an early stage is shown by the similarity between the outline plan, sketched on his first site inspection (SB 1865–77, fol. 121), and that of the final building. He reflected the character and design of the local houses without copying them; for instance, he did not use the local 'kneelers' (stone corbels) and stone 'water tabling' (copings) on the gables. The striking detailing of the projecting ground-floor windows on the south front is entirely Webb's invention.

64. The plan of King's Weston is illustrated in Campbell's *Vitruvius Britannicus*, I, pl. 41.

65. The plan of Bryanston is illustrated, for example, by Saint in *Shaw*, (p. 329, fig. 241), as is that of Alderbrook (p. 105, fig. 87). Lethaby, too, for example, made use of a transverse cross-passage at Avon Tyrell, Hampshire (1891).

66. Winslow Hall, often attributed to Sir Christopher Wren, is illustrated, for example, by Nikolaus Pevsner in *Buckinghamshire*, p. 43.

67. These rods were discovered during alteration work in c. 1980; Clive Cruddas of the architectural practice Dennis Lister and Associates kindly brought them to my attention.

68. The gable is sketched in pencil on the Smeaton Manor contract elevation (E.141–1916). The envisaged cost of educating his many children led Charles North to withdraw his commission for a country house to be built on the site of the old Rougham Hall (demolished c. 1780; North then further enlarged a house he had already created from a laundry building of 1692 into the present Rougham Hall; Mrs Pamela North kindly gave me this information by letter, 19 June 1984). Webb would have destroyed any finished drawings.

69. Webb had used a similar device at Rounton Grange to gain access to the picture gallery from a pavilion roof; during alterations in 1980, another was erected at Smeaton to gain access to the east-wing attics.

70. The manager George Wardle helped Mrs Godman to choose papers and paint colours at Smeaton on 27 March 1880 (Ada Godman Diaries, private collection).

71. Ada Godman Diaries (private collection). The damaged fireplace panels, designed in 1885, are in a private collection; the fireplace is illustrated in Brandon-Jones, 'Notes on the Building of Smeaton Manor', p. 49.

72. Mrs Godman consulted Webb about the hangings on 16 July 1877; he decided their sizes, then Morris designed the pattern. After receiving the design in August, she started working them in September 1877, and the first finished section was exhibited in March 1889 at the Kunst Gewerbe Halle in Dresden (Ada Godman Diaries, private collection). Photographs by Ada Godman show the hangings in the drawing room (private collection); one of them, and her photograph of the hall, are reproduced in Kirk, 'Philip Webb (1831–1915)', vol. 2, figs 87, 89. One piece is now in the Victoria & Albert Museum, the major part is in the Fitzwilliam Museum, and a large section is in a private collection. Morris's design for the embroidery (V&A, W&I, 65–1898) is illustrated in colour in Zaczek, p. 177.

73. The trelliswork is not shown on the contract drawings but photographs taken by Ada Godman in 1894, some time after the climbers and the ivy on the north front had reached the eaves, show that it had been in position for many years. It would not have been installed without Webb's approval.

74. The panelling and seat, now removed, appear on an Ada Godman photograph.

75. It is indicated in pencil on Webb's stable drawing (private collection) and mentioned in Webb to Godman, 24 March and 28 May 1879 (in Brandon-Jones, 'Notes on the Building of Smeaton Manor', pp. 48, 51). The clock was the one for which Webb had added a new upper stage to the tower of Bell's Washington Hall (see chapter 9).

76. As John Brandon-Jones points out, it 'would pass without comment in a collection of Country Houses of the nineteen twenties' ('Notes on the Building of Smeaton Manor', p. 31).

77. Ricardo's entrance is illustrated in Stamp and Goulancourt, p. 198.

78. Houses which reveal the influence of Smeaton include Lutyens' Little Thakeham (1902), Heathcote (1906, a grander version in stone), Middlefield (1908), and Chussex (1909), all illustrated, for example, in Weaver, *Houses and Gardens by E. L. Lutyens*, pp. 103–11, 183–96, 232–4, and 234–6, and Ernest Willmott's Amersfort (1911–12), of which the plan is illustrated in Franklin, p. 232. Webb's disciple Alfred Powell stayed at Smeaton Manor in October 1879, when he also visited Rounton (Rounton Grange Visitors Book, private collection).

79. Brandon-Jones, 'Philip Webb', pp. 255–6.

80. See Webb to Wyndham, 12 December 1876, LB 1, fols 49–50 (Webb's reply to Wyndham's letter of 9 December); Wyndham had decided to found his own seat because he did not get on well with his brother, Lord Egremont, at Petworth. The owner of Wilbury House asked for far more than it was worth, so Wyndham did not buy it (note in rear of AddB). The estate was named Clouds in the sixteenth century, after a former owner.

81. For a full account of the Wyndhams, the designing and building of Clouds, the subsequent history of the house and life in it, see Dakers, *Clouds*. In 1890–93 Wyndham and Webb rescued and repaired the tower of East Knoyle church (see chapter 8). Lethaby discusses Clouds at length (Lethaby (1935), pp. 96–104), and Franklin discusses and illustrates the plan in *The Gentleman's House*, pp.146–50.

82. Webb to Wyndham, 12 and 28 December 1876, LB 1, fols 49–50 and 50–52; SB 1865–77, fol. 124; Webb to Wyndham, 29 and 16 January 1877, LB 1, fols 58–9 and 56–7.

83. This second scheme, which saved many trees (always a matter of concern to Webb), was accepted in October. Ada Godman records that Wyndham had talked to her 'of Rounton which he had been to see' (Ada Godman Diaries, 10 July 1877, private collection). Webb's drawing of the ground-floor plan and two elevations of the first, 1877, scheme (the Yew Tree Court design) is reproduced by Dakers in *Clouds*, p. 58, fig. 29, and his drawing of the other two elevations is reproduced in Farr, pl. 39a (BAL/RIBADC).

84. Smiths used the local stone in their work at Longford Castle (1870–75) for Salvin, and at Fonthill (1847–52) when working for William Burn.

85. Webb to Wyndham, 16 January 1877, LB 1, fols 56–7.

86. On 4 March 1880, Wyndham agreed to have quantities taken for the final design (SB 1878–92); Smith's estimate was £4,375 over the budget figure (letter, Webb to Wyndham, 3 June 1881, LB 1, fols 175–6).

87. Webb investigated recommended builders at Blandford, Frome, Tewkesbury, Oxford, Bristol, and Gloucester.

88. See Dakers, *Clouds*, p. 74. No one was hurt in the fire and most of the contents of the house were saved but some of the reused old fireplaces were destroyed, as was Burne-Jones's cartoon of the 'Annunciation and the Angels', which had hung over the main staircase.

89. Webb mentions having visited the site in his letter Webb to Wyndham, 28 December 1876 (LB 1, fols 50–51), which sets out the conditions under which he would undertake the commission.

90. Webb's four floor plans of the main block, 1881 design, are illustrated in Dakers, *Clouds*, pp. 61–62, figs 32–5 (BAL/RIBADC).

91. Webb's photographs are in a private collection; those of his own buildings and many others were taken for him, including those of Compton Wynyates, which are probably by William Weir.

92. John Howell, the tenant of the brickyard that already existed on the Clouds estate, made most of the bricks, and all the roof tiles except some from the demolished house that were used on the inner roof slopes.

93. Blunt, 'Clouds', p. 740.

94. H Muthesius, *Das englische Haus*, 1979 English edn, p. 19; in this influential book, he illustrates the hall and a perspective view of the house (2nd edn, figs 73 and 74; 1979 edn, figs 12 and 13). Shaw had used transverse arches in the hall of Adcote (designed 1975) but they were pointed and the room had a distinct medieval air (it is illustrated, for example, in Saint, p. 101, fig. 100).

95. See Webb's drawings WEBB [24] 124–28, BAL/RIBADC. Numbers 124–25 are the studies of artichokes, dated 3 August 1884; number 128 carries Webb's instructions to the modeller.

96. See Dakers, *Clouds*, pp. 90–91.

97. See SB 1878–92, 3 October 1883.

98. See Webb's instructions to the modeller on his drawing WEBB [24] 180, BAL/RIBADC; the bookcase drawing is 246–1916, verso, V&A, W&I. The unlikelihood of Byzantine work seen by Webb in Italy having influenced his designs for the Clouds ornament is discussed briefly in chapter 4 of the present volume.

99. See Webb's drawing WEBB [24] 207, BAL/RIBADC, which is reproduced in Dakers, *Clouds*, p. 92, figs 51–2.

100. There was no library at Clouds until 1911–12 when George Wyndham and Detmar Blow created one from the second-floor nurseries. Madeline and Percy Wyndham preferred to have a number of books in every room.

101. Webb mentions the 'little garden house' in his letter to Madeline Wyndham, 30 August 1884 (LB 2, fols 43–5). See chapter 13 for quotations from this letter.

102. Blunt recorded that the garden designer Alfred Parsons designed the layout of the yew hedges (Blunt, 'Clouds', p. 740). Webb's unsolicited design for the gardens is missing.

103. For the Souls, see Abdy and Gere, *The Souls*.

104. Wyndham to Webb, 13 November 1893, Clouds Correspondence (2 bound vols, private collection), quoted in Swenarton, p. 48.

105. For Shaw's admiration see Blomfield, *R. N. Shaw*, p. 12; Lethaby (1935), p. 104.

106. Saint points out that Webb amongst architects of his generation successfully resisted the large scale of practice that made such total designing impossible (*Shaw*, p. 115).

107. See Wyndham to Webb, 2 April 1886 and Webb to Wyndham, 9 July 1886 in the Clouds Correspondence (private collection). Mrs Ramsden was the widow of Ellis Gosling of Busbridge Hall, Surrey, in which house she, Ramsden, and their six children lived before moving into Willinghurst. Caroline Dakers kindly told me of the Ramsden-Muncaster-Wyndham connection.

108. Three local building firms – Mitchell Brothers, W and G King, and E and J H Holden – were each controlled by a family member with whom Webb discussed the drawings before tenders were submitted. He sent Holden and Mitchell to inspect Coneyhurst (built by Kings) so that they would be familiar with his standards.

109. Webb to G Jack, 26 and 30 May 1888 (private collection).

110. The name of the house varied during the design and construction stage between Sparelands, Lapscombe, and finally Willinghurst; Webb agreed to place the stables in this position only after learning that the demolition of an old barn which occupied it was inevitable (Webb to G Jack, 15 May 1888, private collection).

111. During construction, the lean-to roof was extended over the steps down to the garden; judging by the fact that the shutters do not cover the lower part of it, glazed doors were inserted into the west window in the bay at a later date.

112. The various changes can be seen on the drawings in the SPAB Archive.

113. SB 1878–92, 30 October 1889.

114. Webb to Ramdsen, 26 November 1886, LB 2, fol. 71.

115. The carved ornament on this fireplace is a fine example of Webb's custom of designing according to the nature of the material and the tools with which it would be worked.

116. In his letter to Webb, 2 April 1886, Wyndham wrote, 'The Ramsdens came down the other day and were much pleased with the house' (Clouds Correspondence, private collection).

117. Jack's sketch design for the summerhouse, dated 15 October 1906, is in a private collection.

118. Webb to Ramsden, 17 November 1886 (LB 2, fols 66–7), and to G Jack, 10 and 21 May 1888 (private collection).

119. Most of the information in this paragraph came to me from Mrs Elizabeth Motley, a granddaughter of the Beales, in a letter of 8 January 1986.

In the early days, before the house was built, it was referred to as 'Hollybush'. Helen Beale told her niece Mrs Motley that her parents met Webb in this way. Tomes visited Standen with Mrs Beale during its construction (CB, fol. 52); Beale's brother being physician to Bowman comes from 'Funeral of the Late Sir William Bowman at Holmbury St. Mary', *Sussex Advertiser and Country Times*, 2 April 1892. Valpy, a fellow solicitor and the owner of number 19 Lincoln's Inn Fields, probably also recommended Webb to Beale. For more on Standen, see: Garnett, *Standen, West Sussex* (the guidebook for the house); Weaver, 'Standen'; Girouard's article in CL and chapter ?? in *The Victorian Country House*, 1979 edn, pp. 381–9; and John Brandon-Jones's paper 'Arts and Crafts', which includes colour reproductions of two contract drawings (the north and south elevations of the main block, and the elevations of the east wing, BAL/RIBADC). Webb's detail drawing for the porch and staircase of one of the Standen cottages is reproduced in Richardson, pp. 20–21, figs 12–13 (BAL/RIBADC); for a photograph of the cottages, see Kirk, 'Philip Webb (1831–1915)', vol. 2, fig. 125.

120. Peters had displeased Webb by using 'much too much machinery', which had resulted in some work, notably the joinery, being done in a 'rough… and ragged way', so he was not asked to submit a price for the later work (Standen CB, fol. 67). After Webb had retired, Beale asked him to alter some bedrooms to suit changed family circumstances. Webb refused the commission and recommended George Jack, who also panelled the billiard room in 1907 (Webb to G Jack, 3 April 1902, private collection).

121. Webb recorded the Beales' wish in SB 1878–92, 11 April 1891.

122. Until the east wing was reduced in length, bringing the block of lesser offices closer to the morning room, the block was to have been at right angles to the wing. Angling the block also meant that it guided visitors to the entrance court.

123. John Brandon-Jones, consultant architect for Standen for many years, was convinced that this was Webb's intention. Mature trees later obscured this view.

124. In his paper of 1900, 'The House in the Country', in which he uses Standen as a fine example, Halsey Ricardo considers this to be a desirable attribute (p. 107).

125. Motley to Kirk, 8 January 1986.

126. Webb specified that the major parts of the house would be faced in Keymer bricks, but he added a clause that, if Horsham stocks were decided upon instead, Keymers would be used for the dressings. As John Brandon-Jones suggested to me, it seems highly likely that Webb preferred the Horshams from the start, and that Beale thought they would look too undistinguished.

127. This was noted on Webb's drawing (WEBB [42] 31, BAL/RIBADC).

128. Webb's note on his drawing (WEBB [42] 39, BAL/RIBADC); for this being Vanbrugh's way, see Beard, p. 55.

129. On his first visit to the site, Webb noted that because of their exposure, weather-tiling would be necessary on upper walls (SB 1878–92, 11 April 1891); however, the extra height of the tower, an element not initially envisaged, would have made tiles vulnerable to wind damage; the alternative was roughcast, which detracted less from the red-brick porch than tiles would have done, in the entrance court.

130. Weaver, 'Standen', p. 688.

131. Webb to Beale, 20 January 1898, NT Sta/Doc/9. Webb suggested the bay as the only way of achieving the aim without ruining the entrance front and the porch in particular; as he intended, the piano fitted into the bay window perfectly.

132. See Webb to Beale, 20 January 1898, NT Sta/Doc/9.

133. See Webb's drawing, 8 May 1891, NT Collection, Standen. Lutyens' ceiling is illustrated, for example, in *Edwin Lutyens*, ed. by Dunster, p. 54, fig. 5.

134. Helen Beale told Girouard of this promise (Girouard, *Victorian Country House*, p. 388).

135. Webb to Mrs Beale, 7 July 1894, NT Sta/Doc/11.

136. Ricardo, 'The House in the Country', p. 107.

137. See Webb's drawing WEBB [42] 59, BAL/RIBADC. Pearson made seven sconces for the room (CB, fol. 51), and the fender (missing). Many other light-fittings and lamps in the house were by W A S Benson (1854–1924), the architect-designer who specialised in such items and sold them through his London shop.

138. There are 11 Morris & Co. estimates and bills at Standen (NT Sta/Doc/72–83). A few pieces are by the cousins Rhoda and Agnes Garrett, interior decorators known to Webb through their friendship with Lucy Orrinsmith (Charles Faulkner's sister). The embroideries included two panels based on the *Artichoke* pattern designed by Morris for Ada Godman, and worked by Mrs Beale and her three eldest daughters.

139. For an illustrated description and discussion of the gardens see Arthur Hellyer, 'Gardens for a Late-Victorian House: Standen, East Grinstead, West Sussex'. Mrs Beale describes the development of the garden in her diaries (NT Collection, Standen); the gardens are described and illustrated in Garnett, pp. 70-79.

140. Motley to Kirk, 8 January 1986.

141. Ricardo, 'The House in the Country', pp. 105–11, and Weaver, 'Standen', pp. 666–72.

142. The chimney breast and archway are illustrated, for example, in Weaver, *Houses and Gardens by Lutyens*, pp. 23 and 40, figs 43 and 71.

143. These are illustrated in Lionel Lambourne, p. 179, fig. 211.

144. By C H B Quennell, Arthur T Bolton, and Lawrence Weaver in *The House and its Equipment*, ed. by Weaver, pp. 21, 28, 32–3, and 44, figs 28, 40, 49–52, and 67.

145. The final cost of the house, excluding the stables, slightly exceeded the budget

because Miss Cocks requested many extras, including fireplaces, panelling, cupboards in the drawing room and dining room, and a fitted sideboard. Webb's elevation drawing and his design for the stables (from the SPAB Archive) are reproduced in Kirk, 'Philip Webb (1831–1915)', vol. 2, figs 127 and 133. Andrew Robinson kindly supplied useful information about this house.

146. Webb intended it to face due south but, after Miss Cocks urged him to consider shelter from cold winds as well as the aspects of rooms, he turned it a little westwards to match the orientation of Standen (SB 1896–1900, 27 February 1897).

147. The wall from the stables met the blind-arcaded wall from the house at forty-five degrees, not as shown on the contract plan.

148. On the contract plan, the ground-floor passage ran through the kitchen and scullery but during construction a wall was added to separate them from it.

149. SB 1896–1900, 17 September 1897.

150. Webb to A H Powell, 3 December 1898 (quoted in Lethaby (1935), p. 124); the walls were 'rough-rendered … with Portland cement and sand, and then plastered and rough-casted'. Old photographs (private collection) show that though the roughcast was colourwashed a pale shade, the cement-rendered string below it was a still paler shade, and palest of all was the white-painted woodwork.

151. This porch now has a flat roof supported on timber posts.

152. The panelled surrounds have been removed, and the stone surround of the dining-room fireplace is now in what was the hall.

153. SB 1896–1900; see, for example, the entries for 26 April and 13 December 1897.

154. Steep Hill is illustrated, for example, in Blomfield and Newton, p. 55, and Overstrand Hall and the Pleasaunce, for example, in Weaver, Houses and Gardens by Lutyens, pp. 48 and 51, figs 86 and 95.

155. Helen Beale bought the house from the family trust so that she could bequeath it to the nation. The endowment she bequeathed with it was insufficient but the Grogans' payment of a large sum for a long lease of the house, and their undertaking of repairs and renovations, and acting as honorary administrators, made it possible for the National Trust to accept the house.

156. Hussey, 'Joldwynds', p. 276.

CHAPTER 8: THE SOCIETY FOR THE PROTECTION OF ANCIENT BUILDINGS

1. Morris's daughter May Morris in her *DNB* entry on Webb, p. 561.
2. Pugin, *Contrasts*, pp. 19–20.
3. Ibid., p. 22.
4. Ruskin, *Seven Lamps* (1849), chapter 6, subsection xviii.
5. John Ruskin, *The Opening of the Crystal Palace*, pp. 19–20.
6. Lethaby (1935), pp. 6–7. Webb's Account Book shows that he bought *Seven Lamps* in 1856; he might have read it previously, of course.
7. Chris Miele covers the increasing concern about restorations, and this sequence of events, in his informative 'The Conservationist', in *William Morris*, ed. by Parry, pp. 72–87.
8. Morris to the Editor, *Athenæum*, 5 March 1877, quoted in full in Mackail, I, pp. 351–2; see the report of the meeting, SPAB Archive.
9. De Morgan told Mackail of this in a letter (quoted in Mackail, I, p. 356).
10. The manifesto appears in full in Mackail, I, pp. 352–55.
11. Ruskin, *The Opening of the Crystal Palace*, p. 10.
12. See Webb to the Committee of the Ruskin Memorial (Westminster Abbey) Fund, undated [but of 1899], quoted at length in Lethaby (1935), p.152.
13. George Edmund Street, 'Destructive Restoration on the Continent', p. 345.
14. Ian Bradley draws attention to this in *William Morris and his World*, p. 71.
15. For more on this friendship, and for quoted passages from some of Boni's letters to Webb, see Lethaby (1935), pp. 163–71. Boni became the Italian government's Chief Architect for Ancient Buildings and Cultural Monuments. For more on the SPAB's influence abroad, see Chris Miele's 'The Conservationist' (p. 81), to which I am indebted for factual information.
16. During a debate (by correspondence) with Hale White, Webb wrote that the subject was so large 'that I must fail in making my point clear in writing, for which I have no natural aptitude, and have never been taught.' (28 October 1899, MR 10/19, Central Library, Bedford). On being invited to lecture on the SPAB to the students of the Architectural Association, Webb replied that he would adhere to his 'habit of reserve' in promulgating his 'own ideas on art matters'; however, he added that if in this particular case he had 'possessed any clear aptitude for impressing an audience' with what he 'considered the truth of the subject', he might have accepted (Webb to John Hebb, 10 October 1877, LB 1, fol. 104).
17. For example, the 'Thirteenth Annual Report' of the SPAB.
18. See, for example, Webb to Lady Fitzhardinge, 10 May 1877, to Charles Milnes Gaskell, 6 July 1877, and to Salisbury Baxendale, 4 February 1878, LB 1, fols 91–2, 98–9, and 116–17.
19. Lethaby (1935), p. 144.
20. Lethaby (1935), p. 150.
21. Webb to Cockerell, 25 April 1903, in *Friends of a Lifetime*, ed. by Meynell, p. 111; to Hale White, 26 July 1898 and 5 January 1902, MR 10/9, MR 10/21, Central Library, Bedford; to Morris, 17 June 1896, V&A, NAL, 86.TT.13, fol. 76 (quoted by Brandon in 'Philip Webb, the Morris Circle, and Sussex', p. 10); to Cockerell, 20 September 1905, V&A, NAL, 86.TT.16 (quoted in ibid., p. 9).
22. Webb to Hale White, 19 February 1888, MR 10/4, Central Library, Bedford.
23. Webb to Weir, July 1900, V&A, NAL, 86.TT.13.

24. Webb to G Y Wardle, 9 May 1899, SPAB Archive, East Knoyle File (quoted in Drury, *Wandering Architects*, p. 33). Drury's book contains a great deal about Webb and the SPAB and the direct influence he exerted upon the younger architect members of the society.
25. Webb to Hale White, 1 March 1888, MR 10/5, Central Library, Bedford.
26. George Bernard Shaw to Webb, 29 December 1896, and to Ellen Terry, 11 January 1897, published in *Bernard Shaw*, ed. by Laurence, pp. 714–19; the Shaw and Webb letter of protest is the first letter under the heading 'Must Peterborough Perish?', in *Saturday Review*, 2 January 1897, pp. 7–9 (p. 7).
27. Webb to Salisbury Baxendale, 6 July 1877, LB, 1, fols 98–9 (fol. 98).
28. Webb to Salisbury Baxendale, 4 February 1878, LB 1, fols 116–17 (fol. 117).
29. Webb to Howard, 9 September 1875, J22/64, Castle Howard Archives.
30. For more information on the tower see: Rory Spence, 'Theory and Practice in the early Work of the Society for the Protection of Ancient Buildings', pp. 7–9; and Burman, '"A Stern Thinker and Most Able Constructor": Philip Webb, Architect', pp. 17–19; and on the house, G Ll Morris, 'Lake House'. In his paper, Burman discusses Webb's relationship with and work for the SPAB, and his handling of his private repair and enlargement of old buildings. Webb's handling of such commissions is covered in chapter 9 of the present volume, and in Kirk, 'Philip Webb (1831–1915)', vol. 1, part 1 (chapter 3, pp. 64–5) and part 3, (chapter 6, pp. 356–64, 366–8, and 370–84).
31. Ruskin, *The Opening of the Crystal Palace*, p. 10.
32. Webb and George Bernard Shaw, 'Must Peterborough Perish?', p. 8.
33. Webb to G Y Wardle, 9 May 1899, SPAB Archive, East Knoyle File (quoted in Drury, *Wandering Architects*, p. 33).
34. Webb's drawings are in the BAL/RIBADC (Eglwys Brewis, WEBB [11]; Eglwys Cummin, WEBB [12]); and the SPAB Archive (Eglwys Cummin).
35. Hugh Fairfax-Cholmeley, who had worked with C R Asbee's Guild of Handicraft at the Toynbee Hall settlement in London, recognized the influence of Webb in his new house (see Drury, *Wandering Architects*, p. 28).
36. See Drury, 'The Wandering Architects', in *William Morris and Architecture*, ed. by Crawford and Cunningham, pp. 84, 87, and 88. Blow and his career are investigated in Drury's paper and in *Wandering Architects*. Webb helped to arrange Blow's apprenticeship as a stonemason; a note in Webb's hand, 'Blow apprenticed here.1894' in his address book is in reference to Blow's being apprenticed in Newcastle, not to Webb himself as has sometimes been thought (AddB, fol. 89). In 1895, Blow was initiated into the Friendly Society of Stone Masons, Newcastle Lodge (see Drury, *Wandering Architects*, p. 36)
37. See Drury, 'The fall and rise of Stonehenge', pp. 8–9, and *Wandering Architects*, pp. 109–15. The SPAB had been concerned for some years about the condition of several of the stones, and had collaborated on the matter with Webb's client and eminent archaeologist, General Augustus Pitt-Rivers. The society was in favour of re-erecting the fallen stones but in the event this was not done until 1958; all that was done under Blow's supervision in 1901 was to straighten a leaning stone in the inner ring.
38. Lethaby and Sidney Barnsley had set up their practices near Webb's chambers; Gimson shared Barnsley's office that was next door to Webb's. They all visited Webb frequently (Lethaby almost daily in the 1890s), as did Detmar Blow who on occasions was probably accompanied by his friend Lutyens, who also lived near Webb. Troup and Robert Weir Schultz shared an office in Gray's Inn, and would be in frequent touch with Webb, with whom Winmill regularly took evening walks. Thackeray Turner told Lethaby how he used to show Webb his own designs after the SPAB meetings, and to call upon him, when they had 'most interesting talks about building materials and construction', on which subjects his mentor's knowledge was 'wonderful' (Lethaby (1935), p. 150).
39. Lethaby, 'Ernest Gimson: London Days', in *Ernest Gimson*, ed. by Lethaby, pp. 2–4.
40. George Jack also taught woodwork at the Central School of Arts and Crafts, as did Halsey Ricardo, who ran the architectural design classes, and Troup, who taught lead-work. Like Lethaby, they were all deeply influenced by Webb's approach to architectural design and by his work. For more on the Central School of Arts and Crafts, see Rubens, *Lethaby*; for Troup, see Jackson, Troup.
41. [H. Thackeray Turner,] *Notes on the Repair of Ancient Buildings issued by the Society for the Protection of Ancient Buildings.*
42. If indeed he had helped to Turner to write the notes, Webb would not have allowed his name to be appended, and his good friend Turner probably would not have cared to take the full credit.
43. Powys, *Repair of Ancient Buildings*. Burman points out this unfortunate effect of Powys's book in '"A Stern Thinker"' (p. 19).

CHAPTER 9: ALTERATIONS AND ENLARGEMENTS

1. The quoted words are from the account of his fee and expenses for visiting and advising on Moynes House, Suffolk, which Webb sent to Lt. Col. Cecil Ives in December 1881 (LB 1, fol. 218). Webb did nothing more for this client.
2. Webb to George Howard, 18 June 1877, J22/64, Castle Howard Archives.
3. Between 1860 and 1865, Webb added domestic offices and stables (all demolished) to a house at Hatfield for C Drage; this commission was Webb's only alteration and enlargement job of any size before Cranmer Hall. As Jones paid the first instalment of Webb's fee on account in November 1864, the commission must have been received in early 1864 or possibly late 1863 (AB). In 1865, Webb designed the tracery lights of the two MMF&Co windows in All Saints,

Sculthorpe (MMF&Co AB).

4. As Webb almost always submitted his final account six months after the work was finished, and his account for Cranmer was settled in 1867, completion must have been in late 1866 or early 1867 (AB). Sir Willoughby apparently recorded in a notebook that the stables were designed by Webb and built in 1866 (this information and much more was kindly supplied by Josephine de Bono); his grandson Lawrence E Jones writes about Webb's work at Cranmer, and the changes that he (and W Crossman, the next owner, who in 1948 took down most of Webb's clock tower and removed the top storey of the original house) made to it, in *Georgian Afternoon*. The stable block, listed Grade II★, is now a dwelling; most of Webb's exterior features remain, including the entrance archway.

5. Webb's niches appear in an undated photograph of the hall in *Burke's and Savills Guide to Country Houses*, III: *East Anglia*, p. 101.

6. See Jones, *Georgian Afternoon*, pp. 166–67. Jones ignored Henry Stuart Goodhart-Rendel's plea to leave Webb's work untouched but he allowed the drawing room to be photographed before it was dismantled; the photographs, now apparently missing, were given to the V&A in 1930.

7. For Newcastle entrepreneurs being Pre-Raphaelite patrons see, for example, Dianne Sachko Macleod, 'Avant-Garde Patronage in the North East'; Ruskin was on his way to lecture to the Newcastle upon Tyne Literary and Philosophical Society (*The Winnington Letters*, ed. by Burd, p. 413). Lowthian Bell (who appears not to have been related to M A Bell of Winnington) was then mayor of Newcastle, and he and most of his family were members of the society; the family had connections with one London painter, Herbert Menzies Marshall (1841–1913), whose brother had married the sister of Hugh Bell's first wife. It is possible that Webb began work on Washington Hall before enlarging Cranmer Hall (Hugh Bell thought he might have started in 1863 (Sir Hugh Bell to George Jack, 9 June 1915, private collection)) but Cranmer has been covered first because Jones paid Webb on account before Lowthian Bell did so.

8. A drawing relating to the south-western, entrance addition, dated January 1867, shows that this and not the north-eastern enlargement was the second one (ZFK MIC 2129/128–130, NYCRO). In memory of his wife, Lowthian Bell offered to give the hall to the City of Newcastle as a convalescent home but, because of unforeseen financial implications and his own antipathy to the suggestion that the patients should contribute to the cost of their care, with the agreement of the city council he gave it instead to Miss Emma Watson, as a home for destitute boys. Later, it became in succession a Dr Barnardo's Home, a National Coal Board training centre, and a school for maladjusted boys; at present, it is a nursing home.

9. The wall between Webb's dining room and Higham's adjacent room has been removed together with some of the wainscot and the sideboard (which appears on Webb's drawing WEBB [46] 4, BAL/RIBADC).

10. Webb's drawings for the tower-top are missing but it is outlined in pencil on his drawing WEBB [46] 2, BAL/RIBADC and he mentions his drawing for the clock room at Washington in his letter to Godman, 28 May 1879 (see Brandon-Jones, 'Notes on the Building of Smeaton Manor', p. 53). Higham's spire appears in his perspective drawing of the house (photocopy in the author's collection).

11. Webb to Howard, 6 September 1869, J22/64, Castle Howard Archives.

12. In 1865, before being commissioned to design number 1 Palace Green for the Howards, Webb did a small, unidentified job for them, such as a house inspection or the design of a fireplace (AB).

13. The neo-Gothic wing might have been designed by R and R Dickinson of Edinburgh, who added a stair-tower and a Gothic porch, and Gothicized the hall, in 1821 (Cortachy drawings in GD16,Airlie papers, National Archives of Scotland (RHP 5167/1–13)). Mr D L Laird, factor to the Airlie Estate, found no trace of Webb's involvement with Cortachy Castle and the House of Airlie in the Airlie archives.

14. Webb to George and Rosalind Howard, 10 August 1868, J22/64, Castle Howard Archives.

15. Webb was paid in 1869 (AB). Webb's bookcases were replaced in 1949.

16. After the addition to Cortachy of a small Scottish Baronial wing by David Bryce (demolished later), Lady Airlie told her sister that Webb's library was the most satisfactory room in the castle (Blanche Airlie to Rosalind Howard, n.d., J23, Castle Howard Archives). For Lady Airlie's perfidy and a more detailed account of Webb's problems with these clients, see Dakers, 'Castle in the Air', p. 277.

17. Webb confirmed by letter that he would accept the post after his Statement of Business Arrangements, contained in the letter, had been accepted (Webb to Richard Du Cane [the representative of the trustees of the estate], 17 February 1877, C575/7, Howard Papers).

18. Webb's drawing for the clock-face is WEBB [69], BAL/RIBADC; the clock is illustrated in McEvoy, 'Webb at Brampton', p. 44, fig. 6. At this time, Webb also designed several fireplaces for the castle and added double doors with a fixed light above to Belted Will's Room in the Howard Tower (WEBB [69], BAL/RIBADC).

19. Webb's drawings for the Bower are in a private collection. George Jack raised the height of Salvin's crenellations on the Morpeth Tower in 1907 (drawing, private collection).

20. Webb had intimated that if the lower part of the library fittings (on one wall and presumably by Salvin) were not disturbed, he might consider the installing of high-level shelving (Webb to Rosalind Howard, 29 August 1877, J22/64, Castle Howard Archives). Clearly she persuaded him to do so as, during the visit, he

produced the pencil sketch on the reverse of a letter; although unsigned, the technique is typical of Webb's quick sketches and it was entitled, apparently at the time and with the same pencil, 'P. Webb's design for library bookshelves at Naworth Castle September 1877', in what appears to be Rosalind's hand (J22/64, Castle Howard Archives). Perhaps Webb made accurate drawings, and destroyed them after resigning (his designs for the two sets of bookcases, and his plan showing the arrangement of those proposed for the library (on which the two 'future' spiral stairs are indicated), are in a private collection).

21. Webb to George Howard, 8 September 1879, J22/64, Castle Howard Archives.

22. Ferguson's drawings for the fireplace and cupboard doors are in a private collection (they were made known to me after the submission of my doctoral thesis, in which Webb is credited with the arrangement and detailed design). Burne-Jones told Howard by letter (15 January 1885, Castle Howard Archives) that Webb had designed the frame and helped with the drawing. Howard commissioned the large oil painting, *The Sleep of King Arthur in Avalon* from Burne-Jones to hang on the blank wall above the fireplace but, realizing it was Jones's magnum opus, he relinquished it (*Burne-Jones Talking*, ed. by Lago, footnote p. 38) and bought the tapestry instead.

23. Webb to Lady Fitzhardinge, 18 May 1875, LB 1, fols 22–3 (fol. 22). By the later twentieth century, Webb's connection with the castle had been forgotten, and there is no record of it in the Berkeley Archive (this was kindly checked and confirmed in 1985 by the Honorary Archivist for Berkeley Castle, D J H Smith, Gloucestershire County and Diocesan Archivist). This work is referred to in seven letters to the Lord and Lady Fitzhardinge and one to their estate manager J H Cooke in Webb's LB 1, and a few entries about this work in his SB 1865–77. The bench seats and the wainscot were removed, and the fireplace was stripped of its paint or replaced by an older one, in the 1920s.

24. Webb to Lady Fitzhardinge, 25 July 1876, LB 1, fols 40–43 (fol. 42).

25. Webb to Lady Fitzhardinge, 10 May 1877, LB 1, fols 91–2 (fol. 91). The windows were re-glazed, probably with some new as well as the old heraldic devices, between 1918 and 1939, so it is not clear whether or not Morris & Co. executed either of Webb's re-glazing schemes. His designs for the borders and quarries were used in 1884 for a Morris & Co. window at Holmstead, Liverpool (see Sewter, II, pp. 14–15).

26. Possibly Webb had been recommended by Greene's fellow MP, the Hon. Charles Howard (father of George Howard) or by Sir Willoughby Jones of Cranmer Hall. Local historian N R Winwell kindly provided information, including the fact that there was no knowledge locally of Webb's involvement. He is not mentioned in W R Rayner's *The History of Nether Hall and the Various Owners*, an undated booklet published by the Nether Hall Country Club in the late 1970s or 1980s, which contains a reproduction of an old print showing the timber-framed house, with four parallel gabled roofs, and one of a map dated 1620 bearing a sketch of the south front, which by then had been encased in brick, including the gables. For more on Greene, see Wilson, *Greene King*.

27. The map in an 1865 sales brochure for the estate shows the main entrance on the south front (Maps. PS. 18. 120, University Library, University of Cambridge); the term 'Garden Hall' is used on Webb's undated ground-floor plan of the hall, which includes his alterations and additions and, apart from one for the dining-room sideboard, is his only Nether Hall drawing known to have survived (the plan is in a private collection; it is reproduced in Kirk, 'Philip Webb (1831–1915), vol. 2, fig. 210).

28. The wing, water tower, and porch exist but the kitchen yard and minor offices were demolished; a ballroom was added in 1974 when the hall became a country club. The stable block is not by Webb. Nether Hall is now a private residence.

29. In the 1890s, after Greene's death, the house was enlarged and altered for his son by an unidentified architect, who added canted bay windows on two floors to Webb's projections but left the buttresses, gables, and chimneys intact (all remain). A photograph, in the Jarmon Collection (Suffolk County RO) shows this front before the 1890s alteration.

30. On a coloured view of the house from the south, made after Webb's alterations but before the 1890s re-fenestration, his west-front gables and pinnacles can just be seen (the print accompanies 'Nether Hall, near Thurston, Suffolk – Greene', in *County Seats of the Noblemen and Gentlemen of Great Britain and Ireland*, ed. by F O Morris, IV, pp. 56-8, plates and plate pp. not numbered). The unidentified architect, whose work is heavier and less pleasing than Webb's, added mullion-and-transom bay windows to the south front, extended the house on the eastern side (encasing Webb's breakfast bay), removed the butler's pantry from the entrance hall, installed new wainscot and fireplaces in the garden hall, and probably designed the stable block.

31. For the tiles Webb designed for M&Co, see Richard and Hilary Myers, *William Morris Tiles*, in which one of the Nether Hall fireplaces is illustrated (p. 120, fig. 213).

32. Webb's hall fireplace, part of the dining room as decorated by Webb, and a pier, the railings, and gate are illustrated in Austin Caverhill, *Rushmore – then and now* (Amesbury: for Sandroyd School [n.d.]), pp. 23, 25, and 32. For more on the client, see, for example, M W Thompson, *General Pitt-Rivers*. Webb's drawing for the gatehouse (V&A, W&I, E. 163–1916) is reproduced in Kirk, 'Philip Webb (1831–1915)', vol. 2, fig. 221; for more information about Webb's work for Pitt-Rivers, see ibid., vol. 1, pp. 370–72. Neil Jackson discusses Webb's gatehouse, and illustrates the final gates in 'Webb of Intrigue', BD, 17 June 1983, pp. 20–21.

By coincidence, the Sandroyd School for boys moved from Sandroyd, the studio-house Webb had designed for Spencer Stanhope, into Rushmore House (which is listed Grade II), where it remains.

33. For more information on Webb's other alteration and enlargements for his Greek clients, including the work on number 1 Holland Park, see the Catalogue of Architectural Works in the present volume, and Kirk, 'Philip Webb (1831–1915)', vol. 1, part 3, chapter 6; Webb's plan of the gallery and his drawings for A A Ionides's garden room (unexecuted) and smoking room are illustrated in vol. 2 (figs. 208, 218, and 219). For more on the Ionides house, see Day, 'A Kensington Interior'; Crane, *Ideals in Art*, pp. 131 and 258–61; G Ll Morris, 'On Philip Webb's Town Work'; J Gleeson White, 'An Epoch-Making House'.

34. Webb's Site Book 1877–92 and his relevant Certificate Book contain references to this job. Laurence Turner did some carving, and Kate Faulkner some gilding, for the gallery. No. 23 Second Avenue is now divided, with the gallery serving as a snooker-room for the ground floor flat.

35. Jean-Paul Marix Evans kindly provided invaluable information and a copy of the relevant section of his unpublished history 'Journal of an Ancient Manor'. Three articles, with contemporary photographs, are good sources: 'Great Tangley Manor, Surrey, the Country House of Mr. Wickham Flower'; 'Great Tangley Manor, Surrey, the seat of Mr. Wickham Flower'; and Jekyll, attributed to, 'Great Tangley Manor, Surrey, the residence of the Late Mr. Wickham Flower'. The gardens are illustrated and discussed in Hitchmough, *Arts and Crafts Gardens*, pp. 75–84. For a plan and elevation of the cottages, based on Webb's drawing (BAL/RIBADC), see Kirk, 'Philip Webb (1831–1915)', vol. 2, fig. 228. The stables and cottages exist, the latter in separate ownership, one of them considerably enlarged.

36. Webb to Wickham Flower, 11 September 1885, LB 2, fols 47–8.

37. There are several photographic illustrations of the screen, alone and in relation to the covered bridge, in Jekyll, attributed to, 'Great Tangley Manor'.

38. Contemporary photographs of the library and one of the bedrooms above it are reproduced in Cooper, *The Opulent Eye*, pp. 102 and 103 (pls. 50 and 51). The fireplace in the library was amended or replaced, and a bay window was inserted on the east wall, in the twentieth century.

39. SB 1892–96, 8 September 1893 and 7 April 1894.

40. For Webb's belief that nothing more should be added, see Webb to George Price Boyce, September 1894, BL Add. MS 45354, and Jekyll, attributed to, 'Great Tangley Manor', p. 96. In 1948, Jack's bedroom range was demolished, and his music room was divided horizontally; at about the same time Webb's entrance hall was extended into the veranda and made into a full-height pseudo great hall, his and the older offices at the rear of the building were rendered, and the timbers of the 1582 front were painted black. In 1974, a subdued red-brick range containing an indoor swimming pool was added off Jack's music room; in the late 1970s a U-shaped wing of three rooms was built as a link between the original kitchen and Webb's library, at the rear of the house.

41. Webb to George Boyce, 11 September and 23 November 1885, BL Add. MS 45354.

42. Letters, Webb to George Boyce, 23 November 1885, BL Add. MS 45354. Flower certainly asked his opinion about the exact positioning of one yew hedge (Webb to Flower, 11 September, 1885, LB 2, fols 47–8). For a contemporary photograph of the western enclosed garden, see 'In the Garden: Flowers by Water Edge at Great Tangley', p. 420.

43. Webb to George Jack, 23 May 1888, kept loose in LB 2. Cassella was a Maker to the Admiralty & Ordnance, in London. Webb's drawing for the base of the sundial is included on E.107–1916 (V&A, W&I), and that for the dial itself on WEBB [43] 2 (BAL/RIBADC).

44. In the mid-1990s, Jean-Paul Marix Evans replaced this bridge exactly according to Webb's drawing (illustrated in Richardson, p. 18, fig. 9 (BAL/RIBADC)). The original bridge is illustrated in Hitchmough, *Arts and Crafts Gardens*, p. 80.

45. The original pergola and its replacement are illustrated, respectively, in Jekyll, attributed to, 'Great Tangley Manor', p. 94, and in Hitchmough, *Arts and Crafts Gardens*, p. 83.

46. For the history of the house, see, for example, Aslet, 'Forthampton Court', CL, 166 (27 September and 11 October 1979), pp. 938–41 and 1166–9 (Webb's part is covered in the second paper); the illustrations include a watercolour of Keck's front (p. 939, pl. 3). W B Moffat's scheme of 1846 for a complete remodelling of the house was abandoned; in 1860 Armstrong inserted a new main staircase and remodelled the entrance hall in the Jacobean style (the late Gerald Yorke kindly provided this and other information, and permitted the photographing of the papers relating to Webb's work in the Yorke Archive, now in the Gloucester RO).

47. Yorke explained this course of events to Emery Walker, who related what he said in a letter to Lethaby (quoted extensively in Lethaby, p. 105–6); for Webb's full report and passages from other documents in the Yorke Archive, see Helen Smith, 'Philip Webb's Restoration of Forthampton Court, Gloucestershire'. Interestingly, Yorke affirmed that Burges had made a plan for altering the house; probably this would have been around 1863, when he designed the nearby almshouses for Yorke's father.

48. Webb's timber-framed and jettied enlargement of the main bedroom, in elevation and section, and sections through his entrance tower are included on his drawing (E. 251–1916, V&A, W&I), which is reproduced in Helen Smith, pl. 35; the

49. projections can be seen in figure 1 in Aslet, 'Forthampton Court', p. 1166.

A 1903 photograph of the drawing room, with Morris & Co. textiles including a large carpet, is reproduced in Aslet, 'Forthampton Court', p. 1168, fig. 7. The newel stair, seen in elevation and section on Webb's drawing (in Helen Smith, pl. 35), also led to the two servants' rooms he created in the attics above the entrance hall. Gerald Yorke believed that the turret staircase had never been used; it might have been in use, however, until the great hall was returned to its original proportions.

50. One of Webb's drawings (WEBB [15] 5, BAL/ RIBADC) for the new offices forming the court is reproduced in Kornwolf, p. 16, fig. 4. Between 1912 and 1914, Frank S Chesterton removed the floor in the great hall and Webb's wainscot from the upper part, and replaced his timber-framed oriel with a tall stone-mullioned bay window, and made the ground floor of the laundry block, which he refenestrated; in 1958–60, R Blenham-Bull demolished Webb's by then redundant T-plan service block to allow the entrance to be moved to the north-east front, made the great hall into the entrance hall by adding a porch, and turned Webb's study into a neo-Georgian drawing room (information from Gerald Yorke). The demolished offices are on the left in the illustration in Lethaby, 'Philip Webb', B, p. 220, fig. 7. The rest of Webb's work (apart from the main bedroom extension which has been dismantled) remains but the dining room has been subdivided, the billiard room is now detached from the house, and much of his roughcast has been removed.

51. Translated, the inscription reads: 'This house, much deformed by neglect and almost having fallen down with age, was restored and enlarged by John Reginald Yorke helped by his Dutch wife in 1891, aged 55'; the library fireplace and the hall chimneypiece are illustrated in Aslet, pp. 1167–9, pls. 5 and 6. Webb's drawing for the revolving bookcase (WEBB [15] 23, BAL/RIBADC) is reproduced in Lever, p. 89.

52. Yorke introduced Baird to Webb in the latter's office on 19 April 1894, when Baird first consulted him about Exning House (AB). Baird, later a brigadier-general, won the St Leger in 1907 with his horse Woolwinder.

53. Webb underpinned the walls of Jelfe's house, turned its porch into a bay window, inserted a lantern over the main staircase, formed open areas on its long sides to light and ventilate the menservants' bedrooms that he created in the basement, and built a veranda on the south front (now a sun room). Of the later additions, he demolished the library, billiard room, and some offices but retained the game larder and reused many materials and fittings. In the later twentieth century the building housed a home for the aged; listed Grade II★, it has recently been converted into seven self-contained dwellings.

54. The two villas have double-pile plans with six ground-floor rooms, and central halls on their west sides. Though their distance apart and self-contained layout implies two dwellings, it is more likely, if the conservatory already existed, that the second villa's design is merely the result of its unknown architect's belief that a classical-style house should be symmetrical. The two would have been linked behind the conservatory. The main entrance was through the central porch on the west front of the Nash villa.

55. Webb's instructions on drawing WEBB [45] 14, BAL/RIBADC.

56. The Clouds screens were derived from L-plan seats flanking a fireplace in Webb's abandoned scheme for rebuilding Rougham Hall.

57. Webb's work does not remain unaltered as stated in the *Catalogue of the Drawings Collection of the Royal Institute of British Architects: T–Z*, ed. by Lever, p. 192. A photographic record (private collection) was made of his block before demolition (a large chapel added in the 1930s was also removed). In the common room, the Eyre insignia was painted over the chimneypiece c. 1980, and Webb's two small clerestory lights, installed for ventilation, were removed (their dormers remain). The building is a private residence.

58. 'Great Tangley Manor', and 'Great Tangley Manor, Surrey'; Jekyll, attributed to, 'Great Tangley Manor'. Hermann Muthesius illustrates the interior and exterior (*Das englische Haus*, I, pp. 50–51 and 111–12); the English edition from which the quotation is taken (p. 19) has interiors only (pp.18–20, figs 14 and 15).

59. The influence of the staircase can be seen, for example, on Gimson at the White House (1897; illustrated in Lambourne, p. 171, pl. 196), on W H Bidlake at Garth House (1901; illustrated in Stamp and Goulancourt, pp. 214–15), on George Walton at The Leys (1901) and on Mackintosh at number 78 Derngate (1916–17; (illustrated in Pevsner, *Studies in Art, Architecture and Design*, pp. 185 and 173, respectively).

CHAPTER 10: WEBB THE SOCIALIST

1. See George Bernard Shaw's preface to May Morris's *William Morris*, II, ix. In her book, May records that Faulkner, like Webb, was a great help and support to her father (II, p. 174). Morris hoped in vain that more of his close friends would join him in the cause.

2. Pugin, *Contrasts* and *True Principles*.

3. See Lethaby (1979), p. 253, and Webb to William Morris, 17 June 1896, V&A, NAL, 86.TT.13, fol. 76, quoted in Brandon, 'Philip Webb, the William Morris Circle, and Sussex', p. 10. Webb used the last phrase quoted in the sentence to describe Etchingham Church, 'one of those placid fourteenth century Sussex pieces of serious village building'.

4. Webb, 'Thirteenth Annual Report', p. 20 (quoted in Swenarton, pp. 53–4); Webb to Hale White, November 1899, MR 10/20, Central Library, Bedford.

5. Webb to Lethaby, 1903, in Lethaby (1935), pp. 132–4 (p. 133).
6. Webb to Boyce, 4 May 1885, BM Add. MS 45354.
7. Webb to Lethaby, 1901, published in Lethaby (1935), p. 11; Lethaby (1979), p. 244.
8. Ruskin, *Stones of Venice*, II, chapter 6, subsection xvi.
9. Webb to Hale White, 30 January 1899, MR 10/12, Central Library, Bedford, and to Morris, 28 December 1884, V&A, NAL, 86.TT.13.
10. Webb to Hale White, 20 January 1905, MR 10/24, Central Library, Bedford.
11. All the people who attended the inaugural meeting of the college were given a copy of 'The Nature of Gothic', from *Stones of Venice*, in which Ruskin, who lectured at the college, expounds his views on the relationship between art and work most powerfully. See J F C Harrison, A History of the *Working Men's College*, p. 31.
12. In 1874, for example, Webb read the essays in which John Stuart Mill analysed Fourier's system of small communes (Webb to Rosalind Howard, 9 November 1874, J22/64, Castle Howard Archives). Many of Webb's letters contain comments on political matters.
13. See Webb to George Howard, 19 June 1875, J22/64, Castle Howard Archives.
14. Webb to George Howard, 22 April 1879, J22/64, Castle Howard Archives.
15. For the Eastern Question Association and Morris's connection with it see E P Thompson, *William Morris: Romantic to Revolutionary*, pp. 239–63.
16. Probably the most exhaustive account of Morris's political beliefs and activities is E P Thompson's in *William Morris* (it is written from a Marxist viewpoint); May Morris gives a first-hand account in *William Morris*, vol. II. Lethaby's rough draft on Webb and socialism, appended by Godfrey Rubens to the 1979 edition of Webb (as chapter xiii, pp. 239–44) is a valuable and enlightening source of information, and so is Mark Swenarton's 'Philip Webb: architecture and socialism' (chapter 2, in *Artisans and Architects*, pp. 32–60).
17. Morris thus introduced Webb to Henry Mayers Hyndman, the founder of the Democratic Federation (Morris, quoted by Lethaby in Lethaby (1979), p. 241).
18. See Lethaby (1979), p. 240; Lethaby (1935), p. 18.
19. May Morris, *William Morris*, I, p. 55, and II, p. 176; Fairfax Murray informed Lethaby of Rossetti's belief (Lethaby (1979), p. 249).
20. See Mackail, I, pp. 40 and 48–9. In homage to Ruskin, and because it 'kindled the beliefs of his whole life', Morris printed 'On the Nature of Gothic' as the fourth publication of his Kelmscott Press in 1892 (Mackail, II, 289).
21. Burne-Jones informed Lethaby of this (see Lethaby (1979), p. 241).
22. Webb to Howard, 18 June 1877, and another, n.d. but written in 1880 or 1881, J22/64, Castle Howard Archives.
23. See Webb to Howard, 9 December 1878, J22/64, Castle Howard Archives, and Webb to Cockerell, 4 March 1900, in *Friends of a Lifetime*, ed. by Meynell, p. 100.
24. Webb donated £4 a week to the Socialist League between July and November 1888, approximately half his average income (Socialist Archive, Amsterdam, cited by Swenarton in *Artisans and Architects*, p. 51); Walker is quoted in Lethaby (1979), p. 241.
25. For their understanding that medieval life was imperfect, see, for example, Bax, pp.120–21, and Webb to Boyce, 1 October 1881, BL Add. MS 45354.
26. Webb to Boyce, 30 September 1886, BL Add. MS 45354.
27. Webb to Hale White, c. 10 February 1899, MR 10/14, Central Library, Bedford; Lethaby (1979), p. 251.
28. *News from Nowhere, or an Epoch of Rest* first appeared in 1890 as instalments in the Commonweal, 11 January to 4 October 1890, and in book form in the USA in 1890, and in London in 1891. It was reprinted in *William Morris: Stories in Prose, Stories in Verse, Shorter Poems, Lectures and Essays*, ed. and introduced by G D H Cole, pp. 3–197.
29. Morris to Dr Glasse, 23 May 1887, in *Unpublished Letters of William Morris*, introduced by R Page Arnot, p. 5.
30. Quoted in Lethaby (1979), p. 243.
31. See William Morris, 'How the change came', chapter 17, pp. 96–121, *News from Nowhere*, ed. and intro. by G D H Cole, pp. 3–197.
32. See the quotation from Webb's outline paper of c. 1885 in Lethaby (1979), pp. 242–3.
33. Webb's acceptance of Marx's understanding of history as being partially pre-written is demonstrated in his comment to Hale White on the inevitability of industrial squalor: 'it was to be and so it is so' (1 March 1888, MR 10/5, Central Library, Bedford). See also Lethaby (1979), p. 242.
34. See Webb to Morris, 28 December 1884, V&A, NAL, 86.TT.13, and Lethaby (1979), p. 244.
35. Webb to Rosalind Howard, 24 August 1887, J22/64, Castle Howard Archives.
36. For Webb keeping in touch by letter, see the several letters he wrote to Morris and to Kate Faulkner (V&A, NAL, 86.TT.13, 1884–85); Lethaby (1935), p. 184, and (1979), p. 242.
37. For a fuller explanation, see E P Thompson, *William Morris*, pp. 384–421.
38. See Swenarton, pp. 50–51, and for Webb becoming treasurer, Morris to J L Mahon, 7 February 1886, in *Unpublished Letters*, intro. by Arnot, p. 127, and also Lethaby (1979), p. 241. Two of Webb's lectures were 'The necessity for Socialism' and 'Foreigners and English Socialism'; he reflected on the past and present in 'Town and Gown' in the *Commonweal*, 2, no. 47 (4 December 1886), pp. 284–5.
39. See Swenarton, pp. 50–51. Overworking for his two great causes, the SPAB and socialism, and on his architectural work, contributed to this illness.

40. See Swenarton, p. 51; Lethaby (1979), p. 242.
41. Morris told Dr Glasse of his aims by letter on 23 May 1887 (*Unpublished Letters*, intro. by Arnot, p. 5).
42. Webb told Joseph Lane that he agreed with most of his anarchist manifesto (letter, 2 May 1887, BL Add. MS 46345); Lethaby (1979), p. 242. Lethaby's recording of this contradicts E P Thompson's assertion that by this time Webb was active more through loyalty to Morris than by conviction (*William Morris*, p. 610).
43. Hammersmith Socialist Society, Minutes 1890–96, BL Add. MS 45893.
44. *Unpublished Letters*, intro. by Arnot, p. 16; Lethaby recalled Webb's pessimism at this period in a letter to Cockerell, 27 April 1916, *Friends of a Lifetime*, ed. by Meynell, p. 136.
45. Letter, Webb to Morris, 28 December 1884, V&A, NAL, 86.TT.13.
46. Subsequently, Webb apparently ignored competitions until 1886 when he made sketch designs for a cathedral, probably after hearing of the results of the first competition for Liverpool Cathedral.
47. Webb to Hale White, c. 10 February 1899, MR 10/14, Central Library, Bedford.
48. See Charles Handley-Read's 'Jubilee Pyramid', in which Webb's drawing is reproduced (*AR*, 137 (1965), pp. 234–6 (p. 235)). The quoted words in Webb's hand are on the drawing (WEBB [34], BAL/RIBADC).
49. See W Taylor to E R Robson letters, 1863–c. 1867, Fitzwilliam Museum, Cambridge, Burne-Jones Papers, xxiii, 3–27A – for example, the letter of 27 October 1866.
50. E P Thompson, presumably in the belief that Webb was merely a follower of Morris, credits Morris with being the first creative artist to do this (*William Morris*, p. 841).
51. See C R Atlee to Cockerell, 23 November 1953, in *The Best of Friends*, ed. by Meynell, p. 227.
52. Letter, Webb to Cockerell, 4 March 1900, *Friends of a Lifetime*, ed. by Meynell, p. 100.
53. Webb to Hale White, 22 January 1910, MR 10/34, Central Library, Bedford.
54. Lethaby (1979), p. 256.

CHAPTER 11: THE SMALLER HOUSES

1. The contract drawings for the cottage (designed in late 1860) on Gillum's Moated House estate are dated January 1861; the cottage was occupied by 13 April that year (1861 Census Returns, cited by MacGregor, p. 40).
2. MacGregor, pp. 30–34 and 58–9.
3. He had as yet received no fees since setting up practice (AB).
4. MacGregor, pp. 59–60; about sixty per cent of the inhabitants had to find other accommodation (from the 1871 Census Returns, ibid., p. 59).
5. See Harper, p. 31.
6. Ibid., p. 33.
7. Webb penned these instructions on his drawing.
8. Comment upon and exterior perspective of numbers 91–101 Worship Street, *B* (29 August 1863), p. 620; from the Rate Records, 1863, St Leonards, Shoreditch (MacGregor, p. 58).
9. Webb's drawings for the East Rounton terrace are undated (ZFK MIC 2129/113 to 2129/121, NYCRO). The terrace was completed well before January 1878 (see Webb to Godman, 26 January 1878, in Brandon-Jones, 'Notes on the Building of Smeaton Manor', pp. 33 and 35). One of Webb's drawings for the Brampton terrace (from a private collection) is illustrated in Kirk, 'Philip Webb (1831–1915)', vol. 2, fig. 142.
10. Webb to Jane Morris, 24 June 1899, BL Add. MS 453342, Morris Papers, vol. 1.
11. From Morris's poem 'For the bed at Kelmscott' embroidered on the bed-hangings at Kelmscott Manor.
12. See Webb to Jane Morris, 24 June 1899, BL Add. MS 453342, Morris Papers, vol. 1. Webb had inspected the work and workshops of several local builders before selecting Bowley (SB 1896–1900, pp. 20–23 July 1900).
13. Kelmscott CB, 21 May 1900. Jack followed Webb's instructions to the letter and recorded his findings alongside Webb's various points. Webb took no fee for designing the cottages but Mrs Morris possibly paid Jack for supervising their construction. Jack used the notebook for recording his own work after he took over Webb's practice.
14. For sketches of the plan and entrance elevation of the Great Tangley cottages, based on Webb's drawing, see Kirk, 'Philip Webb (1831–1915)', vol. 2, fig. 228.
15. After leaving Bedford Grammar School, White, the son of a bookseller of the town, spent 1848 to 1852 at the Countess of Huntingdon's College at Cheshunt, training to become a minister of the Congregational Church, but he was expelled after expressing doubts about accepting the letter of the Bible.
16. See White's letter to the editor of the *Daily Telegraph*, entitled 'Modern Houses', dated 13 October 1865, published 16 October. He had been driven from two houses in Carshalton because the first was unsatisfactory and the second damp; from another in Epsom because of the noise and vulgarity accompanying the race meetings; and from one in Isleworth by his neighbour's piano playing (see Maclean, pp. 171–3).
17. Ruskin to White, 27 October 1867, quoted in *The Groombridge Diary*, ed. by Dorothy V White, p. 40.
18. Webb took no fee because the construction of the house was supervised by C G Vinall, the architect and surveyor who supervised the completion of several houses after Webb felt bound to withdraw or as in this case was too busy to do it himself.

19. Tomes trained as a doctor in Evesham, and at the Middlesex and King's College hospitals before specializing in dentistry. He enjoyed designing and making furniture and dental instruments and was an expert wood-turner (which would interest Webb), whose love for trees and plants, paintings and music, was shared by Tomes. For more, see Cope, *Sir John Tomes*. As Webb's notes of Tomes's requirements are undated (SB 1865–77, fol. 33), the exact date of commissioning is not known.

20. Webb's drawings for the later, north range are missing but it appears on his drawings for the 1876 enlargements. In 1894, he designed a gardener's cottage but Tomes postponed its construction and the drawing is missing (see SB 1892–96, 21 September 1894); the existing cottage at the entrance to the drive, although altered and enlarged, has many exterior and interior details characteristic of Webb's work, and this fact, with Mrs Tomes's having paid Webb a fee representative of a building costing £280 in 1896 (see Webb's AB), suggests that it was the gardener's cottage.

21. Webb's drawing for the larger garden porch is missing, but the structure appears on photographs taken for him soon after the 1876 work was completed (private collection).

22. Hugh Bell joined the firm in 1862, and subsequently became his father's right-hand man and a leader in the social and public affairs of Middlesbrough and North Yorkshire (see chapter 13). Red Barns is discussed in Curry and Kirk, *Philip Webb in the North*, pp. 18–20, and in Kirk, 'Philip Webb (1831–1915)', vol. 1, pp. 317–22.

23. Lyulph Stanley to Rosalind Howard, 20 April 1871, Castle Howard Archives. Mary (baptized Maria) was the daughter of John Shields, a wealthy merchant of Newcastle upon Tyne.

24. The sites were offered in late 1867 or 1868; Bell leased the ground in three parts, in April 1869, June 1870, and August 1875 (from my photocopy of his 1920 sale agreement). Webb's drawings for the house as first built are missing but he included Red Barns on a sheet of outline plans of houses he had designed in 1868 or earlier (Webb [50], BAL/RIBADC). The sheet also contains a pencilled plan of Joldwynds (designed 1870) but not one of Rounton Grange (designed 1871–72) which suggests that the sheet dates from 1869 or 1870, not c. 1871–72 as suggested in the BAL/RIBADC *Catalogue*, 1984.

25. There is more on Florence Bell, née Olliffe, in chapter 13.

26. Webb designed a sideboard for 'Mr. Bell' in 1870 (MMF&Co AB); as the Washington Hall sideboard had been designed already and Rounton Grange was not yet Lowthian Bell's property, this piece (now missing) must have been designed for Red Barns. For Morris choosing the products, see Mary Trevelyan, 'The Number of My Days', typescript memoirs, fol. 1. Mary, a daughter of Hugh Bell, grew up at Red Barns. In the mid-1860s, Webb had abandoned open grates for the more efficient closed grates developed originally in the 1790s by Count Benjamin Rumford (1753–1814).

27. When seeking exhibits for the 1984 Philip Webb exhibition in Middlesbrough, I found the missing *Redcar* carpet, in a Bell family home where its significance had not been recognized. It was designed by Morris for the Red Barns drawing room of 1868 (the room was not added in 1881–82 as stated in the catalogue of the Morris centenary exhibition, *William Morris*, ed. by Parry, p. 281) and hand-knotted in c. 1881 at Kelmscott House as the hammer trademark demonstrates. It is not known whether it was commissioned by Lowthian Bell, possibly as a belated wedding present for his son Hugh, or by Hugh himself (Morris refers merely to 'Bell's carpet' in his letter of February 1881). It was exhibit 2 in the Webb exhibition (see Curry and Kirk, *Philip Webb in the North*, p. 48, two photographs, and p. 52). Afterwards it was exhibited for a long period at the Laing Art Gallery, Newcastle upon Tyne; at present it is at Kelmscott Manor, on loan to the Society of Antiquaries. Morris's design for the carpet (V&A, W&I, E. 144–1919) is illustrated in Parry, *William Morris Textiles*, p. 95.

28. Most of the local farmhouses dated from the eighteenth century, and were of two types: four-square and hip-roofed, with five sash windows about a central ornamented doorway, or longer and lower with an asymmetrical entrance, horizontally sliding windows, brick dentilated cornice, and end gables with stone kneelers and gable copings.

29. As shown in the advertisement for the sites 'Bird's Eye View and Plan of Villa Sites … to be Leased near Redcar', prepared by Charles J Adams, architect, of Stockton-on-Tees, and dated 1867 (Kirkleatham Hall Archive, 2733–2737, NYCRO).

30. In 1868, Hugh Bell, who was receiving only a small salary from the family firm, could not a have afforded a very large or ornate house but in later years he could have aggrandized Red Barns had he wished. Instead, he and his second wife added only a few essential rooms even though guests often had to sleep in nearby lodging houses.

31. Sackville Cecil's mother, later Mary, Countess of Derby, was the second wife of Robert Cecil; his half-brother, the 3rd Marquess, served three terms as the Prime Minister. After Wellington and Cambridge, Cecil trained as a railway and a telegraph engineer, then served as chief electrician for the laying of the telegraph cable between Marseilles and West Africa before becoming a railway manager, and then a director and chairman of submarine telegraphy companies. Later he became Assistant General and Traffic Manager for Great Eastern Railway, and General Manager of the Metropolitan District Railway, before returning to submarine telegraphy. This information is from Webber, 'Lord Sackville Arthur Cecil', a copy of which was kindly supplied by R H Harcourt Williams, Librarian and Archivist to the Marquess of Salisbury.

32. The site was only a mile from Holwood House, the home of Cecil's mother. As Webb demolished the cottages completely, they must have lacked architectural merit.

33. Webb's letter of 16 April 1873 is missing, but he reiterated its content, including the words quoted, in his letter to Cecil of 11 September 1874 that accompanied the returned cheque (LB 1, fol. 9). In the letter, Webb tells Cecil that if Vinall (and his then partner Goodman) were to be paid the full 5% fee, they would barely be rewarded for their labour. Cecil, clearly a difficult client, was probably emulating his father, who personally directed all building work on his ancestral estate. Webb apparently destroyed all his drawings except a survey sheet that bears outline plans of the house and stables (private collection).

34. The house was illustrated for the first time in 1996, in Kirk, 'William Morris, Philip Webb and Architecture', pp. 39–58 (p. 55, fig. 14). Webb referred to it as Nether Hall Farm in his practice account book. Webb's fee was thought to have been for repair and alteration of the farmhouse near the hall but I found that the fee was too great for the work done. I mentioned my belief that it was for another farm to Richard and Penny Ballard, the new owners of the hall, and subsequently Mr Ballard discovered that Manor Farm in Thurston had been part of the Nether Hall estate until 1920. When I examined this building in 1990 (after submitting my PhD dissertation), it was absolutely clear that Webb had designed it. Fortunately, John Burton, architect of Purcell Miller Tritton and Alan Dodd, designer, having recognized the building as an Arts and Crafts house of quality, had repaired, renovated, and decorated appropriately in the late 1980s, supported by the owners Edward and Muriel Myers, who had joined the SPAB.

35. Almost all Webb's houses have a bay window, and he would have had no hesitation in breaking the symmetry with one here; the horizontal shape of the panes, and the small red tiles on the roof (replaced recently), suggest a post-Webb date and that all the sashes were replaced. The attic window set between chimneys on the south front is by Webb, apparently.

36. Chisolm was the husband of Hale White's sister Mary. Webb's drawings for the houses are missing and no letters from him to Chisolm have been found but it is clear from the building itself that he was the architect. The interior details are very like those of Four Gables, designed the same year, whilst some of the external details resemble those of Upwood Gorse and Oast House. The second owner of the house, on learning that her guest Henry Fletcher intended to become an architect, told him that Philip Webb had designed her house; Miss Blanche Borthwick, governess to the Chisolm children and herself a niece of Hale White or his wife, remembered seeing the builder's board outside the completed building and hearing the name Vinall in connection with final accounts, which indicates that Vinall supervised the construction and explains why Webb received no fee (Fletcher and Borthwick gave this information to John Brandon-Jones, who passed it on to me).

37. Howard's letter is missing; for Webb's reply, see Webb to George Howard, 1 October 1875, J22/64, Castle Howard Archives. Grey sent a plan of the site with his list of requirements but Webb insisted on inspecting the ground before deciding the 'shape and make of the house' (Grey to Webb, 5 October 1875, C575/7/c, Howard Papers). Four Gables is discussed in Brandon-Jones, 'The Work of Philip Webb and Norman Shaw', pp. 12–13; in Curry and Kirk, *Philip Webb in the North*, pp. 34–5; and in McEvoy, pp. 41 and 56–61; illustrations in the last include one of Webb's drawings for Four Gables.

38. Webb to R Du Cane, 14 July 1876, LB 1, fol. 40; on 14 December 1876, Warwick tried to justify the difference between his estimate and the new tenders, chiefly by pointing out that without a specification as guide, he had allowed for expensive finishes ('Explanation of the difference between Estimate and the several Tenders for Mr. Grey's House', 14 December 1876, C575/7/I, Howard Papers).

39. Grey to Du Cane, 12 December 1875, Howard Papers (Grey would have preferred Sproat Brothers, masons, of Talkin, the local firm responsible for the masonry, to construct the entire house, subject to the obtaining of a better joiner, because it had already done good work for the estate); signed but undated contract, C575/7/j, Howard Papers.

40. Grey to Du Cane, 30 March 1877, Howard Papers. On 7 September 1877 Webb noted: 'William Marshall new c. of w.' (SB 1877–92, fol. 4).

41. Pevsner, *Cumberland and Westmorland*, p. 77.

42. Webb to Howard, 9 December 1878, J22/64, Castle Howard Archives.

43. Webb to Stephenson, 12 February 1880, Howard Papers. Stephenson had succeeded Grey as agent before the house was decorated.

44. Webb's letter to Du Cane, 17 February 1877, accepting the post of professional adviser and setting out his conditions, is in the Howard Papers (C575/7) and his copy is in LB 1, fols 65–6. The existing vicarage was out of town and, according to the vicar, uselessly small (copy, Gray to Du Cane, 19 April 1877, C575/6/e (i), Howard Papers). The Vicar's House is discussed in McEvoy, pp. 62–3, and in Curry and Kirk, *Philip Webb in the North*, pp. 36–37.

45. Webb to Howard, 8 September 1879, J22/64, Castle Howard Archives.

46. I am grateful to local historian Richard J Busby and to John A D Cropp, respectively, for information about Dr Webb and about the house.

47. Webb to Arthur Godman, 4 March 1878, in Brandon-Jones, 'Notes on the building of Smeaton Manor', p. 36.

48. Webb sketched the Lindisfarne gable on 6 September 1857 (Webb's Sketch

Book, private collection).

49. Quennell, 'Architectural Furniture', in *The House and Its Equipment*, ed. by Weaver (p. 21, fig. 29).

50. Most of this information comes from the notes taken by Webb before preparing a specification for the cleaning and redecorating of New Place (23 June 1891, SB 1877–92, fols 229–34). Some papers were repeated, others were cleaned; large pieces of furniture are indicated on the preliminary plan. Morris & Co. pieces included the sideboard, Dutch Cabinet, and mahogany chairs purchased by Philip Webb (as recorded in his Morris & Co. AB).

51. From Lawrence Weaver in 'Lesser Country Houses of Today: New Place, Welwyn, Herts., designed by Mr. Philip Webb', a paper printed, complete with illustrations, ready to appear in *Country Life*, 23 July 1910, pp. 7–8 (p. 7), but in fact never published (private collection).

52. In designing Tate's house, Webb was probably obliging his friends the Bells, for whom he was designing the Bell Brothers Offices, Middlesbrough, at the time (chapter 12).

53. The local architect was James Garry of Hartlepool, a neighbour of Tate (information from Mr Benson, a later assistant of Garry).

54. AddB, fol. 67. My further research was kindly aided by the then owners Mr and Mrs T Lumley, local historians Mr and Mrs Eric Smith, solicitor Mr Gilbert Bunting, and Mr Benson. Webb's copy of his letter to Tate of 13 June 1883 (LB 2, fol. 13) confirms that he sent Tate a 'carefully considered arrangement of plan' and a 'sheet of memoranda' to help Tate to get the local architect to fulfil his wishes; in 1972, these sheets were stolen from the car of solicitor Thomas Amos during sale negotiations for the house, and never recovered. The repair and refurbishment was done for new owners Mr and Mrs John Cooke under the guidance of the architects and planners of Cleveland County Council and Hartlepool Borough Council. The house is discussed in Curry and Kirk, *Philip Webb in the North*, pp. 44–5, and in Sheila Kirk, 'Webb's Wonder', pp. 12–13.

55. The original colour was discovered when the roughcast was replaced.

56. Two poor-quality dormers, which were not by Webb but might have been replacements of dormers that he had designed, were copied faithfully during the refurbishment.

57. Webb's explanation of why ornament should be avoided is quoted in chapter 6 of the present volume; Webb had informed Tate that Longdens of Sheffield would supply grates cast from any of his patterns (Webb to Tate, 13 June 1883, LB 2, fol. 13).

58. Miss Ewart was a governor of two London schools for girls, and a member of the councils of Bedford College and of Newnham College to which, and to Somerville College, she gave generous financial support (information from Clough, 'In Memoriam – Miss Mary Ewart'; Ann Philips, Honorary Archivist to the college, kindly supplied a copy). The house is now divided, the parts being Coneyhurst-on-the-Hill and Mendip.

59. Webb told Boyce that he had spent time considering how least to mar the surroundings with the new house, and he informed Miss Ewart that the composition of the house, cottage, and stables required the most careful balancing (Webb to Boyce, 26 September 1883, BL Add. MS 45354, and to Miss Ewart, 23 October 1883, LB 2, fol. 19). Miss Ewart did not purchase the site until Webb had approved it (correspondence between Miss Ewart and R M Gray, Surrey County RO).

60. Webb's stable drawing (BAL/RIBADC) is reproduced in Richardson, p. 17, fig. 8.

61. Against his normal practice of designing each detail afresh, Webb directed that the cove be used again at Coneyhurst (Webb's note, 30 July 1884, on New Place drawing WEBB [47], BAL/RIBADC). As a friend of the family, Miss Ewart would have known New Place, and presumably had admired this feature.

62. The brick is now partly obscured by double glazing.

63. Because of the steeply rising site, the ground floor of the cottage was at the height of the first floor of the house. The outer porch was therefore on three levels; visitors in invalid-chairs could enter on the level through the garden porch into the morning room.

64. For the decoration and furnishings, see SB 1877–92, 9 February 1889, fol. 118, and, including the building itself, the chapter devoted to Coneyhurst in Weaver, *Small Country Houses of Today*, chap. 3, pp. 13–18, pls. 14–16.

65. See Stearn, 'Mrs Robb and "Mrs Robb's Bonnet" (*Euphorbia robbiae*)'. Mrs Robb exchanged plants with leading gardeners, and went on plant-hunting expeditions to the Near East, on one occasion bringing back specimens of *euphorbia robbiae*, which was named after her and given the sobriquet 'Mrs Robb's bonnet' because it had travelled in her hatbox.

66. Webb visited the estate on 19 July 1890, when he took the brief for Mrs Robb's new house, and measured the overall dimensions of the existing Chiltley Farm, a U-plan complex, in which Mrs Robb presumably stayed whilst in Liphook (SB 1877–92, 19 July 1890). There is no further mention of it in Webb's documents; later it was demolished and replaced with a large house by an unidentified architect for Mrs Robb's elder son, John (for the history and contemporary photographs of this house, and the earlier and later history of Mrs Robb and her family, see Anne Silver, *Chiltley Place and Goldenfields* (Liphook: Bramshott and Liphook Preservation Society, 1995), from which some facts have been taken; Anne Silver's discussion of Goldenfields was apparently made without sight of Webb's relevant Site and Certificate Books (private collection)). Goldenfields is discussed and illustrated in Kirk, 'Philip Webb (1831–1915)', vol. 1, pp. 349–52;

vol. 2, figs 195–9. The name Goldenfields refers to the surrounding fields at harvest time; Webb refers to the house as Gardener's Cottage (Mrs Robb's original quarters, apart from the internally galleried room and the tower, form part of the present Lych Gates).

67. Webb noted her requirements in his notebook (SB 1877–92, 19 July 1890). His preliminary designs for the gardener's cottage and the larger house are in the BAL (respectively, WEBB [26] and [61], BAL/RIBADC). A carriage shed and rough stall, and a tiled woodshed, were also built to his design.

68. The room beneath the balcony was extended under it many years later, and the balustrade was probably replaced.

69. Webb measured and sketched the Pembridge bell-house on 17 December 1890 (SB 1878–92); detached bell-houses are more common in Essex than in the west of England. Webb's belvedere resembles the top of the fifteenth-century clock tower in the gardens of Arley Hall, Cheshire, which he would have seen in 1856 when making site visits to the chapel there as Street's assistant, and which Mrs Robb probably knew. The Pembridge bell-house is illustrated, for example, in Pevsner, *Herefordshire*, pl. 35(b); and the Arley clock tower in *The Englishwoman's Garden*, ed. by Lees-Milne and Verey, p. 30.

70. Owen Little apparently added the hip-roofed block between the cottage and the road, and the present porch and entrance, and increased the width of the range flanking the road, probably inserting a floor in the galleried room to create more bedrooms, three having windows in half-hipped gables facing the road. The house has suffered so many changes and most of Webb's drawings are missing; as a result, my present conclusions (apart from Webb having designed the original cottage and enlarged it to suit Mrs Robb) as to who was responsible for the two-storey room and the tower could be wrong. Perhaps Owen Little designed the entire roadside range and the tower, or one of the two. The clock is dated 1905, which seems to suggest the tower is by Little; against this, however, is Webb's memorandum (jotted when on site c. 16 November 1891, in SB 1878–92) to send the clockmaker's address to the builder W & G King. Moreover, the marked resemblance of the clock tower to the Pembridge bell-house, and the facts that Webb saw it in 1890, that Mrs Robb requested a two-storey galleried room, that the £1,900 cost of the house (CB) was sufficient to cover the room and the tower, and that Webb recorded there having been 'various additions since the work was begun', strongly suggest that he designed the room and the tower. If they were by Little, he might have followed suggestions made earlier to the client by Webb. At a later date, Inigo Triggs apparently designed the stone-faced library at the rear of the building, north-west of the tower.

71. Hitchcock, *Architecture: Nineteenth and Twentieth Centuries*, pp. 360–61.

72. Apparently not appreciating the renown of Webb's buildings in England, Kornwolf attributed English interest in barns to that which had arisen in America in the 1880s (see Kornwolf, pp. 39–42).

73. The houses mentioned in this paragraph are illustrated, for example, in Hitchmough, *Voysey*, pp. 34, 32, and 134 (The Cottage, Walnut Tree Farm, and Moorcrag); Weaver, *Houses and Gardens by E. L. Lutyens*, p. 19 (Fulbrook); Hitchcock, *In the Nature of Materials*, pl. 32 (the Nathan Moore house); Girouard, *Sweetness and Light*, p. 124 (Manor Farm).

74. Brandon-Jones, 'Philip Webb', p. 255.

75. The houses mentioned in this paragraph are illustrated, for example, in Hitchmough, *Voysey*, p. 109, 88, 113, and 203 (New Place, Norney, Broadleys, and Brooke End); Weaver, *Houses and Gardens by E. L. Lutyens*, pp. 256, 44, 46 and 47 (the Salutation, Tigbourne Court, and Littlecroft); Haigh, *Baillie Scott*, pp. 15 and 28 (Red House and Blackwell); McKean, 'The Hill House', in *Charles Rennie Mackintosh*, ed. by Kaplan, p. 196; Gray, p. 306 (number 8 Addison Road, London).

76. John Brandon-Jones, who had worked for Voysey's son and knew the father, told me several times of his belief that C F A Voysey had been deeply influenced by Webb's work.

77. See, for example, MacLaren's Tenant Farmer's House (c. 1889) at Glenlyon House, Perthshire, illustrated in Service, 'James MacLaren and the Godwin Legacy', in Alastair Service and others, *Edwardian Architecture and its Origins*, p. 111, and Mackintosh's Windy Hill and Hill House in Steele, pp. 100–1 and 118.

CHAPTER 12: THE NON-DOMESTIC WORK

1. Memorials not discussed include many gravestones, two small mausoleums, memorial conduits and drinking fountains, and the satirical Jubilee Monument of 1886 (for which Webb gives only a rough section, with an elephant bearing the queen at the top) purporting to celebrate Queen Victoria's coming Golden Jubilee, which is mentioned in chapter 10 of the present volume. There are several Webb designs for memorials in the V&A, W&I.

2. For example, Webb told Lowthian Bell to send the drawings to the mason, who should estimate for doing the whole of the work 'in exact accordance with the drawings and the directions thereon written' on a 'carefully selected stone' (Webb to Lowthian Bell, 23 February 1887, LB 2, fols 83–4).

3. Webb's drawing for the Dodgson monument is in the V&A, W&I (E.198–1916); the one for Lady Stanley, dated 24 October 1895, is in the SPAB Archive. Also to be seen at Lanercost Priory are the monumental slab of 1879 to Charles Howard (father of George Howard) and a memorial tablet of 1880 to him and his wife, with portrait medallions by Sir Edgar Boehm and illustrative plaques by Edward Burne-Jones, mounted on Webb's bronze plate in a marble frame; and an effigy by Boehm of George Howard's baby daughter Elizabeth, on a base by

Webb (drawings, respectively: V&A, W&I, E.192-95–1916; E. 196–1916; E.197–1916).

4. Webb to Miss Constance Astley, 21 October 1881, LB 1, fols 199–200 (fol. 200).
5. At Webb's suggestion, Sir Lowthian's shield was done at the same time as his wife's because it would have been difficult to carve later without moving the stone, whereas the necessary inscription could be easily cut *in situ* after his death. The drawings for the gravestone of Sir Lowthian and Lady Bell (d. 1887) are in the BAL/RIBADC (WEBB [39] 1–6, 1887), and those for the graves of the grandchildren Kate (Kitty) Stanley (d. 1884) and Philip Hugh Johnson (d. 1886) are in the V&A, W&I (E.202–1916, n.d., and E.199–1916, n.d.). George Milburn of York, who executed all the carved ornament at Rounton Grange, probably carved these stones. The first tombstone designed by Webb for the Bell family is that of 1871, a few miles away in West Rounton churchyard, for Sir Lowthian's daughter-in-law, the first Mrs Hugh Bell (no drawing has been found). A coped stone, it bears a cross in relief formed by two narrow arris beads at right angles to one another, with simple abstract leaf forms ascending the shaft and raised arabesques of a Celtic character linking the four arms of the cross.
6. Webb's working drawing for Morris's gravestone is in the BAL/RIBADC (WEBB [23]).
7. Webb to Sydney Cockerell, 27 May 1898, in *Friends of a Lifetime*, ed. by Meynell, pp. 97–8. Turner's invoice is in the BL (Add. MS 45346, Morris Papers, vol. IX).
8. Astley and his wife are buried at West Dean, Sussex, and their son at Arisaig. Webb's drawings for the memorial are in the BAL/RIBADC (WEBB [3] 1–2) and the V&A, W&I (E.186-91–1916). Webb had designed a memorial to Mrs Astley's father, Sir Harry D Jones in 1866 (the drawing is in a private collection). When Gertrude and Constance Astley asked Webb's advice about the design of a gravestone to their old gardener, he offered to design the lettering and an upright slab to receive it. The tombstone (in Arisaig churchyard), however, has a small upright slab crowned by a cross surrounded by random rubble walling with ashlar edgings and copings, and another summit cross; with his instructions to Gertrude in his letter of 2 December 1881 (LB 1, fols 215–16), this suggests that one of the sisters designed the rather mean slab and that the memorial was enlarged by Webb to be more in scale with his letter plate. Beatrice's name seldom appears in the family papers; Webb was the most friendly with Constance.
9. Webb told Constance Astley that the chapel would have cost £2,000 in 1866 but that the figure would be much higher in 1881 (Webb to Miss Constance Astley, 14 October 1880, LB 1, fols 170–71).
10. Webb to Miss Gertrude Astley, 29 November 1882, LB 1, fols 1–2.
11. See Webb to Miss Gertrude Astley, 14 October 1882, LB 1, fols 261–3.
12. Webb to Miss Constance Astley, 30 August 1882, LB 1, fols 255–6.
13. Webb to Miss Gertrude Astley, 26 April 1882, LB 1, fols 240–41.
14. Webb's drawings for this final design (dated 1890) and a preliminary scheme (dated 1887) are in the V&A, W&I (E.180–1916 and E.182-184–1916, respectively).
15. Elizabeth Barrett lived from infancy until 1826 at Hope End, a little to the north-east of Ledbury.
16. Webb made a second site visit on 21 January 1892, when he made extensive notes, including his determination that the old timber-framed house should not be pulled down as proposed. Mr Stephens, honorary secretary of the tower committee, accompanied him for at least part of the time, during which Webb expressed his opinions about all the possible sites (SB 1878–92).
17. Pevsner, *Herefordshire*, p. 218.
18. The earlier building was known as the Round School; the National Society for Promoting the Education of the Poor in the Principles of the Established Church was founded in 1811 and was supported by fees, small government grants, and charities. Anglican schools established by the society were known as National Schools, whilst the non-conformist ones established by the British and Foreign School Society, founded in 1814, were known as British Schools.
19. Billing's drawings are in the East Sussex RO (BGP 30/1 and BGP 30/2).
20. Webb's offer is recorded in the minutes of the school management committee, 12 January 1864 (Heathfield National School: minutes of the Management Committee (PAR 372. 25/1/1, East Sussex RO).
21. If Webb made new elevation drawings, they are missing. When the school was pegged out according to Billing's plan, there was insufficient room at each end of the building for a pathway to the playgrounds at the rear. Webb's suggestion of turning the school by ninety degrees was rejected by managers, who wished the building to face the road; fortunately, the owners of the two adjacent properties gave a yard or so to the school, making the pathways possible. Bernard Guile, local historian, provided this information and most kindly loaned me his unpublished illustrated history of the building.
22. Billing's school had a large schoolroom, parallel to the road and aligned a little east of north, with a classroom for infants projecting from the centre of the long west side facing the road and flanked by lean-to porches, one for boys, the other for girls and infants. The earliest addition was a classroom at the rear in 1885–86; it was not by Webb.
23. See Webb to P Cummin, Education Department, Whitehall, 9 June 1876, LB 1 (the approved plans bore the number 76/10836). Webb first inspected the site for the school on 26 October 1875 (SB 1865–77, fol. 104). The drawings, from which the school was built, were prepared for Lowthian Bell, and are dated August 1876.
24. See D A and L T D Heppell, 'The Logbooks of the Hutton Rudby and East

25. Rounton Schools, 1877–1901'.
26. See *Hints to Promoters of Church Schools*.
27. Earth closets in many small schools in the country, including East Rounton, were not replaced by WCs until well after the Second World War. In the 1870s many people regarded ECs as the safer type because there was no danger from sewer gases, which remained a problem until improvements were made in drainage system designs in the 1880s.
28. Elderly villagers have reported that at least part of the walls were in exposed brickwork when they were young.
29. Webb to Lt. Col. Gillum, 13 September 1875, LB 1, fols 27–8.
30. Boys from the Euston Road school made some furniture to Webb's designs (see chapter 3).
31. If Webb did make any changes, the fee is not entered separately in his account book but would have been included in that for the work on the Moated House.
32. From SB 1865–67 (private collection). On a sketch of the Farm School made in 1866, the New Buildings are noted as having been added to the sketch in 1868 (one of the sketches of the Moated House, Tottenham by 'T. H. B.' (1866–68) in the Tottenham Library).
33. From information in Webb to Col. and Mrs Gillum, 20 January 1873 (Barnet Museum) and Webb's SB 1865–67.
34. The Barnet Museum has a printed perspective sketch indicating the date of the various school buildings.
35. There are illustrations of the interiors of the schoolroom and the dormitory in a booklet about the school in the Barnet Museum. Webb was insistent on installing gill stoves because they provided the best ventilation (Webb to Lt. Col. Gillum, 13 September 1875, LB 1, fols 27–8.
36. C G Vinall, Webb's friend, made two designs for a playroom for the school; the first was rejected, the contract for the second was signed in 1878 (it is in the Barnet Museum). In 1865, the school became totally independent from but closely associated with the Industrial School; in the 1930s, it housed an Approved School, which was moved to Godstone, Surrey in 1938, when the immediate surroundings were being developed for housing. The present school, occupying Webb's New Buildings and administered by the public school Mill Hill, is for children who are excluded from normal state education. I am indebted to Dr Gillian Gear, honorary secretary of the Barnet and District Local History Society, for most kindly providing a great deal of information about the Farm School, and advising on my brief account of it. MacGregor's thesis 'Philip Webb' was also helpful.
37. McVarish's estimate was for £390; the final sum appears in roughly jotted figures, apparently in Constance Astley's hand, amongst her papers. The late Miss M J Becher, an erstwhile owner of Arisaig House, kindly allowed me to photocopy the relevant Astley material (inherited from Constance Astley), which includes letters from Webb, various accounts, and the Specification (all now in the BAL/RIBA). There are further papers in another private collection. Susan Forster's thesis 'Philip Webb and the Astleys' contains helpful material and photographs of Webb's drawing. In the BAL Catalogue, Gertrude is given as the client for the village hall but she was no longer *the* Miss Astley.
38. The floor was renewed (1934) and electric light was installed (1936) in memory of Gertrude, her husband Sir Arthur Nicholson, and her sister Constance.
39. Photocopy in the author's collection.
40. Specification (signed by Webb on 29 Jan 1892), p. 6 (now in the BAL/RIBA).
41. Webb to Miss Astley, 22 May 1891 (now in the BAL/RIBA).
42. From information kindly supplied by Ann Martin, secretary to the Astley Village Hall Committee, and by Mandy Ketchim of the Isle of Muck, the architect for the refurbishment, rebuilding, and enlargement.
43. Bell brothers founded their first iron works on Tyneside in 1844 and established their Clarence Works on Teesside in 1851. It became one of the largest iron works in the north-east of England. For more information see, for example, Greville Jones, 'A Description of the Messrs. Bell Brothers' Blast-Furnaces from 1844–1908'; *Description of the Works of Dorman, Long & Co. Ltd. and Bell Brothers Ltd., Middlesbrough*; Edwards, *Chronology of the Development of the Iron & Steel Industries of Teesside*; Almond, B J D Harrison, J K Harrison, and Owen, *Cleveland Iron and Steel, Background and 19th Century History*; J K Harrison, 'Philip Webb's Industrial Buildings for Bell Brothers in their Local Context'.
44. Lowthian Bell to Webb, 7 June 1867 (private collection).
45. Despite Bell's request for a sketch within the week, the tower may not have been built until the early 1870s (the early Bell Brothers records, including Webb's drawings, are believed to have been bulldozed into the ground when the Clarence Offices were demolished in 1970). The clock was purchased sometime between 1 October 1873 and 31 March 1874 (Bell Brothers Private Ledger (no number), Bell Brother Papers, Teesside Archives). The tower appears in the distance in a photograph in *Description of the Works of Dorman, Long & Co. Ltd. and Bell Brothers Ltd.*, p. 47.
46. The bells are not mentioned in Lowthian Bell's letters to Webb but the architect referred to the upper stage as the belfry.
47. Lowthian Bell to Webb, 1873 (private collection). The blowing-engine house must have been built by March 1874 when the first of the engines was purchased. Webb's drawing for the stone-and-brick chimney (dated 1873) is in the V&A, W&I (E.98–1916). A photograph of the engine house is reproduced in *Description of the Works of Dorman, Long & Co. Ltd. and Bell Brothers Ltd.*, p. 53. See also J K

Harrison, *Houses for Steam-Driven Blowing Engines in North-East England*; for Webb's building see pp. 30–33.

47. The blowing-engine house was extended later, following Webb's detailing but with larger windows.

48. It is recorded in the Bell Brothers Limited Director's [sic] Minute Book (Bell Brothers Papers, Teesside Archives), that at the directors' meeting on 9 September 1874 it was decided that an 'estimate of the Clarence Offices [should] be prepared and submitted'; this shows that Webb had designed the building by this date. There are two photographs of the Clarence Offices in the Beamish Museum, one of which (Neg. no. 1917) is reproduced in Curry and Kirk, p. 40; another photograph is reproduced in *Description of the Works of Dorman, Long & Co. Ltd. And Bell Brothers Ltd.*, p. 43.

49. At this time, too, when the family members of the firm were receiving no dividends on their shares, the firm constructed a school, library, RC church and presbytery on the works site for their Irish workforce and their families (Director's [sic] Meeting Minute Book, 1875, Bell Brothers Papers, Teesside Archives). The English workers lived on the south bank of the river in or near Middlesbrough and reached Clarence by Bell Brothers' ferryboat. On 20 January 1876, the directors ordered 'That the Clarence Offices be proceeded with, Cost £3, 500'. Construction began in 1876 and was completed in 1878 (see Bell Brothers Private Ledger No. 2, Bell Brothers Papers, Teesside Archives). All the costs of materials, labour, furniture, etc. are recorded in this ledger. Webb did not receive his fee until 31 March 1880.

50. As previously mentioned, Webb's drawings are believed to have been bulldozed into the ground when the building was demolished in 1970. Fortunately, John K Harrison and a group of his pupils from Eston Grammar School measured the ground floor and the main elevation just before demolition; their drawing is reproduced in J K Harrison, 'Philip Webb's Industrial Buildings', p. 19. The small projections on the north front were probably added later, apparently not by Webb.

51. A K Cumbor and Harry Waller described the first-floor plan to me in 1982.

52. Lattice girders in wood, wrought iron, and mild steel were becoming more widely used but chiefly for bridges (rolled steel joists of sufficient strength were not then available for long spans). The truss was deeply embedded into the wall, which necessitated a blind arch in the centre of the arcade.

53. John K Harrison, who took the interior photograph of the central hall in 1970, and kindly gave me a print of it, has also provided information about the building.

54. For an illustration of the Blenheim turrets, see, for example, Downes, pl. 2.

55. Corner towers with pyramid roofs had long been fairly common on country houses and large stable blocks but not closely grouped round a central turret as on the Clarence Offices. The two projections on the north front, added later, had pitched and gabled roofs that were independent of the pyramids.

56. A K Cumbor and the late Harry Waller, who used to work in the building, expressed their opinions of the building to me during interviews in 1982.

57. A few minor changes were made to the building during its working life, including the insertion of a narrow doorway at the western end of the south front, the widening and lowering of the window to the right of the main entrance, and the insertion of an additional ground-floor window on the east front. The eastern rear projection was extended in the twentieth century when the building became the pay office for all the Bell Brothers' various types of works on Teesside.

58. A considerate employer, Fletcher – a Tory – once voted Labour in the cause of better wages for workmen; as a councillor, he worked tirelessly against smoke pollution (from his obituary, 'Awfully Sudden Death of Mr. Herbert Fletcher', *Bolton Evening News*, 17 September 1895).

59. See Webb to Fletcher, 14 August 1872 (private collection).

60. From the annotation on Webb's drawing (V&A, W&I, E.110–1916, n.d.).

61. Webb to Herbert Fletcher, 14 August 1872 (private collection).

62. For more on the competition see, for example, Saint, pp. 54–8; Brooks, pp. 220–25; and Igor Webb, 'The Bradford Wool Exchange: Industrial Capitalism and the Popularity of Gothic'.

63. As Saint points out, the fact the Ruskin softened his lecture a little by recommending Gothic, and that he drew the audience's attention to the merits of Waterhouse's Manchester Assize Courts, did not appear in the published lecture (Saint, p. 55).

64. For an illustration of the Lockwood and Mawson scheme see, for example, Brooks, p. 224, fig. 89.

65. For an illustration of Shaw's scheme see, for example, Saint, p. 56, fig. 36; Brooks, p. 222, fig. 88; and Stefan Muthesius, pp. 130-31.

66. Minutes of the first meeting of the directors of the Middlesbrough Exchange Co. Ltd., 19 August 1864 (Directors' Minute Book no. 1, 1066/13/16, Teesside Archives).

67. Bell's letter (missing) was read to the directors on 26 January 1865 (Directors' Minute Book no. 1, 1066/13/16, Teesside Archives).

68. The Middlesbrough Exchange Co. Ltd.: Minutes of the Sub-Committee Meeting, 26 January 1865: 'The Secretary … is requested to ask Mr Bell to obtain and kindly give the Directors Information as to the fee demanded by Mr. Webb.' (Directors' Minute Book no. 1, 1066/13/16, Teesside Archives).

69. Several incognito entries were submitted; Charles Adams of London, who had recently established an office in Stockton-on-Tees, was chosen as the winner but was not permitted to take the £100 prize after it was discovered that his name

had been revealed deliberately. However, his design was executed. For the full story of the affair, see Green, 'On Change, Grandeur, and Designs'.

70. Minutes of the Subcommittee on St John's Lane Improvement, 15 December 1866 (Tyne and Wear Archives Service). George Howard knew that 'Bell tried to induce the Newcastle people to employ him to build a new street' (Howard to Lord Airlie, 6 November 1869 (Castle Howard Archives), quoted by Dakers in 'Castle in the Air', p. 276).

71. The final line was very like Webb's but straighter; the upper end of Webb's did line through with Grainger Street, however. On the first of two successive meetings of a subcommittee of the Finance Committee, it was stated that Webb had prepared the Parliamentary plan (which was submitted to Parliament with the application for permission to improve the street), and on the second, that Lamb, the Borough Surveyor, had prepared it (see the *Proceedings of the Newcastle Council* for 1867, Central Library, Newcastle upon Tyne). As there is no mention of this in Webb's papers, the latter would appear to be correct. Irritated by successive delays, some councillors blamed them on Councillor Wilson, who had first suggested approaching an architect from the metropolis, whilst others castigated Bell for involving Webb, whose plan had not been acceptable without amendment.

72. From the notes Webb made on site, it is clear that he intended in his report to make a very strong case for each building being designed individually (SB 1865–77).

73. All quotations in this paragraph are taken from the notes he made for his report (SB 1865–77, private collection).

74. Constantine Ionides, one of its Greek patrons, had introduced Valpy to the circle in the early 1860s.

75. The omission of one floor was considered after the drawings were prepared but in the end the house was built as designed except that the attic floor has a front room only. Valpy and Chaplin moved into 19 Lincoln's Inn Fields in 1871, Valpy having been in practice on his own at 60 Carey Street, and then with Tuke (Tuke and Valpy). In 1871 Webb designed the iron ladder and catwalk which gave access to the chimneys and roof lantern.

76. Webb's preliminary scheme (not identified as being for this building) is in the V&A, W&I (E.203–1916); the others are in the BAL/RIBADC.

77. Similar curves would appear on parapets on some of Webb's later buildings, for example Exning House and St Martin's Church, Brampton (see chapters 9 and 12, respectively).

78. For an illustration of Soane's front elevation, see, for example, Stroud, p. 90, fig. 35. In general Webb disapproved of the architecture of Soane's day but there is no doubt that both men shared a taste for certain building elements. These included bold unadorned geometrical forms (especially for stable-yard entrances), tall sashes in shallow panels, brick pilasters, small pyramid roofs and, in interiors, wide segmental arches, top-lit stair halls with curved staircases, and deep alcoves.

79. For an illustration of such a porch, see for example Condover Hall, Shropshire (c. 1595), in Pevsner, *Shropshire*, p. 45.

80. See Lethaby (1979), pl. 20, for a reproduction of a perspective sketch of the building by W Curtis Green made before it lost the turret and the wrought-iron arches on the balcony. Ashbee was apparently influence by Webb's slender wrought-iron arches. See, for example, his Cheyne Walk houses in Stamp and Goulancourt, pp. 194–5.

81. Warington Taylor to Philip Webb, 1868, quoted in Lethaby (1935), p. 90.

82. For the influence on Shaw's houses see, for example, number 18 Hyde Park Gate (1871) in Saint, p. 137, fig. 116.

83. For St Benet's see, for example, Pevsner, *London: 1*, fig. 70.

84. For illustrations of the use of banding, see, for example: Bodley and Garner, School Board Offices, 1871–77 (in Curl, p. 132, fig. 83); Shaw, Allied Assurance Offices, St James's Street, 1881–88, and New Scotland Yard, Westminster, 1887–90, (Curl, p. 132, fig. 84, and p. 136, fig. 87); MacLaren, numbers 10–12 Palace Court, Bayswater, 1889–90, and Bentley, Westminster Cathedral, 1895–1903 (Service and others, *Edwardian Architecture and its Origins*, p. 113, fig. 16, and p. 257, fig. 11).

85. Sir Sidney Cockerell, at the time Director of the Fitzwilliam Museum, told Webb in a letter of 14 April 1907 that students at Cambridge were studying Webb's work, giving the following as an example: 'He is so much your admirer that he collects photographs of your houses, and goes, as I used to do in my old days, to gaze up at that front in Lincoln's Inn Fields… His name is Goodhart-Rendell…' (Quoted in Brandon, p. 12, from Cockerell to Webb, 14 April 1907, V&A, W&I, 86 TT.16).

86. Pite, p. 90.

87. The details can be found in Webb's letters to Hugh Bell of 10 November 1881, 25 January 1882, and 9 April 1884 (LB 1, fols 207–9 and 230; LB 2, fols 36–7), and in the Directors' Minute Book 2 (Bell Brothers Papers, Teesside Archives). With the first letter, Webb enclosed a rough preliminary plan; a rearrangement of it, embodying Bell Brothers' suggestions, accompanied his second letter; in the third he estimated the cost of the offices to be not less than £8,000, and suggested £200 as his remuneration, the scheme having been put aside. The office block is discussed and illustrated in Curry and Kirk, pp. 41–3.

88. The Bells' private room is marked 'general' office on Webb's plan.

89. Lowthian Bell's office is marked 'Messrs Bell's private office' on Webb's plan.

90. Honan and Rodgers of Manchester installed the steel and concrete floors, using steel joists from Dorman, Long & Co. (CB, and AddB); D Selby Bigge & Co. of

Newcastle upon Tyne installed the electric lighting.

91. Specification, p. 21 (copy in the author's collection).

92. Webb to Hugh Bell, 10 November 1881, LB 1, fols 207–9. The letter is given in full in Brandon-Jones, 'Philip Webb and the Bell Family', p. 12.

93. Pevsner, *Cumberland and Westmorland*, p. 77.

94. The seat was in the building in 1982 but is now missing. Webb's design for it is item WEBB [36] 43, BAL/RIBADC.

95. The late K A S Headlam-Morley, a retired director of Dorman, Long, & Co., told me of Hugh Bell's interest in every detail of the building and in up-to-the-minute office technology.

96. The late R S H Capes, an erstwhile Secretary of Dorman, Long & Co., opined that the standard of building was no longer achievable, and the late Lance Shuttleworth, Manager and a director of Dorman, Long Chemicals, stated that the structure and fittings were exceptionally good and that the accommodation was excellent (in each case in conversation with the author, 1982). Mr Shuttleworth also pointed out that Hugh Bell had a great interest in architecture.

97. See Webb to Boyce, 5 January 1885, BL Add. MS 43534.

98. The dining room was in the part of the building that was demolished in the 1930s. The window can be seen on Webb's 1881 drawing (the accepted scheme), reproduced in Dakers, *Clouds*, pp. 60 and 61, figs 30 and 33, and as built with the upper part amended, in the illustration of the east front in this chapter.

99. For illustrations of Mackintosh's Hill House showing repeated grid patterns, see, for example, Steele, pp. 128–35.

100. For illustrations of the Voysey interiors see, for example, Hitchmough, *Voysey*, p. 197, fig. 13, and p.198, fig. 14.

101. Dorman, Long, & Co., the firm that had taken control of Bell Brothers, had recently bought the houses; a fall in trade necessitated the abandoning of the project. Jack's extension to the east would have repeated Webb's frontage in every detail, with a narrow bay surmounted by a turret between it and the new part. Jack's widow presented the firm with his box of drawings for the project and Webb's original Conditions and Specification, adapted by Jack for the proposed new work (Corus Northern Records Centre).

102. The most significant change came in 1959–60, when local architect Philip Middleton (who kindly provided drawings of his changes) created a new board room on the west side of the ground floor, inserting a long curved timber wall in such a way that it could be removed without trace, as has proved to be the case.

103. After the public inquiry held on 8 January 1974, thanks to the spirited written defence of the building by John Brandon-Jones, the efforts of other defenders, the decision of Geoffrey Rippon, Secretary of State for the Environment, and the recommendation of his inspector V Leslie Nash, the building was saved.

104. Middlesbrough Council extended the renovation of the exterior contract after dry rot was discovered. This work and the conversion of the building into a hostel for use by Toc H, which was funded by the council and the Housing Corporation for the Endeavour Housing Association, was done under the direction of J Stuart Mackie of the local architectural firm Hugh Wilson and Lewis Womersley (Toc H is a charity working to break down the barriers of prejudice which divide individuals and groups in society). The second repair work and conversion was directed by Guy Holmes of the Darlington architectural firm Browne Smith Baker, and funded by the Stonham Housing Association (the present owners of the building) and the Housing Corporation. The two architects kindly provided me with information and drawings of the alterations.

105. Pevsner, *Yorkshire: North Riding*, p. 253; John Brandon-Jones, 'Zetland House, Zetland Road, Middlesbrough', typescript copy (author's collection).

106. Webb's drawing is in a private collection. For the anonymous reviewer's comments in full, see 'The Exhibition of the Royal Academy', p. 306, and 'The Architectural Room at the Royal Academy, 1858', p. 172.

107. See Webb to George Gilbert Scott junior, 6 October 1875, LB 1, fols 11–12. Webb's sheet of sketches, now missing, is reproduced in Brandon-Jones, 'The Work of Philip Webb and Norman Shaw', p. 45. No mention of the project has been found in the Bell family papers.

108. The vicar kindly searched the records for any involvement by Webb.

109. Kennard paid Webb £291 6s 0d (AB).

110. See Pevsner and Hubbard, *Cheshire*, pp. 361–2, and the anonymous reporter's account of the consecration of Pearson's church, 'The Church at Thurston', in January 1886 (from a photocopy in my collection of a page of cuttings from an unidentified local newspaper).

111. For a reproduction of one of Street's drawings see, for example, Stefan Muthesius, p. 97, fig. 62.

112. See Webb to Mrs Oldham, 29 August 1881, LB 1, fols 195–6; he enclosed the drawing, dated the same day, for the church. The drawing is in the V&A, W&I (E.157–1916).

113. Brandon-Jones, 'Philip Webb', p. 254. Webb's drawings are in the BAL/RIBADC (Webb [56]).

114. The altar (W.4–2003) and lectern (W.5–2003), and the cross (M. 34–1970) are in the V&A, FT&F and V&A, SMC&G respectively; Webb's drawings, both of 1897, for the altar and lectern are in the BAL/RIBADC ([31] 2, and [31] 3–4 respectively), and for the chapel itself in the V&A (E.107–1945). Mrs Gilmore asked Webb to design these items as the chapel was being built (4 November 1896, SB 1896–1900); his memorandum of her request makes it clear that he designed the altar table in 1896, its fretted panels and the lectern and cross in

1897; the altar cloth was designed between 1898 and 1899, as a note on the drawing records.

115. The Morris & Co. windows are detailed in Sewter, II, p. 193, and in the English Heritage Listing Database (Clapham Common, 1. 5033, TQ 2775 9/11 and 9/12).

116. Gilmore House and chapel are now owned by Nouettes Investments Limited. I am grateful to Mr G Nawab for information on the recent conversion and present use and condition of the house and chapel.

117. Webb's drawing for the super-frontal, illustrated in chapter 3, is item E.58–1940, the embroidered cloth (illustrated in *William Morris*, ed. by Parry, p. 251) is item T.379–1970, and the altar cross is item M.34–1970, in the V&A, W&I.

118. For illustrations of the interior of Prior's nave, see, for example, Garnham, *St Andrew's Church, Roker*, pp. 42–3.

119. For illustrations of the Voysey buildings, see, for example, Hitchmough, *Voysey*, p. 175, fig. 6, and p. 180, fig. 16.

120. Almshouses, a small grammar school, and a chapel had been built on the site of the existing parish church in 1688 by the then Earl of Carlisle; the chapel was rebuilt as the parish church in 1788 and enlarged in 1828. For a much fuller history of all the successive Brampton parish churches including Webb's, and full descriptions of its M&Co windows, see Penn, *Brampton Church and its Windows*; see also McEvoy, 'Webb at Brampton', and Neil Jackson, 'A church for SPAB?', and Curry and Kirk, pp. 32–3.

121. It is clear from Webb's letter to George Howard of 29 September 1874, from which the quotation is taken, that at some time the two men had discussed the desirability of replacing the existing church; and that whilst in Brampton to examine the site of a proposed terrace of artisans' cottages he was designing for the estate, Webb had examined the existing church and churchyard (Webb to George Howard, 29 September 1874, J22/64, Castle Howard Archives).

122. Henry Whitehead was born in Ramsgate and educated at Oxford. He was a Broad Church man and had worked with the London poor and helped Dr John Snow to prove that contaminated water spread cholera. He left Brampton in 1888 but returned as vicar of nearby Lanercost in 1890.

123. The committee was formed at a public meeting held in June 1874 to consider re-pewing the church. At the September meeting, Charles Howard, the chairman, pointed out that £3,500 had already been promised; he offered to increase his own contribution if Webb were appointed, and intimated that help would be forthcoming for a much-needed tramway and sewerage system for the town (this was duly given).

124. See Webb to George Howard, 29 September 1874, J22/64, Castle Howard Archives).

125. Webb made a copy of his MS report (dated 4 November 1874) and sent it to George Howard (J22/65, Castle Howard Archives); another copy, not in Webb's hand, is item C575/4/a in the Howard Papers.

126. The committee made its decision after Webb had pointed out that he would require payment and George Howard had lauded his design and strongly urged that the church be built but that completion of the tower be postponed for a few years (see Webb to George Howard, 7 May 1875, J22/64, Castle Howard Archives).

127. On 7 February 1877, Webb sent the drawings, specification, contract, and condition to Forster for signing by the builders (see Webb to Thomas Forster, 7 February 1877, LB 1, fol.61). Morland had had experience of church building with Cory and Ferguson of Carlisle. The cost is approximate, as the account of expenses on the church made by C Stephenson, agent to the Naworth Estate, includes estimated figures for the extras, which included the cost of an organ, central heating, and the installation of gas (Howard Papers). When the church was finished in 1878, Webb expressed his hope that George Howard would be 'more or less content with the result of his energetic striving to have something permanently good in the art way done in the north country' (Webb to Rosalind Howard, 2 December 1878, Castle Howard Archives).

128. Webb to Thomas Forster, 23 March 1875, LB 1, fols 18–20 (p. 19). Forster, a local solicitor, was the honorary secretary to the committee.

129. Webb to George Howard, 18 June 1877, J22/64, Castle Howard Archives.

130. There is a copy of Webb's report (dated 15 April 1884), and his original 'Directions for certain repairs …' of the same date, in the Howard Papers (C575/4/h and C575/4/h). The heat generated by the central heating and the gas-lights had drawn up ground water into the floor, necessitating excavation, the construction of sleeper walls, re-flooring, and some draining work along the south front. A few slates of the wrong type were causing leaks in the south aisle; and the gutters above the north aisle were leaking because of shrinkage of the timbers of the lattice girders under them, a matter for which Webb, holding himself partly responsible, tried in vain to pay (see Webb to Christopher Stephenson, Agent to the Naworth Estate, 20 August 1885, Howard Papers).

131. Webb to Stephenson, 13 August 1885, Howard Papers. Opposed to gas lighting because it did 'serious injury to public buildings', in 1877 Webb had nevertheless promised to produce a scheme for its installation; it is not known whether his scheme was executed (see Webb to Forster, 10 and 14 February 1877, LB 1, fols 62–4).

132. Penn quotes Webb on the matter in *Brampton Church*, p. 31. It took some time to amass the necessary funds for the marble.

133. See Webb to George Howard, 2 October 1903, Howard Papers. Evidently Webb had forgotten that, at the beginning of 1878, the committee being 'anxious to

know whether it wd. be possible for them to complete the tower in continuation of the works', he had 'therefore designed the upper part ... on a much reduced scale'; and that he had sent the drawings to Beaty Brothers for an estimate which, if low enough, would decide the committee to go ahead immediately (Webb to Beaty Brothers, 3 January 1878, LB 1, fol. 115). This scheme, with some modification, is the one that was constructed (the 1878 drawings are in the SPAB Archive).

134. Webb made it plain that he did not wish any architect other than George Jack, who understood his work, to carry out his designs and possibly 'make a jumble' of them (Webb to George Howard, 18 November 1904, Howard Papers). Howard, by then the eighth earl, made his subscription conditional on Jack being the supervising architect. Webb chiefly modified the belfry openings and added the spirelet.

135. Webb repeatedly warned George Howard by letter that he was laying himself open to blame for supporting his, a London architect's, design (for example in Webb to Howard, 17 October 1874, J22/64, Castle Howard Archives). In 1879, Howard learnt that the committee *expected* him to pay off the outstanding debts on the church, one of the reasons being that it believed the townsfolk had been induced into having a new church by the Howards (the full text of Howard's response of 30 August 1897 is given in Penn, pp. 21–3). Howard made a large contribution, part to be used to cover Webb's fee (the architect never knew of this).

136. The terracotta was by a Miss Rope, probably Ellen Mary Rope (1855–1934) who designed terracotta panels for the Della Robbia Pottery, Birkenhead. Kate Faulkner possibly worked the gesso panel. A local craftsman, using motifs designed by Webb for the clergy seats, made the large umbrella stand. Charles Ferguson designed the adjacent church hall (1895) in a sympathetic manner, and added wrought-iron gates and a fence (removed).

137. Pugin's convent is illustrated, for example, in Stanton, *Pugin*, p. 154, fig. 131.

138. George Routledge, the publisher and a member of the committee, agreed with Webb that the porch should be built with the body of the church; he offered £100 towards its cost if this were done. Webb sent the working drawings to the builder on 6 November 1877, and the porch was constructed accordingly (see Webb to Forster, 24 October 1877, LB 1, fols 108–9 (fol. 109), and to Beaty Brothers, 6 November 1877, fols 112–13 (fol. 113)).

139. They are shown as being glazed on Webb's 1875 drawings (SPAB Archive).

140. Tracery lights above the lancets were to have lit the clock room but to reduce costs they were omitted and the arch was lowered.

141. On Webb's 1875 plan of the church, the font is in the nave immediately east of the central pillar of the baptistery (SPAB Archive).

142. Penn, p. 16.

143. Webb thought that a pulpit would have to be provided but he readily agreed to its omission at Whitehead's suggestion (Penn quotes from Webb's letter to Whitehead in *Brampton Church*, p. 19).

144. In the 1875 scheme, the lines are broken halfway down the nave by a transverse arch with an open screen above it, but this was one of the omissions made to reduce costs.

145. Webb to George Howard, 14 September 1875, J22/64, Castle Howard Archives. Webb was replying to a letter from the Bishop of Carlisle, in which the latter commented upon and asked questions about Webb's design for the church, including the lack of length in the nave; Howard also enclosed his draft reply, asking Webb to add his own explanations, which he does in this letter.

146. Originating in Burgundy in the eleventh century, this type of stone vault was adopted by the Cistercians in the following century, Fountains Abbey being an early example of its use.

147. Whitewashed plaster walls flush with sandstone dressings were traditional in some parts of Cumberland, and Webb had used them already in Naworth Castle and Four Gables, but his prime motive was to increase the effect of spaciousness.

148. The interior of St Martin's-on-the-Hill is illustrated, for example, in Winpenny, p. 9.

149. Webb to Forster, 24 April 1877, LB 1, fol. 84.

150. Webb to Forster, 24 October 1877, LB1, fols 108–9 (fol. 108); Webb to John Carrick, 16 March 1878, LB 1, fols 123–5 (p. 125).

151. Penn, p. 54.

152. See for example, Webb to John Carrick, 16 March 1878, LB 1, fols 123–5 (fol. 124).

153. The Burne-Jones cartoons are in the Tullie House Museum and Art Gallery, Carlisle (1922.45.1–9). There is not space in the present work to cover any of the windows in detail but Penn and Sewter do so respectively in *Brampton Church* (pp. 53–69) and *Stained Glass of William Morris* (pp. 29–31, and several plates).

154. See Webb to Rosalind Howard, 2 December 1878, and to George Howard, 9 December 1878, J22/64, Castle Howard Archives.

155. Webb to William Weir, 1 March 1902, SPAB Archive.

156. For illustrations of Queen's Cross Church, see, for example, Steele, pp. 32–41.

157. These are illustrated, for example, in Garnham, p. 48 (plans showing the chancel walls) and the plate on pp. 26–7 (showing the battered nave wall).

158. There are several illustrations of the fittings in Garnham, *St Andrew's Church, Roker*. Gimson, one of Webb's friends and disciples, designed those of the chancel.

159. See Garnham, *St Andrew's Church, Roker*, for an illustration of the nave showing the side passages (pl. on pp. 34–5), and of Bodley's nave with passages (p. 14, fig. 28). Garnham points out the likelihood of Bodley's church having inspired Prior in this matter (p. 15).

CHAPTER 13: WEBB AND HIS CLIENTS AND CONTRACTORS

1. Webb to Wyndham, 20 July 1886, LB 2, fol. 61.
2. Webb to W Tatham, 25 July 1874, LB 1, fol. 6.
3. See, for example, *Mary Gladstone: her Diaries and Letters*, ed. by Masterman.
4. Kerr, p. 51. Donald Smith discusses this conditioning through paintings in 'The Work of Philip Webb', p. 17.
5. Hugh Bell to Webb, 25 October 1871 (private collection).
6. Yorke told Emery Walker of the introduction (see Lethaby (1935), pp.105–6).
7. For Howard approaching Webb see Webb to Pitt-Rivers, 12 December 1881, LB 1, fols 217–18 (Pitt-Rivers' wife was Rosalind Howard's sister).
8. For this aspect of Webb's relationships, see Lethaby (1935), p. 111; for his problems with Watts, see Webb to G F Watts, 8, 17, and 18 July 1874, LB 1, fols 1–5, and George Howard to Charles Howard, 25 February1875, J20, Castle Howard Archives, and also Dakers, *The Holland Park Circle*, pp. 150–52; for the refusing of the Oast House fee, see Webb to Lord Sackville Cecil, 11 September 1874, LB 1, fol. 9.
9. See Webb to Fletcher, 1872 (private collection); Fletcher's philanthropic work in London might have brought him into contact with Webb, perhaps via Gillum, or possibly Isaac Lowthian Bell, a fellow colliery-owner, recommended Webb.
10. Webb to Lord Fitzhardinge, 4 May 1877, LB 1, fols 89–90.
11. Webb to W W Cardwell, 19 April and 11 October 1876, LB 1, fols 33–8 and 46–8. Brodie, a distinguished chemist and son of a famous surgeon, probably met Webb through Tomes or Bowman.
12. The Ada Godman Diaries (private collection).
13. Webb to Rosalind Howard, 19 August 1869 and 30 September 1871, J22/64, Castle Howard Archives.
14. Webb to Rosalind Howard, 17 September 1872, J22/64, Castle Howard Archives.
15. Webb to the 'Howards' [George and Rosalind], 12 September 1877, J22/64, Castle Howard Archives.
16. Lyulph Stanley to Rosalind Howard, 1 February 1878, Castle Howard Archives.
17. George Jack, who was often present at Webb's meetings with clients, recorded this (see Lethaby (1935), p. 194).
18. Webb to Lucy Orrinsmith, 22 February 1876, LB 1, fols 31–2.
19. Webb to Frank Faulkner, 24 January 1887, LB 2, fols 79–80.
20. Webb to Wyndham, 28 December 1876, LB 1, fols 50–52.
21. Webb to Miss Ewart, 14 September 1883, 28 February, and 4 or 5 March 1884, LB 2, fols 17–18, 29–31, and 33.
22. Webb to Ramsden, 25 May and 17 and 26 November 1886, LB 2, fols 49–51, 65–7, and 68–71 (the quotation is from the second letter).
23. Webb to Wyndham, 1 July 1884, LB 2, fols 38–9.
24. Webb to Wyndham, 20 November 1879, LB 1, fol. 158. In the event, they were not executed.
25. Webb to Godman, 12 November 1878 (quoted in full by Brandon-Jones in 'Notes on the Building of Smeaton Manor', p. 47).
26. Webb to Flower, 11 September 1885, LB 2, fol. 48.
27. Webb to George Jack, 26 May 1888, kept loose in LB 2.
28. Webb to Pitt-Rivers, 15 December 1882 and 2 January 1883, LB 2, fols 5–6 and 7.
29. Webb to Godman, 27 February 1878 (quoted in full by Brandon-Jones in 'Notes on the Building of Smeaton Manor', pp. 35–6).
30. Webb to Wyndham, 29 January 1877, LB 1, fols 58–9.
31. Webb to Pitt-Rivers, 9 April 1883, LB 2, fols 7–9.
32. George Jack, 'An Appreciation of Philip Webb', p. 5.
33. See note in SB 1896–1900, 17 September 1897.
34. See Max Egremont, *The Cousins* (London: Collins, 1977), p. 145.
35. Webb to Ramsden, 28 November 1886, LB 2, fols 68–71 (fol. 69).
36. See Webb to George Howard, 28 August 1875, J22/64, and to Lowthian Bell, 4 April 1877, LB 1, fols 78–9.
37. Webb to Miss Ewart, 28 February and 4 or 5 March 1884, LB 2, fols 29–33.
38. Webb to Wyndham, 7 and 10 June 1881, LB 1, fols 177 and 178.
39. See, for example, Webb to Ramsden, 14 April 1887, LB 2, fols 86–8 (fol. 87).
40. Webb recounted this in his letter to George Jack, 26 May 1888, loose in LB 2.
41. The snuffbox is in a private collection.
42. Webb to James Simmonds (clerk of works, Clouds), 14 January 1882, LB 1, fols 225–6 (fol. 226).
43. Webb to G Sedger, 14 February and 20 March 1882, LB 1, fols 232–3, 237–8. Webb took Sedger's brother Thomas into his office on a month's trial, but he proved to be insufficiently trained for the work, so Webb advised him to work in a big office where there would be tasks with which he could cope.
44. Jack designed such items for Willinghurst, including some gables that Webb found 'architecturalo'al' (see Webb to G Jack, 10 May to 1 June 1888, loose in LB 2); both Webb and Morris applied this term, coined by Dickens, to pretentious or elaborate buildings and details (see Charles Dickens, *Great Expectations*, chapter 27).
45. Webb to John Tyerman, 2 September 1876, LB 1, fols 45–6.
46. Webb to Wyndham, 17 July 1886, LB 2, fols 56–8.
47. Webb to Edwards (foreman of the works, Willinghurst), and to John Hardy (clerk of works), 3 September 1887, LB 2, fols 97–9.
48. See Webb to Boyce, 23 November 1885, BL Add. MS 45354.
49. See Webb to Lowthian Bell, 4 April 1877, LB 1, fols 78–9.

50. For instance, Webb dined one evening with the Eyres, and selected suitable furniture for Warrens House from their London house (SB 1896–1900).
51. See, for example, Webb to Wyndham, 14 May 1879, LB 1, fols 145–6.
52. Webb designed the decoration (executed by Kate Faulkner, 1884–85) for A A Ionides's piano (Lethaby (1935), p. 189); Webb to Pitt-Rivers, 9 April 1883, LB 2, fols 7–9.
53. Webb to Mrs Beale, 11 and 12 January 1894 (private collection).
54. See, for example, his memorandum about meeting Miss Ewart at Morris & Co. on 9 February 1889 (SB 1877–92), and his letters to Miss Astley, 29 November 1882 (LB 2, fols 1–2), and to the Yorkes, 18 November 1890 (quoted in full by Helen Smith in 'Philip Webb's restoration of Forthampton Court', pp. 98–9).
55. Webb to Madeline Wyndham, 30 August 1884, LB 2, fols 43–5.
56. Webb to Wyndham, 16 August 1886, LB 2, fols 62–3 (fol. 62).
57. Webb to Boyce, 29 August 1884, BL Add. MS 45354.
58. Webb to G Jack, 1 June 1888, kept loose in LB 2.
59. Webb to Boyce, n.d., BL Add. MS 45354 (quoted in Lethaby (1935), p. 93, with the date 15 February 1877).
60. Webb to G Jack, 21 May 1888, kept loose in LB 2.
61. Webb to Boyce, 11 September 1885, BL Add. MS 45354.
62. Webb to George Howard, 6 February 1875, J22/64, Castle Howard Archives.
63. Webb to Godman, 10 December 1879 (quoted in full in Brandon-Jones, 'Notes on the Building of Smeaton Manor', pp. 55–6).
64. Ruskin to Hale White, 27 October 1867, quoted by Hale White in The Groombridge Diary, ed. by Dorothy White, p. 40.

CHAPTER 14: THE LAST YEARS

1. Lethaby (1935), p. 195.
2. Webb to Hale White, 13 May 1899, MR 10/15, Central Library, Bedford.
3. Webb to Hale White, 30 January 1899, MR 10/12, Central Library, Bedford.
4. Lethaby (1935), p. 201.
5. Webb to Cockerell, 23 December 1898, in Friends of a Lifetime, ed. by Meynell, p. 99, and to Hale White, 13 May 1899, MR 10/15, Central Library, Bedford.
6. Webb to Hale White, 13 and 16 May 1900, MR 10/15, 10/16, Central Library, Bedford.
7. I L Bell to Webb, 13 April 1900. For the full letter and a quotation from Webb's reply, see Lethaby (1935), p. 203.
8. Hale White to Webb, 14 June 1900, in William Hale White, Letters to Three Friends, ed. by Dorothy V White, p. 303.
9. For Blunt's romance with Jane Morris, see Elizabeth Longford, 1982 repr. edn, pp. 278–80.
10. Entry for 26 May 1900, in Blunt, My Diaries, 1-vol. edn, 1933, p. 368.
11. Longford, p. 330; Lady Anne Blunt to Cockerell, 14 June 1900, BL Add. MS 52760 (quoted in Brandon, 'Philip Webb, the William Morris Circle, and Sussex', p. 8).
12. Cockerell to Webb, 27 May 1900, in Friends of a Lifetime, ed. by Meynell, pp. 103–4.
13. Webb to Cockerell, 6 July 1900, in ibid., pp. 105–6 (p. 105).
14. Webb to Cockerell, 28 July 1900, in ibid., pp. 106–7.
15. Webb to Sidney Barnsley, 10 August 1900, in Lethaby (1935), pp. 206–7. Bates had hanged himself in the cart-shed; it was moved to another of Blunt's properties before or during Webb's tenancy of the house (Longford, pp. 330–31).
16. Webb to Sidney Barnsley, 10 August 1900 (Lethaby (1935), p. 207); Webb to George Howard, 1 September 1900, J22/64, Castle Howard Archives.
17. SB 1896–1900, and Webb's drawings WEBB [49] 1–6, September to November 1900, BAL/RIBADC.
18. Webb to Mrs Flower and Jane Morris, 1900, BL Add. MS 45343 and 45355; CB. William Dench was the estate carpenter but Webb noted in his Address Book that Benjamin Payne of Three Bridges did some carpentry at Caxtons (February 1901, fol. 111).
19. Cockerell to Webb, 16 December 1900, BL Add. MS 52760. Webb and Cockerell were among the people who regarded 1 January 1901 as the first day of the twentieth century.
20. For the selling of Webb's books, see Lethaby (1935), p. 209; the drawings (receipt in BL Add. MS 52760) are in a private collection.
21. Lethaby (1935), pp. 209 and 219–20, and Surtees, The Paintings and Drawings of Dante-Gabriel Rossetti, pp. 72 and 77. See Webb to Boyce, 18 August 1885, BL Add. MS 45354, for his acceptance of Rossetti's painting. Webb noted on the back of the painting that he gave it to Cockerell on 17 December 1900, after Cockerell promised to dispose of it eventually to a national gallery of English paintings. Cockerell presented it to the Fitzwilliam Museum, Cambridge on 3 June 1937. The sofa sketch is in the Birmingham Museum and Art Gallery Collection.
22. For Morris's explanation of why he printed the books, see Morris to Webb, 27 August 1894, in Mackail, II, pp. 321–2; Webb to the Librarian of Trinity College, 15 December 1902, quoted in Lethaby (1935), p. 220.
23. For example: in 1905 Webb received interest on £1,442 but by the following year his savings were only £1,219 (Bank AB). Sydney Cockerell, one of those who added small sums to Webb's account during the periods when his mind was a little confused, told John Brandon-Jones of this kindly topping-up.
24. All the last figures in the paragraph come from Webb's Bank AB.
25. See Mackail, II, pp. 339–40 and 345; Daily News, 26 June 1909 (from a cutting in Webb's Scrap Book, private collection).
26. As Jack told Lethaby (Lethaby (1935), p. 228); Webb to Cockerell, 4 March 1900, in Friends of a Lifetime, ed. by Meynell, pp. 99–101 (p. 100).
27. Lethaby (1935), p. 209.
28. Webb to Cockerell, 4 March 1900 and 10 January 1901, in Friends of a Lifetime, ed. by Meynell, pp. 100 and 107.
29. See W S Blunt to Cockerell, 26 January 1901, in Friends of a Lifetime, ed. by Meynell, pp. 157–8 (p. 157); Webb to Sidney Barnsley, 25 June 1901, in Lethaby (1935), pp. 214–15.
30. Webb to Cockerell, 10 January 1901, in Friends of a Lifetime, ed. by Meynell, pp. 107–8.
31. Webb to Sidney Barnsley, 11 July 1902, in Lethaby (1935), pp. 218–19 (p. 218).
32. Mrs Dickinson to Lethaby, in Lethaby (1935), pp. 211–13; in 1982 Mr F Hyder, a resident of Worth for over 80 years, told me that when they were boys, he and his friends had found Webb crotchety.
33. See the prefatory note by Cockerell in the bound letters, 'Philip Webb to Mrs Wickham Flower', which he presented to the BL (Add. MS 45355).
34. Webb to G P Boyce, 29 August 1884 (BL Add. MS 45354); Webb to Cockerell, 10 January 1901, in Friends of a Lifetime, ed. by Meynell, pp. 107–8 (p. 107).
35. See Lethaby (1935), p. 212. The Bewick book is Cotes, History of British Birds, illustrated by Thomas Bewick.
36. See Webb's letters to Mrs Margaret Dickinson, 1900–1911, in the Emery Walker Library (cat. 1991 1016 644), Cheltenham Art Gallery & Museum.
37. Webb to Cockerell, 20 November 1902, in Friends of a Lifetime, ed. by Meynell, pp. 109–10 (p. 110); Webb to Hale White, 21 August 1907, MR 10/28, Central Library, Bedford.
38. Lambourne, p. 22 (caption to fig. 18).
39. There is a watercolour by Thomas Rooke at Kelmscott Manor of Webb's parlour in Caxtons (the Collection of the Society of Antiquaries), and others of the house by Rooke in a private collection.
40. Webb to Cockerell, 20 November 1902, in Friends of a Lifetime, ed. by Meynell, pp. 109–10 (p. 110). Webb told Mrs Dickinson by letter, 28 July 1903, that he was her friend as well as her employer (Emery Walker Library, cat. 1991 1016 644, Cheltenham Art Gallery & Museum).
41. See Webb to J R Holliday, 11 June 1902, in Lethaby (1935), p. 217; 'Studio-talk: Birmingham', Studio, 29 (1903), p. 293. Webb's drawings for the mace are WEBB [63] 1–3, dated January–April 1902, BAL/RIBADC. Alice Beale, presented the mace to the university but the commission came to Webb through J R Holliday of Birmingham (see Webb to A H Powell, 7 March 1902, in Lethaby (1935), pp 216–17 (p. 216)).
42. Webb's drawing for these, done on one of Weir's, dated June 1901, is WEBB [12], BAL/RIBADC.
43. See Lethaby (1935), pp. 214–17. The bookplate designed for Cockerell and Walker is probably that for Herbert George Fordham (illustrated in ibid., p. 216). A print from it, and another from St John and Cicely Hornby's Ashendene Press bookplate, which also was probably designed by Webb (dated 19 November 1901 in pencil), are kept with Webb's letters to Hale White (MR 10/37, 38, Central Library, Bedford).
44. See Madeline Wyndham [?] to Cockerell, 15 October 1901, Cockerell Papers, BL Add. MS 52760, and Dakers, Clouds, pp. 148–9 (for the Webb design and sketch, fig. 81).
45. Webb gave his drawing for the panel to George Jack (private collection).
46. See Webb to G Jack, 3 April 1902 (private collection).
47. See Penn, pp. 26–31.
48. See Lethaby (1935), p. 220.
49. Bell to Webb, 1902, in Lethaby (1935), pp. 217–18. The Rounton Grange drawings are now in the NYCRO.
50. W S Blunt to Cockerell, 11 June 1913, in Friends of a Lifetime, ed. by Meynell, pp. 181–2 (p. 181).
51. Webb to Cockerell, quoted in Lethaby (1935), p. 220.
52. Webb to Cockerell, 7 March 1904, in Friends of a Lifetime, ed. by Meynell, pp. 113–115 (p. 114); Webb to Lethaby, 3 July 1904, 8 April 1904, and 21 December 1909, in Lethaby (1935), pp. 138–40 and 129–30.
53. Webb to Lethaby, 5 December 1904, 3 July 1904, and 17 January 1906, quoted in Lethaby (1935), pp. 221, 138, and 221.
54. Webb to Lethaby, 8 February 1908, in Lethaby (1935), p. 224.
55. Winmill, pp. 50 and 51. Webb had advised Winmill on the design of a small house for the 'House and Home' exhibition at the Whitechapel Art Gallery the previous year; Winmill used a Webb design, probably made years before, for the bow-shaped wrought-iron window catches.
56. Webb to Lethaby, 28 August 1905, in Lethaby (1935), p. 141 (for Bentley's request and Webb's refusal, see p. 140).
57. Webb to Jane Morris, 12 November 1903 (BL Add. MS 45343), quoted in Brandon, 'Philip Webb', p. 12.
58. Ibid.. Webb told Mrs Dickinson of Lady Burne-Jones's untiring efforts (letter, 13 November 1903, in the Emery Walker Library (cat. 1991 1016 644), Cheltenham Art Gallery & Museum).
59. Webb to Lethaby, 3 July 1904, in Lethaby (1935), p. 138.

60. See Webb to Hale White, 29 October 1909, in W H White, *Letters to Three Friends*, p. 355.

61. Letters between Webb and I L Bell (private collection); Lethaby (1935), p. 224; see, for example, Webb to Hale White, 16 May 1899 (MR 10/16, Central Library, Bedford) and to Cockerell, 25 April 1903 and 7 March 1904 (in *Friends of a Lifetime*, ed. by Meynell, pp.111–15). Webb made a plan (undated, WEBB [77], BAL/RIBADC) of one of the cells at Mount Grace Priory, presumably while staying at Rounton Grange, and gave a little gratuitous advice about the manor house work, but the architect was Ambrose Poynter, the son of Hugh Bell's and Webb's friend, the painter Edward John Poynter.

62. See Cockerell to Webb, 14 April 1907, V&A, NAL, 86.TT.16, quoted in Brandon, 'Philip Webb', p. 12.

63. Webb to Cockerell, 11 March 1905, quoted by Brandon in 'Philip Webb', p. 12; Wilfrid Scawen Blunt, 'Clouds', 19 November 1904, and Gertrude Jekyll, attributed to, 'Great Tangley Manor', 21 January 1905.

64. See, for example, Hale White to Webb, 15 July 1910, in *Letters to Three Friends*, pp. 371–72, and Blunt, *Cockerell*, pp. 88–9.

65. See Webb to Hale White, 6 April 1909, in *Letters to Three Friends*, p. 350n.

66. Webb to Cockerell, 7 March 1904, in *Friends of a Lifetime*, ed. by Meynell, pp. 113–15 (p. 115). The expression 'shanks' mare' (or 'Shanks's mare') means the use of one's own legs as a means of conveyance.

67. Webb to Lethaby, 29 May 1906, in Lethaby (1935), pp. 221 and 219.

68. See Webb to Hale White, 20 January 1905, 22 January 1910, 2 February 1902, 30 March 1904, 3 February 1905, and 29 October 1909, MR 10/24, 34, 22, 23, 25, and 33, Central Library, Bedford.

69. Webb to Lethaby, and to Alfred Powell, 28 August 1901 and 7 March 1902, in Lethaby (1935), pp. 215–17.

70. Webb to Hale White, 20 January 1905, MR 10/24, Central Library, Bedford.

71. Cockerell to Rooke, 18 June 1898, quoted in Rooke, ed. by Lago, p. 190.

72. Sydney Cockerell, August 1890, quoted in Blunt, *Cockerell*, pp. 85–6.

73. Rooke to Cockerell, and Rooke to Webb, each one of 18 June 1898, quoted by Lago in her 'Conclusion' in Rooke, ed. by Lago, pp. 190–91.

74. Winmill, p. 31.

75. Ibid., p. 53.

76. Ibid., p. 54.

77. W S Blunt to Sydney Cockerell, 16 January 1903, in *Friends of a Lifetime*, ed. by Meynell, pp. 167–8 (p. 167); Blunt, *My Diaries*, p. 520.

78. G Jack, quoted in Lethaby (1935), p. 228.

79. Webb to Cockerell, 7 March 1904, in *Friends of a Lifetime*, ed. by Meynell, pp. 113–15 (p. 115).

80. May Morris to Lethaby, quoted in Lethaby (1935), p. 211.

81. Webb to Lethaby, 2 July 1913, quoted in ibid., p. 229.

82. See G Jack to Lethaby, quoted in ibid., pp. 227–8.

83. See Webb to Hale White, 22 January 1910, MR 10/34, Central Library, Bedford.

84. Webb to Lethaby, 5 November 1907, quoted in Lethaby (1935), p. 233. Webb visited the small group of houses (now the Convent of the Holy Name) in Malvern two or three times to instruct the builder on site, and he advised about the choices of MMF&Co wallpapers and the paint colours, and drew the plan of the servants' hall for one house. The largest house was already inhabited and Webb's design for an additional oriel window for it was not accepted by the owner. Webb apparently refused a fee for his work but Bodley sent him £6 towards his rail fares and time, saying that he knew it was far from enough (see Brandon-Jones, 'Letters of Philip Webb', pp. 63–5). In the letters, Bodley mentions the possibility of asking Webb to go to Wales in connection with an unnamed house (this would have been Cefn Bryntalch in Abermule, Montgomeryshire, designed by Bodley in 1869) but I have found no record of Webb's having done so.

85. Webb to Lethaby, 27 January 1913, quoted in Lethaby (1935), p. 229.

86. Webb to Cockerell, 27 August 1908, in *Friends of a Lifetime*, ed. by Meynell, p. 116.

87. Webb to Hale White, 22 January 1910, MR 10/34, Central Library, Bedford.

88. Lethaby to Cockerell, 16 December 1914, in *Friends of a Lifetime*, ed. by Meynell, p. 131.

89. See Lethaby (1935), p. 230.

90. Quoted by Blunt in *Cockerell*, p. 89. Webb's death certificate records that he died of 'senile decay' – of old age, that is.

91. Mrs Wickham Flower to Cockerell, 17 April 1915, Cockerell Papers, BL Add. MS 52761; Lady Burne-Jones to Cockerell, 19 April 1915, in *Friends of a Lifetime*, ed. by Meynell, pp. 123–4 (p. 123).

92. Lethaby to May Morris, 17 April 1915, BL Add. MS 45347, Morris Papers, vol. 10, fol. 117.

93. Ernest Gimson to May Morris, 22 April 1915, BL Add. MS 45347, Morris Papers, vol. 10, fol. 118.

94. Winmill, pp. 53–4.

95. Blunt, *Cockerell*, p. 89.

96. Webb to Cockerell, 20 November 1902, in *Friends of a Lifetime*, ed. by Meynell, pp. 109–10.

97. Lethaby, 'Philip Webb and his Work', and Lethaby (1935).

98. Mrs Dickinson is quoted in Lethaby (1935), p. 231; Cockerell records her return to service with Mrs Flower in the bound volume of Webb to Mrs Flower Letters, BL Add. MS 45355.

99. From the probate record; Webb's will of 11 January 1903 (private collection); and Sarah Webb to Cockerell, 30 April 1915, Cockerell Papers, BL Add. MS 52761.

100. Lethaby used the material Walker retained in the preparation of 'Philip Webb and his Work'. John Brandon-Jones, who told me of Dorothy Walker's gift, had the greatest admiration for Webb's design approach, his buildings, and his work for the SPAB.

101. Arthur Keen, 'The late Mr. Philip Webb', letter to the editor, *RIBA Jl*, 22, 3rd series (12 June 1915), p. 395.

102. Edwin Landseer Lutyens, 'The Work of the Late Philip Webb', CL, 37 (8 May 1915), p. 618.

103. All quotations in this paragraph are from 'The late Philip Webb', report of a General Meeting, *RIBA Jl*, 22, 3rd series (8 May 1915), pp. 339–41.

104. From G Jack, 'An Appreciation of Philip Webb', pp. 1–6, and pls. (p. 1).

105. G Jack, 'Philip Webb', *RIBA Jl*, 22, 3rd series (22 May 1915), pp. 369–71 (p. 169).

SELECT BIBLIOGRAPHY AND LIST OF SOURCES

PRIMARY SOURCES

MANUSCRIPTS AND DRAWINGS

Details and locations of Webb's MSS are given in the text or the notes. Many of the locations are private collections; most of the owners of these do not wish to be identified but they may be contacted through the author. The locations (in London unless otherwise indicated) in record repositories, museums, art galleries, libraries, and some private and industrial collections are as follows:

Ashmolean Museum, Oxford
Webb drawings for stained glass and decorative panels

Bedford Central Library
Webb's letters to William Hale White, 1888–1812 (MR 10/1–36)

Birmingham Museums and Art Gallery
MS copy, not in Webb's hand, of his account with Morris, Marshall, Faulkner & Co.

British Library, Manuscript Collections
Webb's letters to George Price Boyce, 1865–1895 (Add. MS 45354)
Webb's letters to Mrs Elizabeth Weston Wickham Flower, 1899–1911 (Add. MS 45355)
Webb's letters to William and Jane Morris and family, 1868–1912 (Add. MSS 45342–43, 45346–47)
Webb's correspondence with Sir Sydney Cockerell, 1895–1914, and letters concerning Webb, written after his death to Cockerell (Add. MSS 52760–67)
Letter, Webb to Joseph Lane, 2 May 1887 (Add. MS 46345)
Webb's drawing for the Memorial Cottages, Kelmscott (Add. MS 45344)
Hammersmith Socialist Society Minutes 1890–1896 (Add. MS 45893)

Cambridge University, Fitzwilliam Museum
Webb's letters to Charles Fairfax Murray, 1871–1900
Warington Taylor's letters to E R Robson, 1863–c. 1867

Castle Howard Archives, Castle Howard, North Yorkshire
Webb's letters to George and Rosalind Howard, J22/64, J22/65, J22/83, and sundry letters relating to Webb, 1867–95
Rosalind Howard's diaries

Cheltenham Art Gallery and Museum, Emery Walker Library
Webb's correspondence with a Mr Burbridge, and his letters to Mrs Margaret Dickinson

Corus Northern Records Centre, South Bank, Middlesbrough
Webb drawings for the Bell Brothers Offices, Zetland Road, Middlesbrough
George Jack drawings for the proposed enlargement of the offices and Webb's Specification altered by Jack for use with his (unexecuted) scheme

Courtauld Institute
Papers of Philip Webb, 1882–1907, comprising correspondence concerning building restorations in Italy and the Society for the Protection of Ancient Buildings, and correspondence with Giacomo Boni, and with George Wardle (CI/PW)

Durham University Library, Archives and Special Collections, Palace Green Section
Howard of Naworth Papers: letters, reports, and accounts relating to St Martin's Church, Brampton, and the Howard properties with which Webb was concerned, 1874–1904 (reference: 19–20)

Gloucestershire Record Office, Gloucester
Letters and accounts relating to Webb's alteration and enlargement of Forthampton Court, in the Yorke Archive

National Trust Collection, Standen, East Grinstead
Webb letters, Specification, drawings, and sketches, and contemporary photographs of the house

North Yorkshire County Record Office, Northallerton
Webb drawings for Rounton Grange and ancillary buildings, and three for the enlargement of Washington Hall, in the Bell of Rounton Grange Archive (ZFK)
Webb drawings for the enlargement of Red Barns (from the Trustees of Sir William Turner's Foundation, Redcar; not yet catalogued)

Royal Institute of British Architects Library, Drawings Collection
A large number of Webb drawings, chiefly for architectural works

Royal Institute of British Architects Library, Manuscripts and Archives Collection
Webb's Specifications for Hurlands, number 1 Holland Park Road, and Arisaig Village Hall, and correspondence relating to the hall, 1891–1892
Material, including letters, and notes relating to Webb, assembled by W R Lethaby

Society for the Protection of Ancient Buildings Archive
Early records of the Society, including the Manifesto
Webb drawings and manuscripts: drawings (including contract drawings for Hurlands, Standen, Warrens House, and numbers 91–101 Worship Street, London, and many drawings for Exning House); his initialled MS of the Society's Thirteenth Annual Report; his Site Book 1877–1892; and his letters to several recipients in connection with the society

Teesside Archives, Middlesbrough
Webb drawings for Bell Brothers Offices, Zetland Road, Middlesbrough, and records relating to his work for this firm, in the Bell Brother Papers; planning application drawings for additions to Red Barns

University of Newcastle upon Tyne, School of Historical Studies
Contemporary photographs of Red Barns and Rounton Grange, in the Gertrude Bell Archive

Victoria & Albert Museum, National Art Library
Webb's correspondence, mainly with William Morris, 1884–1896 (Catalogue of English MSS 1975, numbers 731–32)
Webb's correspondence with Sir Sydney Cockerell 1891–1915 (Catalogue of English MSS 1975, number 730)
Warington Taylor's letters to Webb, 1866–1869 (Catalogue of English MSS 1975, number 681)
Letters and accounts in connection with number 1 Holland Park for A A Ionides (Box 111, 86.KK)

Victoria & Albert Museum, Word & Image Department (Prints, Drawings, & Paintings Study Room)
A large number of Webb drawings, chiefly for architectural works

West Sussex Record Office, Chichester
Webb's letters to J S Beale, 1896–1898 (Standen MSS 168–78)

ARTEFACTS DESIGNED BY PHILIP WEBB
In private collections and in the following locations:

Kelmscott Manor, Kelmscott, Oxfordshire (Society of Antiquarians)
Furniture and other items

Red House, Bexleyheath, London (formerly Kent) (National Trust)
Furniture and other items

Standen, East Grinstead, West Sussex (National Trust)
Furniture and other items

William Morris Gallery, Walthamstow, London
Furniture, Metalwork, Ceramics, and Glassware

Victoria & Albert Museum
Department of Furniture, Textiles, & Fashion
Department of Sculpture, Metalwork, Ceramics & Glass

PRINTED WORKS BY PHILIP WEBB
'Ashburnham House'. *Builder*, 41 (2 July 1881), pp. 30–31
'Street, George Edmund (1824–81)'. *Dictionary of National Biography*, pp. 42–5
'Town and Gown'. *Commonweal*, 2, no. 47 (4 December 1886), pp. 284–5
Thirteenth Annual Report of the Society, Report of the Committee and Paper read thereat by Revd W. Cunningham DD, June 1890. London: Society for the Protection of Ancient Buildings, 1890 [page numbers given in notes refer to Webb's initialled MS]
Shaw, George Bernard [and Philip Webb]. 'Must Peterborough Perish?'. *Saturday Review*, 2 January 1897, pp. 7–9

SELECT BIBLIOGRAPHY

UNPUBLISHED WORKS
Brandon-Jones, John. 'Zetland House, Zetland Road, Middlesbrough', typescript copy of his Statement, which was read at the 1974 public inquiry by David Alexander on behalf of the Victorian Society and the Ancients Monuments Society (copy in the collection of Sheila Kirk)
Forster, Susan C. 'Philip Webb and the Astleys: A Re-evaluation of Webb's work at Arisaig'. MA in the History of Art dissertation, University of St Andrews, 1983
Guile, Bernard. 'Old Heathfield School'. MS history with illustrations, 1990
Kirk, Sheila. 'Philip Webb (1831–1915): Domestic Architecture', 2 vols. Doctoral thesis, University of Newcastle upon Tyne, 1990
MacGregor, Scott. 'Philip Webb, Some Aspects of his Early Work and Life'. Dissertation for the Diploma in Architecture, Polytechnic of Central London, 1982
Marix Evans, Jean-Paul. 'Journal of an Ancient Manor'. A history of Great Tangley Manor
Smith, Donald. 'The Work of Philip Webb'. Peter Floud Memorial Essay for the William Morris Society, 1961
Trevelyan, Mary. 'The Number of My Days'. Memoirs, c. 1960 (at Wallington Hall, National Trust)
Weaver, Lawrence. 'Lesser Country Houses of Today: New Place, Welwyn, Herts. designed by Mr. Philip Webb'. Printed ready for inclusion in Country Life (23 July 1910) but omitted from the publication

PUBLISHED WORKS
Abdy, Jane, and Charlotte Gere. *The Souls*. London: Sidgwick & Jackson, 1984
Allibone, Jill. *Anthony Salvin: Pioneer of Gothic Revival Architecture*. Cambridge: Lutterworth Press, 1988
Allibone, Jill. *George Devey, Architect, 1820–1886*. Cambridge: Lutterworth Press, 1991
Almond, J K, B J D Harrison, J K Harrison, and J S Owen. *Cleveland Iron and Steel, Background and 19th Century History*. Middlesbrough: British Steel Corporation, 1979

Anscombe, Isabelle, and Charlotte Gere. *Arts and Crafts in Britain and America*. London: Academy, 1978

'The Architectural Exhibition 1858'. *Ecclesiologist* (February 1858), p. 46

'The Architectural Room at the Royal Academy, 1858'. *Ecclesiologist* (1858), pp. 171–3

Arnold, H Godwin. *Victorian Architecture in Reading*. Reading: by the author, 1975

Aslet, Clive. 'Forthampton Court, Gloucestershire, the Home of Mr and Mrs G. Yorke'. *Country Life*, 166 (27 September and 11 October 1979), pp. 938–41 & 1166–9

'Awfully Sudden Death of Mr. Herbert Fletcher'. *Bolton Evening News*, 17 September 1895

Baldry, A Lys. *Modern Mural Decoration*. London: George Newnes, 1902

Banham, Joanna, and Jennifer Harris, eds. *William Morris and the Middle Ages*. Manchester: Manchester University Press, 1984

Banham, Joanna, Sally MacDonald, and Julia Porter. *Victorian Interior Design*. London: Cassell, 1991

Bax, Ernest Belfort. *Reminiscences of a Mid and Late Victorian*. London: Allen & Unwin, 1918. Reprint, New York: Kelley, 1967

Beard, Geoffrey. *The Work of John Vanbrugh*. London: Batsford, 1986

Bell, Florence. *At the Works*. London: Edward Arnold, 1907. 2nd edn, rev., London: Nelson, 1911

Bird, Margaret. *Holmbury St Mary: One Hundred Years*. Holmbury St Mary: by the author, 1979

Blomfield, Reginald. *R. N. Shaw, R. A., Architect 1831–1912*. London: Batsford, 1940

Blomfield, Reginald, and William Newton Godfrey. *The Work of Ernest Newton, R.A.*. London: Architectural Press, 1925

Blunt, Wilfrid. *Cockerell*. London: Hamish Hamilton, 1964

Blunt, Wilfrid Scawen. 'Clouds, Salisbury, the Residence of the Hon. Mrs. Percy Wyndham'. *Country Life*, 16 (19 November 1904), pp. 738–48

Blunt, Wilfrid Scawen. *My Diaries: Being a Personal Narrative of Events 1888–1914*. 2 vols. London: Martin Secker, 1919, 1920. 1 vol. edn, 1933

Bolsterli, Margaret Jones. *The Early Community at Bedford Park: "Corporate Happiness" in the First Garden Suburb*. London: Routledge & Kegan Paul, 1977

Bradley, Ian. *William Morris and his World*. London: Thames and Hudson, 1978

Brandon, Peter. 'Philip Webb, the William Morris Circle, and Sussex'. *Sussex History*, 2, no. 1 (spring 1981), pp. 8–14

Brandon-Jones, John. 'Arts and Crafts'. In *Masters of Brickwork*, a special supplement of *Architects' Journal* (December 1984), pp. 10–15

Brandon-Jones, John. 'Letters of Philip Webb and his Contemporaries'. *Architectural History*, Journal of the Society of Architectural Historians of Great Britain, 8 (1965), pp. 52–72

Brandon-Jones, John. 'Notes on the Building of Smeaton Manor'. *Architectural History*, Journal of the Society of Architectural Historians of Great Britain, 1 (1958), pp. 31–58

Brandon-Jones, John. 'Philip Webb'. In *Victorian Architecture*, ed. by Peter Ferriday, pp. 249–65. London: Jonathan Cape, 1963

Brandon-Jones, John. 'Philip Webb and the Bell Family'. *Cleveland Industrial Archaeologist*, no. 5 (1976), pp. 11–16

Brandon-Jones, John. 'The Work of Philip Webb and Norman Shaw'. *Architectural Association Journal*, 131 (1955), pp. 9–21 & 40–47

Brandon-Jones, John, and others. *C. F. A. Voysey: architect and designer 1857–1941*. London: Lund Humphries, and the Art Gallery and Museum and the Royal Pavilion, Brighton, 1978

Brooks, Michael W. *John Ruskin and Victorian Architecture*. London: Thames and Hudson, 1989

Brown, Jane. *Gardens of a Golden Afternoon, The Story of a Partnership: Edwin Lutyens & Gertrude Jekyll*. Rev. edn, London and New York: Penguin, 1994

Burke's and Savill's Guide to Country Houses, III: East Anglia. London: Burke's Peerage, 1981

Burman, Peter. '"A Stern Thinker and Most Able Constructor": Philip Webb, Architect'. *Architectural History*, Journal of the Society of Architectural Historians of Great Britain, 42 (1999), pp. 17–19

Burne-Jones, Georgiana. *Memorials of Edward Burne-Jones*. 2 vols. London: Macmillan, 1904. 1 vol. edn, New York: Books for Libraries, 1971

Callen, Anthea. *Women in the Arts and Crafts Movement 1870–1914*. London: Astragal Books, 1980. First published as *Angel in the Studio*, London: Astragal, 1979

Campbell, Colen. *Vitruvius Britannicus or the British Architect*. 3 vols. London, 1715–25. Reprint, introduced by John Harris, 1 vol., New York: Benjamin Blow, 1967

Caverhill, Austin. *Rushmore – then and now*. Amesbury: for Sandroyd School [n.d.]

Cherry, Deborah. 'The Hogarth Club'. *Burlington Magazine*, 122 (1980), pp. 237–44

Clarke, Joseph. *Schools and School Houses: a series of Views, Plans, and details for Rural Parishes*. London and Oxford: Masters, and Parker, 1852

Clough, B A. 'In Memoriam – Miss Mary Ewart'. *Newnham College Roll Letter* (1909), pp. 41–5

Cole, Malcolm. *Whitelands College: the Chapel*. London: Whitelands College, 1985

Collard, Frances. 'Furniture'. In *William Morris*, ed. by Linda Parry, pp. 155–63. London: Philip Wilson in association with the Victoria & Albert Museum, 1996

Collins, Peter. *Changing Ideals in Modern Architecture, 1750–1950*. London: Faber and Faber, 1965. Paperback edn, 1971

Comment upon and exterior perspective of numbers 91–101 Worship Street. *Builder* (29 August 1863), p. 620

Cooper, Jeremy. *Victorian and Edwardian Furniture and Interiors, from the Gothic Revival to Art Nouveau*. London: Thames and Hudson, 1987

Cooper, Nicholas. *Aynho, a Northamptonshire Village*. Banbury: Leopard's Head, with Banbury Historical Society, 1984

Cooper, Nicholas. *The Opulent Eye: Late Victorian and Edwardian Taste in Interior Design*. London: Architectural Press, 1976

Cope, Zachary. *Sir John Tomes, a Pioneer of British Dentistry*. London: Dawsons of Pall Mall, 1961

Cotes, Revd Mr. *History of British Birds, illustrated by Thomas Bewick*. London: 1797

Crane, Walter. *Ideals in Art*. London: George Bell, 1905

Crook, J Mordaunt. *The Dilemma of Style: Architectural Ideas from the Picturesque to the Post-Modern*. London: John Murray, 1987

Crook, J Mordaunt. *William Burges and the High Victorian Dream*. London: John Murray, 1981

'The Cupid and Psyche frieze by Sir Edward Burne-Jones at No. 1 Palace Green'. *Studio*, 15 (1899), pp. 3–13

Curl, James Stevens. *Victorian Architecture*. Newton Abbot and London: David & Charles, 1990

Curry, Rosemary, and Sheila Kirk. *Philip Webb in the North*. Middlesbrough: Teesside Polytechnic and the Royal Institute of British Architects, Teesside Branch, 1984

Dakers, Caroline. 'Castle in the Air: Philip Webb's Rejected Commission for the Earl and Countess of Airlie'. *Architectural History*, Journal of the Society of Architectural Historians of Great Britain, 43 (2000), pp. 271–80

Dakers, Caroline. *Clouds: the Biography of a Country House*. New Haven and London: Yale University Press, 1993

Dakers, Caroline. *The Holland Park Circle: Artists and Victorian Society*. New Haven and London: Yale University Press, 1999

Davey, Peter. *Arts and Crafts Architecture*. London: Phaidon, 1995

Day, Lewis F. 'A Kensington Interior'. *Art Journal*, 1893, pp. 139–44

'Death of F. D. P. Astley Esq., Lord of the Manor of Dukinfield'. *Ashton Reporter*, 28 March 1868, p. 5

Description of the Works of Dorman, Long & Co. Ltd. and Bell Brothers Ltd., Middlesbrough. Middlesbrough: Dorman, Long & Co, 1901

de Zurko, Edward. *Origins of Functionalist Theory*. New York: Columbia University Press, 1957

The Diaries of George Price Boyce. Reprint, ed. by Virginia Surtees. Norwich: Real World, 1980. First edn published by the Old Water-Colour Society in its Nineteenth Annual Volume, London: 1941

Downes, Kerry. *Sir John Vanbrugh, a Biography*. London: Sidgwick & Jackson, 1987

Dresser, Christopher. *Development of Ornamental Art in the International Exhibition*. London: 1862

Drury, Michael. 'The fall and rise of Stonehenge'. SPAB News (autumn 1985), pp. 8–9

Drury, Michael. *Wandering Architects, In Pursuit of an Arts and Crafts Ideal*. Stamford: Shaun Tyas, 2000

Drury, Michael. 'The Wandering Architects'. In *William Morris and Architecture*, Papers from the Annual Symposium of the Society of Architectural Historians of Great Britain 1996, ed. by Alan Crawford and Colin Cunningham, pp. 83–92. London: Society of Architectural Historians of Great Britain, 1997

Dufty, A R. 'Kelmscott: Exoticism and a Philip Webb Chair'. *Antiquaries Journal*, 66 (1986), pt. 1, pp. 116–20 and pls. 22–6

Du Maurier, Daphne. *The Young George Du Maurier: A selection of his letters, 1860–67*. London: Peter Davies, 1951

Eastlake, Charles. *A History of the Gothic Revival*. London: 1872. Reprint, ed. and introduced by J Mordaunt Crook, Leicester: Leicester University Press, 1970

Edwards, K H R. *Chronology of the Development of the Iron & Steel Industries of Teesside*. Middlesbrough: privately printed, 1955

Edwin Lutyens. Ed. by David Dunster, Architectural Monographs, 6. London: Academy Editions, 1979

Egremont, Max. *The Cousins*. London: Collins, 1977

Ellwood, Giles. 'Three Tables by Philip Webb'. *Furniture History*, Journal of the Furniture History Society, 32 (1996), pp. 128–40

'The Exhibition of the Royal Academy'. *Builder*, 16 (8 May 1858), pp. 305–6

Farr, Dennis. *English Art 1870–1940*. Oxford History of English Art Series. Oxford: Clarendon Press, 1978

Ford, Colin. *The Cameron Collection*. London: National Portrait Gallery and Reinhold, 1975

Forrer, L. *Biographical Dictionary of Medallists*, 6 vols (VI). New York: Burt Franklin, 1916, p. 400. Reprint 1970

Franklin, Jill. *The Gentleman's House and its Plan 1835–1914*. London, Boston and Henley: Routledge & Kegan Paul, 1981

'Funeral of the Late Sir William Bowman at Holmbury St. Mary'. *Surrey Advertiser and County Times*, 2 April 1892

Garnett, Oliver. *Standen, West Sussex*. London: National Trust, 1993

Garnham, Trevor. 'Crafts and the Revival of Architecture'. In Neil Jackson, *F. W. Troup, Architect, 1859–1941*, pp. 75–90. London: Building Centre Trust, 1985

Garnham, Trevor. *St Andrew's Church, Roker*. Architecture in Detail Series. London: Phaidon, 1996

Gere, Charlotte. *Nineteenth-Century Decoration: The Art of the Interior*. London: Weidenfeld and Nicolson, 1989

Germann, Georg. *Gothic Revival in Europe and Britain: Sources, Influences and Ideas*, trans.

by Gerald Onn. London: Lund Humphries, 1972

Girouard, Mark. 'Red House, Bexleyheath, Kent'. *Country Life*, 127 (16 June 1960), pp. 1382–5

Girouard, Mark. *Robert Smythson & the Elizabethan Country House*. New Haven and London: Yale University Press, 1983

Girouard, Mark. 'Standen, Sussex, the Home of Miss Helen Beale'. *Country Life*, 147 (26 February and 5 March 1970), pp. 494–7 & 554–7

Girouard, Mark. *Sweetness and Light: The 'Queen Anne' Movement 1860–1900*. Oxford: Clarendon Press, 1977

Girouard, Mark. 'The Victorian Artist at Home'. *Country Life*, 152 (16 and 23 November 1972), pp. 1278–81 & 1370–74

Girouard, Mark. *The Victorian Country House*. New Haven and London: Yale University Press, 1971. Rev. and enlarged edn, 1979

Gladstone, Mary. *Mary Gladstone: her Diaries and Letters*. Ed. by Lucy Masterman. London: Methuen, 1930

Godwin, E W. 'Three Modern Architects'. *Building News*, 13 (30 November 1866), pp. 799–800

Gold, Sidney M. *Biographical Dictionary of Architects at Reading*. Reading: by the author, 1999

Gradidge, Roderick. *Dream-Houses: the Edwardian Ideal*. London: Constable, 1980

Gray, A Stuart. *Edwardian Architecture, A Biographical Dictionary*. London: Duckworth, 1985

'Great Tangley Manor, Surrey, the Country House of Mr. Wickham Flower'. *Country Life*, 4 (6 August 1898), pp. 144–17

'Great Tangley Manor, Surrey, the Seat of Mr. Wickham Flower'. *Country Life*, 4 (30 July 1898), pp. 109–112

Green, Elizabeth M. 'On Change, Grandeur, and Designs: the Early History of the Middlesbrough Exchange'. *50th Bulletin*, Cleveland and Teesside Local History Society (spring 1986), pp. 71–80

Greensted, Mary. *Gimson and the Barnsleys: 'Wonderful furniture of a commonplace kind'*. Stroud: Alan Sutton, 1991

Haigh, Diane. *Baillie Scott: The Artistic House*. London: Academy Editions, 1995

Hall, Michael. 'Simple People and Homely Minds'. *Country Life*, 188 (1994), pp. 58–61

Handley-Read, Charles. 'Jubilee Pyramid'. *Architectural Review*, 137 (1965), pp. 234–6

Harding, James Duffield. *Lessons on Art*. London: Day & Son, 1849

Harper, Roger H. *Victorian Building Regulations: Summary tables of the principal British Building Acts and Model By-laws 1840–1914*. London and New York: Mansell, 1985

Harrison, J F C. *A History of the Working Men's College 1854–1954*. London: Routledge & Kegan Paul, 1954

Harrison, J K. *Houses for Steam-Driven Blowing Engines in North-East England*. Research Report No. 8. Middlesbrough: Cleveland Industrial Archaeologist, 2001

Harrison, J K. 'Philip Webb's Industrial Buildings for Bell Brothers in their Local Context'. *Cleveland Industrial Archaeologist*, no. 5 (1976), pp. 17–20

Harrison, Martin. 'Church Decoration and Stained Glass'. In *William Morris*, ed. by Linda Parry, pp. 106–15. London: Philip Wilson and the Victoria & Albert Museum, 1996

Harvey, Charles, and Jon Press. 'The business career of William Morris'. In *William Morris: Art and Kelmscott*, ed. by Linda Parry, pp. 3–22. London: Boydell Press for the Society of Antiquaries of London, 1996

Hellyer, Arthur. 'Gardens for a Late-Victorian House: Standen, East Grinstead, West Sussex'. *Country Life*, 173 (28 April 1983), pp. 1100–2

Heppell, D A, and L T D Heppell. 'The Logbooks of the Hutton Rudby and East Rounton Schools, 1877–1901'. *Bulletin of the Cleveland and Teesside Local History Society*, no. 36 (spring 1979), pp. 1–11

Hints to Promoters of Church Schools. London: by the National Society for Promoting the Education of the Poor in the Principles of the Established Church [undated but before 1861]

Hitchcock, Henry-Russell. *Architecture: Nineteenth and Twentieth Centuries*. Pelican History of Art Series. New York and Harmondsworth: Penguin, 1958. Reprint, 1977

Hitchcock, Henry-Russell. *Early Victorian Architecture in Britain*. 2 vols. New Haven: Yale University Press, 1954. Abridged 1-vol. edn, New York: Da Capo, 1976

Hitchcock, Henry-Russell. 'G. E. Street in the 1850s'. *Architectural History* (USA), 19, no. 4 (1960), pp. 145–71

Hitchcock, Henry-Russell. *In the Nature of Materials: The Buildings of Frank Lloyd Wright 1887–1941*. New York: Duell, Sloane and Pearce, 1942

Hitchmough, Wendy. *Arts and Crafts Gardens*. London: Pavilion, 1997

Hitchmough, Wendy. *The Arts and Crafts Home*. London: Pavilion, 2000

Hitchmough, Wendy. *C F A Voysey*. London: Phaidon, 1995

Hollamby, Edward. *Red House: Philip Webb*. London: Phaidon, 1991

Honour, Hugh. *Romanticism*. London: Allen Lane, 1979. Reprint, Harmondsworth: Penguin, 1981

Hudson, Kenneth. *Building Materials*. Industrial Archaeology Series, no. 9. London: Longman, 1972

Hunt, John Dixon, and Peter Willis, eds. *The Genius of the Place: the English Landscape Garden 1620–1820*. London: Paul Elek, 1975. 2nd edn, Cambridge, Massachusetts and London: MIT Press, 1988

Hunt, William Holman. *The Story of the Painting of the Pictures on the Walls and the Decorations on the Ceiling of the old Debating Hall (now the Library) in the years 1857–8–9*. London: Henry Frowde, 1906

Hussey, Christopher. 'Joldwynds, Surrey, the Residence of Mr. Wilfrid Greene, K.C.'. *Country Life*, 76 (15 September 1934), pp. 276–81

Hussey, Christopher. *The Life of Sir Edwin Lutyens*. London: Country Life, 1950

Hussey, Christopher. *The Picturesque: Studies in a Point of View*. London: Putnam, 1927. Reprint, London: Cass, 1967

Hutchinson, John, and Paul Joyce. *George Edmund Street in East Yorkshire*. Exhibition catalogue. Hull: University of Hull, 1981

'In the Gardens: Flowers by Water Edge at Great Tangley'. *Country Life*, 20 (22 September 1906), pp. 418–21

Jack, George. 'An Appreciation of Philip Webb'. *Architectural Review*, 38 (1915), pp. 1–6 and pls.

Jack, George. 'Philip Webb'. *Journal of the Royal Institute of British Architects*, 22, 3rd Series (22 May 1915), pp. 369–71

Jackson, Frank. *Sir Raymond Unwin, Architect, Planner and Visionary*. London: Zwemmer, 1985

Jackson, Neil. 'A church for SPAB?'. *Architectural Review*, 161 (August 1977), pp. 69–71

Jackson, Neil. *F. W. Troup, Architect 1859–1941*. London: Building Centre Trust, 1985

Jackson, Neil. 'Webb of Intrigue'. *Building Design*, 17 June 1983, pp. 20–21

Jackson, Thomas Graham. *Modern Gothic Architecture*. London: Graham King, 1873

[Jekyll, Gertrude, attributed to]. 'Great Tangley Manor, Surrey, the Residence of the late Mr. Wickham Flower'. *Country Life*, 17 (21 January 1905), pp. 90–100

Jones, Greville. 'A Description of the Messrs. Bell Brothers' Blast-Furnaces from 1844–1908'. *Journal of the Iron and Steel Institute*, 78 (1908), no. 3, pp. 59–71

Jones, Lawrence E. *Georgian Afternoon*. London: Rupert Hart-Davies, 1958

Jones, Owen. *The Grammar of Ornament*. London: Day & Son, 1856

Jones, Peter Blundell. 'Red House'. *Architects' Journal*, 183 (15 January 1986), pp. 36–51 & 54–6

Keen, Arthur. 'The late Mr. Philip Webb', letter to the editor. *Journal of the Royal Institute of British Architects*, 22, 3rd Series (12 June 1915), p. 395

Kerr, Robert. *The Gentleman's House, or How to Plan English Residences from the Parsonage to the Palace*. London: John Murray, 1864. 3rd edn, 1871

Kirk, Sheila. 'Philip Webb and traditional materials'. In *Architecture 1900*, ed. by Peter Burman, pp. 145–55. Donhead St Mary: Donhead, 1998

Kirk, Sheila. 'Webb's Wonder'. *Building Design* (18 August 1981), pp. 12–13

Kirk, Sheila. 'William Morris, Philip Webb and Architecture'. In *William Morris and Architecture*, Papers from the Annual Symposium of the Society of Architectural Historians of Great Britain 1996, ed. by Alan Crawford and Colin Cunningham, pp. 39–43. London: Society of Architectural Historians of Great Britain, 1997

Kornwolf, James D. *M. H. Baillie Scott and the Arts and Crafts Movement: Pioneers of Modern Design*. Baltimore and London: Johns Hopkins Press, 1972

Lambourne, Lionel. *Utopian Craftsmen: the Arts and Crafts Movement from the Cotswolds to Chicago*. London: Astragal Books, 1980

Langley, Hal. *The Church of St Martin-on-the-Hill, 1863–1988*. Scarborough: by the church, 1988

'The Late Philip Webb'. Report of a General Meeting of the RIBA, *Journal of the Royal Society of British Architects*, 22, 3rd Series (8 May 1915), pp. 339–41

Lees-Milne, Alvida and Rosemary Verey, eds. *The Englishwoman's Garden*. London: Chatto & Windus, 1983

Lethaby, William Richard. 'Philip Webb and his Work'. *Builder*, 128, 129 (1925), passim

Lethaby, William Richard. *Philip Webb and his Work*. Oxford: Oxford University Press, 1935. Reprint, introduced by Godfrey Rubens, containing additional Lethaby material ed. by Rubens. London: Raven Oak Press, 1979

Lethaby, William Richard, ed. *Ernest Gimson, his life and work*. Stratford-on-Avon: Shakespeare Head, 1924

Lever, Jill. *Architects' Designs for Furniture*. RIBA Drawings Series. London: Trefoil Books in association with the RIBA Drawings Collection, 1982

Longford, Elizabeth. *A Pilgrimage of Passion: The Life of Wilfrid Scawen Blunt*. London: Weidenfeld and Nicolson, 1979. Reprint, London: Granada, 1982

Lutyens, Edwin Landseer. 'The Work of the Late Philip Webb'. *Country Life*, 37 (8 May 1915), p. 618

MacCarthy, Fiona. *William Morris: A Life for our Time*. London: Faber and Faber, 1994

Mackail, John William. *The Life of William Morris*. 2 vols. London: Longmans, Green, 1899. Reprint, World's Classics Series, London, New York, and Toronto: Oxford University Press, 1950

Maclean, Catherine Macdonald. *Mark Rutherford, a Biography of William Hale White*. London: Macdonald, 1955

Macleod, Dianne Sachko. 'Avant-Garde Patronage in the North East'. In *Pre-Raphaelites: Painters and Patrons in the North East*, the eponymous catalogue of the exhibition at the Laing Art Gallery, Newcastle upon Tyne, October 1989–January 1990, pp. 9–37. Newcastle: Tyne and Wear Museums Service with assistance from the Paul Mellon Centre, 1989

Macleod, Robert. *Style and Society: Architectural Ideology in Britain 1835–1914*. London: RIBA Publications, 1971

McEvoy, Michael. 'Webb at Brampton'. *Architects' Journal*, 190 (25 October 1989), pp. 40–51 & 56–63

McKean, John. 'The Hill House'. In *Charles Rennie Mackintosh*, ed. by Wendy Kaplan, pp. 175–99. New York, London, Paris: Glasgow Museums, Abbeville Press, 1996

Meynell, Viola, ed.. *The Best of Friends: Further Letters to Sydney Carlyle Cockerell*.

London: Rupert Hart-Davis, 1956

Meynell, Viola, ed.. *Friends of a Lifetime: Letters to Sydney Carlyle Cockerell*. London: Jonathan Cape, 1940

Miele, Chris. 'The Conservationist'. In *William Morris*, ed. by Linda Parry, pp. 72–79. London: Philip Wilson and the Victoria & Albert Museum, 1996

Miele, Chris. 'Introduction'. In *William Morris on Architecture*, ed. and introduced by Chris Miele, pp. 6–15. Sheffield: Sheffield Academic Press, 1996

Mitchell, Charles. 'William Morris at St. James's Palace'. *Architectural Review*, 101 (January 1947), pp. 37–9

Morris, F O, ed.. *County Seats of the Noblemen and Gentlemen of Great Britain and Ireland*. 6 vols. London: William McKenzie [c. 1880], IV

Morris, George Llewellyn. 'Lake House, near Amesbury: an account of its sustentation and repair by Mr. Detmar Blow, with the counsel of Mr. Phillip [sic] Webb'. *Architectural Review*, 5 (1899), pp. 171–9

Morris, George Llewellyn. 'On Philip Webb's Town Work'. *Architectural Review*, 2 (1897), pp. 198–208

Morris, May. 'Philip Speakman Webb'. In *The Dictionary of National Biography: 1912–1921*, pp. 560–62

Morris, May. *William Morris, Artist, Writer, Socialist*. 2 vols. Oxford: Blackwell, 1936

Morris, William. *The Collected Letters of William Morris*. Ed. by Norman Kelvin. 2 vols. Princeton and London: Princeton University Press, 1984, 1987

Morris, William. *The Collected Works of William Morris*. 24 vols. Ed. by May Morris. London: Longman, Green & Co., 1910–15

Morris, William. 'Gothic Architecture'. First delivered as a lecture to the Arts and Crafts Exhibition Society, 7 November 1889. In *William Morris on Architecture*, ed. and introduced by Chris Miele, pp. 143–56. Sheffield: Sheffield Academic Press, 1996

Morris, William. Letter to the editor. *Athenæum*, 5 March 1877, reprinted in J W Mackail, *The Life of William Morris*, I, pp. 351–52

Morris, William. *News from Nowhere, or an Epoch of Rest*. As a series in *Commonweal*, 11 January to 4 October 1890. In *William Morris: Stories in Prose, Stories in Verse, Shorter Poems, Lectures and Essays*, ed. and introduced by G D H Cole, pp. 3–197. London: Nonesuch Press, 1946

Morris, William. 'The Story of an Unknown Church'. *Oxford and Cambridge Magazine*, I (January 1856), pp. 28–33

Morris, William. *Unpublished Letters of William Morris*. Ed. by R Page Arnot. Labour Monthly Pamphlets, Series 6, 1951

Muthesius, Hermann. *The English House*, English 1-vol. edn, ed. and abridged by Dennis Sharpe, translated by Janet Seligman. London: Crosby Lockwood Staples, 1979. First edn, *Das englische Haus*, 3 vols, Berlin: Wasmuth, 1904–05

Muthesius, Stefan. *The High Victorian Movement in Architecture 1850–1870*. London and Boston: Routledge & Kegan Paul, 1972

Myers, Richard and Hilary. *William Morris Tiles*. Shepton Beauchamp: Richard Dennis, 1996

Notes on the Repair of Ancient Buildings issued by the Society for the Protection of Ancient Buildings. London: SPAB, 1903. [Attributed to H Thackeray Turner, probably helped by Philip Webb]

O'Connor, V C Scott. 'Tennyson and his Friends at Freshwater'. *Century Magazine* (1897), pp. 240–68

Opie, Jennifer Hawkins. 'Tiles and Tableware'. In *William Morris*, ed. by Linda Parry, pp. 180–85. London: Philip Wilson and the Victoria & Albert Museum, 1996

Parker, John Henry. *A Glossary of Terms used in Grecian, Roman, Italian and Gothic Architecture*. 3 vols. Oxford: Parker, 1850

Parry, Linda. 'Textiles'. In *William Morris*, ed. by Linda Parry, pp. 224–33. London: Philip Wilson and the Victoria & Albert Museum, 1996

Parry, Linda. *William Morris Textiles*. London: Weidenfeld and Nicolson, 1983

Penn, Arthur. *Brampton Church and its Windows*. Carnforth: by the author, 1993

Pevsner, Nikolaus. 'Art Furniture of the 1870s'. *Architectural Review*, 111 (1952), reprinted in Nikolaus Pevsner, *Studies in Art, Architecture and Design: Victorian and After*, pp. 118–31. London: Thames and Hudson, 1982

Pevsner, Nikolaus. *Buckinghamshire*. Buildings of England Series. Harmondsworth: Penguin, 1960

Pevsner, Nikolaus. 'Colonel Gillum and the Pre-Raphaelites'. *Burlington Magazine* (1953), pp. 76, 78–9, & 81

Pevsner, Nikolaus. *Cumberland and Westmorland*. Buildings of England Series. Harmondsworth: Penguin, 1967

Pevsner, Nikolaus. *Herefordshire*. Buildings of England Series. Harmondsworth: Penguin, 1863

Pevsner, Nikolaus. *London: 1*. Buildings of England Series, 3rd edn, rev. by Bridget Cherry. Harmondsworth: Penguin, 1973

Pevsner, Nikolaus. *Pioneers of the Modern Movement*. London: Faber and Faber, 1936. Rev. edn *Pioneers of Modern Design from William Morris to Walter Gropius*, Harmondsworth: Penguin, 1960

Pevsner, Nikolaus. *Shropshire*. Buildings of England Series. Harmondsworth: Penguin, 1958

Pevsner, Nikolaus. *Yorkshire: North Riding*. Buildings of England Series. Harmondsworth: Penguin, 1966

Pevsner, Nikolaus, and David Lloyd. *Hampshire and the Isle of Wight*. Buildings of England Series. Harmondsworth: Penguin, 1967

Pevsner, Nikolaus, and Edward Hubbard. *Cheshire*. Buildings of England Series.

Harmondsworth: Penguin, 1971

Piper, John. *Buildings and Prospects*. London: Architectural Press, 1948

Pite, Beresford. 'A Review of the Tendencies of the Modern School of Architecture'. *Journal of the Royal Institute of British Architects*, 8 (1900), pp. 77–96

Powell, Christopher G. *An Economic History of the British Building Industry 1815–1979*. London: Architectural Press, 1980

Powys, A R. *Repair of Ancient Buildings*. London and Toronto: Dent & Sons, and Dutton & Co., 1929. Reprint, with added notes, London: Society for the Protection of Ancient Buildings, 1995

Prinsep, Valentine Cameron. 'A Painter's Reminiscences'. *Magazine of Art*, 27 (1904), pp. 167–72

Pugin: A Gothic Passion. Ed. by Paul Atterbury and Clive Wainwright. New Haven and London: Yale University Press and the Victoria & Albert Museum, 1994

Pugin, Augustus Welby Northmore. *Builder*, 1850, p. 134

Pugin, Augustus Welby Northmore. *Contrasts: or a Parallel between the noble Edifices of the Middle Ages, and Corresponding Buildings of the present Day; shewing [sic] the Decline of Taste*. Salisbury: by the author, 1836

Pugin, Augustus Welby Northmore. *The Present State of Ecclesiastical Architecture in England*. London: Charles Dolman, 1843

Pugin, Augustus Welby Northmore. *The True Principles of Pointed or Christian Architecture*. London: John Weale, 1841. Reprint, using the sheets of the 1853 impression, Oxford: St. Barnabas Press, 1969

'"Queen Anne" in America'. *Architect* (24 March 1877), p. 202, reprint of a report in *American Architect and Building News* (USA), April 1877

Quennell, Charles H B. 'Architectural Furniture'. In *The House and Its Equipment*, ed. by Lawrence Weaver, pp. 16–22. London: Country Life, 1922

Rayner, W R. *The History of Nether Hall and the Various Owners*. Booklet published by the Nether Hall Country Club [n.d.]

Ricardo, Halsey. 'The House in the Country'. *Magazine of Art*, 23 (1900), pp. 105–11

Richardson, Margaret. *Architects of the Arts and Crafts Movement*. RIBA Drawings Series. London: Trefoil Books in association with the RIBA, 1983

Roberts, Charles. *The Radical Countess: the History of the Life of Rosalind, Countess of Carlisle*. Carlisle: Steel Bros., 1962

Robinson, Duncan, and Stephen Wildman. *Morris & Company in Cambridge*. Cambridge, London, and New York: Cambridge University Press, 1980

Robson, Edward Robert. *School Architecture*. London: Murray, 1874

Rooke, Thomas. *Burne-Jones Talking: his conversations 1895–1898 preserved by his studio assistant Thomas Rooke*. Ed. by Mary Lago. London: John Murray, 1981

Rossetti, Dante Gabriel. *Letters of Dante Gabriel Rossetti*. 4 vols. Ed. by Oswald Doughty and J R Wahl. Oxford: Oxford University Press, 1965–67

Rossetti, William. *Some Reminiscences*. 2 vols. London: Brown, Langham, 1906

Rossetti, William, ed.. *Ruskin, Rossetti, and PreRaphaelitism: Papers 1854–1862*. London: George Allen, 1899

Rubens, Godfrey. *William Richard Lethaby: His Life and Work 1857–1931*. London: Architectural Press, 1986

Rules of the Hogarth Club and List of Membership. London: 1860

Ruskin, John. *The Opening of the Crystal Palace considered in some of its Relations to the Prospects of Art*. London: Smith, Elder, 1854

Ruskin, John. 'The Poetry of Architecture; or the Architecture of the Nations of Europe considered in its Association with the National Character', a series of articles first published in John Julius Loudon's *Architectural Magazine* in 1837 and 1838. In *Works of John Ruskin*, ed. by E T Cook and Alexander Wedderburn. London: George Allen, 1903, vol. I: *Early Prose Writings*, pp. 1–185

Ruskin, John. *The Seven Lamps of Architecture*. 3 vols. London: Smith, Elder, 1849

Ruskin, John. *The Stones of Venice*. 3 vols. London: Smith, Elder, 1851–3

Ruskin, John. *The Winnington Letters: John Ruskin's Correspondence with Margaret Alexis Bell and the Children at Winnington Hall*. Ed. by Van Akin Burd. London: George Allen & Unwin, 1969

Saint, Andrew. *Richard Norman Shaw*. New Haven and London: Yale University Press, 1976

Scott, George Gilbert. *Remarks on Secular and Domestic Architecture, Present and Future*. London: Murray, 1857

Service, Alastair. 'James MacLaren and the Godwin Legacy'. In *Edwardian Architecture and its Origins*, ed. by Alastair Service, pp. 100–18. London: Architectural Press, 1975

Service, Alastair, with many contributors. *Edwardian Architecture and its Origins*. London: Architectural Press, 1975

Sewter, A Charles. *The Stained Glass of William Morris and his Circle*, 2 vols. New Haven and London: Yale University Press for the Paul Mellon Centre for Studies in British Art (London), 1974, 1975

Shaw, George Bernard. *George Bernard Shaw: Collected Letters 1874–1897*. Ed. by Dan H Laurence. London: Max Reinhardt, 1965

Sheppard, F H W, ed.. *Northern Kensington*. Survey of London Series, vol. 37. London: Athlone Press and University of London for the Greater London Council, 1973

Silver, Anne. *Chiltley Place and Goldenfields*. Liphook: Bramshott and Liphook Preservation Society, 1995

Smith, Helen. 'Philip Webb's Restoration of Forthampton Court, Gloucestershire'. *Architectural History*, Journal of the Society of Architectural Historians of Great Britain, 24 (1981), pp. 92–102, and pl. 35

Smith, Stuart Allen. 'Alfred Waterhouse: Civic Grandeur'. In *Seven Victorian Architects*, ed. by Jane Fawcett, pp. 102–21. London: Thames and Hudson, 1976

Sparrow, W Shaw. *Hints on House Furnishing*. London: Eveleigh Nash, 1909

Spence, Rory. 'Theory and Practice in the Early Work of the Society for the Protection of Ancient Buildings'. In *'A School of Rational Builders'*, exhibition catalogue, pp. 5–9. London: Society for the Protection of Ancient Buildings, 1982

Stamp, Gavin, and André Goulancourt. *The English House 1860-1914: the Flowering of English Domestic Architecture*. London: Faber and Faber, 1986

Stanton, Phoebe. *Pugin*. London: Thames and Hudson, 1971

Stearn, William T. 'Mrs Robb and "Mrs Robb's Bonnet" *(Euphorbia robbiae)*'. *Journal of the Royal Horticultural Society*, July 1973, pp. 306–10

Steele, James. *Charles Rennie Mackintosh: Synthesis in Form*. London: Academy Editions, 1994

Stephens, Frederick. 'Artists' Homes—No. 8: Mr. Val. C. Prinsep's House, Kensington'. *Building News*, 39 (29 October 1880), p. 511 and plate opposite p. 498

Stevenson, John. *House Architecture*. 2 vols. London: James Macmillan, 1880

Stirling, A M Wilhelmina. *A Painter of Dreams and other Biographical Studies*. London: Bodley Head, 1916

Stirling, A M Wilhelmina. *The Letter-bag of Lady Elizabeth Spencer-Stanhope, Compiled from the Cannon Hall Papers, 1806–1873*. 2 vols. London: John Lane, 1913

Stirling, A M Wilhelmina. *Life's Little Day: Some Tales and other Reminiscences*. London: Thornton Butterworth, 1924

Street, Arthur E. 'George Price Boyce, R.W.S.'. *Architectural Review*, 5 (February 1899), pp. 151–60. Published with slight abridgement as the preface (pp. 1–8) to extracts from the Diaries of George Price Boyce in the *Old Water-Colour Society's Club Nineteenth Annual Volume*, ed. by Randall Davies. London: by the Society, 1941

Street, Arthur E. *A Memoir of George Edmund Street, RA, 1824–1881*. London: John Murray, 1888

Street, George Edmund. *Brick and Marble in the Middle Edmund Ages: Notes on a Tour in North Italy*. London: John Murray, 1855

Street, George Edmund. 'Destructive Restoration on the Continent'. *Ecclesiologist*, 18 (1857), pp. 342–5

Street, George Edmund. 'On the Future of Art in England'. *Ecclesiologist*, 19 (1858), pp. 232–40

Street, George Edmund. *An Urgent Plea for the Revival of True Principles of Architecture in the Public Buildings of the University of Oxford*. London: Parker, 1853

Stroud, Dorothy. *Sir John Soane, Architect*. London and Boston: Faber and Faber, 1984

'Studio-talk: Birmingham'. *Studio*, 29 (1903), pp. 291–3

Surtees, Virginia. *The Artist and the Autocrat: George and Rosalind Howard, Earl and Countess of Carlisle*. London: Michael Russell, 1988

Surtees, Virginia. *The Paintings and Drawings of Dante Gabriel Rossetti (1828– 1882): A Catalogue Raisonné*. Oxford: Clarendon Press, 1971

Swenarton, Mark. *Artisans and Architects: the Ruskinian Tradition in Architectural Thought*. London: Macmillan, 1989

Thompson, E P. *William Morris: Romantic to Revolutionary*. London: Lawrence & Wishart, 1955. Rev. edn, London: Merlin, 1977

Thompson, M W. *General Pitt-Rivers: Evolution and Archaeology in the Nineteenth Century*. Bradford-on-Avon: Moonraker Press, 1977

Thompson, Paul. *Butterfield*. London: Routledge & Kegan Paul, 1971

Thompson, Paul. *The Work of William Morris*. London: Heinemann, 1967. Reprint, New York, Melbourne, London: Quartet Books, 1977

Troubridge, Laura. *Memories and Reflections*. London: Heinemann, 1925

[Turner, H Thackeray], *Notes on the Repair of Ancient Buildings issued by the Society for the Protection of Ancient Buildings*. London: by the Society, 1903

Vallance, Aymer. *William Morris, his Art, his Writings and his Public Life: a Record*. London: George Bell, 1897. Reprint, London: Studio, 1986

Walkley, Giles. *Artists' Houses in London 1764–1914*. Aldershot and Brookfield, USA: Scholar Press and Ashgate, 1994

Watkinson, Ray. 'Painting'. In *William Morris*, ed. by Linda Parry, pp. 90–98. London: Philip Wilson in association with the Victoria & Albert Museum, 1996

Watts, Mary S. *George Frederic Watts*. 3 vols. London: Macmillan, 1912

Weaver, Lawrence, ed. *The House and its Equipment*. London: Country Life, 1922

Weaver, Lawrence. *Houses and Gardens by E. L. Lutyens*. London: Country Life, 1913. Reprint, London: Antique Collectors' Club, 1981

Weaver, Lawrence. 'Rounton Grange, Yorkshire, A Seat of Sir Hugh Bell, Bart.'. *Country Life*, 37 (26 June 1915), pp. 906–12

Weaver, Lawrence. *Small Country Houses of Today*. London: Country Life, 1910. Rev. 3rd edn, 1922

Weaver, Lawrence. 'Standen, East Grinstead, a Residence of Mr. James S. Beale'. *Country Life*, 27 (7 May 1910), pp. 666–72

Webb, Igor. 'The Bradford Wool Exchange: Industrial Capitalism and the Popularity of Gothic'. *Victorian Studies* (USA) (Autumn 1976), pp. 45–68

'Webb, Philip Speakman'. In the *Catalogue of the Drawings Collection of the Royal Institute of British Architects: T–Z*, ed. by Jill Lever, pp. 142-99. Amersham: Avebury Publishing, 1984

Webber, C E. 'Lord Sackville Arthur Cecil'. *Journal of the Proceedings of the Institution of Electrical Engineers*, 28 (1899), part 141

Wedgwood, Alexandra. 'Domestic Architecture'. *In Pugin: a Gothic Passion*, ed. by Paul Atterbury and Clive Wainwright, pp. 42–61. London: Yale University Press in association with the Victoria & Albert Museum, 1994

White, J Gleeson. 'An Epoch-Making House'. *Studio*, 12 (1898), pp. 102–12

White, William Hale. *The Groombridge Diary*, ed. by Dorothy V White. New York: Milford, 1924

White, William Hale. *Letters to Three Friends*, ed. by Dorothy V White. London: Humphrey Milford, Oxford University Press, 1924

White, William Hale. 'Modern Houses', a letter to the editor. *Daily Telegraph*, 16 October 1865, p. 5

William Morris. Ed. by Linda Parry. London: Philip Wilson in association with the Victoria & Albert Museum, 1996. Published to coincide with the exhibition at the museum, William Morris 1834–1896

William Morris: Art and Kelmscott, ed. by Linda Parry. London: Boydell Press for the Society of Antiquaries of London, 1996

Willmott, Ernest. *English House Design: A review*. London: Batsford, 1911

Wilson, Richard G. *Greene King, a Family and Business History*. London: Bodley Head and Jonathan Cape, 1983

Winmill, Joyce M. *Charles Canning Winmill: an Architect's Life*. London: J M Dent, 1946

Winpenny, David. *St. Martin-on-the-Hill, A Guide*. Scarborough: by the church [early 1980s]

Wittkower, Rudolf. *Architectural Principles in the Age of Humanism*. London: Warburg Institute, 1949, reprint, London: Academy Editions, 1973

Wordsworth, William. *A Guide through the District of the Lakes in the North of England*. Kendal and London: Hudson & Nicholson; Longman & Co., Moxon, and Whittaker & Co., 1835

Zaczek, Iain. *Essential William Morris*. Bath: Dempsey Parr, 1999

ACKNOWLEDGEMENTS

Inevitably, after such a long period of research, there is insufficient space to mention the names of all the many individuals, organisations, and institutions, without whose help this book could not have been written. I am deeply and sincerely grateful to them all, whether the information or other help they provided was large or small. The unfailing kindness, patience, courtesy, and efficiency with which my queries and requests were answered or fulfilled made the research for this book most enjoyable.

I am profoundly grateful to John Brandon-Jones, for allowing me to study his Webb material and to photocopy much of it, for commenting most helpfully on my PhD thesis, for his unfailing encouragement, and for many stimulating conversations about Webb and his work; to his wife, Helen, for friendship and warm hospitality, and for kindly chauffeuring me to the station, on many occasions; to Peter Willis, for supervising the preparation of the thesis with great skill and commendable patience, and for bringing it to the attention of Michael Spens, then the commissioning editor for Academy Editions; to Colin Cunningham and Hentie Louw, the Examiners of the PhD thesis, for helpful suggestions towards converting it for publication; to T Rory Spence, for providing, at an early stage of the research, a great deal of useful information about Webb and his work; to Norah Gillow of the William Morris Museum, and Linda Parry, of the V&A, for valuable information, and for help with identifying textiles and other artefacts in archival photographs of Webb's houses; to Douglass Wise, for bringing to my attention, in 1979, the surprising fact that very little had been written about Webb, despite his renown; to the staff of the North Yorkshire County Library, of the Stokesley and Thirsk branches in particular, for keeping me supplied with countless books and articles through the Inter Library Loan system; and, of course, to the kindness and cooperation – which was absolutely essential – of the owners, former owners, tenants, and managers of Webb buildings or parts of his buildings, who allowed me to examine their homes and workplaces in detail, to study relevant papers and old photographs in their collections, and to take snap-shots as *aides-mémoire*, and in many cases, they also allowed photography for the book, with its attendant inconveniences (to protect their privacy, they have not been named).

I am profoundly grateful to the following individuals (in many instances, the particular field on which information or other help was provided, is indicated in parentheses):

Richard and Penny Ballard (Nether Hall and Nether Hall Farm); John Bayes (TocH, and Bell Brothers Offices); Lady (Mary) Bell, Mrs (Dorothy) William Babbington Dixon, Mrs (Pauline) John Dower, Lady (Bridget) Plowden, Miles Richmond, Susannah Richmond, and Mrs (Mary) R W Wilson (the Bell family, and their Webb houses); Robert Berwick, of Durham University Library (the Howard Papers); Graham Brown, for producing a large number of prints from my negatives; Sonia Crutchlow (William Morris Society); Keith Coppick and Frank Delany for drawing plans; Peter Cormack, of the William Morris Museum; Caroline Dakers (Clouds); Tim Davies (Courtauld Institute Librarian); A R Dufty, David Gaimster, and Bernard Nurse, of the Society of Antiquaries of London; Susan F Forster, Bernard J Guile, Scott MacRae MacGregor, and Donald Smith, for lending me

their unpublished theses; Robert J Hassall and Elizabeth M Green, of British Steel Co. Northern Region Records Centre (Webb's work for Bell Brothers); Derek Green, of British Steel Co. Legal and Estates Dept., Redcar (Bell Brothers Offices); Cecily Greenhill, Honorary Archivist of the Society for the Protection of Ancient Buildings; Mary Greensted and Sophia Wilson, of the Cheltenham Art Gallery & Museum; Arthur Grogan (Standen); William Grundy, Ruth Gofton, Nicky Ingram, and David Moore (National Trust past and present property staff at Standen); R H Harcourt Williams (Librarian and Archivist to the Marquess of Salisbury); Jennifer Harris, of the Whitworth Art Gallery; John K Harrison (Clarence Works buildings); Ted and Doris Hollamby (Red House); David L Laird (Airlie Estate Papers); the late Lord Howard of Henderskelfe, and archivists Eeyan Hartley and Christopher Ridgway (Castle Howard Archives); the Hon. Philip Howard (Naworth Castle); Dianne Sachko Macleod (19th-century industrialist patrons of the Pre-Raphaelite painters); Ann Martin (Astley Hall, Arisaig); Philippa Martin, of the RIBA Library Drawings Collection; Elizabeth Motley (the Beale family and Standen); Arthur Penn, and Leonard James (St Martin's, Brampton); Margaret Richardson; Eric and Maureen Smith, of the Hartlepool Archaeological & Historical Society (Hill House); Mark Swenarton, for some stimulating debates; Godfrey Rubens (Webb and Lethaby); Mrs F H Towill, née Polly Godman (the Godman and Bell families, and Smeaton Manor); the villagers of East Rounton, chiefly in the 1980s (the Bell family, Rounton Grange, and the estate); N C Wilde, of Bedford Central Library (Webb to W Hale White letters)

My grateful thanks are also tendered to the following individuals, and to the staff of the organisations and institutions:

Nicholas M E Antram; Gilbert Bunting; John Burton; Miss M J Becher; Sir John Bell; K J Burt; Richard J Busby; D J Cann; R S H Cape; Sally Chappell; Neil Charlton; Clive Cruddas; David C Cole; Nicholas Cooper; Arthur K Cumbor; Jim Crow; Josephine De Bono; Alan Dodd; D L Edmonds, Tom E Faulkner; Richard Fellowes; Penelope Fitzgerald; Piers Ford; Wilfrid Garlick; H. Godwin-Arnold; Sidney M Gold; Andrew Hargreaves; Kate Hay; K A S Headlam-Morley; D L and L T D Heppell; Wendy Hitchmough; F Guy Holmes; Margaret Hudson; Malcolm B Kelly; Mandy Ketchin; H L Langley; David Lloyd; Jonathan Lloyd; J Stuart Mackie; Margaret Mackinder, née Bird, and her mother, Constance; Val Martin; Margaret Mawston; John-Paul Marix Evans; Elizabeth Motley; Edward and Muriel Myatt; Roger and Sally Nelson; Ernest Pilling; Aileen Reid; Richard Ricketts; David and Sue Ridley; Andrew Robinson; Tony Rooke; Lance Shuttleworth; D J H Smith; Sister Judith, CHN and Sister Jane Cicely, CHN, Convent of the Holy Name, Malvern; Jeffrey Solomons; Mark Stocker; Virginia Surtees; Alan Swailes; Colin Sylvester; H V C Tarran; Nigel Temple; Colin G Vaux; Ray Watkinson; Owen Wicksteed; Richard G Wilson; N R Winwell; and David T Yeomans

Art galleries and museums: Ashmolean Museum, Oxford; Astley Cheetham Art Gallery, Stalybridge; Beamish Museum; Barnet Museum; Billingham Art Gallery; Birmingham Museums and Art

Gallery; Brighton Art Gallery; Cheltenham Art Gallery and Museum; Fitzwilliam Museum, Cambridge; New Forest Museum, Lyndhurst; National Portrait Gallery; Salisbury & South Wiltshire Museum; Tullie House Museum and Art Gallery, Carlisle; Wandsworth Museum; Watts Gallery, Compton; William Morris Gallery, Walthamstow; Whitworth Art Gallery, Manchester; V&A Museum: Furniture, Textiles, & Fashion Department; National Art Library; Picture Library; Sculpture, Metalwork, Ceramic & Glass Department; Word & Image Department

Colleges & universities: Newnham College, Cambridge; University of Durham (Library, Archives and Special Collections); University of Newcastle upon Tyne (School of Historical Studies, the Robinson Library, and the library of the School of Architecture, Planning and Landscape); University of York (Institute of Advanced Architectural Studies)

National, county, city, and metropolitan borough libraries: Bedford; Birmingham; British Library (Manuscript Collection); Camden; Cheshire; Durham City; Durham County; East Sussex; Gateshead; Gloucester; Hammersmith & Fulham; Hampstead; Haringey; Herefordshire; Hertfordshire; Leeds; Lewes; Manchester; Middlesbrough; Newcastle; Norfolk; Northamptonshire; North Yorkshire; Oxford; Oxford County; Redcar; Surrey; Tameside; Tottenham; Tyne & Wear; Wandsworth; Wantage; Wiltshire

Planning departments: Buckinghamshire; East Hampshire; Hambleton, North Yorkshire; Hammersmith & Fulham; Haringey; Hartlepool; Kensington & Chelsea; Middlesbrough (formerly Cleveland County); Salisbury; Suffolk; Sunderland; Surrey; Wandsworth; Westminster

Record offices (national, city, county, or metropolitan borough, unless stated otherwise): Berkshire; Bolton; British Steel Co. (now Corus) Northern Region Records Centre, Middlesbrough; Buckinghamshire; Cheshire; Chester City; Cumbria; Dorset; Durham County; East Sussex; English Heritage, National Monuments Record; Gloucester; Hampshire; Herefordshire; Hertfordshire; Isle of Wight; Kent; Lambeth; London Metropolitan Archives; National Coal Board Archives Centre; Newcastle; Norfolk; Northamptonshire; North Yorkshire; Public Record Office, Kew, London; Scottish RO; Suffolk; Surrey; Teesside Archives (formerly County Cleveland RO);

Tyne & Wear; Westminster; West Sussex; Wiltshire

Royal Commissions: on Ancient Monuments; on Ancient Monuments in Wales; on Historical Manuscripts

Societies: Barnet & District Local History Society; Bramshott and Liphook Preservation Society; Cleveland & Teesside Local History Society; Cleveland Industrial Archaeological Society; Federation of Sussex Local History Societies; Hartlepool Archaeological & Historical Society; Law Society; Metals Society; Newcastle Literary and Philosophical Society; Old Water-Colour Society; Royal Horticultural Society; Surrey Archaeological Society; Society of Antiquarians of London; Society for the Protection of Ancient Buildings; Surrey Archaeological Society; Victorian Society; Welwyn Archaeological Society; William Morris Society; Yorkshire Archaeological Society.

Abigail Grater, with whom it was a delight to work, earned my boundless gratitude by her never failing encouragement, practical help, enthusiastic championing over several years of the project and later the typescript, and her expert copyediting of the latter. Working with Famida Rasheed, who took over the job of providing practical support some time ago, and with Mariangela Palazzi-Williams, and Helen Castle (all of Wiley-Academy), has also been a pleasure; I am extremely grateful for all their efforts on my behalf and that of my book, as I am also to Paul Nash for the index, and to Liz Sephton for designing the book and taking great pains to put each illustration in the appropriate place in the text. I am greatly indebted to Martin Charles for his kindly co-operation over a long period of time, for his many helpful comments and criticisms, and most of all of course, for his superb photographs.

Finally, but certainly not least, I thank my family: my husband, Harry, for constant encouragement and support in many ways (some of which are mentioned in the Introduction), including preparing plans and sketches; our son, Hilton, and daughter, Hilary, and their spouses, Kate and John, and our grandchildren, for their interest in the project, and their ready acceptance of interruptions to family holidays in order for me to study a Webb building and interview its owners; Hilton, for solving word processor problems, usually arising in the late evening; Hilary, for the church plans and the Rushmore gatehouse drawing; John, for the Thurstaston perspective sketch; our granddaughter Victoria Kirk, for some late research and photography in London; and my cousin, Tony Denton, and his wife, Anthea, for their encouragement and interest, and for hospitality in and near London.

Any mistakes, of course, are my own.
Sheila Kirk

INDEX

Note: *italic numbers* indicate illustrations (and their captions), and **emboldened numbers** are main entry and catalogue listings; 'WM' means 'William Morris', and 'PW' is 'Philip Webb'